TORAH and COMMENTARY

חֲמִשָׁה חֻמְשֵׁי תּוֹרָה
THE FIVE BOOKS OF MOSES

TRANSLATION,
RABBINIC
and
CONTEMPORARY COMMENTARY

TORAH and COMMENTARY

חֲמִשָׁה חֻמְשֵׁי תּוֹרָה
THE FIVE BOOKS OF MOSES

TRANSLATION,
RABBINIC
and
CONTEMPORARY COMMENTARY
by

SOL SCHARFSTEIN

KTAV PUBLISHING HOUSE INC.
Jersey City, NJ 07306

Copyright © 2008 KTAV Publishing House, Inc.

Library of Congress Cataloging-in-Publication Data

Scharfstein, Sol 1921-
 Torah and Commentary: the five books of Moses: Translation, Rabbinic and Cntemporary Commentary / by Sol Scharfstein.
   p. cm.
  Includes index.
  ISBN 978-0-88125-973-5 (hardcover) -- ISBN 978-1-60280-020-5 (pbk) 1. Bible. O.T. Pentateuch--Commentaries. 2. Bible O.T. Pentateuch--Theology. 3. Judaism--Customs and practices. 4. Jewish ethics. I. Title.
  BS1225.53.S355 2008
  222'.1077--dc22

2008015985

Published by
KTAV Publishing House, Inc.
930 Newark Avenue
Jersey City, NJ 07306
Email: bernie@ktav.com
www.ktav.com
(201) 963-9524
Fax (201) 963-0102

TABLE OF CONTENTS

12 **Introduction**

17 **All About the Torah**

    18 Torah History

    22 Torah Scholarship

    23 Two Torah Holidays

    25 Torah Ornaments and Settings

    26 Torah Ceremonies and Honors

    28 Inside the Torah

    30 The Hebrew Calendar

סֵפֶר בְּרֵאשִׁית   32 **Book of Bereshit**

בְּרֵאשִׁית   34 Bereshit

נֹחַ   45 Noah

לֶךְ לְךָ   56 Lech Lecha

וַיֵּרָא   66 Vayera

חַיֵּי שָׂרָה   79 Chayay Sarah

תּוֹלְדוֹת   87 Toldot

וַיֵּצֵא   96 Vayetze

וַיִּשְׁלַח   107 Vayishlach

וַיֵּשֶׁב   119 Vayeshev

מִקֵּץ   128 Miketz

וַיִּגַּשׁ   140 Vayigash

וַיְחִי   148 Vayechi

סֵפֶר שְׁמוֹת 157 Book of Shemot

שְׁמוֹת	160	Shemot
וָאֵרָא	171	Va'era
בֹּא	180	Bo
בְּשַׁלַּח	192	Beshallach
יִתְרוֹ	205	Yitro
מִשְׁפָּטִים	213	Mishpatim
תְּרוּמָה	224	Terumah
תְּצַוֶּה	231	Tetzaveh
כִּי תִשָּׂא	238	Ki Tissa
וַיַּקְהֵל	249	Vayakhel
פְּקוּדֵי	257	Pekuday

סֵפֶר וַיִּקְרָא 263 Book of Vayikra

וַיִּקְרָא	265	Vayikra
צַו	274	Tzav
שְׁמִינִי	281	Shemini
תַזְרִיעַ	288	Tazria
מְצֹרָע	294	Metzora
אַחֲרֵי מוֹת	301	Achare Mot
קְדוֹשִׁים	308	Kedoshim
אֱמֹר	314	Emor
בְּהַר	324	Behar
בְּחֻקֹּתַי	330	Bechukkotai

סֵפֶר בַּמִדְבָּר	336	**Book of Bamidbar**
בַּמִדְבָּר	338	Bamidbar
נָשֹׂא	348	Naso
בְּהַעֲלֹתְךָ	358	Beha'alotecha
שְׁלַח לְךָ	370	Shelach Lecha
קֹרַח	380	Korach
חֻקַּת	388	Chukkat
בָּלָק	397	Balak
פִּינְחָס	406	Pinchas
מַטּוֹת	417	Mattot
מַסְעֵי	424	Massay
סֵפֶר דְּבָרִים	432	**Book of Devarim**
דְּבָרִים	434	Devarim
וָאֶתְחַנַּן	442	Va'etchanan
עֵקֶב	453	Ekev
רְאֵה	462	Re'eh
שׁוֹפְטִים	474	Shoftim
כִּי תֵצֵא	482	Ki Tetze
כִּי תָבוֹא	492	Ki Tavo
נִצָּבִים	502	Nitzavim
וַיֵּלֶךְ	506	Vayelech
הַאֲזִינוּ	510	Ha'azinu
וְזֹאת הַבְּרָכָה	516	Vezot Ha'berachah

521 SPIRITUAL LEADERS and TORAH COMMENTATORS

- 522 Yohanan ben Zakkai
- 524 Hillel
- 526 Rabbi Akiba
- 528 Abba Arikha
- 530 Ezra and Nehemiah
- 532 Judah HaNasi
- 534 Saadia Gaon
- 536 Rabbi Solomon ben Itzhak (Rashi)
- 538 Maimonides (Rambam)
- 540 Rabbi Moses ben Nachman (Ramban)
- 542 Gersonides, Levi ben Gerson (Ralbag)
- 544 Rabbi Obadiah Sforno
- 546 Joseph Karo
- 548 Isaac Abrabanel
- 550 Rabbi Isaac Luria
- 552 Israel ben Eliezer (Baal Shem Tov)
- 554 The Gaon of Vilna

556 BIBLIOGRAPHY
559 BIOGRAPHICAL VIGNETTES
562 INDEX

TO MY WIFE, EDYTHE
Whose patience and support never wavered.
For enduring
"Just give me another ten minutes till I finish this paragraph"–
which often stretched into hours.

In Memorial

In 1921 my parents, Asher and Feiga came to America where they established a Jewish bookstore in the Lower East Side ghetto of New York City. At first we lived in one room in back of the store, with a toilet in the hall. Every Friday we went to the public baths, where we purchased towels and soap for a penny. Sometimes we brought our own towels and soap to save the pennies.

Asher and Feiga were young, intelligent, and not content to just sell books and sundry religious items. So they began to create lead draydels, make Simchat Torah flags, and publish wedding certificates. From this small beginning they began to branch out and publish other books such as siddurim, machzorim, and chumashim. In 1947 my father had a brainstorm and assembled the first-of-its-kind Torah reading text, entitled *Tikkun Torah*. This was an immediate success. This Tikkun, 60 years later has gone through innumerable editions and has helped train tens of thousands of Torah readers. It is still in print and is selling well to this day.

In 1947, after World War II, my father received the devastating news that his brothers and their families in the little town of Dinivetz in Russia were murdered by the Nazis.

In 1950, with tears in his eyes and a quivering hand, he wrote this Hebrew memorial for a new version of the *Tikkun* entitled *Tikkun Encyclopedia*.

continued on page 11

Asher's memorial reads:

In memory of my brother Yosef, son of Dov, and his lovely wife Sara, and their son Yisrael and his wife and their two children, who never even tasted life. They, with all the Jews in the village of Dinivetz, were thrown alive into a mine in the forest by the Nazis and the Polish villagers on the 8th day of the month of Mar Heshvon. May the memory of their murderers be wiped off the face of the earth.

To my nephew Aaron, son of Yosef, the engineer, who was killed in the Russian army during the battle for the city of Varonezh.

To my brother Shmuel and his wife Chava and their two children, who in 1942 were burned alive during a pogrom near the city of Warsaw.

I will never forget them.
Asher son of Dov Scharfstein

DEDICATION

There are times during a restless night, when I see their shadows and hear their cries echo through my dreams. I know that they are reminding me never to forget.

This book is dedicated to my nephews, cousins, aunts, and uncles whose joys I will never share and whose laughter I will never hear.

P.S. I was born in the murderous town of Dinivetz.

INTRODUCTION

The classic book Pirke Avot, *Sayings of the Fathers,* is a tractate of the Mishnah, the Oral Torah of Judaism. It starts with the statement:

"Moses received the Torah at Sinai and handed it on to Joshua. Joshua handed it to the Elders, the Elders to the Prophets, and the Prophets handed it down to the Men of the Great Assembly."

Each of the leaders transmitted the teachings of the Torah not only to the leaders, rabbis, and teachers, but to all Israel. All Israel refers to all generations, directly to you.

The Torah was given on the top of Mount Sinai in a stark, silent wilderness, devoid of life. The cruel, harsh scene epitomizes the state of the world at that time. Nations were ruled by despots, kings, and warlords. Wars, disregard for human life, and the sacrifice of humans to man-made idols were prevalent. There was a complete lack of social justice, lovingkindness, and respect for human life.

In this wilderness, Adonai planted the seed of Torah, which, despite great odds, germinated and grew, spread and became the book of divinity for two other major religions, Christianity and Islam.

When the Torah was offered at Mount Sinai, the people responded, Na'aseh v'nishma. "We will faithfully do and obey all that Adonai has commanded" (Shemot 24:7). The word "do" connotes obedience; "obey" suggests that both the heart and the mind are willing to study and learn and be enlightened.

Even before the Israelites were aware of the contents of the Torah or understood the meaning of the commandments, they accepted a demanding code of conduct for themselves and for future generations. It was the conscious choice of accepting for itself the demands and discipline of the Torah that made Israel into a "holy nation."

As you continue your studies, you will feel the heartbeat of the Torah. You will begin to feel and appreciate the message and mystique of the Torah. The Zohar tells us that the Torah is like a human with a physical body containing a thought system and a moral religious code.

The Torah also has an inward mysterious life composed of spiritual elements, which you can feel but which are difficult to grasp, but if you continue your studies you will begin to sense the divinity of the text.

Why Torah?

Since the revelation at Mount Sinai, Jews have viewed the Torah as the spiritual adventure of a people seeking and learning how to serve Adonai through moral perfection. Possessing its rules and laws, a Jew can learn to live a disciplined and dedicated life.

The Mishnah Teaches:

"There are things of which a man enjoys the dividends in this world while the principal remains for him for the world to come. They are honoring father and mother; deeds of lovingkindness; regular attendance at the house of study and prayer—morning and evening; hospitality to wayfarers; visiting the sick; dowering the bride; attending the dead to the grave; devotion in prayer; and making peace between man and his fellow; but the study of Torah is equal to them all, for it leads to them all."

About the Commentaries

The basic document in the history of the Jewish people is the Torah. The Torah has also been adopted by two other religions: Christianity and Islam. In addition, the Torah has been translated into many hundreds of languages and is the best-selling book in the world. The Torah contains "the greatest story ever told."

Jews as well as other religions draw their moral, social, and religious concepts from the Torah. Throughout Western Europe's entire history, it has maintained the Torah (Bible) as the central document in its religious cultural heritage.

The Torah has been the most popular religious and historical book in Western civilization, and yet in many cases its meaning has been obscured by names, places, and personages. I hope that this translation and the commentaries will illuminate the vague and difficult passages.

The concern for readability goes beyond the sentence structure and vocabulary. The commentaries clarify the historical, religious, and cultural barriers so that the contemporary reader can understand the ancient terms. They provide background and other information about things that are obscure to the modern reader.

The text features more than 2000 commentaries chosen from ancient and modern sources and scholars who provide fascinating insights which enhance our perception of Jewish history and tradition. Explanatory units are indispensable, since the ancients used idioms and thought patterns that are often difficult to follow. Frequently the thought sequence jumps and leaves gaps for the reader to fill in. Often thoughts and events jump or move backwards to something previously mentioned without directing the reader to the reference.

There are instances when a single word or phrase is composed of theological thought which needs clarification and expansion.

The commentaries have been selected to clarify the text and add depth where applicable.

The text especially catalogues some of the 613 commandments and explains their importance in ancient times and their applicability in the twenty-first century.

About The Translation

The Torah is the eternal book of the Jewish people and must be made intelligible to both young and old, both the learned and those who have not yet enjoyed the opportunity to heed the rabbinical injunction to "go and study."

Much effort and time have been expended to make the translation of the Torah—The Five Books of Moses—as simple and comprehensible and as user friendly as possible.

Here are some of the modifications:

1. Besides a simplified translation, the major change is in the usage of the names of God. The original written Torah, which is read in the synagogue, uses three primary names of the Deity: Elohim, El, and most frequently, Adonai.

Elohim and El are found in the Book of Bereshit. The other four books use mostly the name Adonai. But strangely, the word Adonai does not appear in the Torah. Instead the text uses the tetragrammaton YHVH, which in the Torah appears as the Hebrew letters yud, hay, vav, hay. In Jewish tradition, the mysterious Holy Name is forbidden to be pronounced by ordinary laymen or even priests. It was pronounced only by the High Priest on Yom Kippur when he entered the Holy of Holies. Jews have always honored that tradition and read the Holy Name as Adonai. Non-Jewish scholars use the name Jehovah for Adonai.

Why does the Book of Bereshit have a different style than the four other books? Some Bible scholars believe that the scrolls were written by different people at different times. They called the Book of Bereshit the E scroll, referring to the use of Elohim there. The other four books or scrolls are named the J, D, and P scrolls.

The early talmudists were aware of the problem of multiple names and they suggested that the books had been written or edited by Moses during the forty-year trek through the wilderness. They posited that the different styles reflected the different pressures and situations during the wandering.

2. All weights, measures, and monetary units are converted into modern equivalents.
3. The Torah is a male-oriented text. Where possible, without disturbing the meaning of the sentence, the text is modernized by use of the word "person" instead of "man." Sometimes the sentence structure is modified to eliminate the masculine orientation.
4. The text is divided into the traditional sidrot (sections), with both Hebrew and English names.
5. All the *aliyot* are indicated in their proper places. In addition, titles have been added to the aliyot.
6. Most Hebrew place-names appear with English translation, since many of the names record an event or describe the area. The translation will make the text more meaningful.
7. The translation rigidly follows the Masoretic text, but it is not a word-for-word translation, since some phrases have been moved around to simplify the sentence structure and thereby clarify the meaning.
8. The text often joins sentences where continuity is required.

About My Teachers

Unfortunately, I cannot remember all the Hebrew teachers and rabbis who taught me Torah.

Almost every Saturday, my father Asher, after a grueling week of work, summoned the time and energy to review with me portions of the weekly sidrah and, in season, Pirke Avot.

Besides my studies at the five-day-a-week intensive Downtown Talmud Torah, my parents engaged a special tutor named Rabbi Chaim Brecher. Although he was educated in the shtetl, I especially appreciate him now because of his skill in Hebrew, Aramaic, Yiddish, French, Greek, Latin, Russian, mathematics, and science. My father discovered this hidden East Side intellectual pearl, and he soon became a consultant to the Hebrew scholarly elite.

I am eternally grateful to principal Zaslofsky of the Zitomer Talmud Torah located on 8th Street at Avenue B on the Lower East Side of New York. He tamed my youthful exuberance and introduced me to some lifelong friends, notably Rabbi Max Raiskin, who passed away before his time. Mr. Zaslofsky graduated ten of us, who then became students at the Herzlia Hebrew Teachers College.

Max revived the Talmud Torah into a vibrant day school of some three hundred students. Unfortunately, demographics, health, and monetary problems intervened, and the school combined with the Rabbi Arthur Schneier Park East Day School on the Upper East Side of New York City and lives on.

I had some marvelous teachers at Herzlia Hebrew Teachers College. I especially appreciate Mr. Epstein. He was a thin, white-haired, unassuming individual. But in front of a class he assumed the role of the prophet and delivered beautiful introductions to Isaiah, Jeremiah, and Ezekiel in clear concise Hebrew.

Unfortunately, World War II intervened and brought the end of my formal Hebrew studies. During my three and a half years of military service, I was too busy and there was no opportunity for Torah study.

After the war, my education continued with my scholarly editors at KTAV, Mr. Eliahu Persky and Mr. Isaiah Berger. KTAV has published hundreds of books, and every volume has been a learning experience.

Now, fortunately for me, every day is a continuing Torah learning experience.

Pathways Through *Torah and Commentary*

Torah and Commentary is intended to serve the general reader who is interested in learning about the Torah. Besides containing a simple easy-to-read translation of the Torah, this book supplies the following aids.

1. A preliminary illustrated essay (pp. 17-31) called "All About the Torah" provides information about Torah history, scholarship, holidays, settings, ceremonies, Torah honors, writing a Torah, and the 613 mitzvot.
2. Each of the Five Books of Moses has a short introduction summarizing its content.
3. Each of the sidrot contains numerous commentaries, which explain religious, literary, and historical events and place names in the text. The commentaries feature ideas and explanatory units by ancient and modern scholars and sources.
4. A section (pp. 522-555) contains seventeen illustrated biographies of Spiritual Leaders and Torah Commentators whose learned comments are quoted in the texts.
5. A bibliographical section (pp. 556-558) contains the descriptions of the ten major texts that are quoted in the commentaries.
6. A biographical section (pp. 559-561) contains information about the scholars quoted in the commentaries.

Author's Note:

Torah and Commentary, contains more than two thousand different commentaries, was developed over a ten-year period. In the interim, the commentaries were continually revised and modified. Many of the commentaries are ascribed to specific authors and authorities. However, I would be remiss, if I did not admit that in the passage of time, I have accidentally not credited some of the explanatory units to the proper sources or authors. In future editions, I will as soon as alerted credit the proper text or scholar.

I KNOW FIVE

Writing a book is like giving birth. It starts with a gleam. Then there is a period of gestation, which is followed by the long awaited birth. Numerous specialists expend their expertise before the baby sees the light of day.

At the end of the Passover seder we sing Echad Me Yodeah? – Who Knows One? The ditty goes from who knows one to who knows thirteen.

> I know five.
> Five are the books of the Torah.

Five are the specialists and friends who helped me give birth to this volume.

1. Attias, Joan, who for five years tirelessly read my scribbles and transcribed them into a coherent format.

2. McGrath, Ilene, was my morah d'oraitha, my Torah pilot and scholarly lifesaver. I am amazed at her erudition and her patience. She had a steadying effect when I ran out of knowhow. Her encyclopedic knowledge has given the volume validity. Thank you! Todah rabah!

3. Rijo, Oscar, my computer guru. We spent more than five years yoked together by an I Mac. Now at the end of the project, Oscar can quote chapter and verse of the text and commentaries.

4. Scharfstein, Bernard, He spent hundreds of sleepless hours checking, correcting, offering suggestions, and dotting the "i's" and crossing the "t's".

5. Stavsky, Herbert, who checked and double checked the sources and offered numerous scholarly suggestions and revisions.

My heartfelt thanks to the magnificent five. However, in the end, any omissions, mistakes, and scholarly errors are solely my responsibility.

Sol {Shenash} Scharfstein
Shlomo ben Asher
March 1st, 2008

ALL ABOUT THE TORAH

Contents

Page
- **18** Torah History
- **22** Torah Scholarship
- **23** Two Torah Holidays
- **25** Torah Ornaments and Setting
- **26** Torah Ceremonies and Honors
- **28** Inside the Torah
- **30** The Hebrew Calendar

TORAH HISTORY

The Patriarchs and the Matriarchs

The patriarchs and matriarchs of the Jewish people lived in the Fertile Crescent. Ur, the chief city of this region, was a thriving market center visited by merchants from near and far. The people who lived there worshipped many different gods, but Abraham and his wife, Sarah, the parents of the Jewish people, believed in only one God-Adonai. Adonai promised the land of Canaan (Israel) as a homeland for them and for all their descendants.

Abraham and his descendants, Isaac and Jacob, established themselves in the land of Canaan. The Torah tells us that Jacob wrestled with an angel, a messenger of Adonai, who gave Jacob the name of Israel, which means "he struggled with Elohim." Since that time, Jacob's descendants have been called the Children of Israel. They are also referred to as Hebrews.

There was a famine in the land of Canaan, so Jacob sent his sons to Egypt to purchase food. There they encountered their brother Joseph, whom they had sold as a slave. Joseph had risen to a position of great power, second in command only to Pharaoh. At Joseph's invitation, Jacob, his family, and the Children of Israel moved to Egypt.

Moses and Pharaoh

After they had lived there peacefully for about two hundred years, a new Pharaoh came into power who did not remember Joseph's deeds. He enslaved the Children of Israel and issued a decree that all male children born to the Israelites must be killed. Soon after the decree, a male child was born to Jocheved, an Israelite woman, and her husband, Amram, from the tribe of Levi. They placed the baby in a waterproof basket and floated it down the Nile River.

An Egyptian princess found him and named him Moses, which means "I took him from the water." Moses grew up in the palace of Pharaoh as an Egyptian prince. One day, Moses was enraged to see an Egyptian overseer beating an Israelite slave. Moses killed the Egyptian and fled to the land of Midian.

One day, as Moses was caring for his flock, Adonai called to him from the midst of a burning bush. Adonai told Moses to return to Egypt and to free the Hebrew slaves and lead them to freedom. Moses reluctantly agreed and returned to Egypt.

Moses and his brother Aaron again and again confronted Pharaoh and pleaded for the Israelites to be released. After ten miraculous and disastrous plagues, Pharaoh relented and set the Hebrews free.

The Holiday of Passover

The Israelites left Egypt so hurriedly that they had no time to bake their bread. They spread the raw unleavened dough in their kneading bowls and tied them onto their shoulders. The hot desert sun baked the dough into matzot. This was the origin of the custom of eating unleavened bread (matzot) on Passover, the festival that commemorates the victory won for freedom so many centuries ago.

The Israelites Leave Egypt

The great march out of Egypt began with families gathered together, each with its own tribe, twelve tribes in all. Moses did not dare lead them by the established route, which was dangerously near the border forts where Egyptian soldiers might have attempted to prevent their escape. The great throng of people, young and old, carrying their meager belongings, marched slowly eastward, to avoid the border posts. The march was halted suddenly by an obstacle that seemed so great as to be insurmountable. Silent and disheartened they stood, the light of hope slowly fading from their eyes as they gazed at the vast expanse of water that appeared before them. They had come to the end of dry land, to the shores of the "Sea of Reeds" (Yam Suf), the Suez arm of the Red Sea.

Those who looked back uncertainly in the direction of their former homes were greeted by another sight that chilled their already sinking hearts. Bearing down on them from the rear was an army of Egyptian soldiers. Regretting his decision to free the Israelite slaves, Pharaoh

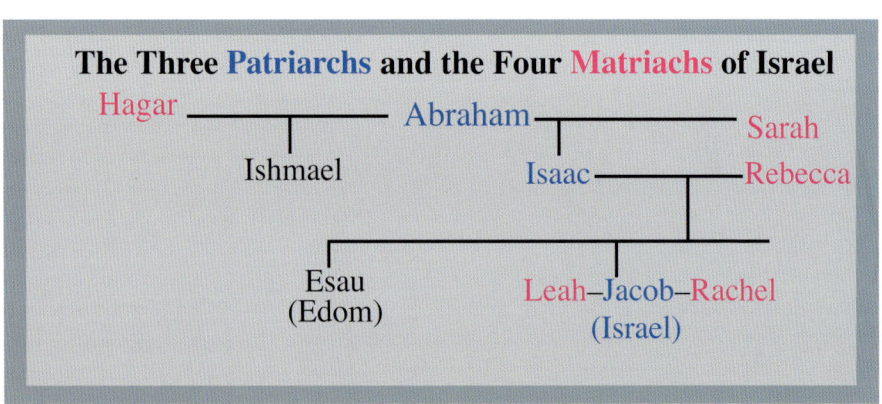

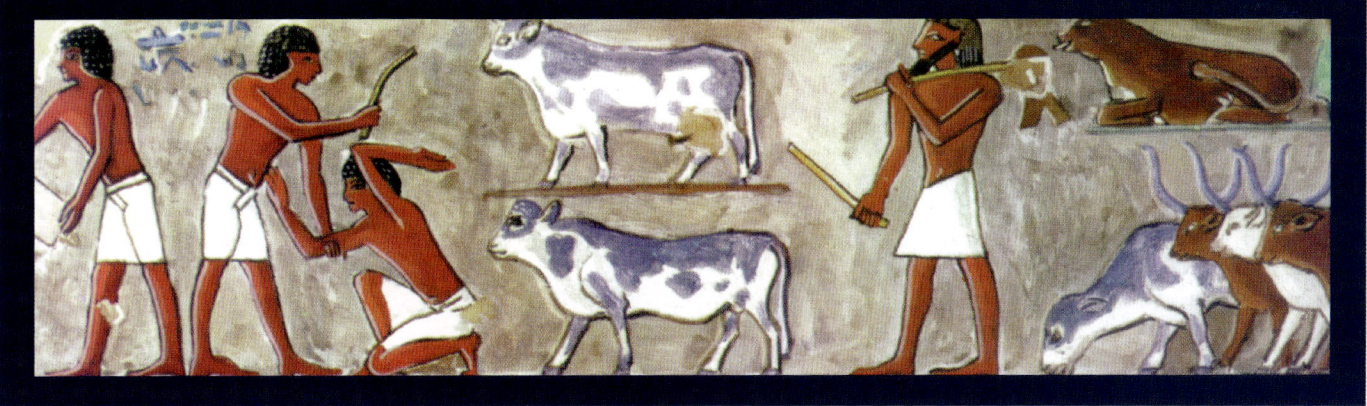
This scene of an overseer beating a slave was found in an Egyptian tomb.

was determined to overtake them. With the sea before them and the charioteers and horsemen of the cruel Pharaoh closing in from behind, the Children of Israel were trapped.

Then, miraculously, a strong easterly wind arose. It drove back the ebbing waters of the sea, making a path of dry sand. Quietly, but with joyful hearts, the throng followed Moses to the opposite shore. In fierce pursuit, Pharaoh's soldiers also took the dry path through the "Sea of Reeds," but the wind had turned and the tide of the sea was changing. Back rushed the waters, engulfing the chariots and drowning the soldiers.

The Bible tells us of the great rejoicing, the ecstatic gratitude that overwhelmed the Israelites when they found themselves safely across the sea. Moses improvised a poem of praise to the Lord. The women also danced joyously to the music of their timbrels and sang a song composed by Miriam, Moses' sister.

Ahead of them lay untold dangers and unreckoned days of weary wandering, but on this great day there was one song in the hearts of the Israelites–a song of gratitude for their newly won freedom.

Moses and the Torah

After the Israelites left Egypt, they camped around Mount Sinai. Moses ascended the mountain and remained there for forty days and nights. God presented the Ten Commandments to Moses during the forty days. Moses then presented them to the people.

Torah is the Hebrew name for the first five books of the Bible. In Hebrew it means "teaching" and "law." The rabbis of the Talmud explained that Moses wrote the Torah under the supervision of Adonai, scroll by scroll. During the forty years of desert trials, Moses recorded the history of Israel as well as his instructions and conversations with Adonai.

During his lifetime of 120 years, Moses had a long and difficult journey. He molded a group of slaves that he had freed from Egypt into a powerful holy nation that was to take center stage in the Middle East and later in world history.

Moses, who was the prophetic leader to his last dying breath, addressed the Israelites and recorded the last section of the fifth scroll of the Torah before he died. His oration starts, "This is the blessing that Moses, man of Adonai, gave to the Israelites just before his death" (Devarim 33:1).

After he finished his oration, Moses handed the completed fifth and last scroll of the Torah to the priests and then climbed Mount Nebo and disappeared.

This picture of Pharaoh Tutankhamen in his chariot was found in his tomb. The chariot reins are tied around the Pharaoh's waist, freeing his arms and enabling him to shoot his arrows. The Bible describes the pursuit of the Israelites by the "chariot of the king of Egypt."

Twelve Tribes

The twelve tribes were descendants of the twelve sons of Jacob-Israel. Each tribe received a portion of land when the Israelites entered Canaan after their Exodus from Egypt and wandering in the desert. The priestly tribe of Levi did not take a portion, but the division into twelve sections was maintained, since the portion of Joseph was divided between his two sons, Ephraim and Manasseh.

THE TRIBES OF ISRAEL

Name	Emblem	Banner	Jewel
Judah	Lion	Sky blue	Emerald
Issachar	Donkey	Black, the sun and the moon	Sapphire
Zebulun	Ship	White	Diamond
Reuben	Mandrake	Red	Sardius (ruby)
Simeon	City of Shechem	Green	Topaz
Gad	Encampment	Gray	Agate
Ephraim	Bullock	Jet black	Onyx
Manasseh	Unicorn	Jet black	Onyx
Benjamin	Wolf	Many-colored	Jasper
Dan	Serpent	Deep blue	Ligure (emerald)
Naphtali	Deer	Wine color	Amethyst
Asher	Woman and an Olive Tree	Pearl color	Beryl
Levi	Urim and Thumim	White, red, and black	Carbuncle

EMBLEMS OF THE TRIBES OF ISRAEL

Judah · Issachar · Zebulun · Reuben · Simeon · Gad

Ephraim Manasseh · Benjamin · Dan · Naphtali · Asher · Levi

The Torah in Israel and Babylon

After the First Temple was destroyed in the fifth century B.C.E., the Israelites lived under Babylonian captivity. Some went to Babylonia and some remained in Israel. During the Babylonian Exile, Ezra the Scribe and the Men of the Great Assembly ruled that a specific sidrah, or portion, from the Torah was to be assigned to each Sabbath, so that all five scrolls (the Five Books of Moses) could be completed in one full year.

The opening words of Psalm 114, which is the Hallel prayer. It begins, "When Israel left Egypt. . . ." This illustrated psalm shows the Children of Israel leaving Egypt. They are led by Moses and are passing through the gate of a medieval town from which the Egyptians are looking down.

They divided the Torah into fifty-four sidrot according to the number of weeks in a leap year.

The Rabbis in ancient Israel disagreed with their colleagues in Babylon. They divided the Torah into 155 smaller portions so that it would take three years to read the whole Torah. This system is called the triennial cycle, and it is now followed in Reform, Reconstructionist, and many Conservative congregations.

Ezra also instituted the reading of short sections of the Torah on Mondays and Thursdays as well as Saturday afternoons. Monday and Thursday were market days, when farmers came to the city to sell their produce and purchase supplies. Ezra recognized that these days were opportunities to assemble a group and teach Torah.

According to the Mishnah, by the end of the second century C.E., there were regular Torah readings on Mondays, Thursdays, Sabbaths, and the festivals, including Hanukah, Purim, and fast days. Today, Orthodox and Conservative synagogues continue the practice and read short sections of the Torah on Mondays, Thursdays, and Saturday afternoons.

The systematic reading of the Torah has had an extraordinary educational and spiritual impact on the life of Jews throughout their history. The Torah is not just read, it is studied and explained and its ethical lessons are applied to the daily life of Jews no matter where they reside. The Torah is the cornerstone of the Jewish religion and has had a profound effect on Jewish survival.

The Five Books of Moses

The Torah is often called the Five Books of Moses. The Torah is the Hebrew book that was revealed to Moses on Mount Sinai in about 1280 B.C.E. It records the beginning history of the Jewish people as well as the basic laws that established the Jewish religion. Hundreds of years later, other religions, notably Christianity and Islam, adapted and interpreted the Torah as their own religious possession.

The Torah has been published in thousands of editions and hundreds of languages. It is by far the best-selling book of all time.

Moses bringing down the Ten Commandments (from the Sarajevo Haggadah).

TORAH SCHOLARSHIP

The Targum

Throughout the Near East, and especially in Babylonia and Syria, Aramaic was the dominant language. After the Israelites returned from the Babylonian Exile, it also became the everyday spoken language of Judea. Since the Torah was written in Hebrew, it was necessary to provide a translation for the many people who were no longer able to understand it.

Ezra solved the problem by providing a translator who stood right next to the Torah reader during services and translated the Hebrew into Aramaic for the congregants. Eventually the oral translations provided in this manner were set down in writing. The Aramaic translation of the Torah is called the Targum. Note the close similarly between the name *Targum* and the word *meturgeman* (translator).

The Talmud mentions that in some synagogues the Torah was read twice: once in Hebrew and once in Aramaic.

There are three major Aramaic translations of the Torah: Targum Onkelos, Targum Jonathan, and the Palestinian Targum (Targum Yerushalmi).

The Septuagint – ca 285–246 B.C.E.

Under Ptolemy II Philadelphus, an Egyptian king of the second century B.C.E., the Bible was translated into Greek. This came about, we are told, because the library at Alexandria had a copy of every book in the world except the Bible. Wanting its collection to be complete, Ptolemy sent to Jerusalem for a Bible and asked the high priest for permission to have it translated. He invited seventy sages to Alexandria and set each of them to work by himself. The seventy sages had no contact with one another, but when they finished, all seventy translations were identical. We do not know whether this story is fact or legend, but whatever may be the case, the first Greek translation of the Bible came to be known as the Septuagint, meaning the translation "by the seventy."

The Septuagint created a great stir. At that time Greek was the most widely used language in the ancient world.

Many Jews in Egypt and other countries no longer knew Hebrew. Their knowledge of Judaism had suffered as a result, but now they were able to read the Holy Scriptures and study the laws of the Torah in Greek.

The Septuagint translation also enabled non-Jews to read the Bible. Before long the entire ancient world became acquainted with the history and ideas of the people of the little land of Judea. Many non-Jews, known as "God-fearers," began attending synagogues or adopting Jewish customs.

A page from the Septuagint, Exodus 19.

The Masoretes

In ancient times every copy of the Bible had to be written by hand. A group of scholars known as Masoretes, in the city of Tiberias in ancient Israel, were aware that over the centuries many errors had been made by the scribes who copied Torah scrolls. They decided to standardize the Torah text so that it could be handed down correctly to future generations. The term *Masorete* means "handed down."

The scribes who copied the text made various errors, which were then copied and thus passed on to later generations. It was important to have an accurate text. The scholars who performed this task of establishing the correct text are called Masoretes. To this day, *soferim* (scribes) follow the Masoretic text when they copy scrolls of the Torah.

In order to preserve the true text and meaning of the Scriptures, the Masoretes carefully compared different versions of each biblical book and decided which corresponded to the pure, original form. They laid down the text word for word, letter for letter, and worked out a system of punctuation. They devised a system of vowel signs to ensure that every word was pronounced properly. They also provided a system of accentuation and punctuation that also serves as musical notation (*trope*) for the chanting of the text in the synagogue.

The Masoretes were active from the seventh through the tenth century. Their most outstanding scholars were Jacob Ben Asher and Ben Naphtali.

TWO TORAH HOLIDAYS

Many kibbutzim in Israel celebrate the wheat and the fruit harvest. The children wear wreaths and carry baskets of fruit and vegetables; the young men and women dance in the fields and the adults cut sheaves of grain. The entire kibbutz gathers and there is a display of the produce of the soil—the fruit of the kibbutz harvest from its orchards, vegetable garden, and field crops.

The Torah is the centerpiece of all synagogue services. It is read and studied every Shabbat and on all Jewish holidays. There are also two holidays, Simchat Torah and Shavuot, that are dedicated to the honor of the Torah.

Simchat Torah

Simchat Torah, the Rejoicing in the Law, is a holiday dedicated to a book—the greatest book of all—the Torah. On this day we come to the end of the reading of the Five Books of Moses in the synagogue and begin again with the wonderful story of creation. The last chapter of Devarim is chanted, and then the first chapter of Bereshit. The cycle of Torah reading continues and the circle of the Torah is eternal, without beginning or end.

In the synagogue, Simchat Torah is celebrated with great merriment. Everybody comes—young and old, men and women.

Torah Procession

On this festive occasion, all the Torah scrolls are taken out of the Ark and carried lovingly around the synagogue in processions known as **hakafot.** Children follow the grown-ups, gaily waving colorful flags. Seven times the procession makes its rounds.

The *hakafot* are introduced by the reading of a collection of biblical verses called *Attah Horeyta*. As each line is read by the cantor or a member of the congregation, it is repeated by the participants. All the members of the congregation are given the opportunity of carrying a Torah scroll during the *hakafot*.

In many synagogues a beautiful ceremony called Consecration is held. The children who will be starting religious school that year are called to the *bimah* (pulpit) and each is presented with a miniature Torah. The rabbi blesses the group and wishes all the children a happy and meaningful Jewish experience in the years of study in the religious school.

Shavuot

Shavuot means "Weeks," and the holiday falls exactly seven weeks after the second day of Passover, on the sixth and seventh days of the month of Sivan. (Reform Jews observe only the first of the two days.) The Greek name for Shavuot is Pentecost, which in Greek means "fiftieth," because it takes place on the fiftieth day after the beginning of Passover.

Shavuot is a triple holiday—a threefold celebration which commemorates the giving of the Torah on Mount Sinai, the harvesting of wheat in Israel, and the ripening of the first fruits in the Holy Land.

The Rabbis declared Shavuot to be the most pleasant of all Jewish holidays. In a way, it is the conclusion of the great festival of Passover, for on Passover the Jews were freed from slavery, and on Shavuot the freed slaves were made into free people by the Ten Commandments.

A Torah Festival

As a Torah festival, Shavuot is also known as **Zeman Matan Torateinu,** which means "The Time of the Giving of Our Law." It was on Shavuot that Adonai spoke to Moses atop Mount Sinai and gave the Israelites the Ten Commandments.

Mount Sinai

When the Israelites reached Mount Sinai, sometime around 1280 B.C.E., Moses ordered them to pitch their tents. Here there would occur the most important moment in Jewish history. Moses was going to receive the Ten Commandments from Adonai and pass them on to the people.

The Ten Commandments

Chapters 19 and 20 of the Book of Shemot vividly tell the story of how Adonai bestowed the Torah on the Jewish people.

In the third month after the Children of Israel left Egypt, they came to the wilderness of Sinai. There they camped in front of the mountain. While they waited, Moses went up to Adonai, and the Eternal called to him from the mountain, "Say to the Children of Israel: 'You saw what I did to the Egyptians, and how I saved you and brought you to Me. Now, if you will listen to My voice and obey My laws, you will be My treasure from among all peoples.'"

Moses told the people what Adonai had said, and the people answered, "All that the Eternal has said, we will do."

The people sanctified themselves and waited for the Ten Commandments. And there was thunder and lightning, and a thick cloud surrounded the mountain. Then the sound of a shofar blowing very loudly was heard and the people trembled. Soon the mountain was completely surrounded by smoke and flames; the shofar became louder and louder, and the whole mountain shook.

Archaeologists unearthed this stone relief of the Holy Ark in the ancient synagogue in Capernaum. The original Holy Ark was built by Moses and was carried from place to place before being permanently enshrined in the First Temple. The Holy Ark safeguarded the Ten Commandments and the Torah during the forty-year journey through the wilderness.

Then God spoke these words, saying:

1. I am the Almighty your God.
2. You shall have no other gods before Me.
3. You shall not take the name of the Almighty in vain.
4. Remember the Sabbath to keep it holy.
5. Honor your father and your mother.
6. You shall not kill.
7. You shall not be unfaithful to wife or husband.
8. You shall not steal.
9. You shall not bear false witness.
10. You shall not desire what is your neighbor's.

The Ten Commandments sealed a covenant between the young nation of Israel and the one God. No other nation had a code of laws so just and humane. The Israelites now truly abandoned the ways of Egypt and dedicated themselves to live by this lofty code.

The Ten Commandments form the basis of Jewish religious and moral law.

Page from a Hebrew Bible with commentaries. The narrow column at the upper left is the Aramaic translation by Onkelos and is the most widely used Targum. It is still printed side by side with the original Hebrew text in some modern editions of the Torah.

TORAH ORNAMENTS AND SETTING

Because the Torah scroll is the most sacred object in Jewish tradition, Jews always try to ensure that it be "clothed" in the most aesthetically pleasing fashion possible. In every generation, among both Ashkenazim (from north and eastern Europe) and Sephardim (from Spain and the Mediterranean), distinctive sets of protective and decorative "garments" have been designed for the Torah, and these can be seen today in any synagogue in the world when the scrolls are removed from the Ark for the public reading of the Torah.

Mantle of the Law
The mantle (*me'il*) of the Law covers the holy scroll when it is not in use. It is usually made of embroidered silk or satin.

Choshen

A choshen.

When the Torah is taken out of the Ark, we see its beautiful breastplate, or *choshen*, suspended by a chain from the top of the rollers. In the center of the breastplate there is frequently a representation of a tiny Ark whose doors are in the form of the two tablets of the Law. The lower part of the breastplate has an area where small plates may be inserted. Each of these plates is engraved with the name of one of the Jewish festivals, to be displayed on the holiday or Shabbat on which the scroll is used.

Atzei Chayyim
The wooden rollers (*atzei chayyim* or "trees of life") on which the Torah scroll is wound are made of hard wood. They have flat round tops and bottoms to support the edges of the rolled-up scroll. The Torah itself is called *Etz Chayyim*, the "tree of life."

Keter Torah

A keter Torah.

Over the upper ends of the *atzei chayyim* is placed the *keter Torah,* the "crown of the Torah." It is usually made of silver and adorned with little bells, and it is one of the scroll's chief ornaments.

Yad
The pointer of silver or olive wood which is used to guide the reading of the Torah is called the *yad,* or "hand." It is shaped like a staff, and its end is narrow and in the form of a closed fist with the forefinger outstretched. When the Torah scroll is rolled, the yad is hung by a chain over the *atzei chayyim* and rests on the silver breastplate.

Yad.

Rimonim
The *rimonim* are the silver decorations with tinkling bells that are placed on top of the two *atzei chayyim* of the Torah scroll. The word *rimon* means "pomegranate." In ancient Israel the robes of the priest were decorated with artistically knotted pomegranates.

Aron Ha-Kodesh
The scrolls of the Torah are safely guarded in the **Aron Ha-Kodesh,** or Holy Ark. This chest is named after the **Aron Ha-Brit,** the Ark of the Covenant, which held the tablets of the Ten Commandments when our ancestors crossed the desert. The **Aron Ha-Kodesh** is usually placed against the synagogue wall facing east or toward Jerusalem.

Parochet
The Children of Israel, while wandering in the desert, hung a curtain before the Ark of the Covenant, and we follow their ancient example in many of our synagogues today. The *parochet,* or curtain, is made of fine material and hangs in front of the **Aron Ha-Kodesh.** It is often embroidered, usually with a rendering of the Ten Commandments.

TORAH CEREMONIES AND HONORS

The honor of lifting the Torah and showing it to the congregation is called hagbah.

Bimah

The *bimah* is the raised platform on which the desk stands for the reading of the weekly portion from the Torah and the prophets. The *bimah* is sometimes placed in the center of the synagogue, where it represents the altar that once stood in the middle compartment of the Temple, and sometimes it is at the front of the synagogue.

The Ba'al Koreh

In ancient times each person who was called to the Torah would read a portion aloud to the congregation. Today, the Torah reading is performed by a master reader called a *ba'al koreh*.

Aliyot

Even Jews who cannot read the Torah want to participate in the reading. This is made possible by calling people to the pulpit to recite special blessings before and after each of the Torah readings. These people are said to have had an *aliyah* (going up), (plural *aliyot*).

Gabbaim

It is customary for two people called *gabbaim (gabbai)* to stand near the *ba'al koreh* as an honor guard and assist the Torah reader. The *gabbaim* are in charge of calling honorees for their Torah *aliyot*. In addition the *gabbaim* follow the reading in a *Humash* (Bible) to assist and correct reading errors of the *ba'al koreh*.

The Trope

The Torah text has been handwritten on the parchment scroll with a feather pen and a special ink. As in the ancient Torah that Moses presented to the Israelites, there is no punctuation and there are no vowel symbols. In the synagogue the Torah is chanted with special musical notes called the *trope*.

The Honors

Aliyot and several other honors are distributed during the Torah service. The honor of opening the Ark and taking out the Torah scroll is called the **petichah**, meaning "opening." The honor of lifting the Torah scroll and showing it to the congregation is called **hagbah**. Another honor is called **gelilah**; the honoree ties and dresses the Torah scroll before it is returned to the *Aron Ha-Kodesh*.

The Order of the Aliyot

In Orthodox and most Conservative synagogues, the first *aliyah* goes to a **kohen**, a person who is descended from the priestly family of Aaron, the brother of Moses. The second *aliyah* is assigned to a **levi**, a descendant of the priestly tribe of Levi. The next five *aliyot* are reserved for Israelites, who are the majority of the Jews.

Some synagogues do not assign the first two *aliyot* to a **kohen** and a **levi**, because they feel that these divisions are outdated and that today all Jews are equal and should be treated equally.

After the reading ceremony, the Torah scroll is opened and raised aloft. This ceremony is called **hagbah**. The Torah scroll is raised in a way that enables the congregation to see three written columns.

Then the honoree takes the scroll and sits down with it. Another honoree binds the Torah with a sash and dresses it with its mantle and ornaments. This honor is called **gelilah**, which in Hebrew means "rolling together."

The Ba'al Maftir

In addition to the seven Torah *aliyot,* there is the honor of reading the haftarah. The person who reads the haftarah is called the *ba'al maftir.* The reading of the haftarah is preceded by and ends with a special blessing.

The Haftarah

The haftarah is a portion from the Prophets that is also read on each Sabbath. The haftarah always has a thematic relationship to the weekly sidrah. The custom of reading the haftarah was instituted during the occupation of ancient Israel by the Greek conquerors. The Greeks forbade the reading of the Torah, so the Rabbis cleverly substituted the reading of a selection from the Prophets. Today, both the Torah sidrah and the haftarah are read on Sabbaths and holidays.

The Sephardic System

Among Sephardim and in the Jewish communities of the East, the preservation and decoration of the Torah scrolls are different from the styles followed by Ashkenazim. The scroll is wound upon two wooden *atzei chayyim,* but these are enclosed within a wooden box, formed by two arch-shaped sections joined to the center by a hinge. The case is flat at the bottom to enable it to stand securely on a table, and when the Torah is read, the box is opened like a book to reveal a column of text, which is read without removing the scroll. The scroll is rolled to the appropriate place by manipulating the *atzei chayyim,* whose ends protrude through the top of the case.

The *atzei chayyim* are usually capped with permanent carved handles, and the box itself is covered in leather or metal engraved with traditional symbols. Inside, colorful and decorative kerchiefs called *mitpahot* are used to protect the part of the parchment that is exposed when the case is opened.

Bar Mitzvah

At the age of thirteen, Jewish boys celebrate their Bar Mitzvah, "Son of the Commandments." In Reform temples and most Conservative synagogues, girls celebrate their Bat Mitzvah, "Daughter of the Commandments."

On the Sabbath following their thirteenth birthday according to the Jewish calendar, the youngsters are called to the Torah and given *aliyot.* They read a section of the weekly Torah portion and also the haftarah. Family members are honored by being given *aliyot* and special honors, such as opening and closing the Ark and dressing the Torah.

According to traditional Jewish law, the thirteen-year-olds can now be counted as part of a prayer *minyan* (quorum) of ten people.

A Sephardic Torah reader.

Zachary Scharfstein reading his Torah portion at his Bar Mitzvah.

INSIDE THE TORAH

The Tanak

The complete Hebrew Bible is called TaNaK. It is divided into three divisions: Torah (the Five Books of Moses), Nevi'im (Prophets), and Ketuvim (Writings).

The name *Tanak* comes from the first letters of each of the three divisions. *T* is for Torah, *N* is for Nevi'im, and *K* is for Ketuvim.

There are a total of thirty-nine separate books in the Tanak. The Torah consists of five books, the Prophets of twenty-one books, and the Writings of thirteen books.

The chapter divisions and the numbering of the verses were introduced into the Tanak to make quoting from it easier.

The language of the Tanak is Hebrew except for portions of the books of Daniel and Ezra, which are in Aramaic.

Writing a Torah Scroll

A Torah scroll must be written in a very special way, by someone who is specially trained. He is called a *sofer* (scribe). The Torah is written by hand in a special script. It is not written on paper but on parchment made from the skins of kosher animals. A special instrument is used to write the Torah. It is a feather pen or quill. The pieces of the scroll are sewn together with thread made from the sinews of kosher animals.

Writing a Torah scroll is long, hard, tedious work. There are very few people today who have the special skill and knowledge that is needed. A properly written scroll is rare. Not only are the words in it very precious, but the scroll itself is precious.

Here are some of the main steps followed by a *sofer* in writing a Torah scroll, or *Sefer Torah:*

For parchment, the *sofer* may use only the hide of a clean animal (one that, according to the Torah, is kosher to eat). With a sharp point, he draws lines on the parchment, dividing each piece into eight sections, with 42 to 72 lines for each section.

A *Sefer Torah* must be written in special black ink only. The pen is a feather of a clean (kosher) fowl, with the tip sliced off at an angle and the point slit. This writing tool can shape thick or thin strokes, as required.

The *sofer* uses a special script. He may not write even one word from memory, and he must pronounce each word out loud before writing it.

אֶת־הַיָּם בְּרוּחַ קָדִים עַזָּה כָּל־הַלַּיְלָה וַיָּשֶׂם אֶת־
הַיָּם לֶחָרָבָה וַיִּבָּקְעוּ הַמָּיִם וַיָּבֹאוּ בְנֵי־יִשְׂרָאֵל
בְּתוֹךְ הַיָּם בַּיַּבָּשָׁה וְהַמַּיִם לָהֶם חוֹמָה מִימִינָם
וּמִשְּׂמֹאלָם וַיִּרְדְּפוּ מִצְרַיִם וַיָּבֹאוּ אַחֲרֵיהֶם כֹּל
סוּס פַּרְעֹה רִכְבּוֹ וּפָרָשָׁיו אֶל־תּוֹךְ הַיָּם וַיְהִי

The sofer uses special script. The decorative little crowns on the top of some letters are called tagim. *These crowns are used on seven letters. The sofer may not write from memory and must pronounce each word before writing it.*

Only seven letters of the alefbet may have the decorative little crowns called **tagim**.

Some sections are written in a special form. For example, the Song of the Red Sea (Exodus 15) is arranged like bricks in a wall, a reminder of how Adonai split the waters so that our ancestors might cross unharmed. The last few lines of the ***Sefer Torah*** are left unfinished. They will be filled in at a synagogue ceremony called the "Completion of the ***Sefer Torah***," or *Siyyum Ha-Sefer.*

The sheets are sewn together with the sinews of kosher animals which are woven into long threads. The sewing must not be visible on the face of the ***Sefer Torah***.

The scroll is attached to two wooden rollers, each called a "Tree of Life," or ***etz chayyim***.

A sofer, or scribe, writing a Torah in the traditional way with a feather pen and special ink.

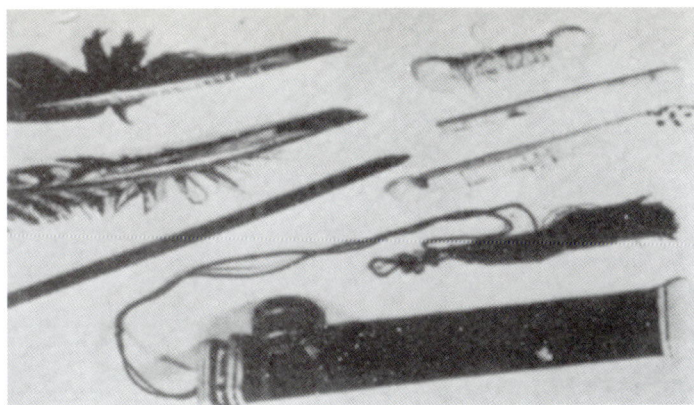

These tools are used in writing a Torah scroll. Here you see the inkwell, the reeds and their case, quills, and sinews (of kosher animals) for sewing parchment sheets together.

The 613 Mitzvot

The Torah comprises the first five books of the Bible, the Five Books of Moses. But the word **Torah** is also a general term for the Jewish way of life. When a Jew lives according to the laws and customs of Judaism, it is said that he or she is living in the way of Torah. To live according to Torah, it is necessary to know what Torah is. Jews have always been encouraged to study Torah—the Jewish way of life.

According to Maimonides, there are 613 mitzvot in the Torah. They are known as the *taryag mitzvot* because the Hebrew letters that spell out the words *taryag mitzvot* have a numeric value of 613. There are 248 yes-do mitzvot. These are the mitzvot that Adonai wants each of us to do, such as praying and honoring our parents. These are called *mitzvot aseh*. There are 365 mitzvot that are of the don't-do kind. These are called *mitzvot lo ta'aseh*. Do not steal and do not kill are just two examples. The mitzvot are associated with every part of life: how a person behaves in school and how a person plays sports; how a person treats friends and family. Mitzvot tell a person how to be a good citizen and how to treat those less fortunate. Mitzvot are an essential part of the cycle of Jewish life: birth, Bar/Bat Mitzvah, marriage, and death. There are mitzvot about the food a person eats and how a person should act as a grown-up in business or in a profession.

Rabbinical Mitzvot

With the development of halachah, the religious tradition of the Jews was separated into two divisions of law: mitzvot **de'oraitha**, meaning Torah commandments, and mitzvot **de'rabbanan**, which is mitzvot developed by the Rabbis.

There are seven mitzvot de'rabbanan that were specifically developed by the Rabbis after the destruction of the Holy Temple.
1. Recitation of the prayer Hallel on certain holidays
2. Reading the scroll of Esther on Purim
3. Lighting Hanukah candles
4. Lighting Shabbat candles
5. Washing of the hands before meals
6. Blessing of Thanksgiving
7. The *eruv* –to be able to carry things on Shabbat from one area to another

Mitzvot of the Sons of Noah

In addition to the 613 mitzvot in the Torah, there are seven mitzvot specifically given to the sons of Noah.
1. Courts of justice
2. No idolatry
3. No cursing
4. No incest
5. No murder
6. No robbery
7. No eating of flesh of live animals

The Names for Adonai

The Torah contains seven names for Adonai. The name that appears most frequently is the tetragrammaton, the four-letter holy name YHWH, which is pronounced **Adonai**. Next in frequency is **Elohim**, followed by **El**. Some scholars believe that the tetragrammaton is derived from the Hebrew root **hayah**, meaning "to be," thus signifying that Adonai is the one who was, who is, and who will be forever.

The ancient Rabbis taught that the tetragrammaton was the true name of Adonai. During the Second Temple period, the name **Adonai** was forbidden to be pronounced out loud except by the High Priest on Yom Kippur.

According to tradition, the Hebrew letters that comprise the tetragrammaton, YHWH, were not to be pronounced. Instead it is customary to substitute the word **Adonai** wherever the tetragrammaton appears in the Tanak, prayerbook, or any other holy text. In the sixth century, when vowels were introduced, Christian scholars placed vowels from **Elohim** under the consonants YHWH of the tetragrammaton and read Adonai's name as "Jehovah." The name "Jehovah" is used in many Christian Bibles, prayerbooks, and religious texts. Today, some non-Jewish scholars also read the tetragrammaton as "Yahweh," again using the vowels from under the Hebrew word for **Adonai.**

THE HEBREW CALENDAR

In the earliest days of our history, in the days of the patriarchs, Abraham, Isaac, and Jacob, the Jewish people were shepherds who wandered in search of green pastures for their flocks. They often went to bed at sunset and got up at sunrise. Men, women, and children thought of the sun as a wonderful friend.

Then someone said, "While you have been sleeping at night, I have been watching the moon and the stars. Sometimes the moon is full and round, sometimes it is only half its size, and sometimes I can't find it at all."

Report to the Sanhedrin

Special observers were placed at stations to wait for the appearance of the new moon. As soon as the slightest crescent showed in the sky, the observers rushed to Jerusalem to the Sanhedrin, the High Court of the Jewish people. "We testify that we have seen the new moon," they swore. They stated the moment it had made its appearance.

It was a moment of high excitement. Once the Sanhedrin had proclaimed the new month, runners were dispatched to light fires on the highest hills ringing the capital city. As soon as these signals were seen by the inhabitants of the next town, they in turn lit a fire on their highest hill. At last the signals reached the farthest communities. The new month had officially begun.

Jews of far-off countries like Persia and Italy and Egypt could not rely on messages that sometimes arrived very late. "We will observe the thirtieth day and the day after it as the new month," they decided. "In that way, we will be certain not to go astray." That is why, according to tradition, our forefathers added an extra day to the Pesach, Shavuot, Sukkot, and Rosh Hashanah holidays.

A Written Calendar

In the year 359 C.E., Hillel the Second—so called to set him apart from the famed Hillel who lived in the days of the Second Temple—set the rules for making a calendar.

Taking quill in hand, he wrote that the length of the Jewish month is the time it takes the moon to go around the earth. This month is 29 days, 12 hours, and 44 minutes. "We must be practical," said Hillel. "We will reckon the months by full days." So the law was laid down that some months should have thirty days and others twenty-nine. From that day Jews everywhere could determine the calendar for themselves and observe the festivals on the same day.

Jews, however, number the years from the time of the creation of the world as accounted for in the Bible. In place of B.C. and A.D., which mean "Before Christ" and "Anno Domini" (in the year of our Lord), we use B.C.E. and C.E., which mean "Before the Common Era" and "Common Era." The latter abbreviations are used in this book.

Originally, the Israelites used numerals to distinguish one month from another. The month in which the spring season began was the first month; the other months were called accordingly the second, third, and so on.

The Hebrew names of the months, as we know them, were adopted when our people lived in the Babylonian Exile after the destruction of the First Temple in 586 B.C.E. The names were derived from the Babylonian calendar.

Now we know about the way our calendar began, but that does not explain how we number our years. Why is the Jewish year called 5718 instead of 1958, or 5719 rather than 1959? The answer to this question lies, as is very often the case, in the lap of Jewish tradition.

From the beginning of recorded time, calendar makers have used events great and small as starting points for

ASTROLOGICAL SYMBOLS FOR THE JEWISH MONTHS

CHESHVAN | IYAR | SIVAN
TISHREI | AV | NISAN
ELUL | TEVET | ADAR
TAMMUZ | SHEVAT | KISLEV

their date guides. The Romans, for example, counted time from the founding of their capital city. Early Christians dated events from the birth of Jesus, which they called "the year 1." Our everyday calendar follows that rule. It is called the Gregorian calendar, because it was revised by Pope Gregory XIII in 1582, and was adopted by England for herself and her American colonies in 1752.

The Hebrew Days

The Jewish week begins on Sunday. It ends on Saturday, or Shabbat. The names of the days are really numbers. They tell what day of the week it is. This is how the days are named in Hebrew:

Sunday—Yom Rishon (The First Day)
Monday—Yom Sheni (The Second Day)
Tuesday—Yom Shelishi (The Third Day)
Wednesday—Yom Revi'i (The Fourth Day)
Thursday—Yom Chamishi (The Fifth Day)
Friday—Yom Shishi (The Sixth Day)
Saturday—Shabbat (The Sabbath)

Observe that the day, in Jewish reckoning, begins at sunset. Saturday, which is the seventh day of the week, begins on Friday evening. That is because the Torah tells us, in the story of the Creation, that "there was evening and there was morning, one day." The very first day, the day of Creation, began not with daybreak but with sunset. All our holidays follow this order and begin at sunset of the day before.

A detailed Jewish calendar tells us when the sun sets on the eve of a Sabbath or holiday; it informs us to light candles about 18 minutes before the sunset.

Look again at the calendar. It will tell you which portion of the Torah and Prophets will be read in the synagogue next Saturday.

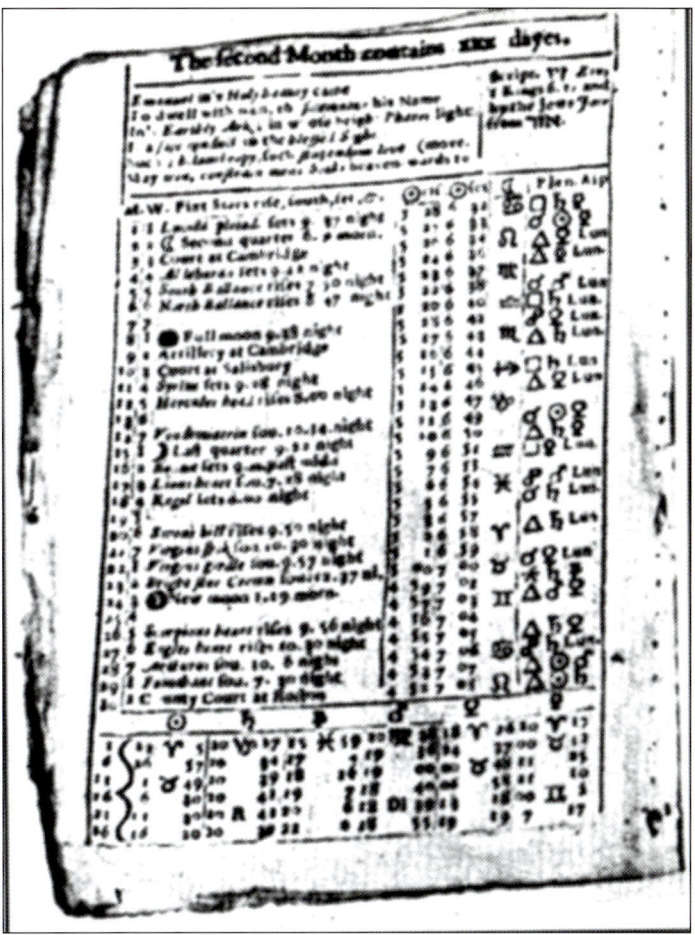

A calendar based on the Bible was introduced by the Pilgrims in Massachusetts, in 1666. The Pilgrims studied and revered the Bible. They used the Hebrew names of the months in this early American calendar.

A page from a Jewish calendar. Notice the variety of information

סֵפֶר בְּרֵאשִׁית

THE BOOK OF BERESHIT

The Hebrew name for the first book of the Torah is Bereshit. The Hebrew word bereshit, which means "in the beginning," is the first word in the Torah. The Greek name of the book is Genesis, which also means "beginning."

The first section of Bereshit (chapters 1–11) starts with the six days during which the world and humanity are created. This event is followed by the story of the first two humans, Adam and Eve, and their expulsion from the Garden of Eden because they disobey Adonai and eat from the Tree of Knowledge. In time the human race becomes so evil that Adonai sends a huge rain and floods the earth, killing every living thing. Only Noah and his family and the animals that Adonai had told Noah to build are spared. At the end of forty days the rain stops and the ark comes to rest on Mount Ararat. From there a new generation spreads out and repopulates the earth.

The second part of the book of Bereshit (chapters 12–24) tells the stories of the patriarchs and matriarchs. According to the Torah, Abraham and his wife, Sarah, were the first Jews and the parents of a new nation. Adonai appears several times to Abraham, concludes a covenant with him, and promises that his descendants will someday be a great nation and inherit the land of Canaan.

Abraham's son Isaac marries Rebecca, who has grown up outside of Canaan. Like Abraham and Sarah, Rebecca uproots herself from her home and its idol-based religion. Adonai also renews the promise of the land of Canaan to Isaac's son Jacob. Jacob leaves Canaan after a bitter quarrel with his twin brother, Esau. Jacob marries his cousins Leah and Rachel, who together with their handmaids bear him twelve sons.

Chapters 25–50 conclude the book of Bereshit. After twenty-five years Jacob returns to his homeland and reconciles with his brother, Esau. On his return to Canaan, after serving his uncle Laban, Jacob meets a man near the River Jabbok. After wrestling with Jacob, the man reveals that he is an angel, a messenger of Adonai. He gives Jacob the name Israel, which means "he who struggles with Adonai." From then on Jacob's descendants were called the Children of Israel.

Jacob is now a rich man with a large family and twelve stalwart sons. His favorite is Joseph.

The brothers resent Joseph and sell him as a slave. A famine in Canaan forces the brothers to go to Egypt to purchase food for the family. Their brother Joseph is now second to the Pharaoh of Egypt. He brings the Children of Israel to live with him in the land of Egypt. Joseph dies at the age of 110, and on his deathbed he says, "When Elohim comes to lead you back to Canaan, you must bring my body out of Egypt (50:25)."

The families of these brothers became the Twelve Tribes of Israel. The Jewish homeland of Canaan, which Adonai promised to the patriarchs and matriarchs and their descendants, is now known as the land of Israel.

סֵפֶר בְּרֵאשִׁית

THE BOOK OF BERESHIT

Masoretic Torah Notes

Here is a list of some of the Masoretic notes for the Book of Bereshit.

1. The Book of Bereshit contains 1,534 verses.
2. The Book of Bereshit contains 50 chapters.
3. The Book of Bereshit contains 12 sidrot.

These are the sidrot in the Book of Bereshit.

סֵפֶר בְּרֵאשִׁית	32	Book of Bereshit
בְּרֵאשִׁית	34	Bereshit
נֹחַ	45	Noah
לֶךְ לְךָ	56	Lech Lecha
וַיֵּרָא	66	Vayera
חַיֵּי שָׂרָה	79	Chayay Sarah
תּוֹלְדוֹת	87	Toldot
וַיֵּצֵא	96	Vayetze
וַיִּשְׁלַח	107	Vayishlach
וַיֵּשֶׁב	119	Vayeshev
מִקֵּץ	128	Miketz
וַיִּגַּשׁ	140	Vayigash
וַיְחִי	148	Vayechi

בְּרֵאשִׁית *Bereshit*

AT THE BEGINNING

1 At the beginning Elohim created the cosmos, which included planet Earth. **2** The earth was shapeless and empty, with darkness on the face of the waters, and life-giving winds from Elohim whooshed over the surface of the water. **3** Elohim said, "Let there be light," and there was light.
4 Elohim saw that the light was good, and Elohim separated the light from the darkness. **5** Elohim called the light "Day," and the darkness He called "Night." And there was evening and there was morning, that very first day.
6 Elohim said, "Let there be a sky in the middle of the water, to separate the waters above from the waters below."
7 Elohim made the sky, and it separated the water below the sky from the water above the sky. And so it was. **8** Elohim named the sky "Heaven." And there was evening and there was morning, on the second day. **9** Elohim said, "Let the waters under the sky be gathered to one place, and let the dry land appear." And so it was. **10** Elohim named the dry land "Earth," and the great pools of water He named "Oceans." And Elohim saw that it was good.

---

4. And Elohim separated the light from the darkness.
The big-bang theory explains that the universe originally consisted of a mixture of a plasma and the light of the primeval fireball. At that time, the universe appeared dark because of the plasma. The sudden transformation of the plasma into atoms shortly after the creation caused the electromagnetic radiation ("light") of the primeval fireball to "separate" from the previously dark universe and shine freely throughout space. This separation is called "decoupling" in scientific terminology.

The passage "Elohim separated the light from the darkness" may be understood as referring to the decoupling of the light from the dark fireball–plasma mixture. This decoupled radiation ("light") was eventually detected 15 billion years later by Penzias and Wilson, earning them the Nobel Prize.
Aviezer

5. And there was evening and there was morning, that very first day.
The word "day" was meant as a period of time. Today, some scientists have theorized that each day or period could be reckoned as millions or billions of years.

5. And there was evening and there was morning, that very first day.
The biblical day begins on the preceding evening. Shabbat and all Jewish holidays begin in the evening and end at the evening of the next day.

5. Elohim called the light "Day," and the darkness He called "Night." And there was evening and there was morning, that very first day.
On the first day, the usual formula, "and Elohim saw that it was good," was omitted. The work that He began was not yet completed since the land and the seas were not finished until the third day. Therefore Elohim's work could not be called "good."

6. Let there be a sky in the middle of the water, to separate the waters above from the waters below.
Here the Torah uses the Hebrew word *rakiah* (sky) as the atmosphere, a gaseous envelope of ozone-oxygen to filter out the harmful ultraviolet rays. The *rakiah* is the barrier between the terrestrial bodies of water and the vapors and gaseous substances emitted from the solar system. Without this protective shield, no vegetable, animal, or human could survive in the solar radiation of heat. The atmosphere (*rakiah*) makes possible organic life, the transportation of sound, and the shading of night and day.

11 Then Elohim said, "Let the earth be filled with vegetation, and plants with seeds and trees that grow all kinds of fruits." And so it happened. **12** The earth was carpeted with vegetation, with plants that produced their own kinds of seeds, and with fruit trees that produced their own kinds of seeds, and Elohim saw that it was good. **13** Then there was evening and it was morning, on the third day. **14** Elohim said, "Let there be bright lights in the sky to separate the day from the night and to mark the time of the holidays, the days, and the years. **15** They shall be lights in the sky, to illuminate the earth." And so it happened. **16** Elohim made two large lights, the stronger light to shine during the day, and the weaker light to shine during the night. He also made the stars. **17** Elohim then positioned them in the sky to illuminate the earth, **18** and to shine by day and by night, and to divide the light and the darkness. And Elohim saw that it was good. **19** And there was evening and there was morning, on the fourth day. **20** Elohim said, "Now let the water be filled with schools of swimming fish. And let birds fly over the land and through the air." **21** Elohim also created huge sea monsters and all kinds of flying creatures. And Elohim saw that it was good. **22** Elohim blessed them all, saying, "Be fruitful and multiply, and fill the waters of the oceans and let the birds fill the air." **23** And there was evening and there was morning, on the fifth day. **24** Elohim said, "Now let the earth give birth to all kinds of tame and wild animals." And so it happened. **25** Elohim made all kinds of wild beasts and tame animals. And Elohim saw that it was good. **26** Then Elohim said, "Let us make a human being in our image like ourselves. Let the human beings be the masters of the fish of the sea, the birds in the sky, the tame animals, and every creature that lives on the earth."

---

14. Let there be bright lights in the sky to separate the day from the night and to mark the time of the holidays, the days, and the years.
Now the sun and the moon are the bearers of light set in the solar system to influence time, to establish the seasons of the year, and to control the stages of the life cycle.

19. And there was evening and there was morning on the fourth day.
Many biblical commentators ranging from the sages of talmudic era down to the present century say that the sixth day refers to six specific phases in the development of the universe-from the initial creation to the appearance of man. According to some scientists much of the biblical text can be understood in its literal sense on the basis of modern science.

26. Let us make a human being.
Now the planet earth has advanced to the point where it is ready to receive the highest form of creation: man and woman. Every need for survival has been met and now the planet stands in readiness to receive its master: humanity.

26. In our image.
There is a relationship between Elohim and humans which other creatures do not share. Humans are able to understand Elohim. Humans are endowed with freedom of intelligence which they can use for the betterment of humankind.

26. Let us make a human being in our image.
The Torah says that man was created in the image or likeness of Elohim. This does not mean that human beings look like Elohim. It means that human beings resemble Elohim's special powers and abilities. Human beings can think, can invent and imagine things, and have a sense of right and wrong.

Because humans have these special abilities, they are Elohim's partners in taking care of the world. We can either pollute the world or clean it up by trying to make the world as clean and beautiful as it was when Elohim created it.

27 Elohim now created a human being to be like himself. In the image of Elohim He created them, male and female.
28 Elohim blessed them. Elohim said to them, "Be fertile and multiply. Settle the land and preserve it. Care for the fish in the sea, the birds of the sky, and every creature that lives on the earth." **29** Elohim said, "I have given you all kinds of seed-producing plants, and trees that produce seed-bearing fruit, for food.
30 And also as food for every beast of the field, every bird of the air, and everything that walks the land and has a living soul." And so it was. **31** Elohim saw that everything that He had created was very good. And there was evening and there was morning, on the sixth day.

2

Heaven and earth, and everything in them were successfully completed. **2** On the seventh day Elohim completed all His work, and on the seventh day He rested from all His work.

---

28. Elohim blessed them. Elohim said to them, "Be fruitful and multiply. Settle the land and preserve it. Care for the fish in the sea, the birds of the sky, and every creature that lives on the earth."
Elohim has made every human a partner in Creation. Elohim created the planet for humans in which they can live and create a civilization. In return, humans must preserve the environment which He created.

We humans are commanded to care for the fish in the sea, the birds in the sky, and every creature, animals and humans. The sages taught the way in which we can care for each other. *Gemilat hasadim* are deeds of loving-kindness extended to another person–the sick, the fallen, the imprisoned, and the dead. You are required to follow Elohim's merciful ways by extending *gemilat hasadim* even when there is no material reward.

28. Be fruitful and multiply.
This is the first mitzvah in the Torah. In essence, it is a mitzvah for people to marry and raise a family. The purpose of this mitzvah is to populate the world with peace- loving families who will make the earth a safer and better place in which to live.

31. Elohim saw that everything that He had created was very good.
The Torah tells us that Elohim created the world in six days.

On the first day He created the light and saw it was good (*tov*). Elohim continued the work of creation for five days. At the end of each day Elohim saw that the day's work was good (*tov*). On the sixth and last day Elohim saw that his work was *tov m'od,* very good.

All the pieces in the creation puzzle fit together and functioned perfectly.

1. Heaven and earth and everything in them were successfully completed.
The evolutionary process which established the cosmos has now been completed. Planet earth has advanced from a terrestrial body devoid of any life and it now overflows with living creatures.

Oceans are filled with fish, jungles resound with roars of animals, birds fly through the air, flowers decorate the earth, and winds rustle through the trees. Now the planet is set for the introduction of the first human created in the *tzelem Elohim*, the image of Elohim. *Aviezer*

2. On the seventh day Elohim completed all His work.
Elohim could have created the cosmos with one single command. Yet he made the world in six days.

The Zohar explains that the six distinct days in the process of creation indicates that Elohim also created the fourth dimension-time.

3 Elohim blessed the seventh day, and He declared it to be holy, because on this day Adonai rested from the work of creation.

The Creation of a Human *2nd Aliyah*

4 This is the account of the creation of the heavens and the earth. **5** All the plants as yet had not emerged out of the ground, and the grasses had not yet sprouted. This was so because Adonai had not yet sent rain to water the soil, and there were no people to farm the land. **6** Then water flowed up from the earth, and it watered the entire surface of the ground. **7** Now Elohim formed a man from the dust of the earth and breathed into his nostrils the breath of life. This is how man became a living person. **8** Now Elohim planted a garden in Eden in the east. There He placed the man that He had created. **9** Elohim planted trees that were beautiful to look at and with fruit that was good to eat, including the Tree of Life in the middle of the garden, and the Tree of Knowledge of Good and Evil. **10** A river flowed out of Eden and watered the garden. From there it divided and became four branch rivers. **11** The name of the first branch river is Pishon. It circles the entire land of Havilah, where gold is found.

---

3. Elohim blessed the seventh day, and He declared it to be holy, because on this day Adonai rested from the work of creation.
Just as creation began with joyous words, "Let there be light," so does the beginning of the Sabbath begin with light. We welcome the Sabbath by lighting the Shabbat candles. The brightly burning candles create an atmosphere of harmony, love, peace, and family togetherness.

Of all the holidays mentioned in the Torah, the Sabbath is the only one mentioned in the Ten Commandments. The laws of Sabbath observance is set down in the Fourth Commandment. The Sabbath is a symbol of freedom and has been given to us to restore the power of the body, mind and soul. It is also a time for us to stop and contemplate the miracle of creation.

7. Now Elohim formed a man from the dust of the earth and breathed into his nostrils the breath of life.
Our sages say that Elohim selected and mixed multicolored earth from all corners of the world, so that no nation, people, or race could claim predominance over another.

Since Elohim blew the breath of life into Adam's nostrils, he became a living creature. A holy divine spark permeates the psyche of every human being. The spark lights up the human personality and allows him to live, love, and learn.

8. Now Elohim planted a garden in Eden in the east.
Eden in Hebrew mans "delight" or "happiness." The Garden of Eden had four rivers flowing through it. The garden was filled with tall trees, green grass, and beautiful flowers. The Garden of Eden was a delightful place in which to live, and at first Adam and Eve found much happiness there.

8. There He placed the man that He had created.
Elohim created one single human so that all of mankind could have one single ancestor. Now, no one could boast and say, "I am more important because my ancestor was more important than yours."

10. A river flowed out of Eden and watered the garden. From there it divided and became four branch rivers.
The main stream divided into four rivers, of which only two, the Euphrates and the Hiddekel (Tigris), are known. The other two, the Pishon and the Gihon, are unknown. Some scholars identify them as the White and the Blue Nile. The two great centers of ancient civilization were the Nile valley and Mesopotamia. The four rivers probably flowed through these two ancient centers.

12 The gold of that land is very pure. Pearls and precious stones were also found there. **13** The name of the second branch river is Gihon. It circles the land of Cush.
14 The name of the third branch river is the Tigris, which flows to the east of Assyria. The fourth branch river is the Euphrates.
15 Elohim placed the man in the Garden of Eden to farm and care for it. **16** Adonai gave the man a warning, saying, "You may eat from every tree of the garden.
17 But you must not eat from the Tree of Knowledge of Good and Evil, for on the day you eat from it, you will surely die." **18** Elohim said, "It is not good for man to be alone. I will make a companion for him." **19** Elohim had created every wild beast and every bird in the air. Now He brought the animals to the man to see what he would name each one. Whatever the man called each living thing would forever remain its name.

The Tree of Knowledge
3rd Aliyah

20 The man named every tame animal and every bird in the air, as well as all the wild beasts. However, the man still did not have a suitable companion for himself. **21** Elohim then made the man fall into a deep sleep, and while he slept, He took one of his ribs and closed the place from which it was taken.
22 Elohim made the rib that he took from the man into a woman, and He brought her to the man. **23** The man exclaimed, "She is bone from my bones and flesh from my flesh: She shall be called WoMan because she was taken from Man." **24** This is why a man leaves his father and mother and marries. So he and his wife can become united as one family. **25** The man and his wife were both naked, but they were not ashamed by each other.

3 The snake was the trickiest of all the wild animals that Elohim had created. The snake asked the woman, "Did Elohim really say that you may not eat from any of the trees of the garden?" **2** The woman answered the snake, "We may eat from the fruit of all the other trees of the garden.
But Adonai warned us 'Do not eat, or even touch, the fruit of the tree that is in the middle of the garden, or else you will die.'"

---

17. But you must not eat from the Tree of Knowledge of Good and Evil, for on the day you eat from it, you will surely die.
Elohim made a beautiful garden as a home for the first man and woman. They were free to use all the powers of their mind and body to enjoy the garden and its fruits, but they also had to exercise self-discipline. They had to restrain themselves by not eating from the fruit of the Tree of Knowledge.

22. Elohim made the rib that he took from the man into a woman.
The first woman was created from the body of a human. Since that moment all humans have been created within the body of a woman.

22. Elohim made the rib that he took from the man into a woman.
Actually, both men and women have exactly the same number of ribs! Even the so-called floating rib, called by this term because it is not connected in the same way as the others, is the same in men as it is in women. Adam was the world's first tissue donor. Today donated body parts from live or dead bodies have helped people live longer and saved numerous lives.
Shenash

1. The snake was the trickiest of all the wild animals that Elohim had created.
In the ancient world, the snake was a symbol of evil. The midrash says that the snake initially had the same upright stature and ate the same food as humans. Only after Adam's sin was it punished with the curse, "You will crawl on your belly all the days of your life."

4 The snake hissed to the woman, "No! You will certainly not die! **5** Elohim knows that on the day you eat from it, your mind will be opened, and you will be like the angels, and you will know good and evil."

6 The woman was convinced that the fruit of the tree was good to eat and that the tree was a way to gain wisdom. She took some of its fruit and ate it. She also gave some to her husband, and he ate it.

7 The minds of both of them were opened, and they became ashamed because they were naked. So they sewed together fig leaves and made loincloths for themselves.

8 Suddenly, toward evening, they heard Elohim moving about in the garden. The man and his wife hid themselves from Elohim among the trees of the garden. **9** Elohim called to the man, and said, "Why are you trying to hide?"

10 The man answered, "I hid because I heard Your voice in the garden, and I was afraid because I was naked."

11 Then Elohim asked, "Who told you that you are naked? Did you eat from the tree from which I warned you not to eat?" **12** The man answered, "The woman that You gave me, she brought me the fruit from the tree and I ate it."

13 Then Adonai said to the woman, "Why did you disobey me?"
The woman replied, "The snake tricked me and I ate it."

14 So Elohim said to the snake, "Because you did this, you will be cursed more than any other animal, of all the wild beasts
You will crawl on your belly, and you will eat dust all the days of your life. **15** From now on, you and the woman will be enemies and your children and her children will also be enemies. He will strike you in the head, and you will bite him in the heel."

---

4. The snake hissed to the woman, "No you will certainly not die!"
The sneaky snake, who at the creation had the power to speak cleverly, charms the woman to defy Elohim and eat from the tree in the middle of the garden.

4. No! You will certainly not die.
The Rabbis tell us that the serpent was jealous of Adam and Eve's happiness and so it decided to lead them to sin.

6. The woman was convinced that the fruit of the tree was good to eat and that the tree was a way to gain wisdom.
Elohim created humans with free will. They could on their own make decisions. They even decided to taste the forbidden fruit to gain knowledge. Since that time snakes-in-the-grass have been tempting people to experience forbidden fruits.

9. Why are you trying to hide?
Elohim asked Adam a number of questions. Each question gave Adam a chance to confess and to repent and resolve not to commit the error again. Instead, Adam offered excuses and showed his guilt by saying he was naked. Finally, he blamed Eve.

14. Because you did this, you will be cursed more than any other animal.
Unfortunately, the snake was clever without being wise. He was determined to use his knowledge for a bad purpose. He proceeded to use his knowledge to mislead Eve.

Knowledge can be used for good or for bad. We can use our knowledge to make life better for others and for ourselves. We can also use knowledge for selfish purposes. One scientist will use knowledge to help human beings. Another scientist may use knowledge only to gain wealth and power.

Had he used his cleverness for good, the snake might have been considered "a wise creature." As it turned out, he used his knowledge to trick poor Eve into doing something she was not supposed to do and he turned out to be "a snake in the grass."
Chiel

16 To the woman He said, "You will give birth in great pain. You will love your husband, but he will be your master." **17** To Adam He said, "Because you listened to your wife, and ate from the tree about which I warned you, saying, 'Do not eat from it,' I have cursed the ground and your life will be a struggle to grow food from the soil.
18 It will grow thorns and weeds for you, and you will be forced to eat wild grass from the field.

> **19** By the sweat of your brow you will eat bread.
> And in the end you will return to the earth dead;
> From the earth you were created.
> You are dust, and to dust you shall return."

20 The man named his wife Eve (Chavah), because she was the mother of all life. **21** Elohim clothed Adam and his wife with leather garments that He made for them.

Expulsion from the Garden *4th Aliyah*

22 Elohim said, "Man has now become like one of us in knowing good and evil. What if he decides to eat from the Tree of Life and live forever?" **23** So Elohim drove man from the Garden of Eden, to farm the earth from which he was created.
24 He drove the man away and stationed cherubim (angels) with the revolving sword at the east of Eden, to guard the path to the Tree of Life.

4 Eve became pregnant and gave birth to Cain. She said, "With Adonai's help I have given birth to a child." **2** Once again, she gave birth, this time to his brother Abel. Abel became a shepherd, while Cain became a farmer.
3 One time, Cain brought some of his crops as an offering to Adonai. **4** But Abel brought some of the finest lambs in his flock. Elohim was pleased with Abel's offering, **5** but He was not pleased with Cain's offering. Cain became very angry and sad.
6 Adonai said to Cain,

> "Why are you so angry and sad?
> **7** If you do good, your future will be special.
> But if you do not do right, Then only sin will be at your door,
> but you can overcome it."

---

20. The man named his wife Eve (Chavah) because she was the mother of all life.
Adonai gave man intelligence and freedom through which he named the animals. But this was not enough. Man needed company for himself as a person, another like him. The one flesh of Adam became two as Adonai created Eve from Adam's rib.

2. Abel became a shepherd, while Cain became a farmer.
The two brothers were given different trades so they would not compete and be jealous of each other.

6. Why are you so angry and sad?
The Rabbis preached, "A mistake can always be corrected."
It does not make any sense to be concerned about an incident that has already occurred. Now, you can learn from your mistake.
Stop being angry, forget the past, and look toward an improved spiritual future.

8 One day when they were in the field, Cain said something to his brother Abel. Cain became angry at his brother Abel, and murdered him.
9 Adonai asked Cain,

"Where is Abel your brother?"
"I do not know," replied Cain.
"Am I my brother's keeper?"

10 Adonai said, "What have you done? Your brother's blood is crying to me from out of the earth. **11** From now on you shall be cursed by the earth that opened up to receive your brother's blood spilled by your hand.
12 When you farm the earth, it will no longer give you new crops. And from now on you will be a fugitive and wander the world." **13** Cain wept and said, "I cannot survive your punishment. **14** Today you have driven me from my land. And also from your presence. Now whoever finds me will kill me." **15** Adonai said to him, "Very well! Then whoever kills Cain will be punished seven times as much." Adonai placed a mark on Cain to prevent anyone from killing him. **16** Cain left Adonai's presence and settled in the land of Nod, to the east of Eden.

---

8. Cain became angry at his brother Abel, and murdered him.
The Hebrew word for Cain is *ky-in*. The Hebrew word *ky-in* also means spear or lance. Is there a connection? Did *ky-in* murder Abel with a *ky-in*?

There are two different scenarios of the quarrel between the brothers. Cain was a farmer and created a successful farm on a fertile piece of land with a good source of water. Abel was jealous and wanted the land and the water for his flocks. Perhaps Cain, to protect his crops from Abel's flock, built a fence around his farm. Now Abel's animals had no source of water, so he broke the fence and his animals destroyed Cain's crops.
Shenash

9. Am I my brother's keeper?
Cain was wrong to ask this question. Humans are not animals. Each human has free will and is held responsible for his brother's welfare.

12 When you farm the earth, it will no longer give you new crops.
Elohim created humans to work for their own existence; he who does not work shall not eat
Midrash Rabbah

12. From now on you will be a fugitive and wander the world.
Adonai gave Cain two punishments because he killed his brother, Abel. He would become a wanderer looking for a hospitable place to live. Also, since he was guilty of murder, his reputation would precede him. "I will mark you with a special mark."

13. Cain wept and said, "I cannot survive your punishment."
The Hebrew words "I cannot survive" can be also be translated as "I cannot be forgiven."

16. In the land of Nod.
The name Nod comes from the Hebrew word *nadah,* meaning isolation or wandering. The land of Nod was east of the Garden of Eden where Cain settled down and married.

16. Cain left Adonai's presence and settled in the land of Nod, to the east of Eden.
Cain carried with him the terrible burden of his crime. He was not a hardened criminal, and he suffered greatly for the wrong which he had committed. On many sleepless nights he wished with all his heart that Abel were alive again. He deeply regretted the terrible wrong which he had done.

When Elohim saw the suffering and sorrow of Cain, He decided that Cain had paid for his crime. And Elohim showed mercy to the unhappy, homeless man. He accepted Cain's plea for forgiveness and put a mark upon Cain's forehead that all who met him might know that he had paid his penalty. Cain was now to be left in peace.
Chiel

17 Cain's wife became pregnant and gave birth to Enoch. Cain founded a city, and he named the city Enoch, after his son.
18 Enoch fathered a son named Irad. Irad fathered a son named Mechuyael. Mechuyael fathered a son named Methushael. Methushael fathered a son named Lemech.

The Family of Lemech   5th Aliyah

19 Lemech married two women. The first one's name was Adah, and the second one's name was Zillah. **20** Adah gave birth to Yaval. He was the ancestor of all those who live in tents and raise cattle. **21** His brother's name was Yuval. He was the first to play the harp and flute. **22** Zillah also had a son called Tuval Cain; he was a maker of copper and iron tools. Tuval Cain's sister was called Naamah.
23 Lemech said to his wives, Adah and Zillah, "Listen to me; listen to my confession. I have killed a man by attacking him, and a child by beating him.
24 If Cain shall be punished seven times, then the revenge against me is that I will be punished seventy-seven times."
25 Adam's wife became pregnant again, and she gave birth to a son. She named him Seth, "Because Adonai has granted me another child in place of Abel, whom Cain killed." **26** A son was also born to Seth, and Seth named him Enosh. It was then that people started to pray to Adonai.

Descendants of Adam   6th Aliyah

5 This is the book of the history of mankind. When Elohim created man, He made him in the likeness of Elohim. **2** He created them male and female. On the day that they were created, He blessed them and named them humans.

---

17. Cain founded a city, and he named the city Enoch, after his son.
Archaeologists often find ancient cities buried on top of one another, forming a big mound. Sometimes many, many cities can be found within such a mound. These little hills are called *tels* as in the name of the modern Israeli city Tel Aviv.

When the archaeologists cut into a tel, they take a slice away and the inside is like a huge layer cake. Naturally the nearer to the top the remains of a city are found, the more recently that city existed; the further down the layer, the older the city.

One such tel is Jericho, situated near very fertile ground. Way down near the bottom of this tel are the remains of one of the oldest cities ever uncovered by man. This could be Enoch, founded by Cain, and according to the Bible, the very first city to be founded by man.

21. His brother's name was Yuval. He was the first to play the harp and flute.
Music had a very important place in the life of ancient times. It provided music for prayer and a rhythmic beat for group activities. Music also played an important role in individual celebrations and national events.

Miriam and the women sang and celebrated with timbrels at the victory at the Sea of Reeds. The Levites played instruments – harps, lyres, drums, bugles, cymbals, and fifes – at ceremonies in Solomon's Temple in Jerusalem.

Among the oldest known musical instruments are the *kinnor*, which is the lyre, and the *ugah*, a kind of fife.

Many of the psalms are introduced by a notation that it was accompanied by a musical instrument.

22. Tuval Cain's sister was called Naamah.
The name Naamah means pleasant, agreeable, charming and sweet.

3 Adam lived 130 years, and he had a son just like himself. He named him Seth. **4** Adam lived 800 years after he fathered Seth, and then he had more sons and daughters. **5** In all, Adam lived 930 years, and he died.
6 Seth lived 105 years, and he fathered a son called Enosh.
7 Seth lived 807 years after he had Enosh, and he had more sons and daughters.
8 Seth lived 912 years, and then he died. **9** When Enosh was 90, he fathered a son called Kenan.
10 Enosh lived 815 years after he had Kenan, and he fathered more sons and daughters.
11 Enosh was 905 years old when he died.
12 When Kenan was 70 years old, he fathered a son called Mahalalel.
13 Kenan lived 840 years after he fathered Mahalalel, and he had more sons and daughters.
14 Kenan was 910 years old when he died. **15** When Mahalalel was 65 years old, he fathered a son called Yered. **16** Mahalalel lived 830 years after he fathered Yered, and he had more sons and daughters. **17** Mahalalel was 895 years old when he died. **18** When Yered was 162 years old, he fathered a son called Enoch. **19** Yered lived 800 years after he fathered Enoch, and he had more sons and daughters. **20** Yered was 962 years old when he died.
21 When Enoch was 65 years old, he fathered a son called Methuselah. **22** Enoch walked with Elohim for 300 years after he fathered Methuselah, and he had more sons and daughters. **23** Enoch died when he was 365 years old. **24** Elohim was pleased with Enoch's way of life. And Enoch disappeared because Elohim had taken him.

The Birth of Noah
7th Aliyah

25 When Methuselah was 187 years old, he fathered a son called Lemech. **26** Methuselah lived 782 years after he fathered Lemech, and he had more sons and daughters.

---

5. In all, Adam lived 930 years, and then he died.
Adam, Seth, Enosh, Kenan, and Jared all lived to be more than 900 years of age.

The Torah lets us know that the first people to walk on the earth lived for hundreds of years. The Torah in its own way is teaching us a hygiene lesson. In the beginning, the air was pure and the streams and rivers were unpolluted. The earth was fertile without impurities. The first humans were vegetarians and hard-working farmers and herders who performed physical tasks. People no doubt had lower levels of LDL (bad cholesterol) and higher levels of HDL (good cholesterol). Is it any wonder that under this ideal regimen, they lived to a ripe old age?

22. Enoch walked with Elohim for 300 years after he fathered Methuselah.
The commentator Onkeles translates the phrase as "Enoch walked in the fear of Adonai for 300 years."

24. Elohim was pleased with Enoch's way of life.
Enoch lived in an evil generation. Despite all the evils, Enoch lived a righteous life.
Rashi

24. Enoch disappeared because Elohim had taken him.
According to tradition, Enoch was taken up to heaven alive as a reward for his piety.

26. Methuselah lived 782 years after he fathered Lemech.
Methuselah lived 969 years, the longest life of any human being in the history of mankind.

27 Methuselah was 969 years old when he died. **28** When Lemech was 182 years old, he fathered a son. **29** He named him Noah, saying, "This one will relieve us from the drudgery and labor of farming the soil that Adonai has cursed." **30** Lemech lived 595 years after he fathered Noah, and he had more sons and daughters.
31 Lemech was 777 years old when he died.
32 When Noah was 500 years old, he had fathered three sons: Shem, Ham, and Yefeth.

6

Humanity began to increase on the face of the earth, and children were born to them. **2** The Nefilim (giants) appeared and saw that the daughters of the humans were beautiful, so they married them. **3** Adonai said, "From now on, I will not tolerate man forever, since he is nothing but flesh. From now on his life span will be 120 years."
4 In those days the giants were on the earth. Afterwards the giants married the daughters of man and they had children. The giants were the strongest ones who ever existed and men of great bravery.

The Wicked People *Maftir*

5 Adonai saw that the people on earth were becoming more wicked. All day long they thought only of evil.
6 Adonai was angry and regretted that He had created man, and He was very sad. **7** Adonai said, "I will erase from the face of the earth the humans, animals, beasts, and birds of the sky that I have created. I am sorry that I ever created them."
8 However, Noah was a special person in the eyes of Adonai.

---

29. This one will relieve us from the drudgery and labor of farming the soil that Adonai has cursed.
Before Noah there were no farming tools, such as rakes, hoes, and shovels. Noah introduced a variety of tools which made life easier for the farmers.
Rashi

30. Lemech lived 595 years after he fathered Noah.
When Noah was born, his father said, "May this child give us a rest from God's curse." And so he named the boy Noah, which is the Hebrew for "rest."

3. From now on his life span will be 120 years.
Adonai gave the people 120 years to stop sinning, but the people only got worse. Noah was the only person who was trying to live a righteous life.

4. The giants were the strongest ones who ever existed and men of great bravery.
Because of their great strength they were successful warriors. The Torah calls these giants Nephilim, but this race of giants soon died out.

5. Adonai saw that the people on earth were becoming more wicked.
Man was created by Adonai to follow His laws. Therefore, when man is unjust to his fellow man, he sins against Adonai and he forfeits the right to exist. As the Rabbis taught, "The world is preserved by three things: by truth, by justice, and by peace."

5. Adonai saw that the people on earth were becoming more wicked.
Rabbis tell us that every person in the world is born with a good side and a bad side. Every person has the freedom to choose between good and evil. The good side is called *yetzer hatov*; the bad side is called *yetzer hara*.

נֹחַ Noah

NOAH'S LIFE

9 This is the story of Noah's life:
Noah was the only righteous man in his generation and lived according to the rules of Elohim. **10** Noah fathered three sons: Shem, Ham, and Yefeth.
11 But the people were evil, and the land was filled with violence. **12** Elohim saw all the evil that was in the world. **13** Elohim said to Noah, "I have decided to destroy all the living creatures that have filled the world with violence. I will therefore wipe them off the face of the earth. **14** Hurry! Make an ark of cypress wood. Divide the ark into compartments. Waterproof the inside and outside with tar.
15 This is how you shall construct it: Make the ark 450 feet long and 75 feet wide, and 45 feet high. **16** Make a skylight for the ark. Make it slanted, so that it is 18 inches wide on top. Construct a door on the side of the ark and build three decks on the inside of the ark.
17 I am about to send a flood, and water will cover the earth and destroy every living creature. Everything that is alive on land will die.
18 But with you I will keep My pledge and keep you safe. Together you and your sons, your wife, and your sons' wives will be safe on the ark.
19 Bring into the ark two of each kind of living creature. They shall be male and female.
20 From each kind of bird, from each kind of cattle, and from each kind of animal, bring two of each kind so they will stay alive. **21** Make sure to take enough food to eat. Enough food for you and the animals."
22 Noah did exactly all that Adonai had commanded him.

---

9. Noah was the only righteous man in his generation.
Noah lived in an evil generation, surrounded by criminals and murderers. Despite the evil surroundings, Noah rose above the population and remained a decent human being. The Torah calls Noah a *tzadik*, meaning a righteous person. The word *tzadik* is related to the word *tzedakah*, meaning righteousness.

9. Noah was the only righteous man in his generation.
Rashi comments that had Noah lived in Abraham's generation he would not have achieved his status. The Torah credits Noah with trying to live righteously. However, Noah never makes an effort or appeals to Adonai to reconsider his verdict.

10. Noah fathered three sons: Shem, Ham, and Yefeth.
Shem was Noah's eldest son. Some believe that it is for this reason that the people and languages are referred to as Semitic. These Middle Eastern languages include Hebrew, Assyrian, Aramaic, and Arabic.

11. The land was filled with violence.
The land was filled with robbery and immorality.
Rashi

14. Hurry! Make an ark of cypress wood.
The Rabbis say that Noah and his three sons worked for 120 years to complete the ark. While the ark was being built, Noah continued to warn the people that their wickedness would bring a great flood and would destroy them. For 120 years the wicked people laughed at Noah and continued to sin. Finally Elohim sent the flood.

The Flood
2nd Aliyah

7 Adonai said to Noah, "Now you and your family must come into the ark. I have seen that you are the only righteous person in this generation. **2** Take seven pairs of every clean animal, each consisting of a male and its mate. Of every animal that is not clean, take two, a male and its mate.

3 Of the birds of the heaven, also take seven pairs, each consisting of a male and its mate. They will remain alive on the face of the earth. **4** For in another seven days I will bring rain on the earth for forty days and forty nights. I will obliterate every living creature that I have made from the face of the earth."

5 Noah did all that Adonai had commanded. **6** Noah was 600 years old when the flood started and water covered the earth. **7** Noah, and his sons, his wife, and his sons' wives, came into the ark ahead of the waters of the flood.

8 The clean animals, the animals that were not clean, the birds, and all that walked the earth **9** came two by two to Noah, into the ark. They were male and female, just as Adonai had commanded Noah.

10 Seven days passed, and the flood waters were on the earth. **11** It was in the 600th year of Noah's life, in the second month, on the seventeenth of the month. On that day all the wellsprings of the great deep burst forth and the floodgates of the heavens were opened. **12** It continued to rain on the earth for forty days and forty nights.

13 On that very day, Noah boarded the ark along with his sons, Shem, Ham, and Yefeth. Noah's wife and the three wives of his sons were with them.

14 They came along with every kind of beast, every kind of livestock, every kind of land animal, and every separate kind of flying creature – every bird and every winged animal. **15** All creatures that had a breath of life came to Noah, two by two into the ark;

---

4. For in another seven days I will bring rain on the earth for forty days and forty nights.
According to Jewish law, we mourn for seven days (*shivah*) when a family member dies. Similarly Adonai waited for seven days before unleashing the flood as a symbol of mourning for His creations which were soon to be destroyed.

5. Noah did all that Adonai had commanded him.
There were many ways in which Adonai could have saved Noah. Why did He put Noah through all the trouble of constructing an ark? He did so in order that the men of his generation might see Noah working at it for many years and might ask him, "What do you need this for?" He would then explain to them that Adonai was about to bring a flood upon the earth. Perhaps then they would repent.

11. On that day all the wellsprings of the deep burst forth and the floodgates of the heavens were opened.
The Zohar states that in the future, the gates of knowledge above ("the heavens") and the fountains of knowledge below ("the great deep") will be opened. The Vilna Gaon takes this passage to refer to the importance of science for the understanding of Torah. He writes that "in order to understand and acquire the wisdom of the Torah, which is bound up with the light of the supreme wisdom, it is necessary to study also the seven wisdoms [branches of science] hidden in the lower world, the world of nature." He greatly encouraged his disciples to engage in scientific studies for this purpose.

12. It continued to rain upon the earth for forty days and forty nights.
Rashi says that initially the rain descended slowly, so if the populace repented, the rain would be a blessing and just water the crops. When the people refused to repent, the rain turned into a flood, which lifted the ark so that it floated on the surface of the water.

16 those that came were male and female living creatures, just as Elohim had commanded Noah. Adonai then sealed them inside.

It Rained for Forty Days and Nights *3rd Aliyah*

17 There was a flood on the earth for forty days. The waters increased and lifted the ark, and it rose from the ground.
18 The waters surged and increased very much, and the ark began to drift on the surface of the water. **19** The waters on the earth flooded upward, and all the high mountains under the heavens were covered. **20** The waters surged upwards to a height of 23 feet, above all the mountains.
21 All the creatures that lived on the earth perished: birds, livestock, wild beasts, and everything that lived on the land, as well as every human being. **22** Everything on dry land whose life was sustained by breathing died.
23 The flood wiped out every creature that had been on the face of the earth: humans, livestock, beasts, and birds of the sky. They were all wiped out from the earth. Only Noah and those with him in the ark survived.
24 The waters flooded the earth for 150 days.

8 Elohim kept watch over Noah, and over all the beasts and livestock with him in the ark. Adonai made a wind blow over the earth, and the waters began to go down. **2** The wellsprings of the deep and the floodgates of heaven were sealed. The downpour from the heavens stopped. **3** The waters receded from the earth. They continued to lessen, and at the end of 150 days the water had decreased.
4 In the seventh month, on the seventeenth day of the month, the ark came to rest on the Ararat Mountains.

---

17. There was a flood on the earth for forty days.
The punishment decreed by Adonai took forty days and forty nights to reach its peak.

18. The waters surged and increased very much, and the ark began to drift on the surface of the water.
The ark was heavily laden, and at first it had much difficulty in floating, but after many days of rain there was enough water to raise the ark and lift it above the earth.

19–20. The waters on the earth flooded upward, and all the high mountains under the heavens were covered. The waters surged upwards to a height of 23 feet, above all the mountains.
The waters covered the mountains 23 feet above the tallest mountain.

23. The flood wiped out every creature that had been on the face of the earth: humans, livestock, beasts, and birds of the sky.
Only the creatures who lived in the water survived, since they had not been corrupted by the land creatures.

23. Only Noah and those with him in the ark survived.
Adonai did not relieve Noah of all cares during the flood. He had to tend the most complete zoo in the world!

1. Adonai made a wind blow over the earth, and the waters began to go down.
As Adonai's anger began to go down, so too did the waters. *Midrash Tanhuma*

4. The ark came to rest on the Ararat Mountains.
Some archaeologists identify this as Mount Ararat, the highest mountain in Turkey.

5 The waters continued to decrease until the tenth month. On the tenth month, on the first of the month, the mountain peaks became visible.

6 After forty days, Noah opened the window he had made in the ark. **7** He sent out the raven, and it departed. It flew back and forth until the water had dried up from the land's surface.

8 He then sent out a dove to see whether the water had disappeared from the land's surface. **9** The dove could not find any place to rest its feet, and so it returned to the ark. There was still water over all the earth's surface. Noah stretched out his hand and brought the dove back into the ark.

10 Noah waited another seven days, and he once again sent the dove out from the ark. **11** The dove returned to him toward evening, and there was a freshly picked olive leaf in its beak. Now Noah knew that the water had subsided from the earth. **12** He waited another seven days and again sent out the dove. This time the dove did not return to him. **13** In the 601st year of Noah's life, in the first month, on the first of the month, the land was drying, so Noah removed the roof of the ark. He saw that the earth's surface was beginning to dry. **14** By the second month, on the twenty-seventh day of the month, the land was completely dry.

Leave the Ark
4th Aliyah

15 Elohim spoke to Noah, saying, **16** "Leave the ark – you, your wife, your sons, and your son's wives. **17** Take with you all the living creatures, birds, livestock, and all the creeping things. Let them populate the land. Let them breed and multiply on the earth." **18** Noah left the ark along with his sons, his wife, and his sons' wives. **19** Every beast, every animal, and every bird – all left the ark by families.

---

5. On the tenth month, on the first of the month, the mountain peaks became visible.
The water started receding after 150 days, or almost half a year after the flood had first begun.

11. The dove returned to him toward evening, and there was a freshly picked olive leaf in its beak.
The fresh green olive leaf was proof that the waters of the flood had receded to the point that plant life could grow.

13. Noah removed the roof of the ark. He saw that the earth's surface was beginning to dry.
Noah just removed a part of the roof so as to get a panoramic view of the area. The waters had not drained completely away. The land was still waterlogged, and it was impossible to find any completely dry ground.

14. By the second month, on the twenty-seventh day of the month, the land was completely dry.
Now the land was dry enough and the animals and the humans on the ark could safely walk on it.

18. Noah left the ark along with his sons, his wife, and his sons' wives.
The midrash says that when Noah left the ark and stepped on dry land, he looked all around him. Wherever he looked there was destruction and desolation from the waters of the flood. Noah was very sad and he cried to Adonai,

"Adonai, you are merciful, but you did not show any mercy for the creatures of the world whom you destroyed." Adonai heard Noah's words and answered, "Noah, you are a foolish man. When I told you there would be a flood, you did not object. When I told you that all living things would die in it, you did not object. When I told you to build an ark so that only you would be saved, you still did not object. Now that the earth has been destroyed and all living beings who were not in the ark have died, you object. Where were you when you could have spoken and saved the world?"

20 Now Noah built an altar to Adonai. He took a few of the clean animals and clean birds, and he sacrificed them as offerings on the altar. **21** Adonai was pleased with the sacrifice, and Adonai said to Himself, "I will never again curse the soil because of man's evil. I will never again strike down all life as I have just done.
22 As long as the earth remains,
>> seedtime and harvest, cold and heat,
>> summer and winter, and
>> day and night, shall never again cease to exist."

9

Elohim blessed Noah and his children. He said to them, "Be fruitful and multiply, and fill the earth. **2** All the wild beasts of the earth, and all the birds of the sky, all creatures on earth and all the fish in the sea, I have placed them in your hands.
3 Every living creature as well as the grain and vegetables are yours to eat as food. I have now given you everything.
4 But you must not eat the flesh of a creature that is still alive.
5 Murder is forbidden. Animals that kill humans must die. Any human who kills another must be punished.
6 Any human who spills the blood of another human shall have his own blood spilled, because Adonai made humans in His own image.
>> **7** Now be fruitful
>> and multiply,
>> populate the earth."

---

20. Now Noah built an altar to Adonai.
Noah was grateful to Adonai for saving him and his family, so he sacrificed birds and animals. Noah was the first to build altars for sacrifices.

21. Adonai was pleased with the sacrifice.
This term is frequently found when the text talks about sacrifices. It means that Adonai accepted the sacrifice.

22. As long as the earth remains, seed time and harvest...shall never cease to exist.
The flood disrupted the climate and the seasons of the year. Now Adonai promises never again to interfere with the balance of nature which existed before the catastrophic flood. *Sforno*

4 But you must not eat the flesh of a creature that is still alive.
From Noah's time onwards, humans were no longer required to be vegetarians. They were permitted to slaughter animals and eat their flesh.

1. Elohim blessed Noah and his children.
After Noah, his family, and the animals left the ark, Adonai blessed them all. He gave Noah seven fundamental laws for human survival. The seven Noahide laws are binding on all human beings, not just the people of Israel. They prohibit 1. idolatry, 2. murder, 3. theft, 4. blasphemy, 5. incest, 6. and eating the flesh of a living animal, 7. and require promotion of justice. The Rabbis say that everyone who observes these laws is worthy of life in the world to come.

6. Any human who spills the blood of another human shall have his own blood spilled, because Adonai made humans in His own image.
Any human who kills another must be punished.

7. Now be fruitful and multiply, populate the earth.
Noah and his family were given the task of rebuilding a new and ethical humanity to take the place of all those people who had been destroyed by the flood.

The Rainbow
5th Aliyah

8 Elohim said to Noah and his sons, **9** "I am now making a covenant with you and with your descendants. **10** And with every living creature, the birds, the livestock, all the beasts of the earth who were with you in the ark.

11 I will make My covenant with you, and with all life. I will never again send a flood to destroy the earth."

12 Elohim said, "This is My sign of the covenant between Me, you, and every living creature that is with you, for all generations: **13** I have placed My rainbow in the clouds, and it shall be a sign of the covenant between Me and the earth. **14** When I send clouds over the earth, the rainbow will be seen among the clouds. **15** I will then remember the covenant that exists between Me, you, and every living creature. Never again will I send a flood to destroy all life. **16** The rainbow will be in the clouds, and I will see it to remember the eternal covenant between Elohim and every living creature on the earth."

17 Elohim said to Noah, "This is the sign of the covenant that I have made between Me and all living creatures on the earth."

The Descendants of Noah
6th Aliyah

18 The sons of Noah who emerged from the ark were Shem, Ham, and Yefeth. Ham was the father of Canaan.

19 These three were Noah's sons, and from them came all the nations of the whole world.

20 Noah began as a farmer, and he planted a vineyard.

21 He drank some of his own wine and became drunk and was naked in his tent. **22** Ham, the father of Canaan, saw his father naked, and he told it to his two brothers.

---

11. I will make My covenant with you and with all life. I will never again send a flood to destroy the earth.
The covenant was between two parties: Adonai and humanity. If humans desist from the spilling of innocent blood by murder, injustice, corruption, violence, and wars, then I, Adonai, will never again send a catastrophe to destroy the earth.

13. I have placed my rainbow in the clouds and it shall be a sign of the covenant between me and the earth.
The sight of the multicolored rainbow stretching across the sky will assure the people that Elohim remembers His promise never to send another terrible flood.

17. Elohim said to Noah, " This is the sign of the covenant that I have made between Me and all living creatures on the earth."
The rainbow is a sign of Elohim's covenant in His lovingkindness and mercy toward the people in the world.

There is a special prayer which is recited when we see the rainbow. "I praise Adonai, who is Ruler over all, who remembers the covenant, is faithful to His covenant, and keeps His promise."

19. These three were Noah's sons, and from them came all of the nations of the whole world.
The term Noachides denotes all of the descendants of Noah, who survived the flood.

21. He drank some of his own wine and became drunk and was naked in his tent.
Some commentators excuse Noah because he was unaware that wine had an intoxicating effect. The text shows how overindulgence in intoxicating liquors can result in sin.

23 Shem and Yefeth took a garment and placed it over their shoulders, and walking backwards, they covered their father's naked body. They looked the other way and did not see their naked father.
24 When Noah awoke from his drunken sleep and understood what his youngest son had done to him, **25** he angrily said, "Cursed be Canaan! He shall be a servant to his brothers!"
26 He then said, "Blessed be Elohim, the Savior of Shem! Let Canaan be his slave!
27 May Elohim bless Yefeth He shall dwell in the tents of Shem and let Canaan be their servant!"
28 After the flood Noah lived for 350 years. **29** Noah was 950 years old when he died.

10

This is the history of Noah's sons, Shem, Ham, and Yefeth. Many children were born to them after the flood.
2 The sons of Yefeth were Gomer, Magog, Madai, Yavan, Tuval, Meshech, and Tiras. **3** The descendants of Gomer were Ashkenaz, Riphath, and Togarmah. **4** The sons of Yavan were Elishah, Tarshish, Kittim, and Dodanim.
5 Their descendants became seafarers. Each one founded a nation and developed its own separate language. **6** The sons of Ham were Cush, Mitzraim, Put, and Canaan:
7 The sons of Cush were Sava, Havilah, Sabtah, Raamah, and Savteca. The sons of Raamah were Sheba and Dedan.
8 Cush was the father of Nimrod, who was a mighty ruler.
9 He was a mighty hunter before Adonai. There is a saying, "Like Nimrod, a mighty hunter blessed by Adonai!" **10** The foundation of his kingdom was in Babylon, as well as the cities of Erekh, Akkad, and Calneh, in the land of Shinar.

---

1. This is the history of Noah's sons, Shem, Ham, and Yefeth.
All the nations of the world are traced to the sons of Noah. The Yefethites formed the Indo-European peoples. The Hamites formed the African People and descendents of Shem became the Semites.

2. The sons of Yefeth were Gomer, Magog, Madai, Yavan, Tuval, … etc.
Archaeological sources have identified Madai (10:2) as the Meder; Yavan (10:2) are the Ionians or Greeks; Ashkenaz (10:3) probably refers to the Scythians; Tarshish is probably Spain.

6. The sons of Ham were Cush, Mitzraim, Put, and Canaan.
Canaan was the son of Ham. His descendants occupied the land of Canaan.

The land of Canaan was about the size of the state of Massachusetts. It was a narrow band of fertile plains, lush valleys, and wooded mountains about 150 miles long and 50 miles wide. Canaan stretched about 50 miles from the Mediterranean Sea to the canyons of the Dead Sea and the Jordan Valley, and 150 miles from Mount Hermon in the north to the Negev in the south.

6. Mitzraim.
This is the Hebrew name for Egypt.

8. Cush was the father of Nimrod, who was a mighty ruler.
Nimrod was a warrior and conqueror who ruled over a large kingdom in the land of Shinar. One of the cities in his kingdom was Erech (Warka). Erech, one of the oldest Sumerian cities, was located about 120 miles south of Babylon on the banks of the Euphrates River. It was a busy commercial center with magnificent, towering temples.

10. In the land of Shinar.
Shinar is the Hebrew name for Babylonia.

11 Asshur left Babylon and built the cities of Nineveh, Rechovoth-Ir, and Calach, **12** as well as Resen, which is between Nineveh and Calach. Nineveh is a great city.

13 Mitzraim was the ancestor of Ludim, the Anamim, the Lehabim, the Naftuchim, **14** the Pathrusim, and the Casluchim from whom the Philistines descended and the Caphtorim.

15 Canaan fathered Sidon (his first-born) and Heth, **16** as well as the Jebusites, the Amorites, the Girgashites, **17** the Hivites, the Arkites, the Sinites,

18 the Arvadites, the Tzemarites, and the Chamathites: Later on the families of the Canaanites became scattered.

19 The Canaanite borders extended from Sidon as far as Gerar until Gaza, and as far as Sodom, Gomorrah, Admah, and Tzevoyim, until Lasha.

20 The descendants of Ham spread into many lands and nations with many languages.

21 Children were also born to Shem. He was the ancestor of all the descendants of Ever and was the older brother of Yefeth. **22** The sons of Shem were Elam, Asshur, Arpachshad, Lud, and Aram. **23** The sons of Aram were Utz, Chul, Gether, and Mash.

24 Arpachshad fathered a son Shelach. Shelach fathered a son Eber.

25 Eber fathered two sons. The name of the first was Peleg, because during his lifetime the world spread out. His brother's name was Yoktan.

26 Yoktan was the father of Almodad, Shelef, Chatzarmaveth, Yerach, **27** Hadoram, Uzal, Diklah,

28 Obal, Abimael, Sheba, **29** Ophir, Havilah, and Yovav. These were all the sons of Yoktan.

30 Their settlements extended from Meshah toward the eastern mountain of Sepher. **31** These are the descendants of Shem, arranged according to their families and languages and by their territories and nations.

32 These were the families of Noah's sons, listed according to their descendants and their nations.

After the flood, these nations spread over the earth.

---

11. Asshur left Babylon and built the cities of Nineveh, Rechovoth-Ir, and Calach.
Nineveh was the capital of the Assyrian Empire. It was located on the Tigris River, in what is now northern Iraq. Tradition names Nimrod (Ber. 10:9–10) as its founder. Excavations have revealed that the city was surrounded by a wall. It also contains the world's first aqueduct.

15. Canaan fathered Sidon (his first-born) and Heth.
Heth was the father of the Hittites. They settled along the Halys River, which is now in central Turkey. The Hittites were one of the three great powers militarily pressuring early Israel. Ten thousand tablets from the ancient Hittite capital of Boghas-Koy confirm Joshua's description of the western fertile crescent as the "land of the Hittites." (Joshua 1:4)

21. Children were also born to Shem. He was the ancestor of all the descendants of Ever.
The word *Ivrit*, meaning the Hebrew language, and *Ivri*, meaning the Hebrew people, both are derived from Ever. The descendants of Shem – the Jews and the Arab peoples – are known as Semitic peoples. The word "Semitic" is derived from Shem.

32. After the flood, these nations spread over the earth.
The Torah tells us that after the flood all nations branched out from the children of Noah. Therefore, it follows that all men – no matter their color, their religion, or their nationality – are brothers.

The Tower of Babel

7th Aliyah

11 During this time the entire world spoke one language. **2** As the population spread eastward, they discovered a valley in the land of Shinar, and they settled there.

3 They said to one another, "Come, let us make strong bricks by firing them." So they made bricks as hard as stone and tar for cement. **4** They said, "Now we can build a city with a tower that reaches the sky. This will keep us together so we will not be scattered all over the face of the earth."

5 Adonai descended to see the city and the tower that the sons of man had built. **6** Adonai said, "They are a single people, all having one language, and this is the first thing they do! Now nothing they plan to do will be unattainable for them!

7 Come, let us descend and confuse their speech, so that one person will not understand another's speech."

8 From that place, Adonai scattered them all over the face of the earth, and they stopped building the city.

9 He named it Babel, because this was the place where Adonai confused the world's language. It was from there that Adonai dispersed [humanity] over all the face of earth.

---

3. Come, let us make strong bricks by firing them.
Our Rabbis tell us that the people of Babel cared more for their bricks than for the lives of their builders. When a brick fell and killed someone, they became angry about the brick and the time lost. They were not concerned about the person who was killed or who was hurt.

The name of the tower was Babel. The word *bavel* means "confused." That is exactly what Adonai did to these cruel people. He confused their language so they could not understand each other.

4. Now we can build a city with a tower that reaches the sky.
There were large towers in most Sumerian and Babylonian cities. There were temples to deities, shaped like stripped pyramids. These pyramids were called ziggurats.

In the sixth century B.C.E. the king of Babylon, Nebuchadnezzer, completed the largest ziggurat ever built. The base was 300 feet square and the temple was 335 feet tall – about the height of a modern forty-story building.

5. Adonai descended to see the city and the tower.
Adonai, who sees everything, did not have to come down to see what was happening. He came down to teach mankind an ethical lesson, not to render a final judgment or to express an opinion on what was not personally seen or heard.

9. He named it Babel because this was the place where Adonai confused the world's languages.
The famous tower of Babel was probably one of the huge structures that the Babylonians used to build. Some of these can be seen today. They were shaped something like the ancient Egyptian pyramids, except that they were built with steps in their sides. And rather than coming to a point on top, they were flat. Such a building is called a "ziggurat."

It seems foolish that men actually thought they could build a ziggurat so tall that it could reach the sky.

Why do we call very tall buildings "skyscrapers"?

Ziggurat   Pyramid

10 These are the chronicles of Shem: Shem was 100 years old when he fathered his son Arpachshad, two years after the flood.

11 Shem lived 500 years after he fathered Arpachshad, and he had more sons and daughters.

12 Arpachshad was 35 years old when he had a son Shelach.

13 Arpachshad lived 403 years after he had Shelach, and he had more sons and daughters.

14 Shelach was 30 years old when he fathered his son Eber.

15 Shelach lived 403 years after he had Eber, and he had more sons and daughters.

16 Eber was 34 years old when he fathered his son Peleg. **17** Eber lived 430 years after he fathered Peleg, and he had more sons and daughters.

18 Peleg was 30 years old when he fathered his son Reu.

19 Peleg lived 209 years after he fathered Reu, and he had more sons and daughters.

20 Reu was 32 years old when he fathered his son Serug.

21 Reu lived 207 years after he fathered Serug, and he had more sons and daughters.

22 Serug was 30 years old when he fathered his son Nachor. **23** Serug lived 200 years after he fathered Nachor, and he had more sons and daughters.

24 Nachor was 29 years old when he fathered his son Terach.

25 Nachor lived 119 years after he fathered Terach, and he had more sons and daughters.

26 Terach was 70 years old when he fathered Abram, Nachor, and Haran.

27 This is the history of Terach: Terach fathered Abram, Nachor, and Haran. Haran had a son, Lot.

28 Haran died in the land of his birth, Ur Kasdim, while his father, Terach, was still alive.

The Descendants of Terach

Maftir

29 Abram and Nachor married.
The name of Abram's wife was Sarai.
The name of Nachor's wife was Milcah,
the daughter of Haran.

---

10. These are the chronicles of Shem.
Now starts the beginning of Jewish history.

Abram, the first patriarch, is traced back to his ancestor Shem, the son of Noah.

The purpose of verses 10–26 is to trace the founders of the Hebrew nation from Shem to Abram. Abram was the first patriarch.

24. Nachor was 29 years old when he fathered his son Terach.
Terach and his family left their home in Ur of the Chaldees and moved to the city of Haran, where they settled. Terach's son Abram left his family to live in Canaan, the land Adonai had promised him.

28. Haran died in the land of his birth, Ur Kasdim, while his father, Terach, was still alive.
The Arabic name of Ur Kasdim is Tel el-Magaiyar, meaning "mound of pitch." Ur, called "of the Chaldees," was a great city and was dominated by a sacred temple of the moon god. Sir Leonard Wooley excavated the city of Ur and found numerous art treasures and historical artifacts in the royal cemetery.

29. The name of Nachor's wife was Milcah, the daughter of Haran.
Milcah was the daughter of Haran, sister of Lot, wife of Nachor, who was the grandfather of Rebecca, Isaac's future wife.

30 Meantime Sarai had no children.
31 Terach took his son Abram, his grandson Lot, and his daughter-in-law Sarai, and he left Ur Kasdim, and he traveled toward the land of Canaan. They came as far as Haran and settled there. **32** Terach was 205 years old when he died in Haran.

---

31. Terach took his son Abram, his grandson Lot, and his daughter-in-law Sarai, and he left Ur Kasdim, and he traveled toward the land of Canaan.
Abram began his journey to Canaan from the now excavated city of Ur Kasdim in southern Babylon. The excavations in the royal cemetery have uncovered art treasures of skill and beauty dating from 2900 to 2000 B.C.E.

THE FERTILE CRESCENT

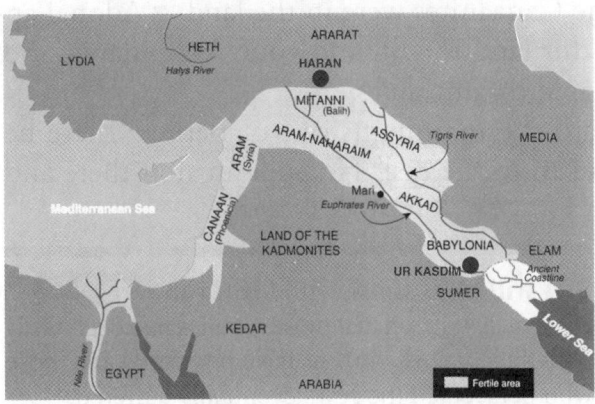

As we trace Abram's journey on the map, we see that he first went to Haran, a flourishing city in the kingdom of Mari. His father and brothers settled there, but Abram moved on. We are told how Abram worshipped and how Adonai promised Abram the land of Canaan as a homeland for him and for all his descendants. With Sarai, his servants, his household goods, and his cattle, Abram pressed on to the Promised Land. His journey covered 600 miles, through the rich lands bordering the great Arabian Desert, from Ur near the Persian Gulf up to Haran and on to Canaan. Following this route carefully on the map, we can clearly see that it forms a crescent, whence comes the name which this area is often called, "Fertile Crescent," to contrast it with the barren desert that borders it.

Rabbis interpreted the words of the Torah in the simple and in the literal sense.

In their classes, on the Sabbath and on the holidays, these sages would preach, using the Torah as their text and revealing their interpretations. These interpretations stressed the moral and ethical principles of Judaism.

So that the average person could understand, our Rabbis used stories to illustrate the ideas they were trying to teach.

Later on, these stories and legends were collected and written down. These are the stories we call *midrashim*.

Some of the most important books containing these *midrashim* are *Midrash Rabbah*, *Midrash Tanhuma*, and the *Yalkut Shimoni*. Many of the midrashim in this book are taken from these books.

This is an example of a midrash.
One day as Abram was watching his father sell an idol, a thought came to him:

"It is silly for people to pray to a god chiseled and formed by my father's hands. Indeed, it would seem more proper for the people to pray to my father, who after all can create idols. He is surely more creative and therefore more godly than his own idols."

Abram repeated the thought to his father. Terach laughed and considered it a great joke but he still continued making and worshipping idols.

TRADITIONAL LINEAGE OF ABRA(HA)M THE HEBREW

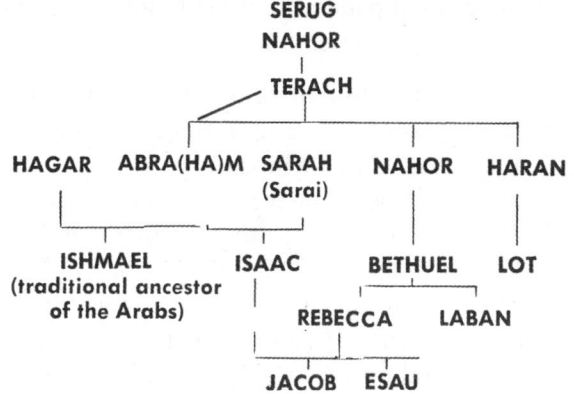

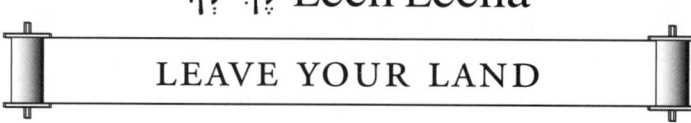

Lech Lecha

LEAVE YOUR LAND

12 Adonai said to Abram, "Leave your land, your birthplace, and your father's house, [and go] to the land that I will show you. **2** I promise to make your descendants into a great nation. I will bless them and make them great. You shall become a blessing. **3** I will bless those who bless you, and curse those who curse you. All the nations of the world will be blessed because of you."

4 Abram went as Adonai had directed him, and Lot went with him. Abram was 75 years old when he left Haran. **5** Abram took his wife Sarai, his nephew Lot, and all their belongings, as well as the people they had gathered, and they left, heading toward Canaan. When they finally came to Canaan, **6** Abram traveled through the land as far as the area of Shechem, coming to the Plain of Moreh. At that time the Canaanites were in the land. **7** Adonai appeared to Abram and said, "I will surely give this land to you and your descendants." So Abram built an altar to Adonai, who had appeared to him there.

8 From there Abram traveled southward toward the mountains east of Bethel. There he pitched his tent between Bethel to the west and Ai to the east. He built an altar there and prayed to Adonai.

---

1. Leave your land, your birthplace, and your father's house.
Under normal phrasing, the order should have been reversed and read as "from your father's house, your birthplace, and your land." A commentator suggests that the original phrase was meant as a spiritual withdrawal. It starts with the two least important spiritual places, country and birthplace. The most important and most difficult place to leave is your father's house.
The three primary influences which molds a persons behavioral patterns are; land, birthplace and fathers (family) house.

1. Adonai said to Abram, "Leave your land, your birthplace, and your father's house, (and go) to the land that I will show you.
Adonai told Abram to leave his father's house because he was in conflict with his father, who was an idol worshipper. By departing, Abram could continue his battle against idolatry without antagonizing his parents. He could continue to respect his parents and resume his ideological mission on another battlefield.

3. I will bless those who bless you.
History has shown that those regimes that dealt fairly with their Jewish citizens have prospered and those who persecuted the Jews eventually suffered.

5. Abram took his wife Sarai, his nephew Lot, and all their belongings, as well as the people they had gathered, and they left.
The midrash says that the phrase "the people they had gathered" referred to the converts which Abram and Sarai had made.

5. Abram took his wife Sarai, his nephew Lot, and all their belongings, as well as the people they had gathered.
Abram led a seminomadic way of life, traveling with his flocks in search of pasturage. His clan was a self-contained community with skilled craftsmen. The group also traded in animals and goods which they accumulated in their travels.

9 Abram then continued his journey, moving steadily toward the south. **10** There was a terrible famine in the land. So Abram traveled south to Egypt to stay there for a while, because the famine in the land had grown very strong. **11** As they approached Egypt, he said to his wife Sarai, "I am aware that you are a beautiful woman. **12** When the Egyptians see you, they will realize that you are my wife and will kill me, while allowing you to live. **13** If you would, say that you are my sister. They will, for your sake, treat me well, and because of you my life will be saved."

Abram in Egypt
2nd Aliyah

14 When Abram came to Egypt, the Egyptians saw that his wife Sarai was very beautiful. **15** Pharaoh's officials saw her and described her to Pharaoh. So Sarai was taken to Pharaoh's palace. **16** Pharaoh treated Abram well because of Sarai. Pharaoh gave Abram many gifts: sheep, cattle, donkeys, male and female slaves, she-donkeys, and camels. **17** But Adonai punished Pharaoh and his palace with plagues because of what he had done to Abram's wife Sarai. **18** Now Pharaoh sent for Abram and angrily said, "How could you do this to me? Why didn't you tell me that she was your wife? **19** Why did you say that she was your sister so that I should take her to myself as a wife? Now here is your wife! Take her and leave my land!" **20** Pharaoh sent Abram and his wife Sarai and all their belongings out of the country.

13
Abram, with his wife and all his belongings, and Lot, headed northward to the Negev. **2** Abram was very rich in livestock, silver, and gold. **3** He continued on his travels from the Negev toward Bethel, until he came to the place where he had originally camped, between Bethel and Ai, **4** the exact place where he had first built an altar. There Abram worshipped Adonai.

---

10. There was a terrible famine in the land. So Abram traveled south to Egypt to stay there for a while.
Whenever a drought and famine desolated the region of Canaan, it was common for whole clans to pick up their belongings and seek refuge in Egypt. There the periodic overflow of the Nile gave life to the land, as it does today, and helped to regulate the agriculture of the country. The Egyptians learned to dig channels for the seasonal flood and to irrigate the grain-producing land. Migration into Egypt was therefore an ancient expedient.

In Canaan, on the other hand, the rains did not always come when needed. Seminomadic inhabitants left their homes in time of drought to come to Egypt to keep themselves alive and to keep their cattle alive. It was famine, too, as the Bible says, that compelled Abraham and Isaac in an early period to go south, and the same reason is given for Jacob's sending his sons to Egypt, where grain could still be procured even in a time of general drought (Ber. 42.2–3). As a result of this mission, the entire family finally settled there.

2. Abram was very rich in livestock, silver, and gold.
Abram was a seminomad who possessed large flocks and skilled craftsmen in his household. As he traveled, he also trafficked in goods and in trade. All of these assets would explain the source of his wealth.

3. He continued on his travels from the Negev toward Bethel.
The regions and cities in Western Asia are associated in the Book of Bereshit with the journeys and sojourns of Abram, Isaac, and Jacob.

Abram and Lot Separate
3rd Aliyah

5 Lot, who accompanied Abram, also had many sheep, cattle, and tents. **6** However, there was not enough grass for both their flocks. **7** There were many quarrels between the shepherds of Abram's flocks and those of Lot. At that time the Canaanites and Perizzites were also living in the land.

8 Abram said to Lot, "We must stop the quarrels between your shepherds and my shepherds. After all, we're from the same family. **9** Look around, all the land is before you. Why not separate from me? If you choose to go to the left, I will go to the right; if you choose to go to the right, I will go to the left."

10 Lot looked around and saw that the entire Jordan Plain was fertile all the way to Tzoar. There was plenty of water. This was before Adonai destroyed Sodom and Gomorrah. It was like Adonai's beautiful garden, like the land of Egypt.

11 Lot chose for his flocks the entire Jordan Valley. And the two separated. **12** Abram remained in the land of Canaan, while Lot settled among the cities of the Plain, near Sodom.

13 But the people of Sodom were very wicked, and they sinned against Adonai.

14 After Lot left, Adonai said to Abram, "Open your eyes, and from where you are now standing, look as far as you can toward the north, toward the south, toward the east, and toward the west.

---

8. We must stop the quarrels.
Abram's men and Lot's men were fighting over fields for grazing cattle and sheep. There was far too much cattle to feed so many animals. So Abram, who was a man of peace, decided that he and his family had to separate from his nephew Lot and his family. He gave Lot first choice to choose the land he wanted.

Abram said, "If you choose to go to the left, I will go to the right; if you choose to go to the right, I will go to the left."

9. Look around, all the land is before you. Why not separate from me? If you choose to go to the left, I will go to the right; if you choose to go to the right, I will go to the left.
Abram had complete faith in Adonai. He showed his complete reliance upon Adonai when he arranged for Lot to choose where he would settle. Lot chose the area, which would support his herd.

Unfortunately Lot's choice brought disaster to his dreams of wealth. Sometimes what you see on the surface can blind your decisions.

Abram was also disgusted with Lot's permissive attitude toward idol worship. He was concerned that Lot's attitude could have a negative effect on his family.

12. Abram remained in the land of Canaan.
The Near East is the region between the Mediterranean, Caspian, and Red Seas and the Persian Gulf. It is in general a barren, arid area. However, in the midst of this uninviting expanse lies a crescent-shaped region of fertile, watered land called the Fertile Crescent. It is in the Fertile Crescent that man made the transition from a hunter of food to an organized, systematic food producer.

The patriarchs traveled extensively through the Fertile Crescent seeking pasturage for their flocks and relief from hunger and drought.

The first great figure to appear on the stage of Jewish history was Abram. Many centuries ago (about 1900 B.C.E.), according to the Bible, Adonai told Abram and his family to leave their native city of Ur and settle in a place that would become their new homeland. Because they crossed the River Euphrates on their journey to the Promised Land, people called them Hebrews (*Ivrim*, "those who came from the other side"), a name that has stayed with the Jews to the present day. In the fertile land of Mesopotamia, where Abram and his wife, Sarai, grew up, a great civilization had developed. Its chief city, Ur, was a short distance from the Euphrates. It was a thriving market center, visited by merchants from near and far.

15 All the land that you see, I will give to you and to your descendants forever. **16** I will make your descendants as many as the dust of the earth. **17** Stand up and explore the length and breadth of all the land, and you will see what I am giving you." **18** Then Abram moved his tents. And he settled in the Plains of Mamre, at Hebron, and there he built an altar to Adonai.

Abram Rescues Lot
4th Aliyah

14 It was about this time that Amraphel king of Shinar, Arioch king of Ellasar, Chedorlaomer king of Elam, and Tidal king of Goyim **2** fought a war against Bera king of Sodom, Birsha king of Gomorrah, Shinav king of Admah, Shemever king of Tzevoyim, and the king of Bela, which is now Tzoar.
3 All of these rulers banded together in Siddim Valley, now the Dead Sea. **4** They had for twelve years served Chedorlaomer, but now, in the thirteenth year, they rebelled. **5** In the fourteenth year, Chedorlaomer and his allied kings arrived. They defeated the Rephaim in Ashteroth Karnaim, the Zuzim in Ham, the Emim in Shaveh Kiryathaim, **6** and the Horites in the hill country of Seir, as far as Eyl Paran, at the edge of the desert.
7 Then they swung around and attacked Eyn Mishpat, now Kadesh, and they defeated the armies of the Amalekites and the Amorites, who lived in Charzatzon Tamar.
8 The armies of Sodom, Gomorrah, Admah, Tzevoyim, and Bela Tzoar prepared for battle. They set up fortified positions in Siddim Valley, **9** against Chedorlaomer king of Elam, Tidal king of Goyim, Amraphel king of Shinar, and Arioch king of Ellasar. There were four kings against the five. **10** The Siddim Valley was filled with tar pits, and when the kings of Sodom and Gomorrah tried to flee, they fell into them. The others escaped to the mountains.

---

18. Then Abram moved his tents. And he settled in the Plains of Mamre, at Hebron, and there he built an altar to Adonai.
The place where Abram pitched his tent is near Hebron. The place is named after one of Abram's allies, Mamre of the Amorites (Ber.14:13).

For "Plains," the Hebrew text reads *elonei*, meaning "plains" and also "oaks." The oaks of Mamre were an oak grove near Hebron. At the time of the Second Temple, there were traditions about an ancient grove in the neighborhood of Hebron.

3. All of these rulers banded together in Siddim Valley, now the Dead Sea.
The five cities of the plain–Sodom, Gomorrah, Admah, Zeboim, and Tzoar–had paid tribute for twelve years to Elam. Now they banded together and refused further payment, and prepared to resist the invaders.

7. Then they swung around and attacked Eyn Mishpat.
Eyn Mishpat means "Well of Judgment." It probably was a place where judges settled disputes between claimants.

7. The Amalekites.
The Amalekites were desert marauders that inhabited the area between Canaan and Egypt. They tried to prevent the Israelites from entering their territory in Sinai.

7. Amorites, who lived in Charzatzon Tamar.
Abram's allies belonged to a tribe that shared the land with the Canaanites. They supported Abram because they themselves had been victims of the attack. Abram's military tactics of speed and surprise guaranteed a victory.

10. When the kings of Sodom and Gomorrah tried to flee, they fell into them.
The armies of the five kings were led by king Chedorlaomer and his allies. In this battle four kings were better than five kings. Two of the kings were sucked into the tar pits. The other three heroic kings left them there and fled into the mountains. The lesson is, sometimes four winning kings are better than five losers.

11 The victorious invaders seized all the goods and all the food of Sodom and Gomorrah, and they returned home. **12** When they left, they also captured Abram's nephew Lot and his possessions, since he had been living in Sodom.

13 A fugitive who escaped came and brought the news to Abram the Hebrew, who was living quietly near the oak grove belonging to Mamre the Amorite, brother of Eshkol and Aner. They were Abram's allies. **14** When Abram heard that his relatives had been kidnapped, he mobilized all his 318 fighting men who had been born in his house. He pursued the kidnappers, catching up to them in Dan. **15** Abram divided his forces, and he and his servants attacked at night. He attacked, and pursued the kidnappers as far as Hovah, which is to the left of Damascus.

16 Abram recovered all the property. He also brought back his relative Lot and all his goods, the women, and all the other people. **17** After he returned from his victory over Chedorlaomer and his allies, the king of Sodom came out to greet him in Shavah Valley, now called King's Valley. **18** Melchi-tzedek king of Salem served bread and wine. He was a priest to Adonai the Most High. **19** He blessed Abram, and said, "Blessed be Abram by El, the most high Creator of heaven and earth. **20** And blessed be El, the most high who helped you conquer your enemies." Abram then gave king Melchi-tzedek a tenth of everything.

I Will Not Take Anything That Is Yours   5th Aliyah

21 The king of Sodom said to Abram, "Give me back my people who were captured, and you can keep the goods that you recovered."

---

12. When they left, they also captured Abram's nephew Lot.
Abram and his nephew Lot did not see eye-to-eye. Lot and Abram separated when his nephew chose to live in Sodom. However when Abram learned that Lot had been kidnapped, he mobilized his 318 fighting men and went to his rescue. Abram forgot his quarrels and differences and rushed to the rescue.

12. When they left, they also captured Abram's nephew Lot and his possessions, since he had been living in Sodom.
Lot was aware that the city of Sodom was filled with criminal gangs. However, he disregarded its evil reputation and decided to live there. Lot was punished because he knowingly chose to live in Sodom.   *Rashi*

13. A fugitive who escaped came and brought the news to Abram the Hebrew.
In this Torah section, Abram is called *Avram Ha-Ivri*, Abram the Hebrew. The Hebrew word *Ivri* comes from *ever*, meaning "on the other side." Abram lived on the other side of the river.

14. He mobilized all his 318 fighting men.
The Torah uses the Hebrew word *chaneechov*, meaning "trained" fighting men. Obviously rich camps were in danger of being raided by marauders. Abram was no softie; he organized a trained fighting force to protect his people and his property.

15. Abram divided his forces and he and his servants attacked at night.
Abram was an excellent military strategist. He divided his forces so he could attack from several sides. He also increased the element of surprise by attacking at night. The result was surely the rout of a superior military force by a small, well-trained troop.

15. He attacked and pursued the kidnappers as far as Hovah, which is to the left of Damascus.
Damascus is believed to be one of the oldest continuously occupied cities in the world. The city is 150 miles north of Jerusalem. Today it is the capital of the nation of Syria.

22 Abram replied to the king of Sodom, "I have sworn in an oath to Adonai Most High, Creator of heaven and earth!
23 I will not take anything that is yours! Not even a thread nor a shoelace! In this way you will not be able to say, 'It was I who made Abram rich.'
24 All I will accept is what my young men have eaten, and a share in the spoils for the young men, Aner, Eshkol, and Mamre, who went with me."

15
After these events, Adonai spoke to Abram in a vision, saying, "Abram do not be afraid, I am your shield. Your reward will be very great."
2 Abram said, "Adonai, what good are Your blessings that You will give me if I remain without a son? Will the heir to my household be my servant, Eliezer of Damascus?"
3 Abram continued, "You have given me no children. A member of my household will inherit what is mine." **4** Then Adonai said to him, "No one else will be your heir! A son born from your own body will inherit what is yours." **5** He then brought Abram outside and said, "Look at the sky and count the stars. See if you can count them." Adonai then said to him, "That is how numerous your descendants will be."
6 Abram believed in Adonai, and Adonai considered Abram righteous because he believed the promise.

Adonai Promises Abram   6th Aliyah

7 Adonai said to him, "I am Adonai, who took you out of Ur Kasdim to give you this land as a possession forever." **8** Abram asked, "Adonai, how can I really be sure that this land will be mine?" **9** Adonai replied, "Bring Me a heifer, a goat, a ram, a dove, and a young pigeon."

---

23. I will not take anything that is yours!
The kings of Sodom and Gomorrah and their allies fought against King Chedorlaomer and his allies.

The king of Sodom and his allies were defeated and fled. The winning side captured the cities of Sodom and Gomorrah and carried away Lot and all his family.

When Abram heard about Lot, he and 318 of his followers went in pursuit. They defeated the armies of Chedorlaomer and freed Lot.

When Abram returned victorious, the king of Sodom said to him, "Keep all of the plunder, and let me keep the people."

Abram answered, "I swear I will not take a thread or a shoestring, lest you should say, 'I made Abram rich.'"

24. All I will accept is what my young men have eaten, and a share in the spoils for the young men, Anev, Eshkol, and Mamre, who went with me.
The three men were obviously the troop commanders. Abram wanted nothing for himself, only for the men who had risked their lives to save his nephew Lot.

5. That is how numerous your descendants will be.
Abram had proven to Adonai that he was a man of faith, of justice, of peace, and of courage. Soon after Abram's victory over the four kings, Adonai revealed to Abram that because of his excellent qualities he was deserving to be the father of a great nation.

But Abram had not yet been blessed with children. He wondered, therefore, how he could be the father of an entire people. Adonai, Creator of the Universe, then commanded Abram to go out of his tent into the night's darkness.

"Look up at the skies," said Adonai to Abram. "What do you see?"

"Stars, O Adonai," replied Abram.

"Even as the stars are too many to be counted," said Adonai, "so large in number shall your descendants be, far beyond counting." This magnificent promise of Adonai gave Abram new courage and hope.

10 Abram brought all of them. He split them in half, and placed one half opposite the other. He did not split the birds.
11 Vultures then came down to feed on the bodies, but Abram chased them away.
12 As the sun was setting, Abram fell into a deep sleep, and he saw a terrifying vision.
13 Then Adonai said to Abram, "You can know for sure that your descendants will be strangers for 400 years in a land that is not theirs, and they will be enslaved and oppressed. **14** But I will punish the nation that enslaves them, and in the end they will leave with great wealth. **15** You will die in peace, and you will be buried at a ripe old age. **16** The fourth generation will return to this land, when the Amorites who are here now will be gone." **17** The sun had set, and it became very dark. A smoking fire pot and a blazing torch passed between the halves of the sacrifice. **18** That day, Adonai made a covenant with Abram, saying, "I have given this land to your descendants, from the border of Egypt as far as the great river, the Euphrates; **19** the lands of the Kenites, the Kenizites, the Kadmonites, **20** the Hittites, the Perizzites, the Rephaim, **21** the Amorites, the Canaanites, the Girgashites, and the Jebusites."

16 Abram's wife Sarai still had not given birth to any children. Sarai had a slave-girl by the name of Hagar.
2 Sarai said to Abram, "Adonai has kept me from having children. Marry my slave, and hopefully she will have sons and they will be like my own children." Abram listened to Sarai.
3 After Abram had lived in Canaan for ten years, his wife Sarai took Hagar the Egyptian, her slave, and gave her to her husband Abram as a wife.
4 Hagar became pregnant. When she realized that she was pregnant, she treated her mistress with contempt.

---

13. Your descendants will be strangers for 400 years in a land that is not theirs, and they will be enslaved and oppressed.
Adonai gave Abram a historical preview of what will happen to his descendants. Notice that he did not reveal the name or location of the country that would enslave them.

18. That day, Adonai made a covenant with Abram.
Because of Abram's goodness, Adonai made a covenant with him and promised that his descendants would inherit the land of Canaan.

That is why eight days after a boy is born his health permitting, he is circumcised in a ceremony called *brit milah*. This ceremony makes every boy a *ben brit* (son of the covenant). And that is why we, the children of Israel, are sometimes referred to as *b'nai brit* (Children of the Covenant). This very same *Brit* has unified our people from the days of Abram to the present.

2. Sarai said to Abram, "Adonai has kept me from having children. Marry my slave, and hopefully she will have sons and they will be like my own children."
Sarai loved Abram and wanted so much for him to be happy that she said to him, "Abram, take my maidservant, Hagar, as your wife. Perhaps she will have the child we want so badly." She was willing to share his love with another woman.

3. Sarai took Hagar the Egyptian, her slave, and gave her to her husband Abram as a wife.
The wealthy people of Canaan preferred Egyptian handmaids because they came from a more advanced and sophisticated civilization. According to the commentators, Sarai herself purchased Hagar. Abram had no claim to Hagar except with Sarai's permission.

5 Sarai said to Abram, "I gave you my slave. Now that she is pregnant, she despises me. Adonai will make you pay for doing this to me!"
6 Abram replied to Sarai, "She is your slave. Deal with her as you see fit." Sarai was cruel to her, and Hagar ran away from her.
7 An angel of Adonai found Hagar near a spring of water in the desert, along the road to Shur. **8** The angel said, "Hagar, maid of Sarai! Where are you coming from, and where are you going?" She replied, "I am running away from my mistress, Sarai." **9** The angel of Adonai said to her, "Return to your mistress, and do what she says." **10** Then the angel of Adonai continued to speak: "I will grant you many descendants. They will be more than anyone can count."
11 Then the angel of Adonai said to her, "You are pregnant and will give birth to a son. You must name him Ishmael, for Adonai has heard about your complaint. **12** He will be like a rebel. His hand will be against everyone, and everyone will fight against him. He will live near all his brothers."
13 Hagar gratefully said to Adonai, who had spoken to her, "You are a God who sees me [El-Ro'i]," for she said, "I saw the One who appeared to me." **14** So she named the oasis, "Oasis to life [and] my vision of the God who sees me [Be'er LaChai Ro'i]." It is located between Kadesh and Bered. **15** Hagar gave birth to Abram's son. Abram named his son, who had been born to Hagar, Ishmael.
16 Abram was eighty-six years old when Hagar gave birth to his son Ishmael.

---

5. I gave you my slave.
Now, Sarai confessed, "I now know that I made a huge mistake. I voluntarily suggested that you take Hagar as your wife and now that she is pregnant, she despises me."

Then she cleverly shifts the blame to Abram and says, "Adonai will make you pay for doing this to me."

10. I will grant you many descendants.
Two great nations are descended from Abram, the Jews and the Arabs. The Jews are the descendants of Abram's second son, Isaac. The Arabs are descendants of Abram's first son, Ishmael.

11. Then the angel of Adonai said to her, "You are pregnant and will give birth to a son. You must name him Ishmael, for Adonai has heard about your complaint."
Ishmael means, "Adonai hears." Adonai heard Hagar's prayer and answered her.

Ishmael, Abram's first-born son, did not inherit his father's estate but led a nomad's life in the desert. Ishmael was a wild donkey of a man. A man or a tribe that cannot fit himself into civilized life is like a wild donkey. Ishmael could not live in the midst of his brethren, but "his hand was against everyone" and he was constantly at war with them.

15. Hagar gave birth to Abram's son. Abram named his son, who had been born to Hagar, Ishmael.
Ishmael gave his name to a group of tribes known as Ishmaelites, who dwelt on the border of the Arabian desert southeast of Canaan. The Israelites recognized the relationship of these Arabian tribes by tracing their descent from Abraham.

The Arabians later came under the influence of Judaism. After the establishment of Islam in the seventh century, they accepted many parts of the Torah and revised the text in Bereshit to suit their religion. They considered themselves to be descended from Abram and Ishmael. The Arabic version of these names, Ibrahim and Ismail, are favorites among Muslims. According to Moslem legend, both Hagar and Ismail are buried in Mecca.

17 When Abram was ninety-nine years old, Adonai appeared to him and said, "I am Adonai Almighty [El Shaddai]. Obey Me and have faith in Me. **2** I will make a covenant between us, and I will make your descendants into a great nation." **3** Abram fell on his face. Elohim spoke to him again, saying, **4** "This is My covenant with you: You shall be the father of many nations. **5** From now on you shall no longer be called Abram. Your name shall be Abraham, for your descendants will become many nations. **6** You will be the father of many nations – kings will be among your descendants.

Adonai's Covenant with Abraham *7th Aliyah*

7 "I will continue the covenant between us and your descendants. This is an eternal covenant; I, Adonai will be with you and your descendants after you. **8** Yes, to you and your descendants I will give the land of Canaan, where you are now living as a stranger. The whole land of Canaan shall be your eternal heritage, and I, Adonai, will be with your descendants."
9 Then Elohim said to Abraham, "You and your descendants must keep My covenant forever. **10** You must keep My covenant between Me and between you and your descendants. You must circumcise every male. **11** You shall circumcise the flesh of your foreskin. This shall be the sign of the covenant between Me and you. **12** Throughout all generations, every male child must be circumcised when he is eight days old. This shall include those born in your household as well as those servants who are purchased – everyone must be circumcised. **13** This shall be My eternal mark on your body.
14 Any male whose foreskin has not been circumcised shall be cut off from the community, for he has broken My covenant."

---

2. I will make a covenant between us and I will make your descendants into a great nation.
Abram refused to believe in gods who acted like human beings. He believed in Adonai, who required people to live a life of justice, freedom, and brotherhood.

Adonai was pleased with Abram's belief and made a covenant with him promising that his descendants would become a great nation.

4. You shall be the father of many nations.
The Arabs are descendants of Abram from his son Ishmael.

5. Your name shall be Abraham, for your descendants will become many nations.
Adonai honored Abram by adding the Hebrew letter *hay* ה to his name. Now his new name is Abraham.

The Hebrew name Abraham is made up of two Hebrew words: *av*, meaning "father," and *hamon*, meaning "a crowd" or "many."

8. The whole land of Canaan shall be your eternal heritage, and I, Adonai, will be with your descendants.
After thousands of years of exile, numerous historical tragedies, and a Holocaust, which murdered 6 million Jews, Abram's dream has become a reality. The modern State of Israel is firmly settled in its Promised Land.

9. You and your descendants must keep My covenant forever.
Every valid agreement depends upon a mutual trust with both sides accepting responsibilities.

Adonai in verse 4 represents Adonai's acceptance. This verse represents Abraham's agreement.

10. You must circumcise every male.
This is mitzvah number 2.

It is a mitzvah that every Jewish male child be circumcised (health permitting) on the eighth day of his life.

The circumcision is to be performed by a specially trained person called a *mohel* to fulfill this mitzvah.

15 Then Elohim said to Abraham, "Sarai your wife shall no longer be called by the name Sarai. From now on she shall be called Sarah. **16** I will bless her, and she will give birth to a son. I will bless her, and she will be the mother of nations – kings will be among her descendants."

17 Abraham fell on his face and laughed. He said to himself, "Can a hundred-year-old man have children? Can Sarah, who is ninety years old, give birth?"

18 To Elohim, Abraham said, "May Ishmael receive a special blessing from you!"

19 Elohim then said, "Soon your wife Sarah will give birth to a son. You must name him Isaac. I will keep My covenant with him and his descendants as an everlasting treaty. **20** I have also heard your request with regard to Ishmael. I will bless him and make him fruitful, greatly increasing his numbers. He will father twelve princes, and I will make him into a great nation.

21 But I will keep my covenant with Isaac, to whom Sarah will give birth at this time next year."

22 When He finished speaking to him, Elohim left, leaving Abraham.

23 Then Abraham, on the very same day that Elohim had spoken to him, circumcised his son Ishmael, and everyone born in his house, and every servant and every male in his household.

Abram and Ishmael Are Circumcised *Maftir*

24 Abraham was ninety-nine years old when he was circumcised.

25 His son Ishmael was thirteen years old when he was circumcised.

26 On the very day that Abraham and his son Ishmael were circumcised, **27** all the men of the household, both those born in Abraham's household and those who were bought, were circumcised with him.

---

15. Then Elohim said to Abraham, "Sarai your wife shall no longer be called by the name Sarai. From now on she shall be called Sarah."
Adonai had decided to make Abraham the father of our people. He added the letter *hay* ה to Abraham's original name, Abram. Adonai also added the same letter *hay* to Sarah's name. In Hebrew the name Sarai means "my princess." The letter *hay* ה is sometimes used to signify the name of Adonai. Now both Abraham and Sarah had blessed names.

16. I will bless her, and she will give birth to a son.
The sages say, "Your wife Sarah will become pregnant and she will be healthy and give birth without pain."

17. Abraham fell on his face and laughed.
Abraham bowed down and thanked Adonai.
Abraham laughed with joy at the miraculous good news. He wondered, "How can a 100-year old man and Sarah, a 90-year old woman, have a child?"

18. To Elohim, Abraham said, "May Ishmael receive a special blessing from you!"
Abraham, already an old man, is aware of his mortality. He is also convinced that he has no worthy successor. Abraham knows that his son Ishmael does not have the intelligence, charisma, or faith to continue the tradition and become his successor as the founder of a great nation. Abraham simply asks Adonai for a special blessing for Ishmael.
Shenash

24. Abraham was ninety-nine years old when he was circumcised.
Visiting the sick, *bikur cholim*, in Judaism is a mitzvah. The sages say that the mitzvah of *bikur cholim* is derived from the fact that Adonai visited Abraham after he was circumcised.

וַיֵּרָא *Vayera*

AND ADONAI APPEARED

18 Adonai appeared to Abraham in the Plains of Mamre while he was sitting at the entrance of his tent in the hottest part of the day. **2** Abraham looked up, and he saw three strangers standing a short distance from him. When he saw them from the entrance of his tent, he ran to welcome them, bowing down to the ground. **3** He said, "My lords, please do not go any farther without stopping here with me. **4** My servants will bring some water to bathe your feet while you rest in the shade of the tree. **5** I will serve some food so you can refresh yourselves. Then you can continue on your journey. After all, you are passing by my house." "All right," they replied. "We will do as you have said."

6 Abraham then rushed into Sarah's tent and said, "Quick! Get two quarts of the finest flour! And bake some bread." **7** Then Abraham ran to the herd and selected a tender, choice calf. He gave it to a young man who rushed to prepare it. **8** Abraham also brought some cheese and milk, and the meat that the servant had prepared, and served his three guests. Abraham served them as they ate under the tree.

---

1. Plains of Mamre.
Mamre is a plain near Hebron where oak trees grew. This place derived its name from the Amorites who lived there. The burial cave of Machpelah is located near Mamre.

1. Adonai appeared to Abraham in the Plains of Mamre while he was sitting at the entrance of his tent in the hottest part of the day.
Wherever Abraham lived, his home was open to strangers. He never failed to show hospitality and kindness to those in need.

Abraham, the great Hebrew leader, showed his concern for humanity and his love of Adonai by practicing hospitality. *Hachnasat orchim* (welcoming guests) is a great mitzvah.

Our sages tell us that when Abraham lived in Mamre, he planted a lovely garden and placed around it four open gates. One gate faced north, one south, one east, and one west. A tired traveler coming from any direction would find an open door into the cool garden, where he could rest, eat and drink.

2. When he saw them from the entrance of his tent, he ran to welcome them.
Abraham did not wait for them to approach. He ran to welcome them into his house.

4. My servants will bring some water to bathe your feet.
The custom of washing feet before entering another person's home was common among ancient Middle Eastern nations. People wore sandals, and their feet were naturally dirtied by sand and debris. Washing the feet before entering a home prevented dirtying the home and also relieved the aches and pains due to walking.

5. I will serve some food.
Abraham provided his guests with a meal of the best flour, calf's meat, and other edibles. On Abraham's orders, Sarah made the guests cakes of the finest flour meal. These were a thin flat cake similar to the matzah baked by the Israelites when they left Egypt.

7. He gave it to a young man who rushed to prepare it.
The young man was Ishmael. The midrash said that Abraham was training him to perform the mitzvah of *hachnasot orchim*, the welcoming of guests.
Rashi

9 They asked him, "Where is your wife Sarah?" "She is here in the tent," he replied.
10 One of the men said, "Next year at this time I will return, and your wife Sarah will have a son." Sarah was listening to the conversation from behind the entrance of the tent.
11 Abraham and Sarah were already old, and Sarah knew that she no longer could have children.
12 Sarah laughed to herself, saying, "I and my husband are very old. How can we possibly have a baby?"
13 Adonai said to Abraham, "Why did Sarah laugh and say, 'Can I really have a child when I am so old?'
14 Is there anything too difficult for Adonai? At this time next year, I will return, and Sarah will have a son."

Adonai Plans to Destroy Sodom
2nd Aliyah

15 Sarah was afraid, so she denied it. "I did not laugh," she said. Adonai said, "You really did laugh." **16** The three strangers got up from their places and continued their journey toward Sodom. Abraham accompanied them part of the way.
17 Adonai said, "Should I hide from Abraham what I plan to do? **18** Abraham's descendants shall become a great and mighty nation, and because of him all the nations of the world will be blessed. **19** I have chosen him so that he will teach his children and his descendants to keep Adonai's laws of doing charity and justice. Adonai will then do for Abraham everything He promised."
20 Adonai continued, "The reputation of Sodom is full of evil, and they are very wicked.
21 I myself must go down to see if the reports are true. Only then can I be sure." **22** The strangers continued toward Sodom. But Abraham was still standing before Adonai.

---

9. They asked him, "Where is your wife Sarah?"
After the strangers had eaten, they asked for Sarah. Then they informed Abraham that Sarah, at this time next year, would give birth to a son.

12. I and my husband are very old. How can we possibly have a baby?
Abraham had faith and rejoiced at the good news. However, Sarah was skeptical and laughed at herself and said, "At my age, impossible."

14. Is there anything too difficult for Adonai?
Adonai promised Abraham and Sarah that their descendants would be as numerous as the stars in the sky. They both asked, "How can this happen? We have no child." But Abraham and Sarah had faith in Adonai. Then the three messengers came to their encampment with the wonderful news: "In one year from now," they informed Abraham, "Sarah will give birth to a son." Abraham assured Sarah, "Have faith and it will happen."

16. The three strangers got up from their places and continued their journey toward Sodom.
The three angels in the form of men were sent to Abraham. The midrash says that the angel Michael was sent to notify Sarah that she would have a son. The second angel, Gabriel, was sent to destroy Sodom. The third angel, Raphael, was sent to save Lot and his family. Each angel was entrusted with only one mission.

20. The reputation of Sodom is full of evil.
Sodom and Gomorrah, the most important of the five Cities of the Plain, were destroyed for their wickedness and inhospitality.

Only the house of Lot, who lived in Sodom, was saved, except for his wife, who was turned into a pillar of salt because she looked back at the destroyed cities when warned not to. The ruins of Sodom and Gomorrah lie at the bottom of the Dead Sea.

23 Abraham approached Adonai and said, "Would You really destroy the innocent together with the guilty? **24** Just suppose there are fifty innocent people in the city. Would You still destroy it, and not save the city for the sake of the fifty good people inside it?
25 I am sure that you will not kill the innocent with the guilty, so that the innocent are punished, and the righteous and the wicked fare alike. It would be sacrilege! Shall the whole world's judge not act justly?"
26 Adonai said, "If I find fifty innocent people in Sodom, I will save the entire area for the sake of them." **27** Abraham continued and said, "I have already said too much before my Lord! I am just dust and ashes!
28 But suppose that there are five missing from the fifty innocent? Would you destroy the entire city because of the missing five?"
"I will not destroy Sodom if I find forty-five innocents there," replied Adonai. **29** Abraham pleaded and said, "But suppose there are only forty there?" "I will not destroy for the sake of the forty innocent."
30 Abraham continued, "Adonai, do not be angry with me, but I must speak up. What if there are thirty innocent there?" "I will not destroy if I find thirty innocent there." **31** "I have already said too much now before my Lord! But what if twenty innocents are found there?" "I will not destroy for the sake of the twenty innocent."
32 Abraham persisted and said, "Adonai, do not be angry with me, but I must speak up just one more time. Suppose ten innocent are found there?" "I will not destroy for the sake of the ten innocent." **33** Adonai left when He finished speaking with Abraham. Abraham then returned home.

---

23. Would you really destroy the innocent together with the guilty?
Abraham begs Adonai not to destroy the city because of the innocent inhabitants. Destroying everyone would equate the innocent with the guilty and violate His quality of mercy.

24. Just suppose there are fifty innocent people in the city.
Abraham argued with Adonai by asking for justice and not mercy. Abraham, acting as defense counsel, stated his plea that if a community of fifty righteous people existed, then the whole city of Sodom deserved to be spared. Such a righteous group can influence the majority of residents to change their behavior patterns.

Abraham kept on bargaining until he almost reached the bottom of the barrel and stopped at ten righteous people. Ten people were an insignificant minority and could never affect any behavioral changes or reform of an evil society.

25. I am sure that you will not kill the innocent with the guilty.
Abraham tries to save the people of Sodom, so he dares to question Adonai's judgment: "Would you really commit a miscarriage of justice and annihilate the whole city of Sodom?"

32. I will not destroy for the sake of the ten innocent.
Abraham was sure that the cities of Sodom and Gomorrah were guilty of committing terrible crimes. But Abraham, the man of peace, courageously tried to save them from destruction. He decided to defend an indefensible case.

Abraham hoped against hope that there might be at least a small group of decent people among the many wicked of the two cities.

He pleaded before Adonai that perhaps He might save the cities for fifty righteous people in those cities. Slowly Abraham pleaded down to ten good people. But there were not ten to be found. And Abraham realized that he could do no more. The case was closed; the verdict had been decided.

The Evil City of Sodom

3rd Aliyah

19 The two strangers came to Sodom in the evening, while Lot was sitting at the entrance of the city. Lot saw them and got up to greet them, bowing to the ground. **2** Lot said, "My lords, please come to my house. Be my guests, bathe your feet, and then in the morning continue on your journey."

"No," they insisted, "we will spend the night in the city square."

3 Lot kept insisting until they finally agreed and came to his house. He made a feast for them and baked matzah, and they ate.

4 Just as they were going to bed, the townspeople, the men of Sodom, surrounded the house. **5** They shouted to Lot and said, "Where are the strangers who came to you tonight? Bring them out to us so that we can molest them!"

6 Lot went out to the mob in front of the entrance, shutting the door behind him. **7** He said, "My brothers, please do not do such an evil thing!

8 I have two daughters who are virgins, and I will bring them out to you. You can do as you please with them. But do not harm these men. After all, they have come into my house, and I am responsible for their safety!"

9 The mob shouted, "Get out of our way!"

They said to Lot, "You came here as an immigrant, and now, all of a sudden, you tell us how to behave. We'll treat you worse than them!"

They pushed Lot, and tried to break down the door.

---

1. Lot was sitting at the entrance of the city.
In Bible days cities were surrounded by walls to protect the inhabitants. The city gates were the gathering place for judges settling problems and for business transactions. The gates were also the place where people came to meet friends and travelers who brought news from other cities.

2. Be my guests, bathe your feet.
Lot welcomes the three strangers by offering them food and a place to sleep. Lot makes them feel at home by preparing the food himself and by serving them personally.

Despite living in Sodom, Lot never forgot the mitzvah of *hachnasat orchim*, the welcoming of guests. Lot was a wealthy man, yet he himself made a feast for them and baked matzot.

5. Bring them out to us so that we can molest them!
Sodom was an ancient city, a great and rich city. Its people should have lived happily. Its people should have been pleased to share their riches. But Sodom was an outlaw city.

It became rich by robbing commercial caravans and travelers. When Lot welcomed the two messengers who had earlier visited Abraham, the Sodomites thought they had a lot of money, and they wanted to rob them or hold them for ransom.

5. Bring them out to us so we can molest them!
Lot thought that his future sons-in-law would help him defend their intended wives. He hoped that a united stand would frighten the mob and he could save his daughters as well as the two strangers.

8. I have two daughters who are virgins, and I will bring them out to you.
Lot, at the risk of his own life, tried to preserve Abraham's righteous way of life by offering hospitality to the strangers. To preserve their lives, he even offered to sacrifice the virginity of his daughters to the mob. The Rabbis condemn Lot for wanting to hand over his daughters to be sexually abused. Lot was trapped in a dilemma and thought nothing of the immorality of his decision, the lesser of the two evils.

10 The two strangers inside the house reached out, pulled Lot into the house, and locked the door. **11** They blinded the Sodomites who were standing at the entrance and trying to find the door. **12** The strangers said to Lot, "Who else do you have in the house? Sons-in-law? Your own sons? Your daughters? If you have any relatives in the city, get them out of Sodom. **13** We are about to destroy the city, for the evil reputation of Sodom is very great. Adonai has sent us to destroy Sodom."

14 Lot hurried and spoke to his sons-in-law, who were married to his daughters. He said, "Quick! Get out of this area! Adonai is about to destroy the city!" But to his sons-in-law, it was a big joke.

15 The next morning, the two angels urged Lot. "Hurry, get moving!" they said. "Take your wife and two daughters who are here! You do not want to be caught in the coming destruction because of Sodom's sins!"

16 Lot still hesitated, so the strangers grabbed him, his wife, and his two daughters by the hand, and rushed them out to the outskirts of Sodom. Adonai had shown pity for Lot and his family.

17 The angel who had led them out said, "Escape for your life! Do not look back! Do not stop anywhere in the valley! Run to the hills, so that you will not die!" **18** Lot said to the strangers, "Please! **19** I know that you have been kind to me and have saved my life! But I cannot reach the hills to escape. The destruction will overtake me and I will die! **20** Please, there is a small village nearby, close enough for refuge! I will escape there and will be safe."

Sodom and Gomorrah   4th Aliyah

21 The angel replied to Lot, "I will accept your suggestion. I will not destroy the city you mentioned. **22** Hurry! Run to the village! I can do nothing until you get there." The village was then called Zoar (Insignificant).

23 The sun was rising as Lot arrived in Zoar.

---

16. Lot still hesitated.
Lot was reluctant to leave because of his property and valuables.

16. Adonai had shown pity for Lot and his family.
Adonai saved Lot and his family because he was related to Abraham.

17. Run to the hills, so that you will not die.
The messengers told Lot to ignore the coming loss of his material possessions and instead run and concentrate on saving his life.

22. The village was then called Zoar.
Zoar was a town in Moab. It was the only one of the five Cities of the Plain, in the Dead Sea region, saved from destruction.

It was saved for the sake of Lot, who found refuge there.

23. The sun was rising as Lot, arrived in Zoar.
Our wise sages tell us that Adonai chose a special day on which to destroy the wicked city of Sodom. It was the sixteenth of the month of Nisan, the day when both the sun and the moon could be seen together.

"If the moon alone were out," said Adonai, "those who worship the sun would say that the sun could have saved them had it been here.

If the sun alone were in the sky, the moon worshippers would cry that the moon could have saved them. Therefore, let both sun and moon be here together when the city is destroyed. Let the people know that the sun and the moon are not gods but creations of Adonai.

24 Now Adonai rained down sulfur and fire from the sky on Sodom and Gomorrah.
25 He destroyed the cities and everything in the entire plain. He destroyed everyone in the cities and every- thing that was growing from the ground.
26 But Lot's wife looked back, and she was turned into a pillar of salt.
27 In the morning Abraham woke up early and hurried back to the place where he had stood before Adonai.
28 He looked toward Sodom and Gomorrah, and all he saw was heavy smoke rising from the earth, like the smoke of a furnace.
29 When Elohim destroyed the cities of the Plain, Adonai remembered Abraham. When He destroyed the cities in which Lot lived, He kept Lot safe from the disaster. **30** Lot and his two daughters left Zoar and settled in the hills, because he was afraid to remain in Zoar. He and his two daughters lived alone in a cave.
31 The older girl said to the younger, "Our father is growing old, and there is no other man that our father will allow us to marry.
32 Come, let's get our father drunk with wine and sleep with him. In this way our family will continue through our father." **33** That night, they got their father drunk with wine, and the older girl went and slept with her father. He was not aware that she had slept with him.
34 The next day, the older girl said to the younger, "Last night it was I who slept with my father. Tonight, let's get him drunk again. Now it is your turn to sleep with him; in this way our family will survive through children from our father."
35 That night, they again made their father drunk. The younger girl got up and slept with him. Again he was not aware that she had slept with him.

---

24. Adonai rained down sulfur and fire from the sky on Sodom and Gomorrah.

The Dead Sea, or Sea of Salt (*Yam Hamelech*) as it is called in Hebrew, is a large lake found in the lowest spot on the surface of the earth. It is some 130 feet below sea level.

The salt content of the Dead Sea is six times that of the ocean. It is so salty that no fish can live in it. It is truly a "dead sea." The saltiness is caused by the minerals that the Jordan River has brought down from the Galilee. The weather is so hot that the seawater evaporates at a greater rate than the rainfall and the salts become concentrated. Even the land nearby cannot be used to grow crops because of the salt.

In its northern half, the Sea of Salt is very deep, some 1,300 feet below sea level, but in the southern portion, down near where Sodom and Gomorrah stood, it is only 3 to 12 feet deep.

Today, along the west shore to the north, at a kibbutz called Ein Gedi, modern Israelis have used a fresh water spring to actually wash away the salt of the land and farm.

There are several chemical factories along the shore which extract minerals and chemicals from the salty waters. These waters contain six times as much mineral salt as the Mediterranean. Among the minerals recovered from the Dead Sea are salt, bromine, iodine, and potash. The salts have made the waters so buoyant that a person can lie on the water and float.

26. But Lot's wife looked back, and she was turned into a pillar of salt.

Lot's wife was warned not to look back but she disobeyed the warning. By looking back at the destroyed evil cities, she betrayed her secret longing for that evil way of life. Therefore she was deemed unworthy to be saved and she was turned into a pillar of salt.

32. Come, let us get our father drunk and sleep with him.

The country of Zoar is mountainous with numerous caves. Caves, in those days and even today, because of their cool and even temperatures, are ideal places in which to store and age wine.

36 Lot's two daughters became pregnant from their father.

37 The older girl gave birth to a son, and she named him Moab. He became the ancestor of the nation Moab that exists today.

38 The younger girl also had a son, and she named him Ben-Ami (Son of My People). He became the ancestor of the people of Ammon who exist today.

20

Abraham journeyed southward to the land of the Negev, and he settled between Kadesh and Shur. He would often visit Gerar.

2 There he announced that his wife Sarah was his sister, so Abimelech, king of Gerar, sent messengers for her and brought Sarah to his palace.

3 Adonai appeared to Abimelech in a dream that night. He said, "You will die because of the woman you took. She is already married."

4 Abimelech had not even touched her. He said, "Adonai, would you kill an innocent person?

36–38. Lot's two daughters became pregnant from their father. The older girl gave birth to a son and she named him Moab…The younger girl also had a son…He became the ancestor of the people of Ammon who exist today.
In Canaan, Abraham's nephew Lot raised a large family, from which developed two related nations of the Hebrews, the Moabites and the Ammonites. These two nations eventually were in conflict with the nation of Israel.

The land of Moab lies off the Jordan and the Dead Sea between the Heshbon River to the north and the Zered River to the south.

The Arnon River divides the land into two. According to the Torah, the Moabites were descendants of Lot, Abraham's nephew.

Because of their close relationship, the Hebrews were forbidden (Dev. 2:9) to wage war on them. There was much hatred between the two nations because of the expansion of the Hebrew tribes in Trans-jordan.

37. The older girl gave birth to a son, and she named him Moab. He became the ancestor of the nation of Moab.
According to Rashi, the older girl boasted that the child was conceived from her father.

38. The younger girl also had a son, and she named him Ben-Ami (Son of My People). He became the ancestor of the people of Ammon who exist today.

The Moabites and the Ammonites, like Israel, worshipped only one god. The Moabites worshipped Chemosh and the Ammonites worshipped the god Malcham, their war god king.

1. Abraham journeyed southward to the land of the Negev.
Abraham deliberately left Mamre to distance himself from Lot. His nephew Lot had an unsavory reputation, so Abraham moved away. *Rashi*

1. He would often visit Gerar.
Gerar was a town in the Negev on an inland caravan route from Palestine to Egypt. Today it is thought to be the modern Tel-ej-Jemmeh. The site has been excavated, uncovering numerous levels of occupation.

3. Adonai appeared to Abimelech in a dream that night. He said, "You will die because of the woman you took. She is already married."
Dreams played an important role throughout the ancient world. The interpretations of a variety of dreams were listed in handbooks for use by interpreters. Abimelech was captivated by Sarah's beauty and brought her into his palace for sexual relations. But Abimelech had a dream in which he was warned that Sarah was a married woman. Abimelech was frightened and confronted Abraham and accused him of lying to him. Conscience stricken, Abimelech confessed his sin and extended the freedom of the land to Abraham. He also gave Abraham a gift to establish peace with Sarah and earn her forgiveness.

5 Her husband told me that she was his sister. She too claimed that he was her brother. I did not harm her in any way."
6 Adonai said to him in the dream, "I realize that you have done this innocently. That is why I prevented you from sinning by not giving you the opportunity to touch her. **7** Now return the man's wife, for he is a prophet. He will pray for you, and you will live. But if you do not return her, then you and your kingdom are doomed."
8 Abimelech got up early in the morning and assembled all his servants. He told them everything that had happened, and everyone was very frightened. **9** Abimelech summoned Abraham and said to him, "What have you done to us?" **10** Abimelech asked Abraham, "Whatever made you think to do such a thing?" **11** Abraham replied, "I realized that the people here do not fear Elohim, and that I could be killed because of my wife. **12** Besides, she really is my sister. We both have the same father but not the same mother, so I married her.
13 When Elohim sent me wandering from my father's house, I asked her to do me a favor. Wherever we were, she was to say that I was her brother."
14 Abimelech took sheep, cattle, and servants, and he gave them to Abraham. He also returned Abraham's wife Sarah to him.
15 Abimelech said, "Travel through my whole land. Settle wherever you choose."
16 To Sarah he said, "I am giving your 'brother' a thousand pieces of silver as payment to you and all who are with you for the violations that have been done to you. This will settle all claims against me."
17 Abraham prayed to Elohim, and Elohim healed Abimelech, as well as his wife and his female servants, so that they would be able to have children. **18** Adonai had made all the women in Abimelech's house infertile, because of what he intended to do to Abraham's wife Sarah.

21

At last Adonai remembered Sarah and His promise to her.
2 Sarah became pregnant, and she gave birth to Abraham's son in his old age, at the exact time that Elohim had promised him.

---

5. "I did not harm her in any way."
Abimelech claimed that he had no intention of hurting Sarah or forcing her to have sexual relations with him.

12. Besides, she is really my sister. We both have the same father but not the same mother, so I married her.
Nachmanides severely criticizes Abraham's conduct, since it endangered the life of Sarah, his wife. He argues that it is inconsequential whether Sarah was really his half sister, but he deliberately lied and did not reveal that she was, his wife. Heroes have virtues and warts, and the Torah openly brings both to the forefront.

16. To Sarah he said, "I am giving your 'brother' a thousand pieces of silver as payment to you."
Abimelech sarcastically reminds Sarah that she was also a part of the deception. He calls Abraham "your brother" instead of "your husband." Abimelech is aware that he was played for a fool and he resents it. *Shenash*

17. Abraham prayed to Elohim and Elohim healed Abimelech.
Abraham first prayed and begged Adonai to heal Abimelech and his family because he was responsible for their sickness. Abraham also prayed and asked Adonai to forgive him for the sins that he committed when he lied to Abimelech.

3 Abraham named his son Isaac, [the son] to whom Sarah had just given birth. **4** When his son Isaac was eight days old, Abraham circumcised him, just as Adonai had commanded.

Isaac Is Born
5th Aliyah

5 Abraham was a hundred years old when his son Isaac was born. **6** Sarah said, "Adonai has made me laugh. All who hear about it will laugh with me."

7 She said, "Who would even have suggested to Abraham that Sarah would be nursing children? But here I have given birth to a son in my old age!"

8 The child grew up and was no longer nursed. Abraham made a great feast on the day that Isaac was three years old.

9 But Sarah saw that Hagar's son was being cruel to Isaac. **10** So Sarah said to Abraham, "Drive away Hagar and her son. The son of Hagar will not share your inheritance with my son Isaac!"

11 This troubled Abraham very much because it involved his son Ishmael.

12 But Elohim said to Abraham, "Do not be upset about Hagar and her son. Do everything that Sarah tells you to do. It is only through Isaac that your descendants will gain nationhood.

13 But I will also make Hagar's son into a nation, because he is your child."

14 Abraham got up early in the morning. He took bread and a leather bag filled with water, and gave it to Hagar, who placed it on her shoulder. He sent Hagar and the boy away. She left and wandered in the desert around Beer-sheva.

15 When the water in the bag was used up, she lay the boy under a shady bush. **16** She walked away, and sat down facing the boy, and she said, "I cannot bear to see my boy die." She sat there facing Ishmael, and wept out loud.

17 Elohim heard the boy crying. Elohim's angel called Hagar from above and said to her, "Hagar, do not be afraid. Elohim has heard the boy's cries.

18 Go and hug your son and comfort him. Keep watch over him, for I will make his descendants into a great nation."

---

3. Abraham named his son Isaac, [the son] to whom Sarah had just given birth.
The name Isaac comes from the Hebrew word *tzechak*, which means "to laugh." The Torah says that Sarah laughed when she heard Adonai promise she would have a child despite her advanced age.

3. Abraham named his son Isaac.
Abraham's hope was for a son who would inherit his faith and carry it forward into the next generation.

At last Abraham's and Sarah's dream of a lifetime was realized. They rejoiced at the arrival of the child of their old age.

Life had real meaning and purpose for them now. They would raise their child to become an honorable heir to honorable parents.

Abraham chose Isaac for the boy's name. Sarah thought to herself that all who heard of his birth would laugh with disbelief.

4. When his son Isaac was eight days old, Abraham circumcised him, just as Adonai had commanded.
Isaac was the first person who was circumcised at the age of eight days. Ishmael was circumcised when he was thirteen years old.

11. This troubled Abraham very much because it involved his son Ishmael.
Obviously Abraham loved Ishmael and was troubled by the whole controversy. Abraham was 100 when Isaac was born and he had a special attachment to the son of his old age.

19 Then Elohim opened her eyes, and she saw a well of water. She went and filled the leather bag with water and gave the boy some to drink. **20** Adonai watched over the boy. The boy grew up and lived in the desert, where he became an expert hunter. **21** He lived in the Paran Desert, and his mother found him a wife in Egypt.

A Peace Treaty
6th Aliyah

22 Around that time, Abimelech and his general, Pikhol, spoke to Abraham, saying, "We are aware that Elohim helps you in everything that you do. **23** Now swear to me in Elohim's name that you will not deal falsely with me, or with my children, or with my grandchildren. Show me and my people the same friendship that I have shown to you."
24 "I swear," replied Abraham.
25 Abraham then complained to Abimelech about the well that Abimelech's servants had taken over from Abraham's servants.
26 Abimelech said, "I have no idea who could have done such a thing. You never told me. I heard nothing about the problem until today."
27 Abraham then took sheep and cattle and gave them to Abimelech, and the two of them made a treaty. **28** Abraham then gathered seven sheep and put them aside. **29** Abimelech asked Abraham, "What is the meaning of these seven sheep?" **30** "Take these seven sheep from me," replied Abraham. "This gift will be my proof that I dug this well." **31** Since then the area has been called Beer-sheva (The Well of the Seven) because the two made peace there and **32** made a treaty in Beer-sheva. Abimelech and his general, Pikhol, then left, and they returned to the land of the Philistines.

---

20. The boy grew up and lived in the desert, where he became an expert hunter.
The Torah describes Ishmael's survival as a sign of divine providence. Ishmael led the typical life of a desert nomad who made a living by hunting and raiding.

In Arab tradition Ishmael occupies the place of Isaac among the Jews. In the Koran, Ishmael and Hagar were taken by Abraham to the valley where Mecca was later built, and there Ishmael grew into a great nation. The well to which the angel Gabriel led Hagar is still shown by Arab guides in Mecca; so is Mount Tabor, where Abraham intended to sacrifice Isaac, and also the tombs of Hagar and Ishmael.

22. We are aware that Elohim helps you in everything that you do.
Abimelech is actually saying, "I am afraid of your connection to your Elohim, who is very powerful."

25. Abraham then complained to Abimelech about the well that Abimelech's servants had taken over from Abraham's servants.
Abimelech concedes that Abraham has a powerful ally in Adonai. Now Abraham has an opening and accuses the king's servants of the crime of stealing the well which his servants had dug.

31. Since then the area has been called Beer-sheva.
The city of Beer-sheva is mentioned frequently in the early sections of the Torah. We are told that Abraham dug a well there and planted a tamarask tree.

Beer-sheva is the city to which Abraham and Isaac returned after Abraham almost sacrificed his son to Adonai.

31. Since then the area has been called Beer-sheva (The Well of the Seven).
The city was named Beer-sheva because Abraham gave Abimelech seven (*sheva*) sheep as proof that he dug a *be'er* (well) there.

33 Abraham planted a tamarask tree in Beer-sheva, and there he prayed to Adonai, Creator of the Universe. **34** Abraham lived in the land of the Philistines for a long time.

Sacrifice Your Son *7th Aliyah*

22 After these events, Elohim tested Abraham's faith. He said, "Abraham!" And Abraham replied, "Hineni, here I am." **2** Elohim said, "Take your only son Isaac, the one you love, and go away to the region of Moriah. And sacrifice him as an offering on one of the mountains that I will show you."

---

33. Abraham planted a tamarask tree in Beer-sheva.
The tree planting was a symbolic gesture.

Abraham was prophetically aware that someday his descendants would inherit the land. The tree represented Abraham, and the roots were his descendants who would embrace the Holy Land.

Beersheva is the northern gateway to the Negev. In biblical times it was the rallying place for the tribes of Israel. When Rome ruled the area, Beersheva was a prosperous caravan station on the route from Eilat to the Mediterranean Sea. After the Arab invasion, it lay desolate for many centuries.

Today Beersheva is a flourishing Israeli city. There are hotels, apartment houses, stores, and a well-known university. Many Israelis and tourists come to visit this modern-ancient city that goes back to Bible times.

33. Abraham planted a tamarask tree in Beer-sheva, and there he prayed to Adonai, Creator of the Universe.
The name Beer-Sheva has a double meaning. The Hebrew word *Beer* means "well" and the word *sheva* can mean "seven" or "swearing." The well of swearing refers to the seven lambs (21:30) that Abraham gave Abimelech as a sworn witness that he dug the well.

34. Abraham lived in the land of the Philistines for a long time.
The Philistines mentioned here later became known as the great enemy of Israel, and they are especially prominent in the lives of Samson, Saul, and David. Goliath, the giant whom David slew with his sling, was fighting for the Philistines.

Actually the Philistines brought many useful things to the land of Israel.

They probably came from Crete, the large island on the route to Greece.

They were originally seafarers and merchants, and settled along the shore south of modern Tel Aviv. Some scholars believe they may have introduced coins, iron weapons, and the chariot to Palestine.

The Torah says they were excellent at making things from iron and jealously guarded their secret for sharpening tools. Also the very name Palestine comes from the name Philistine.

2. Sacrifice him as an offering on one of the mountains that I will show you.
The place where Abraham built the altar to sacrifice Isaac was the same spot where Adam brought his first sacrifice to Adonai, and where Cain and Abel had brought their sacrifices. It was also the same spot where Noah built an altar after he came out of the ark.

On this spot would one day be built the *Bet Hamikdash*, the Holy Temple.

2. Elohim said, "Take your only son Isaac, the one you love, and go away to the region of Moriah. And sacrifice him as an offering on one of the mountains that I will show you."
Artists, authors, and architects are always looking for ways to improve the quality of their creations. Adonai in His own way improves the quality of His creations by challenging His righteous to do His will and perform deeds that will make them even more righteous.

Adonai tested Abraham's faith by asking him to sacrifice his son Isaac and perform an inhuman deed. Adonai never tests the wicked, since they do not obey the commandments.   *Maimonides*

3 Abraham got up early and saddled his donkey. He took two servants and his son Isaac with him. He cut wood for the fire and set out, heading for the place that Adonai had told him.
4 On the third day, Abraham looked up and saw the place from afar.
5 Abraham said to his two servants, "Remain here with the donkey. Isaac and I will go farther, and after we worship we will return to you."
6 Abraham placed the wood on the shoulders of his son Isaac, while he carried the fire and the slaughter knife, and the two of them walked together.
7 Isaac said to Abraham, "Father!" And Abraham answered, "*Hineni!* Here I am." Isaac said, "Here are the fire and the wood. But where is the lamb for the sacrifice?" **8** Abraham replied, "My son, Elohim will provide a lamb for the offering." The two of them continued walking together.
9 Finally they came to the place chosen by Elohim. Abraham built the altar there and arranged the wood. He then tied up his son Isaac, and placed him on the altar on top of the wood.
10 Now Abraham reached out and took the slaughter knife in his hand. **11** At that moment, Adonai's angel called to him from heaven and said, "Abraham! Abraham!" And Abraham answered, "*Hineni!* Here I am."

---

3. Abraham got up early and saddled his donkey. He took two servants and his son Isaac with him.
Abraham was a wealthy man and had many servants. But he was on a holy mission, which was ordered by Adonai. He himself saddled his donkey and he himself cut the wood for the sacrifice.

5. Abraham said to his two servants, "Remain here with the donkey. Isaac and I will go farther, and after we worship we will return to you."
Abraham followed Adonai's instructions exactly. He was also very aware that Adonai was testing him to see if he had complete faith.

6. Abraham placed the wood on the shoulders of his son Isaac, while he carried the fire and the slaughter knife, and the two of them walked together.
Abraham could scarcely believe his ears. Why had God asked him to make such a sacrifice? But Abraham, in his great wisdom, was a man of complete faith. His loyalty to Adonai was to become an example to his descendants, who would be just as loyal, even if it meant losing their homes, their livelihood, and sadly, sometimes their lives.

7. Where is the lamb for the sacrifice?
Imagine asking a father to sacrifice his child.

But Adonai tested Abraham and ordered him to take his only son, Isaac, to Mount Moriah and offer him as a sacrifice.

Abraham proved to be a man of complete faith. His loyalty to Adonai was to become an example to his descendants after him. Even if it meant giving their very lives, the descendants of Abraham accepted Adonai's decisions. Like Abraham, they believed that Adonai acted in His own wisdom and it was not for them to question why. This important lesson that came to Abraham through the test with Isaac was a clear instruction to all the descendants of Abraham. Never, never was human sacrifice to be brought before Adonai. It was strictly forbidden forever.

Judaism in turn brought this important lesson about the value of human life to all the nations of the world. *Chiel*

9. He then tied up his son Isaac, and placed him on the altar on top of the wood.
The Hebrew word *aked* means to "tie up." In Jewish religious literature the sacrifice of Isaac is called the *akedah*.

12 The angel said, "Do not harm your son. Do not do anything to him. For now I know that you have complete faith in Elohim. You have not even withheld your only son from Him."
13 Abraham looked up and saw a ram caught by its horns in a bush. He went and took the ram and sacrificed it in his son's place.
14 Abraham named the place Adonai Yir'eh (Adonai Will See). Today it is called B'har Adonai Yerah (He Will Be Seen on Adonai's Mountain).
15 Adonai's angel called to Abraham from heaven a second time,
16 and said, "Adonai declares, 'I have sworn that because you performed this deed, and did not even hold back your beloved son,
17 I will bless you greatly, and make your descendants as many as the stars of the sky and the sand on the seashore. Your descendants shall conquer their enemies.
18 All the nations of the world shall be blessed because of your descendants – all because you obeyed me.'"
19 Abraham returned to his servants and they went back to Beer-sheva. Abraham remained in Beer-sheva.

The Children of Nachor *Maftir*

20 After this, Abraham received a message: "Milcah has given birth to children by your brother Nachor:
21 Utz, his first-born; Buz, his brother; Kemuel, father of Aram; **22** Kesed, Chazo, Pildash, Yidlaf, and Bethuel.
23 Bethuel has a daughter, Rebecca."
Milcah gave birth to eight sons by Abraham's brother Nachor.
24 Nachor's second wife was named Reumah. She too had children: Tevach, Gacham, Tachash, and Ma'akhah.

---

12. For now I know that you have complete faith in Elohim.
Elohim was testing Abraham's willingness to totally obey Him. Now Elohim was assured that Abraham was truly worthy of being the father of the nation of Israel.

13. He went and took the ram and sacrificed it in his son's place.
The sounding of the shofar, or ram's horn, on Rosh Hashanah serves as a reminder of the horns of the ram that was sacrificed by Abraham in place of Isaac. The practice of sacrificing animals is as old as humankind and is still practiced in some countries.

13. Abraham looked up and saw a ram caught by its horns in a bush.
Abraham did not see the ram before he started his preparations for the sacrifice. Suddenly he looked up and there was the ram. Now Abraham realized that the ram was sent by Elohim and did not belong to any earthly being. *Sforno*

14. Abraham named the place Adonai Yir'eh.
The midrash says that the original name of the place was Shalem (Salem) (Ber. 14:18). When Yir'eh was added to Shalem (Salem), the name became Yir'eh Shalem, Jerusalem.

20. After this, Abraham received a message: "Milcah has given birth to children by your brother Nachor."
Now the Torah is preparing to introduce Isaac's future wife, Rebecca. The four verses following give the genealogy of Rebecca.

23. Bethuel has a daughter, Rebecca.
Rebecca was born before Sarah died. The midrash explains that before a righteous person dies, another special individual is born to replace him or her. Rebecca became the wife of Isaac and one of the "Four Matriarchs" of Israel.

חַיֵּי שָׂרָה *Chayay Sarah*

THE LIFE OF SARAH

23 Sarah lived to be 127 years old. **2** Sarah died in Kiryath Arba, also known as Hebron, in the land of Canaan. Abraham came to mourn Sarah and to cry for her. **3** When Abraham rose from mourning, he spoke to the citizens of Heth. **4** "I am a stranger and a visitor among you," he said. "Please sell me a piece of land for a burial place so that I can bury my dead wife here."
5 The people of Heth replied to Abraham, saying to him,
6 "My lord, listen to us. You are a prince of Adonai among us. Choose our best burial place to bury your wife. No one among us will refuse you a piece of land to bury your wife."
7 Abraham then rose, and he bowed down to the citizens of Heth.
8 He said to them, "If you really want to help me bury my dead, please speak up for me to Ephron son of Zohar. **9** Let him sell me the Cave of Machpelah, which he owns, at the end of his field. Let him sell it to me for its full price, as a burial place for my family."
10 Ephron was sitting among the people of Heth. Ephron the Hittite answered Abraham in the presence of the people of Heth, so that everyone who came to the city gate could hear.
11 "No, my lord," he said. "Listen to me. I will give you the field and the cave that is there. Here, in the presence of my countrymen, I have given you the Cave of Machpelah. Bury your dead."
12 Again Abraham bowed down before the people.

---

2. Sarah died in Kiryat Arba, also known as Hebron.
Hebron (which means "association, group") is a city in Israel 19 miles southwest of Jerusalem. It is situated in a valley and is surrounded by olive groves and vineyards.

It was in the city of Hebron that Abraham bought the family grave, the Cave of Machpelah.

A walled enclosure about 200 by 100 feet has been built on the traditional site of the Cave of Machpelah. The construction is similar to that of the Temple area in Jerusalem. Within the wall is a Moslem mosque. Inside the mosque is the Cave of Machpelah, which contains the graves of the three patriarchs and their wives, except for Rachel.

2. Kiryat Arba.
This name, which means "city of the four," is said to refer to the four couples who are buried there: Adam and Eve, Abraham and Sarah, Isaac and Rebecca, and Jacob and Leah.

2. Abraham came to mourn Sarah.
The account of the death of the matriarch Sarah illustrates the tradition of *kavod ha-met*, respect for the dead. Mourning and lamenting are important aspects of honoring the departed.

Tradition prescribes the proper way to honor the dead. A corpse must not be left unattended and must be watched up to the time of its burial to prevent its desecration by individuals who wish to steal body parts for profit. The body should be washed and cleansed and clothed in shrouds called *tachrichim*. The virtues of the deceased should be eulogized by friends, family, and the rabbi.

The Shulchan Aruch lists many rituals which the family of a deceased should observe.

7. Abraham then rose, and he bowed down to the citizens of Heth.
Bowing was part of ancient Eastern custom. It was a sign of respect for authority. Here, Abraham was also thanking them for their kindness in offering him the burial ground.

13 He spoke to Ephron so that all the people could hear. "Please listen to me," he said. "I will pay you for the field. Take the money from me, so I can bury my dead there."
14 Ephron replied to Abraham, **15** "My lord, listen to me. What is 400 silver coins worth of land between friends? Go ahead and bury your dead."
16 Abraham understood what Ephron meant. Abraham weighed out for Ephron the amount of silver that had been decided in the presence of the citizens of Heth. Abraham paid 400 coins of silver.

Abraham Buys the Cave of Machpelah *2nd Aliyah*

17 Abraham bought Ephron's field in Machpelah facing Mamre. It became Abraham's legal property. The property included the field, the cave, and every nearby tree. **18** It became Abraham's property, and all the people of Heth were eyewitnesses.
19 Abraham then buried his wife Sarah in the Cave of Machpelah, which is near Mamre, which is also known as Hebron, in the land of Canaan.
20 This is how the field and its cave, purchased from the people of Heth, became the uncontested legal property of Abraham as a burial site.

24 Abraham was very old, and Adonai had blessed Abraham with everything. **2** One day Abraham spoke to his trusted servant, who was in charge of all that he owned; he said, **3** "Promise me and swear to Adonai, Creator of heaven and earth, that you will not choose a wife for my son from among the Canaanite girls where I live. **4** Instead, you must go to my homeland, to my relatives' birthplace, and there find a wife for my son Isaac."

---

15. What is 400 silver coins worth of land between friends?
Abraham understood that sly Ephron was playing to the audience who were witnessing the negotiation.

Ephron was aware that Abraham knew he was overpaying for the cave, and he was itching to conclude the deal and see the money.   *Shenash*

16. Abraham weighed out for Ephron the correct amount of silver.
Though Ephron promised much, he did little. Though he originally promised to give Abraham the field, he was easily persuaded to sell it, and for a high price at that.

There were no standard coins in those days, so the merchants would weigh the gold and silver paid to them to establish its value.

Abraham insisted upon paying the full price, since he wanted full and complete rights to the cave.

17. Abraham bought Ephron's field of Machpelah.
Adonai promised Abraham that his descendants would inherit the land of Canaan. Abraham's purchase of the Cave of Machpelah was the first step toward the realization of that promise. The cave became the burial ground for all the patriarchs and matriarchs except Rachel.

Abraham buried his wife Sarah in the Cave of Machpelah.

4. Instead you must go to my homeland, to my relatives' birthplace, and find there a wife for my son Isaac.
There was no difference in the religious faith of the Canaanites, where they were living, and the faith of the Babylonians, where he was sending Eliezer. So why send Eliezer all the way to Babylon to find a wife for Isaac? Abraham calculated that if Isaac married a Canaanite, he would be surrounded by her family of uncles, nieces, and parents and they would soon assimilate into the majority of the population. However, if he married a distant Babylonian girl, she would come alone and would assimilate into Abraham's family of morality and religious beliefs.

The legendary Ten Lost Tribes disappeared by being scattered and so have hundreds or perhaps thousands of tiny isolated Jewish communities disappeared into larger ethnic and religious communities.   *Shenash*

5 "But suppose the girl does not want to return with me to this land?" asked the servant. "Then shall I bring your son back to the land that you left?"

6 Abraham replied, "No you must never do that. Under no circumstances bring my son back there!

7 Adonai, the Creator of Heaven, sent me away from my father's house and the land of my birth. He spoke to me and promised me that He would give this land to my descendants. He will send His angel in front of you, and there you will surely find a wife for my son. **8** But if the girl does not want to return with you, then you will be freed of your promise. But no matter what, you must not bring my son back there!" **9** So the servant promised Abraham, his master, that he would follow his instructions.

Rebecca at the Well *3rd Aliyah*

10 The servant then took ten of his master's camels and brought along some of the precious things that his master owned. He set off and traveled to Aram Naharayim, where Nachor, Abraham's brother lived.

11 When he arrived there, he made the camels rest on their knees outside the city, beside the well. It was in the evening, when women go out to draw water.

12 He prayed, "Adonai, Savior of my master Abraham: Be kind to me today, and also show kindness to my master Abraham.

13 I am now standing by a well, and the daughters of the townspeople are coming out to draw water. **14** If I ask a girl, 'Please let me have a drink from your jar,' and she replies, 'Yes, certainly drink, and I will also water your camels,' then she will be the one whom You have chosen for Your servant Isaac. If there is such a girl, I will know that You have kept Your promise to my master."

15 He had just finished speaking when Rebecca appeared. She was the daughter of Bethuel, the son of Milcah, the wife of Abraham's brother Nachor. Her water jar was on her shoulder.

16 Rebecca was beautiful, and she was untouched by any man. Rebecca went to the well and filled her jar, and started back.

17 At that moment the servant rushed toward her and said, "Please, let me have a drink of water from your jar."

18 Without hesitation she replied, "Drink as much as you want." She quickly lowered the jar and gave him a drink. **19** When he had finished drinking, she said, "Now let me bring some water for your camels, so they too can drink."

---

10. The servant took ten of his master's camels. Aram Naharayim was about 600 miles away, so Eliezer, Abraham's servant, took camels, which were ideal for long-distance travel.

There are two varieties of camels – the single hump and the double hump. The camel's unique physical qualities enable it to survive under harsh desert conditions. It can feed on thorny desert plants and store food and water for several days in its stomach. The thick padding on its paws makes it possible for the camel to walk on the hot, shifting desert sands. The swaying walk had earned the camel the title of "ship of the desert."

11. He made the camels rest. Abraham's camels could easily be identified because they were muzzled. Abraham wanted to prevent his camels from grazing in someone else's field.

19. Now let me bring some water for your camels. Rebecca worked a long time drawing water for all the camels. It was hard work but she asked no reward. She performed the task out of mercy for the camels. Eliezer realized that he had found a fitting wife for Isaac and gave her the presents he had brought with him for the bride-to-be.

20 She quickly emptied her jar into the trough and ran to the well again to bring more water. She brought enough water for all his camels.
21 The man stood there silently staring at her, waiting and wondering if Adonai had miraculously made his journey successful.
22 When the camels had finished drinking, Abraham's servant took out a gold ring weighing half a shekel, and two gold bracelets weighing ten gold shekels, and gave them to her.
23 He then asked, "Whose daughter are you? Also tell me whether there is any place in your father's house for us to spend the night."
24 She replied, "I am the daughter of Bethuel, and my grandparents are Milcah and Nachor."
25 Then she said, "Of course, we have plenty of straw and feed, as well as a place for your people to spend the night." **26** The man bowed low and thanked Adonai.

The Mission Is Successful   *4th Aliyah*

27 He said, "Blessed be Adonai, Savior of my master Abraham, who has been kind to my master. Here I am, and Adonai has led me directly to the house of my master's family!"
28 The girl ran to her mother's home and told the woman what had happened.
29 Now Rebecca had a brother named Laban. He heard Rebecca, and he ran to the stranger at the well. **30** He had seen the ring, and the bracelets on his sister's arms, and had heard his sister Rebecca telling what the man had said to her. He rushed to the stranger, who was standing beside the camels near the well, **31** and said, "Come! You are a man blessed by Adonai! Why are you still standing outside? Come, I have a room for you, and I have prepared a place for the camels."

---

20. She brought enough water for all his camels.
Eliezer had a feeling that Adonai had miraculously directed him to the well. Then he saw Rebecca. Eliezer thought quickly. What could he ask of the young woman at the well? And it came to him. "Please, let me have a drink of water."

Without a moment's hesitation the girl offered the man her pitcher. He drank and thanked her. The she volunteered to bring water for his camels. Without a minute's delay the girl patiently brought jars of water for the camels. Not once, but a second and a third time she moved back and forth to the well, bringing water to the camels.

Eliezer was astonished and sure that Adonai had made his journey a success.

22. Abraham's servant took out a gold ring weighing half a shekel and two gold bracelets weighing ten gold shekels.
The midrash tells us that the two bracelets represented the two Tablets of the Law, while the weight of ten shekels represented the Ten Commandments, which were inscribed on the two Tablets of the Law.

25. We have plenty of straw and feed, as well as a place for your people to spend the night.
Once again Rebecca shows her concern for the animals by mentioning first the food for them and then a place for Eliezer to sleep.

29. Now Rebecca had a brother named Laban. He heard Rebecca, and he ran to the stranger at the well.
Rebecca told her family about the stranger and showed them the gold ring and the bracelets. The mention of gold energized greed in Laban, and he ran to see the wealthy stranger and perhaps also get a gold gift. It was just not his nature to run to welcome him or to offer him or anybody else hospitality.

30. He rushed to the stranger.
Greedy Laban was so impressed with the gifts that Eliezer gave Rebecca that he ran to greet him.

32 So the stranger came into the house and unloaded the camels. Laban gave the camels straw and feed, and brought water for the stranger and the men with him with which to bathe their feet. **33** But when the food was served, the stranger said, "I will not eat until I tell you the reason I came here." Laban replied, "Tell us your mission."

34 The stranger said, "I am Abraham's servant. **35** Adonai has blessed my master, and he is very rich. Adonai has given him many sheep and cattle, silver, gold, servants, camels, and donkeys. **36** In her old age my master's wife Sarah gave birth to a son. And my master has given him everything that he owns.

37 My master made me swear: 'Do not choose a wife for my son from among the daughters of the Canaanites, in whose land I live. **38** Instead, you must go to my father's house, to my family, and there you shall get a wife for my son.'

39 I said to my master, 'But what if the girl will not come back with me?' **40** He said to me, 'Adonai, will send His angel with you and make your mission successful. But you must find a wife for my son from my family and from my father's house.

41 There is only one way that you can be free of your promise. If you go to my family and they do not give you a girl, only then will you be released from your promise.'

42 Now today I came to the well, and I prayed, 'Adonai, Savior of my master Abraham, please make my mission that I have undertaken a success. **43** I will stand by the town well, and when a girl comes out to draw water, I will ask her, "Please let me drink some water from your jar." **44** If she answers, "Not only may you drink, but I will also draw water for your camels," then she is the wife chosen by Adonai for my master's son.'

45 Then, even before I had finished speaking to myself, Rebecca suddenly came by, carrying a water jar on her shoulder. As she went down to the well to fill her jar, I asked her, 'Please give me a drink.' **46** She immediately lowered her jar and said, 'Drink! I will also bring water for all your camels.' I took a drink, and she also brought water for all the camels.

47 I asked her, 'Whose daughter are you?' She replied, 'I am the daughter of Bethuel son of Nachor and Milcah.' I then put a ring on her nose, and bracelets on her arms.

48 I bowed low to Adonai. I blessed Adonai, Savior of my master Abraham, because He led me on the right path to find a wife for my master's son.

---

34 The stranger said, "I am Abraham's servant."
Eliezer makes sure that he is acting as Abraham's servant. Obviously Abraham enjoyed an excellent reputation and Eliezer used it to add worth to the deal.

37. Do not choose a wife for my son from among the daughters of the Canaanites, in whose land I live.
First go to my father's family in Aram Naharayim and see if you can find a proper wife for my son. If she is unwilling to return with you, then we'll fall back and perhaps look for a match among the locals.

47. I asked her, "Whose daughter are you?" She replied, "I am the daughter of Bethuel son of Nachor and Milcah." I then put a ring on her nose and bracelets on her arms.
Diamonds (gold) are a girl's best friend.

It was and still is customary to win a girl's heart with gifts of jewelry. Gold jewelry was widely used in patriarchal times, especially during periods of prosperity. To this day, Bedouin women wear nose rings and bracelets. Modern women also wear bracelets and other types of jewelry.

49 Now if you are willing to do what is kind and right for my master, please tell me. If not, say so, and I will then know my next step whether to go to the right or to the left."
50 Laban and Bethuel both spoke up. "We know that Adonai has purposely sent you here! We have no choice whether it is bad or good. **51** Rebecca is right here in front of you. Adonai has spoken; take her and go. Let her become the wife for your master's son."
52 When Abraham's servant heard these words, he bowed down to Adonai and thanked Him.

Rebecca Meets Isaac *5th Aliyah*

53 The servant then brought out gifts of gold and silver jewelry, as well as articles of clothing, and gave them to Rebecca. He also presented gifts to her brother and mother. **54** Abraham's servants and his men then ate and drank, and they spent the night. When they got up in the morning, the servant said, "It is time for us to go back to our master." **55** The girl's brother and mother replied, "At least allow her to remain with us for another week or ten days, and then she will be prepared to go."
56 "Do not make me stay any longer," said the servant.
"Adonai has already made my mission a success. Let me leave, so that I can return to my master." **57** They replied, "In that case let's call Rebecca and ask her what she wants to do."
58 So they called Rebecca and asked her, "Are you willing to go with this man?" She replied "Yes, I will go."

---

49. Now if you are willing to do what is kind and right for my master, please tell me. If not, say so, and I will then know my next step whether to go to the right or to the left.
Abraham selected Eliezer because he was a tough negotiator. Eliezer exhibits his determination to finalize the deal. "Deal or no deal! Do you intend to let her go so she can marry my master's son, Isaac?"

50. We both know that Adonai has purposely sent you here!
Since it was Adonai who brought you and our daughter together, our personal wishes are not important in this matter.

51. Let her become the wife of your master's son.
When Eliezer, arrived at Rebecca's house, an exciting welcome awaited them. Bethuel, father of Rebecca and Laban, and all the family received him with joy. They soon discovered that Eliezer was the servant of Abraham, uncle to Rebecca's father, Bethuel.

It did not take Eliezer long to get to the matter of Rebecca's marrying Isaac. Bethuel, Rebecca's father, and Laban, her brother, agreed enthusastically to Eliezer's proposal.

For many centuries it was the parents who decided whom their children would marry. It was believed that the parents were much better able to judge who were the best choices for their children as marriage partners. Even today in some Jewish communities marriages (*shidduchim*) are arranged by a rabbi and the parents.

53. The servant brought out gifts of gold and silver jewelry as well as articles of clothing, and gave them to Rebecca. He also presented gifts to her brother and mother.
These presents offered to Rebecca and her family were a reward for accepting the proposal of marriage.

58. So they called Rebecca and asked her, "Are you willing to go with this man?"
Laban and Bethuel loved Rebecca and did not want her to be forced into a marriage. Before they consented to the marriage, they wanted her approval. Good and successful marriage needs the consent of the family as well as the approval and the agreement of both the bride and bridegroom.

59 So Rebecca and her servants left with Abraham's servant, and his men.

60 They blessed Rebecca and said to her, "You are our sister, may you become the mother of millions! And your ancestors triumph over all their enemies."

61 Rebecca and her servants mounted their camels and followed Abraham's servants. **62** Just at that moment Isaac was returning from Beer LaChai Ro'i, since he was then living in the Negev. **63** Toward evening Isaac decided to take a walk in the fields. He looked up and saw camels approaching.

64 When Rebecca looked up and saw Isaac, she stepped down from her camel. **65** She asked Abraham's servant, "Who is this man walking to meet us?"

Abraham's servant replied, "That is my master." Then Rebecca took her veil and covered her face.

66 The servant told Isaac everything that had happened to him.

67 Then Isaac brought the girl into his mother Sarah's tent, and he married Rebecca. She became his wife, and he loved her. She comforted Isaac for the death of his mother.

Abraham Dies
6th Aliyah

25 Abraham married another woman, whose name was Keturah. **2** She gave birth to Zimran, Yakshan, Medan, Midian, Yishbak, and Shuach.

3 Yakshan fathered Sheba and Dedan. The sons of Dedan were the Ashurim, Letushim, and Leumim **4** The sons of Midian were Eiphahl, Epher, Enoch, Avidah, and Elda'ah. All these children were Keturah's descendants.

---

65. Then Rebecca took her veil and covered her face.
The women did not veil themselves. Only aristocratic women in Assyria were in the habit of covering their face. Rebecca came from Aram, so her veiling was a sign of her aristocratic origin.

In many Arab countries it is a rule that women must veil themselves when they leave their home.

67. Then Isaac brought the girl into his mother Sarah's tent, and he married Rebecca.
After weeks of traveling, Rebecca arrived, with Eliezer, in Canaan. At last they approached Abraham's dwelling place and there out in the countryside stood Isaac. Rebecca wondered who the fellow might be. Eliezer understood her curiosity and said to her, "That is Isaac."

And it was love at first sight. Isaac was happy with lovely Rebecca and she was more than pleased to meet her husband-to-be.

For Abraham, Rebecca's coming was a wonderful consolation. Ever since Sarah's death there was a lonely feeling in his and Isaac's life. Now once more their house would be a home. Abraham felt that his life was fulfilled.

67. Isaac brought the girl into his mother Sarah's tent, and he married Rebecca.
Abraham and his beloved wife, Sarah, lived together for many happy years. Our sages tell us that during all of those years a cloud of holiness floated over Sarah's tent, night and day. When Sarah died the cloud disappeared.

Then one day Isaac, son of Sarah and Abraham, brought his bride, Rebecca, to his mother's tent. Lo and behold! The cloud reappeared and once more floated over the tent. Then Isaac knew that Rebecca was truly worthy to be his wife and become a part of the family of Abraham.

1-2. Abraham married another woman, whose name was Keturah. She gave birth to Zimran, Yakshan, Medan, Midian, Yishbak, and Shuach.
The children were brought up in Abraham's house but they were not his children. Abraham fathered only two sons, Isaac and Ishmael.

5 Abraham left everything that he owned to Isaac.
6 To the sons of the concubines, Abraham also gave gifts. Then, while he was still alive, he sent them to the East, far away from his son Isaac.
7 This is the history of Abraham's life. He lived a total of 175 years. **8** Abraham breathed his last and died at a ripe old age. **9** His sons Isaac and Ishmael buried him in the Cave of Machpelah, in the field of Ephron son of Zohar the Hittite, which borders Mamre. **10** The field that Abraham bought from the children of Heth is where Abraham and his wife Sarah were buried.
11 After Abraham died, Adonai blessed Isaac, his son. Isaac now lived near Beer LaChai Ro'i.

The History of Ishmael   *7th Aliyah*

12 This is the history of Ishmael, son of Abraham, whom Hagar the Egyptian, Sarah's slave, bore to Abraham:
13 These are the names of Ishmael's sons in order of their birth: Nebayoth, Ishmael's firstborn, Kedar, Adbiel, Mibsam, **14** Mishma, Duma, Masa, **15** Chadad, Tema, Yetur, Nafish, and Kedmah.

Ishmael Dies   *Maftir*

16 Ishmael's sons founded towns and villages. They became the founders of twelve tribes named after them. **17** This is the history of Ishmael's life. He lived a total of 137 years. and died.
18 His descendants lived in the area from Havilah to Shur, which borders on Egypt, all the way to Assyria. They were always fighting one another.

---

5. Abraham left everything that he owned to Isaac.
The instructions given by a dying person have legal and moral worth and were to be carried out by the survivors. Today people write wills in which they give instructions about what to do with their money and their property after their death.

The Hebrew word for "will" is *tzva-ah*. The root word is *tzaveh*, which means "to command." In a *tzva-ah* we command our family to dispose of our earthly goods in a special way.

6. To the sons of the concubines, Abraham also gave gifts.
Abraham was very well aware of the possible conflicts between his son Isaac and the children of his concubines Hagar and Keturah. So, while he was alive he settled the problems of his inheritance. Abraham deeded his entire estate to Isaac. He also gave enough gifts to the concubines children so as to make it worth while for them to peacefully move away from Isaac.

13. Nebayoth.
Some commentators identify these people with the Nabatians. They were Arabians who between the sixth and fourth centuries B.C.E. seized the mountain stronghold of Edom and Moab. They engineered water conservation devices in the parched Sinai Desert, which produced enough crops to feed a large population.

17. He lived a total of 137 years and died.
People who are near death sometimes have a need to clear the slate. They ask their family and friends to forgive them for their behavior, insults, and lack of self-control. Some clear their conscience and even confess to crimes that they committed. The Rabbis in the Talmud say that Ishmael before he died cleared his conscience and begged his father, Abraham, to forgive him for his actions.

תּוֹלְדֹת *Toldot*

THE HISTORY OF ISAAC

19 These are the chronicles of Isaac son of Abraham: Abraham was Isaac's father. **20** When Isaac was forty years old, he married Rebecca, daughter of Bethuel the Aramaean of Padan Aram and sister of Laban the Aramaean.

21 His wife Rebecca could have no children, and Isaac pleaded with Adonai for her sake. So Adonai answered his prayer, and Rebecca became pregnant.

22 But the twins inside her fought, and when this occurred, she asked, "Why is this happening to me?" She went to seek an answer from Adonai.

23 Adonai said to her, "Two competing nations are in your body. One nation will be stronger than the other. The descendants of the older son will serve the descendants of the younger son."

24 Rebecca gave birth to twins.

25 The first one that came out was covered with red hair. So they named him Esau. **26** The second twin that came out was holding on to his brother Esau's heel (*akav*). So Isaac named him Jacob. Isaac was sixty years old when Rebecca gave birth to Esau and Jacob.

---

21. His wife Rebecca could have no children, and Isaac pleaded with Adonai for her sake. So Adonai answered his prayer, and Rebecca became pregnant.

Isaac was completely in love with Rebecca and prayed that his children would come from her. He recognized her spiritually and was sure that her children would also inherit her holiness.

22. The twins inside her fought.

The two punching children, Esau and Jacob, would become two nations, Edom and Israel. The two children would not be on friendly terms with each other, and neither would the two nations. And so it was, Israel and Edom were constantly at war with each other.

Esau was just a few minutes older than his brother Jacob. Although the two brothers were twins, they were not alike. Esau's arms and body were covered with thick red hair. Jacob's hands and neck were very smooth. Esau grew up to be a strong man, and he loved to hunt for deer in the woods and mountains. But Jacob was quiet and thoughtful, staying at home and caring for the flocks of his father.

25. The first one that came out was covered with red hair.

The name Esau comes from the Hebrew verb *asah*, "to make." Esau was born with as much hair as a "full-made" (mature) man.

His reddish hair was a sign that he and his descendants would shed a great deal of blood.

26. The second twin that came out was holding on to his brother Esau's heel (*akav*). So Isaac named him Jacob (*Ya'akov*).

In ancient times, a large family was considered a great blessing. The Torah says, "Be fruitful and multiply" six times.

When a child was born, a messenger was sent at once to bring the news to the father. "A child is born, to you!" he would cry, and there would be great rejoicing.

In biblical days, a child was given a name that had a definite idea behind it. Joseph was so named because his name derived from the Hebrew word meaning "to add," and his mother said, "Adonai added to me another son." Sometimes a child was named for a living creature or a plant. Deborah means "bee"; Tamar means "palm tree."

Today a Jewish child is usually named after a dear one who has died. In this way the name of the departed is kept alive and is remembered by the family.

27 The boys grew up. Esau became a skilled hunter, a man of the field. Jacob was a quiet man who remained at home.
28 Isaac favored Esau and enjoyed eating Esau's wild game, but Rebecca favored Jacob.
29 Once Jacob was cooking a stew, when Esau came home exhausted from the hunt.
30 So Esau said to Jacob, "I'm famished. Give me some of that red stuff that you are cooking." This is how Esau earned his other name, Edom (Red). **31** Jacob replied, "First sell me your birthright." **32** Esau exclaimed, "I'm about to die of hunger! What good is a birthright to me now?"
33 Jacob answered, "Swear to me right now that the birthright belongs to me." So Esau swore and sold his birthright to Jacob. **34** Then Jacob gave Esau bread and some of the red lentil stew. Esau ate it, drank, got up, and left, not caring that he had rejected the birthright.

26 Once again there was a famine in the land, just like the first famine in the time of Abraham: Isaac went to Abimelech, king of the Philistines, in Gerar. **2** Adonai appeared to Isaac and said, "Do not go down to Egypt. Stay here in this land that I am going to give you.
3 Continue to live in this land. I will protect you and bless you, and I will give all of this land to your descendants. I will keep the promise that I made to your father Abraham. **4** I will make your descendants as numerous as the stars of the sky, and give them all these lands. All the nations on earth will be blessed because of your descendants. **5** I will do this because Abraham obeyed Me and My commandments, and My decrees, and My laws."

---

27. Esau became a skilled hunter, a man of the field. Jacob was a quiet man who remained at home.
The brothers, Esau and Jacob, were rivals. Esau was the vigorous outdoorsman, restless, a hunter by nature, eager for the kill. Jacob, by contrast, was the amiable shepherd, gentle, peace-loving.

To further complicate their relationship was the important matter of the birthright. The first-born son held a special position in the ancient tradition. A double share in the inheritance of whatever his family owned was due to him. But along with this economic advantage there also went something more important in the Hebrew tradition. The first-born son was held particularly responsible for continuing the family's spiritual inheritance. This responsibility was no small obligation for a man to carry through his lifetime.

34. Then Jacob gave Esau bread and some of the red lentil stew. Esau ate it, drank, got up, and left, not caring that he had rejected the birthright.
Esau was a hunter, a man of action. The birthright was a legal term, which meant nothing to him. He used his spiritual birthright for his physical needs. Jacob bought the birthright and became one of the three patriarchs of the Jewish people.

2. Do not go down to Egypt.
In time of famine, it was natural to go down to Egypt, which always seemed to have food to sell. Isaac's father, Abraham, migrated to Egypt during a famine. But now Adonai told him not to go but to remain in the land that "I am going to give you." Adonai said that despite the famine, Isaac's flocks would increase and he would be successful.

3. Continue to live in this land. I will protect you and bless you.
You must continue to live here so as not to forfeit your claim to the land and to establish your rights.
Sforno

5. I will do this because Abraham obeyed Me.
Abraham, the first patriarch, was faithful to Adonai.

Isaac and Abimelech
2nd Aliyah

6 So Isaac settled in Gerar. **7** When the residents asked about his wife, he told them that she was his sister. He was afraid to say that she was his wife, because Rebecca was beautiful, and they would have killed him because of her.
8 Once, after Isaac had been there for some time, Abimelech, king of the Philistines, was looking out the window, and he saw Isaac embracing his wife Rebecca.
9 Abimelech summoned Isaac and asked, "Is Rebecca your wife? Why did you tell me that she is your sister?" Isaac answered, "I was afraid that I would be murdered because of her."
10 "What have you done to us?" exploded Abimelech. "One of my people could easily have molested your wife! You would have made us commit a terrible crime!" **11** Abimelech announced to all his people. "Whoever dares to harm this man or his wife shall die."
12 Isaac farmed in the area. That year he harvested a hundred times more than he planted because Adonai had blessed him.

The Quarrels Over the Wells
3rd Aliyah

13 This was the beginning of his wealth. He continued to prosper until he became extremely wealthy. **14** He had flocks of sheep, herds of cattle, and many servants. The Philistines became jealous of him. **15** They filled up all the wells that his father's servants had dug while Abraham was still alive.
16 Abimelech said to Isaac, "Leave us; you have become too wealthy for us." **17** Isaac left the area and settled in the Gerar Valley.

---

7. When the residents asked about his wife, he told them that she was his sister.
The apple did not fall far from the tree. Isaac does exactly the same as his father did before him. To protect himself against possible enemies, he lies about his true relationship to Rebecca.

10. One of my people could easily have molested your wife! You would have made us commit a terrible crime.
Abimelech was a righteous king and was angry with Abraham for lying to him. He said, the welfare and morality of my people are important to me, and your lies could have corrupted all of us.

12. Adonai had blessed him.
Before Abraham died he, like a good father, distributed his wealth among his children. Now Adonai blesses Isaac and he has a successful harvest. Wealth is a gift from Adonai and is used for the betterment of people and institutions.

14. The Philistines became jealous.
Abraham prospered. He had great harvests and his flocks increased to the point that the Philistines became jealous and stopped up his water supply, the source of his successful harvest. Success due to hard work and ingenuity sometimes breeds jealousy.

16. You have become too wealthy for us.
The midrash reads the verse as "You have become wealthy because of us."

The fact that Isaac used his brains and his brawn to be a success did not mean anything to Abimelech. Now the king accuses Isaac of becoming rich from him and his subjects.

16. Abimelech said to Isaac, "Leave us; you have become too wealthy for us."
Abimelech could have seized all of Isaac's property, and the anti-Isaac subjects would have been happy to seize his wealth. Instead this king, a comparatively decent human being, warns Isaac to "get out of town" before a lynch mob forms.

Thus Abimelech permitted him to leave with all of his assets. Historically, in Jewish history rulers have not been as gracious as Abimelech.

They usually seized all of their property and sent them away just with their clothes on their backs.

This was the first expulsion of many to be suffered by Jews.

18 He opened the wells that had been dug in the days of his father Abraham, which had been closed up by the Philistines after Abraham's death. He gave them the same names that his father had given them. **19** Isaac's servants again dug in the valley and found a new well, overflowing with fresh water. **20** The shepherds of Gerar quarreled with Isaac's shepherds, claiming that the water was theirs. Isaac named the well Esek (Challenge) because the shepherds had challenged him. **21** Isaac's shepherds then dug another well, and again the shepherds harassed them. So Isaac named the well Sitnah (Harassment). **22** He then moved away from there and dug another well. This time it was not challenged, so he named it Rehovot (Wide Spaces). "Now at last Adonai will grant us wide open spaces," he said. "We can be prosperous in this land."

Isaac and Abimelech Make a Treaty   *4th Aliyah*

23 From there, Isaac went to Beer-sheva. **24** That night Adonai appeared to him and said, "I am Adonai of your father Abraham. Do not be afraid, for I am with you. I will bless you and give you very many descendants because of My promise to your father Abraham."
25 Isaac built an altar and worshipped Adonai. He settled there, and his servants dug a well in the area.
26 Abimelech from Gerar, along with a group of friends and his general, Pikhol, came to Isaac. **27** Isaac asked, "Why have you come to me? You hate me, and you drove me away!" **28** They replied, "We have seen that you are blessed by Adonai. We propose that we make a treaty between us, **29** that just as we did not touch you, you will do no harm to us. We will not harm you, and you will not harm us. We will leave you in peace."

The Well at Beer-sheva   *5th Aliyah*

30 Isaac prepared a feast for them, and they ate and drank. **31** They arose early in the morning and exchanged promises. Isaac then said goodbye and they left in peace. **32** On that very same day, Isaac's servants came and told him about the well they had been digging. They announced, "We have found water!" **33** Isaac named the well Shevah. The city is therefore called Beer-sheva (Well of the Seven) to this very day. **34** When Esau was forty years old, he married Judith, daughter of Beeri the Hittite, and Basemath, daughter of Elon the Hittite. **35** His Hittite wives made life bitter for Isaac and Rebecca.

27

Isaac had grown old and his eyesight was almost gone. He called for his elder son, Esau, and said, "My son." Esau answered, "Yes, father, I am here."
2 "I am old, and soon I will die.
3 Take your bow and arrows, and go out into the field and get some deer meat.

---

22. He then moved away from there and dug another well.
Isaac was a stranger in a land ruled by Abimelech. He was well aware that he would not receive any justice if he complained to the ruling authorities. He had no recourse but to move and dig another well.

3. Get some deer meat.
Esau had to go hunting, kill an animal, and bring it home and cook it. Jacob took the animal from his herd and prepared the meal very quickly.

4 Make it into a tasty dish, the way I like it, and bring it to me to eat. Afterwards I will give you the blessing of the first-born."

5 Rebecca had secretly been listening while Isaac spoke to Esau. Esau went out to the field to hunt for a deer and bring it home for Isaac.

6 Rebecca said to her son Jacob, "I just heard your father speaking to your brother Esau. He said, **7** 'Bring me some deer meat and cook it for me. After I eat I will bless you with Adonai's blessing before I die.'"

8 Rebecca continued, "Now, my son, listen to me. Follow my instructions carefully. **9** Go to the herd and choose two lambs. And I will prepare it just the way your father likes.

10 Then you must bring it to your father, so that he will eat it and bless you before he dies."

11 Jacob replied, "But my brother Esau is hairy. I am smooth skinned.

---

4. Make it into a tasty dish, the way I like it, and bring it to me to eat. Afterwards I will give you the blessing of the first-born.
In biblical times, it was customary to finalize a deal or write a treaty by eating a meal. Isaac is preparing to give Esau the blessing, so he sets the stage to bless his spiritual heir with a celebratory meal.

4. Afterwards I will give you the blessing of the first-born.
Isaac grew weak with age. He felt that death was not far off and he was concerned about his family's future. The time had come when he had to make known his last will and testament. In keeping with the then accepted tradition of the birthright, Isaac automatically assumed that Esau would be his spiritual heir. Isaac knew nothing of Esau's disdain of tradition and "sale" of the birthright to Jacob for the price of a mere bowl of pottage. Esau chose to forget his "deal" with Jacob and proceeded enthusiastically to prepare for the blessing transfer by Isaac.

4. Afterwards I will give you the blessing of the first-born.
The instructions given by a dying person have legal and moral worth and were to be carried out by the survivors. Today people write wills in which they give instructions about what to do with their money and their property after their death.

The Hebrew word for "will" is *tzvah-ah*. The root word is *tzaveh*, which means "to command." In a *tzvah-ah*, we command our family to dispose of our earthly goods in a special way.

5. Rebecca had secretly been listening while Isaac spoke to Esau.
Rebecca heard Isaac summoning Esau to prepare the special birthright meal. Long before, Rebecca had become convinced that their son Esau was not the proper successor to the leadership responsibility which had begun with Abraham.

Now that the line of Abrahamic succession was going to pass from Isaac, Rebecca was determined that it go to the son who seemed to her to be the logical heir, Jacob. To Rebecca, who had observed Esau's irresponsibility over the years, the issue had become one of *Worthright vs Birthright*.

In the Esau-Jacob struggle for successorship, this, too, was the issue. Was there to be an automatic transfer of leadership by birthright or was there to be, as Rebecca felt there should be, the important consideration of worthright? As she saw it, Jacob was the truly eligible man for the responsibility. And though Jacob was reluctant to break with the birthright principle, Rebecca persuaded him that it must be done for the future well-being of Abraham and Isaac's descendants.   *Chiel*

7. After I eat I will bless you with Adonai's blessing before I die.
Before I die, I will bless you with the consent and approval of Adonai.   *Rashi*

12 Suppose my father touches me. He will immediately know that I am not Esau! I will earn a curse instead of a blessing!"

13 Rebecca said, "My son, let any curse on you be on me. Listen to me. Go, and do what I said."

14 Jacob went and brought the lambs that his mother had requested. She took the lambs and cooked them, using the same tasty recipe that Jacob's father liked.

15 Rebecca then took some of Esau's clothing and put them on her younger son, Jacob.

16 She also covered Jacob's arms and the hairless parts of his neck with the lambskins.

17 Rebecca gave her son Jacob Isaac's favorite food and the bread she had baked. **18** He approached his father and said, "Father, I am here." Then Isaac asked, "Who are you, my son?"

19 "It is I, Esau, your first-born," said Jacob. "I have done as you asked me. Sit up, and eat the deer meat, so that you can give me your special blessing."

20 Asked Isaac, " My son, how did you find the deer so quickly?"

Jacob answered, "Adonai was with me."

21 Jacob replied, "Then come closer to me. Let me touch you, my son. I must be sure that you are really Esau." **22** Jacob came close, and Isaac touched him. He said, "The voice is the voice of Jacob, but the hands are the hands of Esau."

23 He did not recognize him because Jacob's arms were hairy just like those of his brother Esau.

24 Suddenly Isaac again asked, "Are you really my son Esau?" Jacob answered, "I am."

25 Isaac then said, "Serve me the food. I will eat the deer meat that you hunted and then I will give you my blessing."

Jacob served the food, and Isaac ate. Then Jacob brought Isaac some wine, and he drank it.

26 His father Isaac said to him, "My son, come closer and kiss me."

27 Jacob approached and kissed him. Isaac smelled the aroma of his clothing.

Isaac said, "My son's aroma is like the perfume of a field blessed by Adonai.

---

12. He will immediately know that I am not Esau! I will earn a curse instead of a blessing!
Reluctantly, Jacob followed his mother's command to bring the two lambs which she would prepare for Isaac's "Meal of Blessing." He had protested to Rebecca that this plan would make him "a deceiver" of his own father, but his mother insisted that if the scheme failed, she would take the blame upon herself.

Jacob was torn between his love for his mother plus his own wish to be his father's heir, and his regard for his father. It was a real moral dilemma, and his conscience troubled him deeply. This act of deception which he was about to perform would haunt him through the rest of his life.

22. The voice is the voice of Jacob, but the hands are the hands of Esau.
Much of the history of the Jewish people, and, indeed, of the world, has been a story of conflict between the hands of Esau – the power, strength, and ruthlessness of the mighty empires of the world, and the voice of Jacob – the prayers, the study, and the devotion of the pure, who are less strong in body but all the more mighty in spirit.

The Rabbis say that so long as the voice of the Jews is heard studying and praying, the Children of Israel will never be vanquished by the powers of Esau, be they represented by tyrannies either ancient or modern.

Isaac Blesses Jacob

6th Aliyah

28 "May Elohim grant you the dew of heaven and the richness of the earth and much grain and wine.
29 Nations will serve you;
and people will bow down to you.
You will be the leader of your brothers;
And your mother's children
will bow down before you.
Those who curse you will be cursed,
and those who bless you will be blessed. "
30 As soon as Isaac had finished blessing Jacob, his brother Esau returned from the hunt.
31 He too prepared Isaac's favorite food and brought it to his father. Esau said, "My father, get up and eat your favorite food so that you can give your blessing".
32 Isaac asked,
"Who are you?" Esau replied,
"I am your first-born, Esau."
33 Isaac began trembling.
"Then who just served me my favorite dish?
I ate it all before you came, and I blessed him. The blessing must remain his."
34 When Esau heard his father's words, he broke out into a loud scream.
Esau pleaded, "Father, bless me too."
35 Isaac said, "Your brother came with trickery and he has taken your blessing."

---

28. May Elohim grant you the dew of heaven and the richness of the earth and much grain and wine.
In Canaan, the rains did not always come when needed. In times of drought, tribes came to Egypt to keep themselves and their cattle alive. All three patriarchs at one time or another went down to Egypt in time of a general drought. The threat of drought was a curse and a disaster.

Drought in ancient Israel caused the death of thousands. Ancient Israelites recited special prayers for rain and dew. Even today in modern Israel, with all of its technical expertise, drought is still a huge problem.

One of Adonai's greatest blessings to Israel was His promise to send the rain at the proper time.

Jews all over the world pray for rain and dew in the state of Israel. No matter where Jews live, they are concerned about the well-being of the country and pray for its welfare.

The ancient blessing "You cause the wind to blow and the rain to fall" is recited at the end of Sukkot until the first day of Passover, and the petition "send dew and rain for a blessing on the earth" is recited several weeks later because during this period of time rain is expected in Israel. This prayer is called *tal umatter* – dew and rain.

29. Nations will serve you.
King David conquered many of the surrounding nations. They pledged allegiance to Israel and paid tribute to David.

34. When Esau heard his father's words, he broke out into a loud scream.
Esau pleaded, "Father, bless me too."

Why was Isaac willing to give Esau the divine blessing?

The Torah tells us that Isaac and Rebecca were unhappy that Esau had married Hittite wives. In spite of this, Isaac believed that Esau deserved the blessing.

The commentator David Kimhi suggests that Isaac wished to bless Esau in the hope that the spiritual blessing would change his character and reform him.

Obviously Isaac believed in miracles.

36 Esau said, "No wonder you named him Jacob (Ya'akov)! He tricked (*akav*) me behind my back (*akav*) twice. First he stole my birthright, and now he has taken my blessing!" Esau pleaded, "Haven't you saved a blessing for me too?"
37 Isaac answered, "I have declared that he will be the leader of all his brothers, and I have assured him an abundance of grain and wine. Now what kind of blessing can I give you?"
38 Esau said to his father, "There must be at least one blessing that you have for me? Father, please bless me too!" Esau raised his voice and began to cry.
39 His father Isaac then said,

"Your home will be in fertile places,
they will be watered by dew of heaven.
40 But you shall live by your sword.
You will serve your brother,
but then you will throw off his yoke
and finally be free."

41 Esau hated Jacob because of the blessing that his father had given him. He said to himself, "The days of mourning for my father will be over soon; then I will be able to kill my brother Jacob."
42 When Rebecca heard of Esau's plan, she sent word to her younger son, Jacob. "Your brother Esau is planning to kill you," she said. **43** "My son, listen to me; escape to my brother Laban in Haran. **44** Stay with him until your brother's anger is gone.

---

36. First he stole my birthright, and now he has taken my blessing!
Esau conveniently forgot that he had sold his birthright; he accused Jacob of stealing it from him.

40. But you shall live by your sword.
Isaac, although old and blind, was very well aware of Esau's character. Esau loved to play rough and was comfortable when he could use his bow and arrow as a hunter and his sword as a warrior.

41. Esau hated Jacob because of the blessing that his father had given him.
Hardly had Isaac blessed Jacob, who quickly made his exit from the tent, when Esau arrived with his prepared venison. Esau identified himself to his father. Isaac was stunned. Slowly it dawned upon him that he had been deceived by Jacob. Esau cried out bitterly and pleaded pathetically with Isaac that he bless him as well. Isaac then blessed Esau, but not as the first-born son.

41. The days of mourning for my father will be over soon; then I will be able to kill my brother Jacob.
Jacob was no coward and was ready to face his brother Esau. But Rebecca, who loved both her sons, begged Jacob to run away. She did not want Esau to become a murderer and kill Jacob.

41. The days of mourning for my father will be over soon; then I will be able to kill my brother Jacob.
Esau, out of respect for his father, postponed killing Jacob until Isaac died.
However, Esau knew well that the center of the intrigue was his mother, Rebecca. He hated Jacob and no doubt hated his mother.

42. Your brother Esau is planning to kill you.
In the instance of Jacob outwitting his brother Esau, a wrong has been committed. It therefore brings on the reaction of hatred. Esau in his hatred is determind to get revenge. Jacob has no choice but to run for his life. A negative chain reaction has been started and it must run its unhappy course.

44. Stay with him until your brother's anger is gone.
Rebecca tried to act as a peacemaker. She hoped that in time Esau's anger would disappear and the two brothers would become friends once again.

45 When your brother has calmed down and has forgotten what you have done to him, I will send word and call you home. Why should I lose both of my sons?"
46 Rebecca said to Isaac, "I am sick and tired of those Hittite women. I'd rather die than see Jacob married to a Hittite girl."

28

Isaac summoned Jacob and gave him his blessing and a warning. "Do not marry a Canaanite girl," he said. **2** "Go to Padan Aram, to the house of your mother's father, Bethuel, and marry a daughter from your uncle Laban's family. **3** El Shaddai will bless you and give you many children. You will grow into a great nation. **4** He will grant Abraham's blessing to you and your descendants, and you will rule over the land that Elohim gave to Abraham, where you had lived only as a foreigner."

Jacob Goes to Padan Aram   *7th Aliyah*

5 Isaac then sent Jacob on his way. Jacob headed toward Padan Aram, to Laban son of Bethuel the Aramaean, the brother of Rebecca, Jacob and Esau's mother.
6 Esau saw that Isaac had blessed Jacob and sent him to Padan Aram to find a wife, with the warning, "Do not marry a Canaanite girl."

Esau Marries the Daughter of Ishmael   *Maftir*

7 Esau was aware that Jacob had obeyed his father and mother and had gone to Padan Aram.
8 Esau understood that his father, Isaac, detested the Canaanite girls.
9 Therefore Esau went to Ishmael and married Machlath, daughter of Abraham's son Ishmael, a sister of Nebayoth, in addition to his other wives.

---

45. Why should I lose both of my sons?
A devoted mother will often place her child's happiness before her own.

46. I'd rather die than see Jacob married to a Hittite woman.
Rebecca was also aware that Esau wanted to kill Jacob. So she sent him to Padan Aram to save his life.

46. Rebecca said to Isaac, "I am sick and tired of those Hittite women. I'd rather die than see Jacob married to a Hittite girl."
The Hittites were idol worshippers and Rebecca was concerned about the future of Adonai's promise to Abraham and Isaac that their descendants would eventually establish a homeland in Canaan. Also, Esau's Hittite wife made life bitter for Isaac and Rebecca by praying to idols.

1. Isaac summoned Jacob and gave him his blessing.
Isaac realizes that he has blessed Jacob. Inwardly, he knows that he has blessed the right son and that the future of the Hebrew people is in good hands. Now Isaac once again, and this time knowingly, blesses Jacob.

5. The brother of Rebecca, Jacob and Esau's mother.
Although Esau was the first born, Jacob now takes precedence over Esau.

9. Therefore Esau went to Ishmael and married Machlath, daughter of Abraham's son Ishmael, a sister of Nebayoth, in addition to his other wives.
Esau had many foreign wives. But he also married Machlath to appease his parents, who didn't like his idol-worshipping wives.

וַיֵּצֵא *Vayetze*

JACOB SET OUT

10 Meanwhile, Jacob left Beer-sheva and set out for Haran.
11 He came to a camping place and, because the sun had already set, spent the night there. He took some stones, placed them under his head as a pillow, and lay down to sleep.
12 He had a dream and saw a ladder standing on the ground, with its top way up in the sky. He saw Elohim's angels climbing up and down on it. **13** Suddenly he saw Adonai standing beside him.
Adonai said, "I am Adonai, Lord of your father Abraham, and Lord of Isaac. I will give to you and your descendants the land upon which you are lying. **14** Your descendants will be as numerous as the dust of the earth. Your descendants will cover the earth from the west to the east, to the north and to the south. Every family on earth will be blessed because of you and your descendants. **15** Be assured that I am with you. I will protect you wherever you go and bring you back to this land. I will be with you until I have fully kept My promise to you."
16 Jacob woke up from his dream. He said "Adonai is truly in this place, but I did not know it." **17** He was frightened. And he exclaimed, "This is an awe-inspiring place. It must be Elohim's temple. It is the gate to heaven!" **18** Jacob rose up early in the morning and took the stones that he had placed under his head. He built them into a pillar and poured oil on top of it. **19** He made a pillar with the stones and named the place Adonai's Temple (*Beth El*). The town's former name had been Luz. **20** Jacob made a vow, saying, "If Elohim will be with me, if He will protect me on the journey that I am undertaking, if He gives me food to eat and clothing to wear,

---

11. He took some stones, placed them at his head as a pillow, and lay down to sleep.
The three daily prayers, *Shachrit* (morning), *Minchah* (afternoon), and *Maariv* (evening), were first prayed by the three patriarchs, Abraham, Isaac, and Jacob.

Abraham "rose up early in the morning" so that he might pray before taking Isaac to the altar. Isaac went "to pray in the field toward evening." Jacob prayed at night as he placed the stone for a pillow underneath his head to dream of a ladder with angels climbing on it.

The Torah tells us that Jacob slept on the cold ground with a stone for his pillow.

Our sages say that the moment his head touched the stone, it became as soft as a feather pillow and the ground as comfortable as a couch.

12. He had a dream.
Following the advice of Isaac and Rebecca, Jacob left home to seek refuge from Esau's anger. Rebecca's home town toward which Jacob was headed, was about 400 miles from Beer-sheva. The terrain was rugged and the climate severe – the days were very long and hot, the nights very cold. Out in a lonely field under the sky Jacob fell into a deep sleep and dreamed a remarkable dream, in which Adonai promised to give his descendants the land of Canaan. Adonai also promised to watch over and protect him.

19. He made a pillar with the stones and named the place Adonai's Temple (Beth El). The town's former name was Luz.
The most important towns in Canaan were commercial, and political and also religious centers.

City names that begin with *beth*, meaning "house," such as Beth-shemesh, Beth-dagon, Beth-shean, and Beth-lehem, contained a religious shrine. The patriarch Abraham changed the name of the town of Luz to Bethel, meaning House of Elohim, Adonai's Temple.

21 and if He brings me back in peace to my father's house, then I will dedicate myself totally to Elohim. **22** These stones that I have set up as a pillar will become a temple to worship Elohim. Everything that You give me, I will offer a tenth to charity."

Rachel Meets Jacob
2nd Aliya

29 Jacob set out and traveled toward the land of the Kedemites, the people of the East. **2** From a distance he saw a well. Three flocks of sheep were lying beside it. The mouth of the well was covered with a large, heavy stone. **3** When all the flocks came together there, the shepherds would roll the heavy stone from the top of the well and water the sheep. Then they would replace the stone on the well.
4 Some shepherds were already there, and Jacob asked, "Brothers, where are you from?" They answered, "We are from Haran." **5** Jacob said, "Do you know Nachor's grandson, Laban?" and they answered, "Of course! We all know him." **6** Again Jacob asked, "Is he doing well?" They answered, "Well enough! Here is his daughter Rachel, coming with Laban's sheep."
7 Then Jacob said, "It's still the middle of the day, too early to bring the flocks together. Why not water the sheep and let them go on grazing?" **8** They answered, "We can't until all the shepherds have come together. Only then will we be able to roll the stone from the mouth of the well. Only then will we able to water the sheep." **9** He was still speaking with the shepherds when Rachel appeared with her father's sheep.

---

22. Everything that You give me, I will offer a tenth to charity.
The institution of collecting tithes is linked to Jacob. In ancient Israel the tithes were channeled to the priests and Levites, who in turn distributed the proceeds to the poor.

In ancient days there were several methods for distributing funds to the poor and helpless. Jacob instituted the tithe, a system in which a farmer, a business person, or a herder distributed part of his earnings to the less fortunate. Grain, new wine, new oil, cattle, and sheep were subject to the tithe.

Gleaning was another method for helping the poor. Indigent people, widows, orphans, and other unfortunates were allowed to harvest the corners of the fields and gather the dropped or lost grain.

When the ancient state of Israel was destroyed, these two institutions fell into disuse and were replaced with the institution of *tzedakah*. There are many Jewish organizations that raise *tzedakah* funds for worthwhile causes.

22. Everything that you give me, I will offer a tenth to charity.
Sharing our plenty with less fortunate members of society is very important, but it has to be done in such a way that the other person does not see himself as a beggar. In other words, the other individual should not be made to feel that he is the recipient of a person's charity. Once we understand this, and learn to act accordingly, our contributions will also be accepted more easily. Thus we help prevent society from being divided into two groups, givers and receivers.

Today there are numerous anonymous individuals who set aside ten percent (*ma'aser*) of their earnings to *tzedakah*.

1. Jacob set out and traveled toward the land of the Kedemites, the people of the east.
Jacob had never met his mother's family before. They had always lived several hundred miles from each other. Travel was a major undertaking and there was little or no visiting of one family by the other. And yet, though Jacob had only heard, in conversation, about Rebecca's relatives, now that he met Rachel and the others in Uncle Laban's household, he felt happy. His own parents were far off in Beer-sheva but there was reassurance in the fact that "family" was at hand.

2. The mouth of the well was covered with a large, heavy stone.
The shepherds at the well were waiting for more men to help them remove the large, heavy stone.

10 As soon as Jacob saw his cousin Rachel, who was with his uncle Laban's sheep, he stepped forward and single-handedly rolled the stone from the top of the well and watered his uncle Laban's sheep. **11** Then Jacob kissed Rachel and began to cry. **12** He told her that he was Rebecca's son, and was related to her father. She quickly ran to tell her father the news.
13 When Laban heard that Jacob had arrived, he ran to greet him. He hugged and kissed him, and brought him home. Jacob told Laban everything that had happened to him. **14** Laban said, "Just think, you are my own flesh and blood." Jacob remained with him for a month. **15** Laban then said to Jacob, "Just because you are my close relative, does that mean you must work for me for nothing? Tell me what you want to be paid." **16** Laban had two daughters. The older one's name was Leah, and the younger one was called Rachel.
17 Leah had beautiful eyes, while Rachel was shapely and pretty.

Jacob Marries Leah and Rachel   *3rd Aliyah*

18 Jacob fell in love with Rachel. Jacob said, "I will work for you seven years for Rachel, your younger daughter."
19 Laban replied, "I would rather give her to you than to any other man. You can stay with me."
20 For seven years Jacob worked for Rachel. But he loved her so much that it seemed like no more than a few days. **21** At the end of seven years Jacob said to Laban, "My time is up. Give me my bride so we can be married."
22 Laban invited all of his neighbors and made a wedding feast. **23** In the evening, he took his veiled older daughter, Leah, and in the darkness brought her to Jacob, and Jacob slept with her.
24 Laban gave his servant Zilpah to his daughter Leah to be her handmaid.
25 In the morning, Jacob discovered that he had married the older daughter, Leah. He angrily said to Laban, "How could you do this to me? Why did you cheat me? Didn't I work for you for Rachel?"
26 Laban answered, "In our country it is the custom for the older to marry before the younger. We never give a younger daughter in marriage before the elder.

---

11. Jacob kissed Rachel.
After a long trek from Beer-sheva in the south, Jacob arrived at the outskirts of Haran, in the north. Outside the gates of Haran he freely engaged in conversation with the local shepherds. What were they waiting for when their sheep seemed so much in need of watering? They were unable to remove the large stone covering the well. The Torah says that Jacob was so strong that he easily moved the stone all by himself.

20. But he loved her so much that it seemed like no more than a few days.
Jacob was so much in love with Rachel that the seven years flew by very swiftly.

26. In our country it is the custom for the older to marry before the younger.
Jacob was rudely reminded how the younger supplanted the older and received the birthright which rightfully belonged to Esau. Now the same was done to him. Laban states, "In our country this is the custom."

26. We never give a younger daughter in marriage before the first-born.
From the beginning, Laban was aware that Jacob was a master herder, and his flocks kept increasing. Jacob was his goldmine and he wanted to hold on to him.

27 But wait until the wedding celebrations for Leah are over. Then I will also give you my younger daughter, Rachel, in return for your serving me for another seven years." **28** Jacob agreed and finished the week of celebration for Leah. Laban then gave his daughter Rachel to Jacob as a wife.

29 Laban also gave his servant Bilhah as a handmaid to his daughter Rachel.

30 Jacob also married Rachel, and he loved Rachel more than Leah. He worked for Laban for another seven years.

31 And Adonai saw that Jacob did not love Leah and He made her fertile while Rachel was childless. **32** Leah became pregnant and gave birth to a son. She named him Reuben (Look at My Son), for she said, "Adonai has looked at [i.e., seen my troubles]. Now my husband will love me."

33 She became pregnant again and had a son. "Adonai heard that I was unloved," she said, "and He gave me this son also." She named the child Simeon (Hearing). **34** Leah became pregnant again and had another son. "Now my husband will become attached [*lavah*] to me," she said, "because I have given him three sons." Jacob therefore named the child Levi (Attachment).

35 Leah became pregnant again and had another son. She named the child Judah (Praised be Adonai). She then stopped having children.

30

When Rachel realized that she could not give birth to children, she became jealous of her sister and said to Jacob, "Give me children or I will die!" **2** Jacob became angry with Rachel. He said, "Can I take the place of Elohim? It is He who has made you childless."

---

28. Laban then gave his daughter Rachel to Jacob as a wife.
The ancient Israelite family was patriarchal. The genealogies are given in the father's line and women are rarely mentioned. The father had absolute authority over his children, even over his married sons if they and their wives lived with him.

In ancient times and to this day it has been customary for a suitor to pay a sum of money to the father of a girl who was wanted in marriage. Jacob, who was eager for Rachel's hand, was a poor boy and had nothing to offer her father except his services in labor. Laban knew well Jacob's dependability as a worker and gladly accepted his proposal to work in exchange for Rachel as his wife.

Naturally, Jacob expected Laban to give Rachel in marriage to him at the end of his seven-year contract. But Laban had other ideas. Tradition in Haran required that an older sister must marry before the younger. So Laban passed off Leah in marriage to Jacob instead of Rachel.

Jacob was dismayed at Laban's dishonesty, but there was no way out. Leah had become his wife. Thereupon Jacob put in his bid again for Rachel, whom he loved very much, and he began a new seven-year period of service to Laban. So Jacob also married Rachel.

28. Laban then gave his daughter Rachel to Jacob as a wife.
Jacob had deceived his father, Isaac, and his brother, Esau, at the birthright blessing. Now Jacob was the victim of the very type of wrong that he had committed years earlier. Laban substituted his daughter Leah for Rachel.

1. When Rachel realized that she could not give birth to children, she became jealous of her sister.
Jacob's family was always feuding. He fathered children with two wives and two concubines. Rachel envied her sister Leah. The feuds continued with their sons.

3 Rachel said, "Here is my handmaid Bilhah. Sleep with her and let her give birth to children for me. Then I will also have a son through her." **4** So she gave her handmaid Bilhah to Jacob as a wife.
5 Bilhah became pregnant and gave birth to Jacob's son.
6 Rachel said, "Elohim has judged [*dan*] me and heard my prayer. He has finally given me a son!" She therefore named the child Dan.
7 Once again Rachel's handmaid Bilhah became pregnant and had a second son with Jacob.
8 Rachel said, "I have wrestled with my sister [*naphtuley*], but I have finally won." So she named the child Naphtali (Champion).
9 Leah realized that she no longer could have children. She gave her handmaid Zilpah to Jacob as a wife. **10** Leah's handmaid Zilpah bore Jacob a son.
11 Leah exclaimed, "Good luck [*gad*] has come!" So she named the child Gad.
12 Leah's handmaid Zilpah gave birth to a second son to Jacob. **13** Leah said, "It's my happiness [*asher*]. Women will consider me happy!" She named the child Asher.

Reuben and the Love Flowers   4th Aliyah

14 During the wheat harvest Reuben took a walk, and he found some love flowers in the field. He brought them to his mother Leah.
Rachel said to Leah, "Please give me some of your son's love flowers."
15 Leah angrily said, "Isn't it enough that you have stolen my husband? Now you even want to steal my son's love flowers!" Rachel replied, "All right, I will allow Jacob to sleep with you tonight in exchange for your son's love flowers."
16 That evening, when Jacob came home from the field, Leah went out to meet him and she said, "Tonight you will sleep with me. I have paid for your services with my son's love flowers." So Jacob slept with her that night.
17 Elohim heard Leah's prayer, and she became pregnant, and she gave birth to a fifth son.
18 Leah said, "Elohim has given me my reward [*sachar*] because I have given my handmaid to my husband." She named the child Issachar.
19 Again Leah became pregnant, and she gave birth to a sixth son. **20** "Elohim has given me a wonderful gift [*zeved*]," said Leah. "Now let my husband make his permanent home [*zevul*] with me." She named the child Zebulun (*Zevulun*).
21 Leah then had a daughter, and she named her Dinah.

---

8. Rachel said, "I have wrestled with my sister (*naphtuley*) and I have finally won."
Rachel said that she competed with her sister Leah, who had four children. Now Adonai has heard her prayer and given her a son. So Rachel named Bilhah's son Naphtali, meaning "I have finally won."

14. During the wheat harvest Reuben took a walk, and he found some love flowers in the field.
The technical name for love flowers is mandrakes.

At one time the mandrakes were thought to have aphrodisiac powers.
The root of the mandrake was formerly used to promote fertility, as a cathartic, or as a narcotic. In Hebrew, the mandrakes are called *duda'im*.
Reuben gave the mandrakes to his mother Leah, which she shared with Rachel.
Most of the classical commentators agree that the *duda'im* have the unusual property of promoting conception, but there is no scientific evidence that they do.

22 Elohim remembered Rachel. He heard her prayer, **23** and she became pregnant and gave birth to a son. She said "Adonai has taken away [*asaf*] my sorrow." **24** She named the child Joseph (*Yosef*), saying, "May Adonai grant another [*yosef*] son to me." **25** After Rachel had given birth to Joseph, Jacob said to Laban, "It is time for me to leave. I would like to return to my homeland.

26 Let me have my wives and children, since I have earned them by working for you, and I will leave. You are well aware that I have repaid you by my labor." **27** Laban replied, "Haven't I earned your friendship? I have learned from a fortune-teller that it is because of your presence that Adonai has blessed me."

Jacob and Laban Come to an Agreement   *5th Aliyah*

28 Laban said, "Just tell me how much I owe you. Name your price and I will pay it!"
29 Jacob replied, "You know how hard I worked for you, and how your flocks increased because of me. **30** You had very little before I came, and now your flocks have increased and become very large. Adonai blessed you with my coming. But now I must do something for my own family." **31** Laban asked, "How much should I pay you?" Jacob said, "Do not pay me, just do one thing for me. I will stay and tend your herds and give them the best care. **32** Just let me go through all your flocks with you today and remove every lamb that is spotted or speckled and every sheep that has dark markings and every goat that is speckled or spotted. Those kinds of animals will be my wages.

22–23. Elohim remembered Rachel. He heard her prayer, and she became pregnant and gave birth to a son.
Leah and Rachel contended for Jacob's love and for the future of their children. As in a chess game, Leah is the queen and provides Jacob with six children (pawns). Then when Leah loses the ability for further children, she checks Rachel by providing her maid Zilpah to Jacob to counter Rachel's moves. Fortunately Rachel birthed two boys (towers) to stymie Leah's moves. Unfortunately the chess game ends later on with the death (*met*) of Rachel.   *Shenash*

26. You are well aware that I have repaid you for my labor.
Jacob reminds Laban that his promised seven additional years of service are over. Now he wants to move on with his life.

30. Adonai blessed you with my coming. But now I must do something for my own family.
Jacob honored his agreement with Laban, to work for him the second term of seven years in return for Rachel. At the end of the fourteenth year, Jacob asked Laban to permit him to leave with his growing family, so that he might return to his homeland. But Laban knew Jacob to be a valuable worker and wanted him to stay on.

So he made a new agreement by which Jacob was to be paid a certain portion of the increase of the flock, the portion which by normal expectation would be small. However, success was with Jacob, and the increase in the flock favored him.

32. Remove every lamb that is spotted or speckled and every sheep that has dark markings and every goat that is speckled or spotted. Those animals will be my wages.
Jacob was a very successful herdsman. He had discovered the secret of mating males and female animals to produce spotted and speckled animals.

His father-in-law, Laban, was a deceiver and now Jacob returned the favor and deceived him. The wooden rods fooled Laban and did not influence the birth of speckled animals. Jacob learned the secret of matching DNA genetic bloodlines and kept the finding to himself. Jacob believed in the ancient motto "one bad turn deserves another."   *Shenash*

33 As a sign of my honesty, I will let you inspect all the animals that I have taken as my pay. If you find in my possession any goat that is not spotted or speckled, or any sheep without dark markings, then you will know that I have stolen them from you." **34** Laban replied, "Just as you have said. It's a deal."

35 That day, Laban removed the speckled and streaked male goats, and all the spotted and speckled female goats. He also removed every sheep with dark markings. Those animals he gave to his sons.

36 Laban then moved away from Jacob by the distance of a three-day journey. Jacob was left tending Laban's remaining flocks.

37 Jacob took branches of fresh poplar, almond, and plane trees. He peeled the branches and made white stripes by removing part of the bark.

38 He set up the wooden rods that he peeled facing the animals near the watering troughs where the flocks came to drink. They usually mated where they came to drink. **39** The animals mated in the presence of the rods, and they gave birth to ringed, spotted, and speckled animals. **40** Jacob separated the newborn animals. He made the animals in Laban's flocks mix with the spotted ones and all those with dark markings. Jacob did not allow his own flocks to mix with Laban's flocks. **41** Whenever the stronger females mated, Jacob placed the striped rods before their eyes at the troughs, so that they mated facing the rods. **42** But when the sheep were weak, he did not place the striped rods in front of them. The weak animals went to Laban, while Jacob got the stronger ones. **43** As a result Jacob became very wealthy. He owned many servants, sheep, goats, camels, and donkeys.

31

Soon Jacob began to hear that Laban's sons were complaining, "Jacob has stolen everything that belongs to our father. He has become rich by stealing our father's property!" **2** Jacob saw that Laban was acting very cold toward him. **3** Adonai said to Jacob, "It is time for you to go back to your birthplace in the land of your fathers. I will be with you all the way."

4 Jacob then sent for Rachel and Leah to come to the field where he was with the flock. **5** He said, "Your father is angry at me. He is not treating me in the same friendly way as he used to. But the Elohim of my father has been with me. **6** You know how hard I worked for your father.

---

1. Laban's sons were complaining.
Laban's sons were no different from their father. They were jealous of Jacob's prosperity and accused him of stealing their father's property.

3. Adonai said to Jacob, "It is time for you to go back to your birthplace."
Adonai appeared to Jacob in a dream and told him to return home.

Jacob, you have two strikes against you, and it is time to move out.
  1. Laban's sons say that you are stealing from them.

2. Laban, your father-in-law, is angry at you.

4. Jacob then sent for Rachel and Leah to come to the field.
Jacob was planning to leave without notifying anyone. He was afraid that Laban would forcefully stop him from leaving and steal his cattle.

The open field was the best place for Jacob to meet with his wives and tell them he wished to leave. An open field cannot hide curious eavesdroppers.

Jacob respected the wishes and intelligence of his wives and consulted them on his next move.
Shenash

7 Your father cheated me and broke his agreement about my wages at least ten times, but Elohim would not let him cheat me.
8 If he said, 'Your pay will be speckled ones,' then all the animals gave birth to speckled ones. When he said, 'Spotted ones will be yours,' then all the animals gave birth to spotted ones.
9 It was Adonai who took away your father's herds and gave them to me.
10 One day during the mating season, I suddenly had a vision. I saw the male sheep mating with the ringed, spotted, and speckled sheep. **11** Then an angel called me in Elohim's name, 'Jacob!' – and I replied, 'Yes, here I am.' **12** The angel said, 'Look, and you will see that the male sheep that are mating with the female sheep are ringed, speckled, and streaked. I have seen what Laban is doing to you. **13** I am the Elohim of Beth El, where you set up a pillar and made an agreement with Me. Now get up and leave this land. Return to the land where you were born.'"
14 Both Rachel and Leah spoke up. "We will inherit nothing from our father's wealth. **15** He treats us like strangers! He has sold us and spent our bridal money!
16 Everything that Elohim has taken from our father actually belongs to us and our children. So go ahead and do what Elohim told you to do."

---

7. Your father cheated me and broke his agreement about my wages at least ten times.
The name Laban means "white." Laban always agreed and whitewashed everything. Everything looked and sounded good but on the inside he was a lying, deceptive cheat. Jacob was very much aware of Laban's duplicity. He knew that any of Laban's agreements was in reality a kiss of death.

11. Then an angel called me in Elohim's name, "Jacob"– and I replied, "Yes, here I am."
The angel came to tell Jacob that it was time to return to the land of his father. Before making his decision, Jacob consulted his two wives. When Rachel and Leah heard this, they both agreed and said, "Do whatever Elohim told you to do."

13. Now get up and leave this land. Return to the land where you were born.
Jacob dreamed of a return to the land of his birth. It was a dream that would take hold of his descendants too at various stages in Israel's history. No matter where the people might be exiled, the tiny land on the Mediterranean had a magnetic attraction for the Hebrews.

Jacob was now determined to break away from Laban, who had prevented his departure on several occasions. Jacob felt, after twenty years, that it was a case of now or never. Laban was away in the pasture country during the sheep-shearing season when Jacob decided that the time was opportune to make his departure.

Hurriedly, he gathered his family, his herds, and all his possessions and together they set out on the long journey south.

14. Both Rachel and Leah spoke up. "We will inherit nothing from our father's wealth."
Rachel and Leah were hurt that their father had even profited from their marriages, having sold them for fourteen years of free labor.

15. He treats us like strangers. He has sold us and spent our bridal money!
According to the text, both Leah and Rachel complain that they have equal rights to Laban's inheritance, just like the sons.

15. Our bridal money.
In ancient days it was customary for a groom to pay the parents of the bride for the privilege of marrying their daughter. In certain countries, it is still the custom to provide "bridal money."

Rachel Steals Laban's Idol
6th Aliyah

17 So Jacob put his children and wives on camels and began the journey.
18 He took all his livestock, and took everything that he had earned, including everything that he had bought in Padan Aram, and set off to return to his father, Isaac, in the land of Canaan. **19** While Laban was away, shearing his sheep, Rachel stole the idols that belonged to her father.
20 Jacob secretly left Laban the Aramaean. **21** He left with everything he owned, and crossed the Euphrates River, in the direction of the Gilead Mountains.
22 Three days later, Laban learned that Jacob had fled. **23** He took along his relatives and chased after Jacob for seven days and finally caught up to him in the Mountains of Gilead.
24 That night Elohim appeared to Laban the Aramaean and said, "Be very careful; do not harm or bless or curse Jacob." **25** Laban caught up to Jacob, who had pitched his tents on a hill, while Laban stationed his relatives on Mount Gilead. **26** Laban said to Jacob, "How could you do this thing to me? You went behind my back and stole my daughters away as if they were prisoners of war! **27** Why did you have to leave so secretly? You went behind my back and told me nothing! I would have sent you off with singing and music, with drum and harp!
28 You didn't even let me kiss my grandchildren and daughters goodbye.
What you did was very foolish. **29** I have it in my power to destroy you. But Elohim spoke to me last night and said, 'Be very careful of what you say about Jacob.' **30** I am aware that you are homesick for your parents. But why did you have to steal my idols?"
31 Jacob spoke up. "I left secretly because I was afraid of you. I thought that you might take your daughters away from me by force. **32** However, if you find your idols here, I will punish the person who stole them. Let all our close relatives here be witnesses. If you can find anything here belonging to you, you can take it back." Jacob did not realize that Rachel had stolen the idols.
33 Laban searched the tents of Jacob, Leah, and the two handmaids, but he found nothing. When he left Leah's tent, he went into Rachel's tent.
34 Rachel had taken the idols and hid them inside a camel cushion on which she was sitting. Laban searched the entire tent and found nothing.

---

17. So Jacob put his children and wives on camels and began the journey.
Jacob first took care of the youngest, then the wives. His first thought was to safeguard the women and children.

18. Including everything that he had acquired in Padan Aram.
Padan Aram is a region along the upper Euphrates where the city of Haran was situated. Haran was the home of Rebecca and Laban and his daughters, Leah and Rachel. It is also called Mesopotamia.

19. Rachel stole the idols that belonged to her father.
The midrash says that she stole the idols to prevent Laban from worshipping them.

29. I have it in my power to destroy you.
Laban brought a small army with him, and he boasts that they could easily defeat Jacob.

33. When he left Leah's tent, he went into Rachel's tent.
Each of his wives had separate tents, so that they would not interfere with each other. In this way each of the wives could be alone with Jacob.
Maimonides

35 Then Rachel said to her father, "Do not be angry with me. I cannot get up for you because I am not feeling well." Laban searched, but he did not find the idols.
36 Jacob became very angry, and he argued with Laban. "Have I committed a crime? What terrible thing did I do, that you came chasing me like this? **37** You searched all my belongings. What did you find that is yours? Put it right here, in front of our relatives. Let them decide which of us is right! **38** I worked for you twenty years! During that time, your sheep and goats never lost their young. Never once did I ever take a ram from your flocks as food. **39** I never brought you a goat or a sheep that had been killed by a wild animal. I took the blame on myself. You made me responsible for it whether it was stolen by day or at night. **40** By day I sweated in the scorching heat, and at night I froze in the cold. **41** I have worked for twenty years – fourteen years for your two daughters, and six years for some of your flocks. During this time you reduced my wages ten times!
42 If the Elohim of my fathers – the Elohim of Abraham and the Elohim of Isaac – had not been with me, you would have sent me away empty-handed! But Elohim saw my hard work, and last night He came to a decision!

Jacob and Laban Make a Treaty *7th Aliyah*

43 Laban interrupted Jacob. "Leah and Rachel are my daughters! The children are my grandchildren! The flocks are my flocks! All that you see is mine! As for my daughters…what can I do for them today? Or for the children they have borne?

---

35. Rachel said to her father, "Do not be angry with me. I cannot get up because I am not feeling well."
The Torah mocks the idols. What kind of idols allow themselves to be stolen? Even worse, a sick woman sits atop the idol and it doesn't even scream or come up for air.   *Benno Jacob*

35. Then Rachel said to her father, "Do not be angry with me. I cannot get up for you because I am not feeling well."
In ancient days, a child as a sign of respect had to stand up when his or her father entered the room.

36. Have I committed a crime? What terrible thing did I do that you came chasing me like this?
Jacob became very angry at Laban and exploded. "Am I a criminal that you pursue me? I had plenty of opportunity to rob and cheat you. I watched over your property as I would my own."

36. Jacob became very angry, and he argued with Laban.
Laban searched Jacob's caravan and found nothing.

Jacob thought that the search for the stolen idols was just an excuse to find some stolen property.

43. As for my daughters…what can I do for them today?
Laban said to Jacob, "I will not harm my own children by taking back from you (and them) what rightfully belongs to me." Laban still pretended that Jacob had earned his wealth dishonestly.

43. Leah and Rachel are my daughters! The children are my grandchildren! The flocks are my flocks! All that you see is mine!
Laban still felt that Jacob had grown rich at his expense. Actually, the opposite was true, for Laban had greatly benefited by Jacob's presence in his house.

Why was Jacob eager to get away from Haran? His conscience troubled him. He had wronged his brother Esau long ago and he was determined to have a reconciliation with Esau before it was too late. Likely, too, Jacob had had his fill of Laban's unfair business dealings.

44 Now come on! Let's you and I make a treaty; let us make a peace treaty between us."
45 Jacob took a large stone and set it up it as a pillar.
46 He said to his relatives, "Gather stones!" They took stones and made a large mound. Jacob and Laban and all the relatives then ate a meal of peace beside the large mound. **47** Laban called it Yegar Sahadutha (Witness Mound), but Jacob named it Gal'ed (Witness).
48 Laban said, "This mound shall be a witness between you and me today." That is why it is called Gal'ed. **49** "And let the pillar be called Mitzpah [Watchpost] because Elohim will keep watch between us when we are out of each other's sight.
50 If you mistreat my daughters, or marry other women, I may learn about it, but you must always realize that Elohim is the Witness between you and me."
51 Laban then said to Jacob, "Here is the mound, and here is the pillar that I have set up between us. **52** The mound and pillar shall be witnesses. I will not cross over to attack you and you will not cross over to attack me. We must never break the treaty between us. **53** May the Elohim of Abraham, the Elohim of Nachor, and the Elohim of their fathers be our judge." Jacob made a promise to the Elohim of his father Isaac.
54 He then made a sacrifice, and invited his relatives to eat with him. They ate and spent the night on the hill.

Jacob Camps at Machanayim *Maftir*

32 The next morning Laban got up early and kissed his grandchildren and daughters goodbye. He then blessed them and left to return home.
2 Jacob also continued on his journey, and he met angels of Elohim. **3** When Jacob saw them, he said, "This is Adonai's camp." He named the place Machanayim (Twin Camps).

---

46. Jacob and Laban and all the relatives then ate a meal of peace beside the large mound.
Eating a meal of peace was the ancient way of confirming a meeting of the minds and sealing a pact between adversaries.

47. Laban called it Yegar Sahadutha (Witness Mound), but Jacob called it Gal'ed (Witness).
The name *Gal'ed* is made up of two Hebrew words: *gal*, meaning "pile" or "mound," and *ed*, meaning "witness." Such piles of stones are numerous in trans-Jordan in the area where Jacob and Laban set up their memorial stones.

50. If you mistreat my daughters, or marry other women, I may learn about it.
Jacob promised that he would not mistreat his wives, who were Laban's daughters, and swore that he would not take any more wives. In return, Laban promised not to harm Jacob in any way.

53. May the Elohim of Abraham, the Elohim of Nachor, and the Elohim of their fathers be a judge. Jacob made a promise to the Elohim of his father Isaac.
Laban plays it safe and calls upon two gods to witness the peace treaty. He calls upon Nachor's god and the Elohim of Abraham. Jacob asks only the Elohim of his father Isaac.

1. The next morning Laban got up early and kissed his grandchildren and daughters goodbye. He then blessed them and left to return home.
The next morning Laban says goodbye to his daughters and grandchildren. His departure reminds Laban that he will never see them again. He departed at peace with himself that he followed Adonai's concept of justice.

3. He named the place Machanayim.
Machanayim means "two camps": the camp of the angels and the camp of his father-in-law, Laban.

וַיִּשְׁלַח *Vayishlach*

JACOB SENDS MESSENGERS

4 Jacob sent messengers ahead of him to his brother Esau, to Edom's Field in Seir.
5 He instructed them to deliver the following message to his brother: "Greetings to my brother Esau. Your humble servant Jacob says: I have stayed with Laban and have delayed my return for a long time.
6 I have acquired cattle, donkeys, sheep, servant-girls, and am now sending word to you to welcome me with friendship."
7 The messengers returned to Jacob with an answer: "We met your brother Esau, and he is heading toward you, and he has 400 men with him."
8 Jacob was very frightened, so he divided the people, the sheep, the cattle, and the camels with him into two camps.
9 He said, "If Esau comes and attacks one camp, at least the other camp will escape."
10 Jacob prayed, "Elohim of my grandfather Abraham and Elohim of my father Isaac. You Yourself told me, 'Return to the land where you were born, and I will help you.' **11** I do not deserve all of the kindness and faith that You have shown me. When I left home, I crossed the Jordan. I was alone, with only my shepherd's staff, and now I have grown into two camps.

---

4. Jacob sent messengers ahead of him to his brother Esau, to Edom's field in Seir.
Pirke Avot 32:4 "Do not judge a person until you stand in his shoes." For Jacob this saying meant not to judge Esau from a distance. The now mature Jacob realized that a face-to-face encounter was the right way to test Esau's intentions.

4. Jacob sent messengers ahead of him to his brother Esau.
Twenty years had passed since Jacob fled from Esau's anger. Esau was a warrior and a hunter. Would he take revenge on Jacob? Jacob decides to test Esau and sends him a friendly message.

7. We met your brother Esau, and he is heading toward you.
Upon returning to Canaan, Jacob approaches his brother with great apprehension. He methodically makes plans for the meeting. First he sends messengers to announce his return and is frightened to learn that Esau is coming to greet him with 400 men. Now he decides to shower his brother with gifts of animals so that Esau can forget his promise to kill him.

8. Jacob was very frightened
The midrash says that as Jacob prepared to meet Esau, he was concerned that Esau might now be Adonai's favorite instead of himself. Jacob knew that for the past twenty years Esau had been fulfilling two important commandments that Jacob had unavoidably ignored. Esau had been living in the Holy Land, while Jacob had lived outside it; and Esau had taken care of his elderly parents, Isaac and Rebecca, while Jacob could not because he lived such a distance from them.

10. Jacob prayed.
Jacob does not place "all of his eggs in one basket"; he adopts three methods of defense. First he prays to Adonai for protection. Second, he sends gifts to Esau as tokens of his goodwill and love. His third and last strategy is to stand his ground and fight. He tries to settle his problem by peaceful means, but if all else fails, he is ready, willing, and able to fight.

12 I pray, save me from the anger of my brother – from the hand of Esau. I am afraid of him, for he can come and kill my whole family. **13** You once promised, 'I will make things go well for you, and make your descendants as many as the sand grains of the sea, which are too many to count.'"

Jacob Sends Gifts to Esau *2nd Aliyah*

14 After spending the night there, Jacob assembled a gift for his brother Esau. **15** The gift consisted of 200 female goats, 20 male goats, 200 lambs, 20 rams, **16** 30 nursing camels with their young, 40 cows, 10 bulls, 20 female donkeys, and 10 male donkeys. **17** Jacob put a servant in charge of each herd. He said to his servants, "Move on ahead of me. Make a space between the two herds." **18** He instructed the first group: "When my brother Esau meets you, he will ask, 'To whom do you belong? Where are you going? Who owns all of these animals?'
19 You must reply, They belong to your brother Jacob. It is a gift to his brother. Jacob is following right behind us.'"
20 Jacob gave the same instructions to the second group, to the third, and to all who followed the herd. **21** "You must all say the same thing: 'Your brother Jacob is right behind us.'" Jacob said to himself, "I will quiet him with the gifts that are being sent ahead, and then I will meet him face to face. Hopefully, he will forgive me." **22** Jacob sent the gifts ahead of him, and spent the night in the camp.
23 In the middle of the night, Jacob got up and took his two wives, his two handmaids, and his eleven sons, and sent them across the Jabbok River. **24** After he sent them across, he also sent across all his possessions.
25 Jacob remained alone, when suddenly a stranger appeared and wrestled with him until dawn.

---

12. I pray save me from the anger of my brother, from the hand of Esau. I am afraid of him, for he can come and kill my whole family.
The midrash says that Jacob was never able to enjoy the heritage. He felt guilty all his life because he had deceived his brother and taken his blessing and his inheritance.

The "voice of Jacob" stands for Torah and truth. The "hands of Esau" stand for force and violence. As long as there is Torah and truth in the world, there can be no violence. As long as the Jew allows the "voice of Jacob" to be his guide, the "hands of Esau" cannot harm him.

14. Jacob assembled a gift for his brother Esau.
As Jacob came closer to Canaan, fear and misgiving overcame him. How would Esau react? Did he still carry the grudge of long ago? Jacob decided to face the challenge by sending several messengers ahead to inform Esau of his return.

When Jacob saw Esau's small army he expected a battle with his brother.

25. Jacob remained alone, when suddenly a stranger appeared and wrestled with him until dawn.
Commentators interpret the encounter as an inner struggle between Jacob and his conscience. After this painful inner struggle of self-appraisal Jacob emerges as a stronger human being and becomes a new man. When the contest was over he had won faith in his ability to deal with Esau.

Self-examination is called *heshbon hanefesh*. Jacob is given a new name, Israel, as a symbol of his new, enhanced, and stronger personality. During the The Days of Repentance (Rosh Hashanah and Yom Kippur) Jews are expected to undergo *heshbon hanefesh* and judge themselves. Have I been selfish? Have I distressed anyone? How can I become a better person?

Shenash

26 When the stranger saw that he could not defeat Jacob, he struck Jacob's thigh. Jacob's hip joint became dislocated as he wrestled with the stranger.
27 The stranger said, "Let me leave! Dawn is breaking." Jacob answered, "I will not let you leave unless you bless me."
28 The stranger then asked, "What is your name?" and Jacob answered, "My name is Jacob."
29 "Your name will no longer be Jacob, it is now Israel [*Yisrael*] because you have struggled with angelic beings and you have been victorious."
30 Jacob asked, "Please tell me your name." The stranger replied, "You must not ask my name." Then he blessed Jacob.

Jacob Wrestles with an Angel
3rd Aliyah

31 Jacob named the place Peniel (Divine Face). He said, "I have seen Elohim face to face, and my life has been spared." **32** As he left Peniel the sun rose and shone on him. And he was limping because of his dislocated thigh.

---

26. Jacob's hip joint became dislocated as he wrestled with the stranger.
The Rabbis interpret the struggle as the symbolic struggle between the force of Israel, righteousness, and those of Esau, the forces of evil.

29. Your name will no longer be Jacob, it is now Israel.
As a reward for his victory, the angel changes his name to Israel.

The name Israel is made up of two Hebrew words: *sar* ("prince") and *El* ("Elohim"). It means "prince of Elohim." This is the first time that the name Israel appears in the Torah. Since Jacob's twelve sons became the founders and leaders of the twelve tribes, they came to be called the Twelve Tribes of Israel.

Outside the Torah, the name Israel is not found on many of the documents, walls, or stones that archaeologists have uncovered.

The earliest record of the name Israel is on a victory monument of the Pharaoh Merneptah, who lived about two or three hundred years after Jacob. There the name was found in the ancient Egyptian picture-writing (hieroglyphics).

29. Your name will no longer be Jacob, it is now Israel.
Abraham, the first patriarch, represents the father of the Jews. But Jacob, the third patriarch, was different; his name, Israel, became the name of a nation.

The name Israel refers to the Jews as a covenantal community.
Rabbi Joseph B. Soloveitchik

29. Your name will no longer be Jacob, it is now Israel.
The night before Jacob was to encounter his brother, Esau, was a disturbing one. Many thoughts flashed through Jacob's mind, a review of all the events that had taken place beginning twenty years earlier when he had to run from the home of his parents. Now, with the coming of daylight, he would know whether he had done right to return to Canaan. And Jacob fell asleep.

A mysterious encounter took place during that fateful night. Jacob wrestled with a mysterious stranger on the bank of the River Jabbok. The opponent is wrestled to the ground by Jacob. And so the frightening match goes on for hours. Was it an event that took place with Jacob awake? Was it a dream?

Whatever this experience was, Jacob came out the victor. Now he was given a new name – Israel: "…for you have wrestled with angelic beings and with men, and you have won." No more would Jacob be dogged by a guilty conscience which had troubled him all these years. Now he could start afresh. He could face Esau with a sense of hope instead of defeat.

33 today the Children of Israel do not eat the meat that is attached to the hip joint. This is because the stranger dislocated Jacob's thigh.

33

Jacob looked up, and in the distance he saw Esau approaching with 400 men. He divided the children among Leah, Rachel, and the two handmaids. **2** He placed the handmaids and their children in front, Leah and her sons behind them, and Rachel and Joseph last. **3** Jacob went ahead of them, and he bowed seven times as he approached his brother.

4 Esau ran to meet them. He hugged Jacob and kissed him. They both wept.

5 Esau looked up and saw the women and children, and he asked, "Who are these to you?" Jacob replied, "They are the children with whom Elohim has blessed me."

Jacob and Esau Reconcile
4th Aliyah

6 Then the handmaids approached, along with their children, and the women bowed. **7** Then Leah and her children also approached and bowed. Finally, Joseph and Rachel came forward and bowed.

8 "What were the herds and the people that came to greet me?" asked Esau. "It was my gift to you," Jacob replied. **9** Esau said, "My brother, I have plenty. Let what is yours remain yours." **10** "Please, I beg you!" said Jacob. "If you have forgiven me, please accept this gift from me. After all, you have received me so favorably that seeing your face again is like seeing the face of Elohim.

---

33. Today the Children of Israel do not eat the meat that is attached to the hip joint. This is because the stranger dislocated Jacob's thigh.
This is mitzvah number 3.

Because an angel disguised as a human wrestled with Jacob and dislocated Jacob's hip joint, today we are forbidden to eat the meat of the thigh muscle, the left and right hind legs of an animal. The thigh muscle includes the sirloin area.

If the sciatic nerve is removed, then it is permissible to eat the meat. Outside of Israel, the hindquarters are used by non-Jews. In Israel, there are butchers who can porge (remove the nerve) of the hindquarters.

2. He placed the handmaids and their children in front, Leah and her sons behind them, and Rachel and Joseph last.
Jacob once again plays favorites. He places the handmaids and their children first. Should there be a confrontation, they would be the first to suffer. Then come Leah and her sons. Rachel, the most beloved, is placed last in the safest position.
Shenash

3. Jacob went ahead of them.
Jacob was afraid that Esau still hated him and would attack him and his family. So Jacob went ahead to meet his brother and ask for his forgiveness. Should he fail, Jacob is prepared to sacrifice himself and fight so that his wives and children can escape.

4. Esau ran to meet them.
This is a great surprise. After all of Jacob's fear and the preparations he had made for a possible attack, Esau not only welcomes him but runs to greet him. Jacob's fear led him to imagine danger. His wrestling with the angel had given him back his courage. Now he comes face-to-face with what he fears – and like a bad dream, it disappears.

10. Seeing your face again is like seeing the face of Elohim.
Your kind face and friendly behavior mean that you have forgiven me. I have been in Adonai's presence, and Adonai also has forgiven me.

11 Please accept my welcoming gift exactly as it has been brought to you. Adonai has been kind to me, and I have all I need." Jacob urged him, and Esau finally accepted it.
12 "Let's get going and move on," said Esau. "I will lead the way in front of you."
13 "My brother," replied Jacob, "As you can see, the children are weak, and I have responsibility for the young sheep and cattle. If they are driven hard for even one day, many of the sheep will die.
14 Please move ahead of me. I will lead my group slowly at their own pace, and the pace of the children. I will eventually meet you in Seir."
15 Esau said, "At least let my people help and protect you." Jacob replied, "What for? Just let me remain on friendly terms with you."
16 So on that day, Esau started back to Seir. **17** Jacob moved to Sukkoth. There he built a house for himself and made booths for his livestock. He therefore named the place Sukkoth (booths).
18 Jacob arrived safely at the city of Shechem, which is in the land of Canaan, when he returned from Padan Aram, and he made his camp outside the city.

11. Please accept my welcoming gift exactly as it has been brought to you.
When he was called Jacob, he was known as a deceiver. After he wrestled with the angel, his name was changed to Israel, signifying the change of his character.

Why did it take so long to remove the stain on his character? Because he first had to be forgiven by his brother Esau. He asks Esau to accept his welcoming gift "exactly as it has been brought to you." Esau accepted the gift, exactly as it was brought to him, meaning he had totally forgiven him. Now that Jacob was forgiven, Adonai could provide him with a pure, unadulterated name, Israel.

11. Jacob urged him, and Esau finally accepted it.
It did not need much urging from Jacob to entice Esau to accept the gift. Esau salivated when he mentally calculated Jacob's gift.

14. Please move ahead of me. I will lead my group slowly at their own pace, and the pace of the children. I will eventually meet you in Seir.
In spite of the happy greetings and the warm welcome, Jacob still does not trust Esau. He wanted to disentangle his family from Esau's army of 400 men. Jacob placates and assures Esau that they will eventually meet in Seir.

15. Esau said, "At least let my people help and protect you." Jacob replied, "What for? Just let me remain on friendly terms with you."
The commentator Benno Jacob suspects Esau's hugging and promise of protection. Jacob obviously distrusted Esau and declined his offer to escort him. Jacob's caravan proceeded along and Esau returned to Seir.

17. He therefore named the place Sukkoth.
The city of Sukkoth, which has the same name as the fall festival, is mentioned several times in the Bible. Sukkoth was situated in the Jordan plain and was in a position to control the valley between two important rivers, the Jordan and the Yabbok.

About 4,000 years ago, Jacob built "Sukkoth" for his family after his reconciliation with his brother Esau.

The area around Sukkoth was noted for its high-quality clay. Thousands of pieces of pottery dating back to Bible times have been found in this area. The clay from Sukkoth was also used to make molds for casting copper. It was in this area that the fine copper utensils and adornments for Solomon's Temple were cast.

18. Jacob arrived safely at the city of Shechem.
Despite all the hugging and kissing and friendly discussions, Jacob still distrusts Esau's intentions. Jacob rejects Esau's suggestion that they travel together while accompanied by Esau's band of 400 warriors. After that point the Torah indicates that "Jacob arrived safely." Jacob's fear of Esau's intentions were unfounded and he and his family were safe.

19 Jacob bought a piece of open land for 100 silver coins from the sons of Hamor, chief of Shechem, upon which he set up his tent. **20** He erected an altar there and named it El Elohey Yisrael (Adonai Is Israel's Lord).

Dinah Is Raped *5th Aliyah*

34 Leah's daughter, Dinah, went out to visit some of the girls who lived nearby. **2** Shechem, son of the chief of the region, Hamor the Hivite, saw her, and he raped her. **3** Shechem fell in love with Jacob's daughter, Dinah, and tried to win her affections. **4** Shechem said to his father, Hamor, "I would like to marry Dinah." **5** Jacob learned that his daughter Dinah had been raped. At that time Jacob's sons were in the field with the livestock, and Jacob did not tell them anything.

6 Meanwhile, Shechem's father, Hamor, came to speak to Jacob about the problem. **7** In the meantime Jacob's sons returned from the field. When they learned what had happened, the men became very angry. Shechem had committed a crime by raping Jacob's daughter. Such a criminal act could not be tolerated.

8 Hamor tried to reason with them. He said, "My son Shechem is truly in love with your daughter. Allow him to marry her.

9 Intermarry with us. Our sons will marry your daughters, and our daughters will marry your sons.

10 You will be able to live among us, and our land will be open to you. Settle down, and purchase land among us." **11** Shechem also spoke to Dinah's father and brothers. "I will do anything to regain your respect. I will give you whatever you ask. **12** Set the bridal payment and gifts as high as you like – I will gladly give whatever you demand of me. Just let me have Dinah as my wife."

13 When Jacob's sons replied to Shechem and his father, Hamor, they had a different idea, for they were speaking to the one who had raped their sister Dinah.

14 They said, "We cannot allow our sister to marry an uncircumcised man. It would be a disgrace to us.

---

1. Leah's daughter, Dinah, went out to visit some of the girls who lived nearby.
Dinah was the daughter of Leah and the sister of Simeon and Levi.

2. Shechem, son of the chief of the region, Hamor the Hivite, saw her, and he raped her.
Raping a virgin, especially one from a noble family, was an insult.

12. Set the bridal payment and gifts as high as you like – I will gladly give whatever you demand of me. Just let me have Dinah as my wife.
The Hebrew word *mohar* means "to pay the bride price." This word appears only three times in the Torah. This refers to the money the fiancé had to pay to the bride's father.

A fiancé works for the payment of the *mohar* as Jacob did for his marriages to Leah and Rachel. The *mohar* in reality was compensation to the family. The future husband acquires the right over the woman, but she is not bought or sold.

14. We cannot allow our sister to marry an uncircumcised man.
It is below their dignity to reply to Shechem's offer. An uncircumcised husband for their sister would be a disgrace. Circumcision was a duty of this family to maintain. The prohibition of marrying a Canaanite has a religious foundation. The rape by an uncircumcised man is irreparable.

The brothers secretly plot to revenge themselves against the Canaanites.

15 The only way we can agree is if you will circumcise every male among you. **16** Only then can we give you our daughters and take your daughters for ourselves. Only then will we be able to live together with you and become as a single nation. **17** But if you do not agree to be circumcised, we will take our sister and go."

18 Their terms seemed fair to Hamor and his son Shechem.

19 Because Shechem loved Jacob's daughter, he lost no time and accepted the terms. He was the most respected person in his father's house.

20 Hamor and his son Shechem went to the city gate and spoke to the citizens of the city.

21 They said, "These men are our friends. Allow them to live on the land and earn a living from it. There is more than enough space for them. We will marry their daughters, and they will marry ours.

22 But only if we meet one of their conditions will they agree to live among us and become one nation. Every male among us must first be circumcised, just as they are circumcised.

23 After all, their livestock, their possessions, and their animals will eventually be ours. Let us agree to their condition and live with them."

24 So all the people who came out to the city gate agreed with Hamor and his son Shechem. All the males allowed themselves to be circumcised.

25 On the third day, when the men were in deep pain, Dinah's brothers Simeon and Levi took their swords and sneaked into the city and killed every male.

---

19. Because Shechem loved Jacob's daughter, he lost no time and accepted the terms.
Shechem and the people of Shechem accept the offer. They win over their fellow citizens by emphasizing the material advantage of such a union. It is good business and worth some religious concession.

23. After all, their livestock, their possessions, and their animals will eventually be ours.
Hamor had it all figured out. If his son married Dinah, they would live in the area. They would become a part of our society and everything of theirs would eventually become ours.

24. All the males allowed themselves to be circumcised.
Now Simeon and Levi used deceit to achieve revenge. They demand circumcision of the males in the city.

The assembly of the city elders agree. Then while the males are recovering, the Israelites strike and get their revenge, killing all the males. They rescue Dinah and plunder the city.

Jacob is angry and is worried about the possible consequence by the other Canaanites. He is worried that the family can be attacked and wiped out.

25. Dinah's brothers Simeon and Levi took their swords and sneaked into the city and killed every male.
The brothers obviously loved their sister very much and avenged themselves against all the males in the city. Jacob did not approve of their violent tactics. Later in 49:5, Jacob says, "Simeon and Levi are a pair, men of violence and weapons."

25. On the third day, when the men were in deep pain, Dinah's brothers Simeon and Levi took their swords and sneaked into the city and killed every male.
Initially, Jacob was involved in the negotiations and was willing to solve the problem peacefully. Shechem spoke to Dinah's father (Jacob) and brothers. He said to them, "I will do anything to regain your respect."

However, the brothers Simeon and Levi, without consulting their father, murdered all of the males. *Shenash*

26 They also killed Hamor and his son Shechem, and rescued Dinah from Shechem's house. Then they returned to the camp.
27 Jacob's sons went and plundered the city that had disgraced their sister.
28 They took the sheep, cattle, donkeys, and whatever else was in the city and in the fields.
29 They also took the women and children as captives. They took everything from the houses, plundering the city's wealth. **30** Jacob said to Simeon and Levi, "You have given me a bad reputation among the Canaanites and Perizzites who live in the land. I have only a few men. In revenge they can band together and attack us, and our family will be wiped out." **31** The sons replied, "Should we have allowed them to treat our sister like a prostitute?"

35

Elohim said to Jacob, "Rise up and go up to Beth El. Stay there and erect an altar to Me, the Elohim who appeared to you when you were escaping from your brother Esau."
2 Jacob said to his family and everyone with him, "Get rid of the idols you have. Purify yourselves and change your clothes. **3** We are going up to Beth El. There I will erect an altar to Elohim, who answered my prayers in my time of trouble, and who has watched over me on every journey I have ever taken." **4** The family members gave Jacob all their idols, even the rings from their ears. Jacob buried them under a tree near Shechem.

---

30. You have given me a bad reputation among the Canaanites and Perizzites who live in the land.
Jacob did not want his daughter to marry a Canaanite. The sons then took the delicate problem off Jacob's shoulders, while he remained silent. Jacob realized that he was a stranger and now his reputation as a good neighbor had gone down the drain.

30. Jacob said to Simeon and Levi, "You have given me a bad reputation among the Canaanites and Perizzites who live in the land."
Jacob had a practical reaction to the murders. The brothers had placed the whole family in danger. After all, they were a tiny minority surrounded by hostile neighbors. Besides, he was angry and disgusted by the cruelty of his sons, who had killed people who had done them no harm.

31. Should we have allowed them to treat our sister as a prostitute?
Men of violence react to crimes against their families and relatives. In ancient days violent revenge was common. If you did not react, people would continue to attack you.

1. Elohim said to Jacob, "Rise up and go up to Beth El."
The area was mountainous. The city of Shechem was located about 2000 feet above sea level. Jacob and his family were told to travel upward to the city of Beth El, which was located about 3,000 feet above sea level. It was a difficult march for the women and children.

2. Get rid of the idols you have.
These were the idols that they had taken from the city of Shechem. Now they are going to Beth El, the House of Elohim. Jacob wanted to remove all thoughts of idolatry from their minds and their hearts.

4. The family members gave Jacob all their idols, even the rings from their ears. Jacob buried them under a tree near Shechem.
Jacob was instructed by Adonai to erect an altar in Beth El. As part of the purification process, the members of Jacob's family gave up their idols.

The rings were decorative, holy charms which Jacob buried. By removing the idols, Jacob consecrates (converts) his whole household to the worship of Adonai, who answered his prayers in times of need.

5 Jacob and his family began their journey, and terror from Elohim spread through all the cities in the region, and they were afraid to attack them.
6 Jacob and all the people with him arrived at Luz, now called Beth El, meaning "House of El." **7** Jacob built an altar there and named the place El Beth El (Elohim in Beth El) because it was the place where Elohim had appeared to him when he was escaping from his brother Esau.
8 Rebecca's nurse, Deborah, died, and she was buried in the valley of Beth El, under the oak. It was named Alon Bakhuth (Weeping Oak).
9 When Jacob returned from Padan Aram, Elohim once again appeared and blessed him.
10 Elohim said to him,
"Your name is now Jacob. But your name from now on
will not be Jacob; you will also have Israel as a name."
Elohim named him Israel.
11 Elohim said to him,
"I am El Shaddai, Elohim the Almighty, be fruitful and increase.
A nation and even many nations will come into existence because of you.
Kings will be among your descendants.

The Monument at Beth El
6th Aliyah

12 "I will grant you the land that I promised to Abraham and Isaac; I will also give the land to your descendants who will follow you."
13 Elohim left Jacob in the place where He had spoken to him.
14 Jacob set up a stone pillar in the place where Elohim had spoken to him. Then he poured oil on it.
15 Jacob named the place where Elohim had spoken to him Beth El (Elohim's Temple).
16 They then left Beth El and marched toward Efrat, where Rachel began to give birth. Rachel had great difficulty giving birth. **17** The midwife said to her, "Don't be afraid. You will have a son."
18 As Rachel was dying, she named the child Ben Oni (Son of My Sorrow). But his father called him Benjamin (Son of My Strong Right Hand).

---

6. Jacob and all the people with him arrived at Luz, now called Beth El, meaning "House of El."
Beth El means House of Adonai. Bethel is located about twelve miles north of Jerusalem and is the most mentioned town in the Tanak after Jerusalem. Bethel's Torah history revolves around Abraham, Isaac, and Jacob. Excavations at Bethel have revealed evidence of its destruction by the Israelites during their conquest of Canaan.

10. Elohim named him Israel.
The name Israel occurs 2,355 times in the Bible. The name was given to Jacob and then to the descendants of Jacob. Then it was given to the whole nation, and finally to the northern part of the kingdom when it was split from Judah, the southern part.

10. Your name is now Jacob. But your name from now on will not be Jacob; you will also have Israel as a name.
Jacob's Hebrew name was Ya'akov. The name Ya'akov comes from the Hebrew word *ekev*, meaning "heel."

From now on you have a new name and a changed personality. From now on your Hebrew name is Yisrael, meaning that you are a prince (*sar*) and a leader.
Rashi

19 Rachel died and was buried on the road to Efrat, now called Bethlehem. **20** Jacob set up a monument over her grave. It is the same monument that marks Rachel's grave to this very day.
21 Israel traveled on, and he set up his tent near Migdal Eder (Herd Tower). **22** While Jacob was living in the area, Reuben went and disturbed the sleeping arrangements of Bilhah, his father's concubine. Jacob had twelve sons. **23** The sons of Leah were Reuben, Jacob's firstborn, Simeon, Levi, Judah, Issachar, and Zebulun. **24** The sons of Rachel were Joseph and Benjamin.
25 The sons of Rachel's handmaid Bilhah were Dan and Naphtali. **26** The sons of Leah's handmaid Zilpah were Gad and Asher. These are the sons born to Jacob in Padan Aram.
27 Jacob came to his father Isaac in Mamre, at Kiryath Arba, now called Hebron, where Abraham and Isaac had lived.
28 Isaac lived to be 180 years old. **29** He died at a ripe old age. His sons, Esau and Jacob, buried him.

36

This is the history of Esau, also known as Edom.
2 Esau married girls from the daughters of the Canaanites. His wives were Adah, daughter of Elon the Hittite, and Oholibamah, daughter of Anah, daughter of Ziv'on the Hivite. **3** He also married Basemath, daughter of Ishmael and sister of Nebayoth.
4 Adah gave birth to Esau's son Eliphaz. Basemath gave birth to Reuel.
5 Oholibamah gave birth to Yeush, Yalam, and Korach. These are Esau's sons who were born in the land of Canaan. **6** Esau took his wives, his sons, his daughters, all the members of his household, his livestock, and all the wealth that he had accumulated in the land of Canaan, and he moved away from his brother Jacob.

---

19. Rachel died and was buried on the road to Efrat, now called Bethlehem.
The domed structure known to millions of Jews as the Tomb of Rachel, the favorite wife of Jacob, is situated seven miles from Jerusalem in Bethlehem. This monument was erected by the Crusaders in the twelfth century.

The well-known English philanthropist Sir Moses Montefiore bought the tomb in 1841 and reconstructed it.

20. Jacob set up a monument over her grave.
The Hebrew word for tombstone is *ma-tze-vah*. Today it is customary for Jews to set a *ma-tze-vah* at the head of the grave.
Its purpose is to keep the memory of the dead alive as well as to identify the grave.

The usual practice is to erect a *ma-tze-vah* one year after the death. The stone is covered with a veil. The family conducts a service and the veil is removed. The service is called an unveiling.

29. His sons, Esau and Jacob, buried him.
The death of a beloved family member often brings a reconciliation between quarreling relatives. Now the brothers were united in their sorrow.

Soon after Jacob's return to his homeland, his beloved Rachel died. Not long after, Isaac, his aged father, died. Esau and Jacob together buried their father in the family crypt in the Cave of Machpelah at Hebron.

7 He did so because they had too many animals and not enough grass for both of their herds. **8** Esau moved to the hill country of Seir. There Esau's descendants became the nation of Edom.

9 This is the history of Esau, the ancestor of the nations of Edom who lived in the hill country of Seir:

10 These are the names of Esau's sons: Eliphaz, son of Esau's wife Adah; Reuel, son of Esau's wife Basemath. **11** The sons of Eliphaz were Teman, Omar, Czefo, Gatam, and Kenaz. **12** Timna became the second wife of Esau's son Eliphaz, and she gave birth to Eliphaz's son Amalek. All these children were the descendants of Esau's wife Adah.

13 These are the sons of Reuel: Nachath, Zerach, Shamah, and Mizzah. These are the descendants of Esau's wife Basemath.

14 These are the sons of Esau's wife Oholibamah, daughter of Anah, daughter of Ziv'on: By Esau she gave birth to Yeush, Yalam, and Korach.

15 These are the *alufim* (tribal chiefs) among the children of Esau:

The sons of Esau's first-born, Eliphaz, were: Aluf Teman, Aluf Omar, Aluf Zefo, Aluf Kenaz, **16** Aluf Korach, Aluf Gatam, Aluf Amalek. These were the alufim from Eliphaz in the land of Edom. The above were descendants of Adah.

17 These are the alufim among the children of Esau's son Reuel: Aluf Nachath, Aluf Zerach, Aluf Shamah, Aluf Mizzah These are the alufim from Reuel in the land of Edom. The above were descendants of Esau's wife Basemath.

18 These are the sons of Esau's wife Oholibamah: Aluf Yeush, Aluf Yalam, Aluf Korach. These are the alufim from Esau's wife Oholibamah, daughter of Anah.

19 These are the sons of Esau, and these are their alufim. They are also known as Edom.

The Descendants of Seir *7th Aliyah*

20 These are the sons of Seir the Horite, native to the land of Seir: Lotan, Shoval, Ziv'on, Anah,

21 Dishon, Ezer, Dishan. These were the alufim of the Horites, the descendants of Seir in the land of Edom.

22 The sons of Lotan were Hori and Hemam. Lotan's sister was Timna.

23 These are the sons of Shoval: Alvan, Manachath, Ebhal, Zefo, and Onam.

24 These are the children of Ziv'on: Ayah and Anah. Anah was the one who discovered the hot springs in the desert when he was tending the donkeys for his father, Ziv'on.

25 These are the children of Anah: Dishon and Oholibamah, daughter of Anah.

26 These are the sons of Dishon: Hemdan, Eshban, Yithran, and Keran.

27 These are the sons of Ezer: Bilhan, Zaavan, and Akan.

28 These are the sons of Dishan: Utz and Aran.

29 These are the alufim of the Horites: Aluf Lotan, Aluf Shoval, Aluf Ziv'on, Aluf Anah, **30** Aluf Dishon, Aluf Etzer, Aluf Dishan. These are tribes of the Horites according to their alufim in the land of Seir.

31 These are the kings who ruled the land of Edom before there were any Israelite kings:
32 Bela son of Beer was king of Edom, and Dinhava was the name of his capital.
33 Bela died, and Yovev son of Zerach from Botzrah became king.
34 Yovav died, and Husham from the land of the Temanites became king.
35 Husham died, and Hadad son of Badad, who defeated Midian in the field of Moab, became king. The name of his capital was Avith.
36 Hadad died, and Samlah of Masrekah became king.
37 Samlah died, and Shaul from Rechovoth Hanahar (Rechovoth on the River) became king.
38 Shaul died, and Baal Hanan son of Akhbor became king.
39 Baal Hanan son of Akhbor died, and Hadar became king. The name of his capital was Pau. His wife's name was Meheitaval daughter of Matred, daughter of Me-Zahav.

The Tribes of Esau
Maftir

40 These are the names of the tribes of Esau, according to their families who lived in places named after them: the tribe of Timna, the tribe of Alvah, the tribe of Yetheth, **41** the tribe of Oholibamah, the tribe of Elah, the tribe of Pinon,
42 the tribe of Kenaz, the tribe of Teman, the tribe of Mibtzar, **43** The tribe of Magdiel, the tribe of Iram.
These are the tribes of Esau, who lived in places named after them.
This is how Esau was the ancestor of the Edomites.

---

35. Husham died, and Hadad son of Badad, who defeated Midian in the field of Moab, became king.
Abraham had married a concubine named Keturah, who gave birth to six children (25:2). One of the sons was called Midian and he was the father of the Midianite people. They were a nomadic people, who wandered throughout the Negev and parts of Arabia.

36. Hadad died, and Samlah of Masrekah became king.
Hadad was also the name of the Aramaean storm god. The Canaanites called him Baal.
Hadad was believed to bring rain.

40. These are the names of the tribes of Esau, according to their families who lived in places named after them: the tribe of Timna, the tribe of Alvah, the tribe of Yetheth.
The tribes were unimportant, so they were known only by the areas in which they lived.
Sforno

43. This is how Esau was the ancestor of the Edomites.
Esau defeated the former inhabitants of the mountainous Arabah, the Horites, married their daughter, and settled there. The feud between Jacob and Esau emerged when the Edomites refused passage to the Israelites when the latter invaded Canaan. There was continuous animosity between the Israelites and Edomites. The prophets pronounced doom on Edom for enslaving Israelites. In the post-exile period, because of the pressure of the Nabataean Arabs, the Israelites were pushed north and occupied the southern half of Judea. Judah Maccabee fought them and John Hyrcanus completely conquered them when Rome conquered Jerusalem. Edom ceased to be.

וַיֵּשֶׁב *Vayeshev*

JACOB IN CANAAN

37 Now Jacob settled in the land of Canaan where his father had lived. **2** This is the history of Jacob: Joseph was seventeen years old, and as a young man, he tended the sheep with his brothers, the sons of Bilhah and Zilpah, his father's wives. Joseph tattled to his father about his brothers.

3 Israel loved Joseph more than any of his other sons, because Joseph was the child of his old age. He made Joseph a colorful jacket. **4** When his brothers saw that their father loved Joseph more than all of them, they began to hate him. They could not say a friendly word to him.

5 Once Joseph had a dream, and when he told it to his brothers, they hated him even more. **6** He said to them, "Listen to the dream I had. **7** We were binding sheaves in the field, when my sheaf suddenly stood up and your sheaves formed a circle around my sheaf, and they bowed down to it."

8 The brothers angrily replied, "So you want to be our king? Do you intend to rule over us?" Because of his dreams and his attitude, they hated Joseph even more.

9 Joseph had another dream and once again told it to his brothers. "I just had another dream. The sun, the moon, and eleven stars all bowed down to me."

10 When he told his dream to his father and brothers, his father was angry at him and said, "What kind of dream did you have? Do you expect me, your mother, and your brothers to bow down to you?"

11 His brothers became very jealous of him, but his father silently thought about its meaning.

---

2. Joseph tattled to his father about his brothers.
Joseph's mother, Rachel, had died. So Joseph attached himself to the families of Bilhah and Zilpah. Joseph would report to Jacob what the boys were doing, which, naturally, made them angry.

3. He made Joseph a colorful jacket.
Joseph was considered Jacob's most important descendant. His mother, Rachel, was Jacob's true love, and Jacob had only to look upon Joseph's face to be reminded of his beloved Rachel.

Jacob was showing favoritism to Joseph over all his brothers, which was an unwise thing to do. The tunic that Jacob gave Joseph was a long-sleeved garment which reached down to the ankles.

9. The sun, the moon, and eleven stars all bowed down to me.
In the first dream, only Joseph's brothers were bowing before him. Now, in the second dream, his father and mother, along with his brothers, were doing so.

11. His brothers became very jealous of him.
Jacob's favoritism toward Joseph might have been offset with his brothers had Joseph had the quality of modesty. His brothers might have removed the blame from Joseph. What fault was it of Joseph's that their father was partial to the boy? Unfortunately, Joseph added to his unpopularity. Lacking modesty, he acted superior to his older brothers.

When Joseph dreamed his dreams about ruling the family, he proudly announced them for all to hear. Even Jacob found Joseph's arrogance a little hard to take. But by now it was too late to check him. All the years that Jacob had pampered him had blinded Joseph to other people's feelings.

Joseph Finds His Brothers
2nd Aliyah

12 Joseph's brothers left to graze their father's sheep in Shechem. **13** Israel said to Joseph, "Your brothers are grazing the sheep in Shechem. I would like you to go and see if they are well." "I'm ready," replied Joseph.

14 "Bring me a report and see how your brothers and the sheep are doing," said Israel. Israel sent Joseph from the Hebron Valley to Shechem.

15 A villager found him wandering in the fields. "What are you looking for?" asked the villager. **16** Joseph replied, "I'm looking for my brothers. Perhaps you can tell me where they are grazing their sheep."

17 "They have already left this area," said the villager. "I heard them planning to move to Dothan." Joseph followed after his brothers and found them in Dothan. **18** They saw him in the distance, and they began plotting to kill him.

19 They said to one another, "Here comes the dreamer!

20 This is our chance! Let's kill him and throw his body into one of the wells. We can tell our father that a wild animal ate him. Then we'll see what will come of his fancy dreams!"

21 Reuben heard them and decided to save Joseph. He said to them, "Let's not kill our brother!" **22** Reuben tried to talk sense to his brothers. He said, "At least don't kill him. You can throw him into this well, but do not harm him." He planned to secretly save Joseph and bring him back to his father.

Joseph Is Sold
3rd Aliyah

23 When Joseph came to his brothers, they stripped him of the colorful jacket that he was wearing. **24** They picked him up and threw him into the well. The well was empty; there was no water in it. **25** Then the brothers sat down to eat. In the distance they saw an Ishmaelite caravan coming from Gilead. The camels were carrying spices, balsam, and resin to sell in Egypt. **26** Judah said to his brothers, "What will we gain if we kill our brother and cover up his death?

---

17. "They have already left this area," said the villager. "I heard them planning to move to Dothan."
The villager who knows where the brothers went is not just an ordinary person but a "divine messenger." Only Adonai's plan, working behind the scene, led him to his brothers.
Maimonides

24. They picked him up and threw him into the well. The well was empty; there was no water in it.
It was a dry well, and it was filled with snakes, scorpions and spiders.
Rashi

25. In the distance they saw an Ishmaelite caravan coming from Gilead.
Gilead is the name of a town on the west bank of the Jordan River. The Torah tells us that Gilead was known for its spices.

25. The camels were carrying spices, balsam, and resin to sell in Egypt.
In ancient times trade between Asia and Egypt was carried out by tribes with camels. Experienced camel drivers such as the Ishmaelites monopolized the trade between Canaan and Egypt. Camels are hardy creatures. A pack camel can carry about 500 pounds of goods. The camel requires little food and is capable of storing water for several days.

In ancient times, balm was a familiar spice and was carried by the traders' caravans going to Egypt. The commentator Rashi explains that the balm is a resin which is exuded from the wood of a balsam tree. The balm of Gilead was one of the ingredients of the incense used at the Tabernacle.

27 Let's sell him to the Ishmaelites and not harm ourselves with his blood. After all, he's our brother, he is our own flesh and blood." The brothers reluctantly agreed with Judah. he merchants turned out to be Midianite traders. The brothers pulled Joseph out of the well and sold him to the merchants for twenty pieces of silver. The Midianites intended to bring Joseph to Egypt.

29 Later, when Reuben returned to the well, Joseph was no longer there. Reuben tore his clothes in anger and grief.

830 He returned to his brothers and cried, "Joseph is gone! Now what can I do?" **31** The brothers took Joseph's jacket, and they killed a goat and dipped the jacket in the blood.

32 Then they sent the blood-soaked jacket to their father. When the brothers returned they said to Jacob, "Can you identify the jacket? Is it Joseph's jacket?" **33** Jacob immediately recognized it. He cried, "It is Joseph's jacket. A wild animal must have eaten him! My Joseph has been torn to pieces!"

34 Jacob tore his robes in grief and put on sackcloth and mourned for a long time. **35** His sons and daughters tried to comfort him. He cried, "I will go down to my grave mourning for my son." He wept for his son as only a father could.

---

27. Let us sell him to the Ishmaelites.
Joseph's brothers' hatred for him was so strong that it reached the point where they were ready to kill him. Fortunately, two of the brothers disagreed with the rest. Reuben suggested that they throw him into a pit in the field. It was his plan to free Joseph under the cover of darkness. But Reuben's plan never came off. Along came a trader caravan of Ishmaelites, and Judah, another of the brothers, proposed that they sell Joseph into slavery. To Judah it was the lesser of two evils. At least the brothers would not have Joseph's blood on their conscience.

31. The brothers took Joseph's jacket and they killed a goat and dipped the jacket in the blood.
The brothers sold Joseph to the traders who were on their way to Egypt. Then they slaughtered a goat and dipped Joseph's beautiful coat in the blood.

In this way, the brothers revenge themselves against their father, Jacob, for favoring Joseph and for not giving them the same kind of attention and love.

Joseph deserves the enmity of his brothers. He was a spoiled brat, tattling on his brothers and dressing up in his fancy coat.

32. Then they sent the blood-soaked jacket to their father.
Joseph's brothers were afraid to face their father. They sent the jacket with a messenger.

33. A wild animal must have eaten him! My Joseph has been torn to pieces.
Joseph's brothers were trapped into a series of wrongdoings and lying. Driven by their envy and hatred of their younger brother, they sold him as a slave. That was wrong number one. Next, they had to explain the boy's disappearance to Jacob, their father. They took the colorful coat which they had stripped from Joseph before they threw him into the pit, and they dipped it in animal blood. Bringing the garment as "evidence," they then came to their father, showed it to him, and announced that Joseph had been devoured by a wild animal. This was wrong number two. Now they would have to live a lie for many years to come, fearing that one or another of them might reveal the truth sometime. They each had a guilty conscience. This was wrong number three.

34. Jacob tore his robes in grief and put on sackcloth.
In the biblical period, the wearing of sackcloth and sprinkling of ashes on the head expressed mourning for the dead. The sackcloth was a rough cloth made of goat's hair.

36 In Egypt the Midianites sold Joseph to Potiphar, one of Pharaoh's officers, a captain of the guard.

Judah and Tamar

4th Aliyah

38 About this time, Judah moved away from his brothers. He became friends with a man from Adullam by the name of Hirah. **2** There Judah met the daughter of a merchant named Shua. He married her, and **3** she became pregnant and gave birth to a son. He named the child Er. **4** She became pregnant again, and had another son. She named him Onan. **5** She gave birth for the third time and again gave birth to a son. She named him Shelah. Judah was in Keziv when she gave birth to Shelah.
6 Judah arranged a marriage for Er, his first-born, and the bride's name was Tamar. **7** Judah's first-born, Er, was evil in the eyes of Adonai. And Adonai made him die. **8** Judah said to Onan, "According to the law you must marry your brother's wife. In this way you will then raise children and keep your brother's name alive." **9** However, Onan realized that the children would not carry his name, so whenever he slept with his brother's wife, he let his seed go to waste so as not to have children that did not belong to him. **10** What he did displeased Adonai, and He also made Onan die.

---

1. He became friends with a man from Adullam by the name of Hirah.
Judah was the first of the brothers to become friends with a Canaanite.

2. Judah met the daughter of a merchant named Shua. He married her.
Judah, who had moved away from his brothers, married a Canaanite girl and she gave birth to three sons – Er, Onan, and Shelah.

Later (v. 11) the eldest son, Er, married Tamar, who may also have been a Canaanite. He died young and in accordance with the levirate marriage custom Onan, against his will, married her.

5. She named him Shelah. Judah was in Keziv when she gave birth to Shelah.
The text informs us that Judah for some unexplained reason was not present when the boy was born. The name Shelah, meaning "disappoint me," reflected the attitude of Judah's wife because he was not at her side during Shelah's birth.

6. Tamar.
The Hebrew word *tamar* means "palm tree."

8. Judah said to Onan, "According to the law you must marry your brother's wife. In this way you will then raise children and keep your brother's name alive."
When a brother dies childless, the widow must not be allowed to marry someone outside the family. It is the brother-in-law's responsibility to marry her. Marriage with a brother's childless widow is known as a levirate marriage (*yibbum*). The term "levirate" comes from the Latin word meaning brother-in-law. The purpose of levirate marriage was to perpetuate the name of the deceased and prevent the calamity of the extinction of a family line and also prevent his property from being passed down to children who are not his descendants. Judah asked Onan, the second brother, to perform the levirate. With the abolition of polygamy, levirate marriage has disappeared.

9. However, Onan realized that the children would not carry his name.
Onan was a selfish person. He wanted children of his own. According to the levirate law, the children would carry his brother's name. *Sforno*

10. What he did displeased Adonai, and He also made Onan die.
Onan obeys his father but refuses to have sexual relations with her. So Adonai caused Onan to die. Now the duty reverted back to Shelah, the third brother.

11 Then Judah said to his daughter-in-law Tamar, "You can live as a widow in your father's house until my son Shelah is old enough to marry you." He said that to her because he was afraid that Shelah would also die like his brothers. So Tamar left and lived in her father's house.

12 A long time passed, and Judah's wife, the daughter of Shua, died. When Judah stopped mourning, he went to supervise his sheepshearers in Timna, together with his friend, Hirah the Adullamite.

13 Someone told Tamar that her father-in-law had gone to Timna to shear his sheep. **14** So she took off her widow's robe and disguised herself with a veil. Then she sat at the entrance of Eynayim, which was on the road to Timna. Tamar was angry because she saw that Shelah had grown up and she had not been called to marry him. **15** Judah saw her, and because she was disguised, he thought that she was a prostitute. **16** So he stopped, not realizing that she was his own daughter-in-law. He said, "Hello, I would like to sleep with you." She replied, "How much will you pay me if I sleep with you?" **17** He answered, "I will send you a goat from the flock." She said, "You must give me something to make sure that you will keep your promise." **18** "What do you want?" he asked. "Your ring, your jacket, and the walking stick in your hand," she replied. He gave them to her and he slept with her and she became pregnant. **19** She got up and removed her veil and put her widow's robe back on.

20 As soon as Judah returned home, he sent the young goat with his friend the Adullamite to get back the ring, the jacket, and the walking stick from the woman, but his friend could not find her.

21 His friend Hirah asked the local people, "Where is the prostitute that used to sit near the side of the road in Eynayim?"

"There was no prostitute here," they replied.

---

11. Then Judah said to his daughter-in-law Tamar, "You can live as a widow in your father's house until my son Shelah is old enough to marry you."
Judah got rid of Tamar by telling her to live as a widow until Shelah was grown up.

12. Judah's wife, the daughter of Shua, died.
Tamar wanted to be in charge of the household and she thought that if she married Shelah she could assume this position. When Judah failed to send for her, she devised a substitute plan to terminate her widowhood.

14. Tamar was angry because she saw that Shelah was grown up and she had not been called to marry him.
There was a wide disparity in age between Shelah and Tamar. He was a teenager and Tamar was an adult woman of at least forty. Shelah probably refused to marry her. Judah also realized that the marriage would be harmful to his son Shelah.

15. Judah saw her...and thought she was a prostitute.
She veiled herself so as not to be recognized.

20. As soon as Judah returned home, he sent the young goat with his friend the Adullamite.
Unknowingly, Judah had slept with his daughter-in-law Tamar. He gave her his signet ring, jacket, and walking stick, which were to be redeemed when he sent her a goat in payment for her service. When Judah returned home, he sent his friend Adullamite with a goat in order to redeem his property.

22 Hirah returned to Judah and said, "I couldn't find the woman. The local men said that they never saw a prostitute there."

23 Judah replied, "Let her keep the things. We don't want to look like fools. I tried to send her the goat, but you couldn't find her."

24 Three months later, Judah was told, "Your daughter-in-law has been behaving like a prostitute. She has become pregnant and has no husband."

"In that case take her out and have her burned," said Judah. **25** As she was being dragged out, she sent the ring, jacket, and walking stick to her father-in-law with a message: "The man who made me pregnant is the owner of these articles." When Judah came to see her, she said, "Can you identify these objects. Who is the owner of this seal, this coat, and this staff?"

26 Judah immediately recognized them. "She is more in the right than I am!" he said. "She did it because I refused to marry her to my son Shelah." **27** When her time came, she gave birth to twins. **28** As she was in labor, one of the twins put out an arm. The midwife grasped it and tied a red ribbon on it. She announced, "This one came out first."

29 But he pulled his hand back, and then his brother emerged. She said, "You have pushed [*peretz*] yourself out." So Judah named the child Peretz.

30 Then his brother with the ribbon on his hand was born. Judah named him Zerach (Brightness).

Joseph Is Sold

5th Aliyah

39 Joseph was brought down to Egypt, and Potiphar, one of Pharaoh's Egyptian officers, the captain of the guard, bought him from the Midianites who had brought him there. **2** Adonai watched over Joseph and made him very successful. Soon he was working in his master's own house.

3 His master realized that Adonai was with Joseph and that Adonai brought success to everything Joseph did.

---

24. Three months later, Judah was told, "Your daughter-in-law has been behaving like a prostitute. She has become pregnant and has no husband."
Tamar was sentenced to be burnt, but as she was dragged out she sent her father-in-law his belongings. Now Judah was in a personal ethical dilemma. Would the real father step forward and admit paternity and save Tamar, his daughter-in-law?

26. She is more in the right than I am!
Judah stepped up and assumed the blame and said, "She did it because I refused to allow her to marry my son Shelah. Now she is my responsibility."

27. When her time came, she gave birth to twins.
Judah named the children Peretz and Zerach. Judah, the father-in-law, was the father of the twins of Tamar, his daughter-in-law. Truth is stranger than fiction.

1. Joseph was brought down to Egypt, and Potiphar, one of Pharaoh's Egyptian officers, the captain of the guard, bought him from the Midianites who had brought him there.
The midrash says that it was part of Adonai's plan to get Joseph into Egypt in order that he might in future years be able to save his family. The preference Jacob showed for his son Joseph and the jealousy of the brothers were just disguised means for getting Joseph into Egypt.

3. His master realized that Adonai was with Joseph and that Adonai brought success to everything Joseph did.
His master Potiphar heard Joseph praying and heard him attribute his success in managing his master's affairs to Adonai.

4 Joseph impressed his master and before long was appointed his master's personal servant. His master put him in charge of his household, giving him responsibility for everything he owned.
5 Soon his master had put him in charge of his household and possessions. Adonai blessed Potiphar because of Joseph. Adonai blessed everything the Egyptian owned in his house and in his fields.
6 Potiphar put all his family affairs in Joseph's hands except for the food he himself ate. He did not concern himself with anything Joseph did. Meanwhile, Joseph grew to be a handsome young man.

Potiphar's Wife
6th Aliyah

7 Soon Potiphar's wife took a liking to Joseph. She begged, "Sleep with me!"
8 Joseph refused. He explained to his master's wife, "My master does not even know what I do in the house. He has entrusted me with everything he owns. **9** No one in this house has more authority than I have. He has not held back anything at all from me, except for you – his wife. How could I do such a great wrong? It would be a sin before Elohim!"
10 Every day she propositioned Joseph, but he would not pay attention to her. He did not even stand close to her or spend time near her.
11 One day, Joseph came to the house to do his work. None of the household servants were inside. **12** The woman grabbed him by his cloak. She begged, "Make love to me!" Joseph ran away, leaving his cloak in her hand.
13 When Potiphar's wife realized that he had left his cloak in her hand and fled, **14** she called her household servants and screamed, "Be my witnesses! My husband brought us a Hebrew man to insult us! He tried to rape me, but I screamed as loud as I could! **15** When he heard me scream and call for help, he ran outside and left his cloak with me!"
16 She kept Joseph's cloak with her until her husband came home, **17** then she told him the same story. "The Hebrew slave that you brought us came and molested me! **18** When I screamed and called for help, he escaped, leaving his cloak with me!"
19 When her husband heard his wife's story about what Joseph had done, he became very angry.

---

4. His master put him in charge of his household, giving him responsibility for everything he owned.
Potiphar granted Joseph full authority over everything he owned. Joseph earned his trust, because of his honesty.

6. Potiphar put all his family affairs in Joseph's hands except for the food he himself ate.
The Egyptians refused to eat with foreigners because they believed that foreigners contaminated their food.

8. Joseph refused.
Joseph cites three reasons for his refusal to make love to his master's wife. 1. He did not want to abuse Potiphar's trust. 2. Joseph believed in the sanctity of marriage and did not want to interfere in a family matter. 3. It was against the ethical, moral, and religious principle which he had been taught in his father's house.

19. When her husband heard his wife's story about what Joseph had done, he became very angry.
The sage Arbarbanel says that Potiphar knew Joseph was innocent and he became angry with his wife. He must have shouted, "Not again! Another one of your lies!"

20 Joseph's master had him arrested and thrown into the jail where the king's prisoners were kept. **21** But Adonai was with Joseph, and the warden took a liking to him.

22 In time, the warden put all the prisoners in the jail under Joseph's supervision. Joseph took care of everything.

23 The warden did not have to worry about anything under Joseph's care. Adonai was with Joseph, and Adonai made him successful in everything he did.

The Dream of the Two Prisoners *7th Aliyah*

40 Some time later, the Egyptian king's cup-bearer and the chief baker offended their master, the king of Egypt. **2** Pharaoh was angry at his two officials, the chief wine steward and the chief baker, **3** and he had them arrested. They were put in the same jail where Joseph was imprisoned. **4** They remained in jail for a long time, and the captain of the guards assigned Joseph to care for them. **5** One night, the two of them had dreams. The king's cup-bearer and baker, who were imprisoned in the dungeon, each had a dream that seemed to have a special meaning. **6** When Joseph came to them in the morning, he saw that they were worried. **7** Joseph tried to find out what was bothering Pharaoh's officials who were his fellow prisoners. He asked, "Why are both of you so sad today?"

---

20. Joseph's master had him arrested and thrown into the jail, where the king's prisoners were kept.
The midrash explains that under normal circumstances Joseph would have been immediately executed. However, Potiphar's wife had accused other servants of the same crime. This time the Pharaoh believed him and allowed him to live.

22. In time, the warden put all the prisoners in the jail under Joseph's supervision.
Joseph was challenged by his early experiences in Egypt to grow up fast. He was on his own and he had to sink or swim. The first challenge came to him as a slave in Potiphar's house. He was doing well in growing up to the responsibility of work. But Potiphar's wife, angry with him and vengeful, charged him with wrongdoing. Off to prison he went. It should have broken his spirit but it did not. He was growng up fast to the challenges of life. Very soon, his ability was recognized and Joseph was appointed a prison trustee.

By now he had learned from the bitter experience with his brothers to play fair with people. The warden had confidence in him, and Joseph's fellow prisoners liked and respected him. *Chiel*

4. The captain of the guards assigned Joseph to care for them.
The two new prisoners were noblemen, and so a servant was assigned to them even in prison. Adonai works in mysterious ways. The inmate chosen to be their servant was none other than Joseph.

5. One night, the two of them had dreams.
Among the many interesting things which archaeologists discovered in Egypt was a "dream book" written in the thirteenth century B.C.E. Under the heading, "If a Man Sees Himself in a Dream," there are listed descriptions of all types of dreams, some good, some bad. According to this "dream book," wine usually has a good meaning. But birds are often a bad sign. The word for "bad" is written in this book in red, probably to suggest the color of blood.

Dreams, according to the Torah, were communications from Adonai. This belief was carried forward into the later talmudic period of Jewish history. Rabbi Chisda, one of the great teachers of the Talmud, said, "An uninterpreted dream is like an unread letter."

7. Why are both of you so sad today?
The cup-bearer and the baker were important palace officials. Yet Joseph had the presence of mind to see that the officials were concerned about their dreams. Joseph, the servant, had the audacity to ask the officials, "Why are both of you so sad?"

8 They replied, "We each had a dream, and there is no one here to tell us what they mean."
Joseph replied, "Interpretations are Elohim's business. If you wish, you can tell me about your dreams." **9** The cup-bearer told his dream to Joseph. He said, "In my dream I saw a grapevine right in front of me.
10 The vine had three branches. As soon as its buds formed, its blossoms bloomed and its clusters ripened into grapes. **11** I was holding Pharaoh's cup in my hand. I took the grapes and squeezed them into Pharaoh's cup. Then I placed the cup in Pharaoh's hand."
12 Joseph said to him, "This is what your dream means: The three branches are three days. **13** In three days, Pharaoh will pardon you and give you back your position. You will continue to put Pharaoh's cup in his hand, just as you did before.
14 Please, when things go well for you, just remember that I was in jail with you. Do me a favor and say something nice about me to Pharaoh. Perhaps you will be able to free me from jail. **15** I was kidnapped from the land of the Hebrews and did not deserve to be thrown in jail."
16 The chief baker saw how well Joseph was able to interpret the first dream. He said to Joseph, "I too saw myself in my dream. There were three baskets of fine white bread on my head. **17** In the top basket, there were all kinds of baked goods that Pharaoh likes to eat. But birds were eating it from the basket on my head!"
18 Joseph replied, "This is what your dream means: The three baskets are three days. **19** In three days, Pharaoh will cut off your head! He will hang you from a tree and the birds will eat your flesh."

The Cup-Bearer Forgets Joseph *Maftir*

20 Pharaoh's birthday came three days later, and he made a party for all his officials. At that time he sent for the chief cup-bearer and the chief baker. **21** He returned the wine steward to his position, and he was again allowed to set the cup in Pharaoh's hand. **22** The chief baker was hanged, just as Joseph had predicted.
23 However, the wine steward did not remember Joseph. He forgot all about him.

---

8. They replied, "We each had a dream and there was no one here to tell us what they mean."
The Egyptians had special dream interpreters who were consulted by people who had troubled dreams. The prison had no one who had the professional expertise to interpret dreams.

8. Joseph replied, "Interpretations are Elohim's business. If you wish, you can tell me about your dreams."
Only Adonai can send me the wisdom to interpret your dreams. If you wish, just tell me your dreams. Perhaps Adonai will send me the wisdom to interpret their meanings.

21. He returned the wine steward to his position, and he was again allowed to set the cup in Pharaoh's hand.
The Pharaohs used to commemorate their birthdays with a celebratory and a general amnesty. The cup-bearer was pardoned as predicted by Joseph.

The Pharaohs of ancient Egypt and other Middle Eastern countries were aware of poisons that could be put into their food. The rulers always employed food tasters before eating. One of the duties of the cup-bearer was to sip the Pharaoh's wine before handing him his cup.

Shenash

מִקֵּץ *Miketz*

TWO YEARS LATER

41 Two years later, Pharaoh had a dream. He dreamed that he was standing near the Nile River, **2** when suddenly seven strong, healthy cows came up from the Nile and grazed in the grass.

3 Then another seven, thin, bony cows came up from the Nile and stood next to the strong cows already on the river bank.

4 The thin, bony cows ate up the seven strong healthy, fat cows. Then Pharaoh woke up.

5 Pharaoh fell asleep again and had a second dream. He saw seven large, golden ears of corn growing on a single stalk.

6 Then, suddenly, another seven ears of thin and burnt corn grew up behind them.

7 The seven thin ears swallowed the seven large ears of corn. Pharaoh woke up and realized that it had been a dream.

8 In the morning Pharaoh was very worried, so he sent for his magicians and the wise men of Egypt. Pharaoh told them his dreams, but no one could interpret them for Pharaoh.

9 Then the chief wine steward spoke to Pharaoh. "Today I must recall my sins.

10 Pharaoh was angry at me, and he put me under arrest in the jail of the captain of the guard, along with the chief baker. **11** One night we each had a dream that had its own special meaning.

12 There was a young Hebrew man with us, a slave of the captain of the guard. We told him our dreams, and he interpreted them. He told each of us the meaning of our dreams, **13** and things worked out exactly as he said they would. I was restored to my position, while the baker was hanged."

---

8. Pharaoh told them his dream and no one could interpret them for Pharaoh.
Pharaoh dreamt two dreams. They troubled him. What was their meaning? He consulted the expert dream interpreters of Egypt. They were summoned to the palace one after the other. But none of them could properly interpret Pharaoh's dreams. The experts were stumped!

9. Then the chief wine steward spoke to Pharaoh: "Today I must recall my sins."
First I sinned against Pharaoh and was thrown in jail. I also sinned against my fellow prisoner Joseph the Hebrew. I sinned by forgetting to speak favorably to the Pharaoh about Joseph, the dream interpreter.

12. He told each of us the meaning of our dreams.
Before the wine steward had left prison to take up his work again in the Pharaoh's palace, Joseph had asked the wine steward to help gain his release from prison, where he had been put unjustly.

Likely the wine steward made big promises to Joseph about helping to get him his freedom. "Yet the wine steward did not remember Joseph" (40:23). Only now, when his master Pharaoh was in deep trouble about his dreams, did he suddenly remember the young Hebrew prisoner who had been so helpful to him, and he urged Pharaoh to have him brought from prison to interpret the perplexing dreams.

14 Pharaoh sent messengers to bring Joseph to the palace. They rushed him from the jail. Joseph shaved and changed his clothes, and then appeared before Pharaoh.

Pharaoh's Dream
2nd Aliyah

15 Pharaoh said to Joseph, "I had a dream, and there is no one who can interpret it. I have heard that when you hear a dream, you can explain it."
16 Joseph replied to Pharaoh, "It is beyond my own power. But Elohim will tell me what Pharaoh's dream means."
17 Pharaoh told his dream to Joseph: "In my dream, I was standing on the saore of the Nile River. **18** Suddenly, seven fat, healthy cows came up from the Nile and grazed in the grass. **19** Then, just as suddenly, seven other cows, very thin and bony, came up after them. I never saw such bony cows anywhere in Egypt.
20 The thin and bony cows ate up the seven healthy cows.
21 They were completely swallowed by the thin cows, but the cows looked just as bony as they had at first. Then I woke up.
22 Then I had another dream. There were seven full, golden ears of corn growing on one stalk. **23** Suddenly, seven other stalks of grain grew behind them. The second ones were thin and burnt. **24** The thin stalks of grain swallowed up the seven full stalks of grain.
I told my dream to the magicians, but none of them could interpret it for me."
25 Joseph said to Pharaoh, "Pharaoh's two dreams have a single meaning. Elohim has mercifully revealed to Pharaoh what He is about to do.
26 The seven healthy cows and the seven full stalks of grain are both seven years. It is one dream.
27 The seven thin, bony cows and the seven thin, burnt ears of corn are also seven years, but seven years of famine.
28 It is just as I have told Pharaoh. Elohim has mercifully shown Pharaoh what He is about to do. **29** During the coming seven years, there will be a great abundance of food all over Egypt.

---

14. Joseph shaved and changed his clothes and then appeared before Pharaoh.
Joseph was a prisoner and wore a prisoner's uniform. Now court officials made him presentable to meet the Pharaoh. The aristocracy and the well-to-do used to shave their faces, in contrast to the Semitic Canaanites, who were bearded.

15. I have heard that when you hear a dream, you can explain it.
All of Pharaoh's wise men heard the dream but no one could explain its meaning. Now Pharaoh called upon Joseph to hear the dream and, most important, explain its meaning.

16. Elohim will tell me what Pharaoh's dream means.
Pharaoh had been upset ever since he had the dreams. Now Joseph assures him that with Elohim's help the meaning will become clear and Pharaoh will again have peace of mind.

18. Seven fat, healthy cows came up from the Nile and grazed in the grass.
When the Nile River overflowed in the summer, the land was enriched with fertilizer, which helped produce rich crops.

28. Elohim has mercifully shown Pharaoh what He is about to do.
Joseph shows his humility. He could have made himself look good, but instead he saw fit to give credit to Elohim, who had given him the wisdom to interpret the dream, and thus to teach Pharaoh of His greatness.

30 But these seven years will be followed by seven years of famine, when all the surplus in Egypt will disappear. The famine will devastate the land.

31 The coming famine will be so great that there will be no way of telling that there once was a surplus of food in the land.

32 The reason that Pharaoh had the same dream twice is that the event has already been decided by Elohim, and He will soon make it happen.

33 Now Pharaoh must find a man of wisdom and put him in charge of a national food program for Egypt.

34 Pharaoh must appoint officials over the land. A rationing system will have to be set up in Egypt during the seven years of abundance by collecting one-fifth of all the crops.

35 Let the officials collect all the food during these coming years of plenty, and let them store the grain under Pharaoh's control. The food will be kept in each of the cities under guard. **36** The food will be held in storage when the seven famine years come to Egypt. In that way Egypt will survive the famine."

37 Pharaoh and all his advisers realized that it was an excellent plan.

38 Pharaoh said to his advisers, "Is there any other person who has Elohim's spirit in him as this man does?"

Joseph Becomes Second to Pharaoh   *3rd Aliyah*

39 Pharaoh said to Joseph, "Since Elohim has revealed His plans to you, obviously there is no one as wise as you.

40 You shall be in charge of the project, and food will be distributed to my people only by your orders. Only I will outrank you."

41 Pharaoh then formally declared to Joseph, "I am putting you in charge of food for the entire land of Egypt."

---

30. These seven years of plenty will be followed by seven years of famine.
Besides underground wells and springs, a chief source of water in biblical lands were the rivers. This is true even today. The Nile in Egypt and the Tigris and Euphrates in Iraq are the most important rivers in the area. The crops each year depended on these rivers for water. Each year the river would overflow its banks. The floodwaters irrigated the fields and left a valuable layer of fresh topsoil.

Ancient history records the effect on people who are dependent on nature for every drop of rain or an annual flooding of a river like the Nile to bring water for that year's crops. They, of course, had no way of knowing what the next year would bring, much less the next seven.

33. Now Pharaoh must find a man of wisdom and put him in charge of a national food program for Egypt.
The man chosen by Pharaoh must be able to rule the country fairly and peacefully during the difficult period ahead, and to know how to collect and store the grain so as to preserve it. Joseph hoped Pharaoh would realize that he, Joseph, was a man of wisdom, and that he would appoint him to this high position.

Joseph proved to be not only a clever interpreter of dreams but also a wise adviser on how to act on the message of the dreams. Pharaoh was greatly impressed by Joseph and put him in charge of what was to be done for Egypt's future.

41. I am putting you in charge of food for the entire land of Egypt.
Joseph's interpretation of Pharaoh's dreams made excellent sense to the Egyptian ruler. The two dreams were really messages to the Pharaoh about the future of his land – seven years of plenty followed by seven years of famine. What all the other dream interpreters had failed to see in Pharaoh's dreams, Joseph understood quickly and clearly.

42 Pharaoh took his ring off his own finger and put it on Joseph's finger. He dressed Joseph in the finest linen garments and put a gold chain around his neck.
43 Joseph rode in the second royal chariot, and wherever he went they announced, "Kneel down! Make way for Joseph." Joseph was put in charge of all the food in Egypt.
44 Pharaoh said to Joseph, "I am Pharaoh. Without your permission, no man will lift a hand or foot anywhere in Egypt."
45 Pharaoh renamed Joseph Tzaphnath Paaneach. He gave him Asenath, daughter of Poti Phera, the priest of On, as a wife. **46** Joseph was thirty years old when he was elevated as second to Pharaoh. Joseph left Pharaoh's court and made an inspection tour of the entire land of Egypt. **47** During the seven years of abundance, the land of Egypt produced tons of grain. **48** Joseph collected the food during the seven years of abundance and stored the food in the granaries. The food growing in the fields around each city was put inside warehouses in each of the cities. **49** Joseph stored so much grain, it was like the sand of the sea. They had to give up counting it, because there was too much.
50 Before the famine years came, Joseph fathered two sons with his wife Asenath, daughter of Poti–Phera, priest of On. **51** Joseph named the first-born Manasseh "because Elohim has made me forget [*nasheh*] all my troubles – and even my father's house."
52 He named his second son Ephraim, "because God has made me fruitful [*p'ri*] in the land of my suffering."

---

42. Pharaoh took his ring off his own finger and put it on Joseph's finger.
The person who received Pharaoh's ring was recognized as Pharaoh's chief minister. Pharaoh's ring was a symbol of power.

42. He dressed Joseph in the finest linen garments and put a gold chain around his neck.
Linen in those days was worn only by royalty. The ring, the linen garment, and Pharaoh's gold chain were symbols of authority conferred upon Joseph by the ruler.

45. Pharaoh renamed Joseph Tzaphnath Paaneach.
Joseph bore the impressive title Tzaphnath Paaneach, meaning "sustainer of life." It was the Egyptian title for Pharaoh's prime minister. Joseph left Pharaoh's court and made an inspection tour of the entire land of Egypt.

45. He gave him Asenath, daughter of Poti–Phera.
Poti–Phera was an Egyptian dignitary and priest of On.

45. He gave him Asenath, daughter of Poti–phera, the priest of On.
Some believe that on is the Egyptian city of Heliopolis, which was in northern Egypt about 6 miles from Cairo. In ancient times, it was a religious center and was noted for its Temple of the Sun, dedicated to the sun god Re. References to On can be found in Isaiah 19:18 and Jeremiah 43:13.

49. Joseph stored up so much grain, it was like the sands of the sea.
The Nile River was the life blood of Egypt. But even the Nile sometimes stopped flowing. The Egyptians were very much aware of the moods of the treacherous Nile, so they customarily stored up surpluses in royal storehouses.

Joseph, acting on the advice he had given the Pharaoh, began to store the grain from the years of plenty in royal granaries in all sections of the country.

51. Joseph named the first-born Manasseh "because Elohim has made me forget [nasheh] all my troubles – and even my father's house."
Joseph had forgotten his suffering as a slave and a prisoner. The years had mellowed his anger at his brothers. Joseph was also aware that Adonai had placed him in the position to save his family, and the Egyptian people, from starving to death.

The Brothers Come to Egypt
4th Aliyah

53 Just as Joseph had predicted, the seven years of abundance that Egypt was enjoying finally came to an end.

54 The seven years of famine then began; there was famine in every other land, but in Egypt there was plenty of food.

55 After a while even Egypt began to feel the famine, and the people cried out to Pharaoh for food. Pharaoh announced to all Egypt, "Go to Joseph. You must do whatever he tells you."

56 The famine spread over the entire region. Joseph opened all the storehouses, and he sold food to the Egyptians. But still the famine grew even worse in Egypt. **57** The famine was also becoming more severe in the entire region, and people from all the surrounding countries came to Egypt to buy food from Joseph.

42 Jacob found out that there was food in Egypt, and he said to his sons, "Why are you sitting around doing nothing? **2** I have heard that there is food in Egypt. Go there and buy food so we can live and not starve to death." **3** Joseph's ten brothers went to buy food in Egypt.

4 But Jacob would not send Joseph's younger brother, Benjamin, along with the others because he was afraid that something might happen to him.

5 Israel's sons were among the many who came to buy food because of the severe famine in Canaan. **6** Joseph was like a governor over the land, since he was the only one who distributed food to all the people. When Joseph's brothers arrived, they bowed to him.

7 As soon as he saw them, Joseph recognized his brothers. But he acted like a stranger and spoke harshly to them. Joseph asked, "Where are you from?"

"We are from the land of Canaan, we have come to buy food," they replied.

8 Joseph recognized his brothers, but they did not recognize him.

---

56. The famine spread over the entire region. Joseph opened all the storehouses, and he sold food to the Egyptians. But still the famine grew even worse in Egypt.
Joseph was worried that the Egyptians would riot and storm the food warehouses. He wisely opened the warehouses and showed the people that there was enough food to feed the whole land of Egypt.

1. Why are you sitting around doing nothing?
Despite his old age, Jacob had a very clear and energetic mind. He realized that a solution had to be found or his family would starve to death. Jacob saw grain being brought up from Egypt to Canaan by caravan. He was angry with his sons for not making the effort to go down to Egypt to buy food for their starving families.

6. Joseph was like a governor over the land, since he was the only one who distributed food to all the people.
Joseph had the final say on all sales. All food sales made to foreigners required his personal approval. He would interrogate the purchasers and, if they were enemies of the kingdom, he would refuse to sell them food.

8. Joseph recognized his brothers, but they did not recognize him.
Joseph's brothers came to Egypt to buy grain for their families. When they came before Joseph he recognized them, but the brothers had not the slightest idea that before them sat Joseph.

Joseph determined to put them to various tests, to try them, to see what kind of men they had become, to find out whether they regretted their wrongdoing against him long ago.

9 He remembered what he had dreamed about them years before. "You are spies!" he shouted at them. "You have come to see where Egypt can be attacked."
10 "No, my lord!" they replied. "We are your servants who have come only to buy food.
11 We are all the sons of the same man. We are honest men. We are not spies."
12 "That is not so!" answered Joseph. "You have come to see where Egypt can be attacked."
13 They pleaded, "We are twelve brothers, we are the sons of one father who is in Canaan. Right now our youngest brother is with our father, and one brother is dead."
14 Joseph insisted, "I still say that you are spies. **15** There is only one way to find out who you really are. I swear by the life of Pharaoh that you will not leave this place unless your youngest brother comes here. **16** Let one of you return and bring your brother. The rest of you will remain here in jail. That way I will find out if you are telling the truth. If not, I will know that you are spies." **17** Joseph had them put under guard for three days. **18** On the third day, Joseph said to them, "I respect Adonai, and if you do as I say, you will live.

Benjamin Is Brought to Joseph   *5th Aliyah*

19 "We will find out if you are really telling the truth. I will hold only one of you under arrest. The rest can go and bring food to your starving families. **20** But you must bring your youngest brother here, and only then will I be convinced that you are telling the truth. Then you will not be put to death." The brothers agreed. **21** But they said to one another, "We deserve to be punished because of what we did to our brother Joseph. We allowed him to suffer, and when he begged us we refused to listen. That is why these great troubles have come upon us now."

---

9. He remembered what he had dreamed about them years before.
When Joseph saw his brothers bow before him, he knew that the dream in which his brothers' sheaves had bowed to his sheaf was coming true.

9. He remembered what he had dreamed about them years before. "You are spies!" he shouted at them. "You have come to see where Egypt can be attacked."
Egypt was a fertile country. The waters of the Nile enriched the soil, which produced a great variety of crops. The surrounding countries were in the midst of a drought and their citizens were dying of hunger. The enemies of Egypt continually sent spies to find the soft spots in Egypt's defensive lines. They wanted to capture the food warehouses and feed their people.

21. We deserve to be punished because of what we did to our brother Joseph.
Joseph had his ten bewildered brothers put into prison, having them sample briefly the life he himself had suffered during the years of his imprisonment. But he softened when he thought of their hungry families back in Canaan. He wanted their needs taken care of. He proceeded to release nine of them with the requirement that one remain behind as a hostage.

Moreover, the brothers were to return to Egypt and bring Benjamin, his brother. They blamed themselves for their wrongdoing of years ago. Joseph decided that Simeon would be the brother who would stay in Egypt as the hostage.

21. We allowed him to suffer, and when he begged us we refused to listen. That is why these great troubles have come upon us now.
In Joseph's presence they had a quick discussion. Joseph now got his first clue as to how they felt about the wrong which they had done to him. They spoke in Hebrew, thinking that he did not understand their language. The brothers realized that they had committed a crime, and their consciences bothered them.

The brothers were recalling how cruelly they had treated their brother Joseph. Now they were being repaid for that terrible wrong which they had done.

22 Reuben interrupted them and said, "Didn't I tell you not to commit the crime against the boy? You wouldn't listen. That is why we are now being punished."
23 Meanwhile, the brothers did not realize that Joseph was listening and understood them, because they had spoken to him only through a translator. **24** Joseph left them and wept. When he returned, he spoke to them harshly. He had Simeon taken away and put in chains while they watched.
25 Joseph gave orders that when their bags were filled with grain, each one's money should also be returned in his sack. They were also to be given extra food for the return journey. This was done.
26 The brothers then loaded the food they had bought on their donkeys, and they left.
27 When they camped for the night, one of the brothers opened his sack to feed his donkey. He saw his money at the top of his sack. **28** He called to his brothers, "My money has been returned! It's in my sack!"
Mystified, they said to each other, "What is this terrible calamity that Elohim has brought upon us?" **29** When they returned to their father, Jacob, in the land of Canaan, they told him everything that had happened to them.
30 They said, "The man who was the governor spoke harshly to us, and he accused us of spying on the land. **31** We said to him, 'We are honest men. We have never been spies. **32** We are twelve brothers, all of the same father. One of us is dead, and the youngest is now with our father in Canaan.'
33 The man who was the governor of the land said to us, 'I have a way of knowing if you are honest. Leave one of your brothers with me, and take all the food that you need for your hungry families, and return.
34 Bring your youngest brother back to me, and only then will I know that you are honorable men, and not spies. After that I will return your brother back to you, and you will be able to move freely about Egypt.' "
35 When they began emptying their sacks, they found each one's money was in his sack. The brothers and their father saw the money-bags, and they were frightened. **36** Their father, Jacob, said to them, "You are making me lose my children. Joseph is gone! Simeon is gone! And now you want to take Benjamin!"

---

22. Didn't I tell you not to commit the crime against the boy? You wouldn't listen. That is why we are now being punished.
Reuben argued, "I told you he was just an immature, boastful boy and there was absolutely no reason to sell him to the Midianites. Just think! He was your brother."

24. He had Simeon taken away and put in chains while they watched.
Why did Joseph pick Simeon and throw him into jail? The midrash explains: It was Simeon who threw Joseph into the dry well. Now Joseph revenges himself on Simeon and throws him into jail.

28. My money has been returned! It's in my sack!
They did not know that Joseph had ordered his servant to put the money they had paid for the grain back in their sacks. Now that they had discovered it, they were afraid that they would be accused of dishonesty.

36. Their father, Jacob, said to them, "You are making me lose my children. Joseph is gone! Simeon is gone! And now you want to take Benjamin!"
All of you have your own children. But I, slowly but surely, am losing all of mine.

37 Reuben tried to reason with his father. "If I do not bring Benjamin back to you," he said, "you can put my two sons to death. Let him be my responsibility, and I will bring him back to you."

38 "My son will not go with you!" thundered Jacob. "His brother is dead, and he is all I have left. If something should happen to him along the way, you will bring me down to the grave!"

43

The famine became worse in Canaan. **2** When they had used up all the food that they had brought from Egypt, Jacob said to the brothers, "Go back and get us some food."

3 Judah tried to reason with his father. He said, "The man warned us, 'Do not appear before me unless your brother is with you.' **4** If you agree to send our brother with us, we will go and get you food.

5 But if you will not send him, we cannot go. The man told us, 'Do not appear before me unless your brother is with you.'"

6 Israel said, "Why did you do such a terrible thing to me, telling the man that you had another brother?"

7 The brothers replied, "The man kept asking us about our family. He asked, 'Is your father still alive? Do you have another brother?' We simply answered his questions. How were we to know that he would demand that we bring our brother to Egypt?"

8 "Send the boy with me," said Judah to his father, Israel. "Let us get moving. Let us and our children live and not die.

9 I will be responsible for Benjamin. If I do not bring him back, you can blame me as long as I live. **10** If we had not wasted so much time, we could have been to Egypt and back twice by now!"

---

2. When they had used up all the food they had brought from Egypt. Jacob said to the brothers, "Go back and get us some food."
The Egyptians inhabited an elongated and lush green oasis that slashed through the hot sandy desert formed by the path of the Nile. The source of the Nile lies in the highlands far to the south. Every year between July and November its waters, swollen by tropical rain, loaded with nutritious silt, swept out of their bed down to Egypt to the sea, flooding both sides of Egypt. When they receded, they left behind a layer of fertile soil. The Egyptians simply had to plant, to tend, and to harvest.

5. But if you will not send him, we cannot go. The man told us: "Do not appear before me unless your brother is with you."
Judah is the only son who dares to confront and contradict Jacob. He says to his father, "We cannot return to Egypt unless Benjamin is with us." Now it is up to you. Deal or no deal! We go or we die of hunger!

8–9. "Send the boy with me," said Judah to his father, Israel. "Let us get moving. Let us and our children live and not die. I will be responsible for Benjamin."
"Benjamin must go with us. There is no other source of food. If not, we will all die of hunger." Now Jacob realizes the gravity of the situation and resigns himself to this decision.

10. If we had not wasted so much time, we could have been to Egypt and back twice by now!
Judah criticized his father for wasting time. He said, "If not for your hesitation, we by now could have returned with Simeon, and we and our families would not have suffered from hunger." *Rashi*

11 Their father Israel said to them, "If that's the way it must be, this is what you must do. In your baggage take some of Canaan's special delicacies, perfumes, honey, and some spices, pistachio nuts, and almonds.
12 Take along twice as much money, so that you will be able to return the money that was put in your sacks by mistake.
13 Take your brother with you. Go and return to the man. **14** May El Shaddai (Elohim Almighty) grant that the man have pity on you and release your brothers Simeon and Benjamin. If I must lose my children, then I am prepared to lose them."
15 The brothers took the gifts and also brought along twice as much money as was needed. They set out with Benjamin and returned to Egypt. Once again they stood before Joseph.

Joseph Inquires About Jacob   6th Aliyah

16 When Joseph saw Benjamin, he said to his chief servant, "Bring these men to my palace. Prepare some food. These men will be eating lunch with me."
17 The servant did as Joseph said, and he escorted the brothers to Joseph's palace. **18** When the brothers realized that they were being brought to Joseph's palace, they became terrified. They said, "We are being brought here because of the money that was put back in our sacks the last time.
We will be arrested and our donkeys will be confiscated, and we will be taken as slaves."
19 When they reached the entrance to Joseph's palace, they spoke to the chief servant.

---

11. Take some of Canaan's special delicacies, perfumes, honey, and some spices, pistachio nuts, and almonds.
Canaan delicacies were much appreciated by the Egyptians. So Jacob instructed his sons to take a gift of nuts and spices to the Pharaoh. It was customary (Ber. 42:6) for the inhabitants of Canaan to present gifts and to bow down as a form of respect.

11. Their father Israel said to them, "If that's the way it must be, this is what you must do."
With a sigh, Israel with a voice filled with fear is finally resigned to the inevitable by saying, "That's the way it must be. It is not my decision but we must survive, so go and may El Shaddai be with you."

11. Perfumes, honey, and some spices.
Balm was a pleasant-smelling resin obtained from certain trees and used in perfumes. Honey was made from dates. Myrrh was also a resin from trees that was used in making incense.

12. Take along twice as much money, so that you will be able to return the money that was put in your sack by mistake.
Jacob perhaps does not trust his children, so he reminds them to return the money that was, he thinks, mistakenly placed in their sacks.

13. Take your brother with you. Go and return to the man.
Hunger threatened Jacob's household again.
There was no choice but to go to Egypt once more for fresh supplies. The brothers reminded their father, Jacob, that they could not return unless Benjamin went with them. With a very sad heart Jacob consented to his youngest son's going with them. They set out on their journey with very little enthusiasm.

15. The brothers took the gifts and also brought along twice as much money as was needed. They set out with Benjamin and returned to Egypt. Once again they stood before Joseph.
Joseph was in charge of distributing the stored food to foreigners. Outsiders seeking to purchase food had to present documents and pass inspection by Joseph. Speculators were buying food and reselling it to starving people, reaping enormous profits. Joseph was trying to control the food black market.   *Shenash*

20 "We specially came down to Egypt just to buy food.
21 Then, when we stopped for the night, we opened our sacks, and each man's money was at the top of his sack. It was our own money, in its exact weight. We have brought that money back with us.
22 We have also brought along more money to buy food. We do not know who put the money back in our sacks!"
23 The servant replied, "As far as you are concerned, everything is fine. Do not be afraid! The Elohim you and your father worship must have put a hidden gift in your sacks. I received your money in full." With that, he brought Simeon out to them.
24 The chief servant brought the brothers into Joseph's palace. He gave them water to bathe their feet, and brought food for their donkeys.
25 They readied their gifts to give to Joseph at noon, since they had heard that they would be eating with Joseph.
26 When Joseph came home, they presented him with the gifts they had brought and they bowed down to him.
27 He greeted them and asked, "Is your old father well? Remember, you told me about him. Is he still alive?" **28** They replied, "Our father is well and he is still alive." As in the dream of years before, they bowed their heads to Joseph.
29 Joseph looked up and saw his brother Benjamin, his mother's son. He said, "Is this your youngest brother, about whom you told me?" To Benjamin he said, "May Elohim be gracious to you, my boy."

The Missing Cup   *7th Aliyah*

30 Joseph rushed out because he was overcome with emotion, and he began to cry. He went to another room and there he controlled himself. **31** Joseph rinsed his face and returned, controlling his emotions. He said to his servants, "Serve the meal."

---

21. We have brought that money back with us.
The brothers realized that they were in deep trouble and would be accused of stealing the money. They could not claim innocence, because the Egyptians would just laugh at them. Their only defense was to claim that they had found the money and were returning it to the rightful owner.

23. He brought Simeon out to them.
The brothers were surprised to find Simeon healthy and well fed. He told them that he had been released from prison immediately after they had left and had been given every conceivable comfort.

26. When Joseph came home, they presented him with the gifts they had brought and they bowed down to him.
Joseph arrived at his home at noon. The brothers bowed before their mysterious royal host and presented to him the gifts that they had brought for him.

29. Joseph looked up and saw his brother Benjamin, his mother's son.
Looking at Benjamin, who sat opposite him at the banquet table, Joseph was suddenly overcome. He and this youngest of the brothers were, after all, sons of one mother, Rachel.

30. Joseph rushed out because he was overcome with emotion, and he began to cry. He went to another room and there he controlled himself.
Joseph was an important official, and people respected him for his intelligence and his strong personality. He did not want his attendants to see that he also had a soft side and could be brought to tears.

32 Joseph was served by himself, and the brothers by themselves. The Egyptians who were eating with them could not eat with the Hebrews, since this was against their custom. **33** When the brothers were seated before Joseph, they were placed in order of age, from the oldest to the youngest. The brothers eyed each other in amazement. **34** Joseph sent them delicacies from his table, giving Benjamin five times as much as the others. They feasted and drank with him.

44

Joseph gave his chief servant special instructions. He said, "Fill the men's sacks with as much food as they can carry. Put each man's money at the top of his sack. **2** And put my silver cup and his money at the top of the sack of the youngest brother." The servant did exactly as Joseph instructed him.

3 Early in the morning, the brothers saddled their donkeys and went on their way.

4 The brothers had just left the city and had not gone far when Joseph said to his servants, "Chase after those men. Catch up with them and say to them, 'Why did you repay good with evil?

5 You took my master's personal cup that he drinks from and uses for predicting the future. You have committed a terrible crime.'"

6 The servant caught up with the brothers and repeated Joseph's exact words to them. **7** They said to him, "How can you say such things to us? We would never have done such an evil thing.

---

32. The Egyptians who were eating with them could not eat with the Hebrews, since this was against their custom.
No Egyptians ate with Joseph's brothers, for the Hebrews ate the meat of cows, which the Egyptians regarded as sacred creatures. Others explain that the Egyptians would not eat with the Israelites because Joseph's brothers were shepherds and the people of Egypt despised shepherds as an inferior people.

33. When the brothers were seated before Joseph, they were placed in order of age.
When he returned to the festive table, Joseph reseated them in a remarkable order, each brother next to the other in the order of their age! He was playing a game of suspense with them.

34. Joseph sent them delicacies from his table, giving Benjamin five times as much as the others.
The brothers were jealous of Joseph, so they sold him to the Midianite traders.

Now Joseph tested the brothers by favoring Benjamin.

He carefully watched their reactions to see whether they were jealous of Benjamin because he favored their youngest brother. Obviously, they had learned their lesson and they did not react to Joseph's trap.

1. Fill the men's sacks with as much food as they can carry.
Give them more food than they purchased. When you catch them with the stolen cup, you will also be able to accuse them of stealing the food.

4. The brothers had just left the city.
The city was Memphis, the ancient capital of Egypt. Memphis was located about twelve miles from the present-day Cairo, on the west bank of the Nile River.

5. You took my master's personal cup that he drinks from and uses for predicting the future.
Joseph the dreamer foretold future events by analyzing dreams. Now he uses a special cup for divination. In the ancient Middle East some diviners would put several drops of oil into a cup of water and predict the future from the shapes assumed by the drops of oil.

8 After all, we returned the money we found at the top of our sacks – all the way from Canaan. How could we steal silver or gold from your master's house? 9 If any of us has it in his possession, that person shall die and you can take the rest of us for slaves." 10 The servant replied, "I'll do what you said, but only the one who has the cup will be enslaved. The rest of you will be free."

11 The brothers quickly lowered their sacks, and they all opened their sacks. 12 The servant carefully inspected each of the sacks, beginning with the oldest and ending with the youngest. The silver cup was found in Benjamin's sack. 1

3 The brothers ripped their clothes in despair. Then each one reloaded his donkey, and they returned to the city.

Elohim Has Uncovered Our Guilt *Maftir*

14 Joseph was still there when Judah and his brothers returned to the palace. They threw themselves on the ground before him.

15 Joseph said to them, "What are you trying to do? Don't you know that a person like me has a special way of discovering the truth?"

16 Judah replied, "What can we say to my lord? How can we prove our innocence? Elohim has uncovered our guilt. Let us be your slaves, especially the one who took the cup." 17 Joseph said, "Only the one who took the cup shall be my slave. The rest of you can return to your father in peace."

10. The servant replied, "I'll do what you said, but only the one who has the cup will be enslaved."
The real intention of the servant is to obtain their agreement so that the problem can be solved only by finding the brother with the cup. The servant does not discuss how the cup found its way into Benjamin's sack.

11. The brothers quickly lowered their sacks, and they all opened their sacks.
The brothers knew that they were innocent. They wanted to resume their journey, so they hurriedly open their sacks. They were saying, "Check our bags and let us return to our hungry families."

12. The silver cup was found in Benjamin's sack.
The servant carefully inspected each of the sacks, beginning with the oldest and ending with the youngest. The official proceeded to open their sacks, one by one, until he came to that of Benjamin. They were startled by his finding. There, in Benjamin's sack, was the goblet! Long ago, the brothers had dealt dishonestly in their treatment of Joseph and with their father, Jacob. Now Joseph was putting their honesty to a difficult test.

He wanted to know whether that past experience had made a difference in their thinking and their character. Joseph was putting them through very tough hurdles.

14. Joseph was still there when Judah and his brothers returned to the palace.
Joseph spent his whole day planning how to confront and test his brothers.

16. How can we prove our innocence? Elohim has uncovered our guilt.
We are innocent but we have no way to prove it. Someone purposely placed your silver cup in Benjamin's sack. Elohim knows that we are innocent.

Obviously, the Egyptians were familiar with the word of Elohim.

17. Only the one who took the cup shall be my slave.
Joseph did all this to test his brothers, to learn whether they would be willing to risk danger in order to save their brother Benjamin. Joseph remembered how eagerly his brothers had betrayed him, and he wanted to see whether they would do the same to Benjamin.

וַיִּגַּשׁ *Vayigash*

JUDAH AND JOSEPH

18 Judah went up to Joseph and said, "Your Highness, please let me say something to you. Do not be angry with me, even though you have as much power as Pharaoh.
19 You asked if we still had a father or another brother.
20 We told you, 'We have a father who is very old, and the youngest brother is the child of his old age. He had a brother who died, and he is the only one of his mother's children still alive. He is our father's favorite.' **21** You said to us, 'Bring him to me, so I can see him with my own eyes.'
22 We told you, 'The boy cannot leave his father,' because if he left him, our father would die. **23** But you replied, 'If your youngest brother does not come, do not show your faces to me again.' **24** We returned to our father and told him what you said.
25 Our father told us to go back and buy some food. **26** We replied, 'We cannot go. We can only go if our youngest brother is with us. If he is not with us, we are forbidden to show our faces.'
27 Our father said, 'You know that my wife Rachel gave birth to two sons. **28** One is dead, and I believe that he was torn to pieces by wild animals. I have seen nothing of him ever since. **29** Now you want to take Benjamin from me too! If something were to happen to him, you will have brought me down to the grave.' **30** How can I return to our father if the boy is not with us? His life depends upon the boy!

Joseph Reveals His Identity　　　　　　　*2nd Aliyah*

31 "When he sees that the boy is not with us, he will die! I will have brought our father's life down to the grave.
32 As a guarantee I pledged to my father and I said, 'If I do not bring him back to you, you can blame me for the rest of my life.' **33** Please now, let me remain as your slave in place of the boy. Let the boy return home with his brothers! **34** I cannot return to my father if the boy is not with me. I cannot bear to see my father suffer!"

---

33. Please now, let me remain as your slave in place of the boy.
Of all the brothers, Judah was the one to step forward to offer himself in Benjamin's place. Judah, remember, had urged his brothers not to kill Joseph and had guaranteed Benjamin's return. Judah told Joseph, "I am older and stronger; I would certainly make the more useful slave." He showed kingly qualities–and it was only fitting that King David and King Solomon should be descendants of Judah.

33. Please now, let me remain as your slave in place of the boy.
Frightened by their experience, the brothers were again before Joseph. Why had they betrayed his welcome? Joseph demanded. Judah replied for all of them that if they were at fault they wanted to accept the blame together. Joseph was determined now to test their brotherly love. They had failed to show it to him when he was a youth. Had they come to regret their cruelty to him? Joseph turned down Judah's offer to take the blame. Let the one who had the goblet in his sack pay the penalty of slavery. Let all the others go free and return home to their father.

45 Joseph could not control his emotions. Since his servants were present, he cried out, "Everybody out! Everyone leave my presence!" He wanted to be alone when he revealed himself to his brothers. **2** He began to cry with such loud sobs that the Egyptians throughout the palace could hear his cries. The news of these strange events quickly reached Pharaoh's palace.

3 Joseph said to his brothers, "I am Joseph! Is my father still alive?"

His brothers were amazed and speechless.

4 Joseph said to his brothers, "Please, come close to me."

When they came closer, he said, "Yes, I am Joseph your brother! You sold me to Egypt. **5** Don't worry or feel guilty because you sold me. Elohim is the one who sent me ahead of you to save your lives! **6** There has been a famine in the land for two years, and for another five years no one will be able to plow or harvest grain. **7** Elohim has sent me ahead of you to make sure that you survive and keep you alive through this miraculous event.

Joseph Sends for Jacob *3rd Aliyah*

8 "It is not you who sent me here, but Elohim. He has made me the governor of the entire country. **9** Hurry, return to my father and give him my message: Your son Joseph says, 'Elohim has made me a governor in Egypt. Come down to me immediately.

---

1. Joseph could not control his emotions. Since his servants were present, he cried out, "Everybody out! Everyone leave my presence!"
Joseph dismissed the Egyptians from his presence before he made himself known to his brothers because he did not want them to hear the details of his sale to the caravan by his brothers. He did not want the Egyptians to say, "These Israelites are treacherous people who must not live in our land nor set foot in our palaces. They have dealt treacherously with their brother Joseph and their father. What will they do to the Pharaoh and his people in the land of Egypt?"

Nachmanides

3. I am Joseph.
After all the intrigues and tests, Joseph was finally convinced that brotherly love now existed among them. Now there was no further need to test or challenge the brothers. It was time for him to reveal his true identity. The cat-and-mouse game was over.

5. Don't worry or feel guilty because you sold me.
Observing that his brothers were shocked by his revelation of his identity to them, Joseph urged them to avoid self-blame.

He knew, too, that they might start to quarrel among themselves, shifting the blame from one to the other. Let there be none of this among them. Let bygones be bygones. It was Adonai who had intended for him to come before them to Egypt for the very purpose of saving them from starvation. Joseph proved himself to be a man of rare generosity. He forgave his brothers' unkind acts against him. He was more than willing to share with them his good fortune in their time of need.

Chiel

5. Don't worry or feel guilty because you sold me.
The mature Joseph sees the positive side of their actions: He now understands that he too contributed to their resentment by tattling on his brothers and boasting about his dreams.

5. Don't worry or feel guilty because you sold me.
Joseph consoles the brothers who abused him, imprisoned him, and sold him as a slave. Despite all the pain and degradation, Joseph exercised the divine gift of forgiveness. Jewish ethics makes forgiveness mandatory because humans must emulate the way of Adonai.

Psalm 78:38 says: "He is, full of compassion, He forgives our sins and does not destroy us."

10 You and your children, and your grandchildren, and your sheep, and your cattle, and all that you own will be able to live close to me in the land of Goshen.

11 There I will care for you, since there will still be another five years of famine. I do not want you and your family and all that is yours to go hungry.' "

12 Then Joseph said, "You and my brother Benjamin can see with your own eyes that I am really Joseph. **13** Tell my father all about my high position in Egypt and everything that you saw. You must hurry and bring my father to me."

14 With that, Joseph fell on the shoulders of his brother Benjamin, and he wept with joy. Benjamin also wept on Joseph's shoulders. **15** Joseph hugged all his brothers, and they all wept. After that, the brothers talked with Joseph.

16 The news quickly spread to Pharaoh's palace that Joseph's brothers had arrived. Pharaoh and his advisers were pleased by the news. **17** Pharaoh told Joseph to tell his brothers, "This is what you must do: Load your donkeys and return to Canaan. **18** Bring your father and your families, and come and live with me. I will give you the most fertile land in Egypt. You shall eat the best of the land.

Jacob's Family Comes to Egypt *4th Aliyah*

19 "Now I want you to do the following: Bring wagons from Egypt for your small children and wives, and also use them for your father. Come, **20** and do not be concerned about your belongings, for the best of Egypt will be yours."

21 Israel's sons agreed to do all that Pharaoh instructed. Joseph gave them wagons, and he also supplied them with food for the journey. **22** He gave each of his brothers new clothes. However to Benjamin he gave 300 pieces of silver and five sets of new clothing. **23** As a present Joseph sent his father ten male donkeys loaded with Egypt's finest delicacies, and ten female donkeys loaded with grain, bread, and food for his father's journey. **24** Then he sent his brothers on their way. As they were leaving, he wished them "A safe and pleasant journey!" **25** From Egypt the brothers headed northward, and they returned to their father Jacob in Canaan. **26** They excitedly told Jacob, "Joseph is still alive. He is the governor of all Egypt." Jacob's heart skipped a beat, for he could not believe the news. **27** They repeated everything that Joseph had said to them. When Jacob saw the wagons that Joseph had sent to transport him to Egypt, he felt much better.

---

16. Pharaoh and his advisers were pleased by the news.
Pharaoh was pleased that Joseph would have his family in Egypt and would no longer be a stranger in the land.

Pharaoh depended upon Joseph for his political skills. Now Joseph would have no excuse to leave Egypt.

20. And do not be concerned about your belongings, for the best of Egypt will be yours.
Do not worry about your belongings; you are the important ones. Leave what you can't bring. I have plenty and you will lack for nothing. Just hurry and come.

21. Joseph gave them wagons, and he also supplied them with food for the journey.
Twenty-two years had passed since the brothers had sold Joseph into slavery and told their father the cruel, false tale that an animal had devoured him. Now, more than two decades later, they will return from Egypt with the unbelievable story that "Joseph is still alive and he is the ruler over all the land of Egypt!"

24. A safe and pleasant journey.
Joseph warned his brothers, "Do not begin discussing your selling me into slavery, for that would only lead to arguments. Each of you will blame the other for the deed."

Jacob Journeys to Egypt

5th Aliyah

28. Israel said, "It must be true. My son Joseph is alive! I must go and see him before I die!"

46 Israel assembled all his possessions and began the journey to Beer-sheva. There he brought sacrifices to the Elohim of his father Isaac. **2** That night Elohim spoke to Israel and said, "Jacob! Jacob!" Jacob answered, "Yes, here I am."
3 Elohim said, "I am the Elohim of Isaac your father. Do not be afraid to go down to Egypt, for it is there that I will make you into a great nation.
4 I will go down to Egypt with you, and I will also bring your descendants back again. You will die in Egypt, and Joseph will be at your deathbed." **5** Jacob and his sons set out from Beer-sheva. They brought their father, their children, and their wives on the wagons that Pharaoh had sent to carry them.
6 They brought their livestock and all the possessions that they had acquired in Canaan. Jacob came to Egypt with all his sons **7** and grandsons. He also brought his daughters and his granddaughters.
8 These are the names of the Israelites, the descendants of Jacob, who came to Egypt: Reuben was Jacob's first-born.

---

28. Israel said, "It must be true. My son Joseph is alive!"
The midrash says that when Jacob's sons came back from Egypt and told their father that their brother Joseph was still alive, at first he did not believe them. Years before, they had lied when they told their father that Joseph was dead. That time he did believe them. Now, when they told the truth, he did not believe them. So it is that liars are punished. Even when they tell the truth they are not believed.

Jacob's reaction to the brothers' story was a natural one: "His heart fainted, for he did not believe them."

Jacob found it difficult to accept his sons' latest story. The brothers had to offer proof positive of their dependability. They did so by showing him the Egyptian wagon train filled with supplies which Joseph had sent with them. At last Jacob was convinced that his sons spoke truthfully and he prepared to leave for Egypt with all of his family.

3. Do not be afraid to go down to Egypt, for it is there that I will make you into a great nation.
Jacob did not want to leave Canaan, but Adonai reassured him, "Do not be afraid." Jacob the shepherd feared the sophisticated Egyptian civilization and its dangerous distractions.

He was concerned that his children would become acculturated and assimilated into the newly found Egyptian society.

4. I will go down to Egypt with you, and I will also bring your descendants back again.
Adonai made two promises here: (1) Jacob would be buried in Canaan when he died, and (2) Adonai would someday bring back Jacob's descendants from Egypt to Canaan.

Jacob could die in peace in Egypt, because his beloved son Joseph would be right by him for the rest of his life.

8. These are the names of the Israelites.
The whole family goes down to Egypt. None of them remains. Therefore the list includes all the Israelites. Jacob was included in the list of seventy, counted as the thirty-third person.

8. These are the names of the Israelites.
Now the history of the nation of Israel begins. Until this moment they were a tribe and were known as the Children of Israel. Now they have earned the right to become a nation. From now on, they are to be known as the nation of Israel.

9 Reuben's sons were Enoch, Palu, Hezron, and Carmi. **10** Simeon's sons were Yemuel, Yamin, Ohad, Yakhin, and Zohar, as well as Shaul, the son of a Canaanite woman.

11 Levi's sons were Gershon, Kehath, and Merari. **12** Judah's sons were Er, Onan, Shelah, Peretz, and Zerah, but Er and Onan died in Canaan. The sons of Peretz were Hezron and Hamul.

13 Issachar's sons were Tolah, Puvah, Yov, and Shimron.

14 Zebulun's sons were Sered, Elon, and Yachleel.

15 All the above were from the sons that Leah gave birth to Jacob in Padan Aram, in addition to Jacob's daughter, Dinah. All of his descendants through Leah, including his sons and daughters, totaled thirty-three.

16 Gad's sons were Zifon, Hagi, Shuni, Ezbon, Eri, Arodi, and Areli.

17 Asher's sons were Imnah, Ishvah, Ishvi, and Beriah, also their sister Serach. The sons of Beriah were Hever and Malkiel.

18 These sixteen were the descendants of Jacob through Zilpah, whom Laban gave to his daughter Leah.

19 The sons of Jacob's wife Rachel were Joseph and Benjamin.

20 In Egypt, Joseph's wife Asenath, daughter of Poti Phera, priest of On, gave birth to Manasseh and Ephraim.

21 Benjamin's sons were Bela, Bekher, Ashbel, Gera, Naaman, Echi, Rosh, Muppim, Huppim, and Ard.

22 These fourteen were the descendants of Jacob and his wife Rachel.

23 Dan's son was Hushim.

24 Naphtali's sons were Yachtzeel, Gum, Yezer, and Shilem.

25 These seven were the descendants of Jacob through Bilhah, the servant whom Laban gave to his daughter Rachel.

26 All the blood descendants who came to Egypt with Jacob were sixty-six, not counting the wives of Jacob's sons.

27 Joseph's sons, born to him in Egypt, added another two persons. In total, all of the people in Jacob's family who came to Egypt now added up to seventy.

---

12. Er and Onan died in Canaan.
Er and Onan are mentioned in order to tell that they were not counted among the seventy who came to Egypt.

12. The sons of Peretz were Hezron and Hamul.
The children of Peretz are important because David, king of Israel, was his descendant.

22. These fourteen were the descendants of Jacob and his wife Rachel.
Sixty-six people left Canaan. By the time they reached Egypt, their number had grown to seventy, since Joseph and his two sons, and Yocheved, who was born just as the clan entered Egypt, were added to the original sixty-six. Others explain that Jacob himself was counted as the seventieth person.

26. All the blood descendants who came to Egypt with Jacob were sixty-six, not counting the wives of Jacob's sons.
Leah's descendants were thirty-three, Zilpah's sixteen, Rachel's fourteen, and Bilhah's seven. These add up to seventy. If Er and Onan, who died in Canaan, and Manasseh and Ephraim, who were born in Egypt, are excluded, then the total is sixty-six who made the journey from Canaan to Egypt.

The Children of Israel Settle in Goshen
6th Aliyah

28 Jacob sent Judah ahead of him to make preparations in Goshen. When they arrived in the Goshen district, **29** Joseph himself harnessed his chariot and went to Goshen to greet his father Israel. When they met, they embraced each other and wept with joy.
30 Israel said to Joseph, "Now I can die; I have seen you in person and know that you are still alive."
31 To his brothers and his father's family, Joseph said, "I will go and tell Pharaoh, 'My brothers and my father's family have come to me from Canaan. **32** These men are shepherds. They have brought with them sheep, their cattle, and all their pos- sessions.' **33** When Pharaoh summons you and asks, 'What is your occupation?' **34** you must say, 'We and our fathers have been shepherds all our lives.'
In this way you will be able to settle in the district of Goshen, since shepherds are forbidden in other parts of Egypt."

---

28. Jacob sent Judah ahead of him to make preparations in Goshen.
Judah was the steadiest of the sons, so he was sent to make the arrangements for the move to Egypt.

28. Jacob sent Judah ahead to make preparations in Goshen.
The area of Goshen is located in the northeastern section of the Nile delta. The district is about 900 square miles. Because of the irrigation canals, it was considered and excellent place for cattle raising and agriculture. Goshen contains the cities of Pithon and Rameses, which were built by the Hebrew slaves.

29. Joseph himself harnessed his chariot and went to Goshen to greet his father Israel.
In his eagerness to do honor to his father, Joseph himself harnessed the horses to his chariot.

29. When they met, they embraced each other and wept with joy.
Joseph wept with joy when he saw that his father was healthy and well. Of course Jacob was overjoyed when he saw that his dead son was very much alive. The Rabbis also say that Jacob wept with joy when he realized that his son Joseph, despite the years in Egypt, still retained his ethical and Hebrew heritage.

30. Now I can die; I have seen you in person and know that you are still alive.
Why didn't Joseph get in touch with his father when he became second to the Pharaoh of Egypt? The Torah tells us that as a boy in Canaan, Joseph tattled on his brothers. Now as Joseph matured into an executive, he realized that his tales and dreams brought his problem upon himself.

Now Joseph decides to bury the past and keep the story of crime against him from his father. Even after the reunion there is no mention of his sale into slavery.

In recognition of his own role in the tragedy, Joseph places peace in the family (*shalom bayit*) over his own revenge against the brothers.

31. I will go and tell Pharaoh.
First Joseph will approach Pharaoh and inform him that his brothers have arrived. Then Pharaoh will suggest an area in which to settle them.

34. We and our fathers have been shepherds all our lives.
Joseph instructed his brothers to say this to Pharaoh. He read Pharaoh's mind. When thay say this, Pharaoh will automatically think of Goshen, where his flocks are pastured; Joseph's plan will work.
Shenash

34. Shepherds are forbidden in other parts of Egypt.
People who handle a lot of cattle start to smell like them. People just do not like to live near cattle because of their odors.

47

47 Joseph went to see Pharaoh. He said, "My father and brothers have come from Canaan, along with their sheep, their cattle, and all their belongings. They wish to settle in Goshen." **2** From among his brothers, he selected five men and introduced them to Pharaoh.

3 Pharaoh asked Joseph's brothers, "What are your occupations?"

They replied to Pharaoh, "We are shepherds, just like our fathers before us.

4 We have come to live in your land, because there is a strong famine in Canaan and there is no grass for our flocks. If you permit us, we would like to live in the district of Goshen."

5 Pharaoh said to Joseph, "Your father and brothers have come to you. **6** The land of Egypt is open to them. Settle your father and brothers on the most fertile land. Let them live in the district of Goshen. If there are capable men among them, appoint them to be in charge of my cattle."

7 Joseph brought Jacob, his father, and introduced him to Pharaoh. Jacob blessed Pharaoh.

8 Then Pharaoh asked Jacob, "How old are you?"

9 Jacob replied, "I have lived 130 difficult years. I will not live as long as my ancestors did during their journeys through life."

10 With that, Jacob again blessed Pharaoh and left.

---

1. Joseph went to see Pharaoh.
The Egyptians were very suspicious of foreigners, so Joseph went to Pharaoh to ask permission to bring his family to settle in Egypt in the area of Goshen.

2. From among his brothers, he selected five men and introduced them to Pharaoh.
The midrash says that Joseph selected five of the smallest and weakest of the brothers. He was worried that they would be drafted into the Egyptian army.

6. The land of Egypt is open to them. Settle your fathers and brothers on the most fertile land.
Pharaoh was aware that Joseph had saved the land of Egypt from famine. As a sign of his gratitude, Pharaoh gave the most fertile land to Joseph's family.

6. Let them live in the district of Goshen.
This is exactly the reply Jacob and Joseph wanted. They both realized that the beautiful Egyptian women and the sophisticated life in Egypt would be very attractive to the Israelites and cause intermarriage. Goshen was far from Egyptian centers and the Israelites would be separated there.
Shenash

6. If there are capable men among them, appoint them to be in charge of my cattle.
Now Pharaoh legitimizes the Israelites and grants them legal protection. The brothers become employees of the Pharaoh in charge of livestock.

7. Joseph brought Jacob, his father, and introduced him to Pharaoh. Jacob blessed Pharaoh.
Joseph was proud of his Hebrew birth. Never had he attempted to hide his background or heritage. Even now that he was high in Pharaoh's court, he had no feeling of inferiority about his Hebrew origin. And when his father, a modest shepherd tribesman, arrived in Egypt, Joseph brought him before Pharaoh, the powerful emperor of Egypt.

Pharaoh felt that it was time for Jacob to enjoy what years of life were left to him in peace and security. He instructed Joseph to settle Jacob and all of the family in Goshen, where there were good lands for sheep raising. Jacob was deeply grateful to Pharaoh and he blessed the Egyptian ruler for his kindness.

9. I have lived 130 difficult years.
Jacob answers Pharaoh's question by reciting his life history.

Joseph Saves Egypt
7th Aliyah

11 Joseph found fertile land for his father and brothers to live on. As Pharaoh had ordered, Joseph gave them fertile land in the area around Rameses. **12** Joseph provided all the needs of his father, his brothers, and all his father's family.

13 Meanwhile, the famine was very severe, and there was no bread anywhere. The people of Egypt and Canaan became weak with hunger. **14** Joseph collected all the money that was in Egypt and Canaan in payment for the food the people were buying. Joseph brought all the money to Pharaoh's palace.

15 When their money ran out, people from all over the land of Egypt came to Joseph and complained, "Give us bread! Why should we die just because we have no money?"

16 Joseph replied, "Bring your livestock. If you have no more money, I will give you food in exchange for your animals."

17 From then on they brought their livestock to Joseph, and Joseph gave them bread in exchange for horses, flocks of sheep, herds of cattle, and donkeys. All through that year Joseph gave them bread in exchange for their livestock.

18 The next year they again came back to Joseph and pleaded, "Your Highness, we haven't held anything back from you. Our money and our stock of animals are used up; now there is nothing left for you except our bodies and our land. **19** Why should we die before your very eyes? Buy our bodies and our land in exchange for bread. We will become Pharaoh's slaves, and let our land also be his. Just give us enough food. Let us live and not die! Let the land not be devastated."

20 So Joseph bought up all the farmland in Egypt for Pharaoh. Every farmer in Egypt sold his field because the famine was too much for them, and all the land became Pharaoh's property. **21** Joseph transferred the people from the farms to the cities.

22 But Joseph did not buy the lands of the priests, because they were given food by Pharaoh.

23 Joseph said to the people, "I have bought your bodies and your land for Pharaoh. Now I will give you seeds so that you can plant your fields. **24** When you harvest your crops, you will have to give a fifth of them to Pharaoh. You can keep the other four parts, as seed for your fields, and as food for your families."

Do Not Bury Me in Egypt
Maftir

25 They gratefully exclaimed. "You have saved our lives; we will gladly be Pharaoh's slaves."

26 Joseph passed a law that one-fifth of whatever grew on the farmland of Egypt belonged to Pharaoh. Only the priestly lands did not belong to Pharaoh.

27 Meanwhile, the tribes of Israel lived in the land of Egypt, in the district of Goshen. They bought land there, and their numbers increased very rapidly.

---

11. Joseph found fertile land for his father and brothers to live on.

Joseph gave them fertile land in the area around Ra'ameses. Some historians believe that Ra'ameses II was the Pharaoh who enslaved the Israelites.

17. Joseph gave them bread in exchange for horses, flocks of sheep, herds of cattle, and donkeys.

Egypt was famous for its horses. Pharaoh's army, which will pursue the Israelites into the Sea of Reeds, was equipped with chariots drawn by horses (Shemot 14:23).

The Tanakh tells us that King Solomon had 1,400 horsemen and 12,000 horses.

וַיְחִי *Vayechi*

JACOB'S LAST DAYS

28 Jacob lived in Egypt for seventeen years. And he died at the age of 147 years.
29 Israel felt that he would soon die, so he called for his son Joseph, and said to him, "If you really love me, swear to me that you will not bury me in Egypt. **30** Bury me with my fathers. Carry me out of Egypt, and bury me with my ancestors."
Joseph replied, "I swear to do as you wish."
31 Joseph swore to his father, and from his bed Israel nodded his thanks to Joseph.

48 Some time later Joseph was told that his father was very sick. Joseph took his two sons, Manasseh and Ephraim, along with him and went to see his father. **2** When Jacob was told that Joseph was coming to him, Israel gathered his strength and sat up in bed to greet them. **3** Jacob said to Joseph, "El Shaddai (Elohim Almighty) once appeared to me in Luz, in the land of Canaan. He blessed me **4** and said to me, 'I will give you a large family. They will grow into a mighty nation. I will give this land to you and to your descendants forever.'

---

28. Jacob lived in Egypt for seventeen years.
As long as Jacob lived, the Jews were not enslaved by the Egyptians.

Just as Joseph spent the first seventeen years of his life in the care of his father Jacob, now Jacob spent the last seventeen years of his life in the care of Joseph. The wheel had come full circle.

28. Jacob lived in Egypt for seventeen years.
The seventeen years was the only time in Jacob's life that were quiet and uneventful. These seventeen years were a reward for the tumultuous and difficult years of his long life.

29. Israel felt that he would soon die, so he called for his son Joseph and said to him, "If you really love me, swear to me that you will not bury me in Egypt."
Israel was very much aware that Joseph was the only person who had the power to fulfill his deathbed wish to be buried in the Cave of Machpelah.

30. Bury me with my fathers. Carry me out of Egypt, and bury me with my ancestors.
Jacob affirmed Adonai's promise to his ancestors Abraham (17:8) and his father Isaac (26:3) and to him (35:12) that their descendants would inherit the land of Canaan as their homeland. Eventually that homeland would bear his name, the land of Israel.

1. Some time later Joseph was told that his father was very sick.
Joseph loved his father very much, but he did not visit him very often.

Our sages say that he did not want to be alone with his father so that he would not have to reveal that his brothers had sold him as a slave.

1. Joseph took his two sons, Manasseh and Ephraim, along with him and went to see his father.
The boys Manasseh and Ephraim lived far away from their grandfather and visited only on special occasions. The boys were aware that Jacob was dying, so as a sign of respect they came to see him for the last time. They were also aware that their grandfather was blessed by Adonai. Joseph wanted Jacob to bless his sons before his death. He also wanted to assure Jacob that Ephraim and Manasseh were raised as Israelites.

2. When Jacob was told that Joseph was coming to him, Israel gathered his strength and sat up in bed to greet them.
Jacob did not die suddenly. Adonai allowed Jacob the wisdom and opportunity to instruct and bless his children before his death.

5 Joseph, your two sons who were born to you in Egypt before I came here shall be considered as my own. Ephraim and Manasseh shall be just like Reuben and Simeon to me.
6 Any children who are born later shall be considered yours. They shall inherit only through their older brothers, Ephraim and Manasseh.
7 When I was coming from Padan, your mother Rachel died. It was in Canaan, a short distance before we got to Ephrath. I buried her there along the road to Ephrath, which is now called Bethlehem." **8** Israel, who was almost blind, asked, "Who are these youngsters?"
9 Joseph replied to his father, "They are the sons that Elohim gave me here." Jacob said "Please bring them close to me. I will give them a blessing."

Jacob Blesses Ephraim and Manasseh
2nd Aliyah

10 Israel was almost blind and could hardly see. So Joseph brought his sons near to him. Israel kissed them and hugged them. **11** Israel said to Joseph, "I never thought to see your face again. But now Elohim has even let me see your children."
12 Joseph brought the boys close to his father, and he bowed down to Jacob.
13 Joseph then took the two boys. He placed Ephraim to Israel's left, and Manasseh he placed to Israel's right. He then brought them close to Israel. **14** With his right hand Israel reached out and put it on Ephraim's head even though he was the younger son. He put his left hand on Manasseh's head. Jacob purposely crossed his hands, even though Manasseh was the first-born.

---

5. Joseph, your two sons who were born in Egypt before I came here shall be considered as my own. Ephraim and Manasseh shall be just like Reuben and Simeon to me.
Any children who were born later shall be considered yours. They shall inherit only through their older brothers Ephraim and Manasseh. The Torah hints that Joseph fathered other children. They most likely were assimilated and lost to the Israelite nation. Jacob wanted only his grandsons Ephraim and Manasseh to share his inheritance. Joseph's wealth consisted of palaces, fields, and property which could not be moved.

5. Ephraim and Manasseh shall be just like Reuben and Simeon to me.
The two sons of Joseph who were born in Egypt were not acknowledged as children of Israel until they were adopted by Jacob.

If his sons inherited Joseph's wealth, they would have had to remain in Egypt.

Jacob's wealth was in herds and flocks and was eminently moveable. Jacob had the power of a visionary and could predict future events, such as the Exodus from Egypt.

5. Joseph, your two sons who were born to you in Egypt before I came here shall be considered as my own.
Although Ephraim and Manasseh were Jacob's grandchildren, they were to be considered his sons. They each became heads of a tribe which was allotted a full portion in the land of Canaan.

14. Jacob purposely crossed his hands, even though Manasseh was the first-born.
Joseph was unhappy about this. Manasseh was the first-born and deserved the right hand. Joseph believed that once again Israel was showing favoritism by crossing his hand to bless Ephraim first.

13. Joseph then took the two boys. He placed Ephraim to Israel's left, and Manasseh he placed to Israel's right. He then brought them close to Israel.
Manasseh was the first-born, so Joseph placed him in the position of honor, to Israel's right.

15 Jacob gave Joseph a blessing. He said,
"The Elohim whom my ancestors, Abraham and Isaac, worshipped
is the Elohim who has been my Shepherd all my life.
16 He sent an angel to deliver me from all evil.
May He bless these boys, and let them preserve my name, and the names of my ancestors,
Abraham and Isaac.
May Ephraim and Manasseh increase and became a powerful nation."

Jacob Prophesies the Future *3rd Aliyah*

17 When Joseph saw that his father had put his right hand on Ephraim's head, he was upset. He tried to lift his father's hand from Ephraim's head and put it on Manasseh's. **18** Joseph said, "No, father, that's not the way it should be done. Manasseh is the firstborn. Put your right hand on his head."
19 His father refused and said,
"My son, I know what I am doing
The older one, Manasseh, will become a nation. He will attain greatness.
But his younger brother, Ephraim, will become even greater, and his descendants
will become many mighty nations."
20 Jacob blessed them on that day. He said, "In time to come, the children of Israel will use both of you as a blessing. They will say,
'May Elohim make you like Ephraim and Manasseh.'"
He purposely put Ephraim before Manasseh.

---

15. Jacob gave Joseph a blessing.
Jacob blessed Joseph by blessing his children Ephraim and Manasseh.

16. He sent an angel to deliver me from all evil.
Jacob recognizes that Adonai was with him and protected him all his life. The commentator Abarbanel said that the "angel" was Adonai's influence.

17. When Joseph saw that his father had put his right hand on Ephraim's head, he was upset. He tried to lift his father's hand from Ephraim's head and put it on Manasseh's.
Joseph was aware that his father was blind and he thought that Jacob did not recognize his mistakes. But blind people have a special sense of perception, a type of radar, and can differentiate between people. *Shenash*

19. But his younger brother, Ephraim, will become even greater, and his descendants will become many mighty nations.
Rashi translates "will become many mighty nations" as "rulers of nations."

Onkeles translates the phrase "as destroyer of nations."

20. May Elohim make you like Ephraim and Manasseh.
To this very day Jewish parents on Friday night bless their sons with the words, "May Elohim make you like Ephraim and Manasseh." The blessing for girls is: "May Elohim make you like Sarah, Rebecca, Rachel, and Leah." Though Manasseh was the older brother, Ephraim was mentioned first, because Jacob, having prophetic vision, foresaw that the younger boy would father a mightier and more important tribe than the older. Gideon, a great judge, was descended from Manasseh. Joshua, who was the successor to Moses and conquered the land of Canaan, was of the tribe of Ephraim.

20. In time to come, the children of Israel will use both of you as a blessing.
Jacob blessed each of his grandsons and then predicted their futures. His children played an important part in Jacob's prophecy. Their past determined their present and would shape their future.

21 Israel said to Joseph, "I am dying. Elohim will be with you, and He will bring you back to the land of your fathers.
22 In addition to what your brothers will share, I will give you an extra share. I give you the city of Shechem, which I conquered from the Amorites."

Jacob Blesses His Sons
4th Aliyah

49 Jacob called his sons together. When they came, he said,
"Gather around me,
and I will prophesy what will happen in the future.
2 Come and listen, sons of Jacob;
listen to your father, Israel.
3 Reuben, you are my first-born,
my strength and the child of my youth,
you are first in rank and first in power.
4 But because you were wild as stormy water,
you will no longer be first.
Because you moved your father's bed,
and committed a dishonorable act.
5 Simeon and Levi are a pair, men of violence and weapons.
6 I will never be part of your evil. In anger you have killed men
and abused animals.
7 Cursed be your anger, for it is cruel.
I will scatter your descendants among the tribes of Israel.

---

1. Jacob called his sons together. When they came, he said, "Gather around me and I will prophesy what will happen in the future."
Jacob, who had the gift of prophecy, predicted the future of the tribes. He gathered together all of his children, blessed them, and urged them to develop their own special potentials with which they were created. Here Jacob teaches parents to evaluate the skills and characteristics of their children to allow them to become everything within their own special capabilities.

4. Because you were wild as stormy water, you will no longer be first.
Reuben's position as Jacob's oldest son was never contested, but he proved himself incapable of leadership. The brothers sold Joseph in Reuben's absence; his plan failed. He did not know what to do. The tribe of Reuben produced no remarkable men, no judge, no king, no prophet.

4. Because you moved your father's bed, and committed a dishonorable act.
Reuben was the first fruit of Jacob's marriage. But he lost his preeminence because he defiled his father's wife Bilhah (35:22).

His rejection was motivated by lack of respect for his father. A bad son could command no obedience from his brothers. A man who could not control himself was not fit to control others.

4. You will no longer be first.
Reuben thus lost the rights of the first-born. The Moabites seized the territory of the Reubenites which they had occupied upon entering Canaan.

6. I will never be part of your evil. In anger you killed men and abused animals.
Jacob is referring to Shechem, where Simeon and Levi killed the men. Jacob apologized and is ashamed of his two sons.

7. I will scatter your descendants among the tribes of Israel.
The tribe of Levi was not given its own land holdings as were their brother tribes.

8 Judah, your brothers will praise you. Your strength will defeat your enemies; your father's sons shall bow to you.
9 Judah, you are like a young lion that has eaten its victims; you crouch like a fierce lion. No one will dare challenge you.
10 The power will not depart from Judah, and not from your descendants. Nations will obey you until the final peace comes.
11 You tie your donkey with a single grapevine, you wash your clothes in wine, your cloak in the juice of grapes.
12 Your eyes sparkle like wine, your teeth are whiter than milk.
13 Zebulun, you will live along the seashore; your land will be a harbor for ships; your border shall extend as far as Sidon.
14 Issachar, you are like a strong donkey, lying down among the sheep.
15 When the resting place is good, and the land is pleasant, you will accept the load, and work like a slave.
16 Dan, you will judge your people, just like the other tribes of Israel.
17 Dan, you will be like a snake on the road, a poisonous viper on the path, that bites a horse's heel, so that the rider falls backward.
18 I pray that Adonai will help you.

Jacob Blesses Gad, Asher, Naphtali, and Joseph *5th Aliyah*

19 "Raiders shall attack Gad, but you will rise and defeat them.
20 Asher, you will produce the richest foods, fit for a king's table.

---

8. Your father's sons shall bow to you.
Your brothers will praise you. They will pay homage to you as a leader and a ruler.

9. Judah, you are like a young lion.
Judah, the largest and strongest of the tribes, is compared to a lion, the king of beasts. The tribe of Judah contributed many great kings to the kingdom of Israel.

13. Zebulun, you will live along the seashore; your land will be a harbor for ships.
Zebulun's territory will be along the Mediterranean from today's Haifa northward toward Lebanon.

13. Your border shall extend as far as Sidon.
Sidon was a great Phoenician sea and trade city. Zebulun as a tribe was engaged in trade and was close to Sidon.

14. Issachar, you are like a strong donkey, lying down among the sheep.
Issachar, you are lazy. You know nothing but to rest and sleep.

17. Dan, you will be like a snake on the road.
The tribe of Dan was small but very dangerous. The Danites were clever and preferred ambushes and guerilla raids to mass attacks. Samson, one of the great judges of Israel, was a Danite.

19. Raiders shall attack Gad, but you will rise and defeat them.
Gad will defeat those who attacked him. This tribe for most of its history was engaged in wars with its neighbors the Moabites, Ammonites, and the Arameans.

20. Asher, you will produce the richest foods.
The name Asher means "happy." Historically the territory of Asher was prosperous and produced excellent, highly prized foods.

JACOB'S LAST DAYS • 48

21 Naphtali, you are like a free-running deer with beautiful children.
22 Joseph, you are like a fruitful vine near a fountain,
with branches spreading over the wall.
23 Enemies will attack you and will make you their target.
24 But you will remain strong, with steadfast arms.
From Jacob's Champion, the Shepherd of Israel.
25 The El of your father will help you,
and Shaddai will bless you,
with blessings from heaven above,
and blessings of water below.
26 May your father's blessing, added to the blessing of my parents,
last as long as the eternal hills.
May blessings circle Joseph's head, The leader of his brothers.

Jacob's Final Instructions   *6th Aliyah*

27 "Benjamin is like a hungry wolf. He devours his enemies in the morning, and divides his prey in the evening." **28** All of these sons became the twelve tribes of Israel, and this is what their father said to them when he blessed them. He gave each one of his sons a special blessing.

29 Jacob then gave his sons his final instructions. He said, "I am going to die. Bury me with my fathers, in the cave in the field of Ephron the Hittite.

---

21. Naphtali, you are like a free-running deer.
The blessing of Naphtali also reflects the later life of this tribe. The blessing says Naphtali is like a free running deer and that he will have lovely offspring. Naphtali's territory was in eastern Galilee, which seemed to bound like a deer over beautiful hills and valleys.

22. Joseph, you are like a fruitful vine.
About Joseph, Jacob said he will withstand all attacks. Later, Ephraim and Manasseh, Joseph's sons, were famous for holding off the Philistines in the woods of Ephraim.

22. Joseph, you are like a fruitful vine near a fountain.
Despite all of the disappointments in Joseph's life, he developed into a fruitful vine. His influence and fame were so powerful that they spread beyond the boundaries of Egypt.

23. Enemies will attack you and make you their target.
The enemies are opponents and slanderers, whose verbal arrows can be more dangerous than real arrows.

27. Benjamin is like a hungry wolf.
This was King Saul's tribe, which was famous for its courage, especially when fighting the Philistines.

28. All of these sons became the twelve tribes of Israel, and this is what their father said to them when he blessed them. He gave each one of his sons a special blessing.
Jacob was a keen observer of the strengths and weaknesses of his children. He, like all parents, had hopes and visions for the future of his family. Each of the blessings predicted the future of his children.

28. All of these sons became the twelve tribes of Israel.
Twelve is the traditional number of the tribes of Israel. Joseph's two sons, Ephraim and Manasseh, participate in the division of Canaan in place of Levi and Joseph, thus retaining the number 12.

30 It is the Cave of Machpelah, near Mamre, in the land of Canaan. Abraham bought the field from Ephron the Hittite as a burial place.
31 This is where my grandfather Abraham and his wife Sarah are buried; this is where my father Isaac and his wife Rebecca are buried; and this is where I buried Leah.
32 It is the field and the cave that Abraham legally bought from the children of Heth."
33. Jacob finished his instructions to his sons. He took his last breath and died.

50

Joseph hugged his father and kissed him. **2** Joseph then ordered the morticians to embalm his father. It took forty days to embalm Jacob. **3** All of Egypt mourned Jacob for seventy days.
4 When the period of mourning for Jacob ended, Joseph spoke to Pharaoh's close advisers and said, "Please do me a favor, give my personal message to Pharaoh: **5** 'My father made me swear and said, "I am dying. You must bury me in the grave that I prepared for myself in the land of Canaan." Please allow me to go north and bury my father, and then I will return.'"
6 Pharaoh said, "Go bury your father, just as you swore to him."
7 Joseph headed north to bury his father, and with him went all of Pharaoh's counselors as well as all the leaders of Egypt.
8 All of Joseph's household, his brothers, and his father's family also went. They left their small children, their sheep, and their cattle behind in Goshen. **9** A troop of horsemen accompanied the funeral cortege.

---

31. This is where I buried Leah.
Rachel was buried in Bethlehem, where she died in childbirth. Jacob and Leah are buried together in the Cave of Machpelah. Ironically Rachel, whom Jacob loved dearly, is buried alone. Leah, who gave birth to Jacob's first sons, has now in death once again upstaged Rachel.

2. Joseph then ordered the morticians to embalm his father. It took forty days to embalm Jacob.
Embalming the dead was reserved for the rich and powerful. Jacob, father of Joseph, was given the honor of embalming. As a health precaution, it was important to embalm Jacob since he was to be brought a long distance to be buried.

5. You must bury me in the grave that I prepared for myself in the land of Canaan.
Jacob wanted to be buried next to Leah and his parents in the Cave of Machpelah.

The Hebrews did not embalm the dead; nevertheless it made sense to do so, since Jacob's body was to be brought back a long distance to the Cave of Machpelah near Mamre in Canaan for burial.

6. Pharaoh said, "Go bury your father, just as you swore to him."
Joseph did not immediately agree to Jacob's request because he was not a free agent. Despite his high political office, he still needed Pharaoh's permission to bury his father in the Cave of Machpelah. Finally, Joseph swore he would comply, and Israel nodded his thanks. Later, Joseph explained to Pharaoh that he swore to do so because it was his father's dying request. Pharaoh agreed and said, "Go bury your father, just as you swore to him."

Shenash

9. A troop of horsemen accompanied the funeral cortege.
Jacob was given a state funeral and the cortege consisted of the king's advisers and a military escort. It was customary for the Egyptians to escort the dead to eternal life in the hereafter.

After Jacob's burial in the Cave of Machpelah, the era of the patriarchs and the matriarchs came to an end. No one, not even Joseph himself, was buried there.

10 They came to Goren Ha'atad, meaning The Threshing Floor of Atad on the bank of the Jordan, and there they held a great religious funeral. Joseph observed a seven-day mourning period for his father.

11 When the Canaanites living in the area saw the mourning, they said, "Egypt is in deep mourning here." The place on the bank of the Jordan was therefore called Avel Mitzraim (Egypt's Mourning).

12 Jacob's sons did as he had instructed them. **13** His sons carried him to Canaan, and they buried him in the Cave of Machpelah, near Mamre. This is the field that Abraham bought for a burial property from Ephron the Hittite.

14 After he buried his father, Joseph returned to Egypt along with his brothers and everyone who had gone with him to his father's burial. **15** Joseph's brothers began to be afraid. They said, "What if Joseph is still angry at us? He is sure to pay us back for all the evil we did him."

16 So they sent a message to Joseph: "Before your father died, **17** he told us what to say to you. He said, 'Forgive the crime and the sin your brothers committed against you.' Now we ask you to forgive the terrible wrong that we have done."

When Joseph heard the message he wept. **18** His brothers then came and threw themselves at his feet and cried. "Here!" they said, "We are your slaves!"

19 Then Joseph said to them, "Do not be afraid. I cannot change what Elohim did.

20 You tried to harm me, but Elohim made it come out good. He brought me to Egypt so that I could save you and the lives of our families.

---

10. Joseph observed a seven-day mourning period for his father.
Today, it is customary to observe a seven-day *shivah* period at the death of a close family member.

13. His sons carried him to Canaan.
Only Jacob's sons were allowed to carry his coffin. On his deathbed, Jacob instructed his children not to allow his grandsons who were born from Canaanite women to carry his body. *Rashi*

14. Joseph returned to Egypt along with his brothers and everyone who had gone with him to his father's burial.
The Egyptians, who saw the great respect paid to Jacob by the kings of Canaan, now honored Joseph and his family even more.

15. Joseph's brothers began to be afraid. They said, "What if Joseph is still angry at us? He is sure to pay us back for the evil we did to him."
The brothers felt that they were in danger and their guilty consciences came to the surface.

16. He said, "Forgive the crime and the sin your brothers committed against you."
The brothers feared that Joseph would now take his revenge against them. To his credit, Joseph acted as if he believed his brothers and he forgave them.

18. His brothers then came and threw themselves at his feet and cried. "Here!" they said, "We are your slaves!"
The brothers had sold Joseph as a slave. Now, as repayment for their sin, they offered themselves as slaves.

20. You tried to harm me, but Elohim made it come out good. He brought me to Egypt so that I could save you and the lives of our families.
Adonai helped Joseph lead a charmed life, which had a definite purpose. The evil deed of his brothers brought him to Egypt. The false accusation of Potiphar's wife sent Joseph to jail. The seven years of famine brought Joseph into Pharaoh's palace. Adonai turned all of Joseph's misadventures into one great positive conclusion.

Joseph at Peace with His Brothers
7th Aliyah

21 "Don't worry. I will provide for you and your children," he assured them and made peace with them.

22 Joseph and his father's family continued to live in Egypt. He lived to be 110 years old.

Joseph Dies
Maftir

23 Joseph lived to see Ephraim's grandchildren, and the children of Manasseh's son Makhir.

24 Joseph said to his family, "I am dying. Elohim will remember you and bring you out of Egypt to the land that He swore to give to our ancestors Abraham, Isaac, and Jacob."

25 Then Joseph made the sons of Israel swear, "When Elohim comes to lead you back to Canaan, you must bring my body out of Egypt."

26 Joseph died at the age of 110 years. He was embalmed and buried in a coffin in Egypt.

---

21. "Don't worry. I will provide for you and your children," he assured them and made peace with them.
Joseph even while dying was in complete control of his emotions and his thinking processes. He assures his brothers that he has provided financially for them and their children. He also assures them that he holds no grudges against them, and that he has made peace with them. *Shenash*

24. He swore to give to our ancestors Abraham, Isaac, and Jacob.
Joseph, despite his honored and powerful position in the Egyptian hierarchy, never forgot that he was an Israelite.

As he lies dying, he remembers his heritage and reminds his children and grandchildren that he and they are Israelites. He reminds them that they are Egyptian citizens on the surface, but historically and religiously they are Israelites. *Shenash*

25. When Elohim comes to lead you back to Canaan, you must bring my body out of Egypt.
The years passed by and Joseph, along with his brothers, grew old. When Joseph's time for dying came close, he asked of his brothers that when, some day in the future, they or their descendants returned to the land of their fathers in Canaan, his remains would be taken for burial to the country of their birth.

He remembered Adonai's promise to Abraham, Isaac, and their father Jacob that the Israelites would one day have a country of their own in Canaan. Joseph kept that memory alive and wanted to be buried as an Israelite in Canaan.

Today many Jews specify in their wills that they, like Joseph, wish to be buried in Israel.

26. Joseph died at the age of 110 years.
Death marks the end of the journey called life. It comes to everything in nature: plant life, animal life, human life, to all alike.

The psalmist of the Bible summarized it well when he wrote that man is "like grass which grows up in the morning but with the coming of evening it fades and withers away" (Psalm 90:5–6). Another biblical writer put it this way: "One generation goes and another generation comes but the world continues on" (Ecclesiastes 1:4). Life is a treasure which is passed on to those who follow us.
Chiel

סֵפֶר שְׁמוֹת

THE BOOK OF SHEMOT

The Hebrew name for the second of the Five Books of Moses is Shemot. It comes from the book's second word in Hebrew, shemot, meaning "names." The Greek name of the book is Exodus, meaning "the road out."

The book of Shemot recounts a great variety of important events that lead up to the Exodus from Egypt under the charismatic leadership of Moses. The book of Shemot can be divided into four scenarios.

The first section (1:1–15:21) deals with the miraculous deliverance from Egyptian slavery.

Toward the end of the history related in the book of Bereshit, there was a famine in Canaan, so Jacob (Israel) sent his sons to Egypt to purchase food. There they met their long-lost brother, Joseph, and he brought Jacob and the families of his brothers to live in Egypt. The Israelites lived and prospered there until, after 270 years, a new Pharaoh arose "who did not know Joseph."

The new Pharaoh declares, "The Israelites are becoming too numerous and are a danger to us. We must find a way to deal wisely with them" (1:9–10). He "deals wisely" with the Israelites by enslaving and oppressing them. Adonai sends Moses to free the Israelites from slavery. After nine disastrous plagues, Pharaoh begs the Israelites to leave Egypt. But then he changes his mind, so Adonai sends the tenth plague and all the first-born Egyptian males and animals die. During the plague the holiday of Passover is established and the Israelites make a miraculous escape by crossing the Sea of Reeds.

The Egyptian experience was a decisive factor in the development of Israel as a nation. The purpose of the Exodus was not merely to free a group of slaves but to create a holy nation bound to Adonai. Thus the second scenario (15:22–18:27) finds the Israelites camped at the foot of Mount Sinai, where they enter into a covenant with Adonai.

After forty days on Mount Sinai, Moses returns with the Ten Commandments (20:2–14). These include rules about the observance of Shabbat, the existence of Adonai, reverence for parents, and prohibitions of murder, theft, false testimony, and adultery. The awestricken Israelites pledge, "We will obey all of Adonai's laws and commandments" (19:8). During this period Adonai miraculously provides food for the Israelites by sending them manna and quail.

The third scenario (19:1–24:18) deals with a series of laws and commandments (mitzvot) that transform the Israelites into a holy nation. The commandments sealed the covenant between Israel and Adonai. They dictated Israel's social and ethical behavior and provided for the welfare of the disadvantaged.

Moses is a man of iron who endures constant challenges yet manages to mold a mass of slaves into a strong and God-fearing nation. He faces an endless struggle with rivals who are jealous of his power. Korach and his followers challenge the authority of Moses. Aaron, in a moment of weakness, allows himself to be influenced by backsliders who have lost confidence in Moses and persuade him to build the golden calf. At key moments, many Israelites of weak faith want to return to Egypt because they miss the food there.

The fourth section (25:1–29:46) describes the Meeting Tent and its furnishings and the building of the Holy Ark under the supervision of Betzalel. The priesthood is established under the leadership of Aaron, the first high priest.

The fifth and last section (30:1–40:38) contains a great variety of instructions and laws: instructions for the High Priest, laws for offerings, furnishings for the Meeting Tent, priestly clothing, and instructions for setting up the Meeting Tent.

סֵפֶר שְׁמוֹת

THE BOOK OF SHEMOT

Masoretic Torah Notes

Here is a list of some of the Masoretic notes for the Book of Shemot.

1. The Book of Shemot contains 1,209 verses.
2. The Book of Shemot contains 40 chapters.
3. The Book of Shemot contains 11 sidrot.

These are the sidrot in the Book of Shemot.

סֵפֶר שְׁמוֹת	157	Book of Shemot
שְׁמוֹת	160	Shemot
וָאֵרָא	171	Va'era
בֹּא	180	Bo
בְּשַׁלַּח	192	Beshallach
יִתְרוֹ	205	Yitro
מִשְׁפָּטִים	213	Mishpatim
תְּרוּמָה	224	Terumah
תְּצַוֶּה	231	Tetzaveh
כִּי תִשָּׂא	238	Ki Tissa
וַיַּקְהֵל	253	Vayakhel
פְּקוּדֵי	261	Pekuday

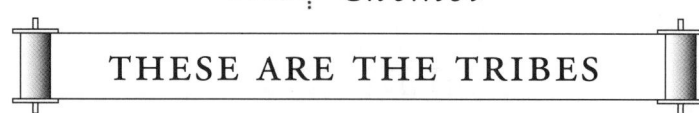

שְׁמוֹת *Shemot*

THESE ARE THE TRIBES

1 These are the names of Israel's sons who came to Egypt with him, each with his own family: **2** Reuben, Simeon, Levi, Judah, **3** Issachar, Zebulun, Benjamin, **4** Dan, Naphtali, Gad, and Asher.

5 The total number of Jacob's direct descendants, including Joseph, who were in Egypt was seventy.

6 Joseph, his brothers, and everyone else in that generation died. **7** The Israelites were fertile and their numbers increased. They became so numerous that Egypt was overrun with them. **8** A new king came to power who no longer remembered how Joseph had saved Egypt. **9** He inflamed his people and said, "The Israelites are becoming too numerous and are a danger to us.

10 We must find a way to deal wisely with them. If we don't, they will increase too much, and if a war breaks out they will join our enemies and fight against us, and drive us from our own country."

---

2. Reuben.
The tribes are listed in the order of their birth, starting with Reuben and ending with Asher.

5. Seventy.
The text repeats the number seventy to emphasize the virility of the men and the fertility of the women. In 210 years, the seventy children of Israel had multiplied and grown into 600,000.

9. He inflamed his people and said, "The Israelites are becoming too numerous and are a danger to us."
Some interpreters blame the victims, the Jews in Egypt. They say that after Joseph died, the Jews in Egypt forgot their heritage. They neglected to circumcise their children and they began to follow the customs of the Egyptians. They moved into upscale Egyptian neighborhoods, attended Egyptian sporting and cultural events, and competed with Egyptian merchants, and some even intermarried.

This alarmed the ruling class and they began to resent and fear the Israelites. For Jews this scenario has been repeated in two historical periods – the expulsion from Spain and the Holocaust in Germany.

Similar events have occurred with successful immigrant populations in other countries.

10. We must find a way to deal wisely with them. If we don't, they will increase too much, and if a war breaks out they will join our enemies.
In about 1500 B.C.E. Hyksos, known as the Shepherd Kings, conquered Egypt, which they ruled until about 1250 B.C.E. During their rule, they were more friendly to foreigners than were later Egyptian dynasties. It is believed that it was in this period that Joseph came to Egypt and rose to his position of power, bringing his family to dwell near the Hyksos capital of Avaris in the Delta. The Hyksos were driven out of Egypt by an Egyptian dynasty unfriendly to foreigners, and from this time, the problem of the Hebrews came to a head.

Nachmanides writes that Pharaoh campaigned against the Israelites for both economic and security reasons. First he was afraid that the Israelites were a fifth column and would rebel and join an invader. Then the Israelites would force them to give up their land and businesses. In addition Pharaoh came to the conclusion that the Israelites would be a cheap source of labor.

11 So the Egyptians appointed taskmasters over the Israelites with orders to crush them with hard labor. The Israelites were forced to build the storehouse cities of Pithom and Ra'amses for Pharaoh. **12** However, the more the Egyptians mistreated them, the more the Israelites increased. **13** The Egyptians forced the Israelites into slavery so as to break their resistance. **14** They made the lives of the Israelites bitter with hard work, making cement and bricks, and doing all kinds of farm labor. The goal was to physically break them.
15 The king of Egypt called the Hebrew midwives, Shifra and Puah.
16 He said to them, "When you help the Hebrew women give birth, if the baby is a boy, kill it; but if it is a baby girl, let it live."
17 The midwives respected Elohim and disobeyed the Egyptian king. They allowed the baby boys to live.

Moses Is Born *2nd Aliyah*

18 The king of Egypt summoned the midwives and angrily demanded, "Why did you disobey me? Why did you deliberately let the baby boys live?"
19 The midwives, Shifra and Puah, replied, "The Hebrew women are not like the Egyptians. They are very healthy. They give birth before we even get to them."
20 Elohim blessed the midwives, and the Israelites continued to increase. **21** And because the midwives feared Elohim, He gave them many children of their own.

---

11. The Israelites were forced to build the storehouse cities of Pithom and Ra'amses for Pharaoh.
Egyptian documents concentrate on how the Pharaohs triumphed over their enemies, never mentioning their slave work groups. The earliest reference to Israel does not occur until the reign of Ra'ameses' successor, Merneptah (1224–1214 B.C.E.). In an inscription Merneptah boasts of all the enemies he has wiped out: "Israel is laid low and his seed is not."

However, some historians assert that the documents from the time of Thutmose III mention a people whose name is spelled Apiru or Habiru that is none other than the Hebrews. In 1444 B.C.E. when Amenhotep II marched up to the Sea of Galilee, he returned with 3,600 prisoners. Other prisoners could also have been captured by Ra'amses.

According to Shemot 1:11 the Israelites "built the storehouse cities of Pithom and Ra'amses for Pharaoh." Ra'amses named the city for himself just as the Torah says.

14. All kinds of farm labor.
Egyptians forced the Israelite slaves to do intensive labor such as digging, plowing, and harvesting.

15. The king of Egypt called the Hebrew midwives, Shifra and Puah.
The midrash states that the two midwives were Jochebed, the mother of Moses, and Miriam, his sister. Shifra and Puah were their nicknames.

16. If the baby is a boy, kill it.
The Egyptian astrologers predicted that a boy would soon be born who would free the Israelite slaves.

20. Elohim blessed the midwives.
The midrash says that for their courage, the midwives were rewarded by Adonai, and they became the founders of the Royal House of Israel and the Priestly family of the Hebrews. Aaron, the high priest, was the son of Shifra (Jochebed), and David was a descendant of Puah (Miriam).

20. And the Israelites continued to increase.
Under a normal course of events, the deaths of the Hebrew children should have led to a reduced population. However, in this case, because of Adonai's intervention, their numbers increased.

22 Pharaoh then ordered his people: "You must throw every newborn baby boy into the Nile, but every girl shall be allowed to live."

2 In this time of trouble, a man and a woman of the tribe of Levi married. **2** The woman became pregnant and gave birth to a son. The child was very healthy and beautiful, and the mother managed to keep him hidden for three months. **3** When she could no longer hide him, she wove a basket of reeds and waterproofed it with tar and pitch. Then, tearfully, she placed the child in it. She put the basket in the reeds on the edge of the Nile. **4** Miriam, the baby's sister, secretly watched from a distance to see what would happen to her brother. **5** At that moment Pharaoh's daughter came to bathe in the Nile, while her maids walked along the edge of the river. The princess saw the basket in the reeds and sent her servant to bring the basket to her. **6** When the princess opened the basket and heard the baby begin to cry, she took pity on it. She said, "It is one of the Hebrew babies." **7** The baby's sister approached and said to Pharaoh's daughter, "Shall I find a Hebrew woman to nurse the child for you?" **8** "Yes, go," replied Pharaoh's daughter. The young girl went and brought the baby's own mother. **9** Pharaoh's daughter said to the mother, "Take this baby and nurse it for me, and I will pay you." The mother took her own child and nursed it for the princess. **10** When the child was old enough, the mother brought him to Pharaoh's daughter. She adopted him as her own son and named him Moses (Moshe) because, she said, "I took [*mashe*] him from the water."

---

21. And because the midwives feared Elohim, He gave them many children of their own.
The midwives were very brave. They feared Elohim and were not afraid of Pharaoh and the Egyptian authorities.

22. You must throw every newborn baby boy into the Nile, but every girl should be allowed to live.
Apparently Pharaoh was informed that Egyptians were intermarrying with Israelite girls and they would be assimilated into the Egyptian population.
Gersonides

1. In this time of trouble a man and a woman of the tribe of Levi married.
Later, in Shemot 6:20, the names of Moses' parents are given as Amram and Jochebed.

3. She wove a basket of reeds.
The reeds, six feet in height, were cut into strips and glued together to form sheets.

These were treated with bitumen to make the sheets watertight. The reeds also had leaves which were used to make paper and mats.

3. When she could no longer hide him, she wove a basket of reed and waterproofed it with tar and pitch.
The reeds acted as a shock absorber. The tar and pitch waterproofed the outside of the basket. The two waterproofing materials were used only on the exterior so that the odor would not make the baby uncomfortable.

9. The mother took her own child and nursed it for the princess.
Not only did Moses' own mother nurse him, she also taught him about Adonai and about the people of Israel. Although Moses resided at the Pharaoh's palace and received an Egyptian education, he never forgot about his own Hebrew people and their faith. But his life as a prince in Egypt also made him a good leader.

10. She adopted him as her own son and named him Moses.
It may be asked why Adonai caused Moses to be raised by an Egyptian princess. The Rabbis tell us that had Moses been brought up among his brethren, he would have had the mentality of a slave and would never have been able to become the liberator of his people.

Moses in Midian
3rd Aliyah

11 When Moses became an adult, he began to be interested in the Hebrews, and he saw how they had to labor as slaves. One day he saw an Egyptian taskmaster kill one of his fellow Hebrews. **12** Moses was very angry. When he thought no one was watching, he killed the Egyptian and buried his body in the sand.

13 The next day Moses went out and saw two Hebrew men fighting. Moses asked one of them, "Why are you beating your brother?"

14 The man replied, "Who appointed you our prince and judge? Do you mean to kill me just as you killed the Egyptian?" Moses became frightened. He said to himself, "Everyone knows what I did." **15** Soon Pharaoh heard that Moses had killed an Egyptian. He ordered Moses arrested and put to death.

But Moses fled from Pharaoh and escaped to the land of Midian. When he reached Midian, Moses sat down to rest near a well.

16 The priest of Midian had seven daughters, who came every day to draw water for their flock. Just as they were starting to fill the troughs to water their father's sheep, **17** other shepherds began to chase them away. Moses stepped up and helped them and then watered their sheep. **18** When they returned home, their father, Reuel, asked them, "Today you came home early. How did you water the sheep so fast?"

19 They answered, "An Egyptian stranger defended us from the shepherds. He also drew water for us and helped water our sheep."

20 The priest asked his daughters, "And where is the stranger now? Why did you leave him at the well? Find him, and invite him to eat with us."

---

11. When Moses became an adult, he began to be interested in the Hebrews, and he saw how they had to labor as slaves.
Jochebed, the mother of Moses, cared for her own child. She obviously told the child that he was an Israelite. Now Moses the adult decides to check on the welfare of his people.

11. He saw an Egyptian taskmaster kill one of his fellow Hebrews.
Moses could easily have played it safe by ignoring the killing of the Hebrew by the Egyptian slave master. But his conscience was stirred, and Moses reacted to that injustice and killed the Egyptian taskmaster.

13. The next day Moses went out and saw two Hebrew men fighting.
Moses was eager to see the condition of his Hebrew brothers. He was shocked to find one Hebrew abusing another and tried to make peace between them.

14. Moses became frightened. He said to himself, "Everyone knows what I did."
According to the sages, Moses was frightened for himself because he realized that the informers would tell the authorities. Moses was also concerned that the Israelites would now not be considered worthy of liberation.

15. But Moses fled from Pharaoh and escaped to the land of Midian.
The tribe of Midian was founded by a son of Abraham from his wife Keturah.

16–17. Just as they were starting to fill the troughs to water their father's sheep, other shepherds began to chase them away.
From the fact that the shepherds drove them away, we may infer that their father had been rejected as priest. The commentator Rashi explains that Reuel had been dismissed as priest of Midian because he had come to realize the foolishness of the Midianite religion and then refused to worship their gods. This fact explains why Moses felt at home with Reuel and his family.

21 Moses decided to live with Reuel and work for him. Reuel gave Moses his daughter Tzipporah as a wife. **22** When she gave birth to a son, Moses named him Gershom, because, he said, "I have been a foreigner (*ger*) there (*shom*) in a strange land." **23** Years passed, and the king of Egypt died. The Israelites were still suffering under their burden of slavery. They cried out for deliverance from their slavery, and their pleas rose up to Adonai. **24** Adonai heard their cries, and He remembered His covenant with Abraham, Isaac, and Jacob. **25** Adonai saw the Israelites and realized that it was time to rescue then.

The Burning Bush
4th Aliyah

3 One day Moses was pasturing the sheep of his father-in-law Yitro, priest of Midian. He drove the flock to the edge of the desert and came to the mountain of Adonai near Sinai.
2 An angel of Adonai appeared to Moses in the midst of a fire, in the heart of a thornbush. As Moses looked, he saw that the bush was on fire but was not being burned up. **3** Moses thought to himself, "I must get closer and find out why the bush does not burn."
4 When Adonai saw that Moses was coming too close, He called from the heart of the bush. He called, "Moses, Moses!" Moses replied, "Yes, I am here." **5** Adonai said, "Do not come any closer. Remove your sandals. You are standing on holy ground."
6 Adonai continued and said, "I am the Elohim of your father, the Elohim of Abraham, the Elohim of Isaac, and the Elohim of Jacob."
Moses was afraid to look at the Divine, so he hid his face. **7** Adonai said, "I have seen the suffering of My people in Egypt. I have heard their cries because of the cruelty of the slave masters. **8** I have decided to rescue them from Egypt's cruelty. I will bring them to their own land, to a land flowing with milk and honey, the territory of the Canaanites, Hittites, Amorites, Perizzites, Hivites, and Jebusites.

---

1. Yitro.
In the Torah, the father-in-law of Moses has seven different names: Reuel, Yetheor, Yitro, Kenite, Hobib, Heber, and Putiel.

2. The bush was on fire but was not being burned up.
The burning bush was on fire but it was not consumed by the flames. This was evidence of the supernatural. Now Moses was positive of the presence of Adonai.

Some commentators say that the fire represents the cruelty of the Egyptians. The bush represents the Israelites who refused to be subjected by their captors and, like the bush, remained whole.

2. An angel of Adonai appeared to Moses in the midst of a fire in the heart of a thornbush.
Adonai chose to appear to Moses out of a simple low thornbush. Why did Adonai choose a scrubby thornbush? The bush, a very small tree, was chosen to indicate His desire to emphasize the virtue of humility.

The thorns were chosen to indicate Adonai's readiness to identify Himself with the Israelites' suffering.

2. The bush was on fire.
The sage Hizkuni says that just as the fire could not destroy the bush, so the enemies will never destroy the people of Israel.

5. Remove your sandals.
Taking off the sandals was considered a form of reverence for a holy place. The Moslems still observe this tradition on entering a mosque.

9 At this moment the cries of the Israelites have reached me. I see, as well, the torture which Egypt is inflicting on them. **10** I am sending you to Pharaoh. Now go, and lead My people, the Israelites, out of Egypt."
11 Moses said to Adonai, "Who am I that I should go to Pharaoh? How can you expect me to lead the Israelites out of Egypt?"
12 Adonai replied, "Have faith, because I will be with you. And this will be your sign that it was I who sent you to lead My people out of Egypt. When you are free, all of you will return to this mountain in Sinai." **13** Moses said to Elohim, "If I go to the Israelites and say, 'Your fathers' Elohim sent me to you,' and they ask me, 'What is His name?' what should I answer them?" **14** Adonai replied to Moses, "*Ehyeh Asher Ehyeh*" (I Will Be Who I Will Be). Adonai then explained, "This is what you must say to the Israelites: '*Ehyeh* [I Will Be] sent me to you.' " **15** Then Adonai said to Moses, "You must say to the Israelites, 'The Adonai of your ancestors, the Adonai of Abraham, Isaac, and Jacob, sent me to you.' This is My eternal name, and this is how I am to be remembered for eternity.

I Will Bring You Out of Egypt   5th Aliyah

16 "Go, assemble the leaders of Israel, and say to them, 'The Adonai of your fathers appeared to me – the Adonai of Abraham, Isaac, and Jacob. He said, "I am aware of what is happening to you in Egypt. **17** I promise that I will bring you out of the slavery of Egypt, to a land flowing with milk and honey, to the land of the Canaanites, Hittites, Amorites, Perizzites, Hivites and Jebusites." '

---

10. I am sending you to Pharaoh. Now go, and lead My people, the Israelites out of Egypt.
I, Adonai am sending you to warn Pharaoh that he must release My people. I will not take no for an answer.

11. Moses said to Adonai, "Who am I that I should go to Pharaoh? How can you expect me to lead the Israelites out of Egypt?"
Moses was an extremely modest person, an *anav*. He was patient with the Israelites and was aware of their shortcomings. Moses was always ready to learn from others – from his father-in-law, Jethro, and from his brother, Aaron. As an *anav*, Moses did not shirk his responsibilities and used his talents for the benefit of his people.

11. How can you expect me to lead the Israelites out of Egypt?
Moses was a realist and came to the conclusion that this was an impossible mission.

Why would Pharaoh listen to him? The Israelite slaves were a great Egyptian asset. Why would he release them and bankrupt the economy and the building program? Pharaoh believed that he was a god, so why would he pay attention to an invisible Adonai?

Moses also weighed the logistical problems of organizing, feeding, and housing 600,000 Israelites. He had no organization, no administrators, no traffic directors. Nothing! So Moses correctly asked himself, "Why me?"   *Shenash*

12. Have faith, because I will be with you. And this will be your sign.
Adonai promised Moses two things. 1. He would come down and rescue the Israelites from slavery. 2. He would help them conquer the land of Canaan.
Nachmanides

12. When you are free, all of you will return to this mountain in Sinai.
Adonai promised Moses that the Exodus and the emancipation were just the beginning of their metamorphosis from a group of slaves into a life of freedom. The sages say that the Israelites were freed from the yoke of slavery to assume the yoke of Torah. The precepts and Torah commandments lead to true freedom of the spirit.

18 They will believe what you say. Then you and the leaders of Israel will go to the king of Egypt. You must tell him,

'Adonai of the Hebrews has met with us. Now we petition that you allow us to take a three-day journey into the desert, to worship Adonai.'

19 I know that the Egyptian king will not allow you to leave unless he is forced to do so. **20** Then I will show my power and punish Egypt with miraculous deeds. Only then will Pharaoh let you go free. **21** I will see that the Egyptians treat you well, and when you finally leave, you will not go empty-handed.

22 Every Hebrew woman should ask for articles of silver and gold, as well as clothing, from her neighbors. In this way the Egyptians will pay you reparations for your (210) years of slavery."

4 Once again Moses asked, "But will the Hebrews believe me? They will not listen to me. They will say, 'Elohim never appeared to you.'"

2 Adonai asked Moses, "What is that in your hand?" Moses answered, "A walking staff."

3 "Now throw your staff on the ground."

When Moses threw it on the ground, it turned into a snake, and Moses was frightened.

4 Then Adonai said to Moses, "Reach out and grab the snake by its tail." When Moses reached out and grabbed the snake, it turned back into a walking staff.

5 Adonai said, "Do this and they will believe that Elohim appeared to you. The Elohim of their ancestors, the Elohim of Abraham, Isaac, and Jacob."

19–20. I know that the Egyptians' king will not allow you to leave unless he is forced to do so. Then I will show my power.
At first Pharaoh will refuse to let you go. However, when I show him my power, he will be happy to see you leave.

22. Every Hebrew woman should ask for articles of silver and gold, as well as clothing, from her neighbors.
When the Israelites leave they will have many things that are too heavy and bulky to take. The gold and silver will be in payment for these belongings that will be left behind. *Abarbanel*

22. Every Hebrew woman should ask for articles of silver and gold.
In Bereshit 15:14 Adonai promised that the Israelites would leave the land that enslaved them, and in the end they would leave with great wealth. Egyptian wealth consisted of much silver and gold from the Nubian gold mines and large quantities of precious metals brought back from successful military campaigns in Asia.

1. They will not listen to me. They will say, "Elohim never appeared to you."
Adonai agreed and immediately responded to Moses by giving him signs to perform.

The commentator Ibn Ezra says that the elders would believe Moses but the ordinary Israelites would react with skepticism.

5. Adonai said, "Do this and they will believe that Elohim appeared to you. The Elohim of their ancestors, the Elohim of Abraham, Isaac, and Jacob."
Abraham, Isaac, and Jacob are the patriarchs and Sarah, Rebecca, Rachel, and Leah are the matriarchs of Israel. The phrase, "the Elohim of their ancestors Abraham, Isaac and Jacob" is recited at the beginning of the *Amidah* prayers.

The sages say that Adonai remembers the faithfulness and the dedication of the patriarchs and matriarchs and continues to show kindness to their descendants because of their merits. This type of merit is called *zechut avot*, or the merit of the founders (parents).

6 Once again Adonai said to Moses, "Now put your hand inside your robe."
Moses put his hand in his robe. When he removed it, it was leprous and as white as snow.
7 Adonai said, "Now put your hand in your robe again." Moses put his hand back into his robe, and when he removed it his skin was as healthy as before.
8 Adonai said, "If they did not believe you, and did not pay attention to the first miraculous sign, then they will surely believe the second sign.
9 And if they do not believe these two miracles, then take some water from the Nile River and pour it onto the ground. The clear water that you took from the Nile will turn into blood on the ground."
10 Now Moses pleaded with Adonai. "Adonai, I beg you, I am not a man of words. I never was, and I am not now. I find it difficult to speak because I have a speech defect."
11 Adonai replied, "Who makes people speak? Who makes a person deaf? Who gives a person sight or makes him blind? I do. **12** Now go! I will be with you and will teach you what to say."
13 Moses pleaded, "Adonai, I beg you! Please send someone else."
14 Adonai was angry with Moses. He said, "Is Aaron the Levite your brother? I know that he is a good speaker. He is coming to meet you, and when he sees you, he will be happy.
15 You will tell him to speak for you, and you will put the right words in his mouth. I will be your mouth and his mouth, and I will direct you what to say.
16 He will be your spokesman. He will speak to the people for you, and you will be his guide.
17 Make sure you take your staff with you, in order to perform the miracles with it."

---

7. Adonai said, "Now put your hand in your robe again." Moses put his hand back into his robe, and when he removed it his skin was as healthy as before.
Leprosy was a deadly disease and numerous Egyptians were afflicted with it. The ability of Moses to cure this disease impressed the royal audience. '

10. I am not a man of words. I never was, and I am not now. I find it difficult to speak because I have a speech defect.
Some say that Moses had a speech impediment or he was not good at putting words together and expressing his thoughts. Others say he meant, "I have forgotten how to speak Egyptian fluently."

Moses stuttered. According to legend, this impediment came about in the following manner: As a small child, Moses, while sitting at the king's table in the presence of the princes and counselors, removed the crown from Pharaoh's head and placed it on his own. The princes feared that this was the same boy who, in accordance with the predictions of the astrologers, would destroy the kingdom of Pharaoh and liberate Israel. In order to see whether the act was significant or merely accidental, they decided to test him.

They placed a shining piece of gold and a hot coal on a plate before the boy, waiting to see which piece he would choose. The angel Gabriel guided his hand to the coal, which he took up and put into his mouth. It burned his tongue, causing him to stutter.

11. Adonai replied, "Who makes people speak? Who makes a person deaf? Who gives a person sight or makes him blind? I do."
Adonai said to Moses, "I helped you escape Pharaoh's soldiers who were hunting for you. I made them deaf so they could not hear the Pharaoh's order. I made them blind so they could not find where you were.

Now stop looking for excuses. I will be with you and tell you what to say."

Moses Leaves Midian

6th Aliyah

18 With that Moses left and returned to his father-in-law, Yitro. Moses said to him, "I must leave and return to my people in Egypt, to see how they are getting along."

Yitro said to Moses. "Go in peace." **19** While Moses was still in Midian, Adonai said to him, "It is now safe to return to Egypt. The Egyptians who wanted to kill you have died." **20** Moses took his wife and sons, mounted them on a donkey, and set out to return to Egypt. He took the miraculous walking staff in his hand. **21** Adonai instructed Moses, "On your way back to Egypt, keep in mind the miraculous powers that I have taught you. Use them before Pharaoh. However, I will make him stubborn, and he will refuse to allow the Israelites to leave. **22** Then you must say to Pharaoh, 'This is what Adonai says: Israel is My son, My first-born. **23** Let My son go to worship Me. If you refuse to let them leave, I will kill your first-born son.'" **24** Moses and his family came to a place where they camped for the night. Adonai confronted Moses and wanted to punish him because he had not circumcised his son Gershom. **25** His wife, Tzipporah, took a knife and circumcised her son. She said to the child, "Now you are safe because you are circumcised." **26** After that Adonai did not punish Moses. **27** Now Adonai said to Aaron, "Go and meet Moses in the wilderness." Aaron went, and when he met Moses near the Mountain of Elohim, he hugged him. **28** Moses repeated to Aaron everything that Adonai had told him about his mission, as well as the miracles that He had instructed him to perform. **29** Moses and Aaron went to Egypt, and they assembled all the leaders of Israel.

---

19. It is now safe to return to Egypt. The Egyptians who wanted to kill you have died.
Moses was an Egyptian prince and was raised in the palace. The headhunters who knew him and could recognize him had died. Now nobody who had witnessed the slaying knew who he was and what he looked like. Now it was safe to return to Egypt. *Shenash*

20. Moses took his wife and sons, mounted them on a donkey, and set out to return to Egypt.
Moses lived in Midian as a free man in his own house with his own family. He would never return to Egypt with his family to become a slave. Moses was positive that Adonai would redeem the Israelites in the near future. They left Midian so he would not have to return to pick them up when the Israelites were freed. *Nachmanides*

21. On your way back to Egypt.
Tzipporah and Gershom went back to Midian and Moses went down to Egypt all by himself. Eliezer had not yet been born.

22–23. This is what Adonai says: "Israel is My son, My first-born. Let my son go to worship me."
All nations in the world are Adonai's children and creations. Israel spiritually is Adonai's first-born.

25. His wife, Tzipporah, took a knife and circumcised her son.
For some unknown reason, Moses had failed to circumcise his son Gershom. Adonai confronted Moses and wished to punish him. However, Tzipporah solved the problem and circumcised Gershom. Curiously, the generation of the desert also was not circumcised after birth (Josh. 5:1–8).

27. Go and meet Moses in the wilderness.
Aaron, who was in Egypt, was instructed by Adonai to go to Mount Sinai, where he would meet Moses and get instructions about their mission to Pharaoh.

30 Aaron repeated everything that Adonai had told Moses and performed the miracles before the people. **31** The people believed that Adonai had visited them and had seen their misery. They bowed their heads and prayed.

Let My People Go *7th Aliyah*

5 Then Moses and Aaron went to Pharaoh and said, "This is what Adonai demands: Let My people go, so that they can worship Me in the wilderness."
2 Pharaoh replied, "Who is Adonai that I should obey Him and let the Israelites go? I do not know Adonai. Nor will I allow the Israelites to leave."
3 "The Adonai of the Hebrews has revealed Himself to us," said Moses and Aaron. "Please allow us to take a three-day journey into the wilderness to worship Adonai. Otherwise He will punish us."
4 The Egyptian king shouted, "Moses and Aaron, why do you bother the people when they are working? Go away and mind your own business!"
5 Pharaoh said, "The slaves are increasing, and you want to stop them from their work!"
6 That very day, Pharaoh met with his slave masters and the Hebrew foremen. He said,
7 "From now on, do not supply the slaves with straw for bricks as before. Let them find and gather their own straw. **8** However, they must still produce the same amount of bricks. Do not reduce the quota. They are lazy, and that is why they want to go to worship Adonai.
9 Increase the workload for the men, and make sure they do it. Then they will stop paying attention to what Moses and Aaron tell them."

---

1. Then Moses and Aaron went to Pharaoh.
Moses and Aaron went to Egypt and assembled the leaders of Israel and told them that they were going to confront Pharaoh and ask to be free. Some commentators surmise that Moses and Aaron asked the leaders to accompany them. As they approached the palace, the leaders became afraid and one by one quietly slipped away. Now Moses and Aaron came to the palace by themselves.

2. Who is this Adonai that I should obey Him and let the Israelites go?
"I am the god and king of Egypt. There is no god bigger and more important than me. Do you expect me to obey your Adonai?"

3. The Adonai of the Hebrew has revealed Himself to us.
Obviously, the Egyptians were familiar with the term "Hebrews." The Hebrews, Abraham, Isaac, and Jacob, had often visited and lived in Egypt.

3. Please allow us to take a three-day journey into the wilderness.
The destination of the three-day journey was Mount Sinai.

7. "From now on, do not supply the slaves with straw for bricks as before. Let them find and gather their own straw.
Mud bricks are made by mixing soil and water, frequently with the addition of some straw, and then packing and tamping the mixture into wooden frames, forming mud cakes. The cakes are placed in a sunny spot for drying and curing. The dried mud makes an excellent insulator, keeping the summer's heat out and retaining the warmth of the furnace or fireplace in winter. Archaeologists had found and identified storage buildings and other structures in Pithom which attests to the durability of mud bricks. *Sturm*

9. Increase the workload for the men, and make sure they do it. Then they will stop paying attention to what Moses and Aaron tell them.
Tell them to stop paying attention to the two agitators who are spouting nonsense. Now they can spend their energy on the increased workload.
Shenash

10 The slave masters and foremen went out and told the Hebrews, "Pharaoh has ordered us to stop supplying you with straw. **11** From now on you must go and find your own straw wherever you can find it. But remember, you must still produce the same amount of bricks as before." **12** The Israelites scattered all over Egypt to find straw for the bricks. **13** The slave masters brutally said to them, "You must make the same number of bricks as before." **14** The Israelite foremen, whom Pharaoh had appointed, were whipped. They were told, "Yesterday and today you did not complete your quota of bricks." **15** The Israelite foremen complained to Pharaoh, "Why are you punishing us? **16** You no longer give us straw, but we are told to make bricks. We are the ones being whipped, but it is the fault of your slave masters." **17** Pharaoh angrily replied, "You are all lazy! You say you want to sacrifice to Elohim, but it is just an excuse. **18** Now go! Enough talk! We will not give you any straw, but you must still produce the same amount of bricks." **19** The Israelite foremen realized that they were in serious trouble. Clearly there was no chance of the daily brick quota being reduced. **20** When they left Pharaoh, the foremen met Moses and Aaron, who were waiting for them. **21** They said, "May Adonai punish you. You have destroyed our influence with Pharaoh and his advisers. You have given them an excuse to kill us."

Pharaoh Will Drive Them Out of Egypt *Maftir*

22 Moses returned to Adonai and said, "Adonai, why have you punished Your people? Why did You send me? **23** Ever since I first went to Pharaoh to speak in Your name, he has become more cruel. You have done nothing to save Your people.

6 Elohim said to Moses, "Soon I will show you how I will punish Pharaoh. He will gladly let them go. In fact he himself will drive them out of Egypt."

---

12. The Israelites scattered all over Egypt to find straw for the bricks.

Brick-making, as shown on an Egyptian monument

19. The Israelite foremen realized that they were in serious trouble.
These men, who were in direct charge of the labor gangs, were Hebrews themselves. They were responsible, in turn, to the Egyptian taskmasters. The Hebrew supervisors held Moses and Aaron responsible for their present troubles. The Hebrew foremen complained to Moses and Aaron.

Then Moses complained to Adonai.

Adonai assured Moses that His promise of redemption was near.

22. Adonai, why have you punished Your people? Why did You send me?
Moses had two complaints. One, since he spoke to Pharaoh, the working conditions of the Israelites worsened. Now they had to find their own straw and produce the same number of bricks.

Two, why did Adonai choose him to cause all of this trouble?

1. He will gladly let them go. In fact he himself will drive them out of Egypt.
They will be forced to leave – whether they want to or not. They will have to leave so fast that they will not even have time to prepare food for the journey.

Rashi

וָאֵרָא *Va'era*

ADONAI REVEALS HIMSELF

2 Adonai spoke to Moses and said to him, "I am Adonai. **3** I appeared to Abraham, Isaac, and Jacob as El Shaddai, but I did not reveal to them My name Adonai. **4** I established My covenant with them and promised to give their descendants the land of Canaan, where they lived as foreigners. **5** I have heard the suffering of the Israelites, whom the Egyptians have enslaved, and I have remembered My covenant.

6 Moses, I command you to assure the Israelites that I will free them from forced labor in Egypt, and that I will liberate them with power and great miracles.

7 Tell them, I will adopt you as My people, and Elohim will always be with you. Know that I, Adonai, will bring you out from under the Egyptian slavery. **8** I will bring you to the land that I swore I would give to Abraham, Isaac, and Jacob. I will give it to you as your own. I am Adonai."

9 Moses told all of this to the Israelites, but because they were demoralized by hard work, they refused to listen to him.

10 Adonai spoke to Moses, saying, **11** "Go back again and speak to Pharaoh, king of Egypt, and tell him to let the Israelites leave Egypt."

12 Then Moses spoke and said, "Now even the Israelites will not listen to me. How can I expect Pharaoh to listen to me? Besides, I have a problem speaking clearly."

13 Adonai then spoke to both Moses and Aaron. He told them what to say to Pharaoh, king of Egypt, demanding that he let the Israelites leave Egypt.

The Ancestors of the Tribes of Israel *2nd Aliyah*

14 These are the ancestors and families of the tribes of Israel. The sons of Israel's first-born, Reuben, were Hanoch, Pallu, Hezron, and Carmi. Their descendants became the tribe of Reuben.

---

6. I will liberate them with power and great miracles.
If I, Adonai, had decreed it, Pharaoh would have immediately released them. But I wish to punish him for enslaving my people.

7. Tell them, I will adopt you as My people and Elohim will always be with you.
Know that I, Adonai, will bring you out from under Egyptian slavery.

These verses are the start of the Exodus drama. Adonai assures Moses what He will do, with four promises.
1. Will free them from forced labor.
2. Will liberate them.
3. Will adopt them.

4. Will always be with them.

At the Passover seder, the four liberation promises are symbolized by means of the four glasses of wine.

9. They refused to listen to him.
The Israelites refused to listen because, despite the promises, they were still being punished by hard labor.

They were so physically and spiritually demoralized from the cruel slavery that words of revolt and redemption did not appeal to them. Moses was aware that in order to be able to appear before Pharaoh with demands, he first had to unite the slaves into one homogeneous nation and to represent them to Pharaoh.

15 The sons of Simeon were Yemuel, Yamin, Ohad, Yakhin, and Zochar, as well as Saul, son of the Canaanite woman. Their descendants became the tribe of Simeon.
16 According to their family records, these are the descendants of Levi. Gershon, Kehoth, and Merari are the names of Levi's sons. Levi lived to be 137 years old.
17 The descendants of Gershon were Livni and Shimi.
18 The descendants of Kehoth were Amram, Izhar, Hebron, and Uzziel. Kehoth lived to be 133 years old. **19** The descendants of Merari were Machli and Mushi. These are the families of Levi and their descendants.
20 Amram married Jochebed, and she gave birth to Aaron and Moses. Amram lived to be 137 years old. **21** The sons of Izhar were Korach, Nefeg, and Zikri.
22 The sons of Uzziel were Mishael, Eltzafan, and Zithri.
23 Aaron married Elisheva, Nachshon's sister, daughter of Aminadav. She gave birth to Nadav, Abihu, Elazar, and Ithamar.
24 The sons of Korach were Assir, Elkanah, and Aviasaf. These descendants became the Korachites.
25 Elazar, Aaron's son, married one of the daughters of Putiel, and she gave birth to Pinchas. The above are the ancestors of the Levite clans listed according to their families.
26 This is the family tree of Moses and Aaron, to whom Adonai said, "Bring the Israelites out of Egypt." **27** Moses and Aaron were the ones who spoke to Pharaoh, king of Egypt, for permission to lead the Israelites out of Egypt.
28 Yet on that day in Egypt, Adonai spoke only to Moses.

Pharaoh Refuses for the Second Time *3rd Aliyah*

29 Adonai said to Moses, "I am Adonai. Tell Pharaoh, king of Egypt, everything that I tell you." **30** Then Moses said, "Adonai, I do not have the confidence to speak. Pharaoh will never listen to me because I do not speak well."

7

Then Adonai said to Moses, "Watch! I will make you seem like a god to Pharaoh; Aaron, your brother, will be your prophet, and he will speak for you.

---

18. The descendants of Kehoth were Amram, Izhar, Hebron and Uzziel. Kehoth lived to be 133 years old.
His life span is given because he was the father of Amram, who was the father of Aaron, Moses, and Miriam.

23. Aaron married Elisheva, Nachshon's sister, daughter of Aminadav. She gave birth to Nadav, Avihu, Elazar, and Ithamar.
Nadav and Avihu died when they led a revolt against Moses. Elazar and Ithamar survived to be the ancestors of two priestly families. Aaron was the first High Priest, and he was succeeded by his son Elazar and then by his grandson Pinchas. Ithamar, the youngest, supervised the Gershonites and the Merarites. He founded a priestly family to which Eli and his descendants belonged.

23–25. Elisheva…gave birth to Nadav, Avihu… and one of the daughters of Putiel…gave birth to Pinchas.
Nadav and Avihu, Aaron's sons, died on the altar because they and 250 followers offered "unauthorized fire that Adonai had not commanded." (Vayikra 10).

When Elazar died, Pinchas inherited the position of High Priest.

2 You must repeat everything that I tell you, and then your brother Aaron will repeat it to Pharaoh. Then Pharaoh will allow the Israelites to leave Egypt.
3 I will make Pharaoh stubborn, and then you will have the opportunity to show My miraculous signs and wonders in Egypt. **4** Even then Pharaoh will refuse to listen to you. Then I will show My power against Egypt. With powerful acts and deeds, I will bring My armies – My people, the Israelites – out from Egypt. **5** When I show My power and bring the Israelites out from among them, Egypt will be certain that I am Adonai." **6** So Moses and Aaron did exactly as Adonai had instructed them.
7 When they confronted Pharaoh, Moses was eighty years old, and Aaron was eighty-three years old.

The Staff Turns into a Snake
4th Aliyah

8 Adonai said to Moses and Aaron, **9** "When Pharaoh speaks to you, he will ask you to prove who you are by performing a miraculous sign. You, Moses, must then tell Aaron to take your walking staff and throw it down in front of Pharaoh. It will became a snake."
10 So Moses and Aaron went to Pharaoh. They did exactly as Adonai had instructed them. Aaron threw his staff down before Pharaoh, and it became a snake.
11 Pharaoh summoned his wise men and magicians. The magicians were able to do the same thing with their mumbojumbo. **12** Each magician threw down his staff, and they all turned into snakes. Then Aaron's staff swallowed up their staffs. **13** But Pharaoh remained stubborn, and just as Adonai had predicted, he refused to listen to them. **14** Adonai said to Moses, "Pharaoh is still stubborn and refuses to let the people leave.
15 In the morning meet Pharaoh when he goes down to the Nile. Hold in your hand the staff that was changed into a snake.

---

3. I will make Pharaoh stubborn, and then you will have the opportunity to show My miraculous signs and wonders in Egypt.
Adonai has taught humans what is right and what is wrong, and allowed them to choose between the alternatives and deal with the consequences. The Torah states, "I have given you the choice of life or death, blessing or curse. Choose life so that you and your descendants will live" (Dev. 30:19).

Adonai does not predetermine a person's actions, good or bad. The choice is man's. Maimonides regards the Jewish doctrine of free choice as a pillar of the Torah. He states, "Every person is capable of being as upright as Moses and as wicked as King Jereboam."

7. When they confronted Pharaoh, Moses was eighty years old and Aaron was eighty three years old.
The Torah mentions their age to point out how brave they were. Although they were no longer young, they believed in their mission and undertook their difficult roles. Despite their old age, they had the energy and the strength to confront the Pharaoh. The Egyptians respected them because of their age, audacity, and wisdom.

Shenash

11. The magicians were able to do the same thing with their mumbojumbo.
Egypt was a country whose people had great faith in magic, and they had magicians who could perform many tricks. The magicians were so ashamed of being afflicted by the boils that they would not appear in public.

12. Each magician threw down his staff, and they all turned into snakes. Then Aaron's staff swallowed up their staffs.
The snakes of the magicians were an illusion and motionless, but Aaron's snake was very much alive and quickly swallowed the lookalike snakes.

16 Say to him: 'Adonai has sent me to you with this message: "Let My people leave, so they can worship me in the wilderness. So far, you have not listened to us. **17** Now Adonai says:

By this miracle you will surely find out that I am Adonai. I will strike the water of the Nile with the staff in my hand, and the waters will turn into blood. **18** The fish in the Nile will die, and the river will become polluted, and the Egyptians will have to stop drinking water from the Nile."' " **19** Adonai said to Moses,

"Tell Aaron to take your staff and point it toward the waters of Egypt – over their rivers, their canals, their reservoirs, and every place where water is stored – and the water shall turn into blood. There will be blood throughout all Egypt, even in the wooden barrels and stone pots."

20 Moses and Aaron did exactly as Adonai had commanded. Aaron raised the staff and struck the Nile in the presence of Pharaoh and his officials. The waters of the Nile were changed into blood.

21 The fish in the Nile died, and the river smelled so bad that the Egyptians were no longer able to drink its water. There was blood throughout the land.

22 However, when the magicians of Egypt were able to produce the same effect with their magic, Pharaoh continued to be stubborn, just as Adonai had predicted, and he refused to listen to Moses and Aaron. **23** Pharaoh turned around and returned to his palace. Even this miracle did not impress him.

24 Since they could not drink any water from the river, the Egyptians dug wells close to the Nile for fresh drinking water.

25 After Adonai struck the Nile, it remained polluted for seven full days.

26 Now Adonai said to Moses, "In My name, go to Pharaoh and say to him: 'Let My people leave so they can worship Me.

27 If you refuse, I will flood the land of Egypt with frogs.

28 The Nile will swarm with frogs, and when they emerge, they will jump into your palace, into your bedroom, and even into your bed. They will also be inside the homes of your leaders and people, even in your ovens and your bread-making bowls.

---

17. I will strike the water of the Nile with the staff in my hand, and the waters will turn into blood.
The Nile is the world's longest river. It starts deep in the heart of Africa and flows northward for 4,180 miles to the Mediterranean Sea. The life-giving waters of the Nile have created a farming area about 15 miles wide where people and plants thrive. Egypt is completely surrounded by deserts except for this fertile strip of land.

The Egyptians worshipped the Nile since it was the life blood of the country. There was almost no rain in Egypt, but the waters of the Nile made Egypt a prosperous agricultural country. That is why Adonai decided to make the Nile his first target.

17. I will strike the waters of the Nile with the staff in my hand, and the waters will turn into blood.
According to an old Egyptian legend a god sneezed and the world was born. Then a goddess cried, and her tears fell upon the earth and the Nile River was created.

20. Aaron raised the staff and struck the Nile.
Aaron borrowed the miraculous staff from Moses and struck the Nile. The Rabbis say Aaron was given this task because the Nile had saved Moses as a child. Now, it was inappropriate for Moses to strike his savior.

29 When the frogs emerge, they will jump and hop all over you, your people, and your leaders.'"

8 Adonai said to Moses, "Tell Aaron to point the staff at the rivers, canals, and reservoirs, and he will make frogs swarm all over Egypt." **2** Aaron extended his staff over the waters of Egypt, and the frogs jumped out and covered Egypt.
3 The magicians were also able to produce even more frogs, which blanketed Egypt.
4 Pharaoh hurriedly summoned Moses and Aaron, and said, "Pray to Adonai! Please ask him to remove the frogs from me and my people. Then I will let the Hebrews leave to worship Adonai." **5** Moses replied, "Test me. Tell me exactly when I should remove the frogs from you and your homes and return them to the Nile."
6 Pharaoh begged, "Please remove them tomorrow!" And Moses replied, "Just as you say. Now you will know that there is none like Adonai.

Frogs and Lice
5th Aliyah

7 "The frogs will disappear from your houses, your leaders, and your people. They will remain only in the Nile."
8 Moses and Aaron left Pharaoh, and Moses pleaded with Adonai to remove the frogs He had brought upon Pharaoh.
9 Adonai did just as Moses requested, and the frogs in the houses, courtyards, and fields died. **10** The Egyptians shoveled them into big piles, and the land of Egypt stank.
11 When Pharaoh saw that the frogs were gone, he once again became stubborn, and again would not listen to them, just as Adonai had predicted.
12 Adonai said to Moses, "Tell Aaron to raise his staff and strike the dust of the earth. It will turn into lice that will infest all of Egypt."

---

2. Aaron extended his staff over the waters of Egypt, and the frogs jumped out and covered Egypt.
The decay of the dead fish polluted the waters of the Nile. The frogs in the river began searching for clean water, so they jumped out of the river into the fields, cities, and homes hunting for fresh drinking water. The natural enemy of the frog was the ibis bird who feasted on them.

Even these birds could not control the astronomical increase of the frogs.

5. Test me. Tell me exactly when I should remove the frogs.
I am not playing games with you. I'm holding all the cards. Tell me when to show you my power.

The midrash says that Moses wanted to impress the Pharaoh that the plague of frogs was not an accidental occurrence.

Moses asked Pharaoh to name a specific time for their removal. By this time, Pharaoh began to understand that he was dealing with a heavenly force.

6. Pharaoh begged, "Please remove them tomorrow."
When Pharaoh saw the difference between what his magicians could do and what Moses and Aaron did, he began to treat them more seriously and asked them to seek Adonai's mercy on his behalf.

12. Tell Aaron to raise his staff and strike the dust of the earth.
It is Aaron who does the striking of the earth and not Moses, because the earth had saved Moses' life when he hid the body of the Egyptian in the sand. Once again, the overriding importance of the principle of gratitude is shown by Adonai's command that Aaron perform this miracle.

13 Aaron did this. He raised his hand with his staff and struck the dust of the earth. Suddenly the lice appeared, attacking humans and animals. All over Egypt, the dust turned into lice. **14** The magicians tried to produce lice with their mumbo-jumbo, but they could not. Meanwhile, the lice attacked and itched the Egyptians and their animals. **15** The Egyptians said it must be the finger of Elohim. Still Pharaoh remained stubborn and, just as Adonai had predicted, refused to listen. **16** Adonai said to Moses, "Get up early in the morning, and meet Pharaoh when he goes down to the Nile. In My name say to him: 'Let My people go and worship Me. **17** If you do not let My people leave, I will send swarms of wild animals to attack you, your leaders, your people, and your homes. The houses of Egypt, and even the ground upon which they stand, will be filled with wild animals. **18** On that day, I will isolate the district of Goshen, where the Israelites live, so that there will not be any wild animals there. Then you will realize that I, Adonai, am right here in Egypt.

Cattle Plague and Boils *6th Aliyah*

19 "'I will separate My people from your people. This miracle will take place tomorrow.'" **20** Adonai did this, and huge packs of wild animals attacked the palaces of Pharaoh and his officials. Throughout all Egypt, the land was devastated by the animals. **21** Pharaoh hastily summoned Moses and Aaron and begged, "Leave! You have permission to worship Adonai here in Egypt." **22** "That is not acceptable," replied Moses. "What we will sacrifice to Adonai is holy to the Egyptians. We cannot sacrifice the sacred animal of the Egyptians in their presence, because they will kill us.

---

14. The magicians tried to produce lice with their mumbo-jumbo, but they could not.
The commentator Hizkuni says they tried to remove the lice because they had attacked the magicians, who were scratching all over.

15. The Egyptians said it must be the finger of Elohim.
The Egyptian magicians were finally convinced that the plague was performed by the finger of Elohim.

19. I will separate my people from your people. This miracle will take place tomorrow.
The swarms of insects will be able to distinguish between the Israelites and the Egyptians. This distinction applies even to the Israelites who were living among or closest to the Egyptians. There could be no doubt about who would be afflicted.

19. This miracle will take place tomorrow.
Adonai was giving Pharaoh time to think of the consequences and change his mind.

Pharaoh and his advisers thought that the plagues happened just haphazardly.

So this time, to convince Pharaoh that a higher force was sending the plagues Moses set a specific time for the plagues, to come.

21. You have permission to worship Adonai here in Egypt.
Moses asked Pharaoh for permission to sacrifice in the wilderness. Pharaoh gave them permission. This is the first sign that Pharaoh's confidence is beginning to erode.

21. You have permission to worship Adonai here in Egypt.
Pharaoh finally came to the conclusion that a superior force was sending the plague. Like a diplomat, he decided to compromise. He said to Moses, "Yes you can sacrifice, but you must do it in Egypt. I will not allow you to leave the country."

23 What we must do is make a three-day journey into the desert. There we will be able to worship Adonai, just as He wants us to."
24 "I will allow you leave," said Pharaoh, "as long as you do not go too far away. You can sacrifice to Adonai in the desert. But remember to pray for me!"
25 Moses replied, "When I leave your presence, I will pray to Adonai. Tomorrow the animals will disappear from Pharaoh, his servants, and his people.
But let Pharaoh never again deceive us by refusing to let the people sacrifice to Adonai."
26 Moses left Pharaoh and prayed to Adonai. **27** Adonai did just as Moses requested. Adonai caused the animals to leave Pharaoh, his servants, and his people. Not a single one remained.
28 But once again Pharaoh became stubborn and would not allow the Israelites to leave.

9 Once again Adonai told Moses to go to Pharaoh and, in the name of Adonai, say to him, "Let My people leave to worship Me.
2 If you refuse to let them leave, and continue holding them, **3** the power of Adonai will strike your livestock in the field. Your horses, donkeys, camels, cattle, and sheep will die from a very deadly epidemic.
4 Once again Adonai will separate Israel's livestock from Egypt's livestock. Not a single animal belonging to the Israelites will die.
5 Adonai has announced that the plague will begin the very next day." **6** The next day, all the cattle in Egypt began to die, but not a single one of the Israelite animals died. **7** Pharaoh investigated and discovered that not a single one of the Israelites' animals had died. But Pharaoh remained stubborn and still would not let the people leave.
8 Then Adonai said to Moses and Aaron, "Take a handful of ashes and throw it up in the air in front of Pharaoh's eyes.
9 It will spread out like dust all over Egypt, and when it touches a man or a beast, it will cause a rash and boils will break out." **10** So they took some ashes and stood before Pharaoh. Moses threw the ashes up in the air, and they caused boils in people and animals.

---

25. But let Pharaoh never again deceive us by refusing to let the people sacrifice to Adonai.
Moses made this statement because Pharaoh had promised to let them leave if the frogs were removed.

3. The power of Adonai will strike your livestock in the field.
Sheep were sacred animals to the Egyptians, objects of worship. The Egyptians therefore sent their sheep to graze in the distant province of Goshen, for it was rich in pasture land and unaffected by the plague. They were now warned however, that these cattle, too, would be affected by the plague.

9. It will spread out like dust all over Egypt, and when it touches a man or a beast, it will cause a rash and boils will break out.
The sages say that the weather was very hot and dry, and the hot burning soot polluted the air. The hot dirty dust infected the skin and caused pus filled boils on the Egyptians and their livestock.

10. So they took some ashes and stood before Pharaoh. Moses threw the ashes up in the air, and they caused boils in people and animals.
Verse 6 states that "all the cattle in Egypt began to die." Verse 3 tells us that only the "livestock in the field" died. The Egyptians who now believed Moses pushed their animals into shelter and their cattle survived. The remaining animals were covered with boils.

11 Even the magicians were too sick to stand before Moses because of the boils, since the boils attacked the magicians as well as every other living thing in Egypt. **12** This time Adonai made Pharaoh even more stubborn. Just as Adonai had predicted, this time too Pharaoh refused to listen to the warning of Moses and Aaron. **13** Adonai told Moses to get up early in the morning and stand before Pharaoh, and say to him in the name of Adonai, "Let My people go, so that they can worship Me. **14** This time, I am going to send a plague against your whole land. It will infect your leaders and your people, and prove that there is no one as powerful as Me in all the world.

15 I could have killed you and your people with the epidemic. **16** But I let you survive to demonstrate My power to you and to the whole world.

The Plague of Hail *7th Aliyah*

17 "But now you are still enslaving my people, refusing to let them leave. **18** Tomorrow at this time I will bring a very powerful hailstorm. Never before, since the day it was founded, has Egypt suffered such a hailstorm. **19** Quick! Warn the people to shelter their livestock and everything else you have in the field. Any person or animal who remains outdoors and does not find shelter will be crushed by the hail and will die."
20 Some of the Egyptians believed Adonai, and they brought their slaves and livestock indoors. **21** But those who did not fear Adonai's warning left their slaves and livestock in the field.
22 Now Adonai said to Moses, "Raise your hand toward the sky, and hail will fall over Egypt. It will fall on people and animals and on all the growing things throughout Egypt."
23 So Moses raised his staff toward the sky, and Adonai sent a hailstorm with thunder and lightning. Adonai sent a hailstorm all over the land of Egypt.
24 There was hail, with flashes of lightning. It was the heaviest Egypt had experienced since it was founded. **25** Throughout all Egypt, the hail killed every human and animal that was outdoors. The hail destroyed all the outdoor plants, and smashed every tree in the fields. **26** Only in Goshen, where the Israelites lived, was there no hail.

---

11. Even the magicians were too sick to stand before Moses.
The magicians were covered with boils dripping with pus. They were too sick and ashamed to appear in public or face Moses.

15-16. I could have killed you and your people with the epidemic. But I let you survive to demonstrate My power to you and to the whole world.
During the epidemic, only the cattle died. I also could have infected and killed you and your people. I saved you, so that you could be witnesses and tell the world of My power.

18. Tomorrow at this time I will bring a very powerful hailstorm.
Moses made a line on the wall and warned Pharaoh, "Tomorrow at this time, when the sun on the sundial reaches this mark, the hailstorm will smash trees and kill numerous Egyptians."

18. Tomorrow at this time I will bring a very powerful hailstorm.
Hailstorms are very rare in Egypt. When they do occur, it is usually in January. The hailstorm was the seventh plague.

19. Any person or animal who remains outdoor, and does not find shelter will be crushed by the hail and will die.
The purpose of this command was to save the slaves, since they had to attend to the cattle. The warning was given to the owners so their slaves would seek shelter and not be struck down by the hail. Some of the slave owners did not believe the warnings, so they left their slaves and cattle in the field.

27 Pharaoh hurriedly summoned Moses and Aaron. He said to them, "This time it is my fault. Adonai is right! I and my people are wrong!
28 Please pray to Adonai for me. There has been enough of this thunder and hail. I will let you leave. You will not be stopped again."
29 Moses said to Pharaoh, "When I leave the city I will raise my hands to Adonai. Then the thunder will stop, and there will be no more hail. By this sign you will understand that the whole world belongs to Adonai.
30 I am aware that you and your subjects still do not fear Adonai. **31** All your flax and barley plants have been destroyed, since the barley was ripe, and the flax was full-grown. **32** But the wheat and spelt seeds have not been destroyed, since they are still in the ground."

Pharoah Remains Stubborn
Maftir

33 Moses left Pharaoh and went out of the city. Just as soon as he raised his hands up to Adonai, the thunder and the hail and rain stopped. **34** But when Pharaoh saw that there was no longer any rain, hail, or thunder, he and his officials continued their stubborn behavior. **35** Just as Adonai had predicted, Pharaoh continued to be stubborn and did not let the Israelites leave.

27–28. This time it is my fault, Adonai is right. I and my people are wrong. Please pray to Adonai for me.
For the first time Pharaoh shared the blame with his people. Then he admitted that he miscalculated and he begged Moses to pray for him.

Sinners and even career criminals will for the moment confess and repent but will in a short time continue their old ways. This was just a half-hearted temporary repentance and reform.

29. Moses said to Pharaoh, "When I leave the city I will raise my hands to Adonai. Then the thunder will stop, and there will be no more hail. By this sign you will understand that the whole world belongs to Adonai."
Moses was aware that the city was filled with idols, and so Adonai would not speak to him within its limits. Moses had to leave the city to speak to Adonai, and then the rain, thunder, and hail stopped.

30. I am aware that you and your subjects still do not fear Adonai.
I am fully aware that you and your subjects fear Adonai while the plague is in progress, but as soon as it disappears you go back to denying His power.

32. But the wheat and spelt seeds have not been destroyed, since they are still in the ground.
Moses and Pharaoh were in a poker game.

Moses told Pharaoh, "You bet your flax and your barley and you lost, but you still have your wheat and spelt in your pot. Do you want to continue and bet the limit and lose them too? I dare you! Challenge me!"
Shenash

32. But the wheat and spelt seeds have not been destroyed, since they are still in the ground.
Adonai did not destroy all the plants because he wanted to use the wheat and the spelt as a threat. You cannot threaten someone when he has nothing to lose, because he will not be afraid. But a person who still has some possessions realizes his dangerous position and will be moved from being so adamant.

35. Pharaoh continued to be stubborn and did not let the Israelites leave.
Pharaoh was a poor poker player and did not realize that he was overmatched. He continued his irrational bets and lost.

בֹּא *Bo*

GO AND WARN PHARAOH

10 Adonai said to Moses, "Go to Pharaoh! I have made him and his advisers stubborn, so that I will be able to demonstrate my miraculous powers to them. **2** Now you will be able to tell your children and grandchildren how I performed miracles among them and how I proved that I am Adonai."

3 Moses and Aaron went to Pharaoh and said to him in the name of Adonai, "How long will you refuse to submit to Me? Let My people leave to worship Me.

4 If you refuse to let My people leave, tomorrow I will cover Egypt with locusts. **5** They will cover every visible spot of land, so that you will not be able to see the ground, and they will devour everything that remained after the hail. They will eat every tree in the land. **6** They will overrun your palaces and the houses of your leaders. Never did your fathers and your fathers' fathers see so many locusts." With that, Moses turned his back and left Pharaoh.

7 Pharaoh's officials said to him, "How long will you allow the Israelites to be a problem to us? Let the Israelites go and allow them to worship Adonai. Don't you see that Egypt is being ruined?"

8 Moses and Aaron were brought back to Pharaoh. He said, "All right! Go worship Adonai. But I must know exactly who will be going."

9 Moses replied, "Young and old alike will go. We will take our sons and our daughters, our sheep and our cattle. For us it is a festival in honor of Adonai."

---

3. How long will you refuse to submit to Me?
It was a battle of wills. Pharaoh's heart was still hardened and he stubbornly refused to admit that Adonai was a super power.

3. Moses and Aaron went to Pharaoh and said to him in the name of Adonai, "How long will you refuse to submit to Me?"
Moses and Aaron in the name of Adonai begged Pharaoh to reconsider. Moses said, "Egypt has been disastrously affected by plagues. Egypt and your people have suffered greatly: the Nile has turned into blood; in addition I sent frogs, lice, wild animals, cattle plague, boils, disease, and hail. How much more suffering can the Egyptians tolerate? Let the Israelites leave."

4. I will cover Egypt with locusts.
Locusts have an insatiable appetite and eat everything in their way. They come in swarms like a cloud and blot out the sun. In the Middle East, locusts usually come from Saudi Arabia. Often, a southeasterly wind will carry them to the lands of the fertile crescent- that is, Iraq, Syria- Lebanon, and Israel; or to the lush Nile Valley. In the past, when the food could not be transported quickly over long distances, a sizeable locust invasion was often the cause of famine.

In Hebrew, the word for locusts is *arbeh*, closely related to the Hebrew word *harbeh*, which means "many". Swarms have been observed covering an area of more then 1,000 square miles in flight- that is, about the size of the state of Delaware. *Sturm*

7. Don't you see that Egypt is being ruined?
Pharaoh's advisers saw the futility of his refusals and urged him to submit and admit defeat.

9. All right! Go worship Adonai. But I must know exactly who will be going.
Pharaoh's resolve was weakening, so he sent messengers to bring the brothers back to the palace. Pharaoh wanted the Israelites to continue with their building projects, but he wanted only the leaders and elders to go. Moses refused the offer. He said, "Young and old alike will go."

10 Pharaoh replied, "You will need Adonai to be with you if you intend to leave with your children! I know that you are looking for trouble. **11** No, I will not permit it! If that's what you really want, only the males may go and worship Adonai." With that, Pharaoh threw them out of the palace.

Locusts and Darkness
2nd Aliyah

12 Adonai said to Moses, "Raise your hand toward Egypt to bring the locusts over Egypt. They will eat whatever growing things still remain in the land after the hail."
13 Moses raised his hand over Egypt, and all that day and night Adonai sent an east wind to blow over Egypt. When morning came, the east wind had brought the locusts. **14** The locusts swarmed all over Egypt. It was a terrible plague. In Egyptian history, there had never been such a plague of locusts.
15 The locusts covered the entire surface of the land, making the earth look black. They ate all the plants on the ground and all the fruit on the trees, and anything that had survived the hail. Throughout all of Egypt nothing green remained on the trees and plants.
16 Pharaoh hurriedly called for Moses and Aaron and said, "I have committed a sin against you and Adonai. **17** Forgive me just this one more time. Pray to Adonai, I beg you! Just take this plague away from me!"
18 Moses left Pharaoh and prayed to Adonai. **19** So Adonai sent a very strong west wind, and it carried away the locusts and drowned them in the Sea of Reeds. Not a single locust remained in all of Egypt.
20 But once again, Adonai made Pharaoh stubborn, and he would not allow the Israelites to leave.

---

10. You will need Adonai to be with you if you intend to leave with your children! I know that you are looking for trouble.
Pharaoh wished to hold the children as hostages so as to make sure that Moses and the people would return. Pharaoh was sure that the men would not abandon their families and would return. However if they did not return he still had the women and children as slaves. Half of a nation of slaves is better than none.

10. You will need Adonai to be with you if you intend to leave with your children!
Everybody knows that children do not offer sacrifices. Anyone who says he is taking children with him to offer sacrifices obviously wants to escape and not return. *Nachmanides*

15. The locusts covered the entire surface of the land, making the earth look black.
The locusts were so numerous that they resembled a huge black cloud which blacked out the rays of the sun.

17. I beg you! Just take this plague away from me!
Pharaoh was an economic realist who finally realized that the locusts could destroy Egypt's richest asset – agriculture. Not only would the present harvest be doomed, but he was aware that the eggs of the locusts could hatch in the near future and destroy other harvests.

19. So Adonai sent a very strong west wind, and it carried away the locusts.
Pharaoh pleaded with Moses and Aaron after the locust plague struck Egypt. He asked them to pray to Adonai to lift the punishment of this plague.

19. Not a single locust remained in all of Egypt.
The Egyptians evidently liked the taste of locusts and attempted to preserve some by salting them. Even these were swept away by the west wind. Today in some near-Eastern countries, pickled or salted grasshoppers are a delicacy.

Some grasshoppers are kosher and can be eaten.

21 Adonai said to Moses, "Raise your hands toward the sky, and darkness will cover Egypt. The darkness will be very strong."
22 So Moses raised his hand toward the sky, and there was a deep darkness all over Egypt, which lasted for three days. **23** People could not see each other, and no one left his home for three days. Where the Israelites lived, however, there was light.

Pharaoh's Last Chance
3rd Aliyah

24 Once again Pharaoh called for Moses, and said, "Go! Worship Adonai! You can go, and even your children can go with you. Just leave your sheep and cattle behind."
25 Moses replied, "No! You have to provide us with sacrifices and burnt offerings so that we can offer them to Adonai.
26 Our own livestock must also go along with us. Not a single animal can be left behind. We must take them to worship Adonai, since we will not know how to worship Adonai until we get there."
27 Again Adonai made Pharaoh stubborn, and he refused to allow the Israelites to leave.
28 Pharaoh shouted at Moses, "Leave my presence! Don't dare show your face to me again. The moment you appear before me, you will die!"
Moses replied, "Just as you say. I will never see your face again."

11 Adonai said to Moses, "There is one more plague that I will send against Pharaoh and Egypt. After that, he will let you leave this place. When he lets you leave, he will actually drive you out of here.

---

23. People could not see each other, and no one left his home for three days.
The darkness was extremely thick. The cloud of darkness (fog) prevented the light from penetrating and made it inpossible both to see and to move.
Nachmanides

24. You can go, and even your children can go with you. Just leave your sheep and cattle behind.
Pharaoh again was testing Moses to see if he really meant to return after the offering of sacrifices to Adonai. His willingness to leave the flocks and herds behind would be proof of his intentions to bring the people back to Egypt after the religious exercises in the desert were completed.

25. You have to provide us with sacrifices and burnt offerings.
We are slaves; we have no animals to sacrifice. You kept us in slavery and now it is your responsibility to provide us with animals for our sacrifices.

27. Adonai made Pharaoh stubborn.
Maimonides writes that every evil act makes a person stubborn and hardens a person's heart, which prevents the person from making intelligent choices. Pharaoh, because of his hardened heart, did not have the moral strength and the courage to change. Pharaoh's heart was so hardened that he could not reverse his decrees as he fell victim to his own ego, and he continued the persecutions.

28-29. Pharaoh shouted at Moses, "Leave My presence! Don't dare show your face to me again. The moment you appear before me, you will die!" Moses replied, "Just as you say. I will never see your face again."
Moses replies, "Just remember, you said, 'Don't dare show your face to me again!' I will not come to you. Next time you will come to me."

2 Now speak to the people quietly, and let each man request from his friends gold and silver articles. Let every woman make the same request of her friends."
3 The Israelites were respected by the Egyptians. Moses was also admired, both by Pharaoh's officials and the Egyptian people.

Death of the First-born
4th Aliyah

4 Moses said to Pharaoh in the name of Adonai, "About midnight I will pass over Egypt **5** Every first-born in Egypt will die, from the first-born of Pharaoh sitting on his throne, to the first-born of the slave girl. Every first-born animal will also die. **6** There will be a great cry of mourning throughout all Egypt. Never before has there been so much sadness, and never again will it happen. **7** Among the Israelites, however, not even a dog will bark. Then you will know that Adonai has made a miraculous distinction between the Egyptians and the Israelites. **8** Then all your leaders will come and bow down to Me. They will beg, 'Please leave! You and all your followers!' Only then will I leave." Moses left Pharaoh in great anger. **9** Adonai said to Moses, "Pharaoh will still not listen to you, so I will have to perform more miracles in Egypt." **10** Moses and Aaron had performed all these wonders before Pharaoh. Yet because Adonai had made Pharaoh stubborn, he would not allow the Israelites to leave Egypt.

12 Adonai said to Moses and Aaron: **2** "This month (Nisan) shall be the first month of the year to you. **3** Speak to the community of Israel, saying: 'On the tenth of this month, every person must choose a lamb for each family. **4** If the family is too small for a whole lamb, then they and a neighbor can share a lamb together. **5** You must choose a healthy, one-year-old male lamb or goat.

---

2. This month (Nisan) shall be the first month of the year.
Before the invention of the calendar, it was a mitzvah for the Sanhedrin in Jerusalem to certify Rosh Chodesh, the new moon, on the testimony of two reliable witnesses who had seen the new moon. This declaration set the dates for all the holidays. Rosh Chodesh means the beginning of the month.

The proclamation of the Rosh Chodesh was signaled from mountaintop to mountaintop by beacon fires. Today, the beginning of each Rosh Chodesh is announced in the synagogue and special prayers are recited. In the Rosh Chodesh prayers we ask Adonai to make the new month a time of happiness, joy, and gladness.

4. If the family is too small for a whole lamb, then they and a neighbor can share a lamb together.
Eating together is a great medium of communication between individuals – everything is shared. The Passover seder starts with the declaration, *Ha lachma anya*, "This is the bread of affliction." Whatever we possess, even if it is a crust of matzah, we invite all to come and share with us: " Let all who are hungry come and eat."

Planned meals are those in which many participate and help mold togetherness and community-mindedness. *Rabbi Joseph B. Soloveitchik*

4. If the family is too small for a whole lamb, then they and a neighbor can share a lamb together.
The Torah contains many mitzvot about sharing and helping. The Torah is concerned about the welfare of the poor, and the sages have recommended that funds be established to help share the costs of the Passover celebration with the less fortunate.

The fund known as *Ma'ot Chittim* ("wheat money") is set up in most communities. The fund provides Passover provisions for the poor and the needy. We can participate in the mitzvah of *tzedakah* by contributing to the *Ma'ot Chittim* fund.

6 Watch over it until the fourteenth day of this month.'

Then, in the evening, the entire community of Israel shall slaughter their sacrifices.

7 They must take the blood and smear it on the two doorposts and the beam above the door of the house where they will eat the sacrifice.

8 You must eat the sacrificial meat during the night, roasted over a fire. Eat the roasted meat as a sandwich with matzah and bitter herbs.

9 Do not eat it raw or boiled in water, but only roasted over a fire, and include all of it. **10** Do not leave anything over until morning. Whatever is left over that night must be burned in fire.

11 You must eat it in your marching clothes, with your shoes on your feet, and your walking staff in your hand, and you must eat it quickly, for it is the Passover offering to Adonai.

12 On that night I will pass over Egypt, and I will strike down every first-born in Egypt, man and beast. I will punish all the gods of Egypt. I alone am Adonai.

13 The blood on the doorposts will be a sign where you are staying. I will see the blood and pass over that home. There will be no deadly plague among the Hebrews when I punish Egypt.

---

7. They must take the blood and smear it on the two doorposts and the beam above the door of the house where they will eat the sacrifice.
Adonai tells the Israelites to mark their homes distinctly with blood so that the deathly sickness or plague would not affect the first-born males in their homes. The death of the first-born finally persuaded Pharaoh to allow the Israelites to leave.

8. Eat the roasted meat as a sandwich with matzah and bitter herbs.
This is mitzvah number 6.

In ancient times the Israelites celebrated Passover by sacrificing a lamb and eating the roasted lamb with *maror* (bitter herbs) and matzah. This ceremony has now evolved into the home ritual called the *seder*. The Hebrew word *seder* means "order." It is called *seder* because the ceremonial order consists of fourteen steps.

8. Eat the roasted meat as a sandwich with matzah and bitter herbs.
The ninth step in the seder ceremony is *korech*: the sandwich. In this ceremony you make a sandwich of *maror*. No blessing is recited. The lives of the Jews in Egypt were filled with *maror*, bitterness.

After the tenth plague, they left Egypt in a great hurry. The raw dough had no time to rise and turn into bread. So our ancestors strapped the raw dough to their backpacks, and let the hot desert sun bake the dough into matzot. According to the sage Hillel, matzah, *maror*, and the Pascal lamb were eaten together in a sandwich. Other rabbinic authorities disagree and suggest that the three foods were eaten separately.

11. You must eat it in your marching clothes, with your shoes on your feet, and your walking staff in your hand, and you must eat quickly, for it is the Passover offering to Adonai.
The Israelites were still slaves and had completed a full day's work. Now, they were asked to have complete faith in Adonai and prepare to move out.

12. I will strike down every first-born in Egypt.
Adonai wanted Pharaoh to allow the Israelites to leave peacefully, so He sent minor plagues to convince him to change his mind. Adonai did not wish to punish the innocent people of Egypt, but after the ninth plague Adonai's patience was exhausted. Now, Adonai was forced to impose the tenth and worst plague, the death of the first-born males.

13. I will see the blood and pass over that home.
The Hebrew verb *pesach* means to "jump past, or pass over." That is why the holiday is called *pesach* or Passover, because Adonai passed over the homes of the Israelites.

14 This day will be one that you will long remember. You must observe it as a festival to Adonai in every generation, and you must celebrate it as a law forever.

15 You must eat matzot for seven days. On the first day, you must clean your homes and remove all leaven. Whoever eats leaven from the first day until the seventh day will be cut off from the community.

16 The first day and the seventh day shall also be a sacred holiday. No work shall be done on these two days. The only work that you may do is the preparation of food so that everyone will be able to eat.

17 You shall observe the Festival of Matzot, for on this very day I brought your people out of Egypt. In every generation you must carefully observe this festival.

---

14. This day will be one that you will long remember. You must observe it as a festival to Adonai in every generation.
The Talmud says that your ancestors were idolaters, and on Passover you celebrate their liberation from idolatry. In this view the real shame in Egypt was not the physical servitude but the spiritual enslavement.

The Israelites were so strongly influenced by the idolatrous practices of the Egyptians that they did not truly believe in Adonai. The triumph of the Exodus, then, celebrates our being set free to become worshippers of Adonai. *Chiel*

14. This day will be one that you will long remember.
"Remember" is the keyword of the first instruction by Adonai to His people Israel through Moses, their teacher. All that had gone before were predictions, promises, warnings, and the preparation for a long and eventful journey. Now as they leave Egypt, the House of Bondage, on their way to the Promised Land, Adonai begins guiding His people into nationhood.

The holy days of Passover are the first days that unite Israel as a nation under Adonai.

In a sense, Passover is two holidays – it is Independence Day and it is the day of the affirmation of the *brit*, the covenant between Adonai and Abraham, Isaac, and Jacob. The emphasis is – remember!

14. You must observe it as a festival to Adonai in every generation.
The seder is celebrated as a family community in which one shares not only material goods, but also spiritual treasures, knowledge, experiences, aspirations, and hopes.

The narration of the events of the Exodus is that of inquiry, questions, answers, and explanations.

On the seder night every Jewish home becomes a teaching community, a school, where a class of disciples is instructed in Judaism and meets with and feels the pain of slavery.

15. On the first day, you must clean your homes and remove all leaven.
This is mitzvah number 9.

Traditionally, there must not be any *chametz* (leaven products) in Jewish homes on Passover. Orthodox and Conservative Jews perform a ceremony known as the *mechirat chametz*, several days before the holiday. A bill of sale is written out and all the *chametz* is "sold" to a non-Jew for the duration of Passover. This transaction is handled as a collective sale by the rabbi as their agent. The bill of sale is prepared with the understanding that the *chametz* will be returned after Passover.

15. You must clean your homes and remove all leaven.
The Rabbis instituted a search for leaven called *bedikat chametz* on the evening preceding Passover. To symbolize the change from the old to the new, from leavened to unleavened bread, a family member takes ten crumbs of bread and burns the *chametz* with a wooden spoon.

18 From the fourteenth day of the month of Nisan in the evening, until the night of the twenty-first day of the month, you must eat matzot. **19** During these seven days, no leaven shall be found in your homes. If someone eats any leaven during this period, he shall be cut off from the community of Israel. It is a law for the stranger as well as for Israelites. **20** It is forbidden to eat anything leavened. Wherever you live, you must eat matzot."

The First Passover
5th Aliyah

21 Moses gathered the leaders of Israel and said to them, "Assemble the people and tell them to choose a lamb for each of their families, for the Passover sacrifice.

The Final Plague
6th Aliyah

22 Also, take a bunch of hyssop plants and dip it into the blood that is in a basin. Smear the blood on the beam of the door and the two doorposts. Remember, none of you is allowed out of the door of your house until morning.

23 Adonai will then pass over and punish Egypt. When He sees the blood above the door and on the two doorposts, Adonai will pass over that door and not let the plague strike your houses.

---

18. From the fourteenth day of the month of Nisan in the evening, until the night of the twenty-first day of the month, you must eat matzot.
Matzah represents the poor bread that the Israelites ate in Egypt. Matzah also represents the bread of freedom when the Israelites left Egypt. The Zohar suggests a third interpretation. Matzah represents the bread of faith that they took with them when they followed Moses into the unchartered desert.

19. During these seven days, no leaven shall be found in your homes.
According to a rabbinic ruling, you must clear out the homes under your control. However leaven owned by a non-Jew is permissible.

21. Assemble the people and tell them to choose a lamb for each of their families, for the Passover sacrifice.
In ancient times the Israelites celebrated Passover by sacrificing a lamb and then eating the roasted lamb with *maror* (bitter herbs) and matzah.

This ceremony has evolved through the ages into the beautiful and elaborate home ritual we call the seder, which is celebrated by Jews all over the world. The Hebrew word *seder* means "order." The seder is celebrated in a prescribed order.

21. Assemble the people and tell them to choose a lamb for each of their families for the Passover sacrifice.
The Samaritans were once a fairly sizable religious community. Today only about 600 people still accept the Samaritan faith. Half of them live in the town of Nablus, near Mount Gerizim. The other half live in Holon near Tel Aviv.

In ancient times the Samaritans were often in conflict with the Jews. They acknowledge Moses as a prophet and claim to be descended from Ephraim and Manasseh, the two sons of Joseph. They accept the Torah and the Book of Joshua as holy, but not the rest of the Bible.

Passover is the Samaritans: most important holiday. It is celebrated on top of Mount Gerizim. The Passover feast is celebrated just as it was thousands of years ago. A lamb is sacrificed and matzot are baked in the ancient way.

23. Adonai will then pass over and punish Egypt.
Egypt is an ancient country whose recorded history goes back about 6,000 years. The patriarchs Abraham and Jacob visited Egypt; Joseph was the vizier of Egypt; and Jewish history began in Egypt.

King Solomon, in the tenth century B.C.E., married an Egyptian princess and made a treaty with Egypt. The prophet Jeremiah founded Jewish colonies in Egypt. After Alexander the Great conquered Egypt in 333 B.C.E., many Jewish immigrants settled there. Jews continued to live in Egypt throughout the centuries. In the Middle Ages the great scholar Maimonides was the doctor to the Egyptian Sultan Saladin.

24 You must observe this custom as a law for you and your descendants forever.
25 When you come to the land that Adonai will give you, you must also keep this custom.
26 When your children ask, 'Why are you observing this custom?'
27 You must answer, 'It is the Passover service to Adonai. When He struck the Egyptians, He passed over the houses of the Israelites in Egypt, and spared our families.' "
The people bowed their heads and worshipped.
28 The Israelites did as Adonai had instructed Moses and Aaron. They did it exactly.
29 At the stroke of midnight Adonai killed every first-born in Egypt, from the first-born of Pharaoh, who ruled the country, to the first-born of the prisoner in jail, as well as every firstborn animal.

---

24. You must observe this custom as a law for you and your descendants forever.
On Passover, Adonai meets a community in its entirety. No individual is singled out; no person, however great and spiritually mighty, stands out; no leader, however inspiring and impressive, is treated differently than the rest of the community. Therefore, it seems fitting that the name of Moses does not appear in the Haggadah. On that mysterious night of revelation, Adonai enveloped in glory and majesty appears to the whole community. Everyone rich or poor, simpleton or genius, sees Adonai and worships him.
Rabbi Joseph B. Soleveitchik

24. You must observe this custom as a law for you and your descendants forever.
The text refers to the celebration of Passover and not to the sprinkling of blood. The sprinkling was confined to the escape from Egypt.

27. The people bowed their heads and worshipped.
Rashi explains that the Israelites bowed in gratitude to Adonai for the announcement that they would be redeemed, for the promise that they would enter the Holy Land, and finally for the tacit blessing that the Israelites would have their own country.

29. At the stroke of midnight Adonai killed every first-born in Egypt.
At the Passover seder we celebrate the freedom of our ancestors from Egyptian slavery. Each person at the seder spills out a drop of wine at the mention of each of the plagues. There were ten plagues, so each person spills out ten drops of wine.

Rabbi Judah was a wise and gentle scholar. He could not bring himself to recite the plagues.
The rabbi felt that even though the Egyptians were our enemy, they were still Adonai's creations. It pained him to recite plagues that killed people. So Rabbi Judah formed the first Hebrew letter of each of the ten plagues in three-word combinations: D'TZACH, ADASH, B'ACHAV.

29. At the stroke of midnight Adonai killed every first-born in Egypt.
Pharaoh himself was a first-born but he was spared. Adonai wanted to punish Pharaoh by having him witness the destruction of his army and then drowning in the Sea of Reeds.
Rashi

29. At the stroke of midnight Adonai killed every first-born in Egypt.
The plagues sent by Adonai to punish the Egyptians corresponded to the cruel actions of the Egyptians against the Israelites. Because the Israelites were forced to draw water for the Egyptians, the water was changed to blood. Because the Egyptians forced the Israelites to catch fish for them, the rivers were filled with frogs. Because the Israelites were forced to sweep the Egyptian houses, the dust of the air was changed to lice. Because the Egyptians forced the Israelites to take care of their sheep, the sheep were struck down by disease, and so on. The tenth plague, the killing of the first-born, was a punishment for Pharaoh's order to murder the male children of the Israelites at their birth.

30 Pharaoh, along with all his officials and all the rest of Egypt, stayed up that night. There was much mourning because there was not a single Egyptian house where there were no dead. **31** Pharaoh sent for Moses and Aaron during the night and pleaded, "Get moving! You and the Israelites, get out from among my people! Go! Worship Adonai just as you demanded! **32** Take your flocks and your cattle and leave us. Go! But as you leave, bless me!"
33 The Egyptians also urged the Israelites to hurry and leave Egypt. They kept crying, "If you don't leave us, we will all surely die!"
34 The Hebrews took their unleavened dough, which had not had time to rise. They wrapped the bread bowls of unleavened dough with robes and carried them on their shoulders. **35** The Israelites also did as Moses had suggested. They asked for silver and gold articles and clothing from the Egyptians.
36 Adonai made the Egyptians respect the Israelites, and they gladly granted their requests. In this way the Israelites were paid reparations for their (210) years of slavery in Egypt.
37 That night the Israelites marched from Ra'amses toward Sukkot. There were about 600,000 adults besides the children.
38 Many non-Israelites left with them. There were also many sheep and cattle.
39 When the Israelites stopped, they baked the unleavened dough, which had not risen, into matzah cakes. They had been driven out of Egypt, and there had been no time for the dough to rise, and no time to prepare any other food for the journey.

---

30. There was much mourning because there was not a single Egyptian house where there was no dead.
Until now all the plagues involved natural disasters, now Adonai punished Egypt directly.

32. Take your flocks and your cattle and leave us. Go! But as you leave, bless me!
Finally, after ten plagues which almost destroyed all of Egypt, Pharaoh begged them to leave. Nachmanides says that Pharaoh finally realized the strength of Adonai.

32. Go! But before you leave, bless me!
For the moment, Pharaoh became a believer in the power of Adonai. Since Pharaoh, too, was a firstborn son, he was very much afraid of dying. He therefore begged them to bless him and thereby to spare his life.

34. The Israelites took their unleavened dough, which had not time to rise.
Despite the many miracles, the Israelites still did not believe that the Egyptians would allow them to go free. They were completely caught unawares, and had not prepared for the sudden exodus.

38. Many non-Israelites left with them.
Not all who joined Moses and Aaron in the exodus from Egypt were Israelites; there were also converts from other religions, as well as slaves who were captured from many wars.

39. They baked the unleavened dough, which had not risen, into matzah cakes.
Matzah is called *lachma anya* (poor man's bread) because, like a poor person's bread, it is made only with flour, without nourishing ingredients such as oil, eggs, or milk. And like a poor person's bread, it is hard to eat and digest. The economic status of the poor person is like matzah. Like matzah, he has also not risen to the point where he can by himself easily support himself and his family.

40 The Israelites had lived in Egypt for 430 years.
41 At the end of the 430 years, the children of Israel left Egypt in broad daylight.
42 The last night in Egypt was the night of freedom in which Adonai saved the Israelites. This event was a night for the Israelites to remember for all generations.
43 Adonai said to Moses and Aaron, "This is the law of the Passover offerings: No foreigner may eat it. **44** If a person purchases a slave and circumcises him, then the slave can eat it.
45 No foreigners or hired workers may eat the Passover sacrifice.
46 The whole lamb must be eaten by a single group at once. Do not take any of its meat out of the house. Do not break any of its bones.
47 The entire community of Israel must celebrate this festival at the same time. **48** When a stranger joins you and wants to celebrate the Passover with you, then each male must be circumcised. Only then may he join in the observance and be counted as if he had been born an Israelite. But no uncircumcised man may eat the sacrifice. **49** This law applies to the native-born Israelite and to the stranger who settles among you."
50 All the Israelites did exactly as Adonai had instructed Moses and Aaron. **51** On that very day, Adonai led the Israelites out of Egypt tribe by tribe.

Remember the Exodus   *7th Aliyah*

13 Adonai spoke to Moses: **2** "Dedicate to Me every first-born among the Israelites. Both man and beast are Mine."

---

42. This event was a night for the Israelites to remember for all generations.
The day of the liberation of the Israelites from Egypt is to be remembered every day. Therefore, in our prayers, every morning and every evening, we recite the following: "I am the Adonai, your God, who took you out of the land of Egypt."

46. The whole lamb must be eaten by a single group at once.
The lamb was a sacred symbol to the Egyptians. The slaying of the lamb as a sacrifice to Adonai showed the Egyptians how foolish their beliefs were.

The Israelites were finally feeling a surge of freedom, and the slaying of the lamb sent a message of strength and defiance.

48. When a stranger joins you and wants to celebrate the Passover with you, then each male must be circumcised.
The stranger must, on his own request, agree to be circumcised. He must not be forced to undergo circumcision.

Jews do not recruit or proselytize for converts. The Rabbis believed that people who wish to convert must be sincere and not persuaded by outside forces.

2. Dedicate to Me every first-born among the Israelites. Both man and beast are Mine.
The Hebrew term *b'chor* is used to refer to the first-born men and animals. The eldest son received the right to inherit a double portion of his father's estate as well as family leadership. One of the reasons for this distinction was the fact that Adonai, when liberating the Hebrews from Egyptian slavery, saved the first-born of the Hebrews from the tenth and last plague. The sanctification of every first-born was designed to keep the memory of the Exodus fresh in every home. Traditionally in commemoration of the miraculous deliverance, the day before Passover is observed as a fast by the first-born. This fast is known as *ta'anit b'chorim*, the fast of the first-born.

3 Moses said to the people, "Remember this day on which you left Egypt, the land of slavery, when Adonai brought you out of Egypt with a show of force. Always remember that no leaven may be eaten during this festival.
4 You were freed on this day in the month of Nisan. **5** A time will come when Adonai will bring you to the land of the Canaanites, Hittites, Amorites, Hivites, and Jebusites, which He swore to your ancestors that He would give you – a land flowing with milk and honey. There too you will have to observe this festival in this way. **6** For seven days eat matzot, and make the seventh day a festival to Adonai. **7** Since matzot must be eaten for these seven days, no leaven may be seen in your possession. No leaven may be seen in all your territories.

---

3. Moses said to the people, "Remember this day on which you left Egypt, the land of slavery."
The Torah tells us that Passover is *Zeman Cheruteinu* (Season of Our Freedom). The Roman conquerors of Israel in the first century C.E. were very much aware of the Jewish thirst for freedom and were especially alert during the Passover pilgrimage. At Passover time, when the city was crowded with pilgrims, Jerusalem became a hotbed of revolt. Roman spies searched the crowds for rebels. Agitators who were caught preaching rebellion were condemned to death by crucifixion.

4. You were freed on this day in the month of Nisan.
During the month of Nisan the barley starts to sprout. Shavuot is the beginning of the wheat harvest. Sukkot will occur at the time of the ingathering at the end of the agricultural year, when the farmers are free from their labors.

These three holidays are the pilgrimage holidays, when the Israelites traveled to Jerusalem with their *bikkurim*, first fruits.

4. You were freed on this day in the month of Nisan (Aviv).
Aviv is an example of the names of the months used by the Israelites in pre-Exilic times. The word *Aviv* means a kernel of grain and describes the time of the year when the wheat begins to ripen.

During the Babylonian Exile, the Jews adopted the names on the Babylonian calendar, and we use those names today in our calendar.

5. A time will come when Adonai will bring you to the land of the Canaanites, Hittites, Amorites, Hivites, and Jebusites which He swore to your ancestors that He would give you.
Canaan was the land of seven nations. Only five nations are mentioned here because only the lands of these five nations were "flowing with milk and honey."

Nachmanides says that all seven nations were Canaanites and they are all descended from Ham's son Canaan.

7. Matzot must be eaten for these seven days.
The holiday of Passover was used by anti-Semites to spread the rumor that the Jews used the blood of Christian children to make matzot. The first pogrom caused by this libel occurred in 1171 C.E. in the city of Blois in France. Thirty innocent Jews were burned at the stake. In 1475, in the city of Trent, Italy, after questioning under torture, 17 Jews confessed and were executed. In 1903, a massacre occurred in Kishenev, Russia. Forty Jews were murdered and hundreds injured. In 1993, the blood libel once again raised its ugly head in Lyon, France. Unfortunately, the lie is still disseminated today.

7. Matzot must be eaten these seven days.
This is mitzvah number 20.

It is forbidden during Passover to eat any food that contains leaven. This mitzvah is the same as mitzvah number 11 in Shemot 12:19.

There is a special kind of matzah called *shemurah matzah* ("guarded matzah"). Orthodox Jews use it, particularly on seder nights. *Shemurah matzah* is made from wheat that is watched from the time of harvesting, through milling and baking. The wheat is carefully protected against leavening, either by rain swelling the grain or dampening the flour, or by too much kneading or slow baking.

8 On that day, you must explain to your children, 'It is because of what Adonai did for me when I left Egypt.'
9 These words shall be a sign on your arm and a reminder in the center of your head. Adonai's teaching will then be in your mouth: that it was with a show of strength that He brought you out of Egypt.
10 You must observe this law at the same time each year.
11 The time will come when Adonai will have brought you to the land of the Canaanites, which He promised you and your ancestors. **12** There you will also bring to Adonai every first-born. All first-born males belong to Adonai.
13 Every first-born donkey must be redeem with a sheep. If it is not bought back, you must kill it. You must also redeem every first-born among your sons.

If Your Childs Asks *Maftir*

14 "Your child should later ask, 'Why do you observe this custom?' You must answer him, 'Adonai brought us out of Egypt,
the place of slavery, with a show of power. **15** When Pharaoh stubbornly refused to let us leave, Adonai killed all the first-born in Egypt, both man and beast.
That is why we sacrifice to Adonai all the male first-born animals, and reedem all the first-born of our sons.'
16 These words shall also be a reminder on your arm and a sign in the center of your head. We do this because Adonai brought us out of Egypt with a show of strength."

---

8. On that day, you must explain to your children, "It is because of what Adonai did for me when I left Egypt."
This is mitzvah number 21.

14. If your child should later ask, "Why do you observe this custom?"
The obligation to retell the Exodus story to one's children lies at the heart of the Passover seder. The name *Haggadah* means "a retelling." The seder is a family or communal affair whose primary purpose is to teach and inspire the next generation. The Torah instructs us to observe Passover in groups that include family, children, and friends. During the talmudic period, many rituals were incorporated into the seder to ensure the participation of children, such as the Four Questions and later the *afikomen* and numerous songs.

16. These words shall also be a reminder on your arm and a sign in the center of your head. The Rabbis interpreted this phrase to mean *tefillin*.

The *tefillin* are worn by Jewish males from the age of thirteen during the daily morning (*shacharit*) services. Tefillin are not worn on the Sabbath and Jewish holidays.

The *tefillin* consist of two leather capsules which contain four biblical passages. The *shel rosh*, head phylactery, contains four strands of parchment with four handwritten passages.

The *shel yad*, hand phylactery, contains the same four biblical passages handwritten on a single piece of parchment.

The *shel rosh* is attached to the head by a leather band called *retzuah*. The *shel yad* is wound around the left hand with the leather strap.

Shel Rosh

Shel Yad

בְּשַׁלַּח *Beshallach*

THE ISRAELITES LEAVE EGYPT

17 When Pharaoh finally allowed the Hebrews to leave, Adonai did not lead them through the land of the Philistines even though it was the shorter route. Adonai realized that if the people met with armed resistance, they would become discouraged and return to Egypt. **18** Therefore Adonai led the people on a roundabout route, through the desert to the Sea of Reeds. The Israelites were well armed when they left Egypt. **19** Moses remembered and took Joseph's body with him. Joseph had made the Israelites swear, saying, "Adonai will remember you, and then you must bring my body with you out of Egypt."
20 The Israelites marched from Sukkot and camped in Etham, at the edge of the wilderness. **21** By day Adonai guided them with a pillar of cloud. By night a pillar of fire guided them with light. In this way they were able to move forward by day and by night. **22** The pillar of cloud by day and the pillar of fire at night were never out of sight.

---

17. Adonai did not lead them through the land of the Philistines even though it was the shorter route.
Adonai guided them on a much longer route, bypassing hostile areas. He was afraid that the freed slaves would panic at the first sign of danger or conflict and would hurry to return to Egypt.

17. Adonai did not lead them through the land of the Philistines even though it was the shorter route.
If the Israelites had taken the shorter route, there would have been no Sea of Reeds in which to annihilate the Egyptian pursuers. The miracle at the Sea of Reeds was a visual lesson to the enemy: "Do not intimidate My people."

18. The Israelites were well armed when they left Egypt.
The Hebrew word *chamushim* is translated as "armed." Some believe that *chamushim* means "loaded." The Israelites were leaving with all of their possessions – utensils, clothing, and food loaded on their animals. These freed slaves had no arms. The Israelites had been slaves for 210 years, and their Egyptian masters would never have permitted them to carry arms. Pharaoh had enslaved them because he was afraid that "they will join our enemies and fight against us" (1:10). They could certainly not defend themselves without arms. So the pillar of cloud led them into the desert, where there were no potential enemies.
Shenash

19. Moses remembered and took Joseph's body with him.
Long ago, Joseph's brothers had promised to take his bones from Egypt for reburial in their own land (Ber. 50:25). He made his family promise that they would bury him there. Now they took his bones for reburial in the Promised Land.

21. By day Adonai guided them with a pillar of cloud. By night a pillar of fire guided them with light.
The cloud had two functions: it was a guide and it also acted as a screen. The pursuing Egyptians could not see the escaping Israelites. There are many extinct volcanoes along the edge of the Red Sea, in what is today Saudi Arabia. If one of these erupted in 1300 B.C.E., the glow of its flames might have been visible to the Israelites. One day geologists may study the extinct volcanoes of Saudi Arabia and determine their dates of formation. If one of these turns out to have been active in 1300 B.C.E., it may furnish us with a perfect reference point regarding the actual direction of the initial exodus march.
Sturm

14 Adonai spoke to Moses, saying, **2** "Speak to the Israelites and tell them to turn back and march to Pi-hahiroth (Freedom Valley), between Migdal and the sea, before Baal-zephon, meaning Lord of the North. **3** In this way Pharaoh will think that the Israelites are lost and trapped in the wilderness.

4 One last time I will make Pharaoh stubborn, and he will chase after you. I will be victorious over Pharaoh and his entire army, and once again Egypt will realize that I am Adonai." The Israelites did as they had been instructed.

5 When the king of Egypt learned that the Israelites were escaping, Pharaoh and his officials again changed their minds, and said, "Look what we have done. How could we have freed the Israelites from doing our work?"

6 Pharaoh harnessed his chariot and alerted his troops to go with him. **7** He mobilized 600 chariots with armed troops, as well as the rest of the chariot corps of Egypt, with supporting cavalry. **8** Adonai again made Pharaoh, king of Egypt, stubborn, and he pursued the Israelites. Meanwhile, the Israelites were leaving in triumph.

Do Not Be Afraid
2nd Aliyah

9 The Egyptians caught up to the Israelites while they were camping by the sea, at Pi-hahiroth opposite Baal-zephon. All of Pharaoh's chariots, cavalry, and infantry were there. **10** As Pharaoh's army approached, the Israelites looked up and saw the Egyptians marching after them, and the Israelites were very frightened.

The Israelites cried out to Adonai.

2–3. Speak to the Israelites and tell them to turn back and march to Pi-hahiroth (Freedom Valley), between Migdal and the sea, before Baal-zephon, meaning Lord of the North. In this way Pharaoh will think that the Israelites are lost and trapped in the wilderness.

Egocentric Pharaoh did not realize that he was being drawn into a trap. He reasoned that the Israelites who were now camped on the shore of the Sea of Reeds had nowhere to go, either backward or forward. Now they were trapped. The Israelites were themselves puzzled by the maneuver but they bravely followed orders. Now the trap was ready to snap shut.

Shenash

2. Tell them to turn back and march to Pi-hahiroth (Freedom Valley).

Rashi says that Pi-hahiroth was originally called Pithom, the store city they had originally built for Pharaoh. The Israelites renamed it Freedom Valley because it was there that they became a free nation.

5. When the king of Egypt learned that the Israelites were escaping.

According to the Rabbis, Pharaoh had sent spies to accompany the Israelites on their journey. They reported back to him that the Israelites had no intention of returning to Egypt.

5. How could we have freed the Israelites from doing our work?

Suddenly, Pharaoh and his ministers were struck by the lack of noise and activity in the brickyards. There was no movement and no construction. The economy of Egypt was paralyzed. After several emergency meetings the decision was made to bring the slaves back.

10. The Israelites were very frightened.

The Israelites had been slaves and beaten down by the Egyptian taskmasters. They still felt the sting of the whips and the blows of their tormentors. Now they looked and saw an army of chariots and soldiers chasing after them. To their credit, they believed that Adonai would save them and they awaited a miraculous rescue. But they still shivered in fright.

11 They complained to Moses, "Aren't there enough graves for us in Egypt? Why did you have to bring us out here to die in the wilderness? How could you do such a thing to us, bringing us out of Egypt?
12 Didn't we tell you in Egypt to leave us alone and let us slave for the Egyptians? It would have been better to be slaves in Egypt than to die here in the wilderness!"
13 Moses replied to the people, "Do not be afraid. Be strong, and you will see that Adonai will rescue you. Today you see the Egyptians, but you will never see them again. **14** Adonai will fight your battle, and you will not even lift a finger."

Crossing the Sea of Reeds
3rd Aliyah

15 Adonai said to Moses, "Why are you wasting My time by crying to Me? Speak to the Israelites, and tell them to start moving. **16** Raise your staff and stretch your hand over the sea, and you will split the sea, and the Israelites will be able to pass over to dry land.
17 I will make the Egyptians stubborn so that they will chase after you. In this way I will defeat Pharaoh and his entire army, his chariot corps, and his cavalry. **18** When I have defeated Pharaoh, his chariot corps, and his cavalry, then the Egyptians will know that I am Adonai."
19 An angel of Adonai had been in front of the Israelite camp, and now the angel moved behind it. The pillar of cloud shifted from in front of them and now stood behind them.
20 It stood between the Egyptian and Israelite camps. That night there was cloud and darkness, and no one could see. All that night the Egyptians and the Israelites could not see each other.
21 Then Moses raised his hand over the Sea of Reeds. During that whole night, Adonai drove back the sea with a powerful east wind, which drove back the waters till the sea bed became dry land. The waters in the sea were split.
22 The Israelites marched into the dry land in the sea bed. There was a wall of water on their right and a wall of water on their left.

---

15. Adonai said to Moses, "Why are you wasting My time by crying to Me?"
The sages say that it was Moses who was crying to Adonai. At this moment, the iron resolve of Moses was weakening and he did not know what to do. So Adonai stiffened his resolve and reassured him that He would split the sea so the Israelites could escape the oncoming Egyptians.

22. The Israelites marched into the dry land in the sea bed. There was a wall of water on their right and a wall of water on their left.
The sea did not part as soon as the Israelites stepped into it. It did not part until they were in water up to their nostrils and in danger of drowning. Adonai did this to test the faith of the people.
Midrash

22. The Israelites marched into the dry land in the sea bed.
The most dramatic miracle recorded in the Torah is the splitting of the Sea of Reeds. However, even the greatest of miracles did not involve a deviation from the laws of nature. We are told that a strong east wind (hurricane) struck the Sea of Reeds, drawing the waters from the sea bed and leaving a path of dry land. This is a natural event that has occasionally been observed in various bodies of water.

Therefore, what is the miracle here?

The miraculous aspect of the splitting of the Sea of Reeds is in the timing of the event. With the Egyptian army fast approaching and the Israelites trapped by the Sea of Reeds, a strong wind suddenly occurred to create a path of dry land in the midst of the waters.

23 The Egyptians chased after the Israelites. All of Pharaoh's horses, chariot corps, and cavalry drove into the middle of the sea. **24** In the morning Adonai struck the Egyptian army with a pillar of fire and cloud. The Egyptian army panicked. **25** The chariot wheels became stuck in the mud of the sea bed and they could hardly move. The Egyptians shouted, "Let us get away from the Israelites, for Adonai is fighting for them against us!"

The Song of Victory
4th Aliyah

26 Now Adonai said to Moses, "Raise your hand toward the sea. The walls of water will break and rush back over the Egyptians and drown their chariots and cavalry." **27** Just as the sun rose, Moses raised his hand toward the sea, and the walls of water broke and flooded back to their usual place. The Egyptians tried to escape the rushing waters, but they were drowned in the middle of the sea.

28 The waters rushed back and completely covered the cavalry and chariots. Of all Pharaoh's army that chased after the Israelites into the sea, not a single man remained alive.

29 Meanwhile, the Israelites had marched in the midst of the sea on dry land. There was a wall of water on their right and a wall of water on their left.

30 On that day, Adonai freed the Israelites from Egypt. From the dry land on the other side, the Israelites saw the Egyptians dead in the sea.

31 When the Israelites saw the mighty power that Adonai had displayed against Egypt, they were in awe of Adonai. They believed in Adonai and in his servant Moses.

---

23. The Egyptians chased after the Israelites. All of Pharaoh's horses, chariot corps, and cavalry drove into the middle of the sea.
The Torah says that Pharaoh assembled a force of 600 chariots. Chariots were the armored cavalry and the spearhead of the Egyptian army. The chariot was a wheeled vehicle drawn by two horses, and its fire power was an archer riding next to the charioteer. The chariot was an ideal mobile weapon for pursuit of a retreating enemy and for covering long distances.

Pharaoh himself led the chariots into the Sea of Reeds and was drowned with the rest of his unfortunate army.

25. The chariot wheels became stuck in the mud of the sea bed and they could hardly move. The Egyptians shouted, "Let us get away from the Israelites, for Adonai is fighting for them against us!"
The Egyptian soldiers were acquainted with the power of Adonai. They were aware that Adonai had inflicted ten plagues against the land of Egypt.

28. The water rushed back and completely covered the cavalry and chariots.
Adonai saved the Israelites from the pursuing Egyptian army by drowning the Egyptians in the rushing waters of the Sea of Reeds.

30. The Israelites saw the Egyptians dead in the sea.
The Israelites were not convinced that they were free men until they actually saw the Egyptian bodies washed up on the seashore.

30. From the dry land on the other side, the Israelites saw the Egyptians dead in the sea.
The midrash says that Pharaoh was the last Egyptian to drown in the waters of the Sea of Reeds. It was part of his punishment to witness the death of all his soldiers and servants before he himself died.

31. They believed in Adonai.
The Haggadah continually emphasized Adonai's role in freeing the Israelites from Egyptian slavery. Curiously, Moses the leader, the driving force of the Exodus, appears only once in the Haggadah. Why? The sages who composed the Haggadah wanted to make sure that succeeding generations seeking freedom would not wait for a leader comparable to Moses. Each generation, in each period, has the ability to generate its own political and religious freedom fighters.
Shenash

15

Moses and the Israelites sang this song to Adonai:
"I will sing to Adonai for His great victory,
Horse and rider He has thrown into the sea.
2 Adonai is my strength and my song,
He is my deliverer;
Adonai is mine, I will adore Him.
I will praise the Adonai of my ancestors.
3 Adonai is the Master of war, Adonai is His name.
4 Pharaoh's chariots and army He has thrown into the sea;
The best of his officers were drowned in the sea.
5 The waters of the deep covered them;
They sank to the bottom like a stone.
6 Adonai, Your right hand is awesome in power;
Adonai, Your right hand crushes the enemy.
7 In triumph You shattered Your enemies;
You sent forth Your anger;
it burned them like dried straw.

---

1. Moses and the Israelites sang this song to Adonai.
The midrash says that while the Egyptian army was drowning, the angels in heaven also wanted to sing in triumph.

Adonai immediately silenced them and said, "The Egyptians are also my creations. You must not celebrate their destruction."

1. Moses and the Israelites sang this song to Adonai.
The hymn of praise chanted by Moses and the Israelites on the shores of the Sea of Reeds (Shemot 15:1–18) expresses the fear and gratitude of the freed slaves as they witnessed the destruction of Pharaoh and his army.

This hymn of praise forms part of the daily morning service (*Shacharit*).

1. Moses and the Israelites sang this song to Adonai.
After more than 210 years of slavery the Israelites celebrated their freedom by singing this song.

1. Horse and rider He has thrown into the sea.
According to the commentator Sforno, horse and rider specifically refers to Pharaoh and his chariot.

Pharaoh, the king of Egypt who subdued countless other rulers, who boasted that he was a god, had met his match. Now Adonai demonstrated to the Egyptians and the Israelites that He was the Ruler of kings.

2. I will praise the Adonai of my ancestors.
Adonai is the same God that my ancestors, the patriarchs and matriarchs, worshipped.

3. Adonai is the Master of war.
Adonai fought the battle of freedom and liberated the slaves from Egyptian cruelty.

4. Pharaoh's chariots and army He has thrown into the sea; The best of his officers were drowned in the sea.
At the Passover seder we celebrate the freedom of our ancestors from Egyptian slavery.

Each person at the seder spills out a drop of wine from his or her wine cup at the mention of each of the plagues. Some say that the ten drops of wine are tears of regret that freedom had to be obtained through the death of Egyptians.

1. BLOOD 2. FROGS 3. LICE 4. FLIES 5. CATTLE DISEASE 6. BOILS 7. HAIL 8. LOCUSTS 9. DARKNESS 10. SLAYING OF THE FIRST-BORN.

8 At the blast of Your breath
The waters became tall like towers.
Flowing waters stood tall like a wall.
The waters of the deep
Froze in the heart of the sea.
9 The enemy said, 'I will pursue;
I will catch them,
I will divide their riches,
I will satisfy my hunger.
I will draw my sword;
My hand will destroy them.'
10 But You made Your wind blow;
The sea drowned them.
They sank like lead
In the mighty waters.
11 Adonai, no one is like You among the powerful.
There is no one so majestic in holiness as You.
You are awesome, doing wonders.
12 You just raised Your right hand,
and the earth swallowed them.
13 With love, You led Your people,
You freed them with might,
You led them to Your holy shrine.
14 Nations heard and trembled;
Terror crippled the Philistines;
15 The leaders of Edom panicked;
The bravest of Moab trembled;
The people of Canaan melted with fear.
16 Fear and terror overcame them
Because of the strength of Your arm.
They were motionless like stone
Till Your people crossed the sea,
Till the people You saved passed over.
17 You will bring them
and plant them on Your mountain,
In the sanctuary of Adonai which You have established.

11. Adonai, no one is like you among the powerful.
A theocracy is defined as a government in which the deity is the ruler. Israel was initially a true theocracy. It was a confederation of tribes with no central authority. Israel was a nation with creed, and conduct detailed by the Torah.

Adonai and loyalty to the commandments were unifying factors. In time, the confederation began to falter and the people demanded a king.

13. With love, You led Your people.
Just as a shepherd leads and protects his flock, You led us, You protected us, You saved us, and You freed us.

18 Adonai will rule for ever and ever."

19 This song was sung when Pharaoh's army, along with his chariot corps and cavalry, marched into the sea, and Adonai made the sea return and cover them, while the Israelites walked on dry land in the midst of the sea.

20 Aaron's sister, Miriam the prophetess, took a tambourine, and all the women followed her with drums and dancing. **21** Miriam led them in the response:

"Sing to Adonai for His great victory, horse and rider He has thrown into the sea."

22 Moses led the Israelites away from the Sea of Reeds, and they marched into the wilderness of Shur. They marched for three days in the wilderness but could not find any water.

23 Finally they came to Marah, but they could not drink any of the water. The water was bitter [*marah*], and that is why the place was called Marah.

24 The people complained to Moses. They cried, "What can we drink?"

25 Then Moses asked Adonai, and He showed him a certain bush; Moses threw it into the water, and the water became drinkable.

It was there at Marah that Adonai gave them rules and laws to test their faith in Him.

---

20. Aaron's sister, Miriam the prophetess, took a tambourine, and all the women followed her with drums and dancing.
The women of Israel had such strong faith in Adonai that before they left Egypt they had already prepared musical instruments to celebrate the miracles that Adonai would perform for them. Miriam was the soloist and the women were the chorus.

22. Moses led the Israelites away from the Sea of Reeds.
Many of the Israelites wanted to stay and celebrate their miraculous escape. Some even wanted to remain to see what Egyptian goods they could find floating on the water or swept onto shore. Moses insisted that they keep moving.

22. Moses led the Israelites away from the Sea of Reeds, and they marched into the wilderness of Shur.
Shur was located close to the northeast border of Egypt at the top of the Sinai Peninsula. The angel of Adonai found Hagar between Shur and Kadesh. The wilderness of Shur was adjacent to the land of the Ishmaelites, which Israel crossed after passing over the Sea of Reeds.

23. The water was bitter *(marah)* and that is why the place was called Marah.
Ibn Ezra says that the waters at Marah were really not bitter. Because of the Israelites' fears and problems, everything they ate and drank tasted bitter to them.

24. The people complained to Moses.
Moses led them on the march and they complained because they thought he did not know what he was doing and where he was going.

25. Then Moses asked Adonai and he showed him a certain bush. Moses threw it in the water and the water became drinkable.
The difficult journey now began for Israel – a nomadic existence in dry, sandy scrub land which would last for nearly forty years. It would be a time for hard testing of the former slave people. With donkeys, goats, and sheep, only short distances of perhaps twelve miles a day could be traveled. And the goal always was to reach the next water hole. For forty long years Israel wandered around the edge of the desert country from well to well, from watering place to watering place.

Water was crucial to their survival. When they arrived at Marah in the Wilderness of Shur and they found the water to be bitter to their taste, they were angered. But Adonai gave Moses the knowledge with which to sweeten the waters. Such "water treatment" is carried out to this day in various parts of the world. This bitter-water incident was the beginning of the challenge to Moses' leadership ability. It was also an indication of the impatient character of the Israelites.

26 He said, "If you obey Adonai and do what is right in His sight, carefully obeying all His commandments and keeping all His laws, then I will not afflict you with any of the diseases that I sent on Egypt. I am Adonai who heals you."

The Oasis of Elim
5th Aliyah

27 From Marah they marched to Elim, an oasis where there were twelve springs of water and seventy date palms. They camped near the water.

16 From Elim the entire community of Israel marched to the wilderness of Sin, which is between Elim and Sinai. They arrived on the fifteenth of the second month after they had left Egypt.
2 There in the desert, the entire Israelite community began to complain against Moses and Aaron.
3 The Israelites said to them, "We would have been better off if we had died by the hand of Adonai in Egypt! At least there we could smell pots of meat and stuff ourselves with bread! But you had to bring us into this desert and starve our whole community to death!"

---

27. From Marah they marched to Elim, an oasis where there were twelve springs of water and seventy date palms.
The twelve springs correspond to the twelve tribes of Israel, and the seventy palm trees to the seventy elders of Israel.

An oasis, where caravans and tribes could pause to rest and replenish their water supplies, are places of importance. Most of the water found in a desert oasis originates as rain. The rainwater trickles through the soil and onto bedrock, where it is stored. In places where the rock is exposed one can find springs. These are the locations of oases or wadis, of islands of greenery in the gray desert landscape.

It is impossible to identify the location of Elim, which was an extremely fertile oasis with numerous springs and palm trees.

2. The entire Israelite community began to complain against Moses and Aaron.
This was now the second time that the Israelites complained about their situation. Unfortunately, they would continue to complain during all the years of their wandering in the wilderness. Moses certainly had his problems as a leader.

2. There in the desert, the entire Israelite community began to complain against Moses and Aaron.
It took only one month after they left the brickyards of Egypt for the complaints to start against the leadership of Moses.

The desert heat, the constant movement, and the fear of attack had a demoralizing effect on the freed slaves.

3. At least there we could smell pots of meat and stuff ourselves with bread.
This statement leads to an important understanding of the history of Israel. It shows the choices a person has and their values and consequences. Some sought comforts and could not delay their satisfaction. They suffered both in lust and in their punishment. Others lifted themselves above their own personal desires and were concerned for the people and their future according to the divine plan. They became leaders, even prophets.

Moses welcomed these men and wanted to share his leadership and his responsibility with them. The democracy of the Jewish people is very ancient. In the end, no single man, not even Moses, could take sole responsibility for a great and numerous people. The potential responsibility of each Jew for his or her people derives from the same Moses who stated, "I wish that all of Adonai's people were holy enough to have the gift of prophecy!"

4 Then Adonai said to Moses, "I will make bread rain down for you from the sky. Everyone must go out and gather just enough for each day. I will test them to see whether or not they obey My instructions.
5 On Friday, they will have to gather twice as much as they gather every other day."
6 Moses and Aaron said to the Israelites, "By evening you will realize that it was Adonai who brought you out of Egypt;
7 and in the morning, you will see Adonai's presence. He has heard your complaints, which are against Him, and not against us."
8 Moses said, "In the evening, Adonai will give you meat to eat, and in the morning, there will be enough bread to fill your stomachs. Adonai has heard your complaints, which are really against Him. Who are we? Your complaints are not against us, but against Adonai!"
9 Moses said to Aaron, "Tell the entire Israelite community to assemble before Adonai, for He has heard their complaints."
10 As Aaron spoke to the Israelite community, they turned toward the desert and saw Adonai's divine light shining in the clouds.

Manna and Quail   *6th Aliyah*

11 Adonai spoke to Moses, saying,
12 "I have heard the complaints of the Israelites. Reassure them and say, 'In the evening you will have meat to eat, and in the morning you will have your fill of bread. Then you will know that I am Adonai.'"
13 That evening, a flock of quail flew in and covered the camp. Then, in the morning, there was a layer of dew around the camp.

---

4. I will make bread rain down for you from the sky.
To this day when someone talks about something good coming in abundance and completely unexpectedly, almost out of the air, so to speak, they say it was like "manna from heaven." The Torah says that when the Israelites awoke, the ground was covered with it. What is manna, the bread from heaven? One theory is as follows:

A certain scalelike insect that lives on trees gives off a large transparent drop of liquid from its egg sac. When it first comes out it is very white; after the drops are exposed to the air, however, they begin to turn brown and become brittle. The taste of these grains is very sweet. Thus it closely fits the description of the manna given in the Torah: it was like coriander seed, white, and the taste of it was like water with honey.

Interestingly, the Arabs who live in the desert today call this substance *man min sama*. In Hebrew that would be *mannah min ha-shamayim*, or manna from heaven.

4. Everyone must go out and gather just enough for each day.
If they wanted to save some of the manna for the next day, they would be demonstrating their lack of trust in Adonai that more would come.

7. He has heard your complaints, which are against Him and not against us.
Moses was annoyed with them, not because they had accidentally left over some of the manna, but because they may have been deliberately testing Adonai to supply more.

13. That evening, a flock of quail flew in and covered the camp.
The arrival of the quail was just one single event. However, the "manna from heaven" was continuous during their forty-year sojourn in the desert.

14 When the layer of dew evaporated, there were tiny balls covering the surface of the desert. It looked like frost on the ground.
15 The Israelites looked at it, and they had no idea what it was. They asked each other, "*Man-hu?*" (What is it?). Moses said to them, "This is the bread that Adonai is giving you to eat.
16 Adonai has instructed that each person is to gather only as much as each person needs. There will be an omer (**2** quarts) for each person."
17 When the Israelites did so, some gathered more and some gathered less.
18 But when they measured the manna with an omer, the one who had gathered more did not have any extra, and the one who had gathered less did not have too little. Each one had gathered exactly enough to eat.
19 Moses warned them, "Do not leave any manna over until the morning."
20 Of course some people did not listen to Moses and left a portion for the morning. It became smelly and filled with worms. Moses was angry with those Israelites. **21** Each morning the people gathered as much as they could eat. Then, when the sun became hot, the manna melted. **22** When Friday came, they gathered a double portion of manna, four omers for each person. The leaders of the community were puzzled. They asked Moses, "Why did this happen?"
23 Moses explained, "This is what Adonai has said: 'Tomorrow is a day of rest, Adonai's holy Sabbath. Bake what you want to bake, and cook what you want to cook today. Whatever is left over, carefully set it aside until morning.'"
24 The next morning, as Moses had instructed, they saved the food until Saturday, and it was not smelly, and there were no worms in it.
25 Moses instructed them, "Eat it today, for today is Adonai's Sabbath. Today you will not find any manna in the field.
26 On the six weekdays you are to gather this food, but the seventh day is the Sabbath, and on that day there will not be any manna."

---

15. They asked each other, "*Man–hu?*" (What is it?)
In Hebrew: *Man-hu?* Thus the name *man*, or manna. It is believed by some to have been a sweet, sticky, honey juice that exudes from a shrub which grows in the Sinai Peninsula. It crystalizes and turns white.

20. Moses was angry with those Israelites.
Moses was angry with the Israelites because they had no faith and disobeyed Adonai's command.

22. The leaders of the community were puzzled. They asked Moses, "Why did this happen?"
The people could not comprehend the reason for the double portion, and so the elders came to Moses and asked why this day was different from the other days.

23. Tomorrow is a day of rest, Adonai's holy Sabbath. Bake what you want to bake, and cook what you want to cook today. Whatever is left over, carefully set it aside until morning.
When Adonai gave the Israelites twice as much manna on the sixth day and it had not spoiled by the next morning, they understood the meaning of the Sabbath even better. Adonai said to them, "I want you to rest and make this day holy to me and I in turn will provide for you on the seventh day without any effort on your part." In the years that followed, Israel realized that it was always possible to have a surplus for the Sabbath and that if they obeyed His command, Adonai would assure them that the surplus would permit them to rest and make the day holy. If people are replenished physically and spiritually on the Sabbath, they will be able to produce more during the week.

27 Nevertheless, some people went out to gather manna on Saturday, but they did not find anything.
28 Adonai said to Moses, "Say to the Israelites: 'How long will you refuse to observe My commandments and My laws?'
29 They must understand that Adonai has given them the Sabbath, and that is why He sent you food for two days on Friday. On the Sabbath you must all remain at home, and no one is to gather manna on Saturday."
30 And so the Israelites rested on Saturday. **31** The Israelites called the food manna. It looked like coriander seeds, except that it was white, and it tasted like honey bread.
32 Moses said, "This is what Adonai has commanded: Fill an omer measure with the manna as a sacred reminder for your descendants. Then they will be able to see the food that I fed you in the desert when I brought you out of Egypt."
33 Moses said to Aaron, "Take a jar and fill it with two quarts of manna. Set it before Adonai as a sacred reminder for your descendants."
34 Just as Adonai commanded Moses, Aaron later set the jar of manna before the Ark of the Covenant as a sacred reminder.
35 The Israelites ate the manna for forty years, until they came to a fertile land. The Israelites ate manna until they reached the land of Canaan, where there were growing things to eat.
36 An omer (two quarts) is a tenth of an ephah.

Water from the Rock at Horeb

7th Aliyah

17 According to Adonai's plan, the entire Israelite community marched from the wilderness of Sin until they reached Rephidim. When they arrived, there was no water for the people to drink.

---

27. Nevertheless, some people went out to gather manna on Saturday, but they did not find anything.
Some people went out to test Moses and to see whether Moses' words, that no manna would fall on the seventh day, were true.

30. And so the Israelites rested on Saturday.
The nation now took it upon itself to rest not only on this Sabbath but on every Sabbath thereafter.

31. It looked like coriander seeds.
The seeds of this plant are in the carrot family and are about the size of a peppercorn. They grow wild in the Holy Land and the seeds are used in cooking and for medicinal purposes.

32. Fill an omer measure with the manna as a sacred reminder for your descendants. Then they will be able to see the food that I fed you in the desert.
After the tabernacle was built, Moses told Aaron to take an earthen jar, fill it with an omer of manna, and place it in the Holy Ark. This verse is anachronistic, meaning that it is out of sequence. The Holy Ark had not been built yet, but since this chapter is concerned with the manna, the verse was placed here even though it was said by Moses later.

33. Moses said to Aaron, "Take a jar and fill it with two quarts of manna. Set it before Adonai as a sacred reminder for your descendants."
The jar was made of glass so it could be viewed by the Israelites.   *Abarbanel*

1. According to Adonai's plan, the entire Israelite community marched from the wilderness of Sin until they reached Rephidim.
Rephidim was the third stage of the journey. The other two encampments were Dophkah and Alush. The text does not mention them because nothing special happened there.

2 Once again the Israelites complained to Moses. "Give us water to drink!" Moses asked, "Why are you complaining to me? You are just wearing out Adonai's patience."
3 Because of the lack of water, the people were suffering from thirst, and they began grumbling against Moses. Their leader shouted, "Why did you bring us out of Egypt? Do you want to make me, my children, and my cattle die of thirst?"
4 Moses pleaded, "Adonai, what shall I do with these people? Before long they will stone me!" **5** Adonai said to Moses, "Take the staff with which you struck the Nile and, with the leaders of Israel, march in front of the people. **6** I will stand beside you on the rock at Horeb. Strike the rock, and water will stream out of it for the people to drink." Moses did this in the presence of the leaders of Israel.
7 Moses named the place Massah and Merivah (Testing and Quarreling) because the people had tested and quarreled with Adonai, and because they had asked,
"Is Adonai going to take care of us, or is He against us?"
8 Now the army of Amalek came and attacked the Israelites in Rephidim.

---

2. Once again the Israelites complained to Moses, "Give us water to drink!" Moses asked, "Why are you complaining to me? You are just wearing out Adonai's patience."
Moses realized that the problem was not a lack of water but a lack of faith and resolve. There they were, surrounded by miles of endless sand, surrounded by hostile marauders, trapped with a leader who receives orders from outer space. They were frightened and wondered why they had allowed this mysterious, invisible entity to kidnap them. *Shenash*

6. Strike the rock, and water will stream out of it.
That the water supply was a steady problem in the desert country through which they moved is understandable.

But the Israelites continuing to "murmur" showed that they still had little faith in Adonai and in His appointed leader, Moses. After all, the Marah bitter-water incident should have shown them that Adonai cares and provides for them. But no! They had quickly forgotten and they griped once more at Rephidim. So Adonai gave Moses the knowledge to seek out a certain rock at Mount Horeb. Moses tapped the rock with his rod and, miracle of miracles, water did begin to flow.

Once more Israel's need is taken care of. Again they have tested Adonai's dependability, and again He has demonstrated it to them.

6. I will stand beside you on the rock at Horeb.
Horeb was in the area where Adonai had first revealed Himself to Moses when he was a shepherd (Shemot 3:1).

6. Moses did this in the presence of the leaders of Israel.
The elders will be witnesses to the fact that it is because of you that water will come from the rock and that there were no springs of water hidden underneath.

8. Now the army of Amalek came and attacked the Israelites in Rephidim.
The Amalekites were a nomadic tribe of desert raiders in the vicinity of Kadesh. They attacked the Israelite stragglers.

Arab genealogists list Amalek as a grandson of Shem. The Torah lists Amalek (Ber. 36:12) as the first born of Eliphaz, the son of Esau. The history of the tribe of Amalek was supposed to have been brought to an end at the time of Mohammed. According to the Koran, the tribe was exterminated because of their refusal to accept Allah as their god.

9 Moses instructed Joshua, "Select fighters, and prepare them to battle against Amalek. Tomorrow, I will station myself on top of the hill with the staff of Adonai in my hand." **10** Joshua did as Moses had told him. He and his warriors battled Amalek. Meanwhile, Moses, Aaron, and Hur had climbed to the top of the hill. **11** As long as Moses held his hands outstretched, Israel won, but as soon as he let his hands down, the battle turned against Israel. **12** When the hands of Moses became tired, they took a stone and placed it so that he could sit. Aaron and Hur each supported one of Moses' arms so that they remained outstretched until sunset. **13** As a result Joshua was able to defeat Amalek and his allies.

I Will Destroy Amalek
Maftir

14 Adonai instructed Moses, "Record this as a permanent reminder, and carefully repeat it to Joshua. I will totally wipe out the memory of Amalek from under the heavens." **15** Moses built an altar there, and he named it Adonai Nissi (Adonai Is My Banner). **16** He said, "Adonai has sworn that in every generation He will battle against Amalek."

---

9. Moses instructed Joshua.
Joshua was Moses' trusted military aide. He is mentioned on a number of occasions.

9. Tomorrow, I will station myself on top of the hill with the staff of Adonai in my hand.
I will raise this staff high as I pray, and the brave men who are fighting against the Amalekites will know I am praying; it will give them courage to continue fighting.

The miraculous staff had performed miracles in Egypt and had also split the Sea of Reeds. The staff was also used to produce water for the thirsty Israelites.

9. Moses instructed Joshua.
Moses changed the name of Hosea son of Nun to Joshua. The midrash say that Moses changed his name to make it a prayer. The Hebrew name *Joshua* means "Adonai will help."

10. Moses, Aaron, and Hur had climbed to the top of the hill.
The Israelites prepared for the battle by fasting. Since then, it has now become customary for three people to lead the prayers before the Aaron Kodesh on fast days.   *Rashi*

11. As long as Moses held his hand outstretched, Israel won, but as soon as he let his hands down, the battle turned against Israel.
Hizkuni says that Moses would hold up one hand, and when it tired he would hold up the other hand. Eventually, both hands became tired.

The Israelites regarded this lowering of hands as a sign of defeat, so they retreated. When Moses raised his hands again, they were inspired and once again attacked and surged forward, defeating the Amalekites.

12. They remained outstretched until sunset.
This was no small skirmish. This was a battle for survival, which lasted all day. A defeat would have destroyed the Israelite nation forever.

16. He said, "Adonai has sworn that in every generation He will battle against Amalek."
As the Israelites left Egypt, the desert marauders attacked the stragglers. Adonai instructed the Israelites to wipe out the Amalekites at every opportunity.

Throughout the generations Amalek has earned the well-deserved hatred of the Jews. Hundreds of years later in Persia, Haman, a descendant of King Aga the Amalekite, tried to initiate a pogrom against the Jews.

Abarbanel laments that neither Joshua, King Saul, nor Mordecai and Esther were able to completely destroy Amalek's influence.

יִתְרוֹ *Yitro*

YITRO, FATHER-IN-LAW OF MOSES

18 Yitro, the sheikh of Midian and Moses' father-in-law, heard about the miracles that Adonai had performed for Moses and the Israelites when He brought them out of Egypt. **2** So Yitro brought Tzipporah, the wife of Moses, and her two sons, who had earlier been sent home. **3** The name of the first son was Gershom, because Moses had declared, "I was a foreigner [*ger*] there [*shom*] in a foreign land." **4** The name of the second son was Elazar, because "My father's *El* [Elohim] was my helper [*ezer*] and rescued me from Pharaoh's vengeance."

5 Yitro, accompanied by Moses' wife and sons, came to the wilderness, where Moses was camped, near the mountain of Elohim. **6** He sent word to Moses: "I, your father-in-law Yitro, with your wife and your two sons, am on my way to see you." **7** Moses went out to meet his father-in-law and greeted him by bowing and hugging him. They asked about each other's health and went into a tent to talk.

---

1. The miracles that Adonai had performed for Moses.
Moses escaped Pharaoh's soldiers, who were searching for him. Pharaoh listened to Moses and did not harm him. In fact, Moses was respected by Pharaoh and his advisers. In addition Adonai had performed miracles through Moses.

2. So Yitro brought Tzipporah, the wife of Moses, and her two sons, who had earlier been sent home.
The midrash tells us that when Adonai ordered Moses to return to Egypt, he took his wife, Tzipporah, and her two sons, Gershom and Elazar, with her. When Aaron saw them he said, "Our wives and our children here in Egypt are in trouble. Send them back." So Moses took Aaron's advice and sent them home to his father-in-law, Yitro. Now Yitro brought the family back to Moses.

3. The name of the first son was Gershom.
The Hebrew word *ger* means "stranger" and the word *sham* means "there." Moses named his son Gershom because he was a stranger in a foreign land. Moses was always aware that his eventual destination and that of the Israelites was Canaan.

4. The name of the second son was Elazar.
This is the only mention of Elazar, the second son of Moses.

The name Elazar "The El means (Elohim) God of my ancestors was my help."

5. Where Moses was camped, near the mountain of Elohim.
Where he usually camped when he had been a shepherd for Yitro's flocks.

5. Yitro, accompanied by Moses' wife and sons, came to the wilderness, where Moses was camped, near the mountain of Elohim.
The text teaches respect (*derech eretz*). Notice the progression. First came Yitro, then the wife of Moses, and then the children of Moses.
The mountain of Elohim was Mount Sinai, where Moses received the Ten Commandments.

6. He sent word to Moses.
Yitro sent a messenger to Moses. *Rashbam*

7. Moses went out to meet his father-in-law and greeted him by bowing and hugging him.
This was a sign of respect. Yitro had welcomed Moses into his home and Moses genuinely liked him. Moses was aware that Yitro was an *ohev Yisrael*, a person who liked the Israelites. Moses and the Israelite leaders shared a sacrificial meal with Yitro, their friend and admirer.

8 Moses told his father-in-law everything that Adonai had done to Pharaoh in Egypt to free Israel, as well as all the problems they had experienced, and how Adonai had saved them from their troubles.
9 Yitro was happy for all the good things Adonai had done for Israel by rescuing them from Egypt. **10** Yitro said, "Blessed be Adonai, who rescued you from the power of Egypt and from Pharaoh. **11** Now I know that Adonai is greater than any other deity. Despite all their schemes, He defeated them." **12** Yitro brought sacrifices to Adonai. Aaron and the leaders of Israel shared the sacrificial meal with Moses' father-in-law in the presence of Adonai.

Moses the Judge
2nd Aliyah

13 The next day, as usual, Moses went out to judge the people. They surrounded Moses from morning to evening.
14 When Moses' father-in-law saw that Moses was doing this for the people all by himself, he said, "Why are you the only judge? Why do you sit all by yourself while people crowd around you from morning until evening?"
15 Moses replied to his father-in-law, "The people come to me and ask Adonai's advice. **16** Whenever they have a dispute, they come to me, and I settle the problems between them, and I also teach them Elohim's rules and laws."
17 Moses' father-in-law said to him, "What you are doing is not right. **18** The responsibility will exhaust you and will harm the nation. You are going to wear yourself out. You cannot do it all alone.
19 Now listen to me. Let me give you some advice, and may Elohim be with you. You must continue to be the representative who brings the people's problems to Elohim. **20** Explain the rules and laws to the people. Show them the right path to take, and the rules to follow.
21 But most important, find among the people capable, honest men who hate injustice and fear Adonai.
Appoint them as leaders of thousands, leaders of hundreds, leaders of fifties, and leaders of tens.

---

8. Moses told his father-in-law everything that Adonai had done to Pharaoh in Egypt to free Israel.
At first Yitro had heard only about the plagues and the death of the first-born and was horrified. However, when Moses told him about the complete sequence of events, Yitro realized that Adonai had acted justly.

Gersonides

10. Yitro said, "Blessed be Adonai, who rescued you from the power of Egypt and from Pharaoh."
It was a miracle that none of the Egyptian guards or Pharaoh himself did not kill you, because of the catastrophes you brought to the land of Egypt.

11. Now I know that Adonai is greater than any other deity. Despite all their schemes, He defeated them.
Yitro was the priest of the Midianite tribe called Kenite. After Moses tells him how the Israelites escaped from Egypt, Yitro in admiration states that Adonai is the greatest of all gods. The midrash says that Yitro became a true believer and gave up idol worship. He also celebrated his conversion by bringing sacrifices to Adonai.

15. Moses replied to his father-in-law, "The people come to me and ask Adonai's advice."
Moses was occupied by three different tasks.
   1. Public business (v.15); 2. Disputes between leaders (v.16); 3. Instructing the Israelites about Elohim's rules and laws (v.16).

22 Let them regularly judge the people. Have them bring you all the important cases, but let them judge the minor cases by themselves. In this way, they will share the burden, and make things easier for you. **23** If you follow this advice, and Elohim agrees, then you will be able to survive. The entire nation will be able to reach their goal in peace."

Moses Takes Yitro's Advice *3rd Aliyah*

24 Moses took his father-in-law's advice and followed all of his suggestions. **25** Moses picked capable people from all the tribes of Israel, and he appointed them as chiefs over the people, leaders of thousands, leaders of hundreds, leaders of fifties, and leaders of tens.
26 They regularly dispensed justice, bringing the difficult cases to Moses, and settling the simple cases by themselves.
27 After a while Moses let his father-in-law return to his homeland in Midian.

A Kingdom of Priests *4th Aliyah*

19 Exactly three months after the Israelites left Egypt, on the first day of the month (Sivan), they arrived in the wilderness of Sinai. **2** They left Rephidim and entered the wilderness of Sinai, camping in the wilderness, at the base of the mountain. **3** Moses went up to meet Adonai. Adonai called to him from the mountain and said, "This is what you must say to the family of Jacob, the Israelites: **4** 'You witnessed what I did in Egypt, and how I carried you on wings of eagles and brought you to Me. **5** Now, if you will obey Me and keep My covenant, you shall be My special treasure among all the nations of the world. **6** You will be a kingdom of priests and a holy nation to Me.' These are the exact words that you must repeat to the Israelites."

---

23. If you follow this advice, and Elohim agrees, then you will be able to survive. The entire nation will be able to reach their goal in peace.
The decision-making process will be streamlined. Each of the districts in the camp will have its own court and judges. The judges will in most cases be able to render quick decisions, thereby allowing the litigants to return to their families in peace.

26. They regularly dispensed justice, bringing the difficult cases to Moses, and settling the simple cases by themselves.
Yitro urged Moses to decentralize the decision-making process. In this way people would not have to wait in line for hours and perhaps days for a simple judgment.
In modern times Yitro's advice would probably have been given by an MBA. *Shenash*

2. They left Rephidim and entered the wilderness of Sinai, camping in the wilderness, at the base of the mountain.
The specific purpose of the journey was to reach Mount Sinai, where they would receive the Torah.

The midrash says that Adonai gave the Israelites the Torah on Saturday.
The prayer *Yismach Moshe* (Moses was overjoyed) is recited on the Sabbath because the Torah was given to Moses, who immediately transmitted it to the Israelites, on the Sabbath.

4. You witnessed what I did in Egypt, and how I carried you on wings of eagles and brought you to Me.
I carried you high above the earth, to separate you from the idol worshippers so that you could be Mine.
 Sforno

5. Now if you will obey Me and keep My covenant, you shall be My special treasure.
The covenant lays down the rules for all Israelites. These rules are the vehicle for both the community and individuals to enter into a convenantal relationship with Adonai.
Adonai's commandments from Mount Sinai oblige each person to obey His rules and the laws. When people break the rules, the action rejects Adonai and endangers the fabric of the nation.

Israel at Sinai
5th Aliyah

7 Moses came down the mountain and assembled the leaders of the people and repeated to them everything Adonai had said to him.

8 In one loud voice, all the people answered and said, "Everything that Adonai has spoken, we will do." Moses reported the Israelites' reply to Adonai.

9 Adonai said to Moses, "I will return to you in a thick cloud, so that all the people can hear when I speak to you. Then they will completely trust you forever."

Then Moses repeated the people's response to Adonai. **10** Adonai said to Moses, "Go to the people, and sanctify them today and tomorrow. Tell them to clean their clothes. **11** Tell them to be ready for the third day, because on that day Adonai will come down upon Mount Sinai, as everyone will see. **12** Set a boundary line for the people, and warn them not to climb the mountain, or even come close. Anyone touching the mountain will die. **13** You will not have to touch him, for he will be stoned or shot by an arrow. Neither man nor beast will be allowed to live. Only when a long blast is sounded on the shofar will they be allowed to climb the mountain." **14** Moses went down to the people from the mountain.

He sanctified them, and they purified themselves and their clothing. **15** Moses said to the people, "Prepare yourselves for three days. Do not go near a woman."

16 On the third day, there was thunder and lightning in the morning, and a heavy cloud covered the mountain, and there was a loud shofar blast. All the Israelites trembled. **17** Moses led the people from the camp toward the Divine Presence. They stood frozen at the foot of the mountain.

18 Now Mount Sinai was covered in smoke because of the Presence that had come down on it. Adonai was in the fire, and smoke rose up like the smoke from a furnace. The whole mountain quaked violently.

19 Then there was a loud shofar blast. Moses spoke, and Elohim answered.

The Ten Commandments
6th Aliyah

20 Then Adonai came down to the top of Mount Sinai, and He called Moses to climb up to the peak. Moses climbed up.

---

7. Moses came down the mountain and assembled the leaders of the people and repeated to them everything Adonai had said to him.
Moses reported to the leaders, and they reported to the people.

Nachmanides points out that Moses did not tell them that they must accept the Torah. He left it to them to decide whether or not they wished to take it upon themselves. Now they had a choice and they unanimously accepted the mission of Adonai and became a nation of priests and a holy nation to Adonai.

This was democracy in action.

8. In one loud voice, all the people answered and said, "Everything that Adonai has spoken we will do."
They all answered together as if they were one.

16. There was a loud shofar blast.
The shofar in ancient days was used for numerous purposes. It was used as a signal to alert the Israelites that they were being invaded. In the military, it was used to signal the movements of soldiers. In religious life the shofar was used in public and political events. It was also used to inaugurate a king. On Rosh Hashanah and Yom Kippur it is used during prayer services. On Mount Sinai, it was used to announce that the Israelites were now a free people.

21 Adonai said to Moses, "Go back and warn the people not to cross the boundary line to see the Divine, because they will die.
22 Even the priests, who usually come near Adonai, must sanctify themselves, or else Adonai will destroy them."
23 Moses protested to Adonai "The people cannot climb Mount Sinai, because You have already warned them to set a boundary line around the mountain and declare it holy." **24** So Adonai said to him, "Go down and return with Aaron. However, the priests and the other people must not cross the boundary line to go up to Adonai. If they do, He will punish them." **25** Moses went down to the people and told them what Adonai had said.

20
Elohim gave the Israelites these Ten Commandments:
The First Commandment
2 I am Adonai, who brought you out of Egypt, from the land of slavery.

---

22. Even the priests, who usually come near Adonai, must sanctify themselves.
These were the elders, all of whom were first-borns. The commentator Hizkuni says that "priests" had not yet been ordained.

24. Go down.
Go down and warn them again. Adonai wanted to be absolutely certain that nothing would interfere with the giving of the Ten Commandments.

25. Moses went down to the people and told them what Adonai had said.
Moses warned them that if they disobeyed, the punishment (v. 21) would be death.

1. Elohim gave the Israelites these Ten Commandments.
The midrash tells us that Adonai first offered the Torah to other nations around the world, but they all refused it. Adonai asked the first nation, "Will you accept and obey the laws and rules of the Torah?" "What does it say?" they asked. "It says, 'You shall not kill,'" answered Adonai. "Oh no!" they replied angrily. "We live by war and by killing, and we cannot accept your Torah."

Then Adonai approached another nation and offered them the Torah. They too asked, "What does this Torah of yours say?" "It says, 'Honor your father and your mother.'" "Definitely not," replied the people, "we throw out and reject our parents when they become poor, old, and useless."

Adonai continued asking all the nations of the world, and they all found something in the Torah that they did not like.

Lastly, Adonai approached Israel, and asked them. They replied without hesitation and in one loud voice, "All that Adonai has spoken we will do."

1. Elohim gave the Israelites these Ten Commandments.
Adonai gave us the commandments, but each one of us can decide whether or not to obey them. Adonai created all humans with free will. Each person has the ability to obey or disobey. The power whether or not to be righteous is in the minds of the individual.

1. Elohim gave the Israelites these Ten Commandments.
The midrash says that when Adonai gave the Ten Commandments to Israel, the whole world was quiet. No birds sang or flew. No lion roared, no angels flew, the seas were calm and no creature spoke, and Adonai said, "I am Adonai." The divine voice spoke in all languages, so that everyone in the world could understand the commandments.

2. I am Adonai, who brought you out of Egypt.
This is mitzvah number 25.

It is a mitzvah to believe in Adonai. This mitzvah is the fundamental belief in Judaism.

The Second Commandment

3 You shall not have any other gods except Me. **4** Do not make any carved statues or pictures of anything in the heavens above, or on the earth below, or in the water below. **5** Do not bow down to such idols or pray to them. I, Adonai, am jealous, and I demand total loyalty. As for My enemies, I will remember the sins of the fathers up to the third and fourth generations. **6** But for those who love Me and keep My commandments, I will show them kindness for thousands of generations.

The Third Commandment

7 Do not misuse the name of Adonai. He will not allow anyone who misuses His name to go unpunished.

The Fourth Commandment

8 Remember to observe the Sabbath and keep it holy. **9** You shall do all your regular work during the six days of the week. **10** But the seventh day is the Sabbath to Adonai, your Lord. Do not do any kind of work. This includes you, your son, your daughter, your slave, your maid, your animal, and the strangers in your country. **11** It was during the six weekdays that Adonai created the cosmos, which includes planet earth, the sea, and everything that is in them, but He rested on the Sabbath. Therefore Adonai blessed the Sabbath and made it holy.

---

3. You shall not have any other gods except Me.
The Israelites were continually warned in the Torah against *avodah zara*, the worship of other gods. The second commandment clearly prohibits the Israelites from making any visible representation of Adonai. Elimination of *avodah zara* from among the Israelites was the most formidable task that confronted Moses. The Israelites frequently lapsed into *avodah zara* during the era of the Judges and Kings. Judaism was also under the threat of extinction under the influence of the Greeks and Romans. A whole volume of the Talmud is devoted to the problem of *avodah zara*.

4. Do not make any carved statues or pictures of anything in the heavens above, or on the earth below, or in the water below.
Do not even make statues to use in honoring and worshipping Me.

Synagogues, in contrast to other places of worship, contain no statues. The complete attention of the worshippers must be on the *Aron Kodesh* and the Torah. *Bekor Shor*

4. Do not make any carved statues or pictures of anything in the heavens above.
The ancients worshipped the stars and all the other heavenly bodies. They believed that the movements of the planets and stars could predict events in their lives. The Babylonians, who were skilled astronomers, believed in astrology. Maimonides, an enemy of astrology, declared, "Astrology is a disease, not a science; only fools lend value to it."

6. But for those who love Me and keep My commandments, I will show them kindness for thousands of generations.
Adonai's kindness is called *middat ha-rach-amim*. Adonai created the world with the qualities of justice and kindness. Our civilization would be completely destroyed without these two elements. Humans can always appeal to the *middat ha-rachamim* of Adonai, no matter how undeserving they may be. His kindness motivates His justice.

10. This includes you, your son, your daughter.
The commentators state that the Sabbath was given not only to the adults, but also to the children. They too must be taught to observe the Sabbath as a day of rest.

The Fifth Commandment

12 Honor your father and your mother. If you do, you will live long on the land that Adonai is giving you.

The Sixth Commandment

13 You must not murder.

The Seventh Commandment

You must not commit adultery.

The Eighth Commandment

You must not steal.

The Ninth Commandment

You must not act as a false witness against your neighbor.

The Tenth Commandment

14 You must not be jealous of your neighbor's wealth. You must not be jealous of your neighbor's wife, his slave, his maid, his ox, his donkey, or anything belonging to your neighbor.

---

12. Honor your father and your mother.
This is the Fifth Commandment and mitzvah number 33. To honor means to provide your parents with food, clothing, and shelter. Keep in touch and, if need be, do errands and see that they have adequate medical advice and care.

Abarbanel provides two reasons for honoring our parents. They have given us an education, talents, and capacities (DNA) which enhance our lives. Second, by honoring our parents we set an example for our children to honor us.

12. Honor your father and your mother.
The first five commandments reflect on the relationship between a person and Adonai.

The last five commandments deal with the relationship between people.

The fifth commandment, "honor your father and your mother," is the link between these groups of mitzvot. When one honors one's parents, the person is also honoring Adonai.

12. Honor your father and your mother. If you do, you will live long on the land that Adonai is giving you.
The sages say that the phrase "you will live long" refers to your life in this world.

13. You must not murder. You must not commit adultery. You must not steal.
I, the Creator of the world, have given humanity a perfect world. Do not in word or deed maliciously debase My world. Do not spill human innocent blood. Do not vandalize parenthood. Do not steal what My creatures have earned by the sweat of their brows and the intelligence of their minds. To respect Me, respect My creations.

13. The eighth commandment: You must not steal.
This is mitzvah number 22.

Theft is a very serious sin. It makes no difference if someone steals something from a store, money from a wallet, a thesis from the Web, an answer on a test, or a business plan. It is a sin to steal. There is another type of stealing called *genevat da'at*, meaning intellectual stealing. *Genevat da'at* can involve stealing patent information, breaking into a business website for customer or financial information, or stealing musical files for your computer.

Abarbanel says that in case of a theft, the accused must make restitution of double the value. Aside from the punishment, the thief must suffer the humiliation of being caught and public exposure.

14. You must not be jealous of your neighbor's wealth.
When you feel envious of your neighbors' wealth or possessions, just remember that if you accept their good fortune, you must also accept their miseries.

The Israelites Are Awed
7th Aliyah

15 When the Israelites heard the sounds, and saw the flames, and heard the blast of the shofar, and saw the mountain smoking, they trembled with fear and kept their distance. **16** They said to Moses, "You teach us what Adonai said, and we will listen and do. But don't let Adonai speak with us any more, for if He does we will die." **17** Moses assured the people, "Have no fear. Elohim only came to show you His power. From now on you will obey Him and you will not sin."

18 The people kept far away while Moses entered the cloud where Elohim was.

I Will Bless You
Maftir

19 Adonai said to Moses: "This is what you must tell the Israelites: You were witnesses that I spoke to you from heaven. **20** Remember, do not make a statue that represents Me. Do not make silver or gold statues for yourselves. **21** Make a simple earthen altar for Me. On it you can sacrifice your burnt offerings and your peace offerings, your sheep and your cattle. Wherever you build a sanctuary, I will come and bless you. **22** When you build a stone altar for Me, do not build it out of stone that has been cut by metal. If you use metal on your altar, it will not be holy. **23** Do not build My altar with steps, for someone might look up and see your nakedness."

---

16. You teach us what Adonai said, and we will listen and do.
The commandments given to Israel at Mount Sinai were like instructions given to farmers:

If the instructions are followed, the crops will grow in abundance. If not, there will be very little to harvest.

16. You teach us what Adonai said, and we will listen and do.
No individual is considered free as long as he is under the influence of a foreign yoke or ideology. People are free only when they live in a society not subject to foreign dictates. The Israelites were not given the Torah and commandments until they physically escaped the yoke of servitude, and were freed from Egyptian influence.

Now the slaves followed the freedom trail to Sinai, where they received a physical and spiritual awakening. *Shenash*

20. Remember, do not make a statue that represents Me. Do not make silver or gold statues for yourselves.
The Torah was aware that the Israelites had lived for more than two hundred years in Egypt, an idol-worshipping country. Idol worship was an ingrained habit. They knew and saw nothing else. Now, they were asked to worship an invisible deity which demanded that they conform to a set of ethical and moral standards.

22. When you build a stone altar for Me, do not build it out of stone that has been cut by metal.
This is mitzvah number 40.

Iron is used to make military implements, such as swords and spears, which kill and destroy. Any stone that has been touched by a metal tool must be replaced. Nachmanides points out that tools of other metals such as silver may be used. The midrash suggests the use of the *shamir*, a worm that is reputed to bite through stone as a diamond does, but it became extinct after the destruction of the Temple.

22. When you build a stone altar for Me, do not build it out of stone that has been cut by metal.
If the altar is made of stone, that stone must not be trimmed by a metal chisel. The sages offer several explanations for this precept:

1. The altar is for forgiving, and iron is for punishing. 2. The altar prolongs life, but iron cuts it short. 3. Iron desecrates stone: meaning that things used for the service of Adonai should be used only in their natural state, before they have been changed in any way by man.

מִשְׁפָּטִים *Mishpatim*

THESE ARE THE LAWS

21 These are the laws that the Israelites must obey. **2** If you buy a Hebrew slave, he shall serve for six years, but in the seventh year he is to be set free without paying for his freedom. **3** If he was unmarried when he entered slavery, he shall leave by himself. However, if he was a married man, his wife must leave with him.

4 But if his master gives him a wife, and she gives birth to sons or daughters, the woman and her children shall remain her master's property. The slave must leave by himself. **5** If the slave on his own says, "I like my master, and my wife and my children; I do not wish to go free," **6** then his master must bring him to court, and stand the slave next to a door or doorpost, and then his master must pierce his earlobe with an awl. Then the slave shall serve his master forever.

7 If a man sells his daughter as a maidservant, she shall not be released the same way as the male servants. **8** If she displeases her master, then he should allow her to be redeemed. Since he is considered to have broken the agreement with her, he does not have the right to sell her to anyone else.

9 If the master chose her as a bride for his son, she must be treated exactly the same as any free girl.

---

1. These are the laws that the Israelites must obey.
The revelation at Sinai, like the Declaration of Independence, established the foundation of the law. The Torah portrays the establishment of the law as the true beginning of Israelite history. Now Israel can function as a state, with a leader, a legal system, and rules regarding war, commerce, and property. All that is missing is land.

2. If you buy a Hebrew slave, he shall serve for six years, but in the seventh year he is to be set free without paying for his freedom.
Slavery, until Lincoln freed the slaves, was a common practice in the United States. In some Eastern countries slavery is still practiced. Slavery was a legitimate institution throughout the ancient world. At the same time, the Israelite codes had numerous clauses spelling out the rights of slaves.

2. If you buy a Hebrew slave, he shall serve for six years, but in the seventh year he is to be set free without paying for his freedom.
Israelites rested on the seventh day because Adonai created His world in six days and rested on the seventh day, the Sabbath. Hebrew slaves shall serve their master for six years, and on the seventh year they shall rest from their slavery to go free.

Tzeena Urenah

5–6. If the slave on his own says, "I like my master, and my wife and my children; I do not wish to go free," then his master must bring him to court, and stand the slave next to a door or doorpost, and then his master must pierce his earlobe with an awl. Then the slave shall serve his master forever.
If the slave rejects his freedom because of his love for his wife and his children, then he must bring himself before a court. He must with his own words convince the judges that he was not coerced or brainwashed.

Then, the slave is brought to a doorpost, which symbolically stands for freedom. The slave now has a choice to step out and go free, or to step in and remain a slave. If he chooses the latter, then his earlobe is pierced, and he must remain a slave until the Jubilee Year. At that time he again is given the opportunity to go free.

10 Also, if the master marries another wife, he must not reduce her allowance or clothing or shelter rights. **11** If he fails to provide these three things to the slave girl, then she shall be free without any payment.

12 If one person deliberately strikes another and the victim dies, the murderer must be put to death.

13 If he did not deliberately plan to kill his victim, but it happened accidentally, then I will provide a refuge where the killer can find safety **14** If a person intentionally plots to kill his neighbor, then you must drag him even from My altar to put him to death.

15 Anyone who deliberately harms his father or his mother must be put to death.

16 If someone kidnaps and sells another person, and is found with the victim, then the kidnapper shall be put to death.

17 Whoever insults his father or mother must be put to death.

18 When two people fight, and one hits the other with a stone or with his fist, and the victim does not die but is bedridden, **19** and later gets up and can walk under his own power, then the one who struck him must not be punished. But he must pay for the victim's loss of earning power, and must also pay for his medical expenses.

Injuries and Penalties
2nd Aliyah

20 If a man hits his male or female slave with a stick, and the slave dies, the death must be avenged.

21 However, if the slave lives for a day or two, then his death shall not be avenged, because he is his master's property.

22 When two men fight and accidentally harm a pregnant woman and cause her to miscarry, but there is no fatal injury to the woman, then the guilty party must pay a monetary penalty. The woman's husband must sue, and the amount will be determined by the court.

23 However, if the woman is fatally injured, then he must pay full compensation for her life.

24 Compensation must be paid for the loss of an eye, a tooth, a hand, or a foot.

---

14. You must drag him even from My altar to put him to death.
The Talmud says if the death was a deliberate deed, then the killer, even if he is a priest at the altar, is to be punished.

15. Anyone who deliberately harms his father or his mother must be put to death.
The Ramban said that anyone who curses his or her parents commits a greater sin than striking them. The Gaon from Vilna said that physical abuse will heal and disappear, but verbal abuse and insults remain forever.

18. When two people fight, and one hits the other with a stone or his fist, and the victim does not die but is bedridden.
It is a mitzvah for the Beth Din to penalize the person who injures his opponent.

This is mitzvah number 49.
The injured individual may be entitled to damages and payment of medical expenses as well as payment for loss of earnings.

24. Compensation must be paid for the loss of an eye, a tooth, a hand, or a foot.
The reason each injury is mentioned is that the value of the compensation for each is different. Losing a tooth is entirely different from losing a hand or a foot. In addition, the compensation also depends on the job or occupation of the individual. For a woodcutter, it is catastrophic to lose an arm, while losing a tooth is negligible. There are numerous variations and scenarios, and a compensation trial can be very difficult. The eye, tooth, hand, and foot are specifically mentioned because they are most commonly damaged.

25 Compensation must also be paid for a burn, a wound, or a bruise.

26 If a person strikes his male or female slave in the eye and blinds it, he shall set the slave free in compensation for the loss of his eye.

27 And if he knocks out the tooth of his male or female slave, he must set the slave free in payment for the tooth.

28 If an ox injures a man or woman, and the victim dies, the ox must be stoned to death, and its flesh must not be eaten. The owner of the ox shall not be punished.

29 However, if the ox had a history of hurting people, and the owner was warned and failed to take precautions, and it kills a person, then the ox must be stoned, and its owner, too, must be put to death.

30 As a redemption for his life, an atonement fine can be imposed, and he must pay a redemption for the lost life.

31 The same law also applies if the ox injures a young boy or a young girl.

32 But if the ox injures a male or female slave, its owner must give thirty silver coins to the slave's master, and the bull must be stoned.

33 If a person digs a hole in the ground, or opens a hole, and does not cover it, and an ox or a donkey falls into it,

34 the person responsible for the hole must pay the full value of the animal to its owner, and the dead animal becomes his property.

35 If a person's ox injures the ox of another person, and it dies, they must sell the live ox and share the money received for it. They shall also share the dead animal.

36 But if the ox was known to injure people on previous occasions, and its owner did not control it, he must pay the full price for the dead ox. The dead animal still remains the property of its owner.

37 If a person steals an ox or a sheep and then kills it and sells it, he must be fined five oxen for each stolen ox, and four sheep for each sheep.

---

28. If an ox injures a man or a woman, and the victim dies, the ox must be stoned to death, and its flesh must not be eaten.
It makes no difference if it is a large animal, like an ox, or a small animal such as a dog. The text just posits a likely situation. The animal can cause injuries by pushing, biting, crushing, or kicking.

The same rules can apply to any loose pet.

The ox must not be eaten because it was not ritually slaughtered.

29. Its owner, too, must be put to death.
If the ox has injured people three times, and the owner has not taken steps to prevent a reoccurrence, then the owner is guilty and should be put to death. In some instances, an atonement fine can be imposed for the lost life.

37. If a person steals an ox or a sheep and then kills it and sells it, he must be fined five oxen for each stolen ox, and four sheep for each sheep.
Why the disparity between stealing an ox and a sheep?

Ibn Ezra says that the penalty for stealing an ox is heavier than for stealing other animals, because the thief must be an expert since an ox is very difficult to conceal.

The ox contributes more to the man than the sheep does. The sheep provides four benefits: milk, cheese, wool, and lambs. The ox provides plowing and threshing and is useful in many other capacities so the thief most pay five times the value of the theat.

On the other hand, a sheep does not work, so the thief is fined only four times the value of the theft.

22

1 If a thief is caught in the act of breaking in, and is struck and killed by the owner, it is not considered an act of murder. **2** However, if it is broad daylight when the thief breaks in and is struck and killed, the one who killed the thief is a murderer. Every thief must make full restitution. If he does not have the means, he must be sold into servitude to pay for what he has stolen. **3** If the stolen animal is found in his possession, and it is an ox, a donkey, or a sheep, he must repay double.

Crimes and Damages
3rd Aliyah

4 If a person lets his animal loose so that it grazes in someone else's field, he must pay for the damages to the field or vineyard. **5** If fire breaks out and spreads to weeds, so that it burns stacks of grain, then the one who started the fire must pay for the damages. **6** When a person entrusts money or goods to someone for safe-keeping, and they are stolen from the house of that person, then if the thief is caught, the thief must repay double the amount. **7** But if the thief is not found, the owner of the house shall be brought to court and he must swear that he did not steal the property given into his care.

---

1. If a thief is caught in the act of breaking in, and is struck and killed by the owner, it is not considered an act of murder.
It is not considered an act of murder to kill the thief if he breaks in at night. He has forfeited the right to be protected by the courts and society by his own intentions.

3. If the stolen animal is found in his possession, and it is an ox, a donkey, or a sheep, he must repay double.
The rule applies to all stolen animals. The animals must be returned alive, and the thief is fined double the value of the stolen animals.

4. If a person lets his animal loose so it grazes in someone else's field, he must pay for the damages to the field or vineyard.
It is the responsibility of the owner of an ox, or other animals, to restrict their movements to his own property. If his animals wander into his neighbor's fields, then he is responsible for any damages they may cause.

5. If fire breaks out and spreads to weeds, so that it burns stacks of grain, then the one who started the fire must pay for the damages.
This is mitzvah number 56.

When anyone starts a fire, it is his or her responsibility to ensure that the fire is contained. Should the fire spread because of negligence or some unforeseen problem such as heavy winds, then he or she is liable for the damages. The fire setter must reimburse the neighbors for the house, field, or any property destroyed by the fire.

7. But if the thief is not found, the owner of the house shall be brought to court and he must swear that he did not steal the property given into his care.
This is mitzvah number 57.

This is a case of a *shomer chinom*, an unpaid guard. The person who agrees to accept someone else's property for safekeeping without accepting payment for the service is obligated to make sure that the item is not stolen. Should the item be stolen or lost, then he must swear that the missing object is not in his possession and that he was not irresponsible in its safekeeping. However if the *shomer chinom* stole the article, he must repay double its value. Maimonides says that a person who accepts an item for safe-keeping is doing a mitzvah.

Now, the owner of the property is free to attend to his business or social affairs without worrying about his property. If anything happens to the property, the *shomer chinom* is not liable, because he has not benefited from the arrangement.

8 In every case in which an ox, a donkey, a sheep, a garment, or anything else is lost, and witnesses testify that it was seen, the claims of both parties must be brought to the court. The guilty person must pay double damages to the other.

9 If one person asks another to watch a donkey, an ox, a sheep, or any other animal, and it dies or is hurt or is stolen, without any eyewitnesses,

10 then the case between the two must be decided by taking an oath to Adonai. If the person watching the animal did not make use of the other's property, the owner must take his word, and the person watching the animal need not pay.

11 However, if it was stolen from the keeper, then he must repay the animal's owner.

12 But if the animal was killed by a wild beast and the keeper can prove it, he need not pay for the dead animal. **13** If a person borrows an animal from another, and it becomes injured or dies while the owner is not with the borrower, then the borrower must make full payment.

14 But if the owner was present with him, then the borrower need not make any payments. If the animal was hired, the loss is guaranteed by the rental price.

15 If a man sleeps with a virgin who is not engaged to anyone, he must pay a dowry and must marry her. **16** If her father refuses to let him marry her, then he must pay the father the usual dowry money for virgins.

17 Do not allow a witch to live.

18 Whoever has sexual relations with an animal must be put to death.

19 Whoever worships any god other than Adonai must be condemned to death.

---

8. The guilty person must pay double damages to the other.
If the stolen or lost article or animal has been positively identified as belonging to the claimant and has not been damaged, then the person who falsely claimed ownership must pay double.
(Shemot 22:3)

11. However, if it was stolen from the keeper, then he must repay the animal's owner.
If a guard (Shemot 10) was not paid to watch the animal, then he simply swears that he did not steal it, and he is innocent. He was a *shomer chinun* and he is not liable.

12. But if the animal was killed by a wild beast and the keeper can prove it, he need not pay for the dead animal.
Let him bring witnesses to prove that the loss of the animal was not due to his negligence.

13. If a person borrows an animal from another, and it becomes injured or dies while the owner is not with the borrower, then the borrower must make full payment.
The borrower is completely responsible for the condition of the animal. *Rashi*

15. If a man sleeps with a virgin who is not engaged to anyone, he must pay a dowry and he must marry her.
This is mitzvah number 61.

A man who seduces a virgin who willingly consents has to marry his victim and pay an increased *mohar* (dowry). He also forfeits the right to divorce her (Dev. 23:28)

17. Do not allow a witch to live.
This is prohibitive mitzvah number 62.

The Torah tells us that we are ordered to execute witches and sorcerers who mislead people to believe that there are "powers" other than Adonai.

Gersonides says that this prohibition applies to black magic and not to tricks done with cards, mirrors, or sleight of hand.

20 Do not abuse a foreigner or oppress him, for you must remember that you were foreigners in Egypt.
21 Do not abuse a widow or an orphan. **22** If you abuse them, and they cry to Me for help, I will hear their cry.
23 And then I will hear and I will punish you, so that your wives are widowed, and your children are orphaned. **24** When you lend money to the poor among you, do not threaten him for repayment. And do not take interest from him.
25 If you accept your neighbor's garment as security for a loan, you must return it to him before the sun goes down.
26 Remember, this is his only warm covering for his body.
How can he sleep without his covering? If he cries out to Me, I will listen, for I am merciful.

---

20. Do not abuse a foreigner or oppress him, for you must remember that you were foreigners in Egypt.
Remember, study your history. At one time your ancestors were strangers (*gerim*) in the land of Egypt, and they are now in many far-flung lands. You know the bitterness of a *ger* living in a foreign country. Just as you wished that the Egyptians, Russians, Arabs, and Europeans had not embittered and humiliated and terminated the lives of your ancestors when you lived among them, do not do the same to them. Jews, because of their long-term history of persecution in Europe, and Middle Eastern countries, must be aware of and alert to respect human rights.

Rabbi Samson Raphael Hirsch says that respecting human rights is a special test of living ethically as a Jew.

20. Do not abuse a foreigner or oppress him, for you must remember that you were foreigners in Egypt.
A *ger* is a foreigner who lives in the midst of another community where he is accepted and enjoys certain rights.

Abraham was a *ger* in Hebron, as was Moses in Midian. The Israelites were *gerim* in Egypt. When the Israelites settled in Canaan, they considered themselves the legitimate owners of the land, and the former owners became the *gerim*.

The *gerim* were free men but did not possess the full civil rights of Israelites. All the properties belonged to the Israelites, and the *gerim* hired out their services.

They shared in tithing every third year and the produce of the tithes in Sabbatical years. The cities of refuge were open to them. In legal actions they were entitled to the same justice as were the Israelites. The *gerim* had to observe the Sabbath and fast on Yom Kippur. They could offer sacrifices and take part in religious festivals. If they were circumcised, they could also celebrate Passover with the Israelites. Many of the *gerim* were absorbed into the Israelite population. They paved the way for the "proselytes."

21. Do not abuse a widow or an orphan.
Mitzvah 65 warns us to be especially considerate of the widow and orphan. The widow and orphan were particularily vulnerable and too weak to defend themselves against injustice.

24. When you lend money to the poor among you, do not threaten him for repayment. And do not take interest from him.
Mitzvah 67 cautions us not to pressure a borrower to repay his loan. This is especially true if you know that the indebted is in financial trouble. It is important for humans to feel kindness and compassion for each other.

It is a mitzvah (number 66) to ease the burden of a person in need by lending him money. Our sages say that lending money is a greater mitzvah than giving it as a gift. An individual who accepts charity feels a sense of shame. Accepting a loan, however, bolsters the dignity of the borrower and may help him start a new business or pay off some long overdue debts.

Authority and Justice
4th Aliyah

27 You must not curse the judge. You must not curse a leader of your people. **28** You must bring your offerings of newly ripened produce and your agricultural offerings on time. You shall redeem the first-born of your sons. **29** You must also redeem your first-born ox and sheep. It must remain with its mother for seven days, but on the eighth day you must give it to Me. **30** You are My holy people. You must not eat the flesh of a torn animal killed in the field by a wild beast. Let the dogs eat it.

You must not listen to false rumors.

23 You must not cooperate with a wicked person and become a false witness. **2** You must not join a mob to do evil. You must not lie in court to deny justice. A court case must be decided by a majority.
3 Do not slant your testimony to favor the poor man in his lawsuit.
4 If you come across your enemy's ox or donkey that has wandered away, you must bring it back to him. **5.** If you see an overloaded donkey that belongs to someone who hates you, you may not want to help him unload it, but nevertheless you must do so.

Keep Away from Evil
5th Aliyah

6 You are not permitted to treat someone unfairly in a lawsuit simply because he is poor.

---

28. You must bring your offerings of newly ripened produce and your agricultural products on time.
This is mitzvah number 72.

The Torah insists that the offering be brought in the proper order and on time. The order includes some of the following:

1. *Bikkurim* – The first fruits to ripen are brought to the Temple for a *kohen*.

2. *Terumah (gedolah)* – 1½–2½ percent of the total harvest is presented to a *kohen*.

3. *Ma'aser rishon* – First tithe; ten percent of the harvest is given to the Levites.

Terumat ma'aser – The Levitical recipient tithes his *ma'aser rishon* and gives this share to a *kohen*.

4. *Ma'aser sheni* – Second tithe – one tenth of what remains of the harvest after all the above deductions. This *ma'aser sheni* was brought to Jerusalem, where the owner was to eat it.

30. You must not eat the flesh of a torn animal killed in the field by a wild beast.
Animals or birds, kosher or nonkosher, that have been killed by another animal are forbidden to be eaten. The flesh of even a kosher animal that was killed in the field and was not slaughtered by a *shochet* (ritual slaughterer) is forbidden food.

Under Jewish law such an animal was *terefah* (unclean) or unfit for consumption.

3. Do not slant your testimony to favor the poor man in his lawsuit.
The Torah provides a structure for all elements of society. The legal code sets the basic rights and protections for all inhabitants of the land. Although the Torah acknowledges the practice of slavery, it emphasizes the rights of slaves after their servitude and mandates the release of slaves every seven years. The Torah also imposes the same responsibilities upon rich and poor, the powerful and the weak, demanding that the weakest members of society receive the same justice as the strong. Biblical law requires that justice be carried out fairly and impartially.

4. If you come across your enemy's ox or donkey that has wandered away, you must bring it back to him.
Even though your neighbor may have wronged you, and you may dislike him, you must do what is right for him and for his animals in spite of your feelings.

7 Keep far away from accusing anyone falsely.

Do not kill a person who is innocent or one who has been found innocent by a court. But take care not to allow a guilty person to escape punishment.

8 You shall not accept bribes. Bribery blinds your fairness and destroys the words of an honest person. **9** You shall not oppress a foreigner. You know how it feels to be a foreigner, for you were foreigners in the land of Egypt.

10 Plant your land for six years and harvest its crops. **11** But during the seventh year, let the land rest. This will allow the poor among you to glean from your fields, and whatever is left over can be eaten by the wild animals. The same rule applies to your vineyard and your olive grove.

12 Work on the six weekdays, but you must stop and rest on the Sabbath. In this way your donkey and ox will be able to rest, and your servants and the foreigner will also be reinvigorated. **13** Be sure to obey all My instructions. Do not mention the name of any other god. Their names must never pass your lips.

14 Three times each year bring a sacrifice to Me. **15** Observe the Festival of Matzot (Passover). You must eat matzot for seven days, as I commanded you, during the set time in the month of Aviv, because this was the time when you left Egypt.

You must not come to me empty-handed without a sacrifice!

16 You must observe the Festival of Harvest (Shavuot) and bring Me the first fruits of what you have planted in the field. Also observe the Festival of Ingathering (Sukkot) at the end of the year, when you gather what you have grown from the field.

---

11. But during the seventh year, let the land rest.
Ecologically, the land will have time to rest and recover its power to produce new crops. Not only will the land rest, but the animals that plow and harvest will also rest. The farmer, his family, and workers or slaves will also enjoy a full year of rest.

12. Work on the six weekdays, but you must stop and rest on the Sabbath.
Judaism has always demanded a humane attitude toward animals. The attitude is highlighted in the biblical account of the creation of living creatures. "Elohim saw that it was good. And Elohim blessed them."

The Rabbis pointed to Elohim's kindness to animals as a model for man to follow. "Just as the Almighty is merciful to man, so be merciful to animals." Biblical consideration for animals was the basis for the following laws.

1. A passerby who comes across a fallen beast of burden must stop to help. (Shemot 23)
2. Animals must be permitted to search for food in fields or farms in a sabbatical year. (Shemot 23:11)
3. Beasts of burden must be permitted to rest on the Sabbath. (Shemot 23:12)
4. Animals of different species must not be harnessed together for the performance of labor. (Dev. 22:10)
5. Animals must be slaughtered by a *shochet* to minimize pain. (Dev. 14:21)

14. Three times each year bring a sacrifice to Me.
The three Pilgrimage Festivals were holidays of thanksgiving to Adonai for the successful harvests which the Israelites had in the spring (Passover), early summer (Shavuot), and fall (Sukkot).

16. You must observe the Festival of Harvest (Shavuot) and bring Me the first fruits of what you have planted in the field.
In the synagogue, besides the regular Shavuot service, the Book of Ruth is read. The reason is, that this beautiful story of faith and devotion took place during the harvest season. King David was descended from Ruth. It is said that he was born and died on Shavuot.

17 Three times each year, every man in Israel must appear before Adonai, Master of the universe!
18 Do not offer the blood of My Passover offering in the presence of matzot. Do not keep the fat of the festival sacrifice to remain overnight until morning.
19 Bring the best of your first fruits to the House of Adonai. You must not cook a goat in its mother's milk.

My Angel Will Protect You *6th Aliyah*

20 Be aware that I will send an angel to safeguard you on your journey and bring you to the land I have prepared for you.
21 Be respectful to the angel and listen to his advice.
Do not defy him, for he is My messenger. He will not forgive your disobedience.
22 But if you listen to him and do everything I say, then I will be an enemy to your enemies.
23 My angel will go before you and lead you to the lands of the Amorites, Hittites, Perizzites, Canaanites, Hivites, and Jebusites, and I will destroy them. **24** You must not bow down to their gods and worship them. You must not follow the evil customs of these nations. You must smash their idols and destroy their sacred pillars.
25 You must worship Adonai, and He will bless you with food and with drink. I will remove sickness from among you.

In the Land of Israel *7th Aliyah*

26 No woman in your land will suffer miscarriages or remain childless. I will give you long, healthy lives.
27 I will confuse the enemies who stand in your path, and they will be terrified of Me; I will make your enemies turn and run away in a panic.
28 I will send deadly hornets ahead of you to drive out the Hivites, Canaanites, and Hittites from your path. **29** I will not drive them out in just one year; otherwise the land will be deserted and the wild animals will become too numerous for you to control. **30** Little by little I will drive out the inhabitants and give you the opportunity to increase in numbers and fully occupy the land.

---

17. Three times each year, every man in Israel must appear before Adonai, Master of the universe!
Women were not obligated to appear because they could not be expected to leave their children for the journey.

19. You must not cook a goat in its mother's milk.
This phrase is mitzvah number 92.
   Mixing meat and dairy foods is strictly forbidden by Jewish religious law. The Torah says, "You shall not cook your goat in its mother's milk." This regulation was applied to all manner of meat and dairy products. It was also extended to utensils. Every kosher home has two sets of dishes, pots, and other food utensils, in order to make the distinction between meat and dairy. Observant Jews wait six hours after eating meat before eating dairy food.

25. You must worship Adonai, and He will bless you with food and with drink. I will remove sickness from among you.
This verse contains the assurance that if one recites a blessing before eating and drinking, he or she will be rewarded with abundant fare and good health.

28. I will send deadly hornets.
Adonai would send swarms of stinging hornets, which would weaken the resistance of the enemy.

31 I will establish your borders from the Red Sea to the Mediterranean Sea, from the desert to the river. I will defeat the inhabitants, and you will drive them before you.

32 Do not make a peace treaty with these nations or with their gods. **33** Do not allow them to live in your land, because they will then make you sin against Me. You may even end up worshipping their gods, and it will be a disaster for you.

24

Adonai said to Moses, "Come up to Me along with Aaron, Nadab, and Avihu, and seventy of the leaders of Israel. All of you must worship at a distance. **2** Only Moses shall approach Me. The others must not come close, and the people are not allowed to go up to the mountain with him."

3 Moses came and repeated to the people all of Adonai's teachings and laws. The Israelites responded with a single voice: "We will treasure and obey every word that Adonai has spoken."

4 Then Moses wrote down all of Adonai's words. He rose up early the next morning and built an altar at the foot of the mountain, along with twelve stone pillars, one for each of the twelve tribes of Israel. **5** He sent the first-born young men from among the Israelites, and they sacrificed oxen as burnt offerings and peace offerings to Adonai. **6** Moses took half the blood of these offerings and poured it into large bowls; the other half he sprinkled on the altar. **7** He took the Book of the Covenant and read it to the people. They replied, "We will faithfully do and obey all that Adonai has commanded."

8 Then Moses took the rest of the blood and sprinkled it on the people. He said, "This blood confirms the covenant that Adonai has made with you regarding all of these laws."

---

31. I will establish your borders from the Red Sea to the Mediterranean Sea, from the desert to the river. I will defeat the inhabitants, and you will drive them before you.

The river is the Euphrates River, the longest river of southwest Asia. It was the boundary between the kingdoms of Egypt and Babylonia. Kings David and Solomon extended Israel's border over all the kingdoms, from the Euphrates to the land of the Philistines and the boundaries of Egypt.

32. Do not make a peace treaty with these nations or with their gods.

This is mitzvah number 93.

Adonai warns the Israelites against foreign entanglements and alliances with idol-worshipping nations. Close friendships can lead to idol worship. The history of Israel in Canaan proves that the warnings of the prophets were correct. Alliances often led to idolatry among the Israelites.

4. Twelve stone pillars, one for each of the twelve tribes of Israel.

Three pillars on each side, in the same positions in which they camped around the Tabernacle.

The twelve pillars represented the unity of Israel.

Hizkuni

7. He took the Book of the Covenant and read it to the people.

The commentator Rashi says that at this point the Book (Torah) consisted of Bereshit, half of Shemot, and the Ten Commandments.

8. Then Moses took the rest of the blood and sprinkled it on the people.

The commentator Abarbanel says that Moses dashed the blood on the twelve pillars, which represented the people. Onkeles translates: "He dashed it on the altar to make atonement for the people."

9 Moses, along with Aaron, Nadav and Avihu, and the seventy leaders, went up the mountain, **10** and there they saw a vision of Adonai, and under his feet there was a floor decorated with sapphire jewels as clear as the heavenly skies. **11** Adonai did not harm the leaders of the Israelites. They had a vision of Elohim, and they celebrated and they ate and drank.
12 Adonai said to Moses, "Come up to Me, to the mountaintop, and wait there until I give you the stone tablets, the Torah and the commandments that I have written for you to teach the people." **13** Moses and his assistant, Joshua, set out and ascended the Mountain of Adonai. **14** Moses said to the leaders, "Wait for us here until we return to you. Aaron and Hur will remain with you. Anyone who has a problem can consult with them."

On Top of Mount Sinai *Maftir*

15 As soon as Moses reached the mountaintop, a cloud covered the mountain. **16** Adonai's glorious presence rested on Mount Sinai, and for six days it was covered by the cloud. On the seventh day, Adonai called to Moses from the midst of the cloud.
17 To the Israelites, the appearance of Adonai on the mountaintop was like a brilliant flame.
18 Moses climbed up to the mountaintop and disappeared into the cloud, and Moses remained on the mountain for forty days and forty nights.

---

12. Adonai said to Moses, "Come up to Me to the mountaintop and wait there."
This sentence tells us that Moses escorted the elders down the mountain and then Adonai said to him, "Come up to me."

12. Wait there until I give you the stone tablets.
Moses was told to stay on the mountaintop until Adonai had given him the stone tablets.
Nachmanides

13. Moses and his assistant, Joshua, set out and ascended the Mountain of Adonai.
Joshua accompanied Moses up to the boundary. He was not authorized to go any farther. Joshua waited there until Moses descended.

14. Aaron and Hur will remain with you. Anyone who has a problem can consult with them.
Moses was aware that he would stay on the mountain for a long period of time. So like a responsible leader, he set up a group of problem-solvers who had the power to settle legal matters.

14. Aaron and Hur will remain with you.
Here Moses informs the Elders of Israel that Aaron and Hur are to be the leaders in charge of the people during his forty days absence. Later, when Moses is gone, we are informed that a majority of the Israelites demanded of Aaron, "Make us a god who shall go before us." What happened to Hur, who was supposed to be a co-leader with Aaron? The Rabbis of the Talmud suggest an answer. Hur, they say, stood up and condemned the Israelites for their wrongdoing. Unlike Aaron, who stalled for time in hope that Moses might soon return, Hur spoke out. He would not compromise. The people were angered by him and they killed him.

18. Moses climbed up to the mountaintop and disappeared into the cloud.
Moses remained on the mountaintop for forty days and forty nights to receive the first set of stones. In Devarim 9:9, Moses says, "For forty days and forty nights I remained on the mountain without food or water."

תְּרוּמָה *Terumah*

OFFERINGS FOR THE TEMPLE

25 Adonai spoke to Moses, saying, **2** Speak to the Israelites, and have each one bring Me a gift. Accept the gifts from everyone who wants to give willingly. **3** The gifts that you accept from them shall consist of the following: gold, silver, copper, **4** blue wool, dark red wool, and crimson wool, linen, goats' hair, **5** tanned rams' skins, dyed blue sealskins, acacia wood, **6** olive oil for the lamp, spices for the anointing oil and the sweet-smelling incense, **7** and onyxes and other precious stones for the ephod and breastplate.

8 The Israelites shall make Me a Tabernacle in which I will live among them.

9 Make the Tabernacle and all its furnishings according to the construction plan that I am showing you.

---

1. Adonai spoke to Moses.
When Moses went up to Sinai, Adonai instructed him how to build the Tabernacle. Adonai wanted him to build it so He could speak to Moses whenever He wanted to.

Ibn Ezra

2. Accept the gifts from everyone who wants to give willingly.
No compulsory levy was to be put on the people. The gifts had to be purely voluntary.

3–4. The gifts that you accept from them shall consist of the following: gold, silver, copper, blue wool, dark red wool, and crimson wool, linen, goats' hair.
The word *terumah* (offering) is used three times and refers to three different offerings. One was of silver, out of which the sockets of the Tabernacle were made; the second was an offering for the altar; and the third was an offering of money for the many needs of the Tabernacle.

4. Blue wool.
The Rabbis say that the wool was dyed from the blood of shellfish found in the Mediterranean Sea. In 15:38, the Israelites were told to place fringes (*tzitzit*) on the corners of their garments, with a blue thread at each corner. The dye of the blue wool and the blue thread in the *tzitzit* were from the same type of shellfish. The Torah calls the blue thread *p'seel t'chayles*. The shellfish was called *chilazon*.

8. The Israelites shall make me a Tabernacle in which I will live among them.
Adonai spoke to Moses and told him to erect the Tabernacle according to the construction plans He showed to Moses. He transmitted to Moses the exact details and measurements.

Before the Tabernacle was built, there was no need for a central worship area. The families traveled throughout the area and prayed wherever they encountered Adonai.

Adonai met with Abraham and Isaac on Mount Moriah. Jacob encountered Adonai's angels climbing a ladder somewhere in the loneliness of the desert. Adonai met Isaac and promised to give his descendants, who would be as numerous as the stars in the sky, the land of Canaan. Now the Tabernacle was to be the center of prayer.

9. Make the Tabernacle and all its furnishings according to the construction plan that I am showing you.
The Tabernacle was the portable sanctuary built by the Hebrews in the desert at Adonai's command. It was the first synagogue, the institution that has preserved Judaism through the ages.

The chief architect of the *mishkan* (Tabernacle) was Betzalel, who was assisted by Oholiab and a group of skilled artisans. As soon as the mishkan was completed, the cloud of Adonai covered the Tent of Meeting. The Tabernacle occupied a central position in the Israelite camp.

10 Make an ark of acacia wood, 3.5 feet long, 2.25 feet wide, and 2.25 feet high.
11 Cover it with a layer of pure gold on the inside and the outside, and make a gold molding all around the top.
12 Cast four gold rings for the ark, and attach them on its four corners, and attach two rings on one side, and attach two on the other side. **13** Make two carrying poles of acacia wood and coat them with a layer of gold. **14** Fit the poles into the rings on the sides of the ark, so that the ark can be carried with them. **15** The poles must remain in the rings and not be removed. **16** Inside the ark place the engraved tablets with the Ten Commandments that I will give you!

Make the Ark
2nd Aliyah

17 Make a golden cover for the ark out of pure gold. Make it 3.75 feet long and 2.25 feet wide. **18** Make two golden cherubs, hammering them out from one piece of gold, and place them on the two ends of the cover.
19 Put one cherub on one end, and one cherub on the other. Make the cherubs from the same piece of gold as the cover on its two ends. **20** The cherubs shall spread their wings outward so that their wings shield the cover. The cherubs shall face one another and downward toward the cover of the ark.
21 Set the ark cover on top of the ark after you put the Ten Commandments that I will give you into the ark.
22 There I will meet with you and speak to you from the ark cover, from between the two cherubs that are on the ark. This is how I will pass along My instructions for the Israelites.
23 Make a table out of acacia wood, 3 feet long, 1.5 feet wide, and 2.25 feet high. **24** Cover it with pure gold, and make a gold rim all around it. **25** Make a 3-inch-wide rim around the edge of the table, and put a gold molding on the rim.
26 Make four gold rings for the table, and set the rings on the four corners next to the four legs. **27** The rings shall be close to the frame; they will hold the poles with which the table is carried. **28** Make the poles of acacia wood, and cover them with a layer of gold. The poles will be used to carry the table.
29 For the table make bread pans, ladles, incense bowls, and gold pitchers for pouring the liquid offerings.

---

10. Make an ark of acacia wood.
Adonai ordered that acacia wood was to be used in building the Tabernacle. The acacia tree is not a fruit-bearing tree. Adonai wanted to set an example that wood from fruit-bearing trees should not be cut down for building.

11. Cover it with a layer of pure gold on the inside and outside.
Adonai ordered that the ark be covered inside and outside with gold in order to teach us that if a person just seems wise on the outside, he is not totally wise. He must be wise inside as well. *Talmud*

18. Make two golden cherubs, hammering them out from one piece of gold, and place them on the two ends of the cover.

The Torah refers to supernatural beings as cherubim or seraphim, which are winged creatures with a human likeness. The fittings of the Tabernacle included two types of cherubim. The covering of the mercy seat had two gold cherubim. The curtains of the Tabernacle had cherubim woven into them.

The cherubim on the mercy seat symbolize Adonai's throne.

30 The showbread shall be placed before Me at all times on this table.

Make a Menorah

3rd Aliyah

31 Make a menorah out of pure gold. The entire menorah – its base, stem, decorative cups, buds, and flowers – must be hammered out of a single piece of gold. **32** Six branches shall extend from its sides, three branches of the menorah on one side and three branches on the other side.

33 Each branch shall hold one embossed cup, as well as a bud and a flower. All six branches extending from the menorah's stem must be the same.

34 The center of the menorah shall be decorated with four embossed cups along with its buds and flowers. **35** A bud shall serve as a base for each pair of branches extending from the center. All six branches extending from the center must be the same.

36 The buds and branches must all be a part of the menorah. They shall all be hammered out of a single piece of pure gold.

---

30. The showbread shall be placed before Me at all times on this table.
This is mitzvah number 97.

This showbread was required to be constantly in the presence of Adonai. Each Sabbath, fresh loaves replaced the old, which then belonged to the priests, who ate them in a holy place, because they were regarded as a holy offering. They were baked on Friday and were placed on the holy table on Sabbath morning, six in a row, one loaf leaning against the other. On the top of each row, two golden cups of frankincense were placed. They remained there until the next Sabbath, when the fresh loaves were brought and the loaves were given to the priests. The frankincense was burned in the sacred fire, and a new supply was placed upon the fresh loaves.

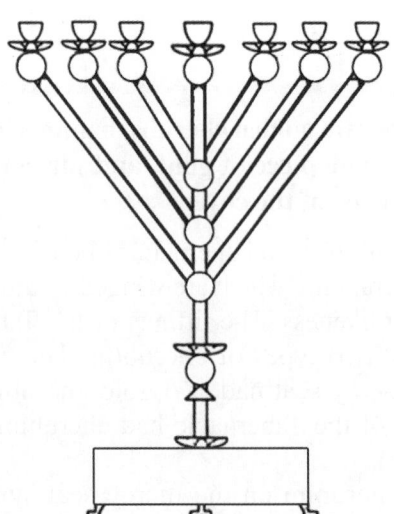

31. Make a menorah out of pure gold. The entire menorah – its base, stem, decorative cups, buds and flowers – must be hammered out of a single piece of pure gold.
The Torah provides the construction details of the Temple menorah. It was made by Betzalel and hammered out of a solid slab of gold. According to the Torah, it stood 7 feet tall, weighed 100 pounds, and was seven-branched.

The midrash says that the construction details were too difficult for Moses to understand so Adonai revealed a fiery picture of the finished menorah to him.

According to some commentators, the seven-branched menorah represents the creation of the world in seven days, and the center light is for the Sabbath.

Our sages say that the original Mosaic menorah was hidden by the priests just prior to the destruction of the First Temple and has never been found.

The menorah of the Second Temple was made to resemble that in the Tabernacle. The relief on the Arch of Titus in Rome shows the menorah from the sacking of Jerusalem being carried on poles by the Roman soldiers. Today the descendants of the vanquished who carried the menorah have rebuilt Jerusalem in the State of Israel.

37 Make seven lamps for the menorah. The lamps are to be attached in such a way as to shine toward the center of the menorah.
38 The tongs and the ash shovels for the menorah shall also be made out of pure gold.
39 The menorah, including all its parts, will require an ingot of pure gold weighing 75 pounds.
40 Carefully observe the model that you will be shown on the mountain, and make the menorah exactly the same.

26

Construct the Tabernacle out of ten large tapestries woven of fine linen with blue, purple, and scarlet wool, with a pattern of cherubs woven into them. **2** Each of the ten hanging tapestries shall be 42 feet long and 6 feet wide. Make each tapestry the exact same size.
3 The first five tapestries shall be sewn together, and the second five tapestries shall also be sewn together.
4 Sew loops of blue wool at the edge of the last tapestry of the first group. Do the same on the edge of the last tapestry of the second group. **5** Sew fifty loops on the edge of one tapestry, and fifty loops on the edge of the tapestry in the second group. The two sets of loops shall be made so that the loops are exactly opposite one another.
6 Make fifty golden fasteners: The fasteners will join together the two groups of tapestries so that the Tabernacle will be one piece.

---

1. Construct the Tabernacle.
Before the creation of the first *mikdash*, or "sanctuary," the Hebrews worshipped Adonai on hilltops, beside streams, or wherever they felt moved to pray. Abraham and Isaac traveled to Mount Moriah; Jacob encountered Adonai in a lonely place on the desert and near the river Jabbok; Moses met Adonai at the burning bush and at the top of Mount Sinai. Now, after their liberation from Egypt and the acceptance of the laws given to them at Mount Sinai, the people are commanded to build a sanctuary.

The sanctuary is to contain the Ark of the Covenant with its sacred stones on which the Ten Commandments are inscribed. It is to be placed in the Holy of Holies chamber inside the inner Tabernacle.

The opening of the Holy of Holies chamber is to be covered by a curtain. Outside the curtain is a special altar for incense, a table for the showbread, and a gold *menorah*, or "lampstand."

In front of the inner Tabernacle is another curtain, outside of which are the laver and an altar for burnt offerings. Clearly, the sanctuary is designed for offering sacrifices and prayers to Adonai.

6. The fasteners will join together the two groups of tapestries so that the Tabernacle will be one piece.
The individual pieces of the curtain were joined to form a single covering of the Tabernacle.

Ibn Ezra says that the tribes, clans, and individual families must also be linked together into one unified nation living together in peace and security.

An artist's rendition of the Tabernacle

7 Weave goats' wool into sheets to cover the roof of the Tabernacle. Weave eleven such sheets. **8** Each sheet shall be 45 feet long and 6 feet wide. Make sure that all eleven sheets are exactly the same size.

9 Sew together the first five sheets, and sew together the remaining six sheets. Half of the sixth sheet shall hang over the front of the Tabernacle.

10 Sew fifty loops on the edge of the last sheet of the first group, and sew fifty loops on the edge of the last sheet of the second group. **11** Make fifty copper fasteners. Put the fasteners in the loops, and join the sheets together, making the Tabernacle into one piece.

12 Hang the remaining extra half of this sheet over the back of the Tabernacle.

13 The extra 18 inches on both sides of the tent will hang down over the sides of the tapestries of the Tabernacle to cover them on both sides.

14 Make the roof for the tent out of tanned rams' skins. Above the rams' skins add the tanned waterproof blue sealskins.

Make the Frames
4th Aliyah

15 Out of acacia wood make upright frames for the Tabernacle. **16** Each frame shall be 15 feet long and 2.25 feet wide.

17 Each frame shall have two matching square pegs carved out at the bottom. All the frames for the Tabernacle must be made exactly the same way.

18 Make twenty frames for the southern side of the Tabernacle. **19** Set forty silver bases under the twenty frames – two bases under each frame, one for each peg.

20 For the northern side of the Tabernacle, set the twenty frames **21** and the forty silver bases with two sockets under each and every frame.

22 Make six frames for the western side of the Tabernacle, **23** and place an extra frame at the corners. All the frames must be exactly next to each other on the bottom. **24** Every pair must be joined together evenly on top with a square ring making a single unit. This shall also be done with the two frames at the two corners.

25 On the western side there will be a total of eight frames and sixteen silver bases, two bases under each and every frame.

26 Make crossbars out of acacia wood. There shall be five for the frames of the first side of the Tabernacle to the south.

27 There shall also be five for the frames of the second side to the north, and five for the frames of the Tabernacle on the western wall. **28** The center crossbar shall go through the middle of the frames, from one end of the Tabernacle to the other.

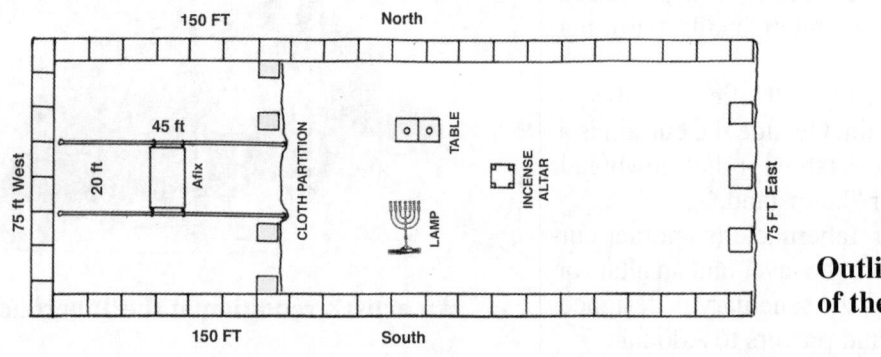

Outline drawing of the Tabernacle

29 Cover the frames with a layer of gold. Also make gold rings on the frames to hold the crossbars. The crossbars shall also be covered with a layer of gold.
30 You will then be ready to set up the Tabernacle exactly as you were shown on the mountain.

The Partition
5th Aliyah

31 Weave a cloth partition out of blue, purple, and scarlet wool, woven together with fine linen. Cherubs shall be woven into it so that they can be seen on both sides. **32** Hang it on four gold-covered acacia pillars fitted with gold hooks. The pillars shall be set in four silver sockets.
33 Place the cloth partition directly under the fastenings holding the tapestries together. In the space behind this curtain you will place the ark. The curtain will serve as a partition between the sanctuary and the Holy of Holies. **34** Put the cover on the ark in the Holy of Holies.
35 Place the table outside the curtain, near the northern wall of the Tabernacle. The menorah shall be opposite the table, near the southern wall of the Tabernacle.
36 Weave a screen for the entrance of the tent out of blue, purple, and scarlet wool, and twined linen. It shall be embroidered work. **37** Make five acacia pillars to hold the screen. Cover the pillars with a layer of gold and attach golden hooks to them. Cast five copper bases for the pillars.

The Altar
6th Aliyah

27 Build the altar out of acacia wood. The altar shall be square, 7.5 feet by 7.5 feet, and 4.35 feet tall. **2** Make horns on all four sides of the altar. Then cover the altar with a layer of copper.
3 Make pails to remove the ashes, as well as shovels, basins, hooks, and fire pans for the altar. All these altar instruments must be made of copper.
4 Make a grating out of copper net to go around the altar. Fasten four copper rings on the four corners of the grating. **5** Put the grating below the decorative border of the altar, extending downward until the middle of the altar.
6 Make carrying poles for the altar from acacia wood covered with a layer of copper.

---

33. The curtain will serve as a partition between the sanctuary and the Holy of Holies.
The Holy of Holies was the holiest place in the Tabernacle, and later in the Temple, where the Ark of the Covenant was kept. The Holy of Holies was entered only once a year, and only by the High Priest, on the holy day of Yom Kippur.

1. Build the altar out of acacia wood.
The burnt offerings were placed on the altar. It was of light construction so that it could be carried easily, a hollow frame of acacia wood, covered with bronze.

1. Build the altar out of acacia wood.
The Tabernacle had two altars: the altar for burnt offerings and the altar for incense (Shemot 30:1-5)

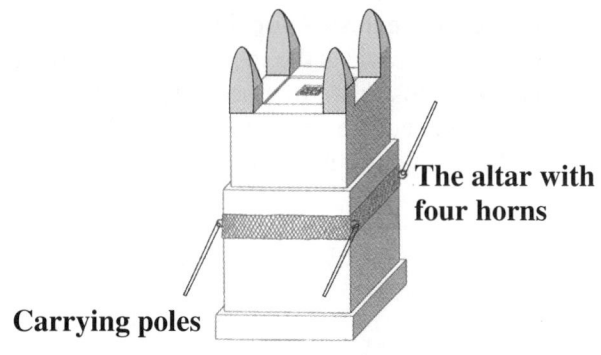

The altar with four horns

Carrying poles

7 Insert the poles into the rings so that the poles will be secured on both sides of the altar when it is carried.

8 Make the hollow altar out of boards. Make it exactly like the model you were shown on the mountain.

Make the Enclosure *7th Aliyah*

9 Make the enclosure for the Tabernacle in this manner: On the southern side will be hangings made of woven linen. It shall be 150 feet long **10** and shall have twenty pillars and twenty copper bases. The hooks and clasps for the pillars shall be made of silver.

11 The same shall be done on the northern side. The curtain hangings shall be 150 feet long, with twenty pillars and twenty copper bases, with silver hooks and clasps for the pillars.

12 The width of the curtain hangings at the western end of the enclosure will be 75 feet, and it shall have ten pillars and ten bases.

13 The width of the enclosure at its eastern end shall also be 75 feet.

14 The curtains on one side of the entrance shall be 22 feet long, with three pillars and three bases.

15 On the other side, the curtain shall also be 22 feet long, with three pillars and three bases.

16 The entrance of the courtyard shall be covered with a 30-foot embroidered drape made of blue, purple, and scarlet wool together with woven linen. It shall have four pillars and four bases.

The Courtyard *Maftir*

17 All the pillars of the courtyard will have silver rings, silver clasps, and copper bases.

18 The courtyard shall be 150 feet long and 75 feet wide. The pillars holding the hangings of woven linen shall be 7.5 feet high, and their bases shall be made of copper. **19** All the tools used to make the Tabernacle shall be made out of copper. The pegs for the Tabernacle and all the pegs for the courtyard shall also be made of copper.

---

8. Make the hollow altar out of boards.
The boards were made of acacia wood on all four sides and was hollow in the middle. The altar was easily portable. The Rashbam says that before they offered sacrifices on it, they filled the hollow center with sand. When they picked up the altar, the sand would fall out.

9. Make the enclosure for the Tabernacle.
Now Adonai provides the instructions for how to make the enclosure for the sacred Tabernacle. The Tabernacle needed a fence to safeguard the holy from the everyday activities.

10. Twenty pillars and twenty copper bases.
The copper bases, which did not rust, were securely placed on the ground and the pillars were inserted into them.

12. The width of the curtain hangings at the western end of the enclosure will be 75 feet, and it shall have ten pillars and ten bases.
The enclosure of the Tabernacle was 150 feet long and 75 feet wide. There were 20 pillars at the northern and southern sides. There were 10 pillars and 10 bases at the western side.

תְּצַוֶּה Tetzaveh

INSTRUCT THE ISRAELITES

20 Moses, you must instruct the Israelites to bring clear illuminating oil, made from crushed olives, to keep the menorah constantly alight. **21** Aaron and his sons shall care for the burning lamps from evening until morning in the presence of Adonai, in the Meeting Tent, outside the cloth partition that conceals the ark. It is a permanent rule for all time that this oil shall be given by the Israelites.

28 Ordain your brother Aaron and his sons Nadav, Avihu, Elazar, and Ithamar from among the Israelites, and bring them close to you so that Aaron and his sons can serve Me as priests. **2** Make sacred garments that will add dignity and honor for your brother Aaron.

3 Find talented weavers and tailors to make Aaron's garments. These special garments will be used to ordain Aaron and make him a priest to serve Me. **4** These are the garments that they shall make: a breastplate, an ephod, a robe, a knitted tunic, a headdress, and a sash. They will be designed as sacred garments for Aaron and his sons so that they will be able to officiate as priests before Me.

---

20. Moses, you must instruct the Israelites to bring clear illuminating oil, made from crushed olives.
The Hebrew expression for the special olive oil is *shemen zayit zach*. The Talmud explains: "The oil was to be clear, free of sediment. The ripe olives were to be pounded in a mortar."

The Talmud (Menahoth 86a) adds the following details regarding the production of the holy oil: There are three periods of gathering olives and each crop gives three kinds of oil. For the first crop, the olives are picked from the top of the tree, then pounded and placed into the basket. This gives the first oil. They are then pressed with the beam. This gives the second oil. They are then ground and pressed again. This gives the third oil. The first (oil) is fit for the candlestick and the others for meal offerings.

20. Keep the menorah constantly burning.
Even though the Temple was destroyed and the menorah was stolen, Jews have never allowed the light to stop shining. We have synagogues, "miniature temples" which perpetuate the light of Torah prayer, wisdom, and spiritual treasures.

21. Aaron and his sons shall care for the burning lamps from evening until morning.
Although all seven lights of the menorah burned from morning to evening, only one of them was refilled for night time burning.

From its light the other six were rekindled every morning. Centuries later a separate lamp was made that came to be known as the *ner tamid*, or "perpetual lamp" (Eternal Light), which hangs above the *Aron Kodesh*.

Aaron, the brother of Moses, was given the special privilege of being the first to light the menorah that Betzalel built. Adonai told Moses to reveal the following secret revelation to Aaron: "The sanctuary, at another time (many years from now), will also be dedicated by the lighting of a menorah. The lighting will be performed by Aaron's descendant, a Hasmonean, for whom I will perform miracles.

2. Make sacred garments that will add dignity and honor for your brother Aaron.
The Meeting Tent was to be a place of beauty and splendor, and the priest was also beautifully attired.

He is a representative of Adonai, and his regalia must reflect his position of honor and dignity. Twelve precious stones engraved with the tribal names point to him as official representative of the tribes.

5 The skilled workers shall embroider the gold thread, the blue, purple, and scarlet wool, and the fine linen. **6** The embroiderer shall make the ephod out of gold thread, blue, purple, and scarlet wool, together with fine twined linen.
7 Make two attached shoulder pieces at its two corners, and attach them to the ephod.
8 Make the sash the same way as the ephod. Weave it out of gold thread, blue, purple, and scarlet wool, and fine linen.
9 Take two onyx stones and engrave them with the names of Israel's sons. **10** There shall be six names on one stone, and six names on the second stone, inscribed in the order of their birth. **11** The names of Israel's sons shall be inscribed by a skilled engraver, like the engraving on a signet ring.
Mount these stones in gold settings. **12** Attach the two stones on the two shoulder pieces of the ephod as a reminder of Israel's history. Aaron shall carry the engraved names on his two shoulders as a remembrance before Adonai.

Make a Judgment Breastplate
2nd Aliyah

13 Make gold settings. **14** Also make matched chains of pure gold, braided like cord. Attach the braided chains to the settings on the shoulders of the ephod.
15 Make a judgment breastplate. It shall be embroidered like the ephod. Make it out of gold thread and blue, purple, and scarlet wool, and fine linen.
16 When folded over, it shall be 9 inches long and 9 inches wide.
17 Set it with four rows of mounted, precious jewels.
The first of these rows shall contain a ruby, an emerald, and a topaz.
18 The second row: carnelian, sapphire, and a diamond.
19 The third row: amber, agate, and jasper.
20 The fourth row: beryl, onyx, and amethyst.
All of these stones shall be mounted in gold settings.
21 The twelve stones shall contain the names of the twelve sons of Israel. Each one's name shall be engraved as on a signet ring, to represent one of the twelve tribes. **22** For the breastplate make matched chains out of pure gold, braided like cords. **23** Make two gold rings for the breastplate, and attach them to the two upper corners of the breastplate. **24** Attach the two gold braids to the two rings on the two corners of the breastplate. **25** Attach the two chains on the two corners to the two settings; then attach them to the two shoulder pieces of the ephod, toward the front. **26** Make two gold rings, and attach them to the two lower corners of the breastplate, toward the inside of the ephod.
27 Make another two gold rings, and attach them to the bottoms of the two shoulder pieces, toward the front, above the ephod's sash.

9–10. Take two onyx stones and engrave them with the names of Israel's sons. There shall be six names on one stone and six names on the second stone.
The names of the tribes were imprinted on two onyx stones that were on the shoulder pieces of the ephod. Additionally, the tribal names were also found on the *hoshen*, where each tribe had its name on one of the twelve stones.

The second set of stones were to remind the *kohen gadol* (High Priest) that he carried on his shoulders a responsibility to all the tribes.

28 Attach the lower rings of the breastplate to the lower rings of the ephod with a cord of blue wool. **29** In this way, when Aaron comes into the sanctuary, he will carry the names of Israel's sons on the judgment breastplate over his heart. It will be a constant reminder to Adonai of His people.

30 Place the Urim and Thumim in the judgment breastplate, over Aaron's heart, whenever Aaron enters into the presence of Adonai. He must always carry the judgment-making device for the Israelites at all times when he enters Adonai's presence.

Make a Robe   *3rd Aliyah*

31 Make the robe that is worn under the ephod out of blue wool. **32** It shall have an opening for the head in the middle, and this opening shall have a woven border all around it, so that it does not tear. **33** Fasten pomegranates made of blue, purple, and scarlet wool on the bottom of the robe, all along its lower border, and put gold bells in between the pomegranates. **34** There shall be a gold bell and a pomegranate, a gold bell and a pomegranate, all around the lower edge of the robe.

35 Aaron is to wear this robe whenever he officiates at a divine service. The tinkling of the bells will be heard when he enters Adonai's sanctuary, and when he goes out, to ensure that he does not die.

36 Make a medallion of pure gold, and engrave on it, in the same manner as a signet ring, the words "Holy to Adonai."

---

30. Place the Urim and Thumim in the judgment breastplate.
The judgment breastplate carried the Urim and Thumim, which consisted of inscribed stones. The stones may have been inscribed with Hebrew letters. The first Hebrew letter of *Urim* is the *alef*, the first letter in the Hebrew alphabet. The first letter in *Thumim* is the Hebrew letter *tav*, the last letter in the alphabet. Together the two letters spell the Hebrew word *ot*, meaning "sign." There may have been other stones inscribed with Hebrew letters.

When the High Priest needed a decision, the inscribed stones were cast as lots, and the stones were read to provide answers.

Shenash

35. The tinkling of the bells will be heard when he enters Adonai's sanctuary, and when he goes out.
The tinkling of bells announces the entrance of the High Priest. This teaches us that it is good manners not to surprise and arrive unexpectedly.

Bekor Shor

36. Make a medallion of pure gold, and engrave on it, in the same manner as a signet ring, the words "Holy to Adonai."
This medallion was a gold forehead plate 1½ inches wide, which Aaron wore over his headdress. Three blue threads, one at each end and one at the center, held it in position.

The blue threads may have been dyed with the same *chilazon* dye used in the threads of the *tzitzit*.

37 Attach a cord of blue wool to it, so that it can be worn at the front of the headdress.
38 This medallion shall be worn on Aaron's forehead. Thus Aaron will carry the medallion that removes sin from the sacred offerings that the Israelites bring as holy gifts. It shall always be on Aaron's forehead when he makes the offerings of the Israelites acceptable before Adonai. **39** Weave the tunic out of linen. Also make the headdress and the embroidered sash out of linen.
40 Make tunics and sashes for Aaron's sons. Also make dignified and beautiful headdresses for them.
41 Clothe Aaron and his sons in these garments. Then anoint and ordain them to serve as priests before Me.
42 Make linen undergarments for them, reaching from their hips to their thighs.
43 Aaron and his sons must wear all these garments whenever they enter the Meeting Tent or offer sacrifices on the altar, in the sanctuary; otherwise they will have committed a sin and they will die. For all time, this shall be a law for Aaron and his descendants after him.

Ordain Aaron and His Sons *4th Aliyah*

29 Moses, this is what you must do to ordain Aaron and his sons as priests to Me. Take a young bull, two perfect rams, **2** loaves of unleavened bread, unleavened loaves mixed with olive oil, and flat matzot brushed with olive oil. All the loaves must be made of fine wheat flour.
3 Place all the loaves in a basket, and present them in the basket along with the young bull and the two rams.
4 Bring Aaron and his sons to the door of the Meeting Tent, and cleanse them with water.
5 Clothe Aaron in the tunic, the ephod's robe, the ephod, and the breastplate, and bind him with the ephod's sash.
6 Then place the headdress on Aaron's head, and attach the sacred medallion to the headdress.
7 Take the holy anointing oil, and pour a little on Aaron's head. **8** Next, clothe Aaron's sons in their linen tunics, **9** sashes, and headdresses.
You shall ordain Aaron and his sons as priests, and their descendants shall be priests forever.
10 Bring the young bull before the Meeting Tent, and have Aaron and his sons place their hands on the bull's head.

---

41. Clothe Aaron and his sons in these garments. Then anoint and ordain them to serve as priests before Me.
This sacred anointing oil was blended by a skilled perfumer (Shemot 30:25).

2. Loaves of unleavened bread, unleavened loaves mixed with olive oil.
Yeast was excluded from meal offerings. Yeast when mixed with dough causes the mixture to rise. Symbolically some humans behave as if their ego has been fortified with yeast, and they become inflated with their own importance. In time yeast came to represent corruption. *Shenash*

9. You shall ordain Aaron and his sons as priests, and their descendants shall be priests forever.
This is the beginning of the priesthood dynasty. Future generations will automatically become priests.
However, each new High Priest would still need to be anointed since only one of the High Priest's sons could assume this position. There could be only one High Priest at a time. *Gersonides*

11 Then slaughter the bull at the door of the Meeting Tent. **12** With your finger, smear some of the bull's blood onto the horns of the altar. Pour the remaining blood at the base of the altar.
13 Remove all the organs of the bull and burn them on the altar.
14 Burn the bull's flesh, outside the camp, as a sin offering.
15 Have Aaron and his sons place their hands on the head of the first ram. **16** Then slaughter the ram, and sprinkle its blood on all sides of the altar. **17** Cut the ram into pieces and cleanse the internal organs and legs. Place them near the head and the other body parts.
18 Burn all the parts of the ram on the altar as a burnt offering to Adonai. This offering will be a sign of faith in Adonai.

The Wave Offering
5th Aliyah

19 Take the second ram, and have Aaron and his sons place their hands on its head.
20 Slaughter the ram, and place a drop of its blood on the right earlobes of Aaron and his sons, as well as on their right thumbs and right big toes. Sprinkle the remaining blood on all sides of the altar.
21 Collect the blood that is on the altar, and together with the anointing oil, sprinkle it on the garments of Aaron and his sons. This will ordain Aaron and his sons and their garments.
22 Burn the organs of the second ram, as an ordination offering.
23 Take one flat unleavened loaf of bread, one loaf of oil bread, and one flat cake from the basket of unleavened bread that is before Adonai.
24 Put all these items into the hands of Aaron and his sons, and have them offer them as a wave offering before Adonai.
25 Then take these items and burn them on the altar as a fragrant burnt offering to Adonai. This offering will be a sign of faith in Adonai.
26 Remove the breast of Aaron's dedication ram, and wave it before Adonai as a wave offering. Moses, afterwards you may keep that portion for yourself.

---

20. Slaughter the ram, and place a drop of its blood on the right earlobes of Aaron and his sons, as well as on their right thumbs and right big toes.
The midrash says that placing a drop of its blood on the three parts (ear, toes, thumb) of the body of the *kohen* is to make sure that the *kohen* mingles (toe) with the people, listens (ear) to their complaints, and reacts (thumb) to their suggestions or complaints.

20. Place a drop of its blood on the right earlobes of Aaron and his sons, as well as on their right thumbs and right big toes.
The earlobes, thumbs, and toes are symbols of service to Adonai. The earlobes are made holy to hear Adonai's message properly.

The hand is to perform the duties of the priesthood properly. The toes are to walk and follow the laws of the Torah.

24. And have them offer them as a wave offering before Adonai.
It was waved back and forth in all four directions and then up and down.
Rashi

25. This offering will be a sign of faith in Adonai.
When one is offering a sacrifice to Adonai, it is not important whether one offers a little or a lot. What is important is that whatever is offered is given with a full heart and that the offerer's thoughts and feelings are directed to Adonai.

27 Dedicate the breast that was offered as a wave offering and the hind leg of the wave offering from the ram of ordination.
28 It shall be a law for all times that the breast and the thigh shall be a gift offering for Aaron and his sons from the Israelites, taken from their peace offerings to Adonai.
29 Aaron's sacred garments shall be preserved and passed down to his descendants so they can be ordained in them.
30 The descendant who takes Aaron's place in the Meeting Tent must first put on these garments for seven consecutive days before performing the divine service in the inner sanctuary.
31 Take the rest of the dedication ram and cook its flesh in a sacred area. **32** Then Aaron and his sons shall eat the rams' meat and the bread from the basket near the door of the Meeting Tent. **33** They are the only ones permitted to eat the meat and bread used to make atonement in the dedication ceremony. These offerings are sacred and must not be eaten by nonpriests. **34** You must burn any meat or bread of the dedication offering that is left over until morning. Since it is holy, it must not be eaten. **35** Do exactly as I have instructed you to ordain Aaron and his sons. The ordination ceremony shall take seven days. **36** Each day you shall sacrifice a young bull as a sin offering to make atonement. Afterwards you shall purify the altar by sprinkling it with oil. **37** For seven days, you shall purify the altar and sanctify it, making the altar very holy. Anyone who touches the altar will be sanctified.

The Sacrifices
6th Aliyah

38 This is what you must sacrifice on the altar:
Sacrifice two lambs each day. **39** The first lamb shall be sacrificed in the morning, and the second lamb in the late afternoon. **40** Offer two quarts of fine flour mixed with one quart of olive oil, and a liquid offering of wine, with the first lamb. **41** In the late afternoon, sacrifice the second lamb along with a meal offering and a liquid offering like the one offered in the morning. It shall be a fragrance offering to Adonai. **42** There shall be a daily burnt offering throughout the generations. It shall be offered to Adonai at the entrance of the Meeting Tent, the place where I will meet with the people and also speak to you. **43** It is there that I will meet with the Israelites, and the Tabernacle will be sanctified by My presence.

---

28. It shall be a law for all times that the breast and the thigh shall be a gift offering for Aaron and his sons from the Israelites, taken from their peace offerings to Adonai.
The sacrifices are called *shelemim* because they are offer for the *shalom*, wellbeing, of those who offered them.
Ibn Ezra

29. So that they can be ordained in them.
All future High Priests will in the future be ordained in these same holy garments.

33. These offerings are sacred and must not be eaten by nonpriests.
This is mitzvah number 102.

It is a mitzvah for the priests to eat from the sin and guilt offerings. The atonement of the individual seeking forgiveness is completed when the priests consume the offerings.

35. The ordination ceremony shall take seven days.
During the seven days Aaron and his sons must remain in place and may not leave the Meeting Tent.

36. Each day you shall sacrifice a young bull as a sin offering to make atonement.
The sin offering to make atonement was necessary in case the contributor dishonestly obtained any of the contributions. To steal and rob in order to give *tzedakah* is insulting.
Rashi

44 I will sanctify the Meeting Tent and the altar, and I will also sanctify Aaron and his sons, so that they will become priests and serve Me.
45 I will live among the Israelites. **46** They will know that I, Adonai, liberated them from Egypt so that I could live among them. I am Adonai.

The Incense Altar
7th Aliyah

30 Make an altar of acacia wood on which to burn incense. **2** Make it square, 18 inches long and 18 inches wide, and 36 inches tall, with horns at the corners. **3** Cover it with a layer of pure gold, on its top, its sides all around, and its horns. Make a gold molding all around the altar. **4** Attach two gold rings under the altar's molding on its two opposite sides. These rings will hold the carrying poles.
5 Make the carrying poles from acacia wood and cover them with a layer of gold.
6 Set the incense altar in front of the cloth curtain concealing the ark – before the cloth curtain where I will meet with you.
7 Each morning Aaron will burn incense on this altar when he cleans the lamps.

The Atonement Sacrifices
Maftir

8 Aaron shall also burn incense in the evening when he lights the lamps. In every generation, at all times, there must be incense before Adonai.
9 Do not burn any foreign incense on it. And do not offer any animal sacrifice, meal offering, or liquid offering on it. **10** Once each year Aaron shall sanctify the horns of the altar. Once each year, throughout the generations, he shall sanctify the altar with the blood of the sin sacrifice. This altar is the most holy to Adonai.

---

44. I will sanctify the Meeting Tent and the altar.
Jews build synagogues and temples of worship. However, Adonai sanctifies only those that are committed to observance of commandments and mitzvot.

45–46. I will live among the Israelites. They will know that I, Adonai, liberated them from Egypt, so that I could live among them. I am Adonai.
Adonai said to the Children of Israel: "I have given you my precious Torah, but I cannot part with it. So I ask you – make a sanctuary for me, where my presence will exist among you." So it is written: "Let them make a sanctuary, so I will live among the Israelites."

1. Make an altar of acacia wood on which to burn incense.
Incense was burnt on this special altar in the Tabernacle. The incense was made of fragrant oils mixed with salt. When burned, it gave off a fragrant smoke. The altar for incense stood before the entrance to the Holy of Holies.

It was 1½ square feet, and stood 3 feet high. A rim of gold ran round it, near the top. One of the altar was for burnt offerings and one was for incense (Shemot 30:1–5).

4. Attach two gold rings under the altar's molding on its two opposite sides.
There were four rings, one at each corner.
The rings held the poles which were used to carry the altar.

7. Each morning Aaron will burn incense on this altar when he cleans the lamps.
Aaron's task was to remove from the dishes of the lampstand the remains of the wicks from the previous night.
Aaron would do this every morning. Then he would relight the lamps.

9. Do not burn any foreign incense on it.
Any incense made with unauthorized ingredients.

כִּי תִשָּׂא *Ki Tissa*

TAKE A CENSUS

11 Adonai spoke to Moses, saying: **12** Whenever you take a census of the Israelites, each one that is counted shall donate a ransom offering to Adonai for his life, so that they will not be stricken by the plague when they are counted. **13** Every person included in the census must pay a half-shekel (one-fifth of an ounce of silver), as measured by the sanctuary weight standard, whereby a shekel is twenty gerahs. The half-shekel must be given as a donation to Adonai. **14** Every man over twenty years of age shall be included in the census and must give this donation to Adonai. **15** The rich may not give more than a half-shekel, and the poor may not give less. It is an offering to Adonai to atone for your lives. **16** You will take this atonement money from the Israelites and use it for constructing the Meeting Tent. It will be a reminder for the Israelites before Adonai to atone for their lives. **17** Adonai spoke to Moses, saying: **18** Make a copper washbasin with a copper base. Put it between the altar and the Meeting Tent, and fill it with water for cleansing. **19** Aaron and his sons must cleanse their hands and feet in this washbasin. **20** They must cleanse themselves with the water in the washbasin before entering the Meeting Tent or approaching the altar to perform a divine service to Adonai. **21** They must first cleanse their hands and feet, or they will die. This shall be a law for Aaron and his descendants for all time, throughout the generations. **22** Adonai spoke to Moses, saying, **23** You must collect the following spices: 12 pounds of pure myrrh, 6 pounds of cinnamon and 6 pounds of aromatic cane, **24** and 12 pounds of cassia, all measured by the sanctuary weight standard along with a gallon of olive oil.

---

12. Each one that is counted shall donate a ransom offering to Adonai for his life.
This is mitzvah 105.

The ransom money refers to the money paid by one who is guilty of taking a human life under conditions that do not constitute deliberate murder.

The soldier who is ready to march into battle will ultimately kill someone. He pays the ransom before going into the front lines, because his killing is a necessary evil. He is defending his country, his family, and his right to practice his religion.

13. Every person included in the census must pay a half-shekel.
This coin of one-half shekel is designed as a token payment for the customary Purim collection, in the month of Adar (February to March), which every male Jew over 20 years of age had to pay to the Temple treasury.

The custom has not been required since the Temple's destruction in 70 C.E., but has been continued. The money in most cases was sent to the Holy Land for the preservation of learning, thus following the custom that prevailed in the time of the second Jewish commonwealth. Then, the half-shekel was collected outside the country and sent to Jerusalem as a contribution to the Temple.

13. Every person included in this census must pay a half-shekel.
Why only a half-shekel? Adonai wanted to demonstrate that everyone, regardless of his position, was equal in the eyes of Adonai. Every person is an important part of the Jewish community and does his or her best to continue to work for the common good of the nation.

25 Blend it into the sacred anointing oil. It must be blended by a skilled perfumer into the sacred anointing oil.
26 Then use it to anoint the Meeting Tent, the ark, **27** the table and all its utensils, the menorah and its utensils, the incense altar, **28** the sacrificial altar and all its utensils, the washbasin and its base. **29** You will sanctify them, making them holy, so that anything touching them also becomes holy. **30** You must also anoint Aaron and his sons, ordaining them as priests to serve Me.
31 And you shall speak to the Israelites and tell them, "This shall be the sacred ordaining oil to serve Me for all generations. **32** Do not pour it on the skin of any unauthorized person, and do not make any of it for your own use. It is holy, and it must remain sacred. **33** If a person blends the same mixture, or puts it on an ordinary person, he shall be cut off from his people."
34 Adonai instructed Moses: Take aromatic spices, such as balsam, onycha, galbanum, and an equal amount of frankincense.
35 Let a master perfumer blend the mixture into a holy incense.
36 Grind it finely, and place it before the ark in the Meeting Tent where I meet with you. This shall be holy to you.
37 Do not blend the same incense for your own personal use. It must remain sacred to Adonai.
38 If a person blends it to enjoy its fragrance, he shall be cut off from his people.

31

Adonai spoke to Moses, saying:
2 I have chosen Betzalel son of Uri, son of Hur, of the tribe of Judah.
3 I have filled him with a special spirit, with wisdom, understanding, and knowledge, and with skills to perform all types of craftsmanship.
4 He will be able to create plans as well as work in gold, silver, and copper, **5** cut stones to be set, carve wood, and do other work.
6 As his assistant I have assigned Oholiav son of Achisamakh of the tribe of Dan. Besides this, I have also granted wisdom to every talented Israelite. They will construct everything that I have ordered:

---

32. Do not make any of it for your own personal use.
This is prohibitive mitzvah number 110.

It is forbidden to formulate the same incense mixture for personal use. The art of formulating the incense was the secret of a family living in Jerusalem. No bride from this family ever went to her wedding wearing perfume.

2. I have chosen Betzalel son of Uri, son of Hur, of the tribe of Judah.
The sages say that the Torah teaches that when a person possesses talent, it is a gift from Adonai. It is a gift not only for him, but also for the community of Israel and for the welfare of the world.

3. I have filled him with a special spirit, with wisdom, understanding, and knowledge, and with skills to perform all types of craftsmanship.
The Israelites were slaves and not one of them was ever trained in construction of a completed structure like the Tabernacle. Adonai gave Betzalel the special wisdom and skills necessary to build the Tabernacle.

6. I have granted wisdom to every talented Israelite.
Israelites were employed in every phase of the Pharaoh's building program. Now Moses is told to find and utilize these individuals in building the Tabernacle.

7 The Meeting Tent, the ark, the ark cover to go on it, all the utensils for the tent, **8** the table and its utensils, the pure gold menorah and all its utensils, the incense altar, **9** the sacrificial altar and all its utensils, the washbasin and its base, **10** the packing cloths, the sacred garments for Aaron the priest, the garments that his sons wear to serve as priests, **11** the anointing oil, and the incense for the sanctuary. Now they will have the skills to follow all My instructions.

12 Adonai instructed Moses **13** to speak to the Israelites and say to them:

You must observe My Sabbaths. This is a sign between Me and you throughout the generations, to make you realize that I, Adonai, have made you holy.

14 Therefore observe the Sabbath as something sacred. Anyone who does not observe the Sabbath shall be cut off from his people, and therefore anyone violating the Sabbath shall be put to death. **15** Do your work during the six weekdays, but observe the Sabbath as holy to Adonai. Whoever works on the Sabbath shall be put to death.

16 The Israelites shall observe the Sabbath eternally throughout the generations. **17** It is a sign between Me and the Israelites that during the six weekdays Adonai created planet Earth and the rest of the universe, but on the Sabbath He stopped working and rested.

The Golden Calf
2nd Aliyah

18 When Adonai finished speaking to Moses on Mount Sinai, He gave him two tablets. They were stone Ten Commandments tablets, written by the finger of Adonai.

32 Meanwhile, the people saw that Moses was taking a long time to come down from the mountain. They gathered around Aaron and demanded, "Make us a god to lead us. Moses, the man who brought us out of Egypt, has disappeared. We have no idea what happened to him."

---

13. You must observe My Sabbaths.
The building of the Tabernacle does not in any way supersede the observance of the Sabbath. The word "Sabbath" also includes the festivals.

13. You must observe My Sabbaths.
When Adonai created Sabbath, it complained that everything else that had been created had a partner. Only the Sabbath did not have a partner.

"Do not worry," said Adonai. "You too will have a partner. The entire nation of Israel will be your partner. Throughout the ages Israel will watch over you and love you."

14. Anyone violating the Sabbath shall be put to death.
This death penalty was to be inflicted only if the individual violated the Sabbath in front of two witnesses. The witnesses had to have warned the culprit that he or she was violating the Sabbath. This rule was important because some absent-minded people may not be aware that it is the Sabbath.
Shenash

1. Make us a god to lead us.
Moses was gone for forty days on his holy mission to bring the Israelites the Commandments, and they already had lost patience. Brought up among idol worshippers in Egypt, they were unable to understand the idea of an Adonai who was not visible and who was everywhere. They returned to the idea of the Adonai-Pharaoh. Also, they could not tolerate even a short delay or a brief period of anxiety and worry. As they had acted previously in regard to food and water, they now concluded that all was lost and that Moses was dead.

The ability to think of a lofty, abstract Adonai was beyond them, and the ability to exercise patience was also beyond them. They immediately demanded a new and visible god, someone to protect them. So they demanded an idol, and Aaron was forced against his will to provide one.

2 Aaron replied, "Remove the rings from the ears of your wives and children and bring them to me."
3 All the people removed their earrings and brought them to Aaron. **4** He melted the golden rings, and molded them into a golden calf. Some of the people said, "This is the god who brought us out of Egypt."
5 When Aaron saw the mood of the people, he built an altar. Aaron said, "Tomorrow there will be a festival to Adonai."
6 Early the next morning, the people sacrificed burnt and peace offerings. The Israelites sat down and feasted, and then they began to dance. **7** Adonai said to Moses, "Hurry! Go down, for the Israelites whom you brought out of Egypt, they have abandoned My teachings and are acting like wild people. **8** They have so quickly abandoned the laws that I ordered them to follow, and they have made themselves a golden calf. They have worshipped and sacrificed to it, boasting, 'This is the god of Israel, who brought us out of Egypt.' "
9 Adonai said further to Moses, "I have closely watched the people, and they are a rebellious, stubborn bunch.
10 Now do not try to stop Me when I become angry and destroy them. Then I will make you, Moses, and your descendants into a great nation."
11 Moses began to plead and beg Adonai. He said, "Adonai, why are You angry against the people whom You freed from Egypt with Your great power and miracles?
12 Do You want the Egyptians to say that You deliberately took them out to kill them in the mountains and erase them from the face of the earth? Turn back Your anger, and do not punish the Israelites.

---

2. Aaron replied, "Remove the rings from the ears of your wives and children and bring them to me."
Aaron was certain that the women would not to part with their jewelry. He felt that he ought to delay the people as long as possible, for Moses was bound to appear sooner or later. However, his plan was foiled by the men, who also took off their own ornaments.

4. He melted the golden rings and molded them into a golden calf.
In Egypt the Israelites had seen the worship of bulls by the Egyptians. Bulls were worshipped in other ancient lands, too. With this form of worship so common, the Israelites, in their weakness, imitated the other peoples around them.

5. When Aaron saw the mood of the people, he built an altar.
Aaron saw that they believed in the golden calf. In order to delay their worshipping of this animal, he built an altar, hoping that Moses would arrive by the time he finished and that they would celebrate with a feast to Adonai.
 Perhaps, Aaron acquiesced to those Israelites who wanted to worship the Golden Calf because he feared that his refusal would result in bloodshed.

8. This is the god of Israel who brought us out of Egypt.
The episode of the golden calf raises the question of why a calf? Of all the graven images that people at that time worshipped, why did the Israelites make this kind of animal? What god did it represent?

Archaeologists feel it was one of two gods: some say the sun god of Egypt, some say the moon god of Canaan and Babylon. In Egypt there was a sacred bull, Apis, often cast in metal and often pictured with a sun disk between its horns.

The bull was also a symbol of the moon god of Sin, which was a very popular god in the land of Canaan.

The molding of the golden calf meant the people wished to go back to a form of worship that they had seen in Egypt.

13 Remember Your promises to Abraham, Isaac, and Jacob. You swore, and promised that You would make their descendants as numerous as the stars of the sky and give them the land You promised, so that they would be able to live in it forever."

14 Adonai relented and postponed the punishment He had planned.

15 Moses went down the mountain holding the two stone tablets with the Ten Commandments. They were two stone tablets written on both sides, with the writing visible from either side. **16** The tablets had been made by Adonai, and Adonai Himself had written on them.

17 When Joshua heard the sound of the people partying, he said to Moses, "It sounds as though there is a battle going on in the camp!"

18 Moses replied,

> "It is not a song of victory,
> nor the sound of defeat.
> That I hear. It is just plain singing."

19 As Moses approached the camp and saw the golden calf and the dancing, he lost his temper and threw down the Ten Commandments that were in his hands, shattering them. **20** He removed the golden calf that the people had made, and melted it in fire, and ground it into a fine powder. He mixed the powder in water, and made the Israelites drink the mixture.

21 Now Moses angrily said to Aaron, "How could you have permitted the people to commit such a great sin?"

---

14. Adonai relented and postponed the punishment He had planned.
Adonai loved the Israelites.

The original intent was to dwell in the midst of the Israelites without the intermediary of a sanctuary between Him and His people. However, the sin of the golden calf torpedoed His plan. Adonai even refused to dwell in the sanctuary until Moses prevailed upon Him to reside in their midst.

15. They were two stone tablets written on both sides, with the writing visible from either side.
The tablets could be seen by all the Israelites because the writing was visible from all sides. The Rabbis interpret this visual miracle to demonstrate that Adonai's commandments are visual and active in every facet of one's life, from the mundane, everyday pursuits to one's religious activities.

17. When Joshua heard the sound of the people partying, he said to Moses, "It sounds as though there is a battle going on in the camp!"
Moses left Joshua to wait and to escort him back to camp. Sounds in the desert can travel very far. He heard the noise, but he could not see the commotion swirling around the golden calf.

19. He lost his temper and threw down the Ten Commandments that were in his hand, shattering them.
Moses threw down the tablets because he felt that a people who could betray Adonai so quickly were not worthy of receiving them.

19. As Moses approached the camp and saw the golden calf and the dancing, he lost his temper and threw down the Ten Commandments that were in his hands, shattering them.
The midrash says that the broken stones of the Ten Commandments were saved and stored in the Ark of the Covenant.

20. He removed the golden calf that the people had made, and melted it in fire.
This was the demonstration of the futility of idol worship. Moses did all these things to the calf to show the people how easily it could be destroyed and made into nothing.

21. Now Moses angrily said to Aaron, "How could you have permitted the people to commit such a great sin?"
How did the people torture you to the point that you helped bring this sin upon them? *Rashi*

22 Aaron replied, "Do not be angry, my lord, but you must be aware that the people have evil in their blood. **23** They insisted and said to me, 'Make a god to lead us, since the man who took us out of Egypt has disappeared.'
24 When I asked them, 'Who has gold to contribute?' they willingly took off their gold jewelry and gave it to me. I threw the gold jewelry into the fire and out came a golden calf."
25 Moses realized that the people were out of control: Aaron had been unable to restrain them, and they were a danger to those who would try to control them.
26 Moses stood up at the camp's entrance and shouted, "Whoever is on Adonai's side, join me!" All the Levites immediately gathered around him.
27 Moses said to them, "This is what Adonai says: Let each man buckle on his sword, and go from one end of the camp to the other. Let each one execute all the idol worshippers, even his own brother, close friend, or relative." **28** The Levites did as Moses ordered, and about three thousand Israelites were killed.
29 Moses said, "Today, Adonai has ordained you with a special blessing as a nation dedicated to Adonai. At Adonai's command you have been willing to kill your own sons and brothers."
30 The next day, Moses said to the people, "You have committed a terrible sin. Now I will return to Adonai and try to gain forgiveness for your crime." **31** Moses returned to Adonai and said, "The people have committed a terrible sin by making the golden calf. **32** Please forgive their sin. If not, You can erase me out of the future You have written."
33 Adonai replied to Moses, "I will erase from My history those who have sinned against Me. **34** Now go; you still have to lead the people to the land I have given to you. I will send My angel to lead you. But when I make My final decision, I will take their sin into account."

---

26. Moses stood up at the camp's entrance and shouted, "Whoever is on Adonai's side, join me!" All the Levites immediately gathered around him.
Moses was from the tribe of Levi. The Levites without hesitation immediately joined Moses. The Levites remained faithful and observed the laws of the covenant.

27. Go from one end of the camp to the other. Let each man execute all the idol worshippers.
The Israelites were out of control, and it was necessary to support the Levites and punish the sinners. That is why the punishment had to be carried out immediately and openly, so that everyone could see the punishment. *Sforno*

30. Now I will return to Adonai and try to gain forgiveness for your crime.
Moses was the first biblical figure to assert the crucial importance of forgiveness in Adonai's relationship with man.

The worshippers of the golden calf were initially condemned to death by Adonai.

Moses was distressed by Adonai's decree, which did not leave the door open to forgiveness. Addressing the people, he said: "You have committed a terrible sin…I will…try to gain forgiveness for your crime." Moses, forceful argument and his pleas to Adonai formulated the theological doctrine of forgiveness as a permanent factor in divine judgment.

34. Now go; you still have to lead the people to the land I have given to you.
I have forgiven their sin on account of your entreaties and prayers. Now, if you love them so much, get up and get moving and lead.

34. But when I make My final decision, I will take their sin into account.
I eventually will make a full and final accounting if they sin again.

35 Then Adonai sent a plague among the Israelites because of the golden calf Aaron had made.

33
Now Adonai said to Moses, "You and the people you took out of Egypt will have to leave this place and go to the land I swore to give to Abraham, Isaac, and Jacob and to their descendants. **2** I will send an angel ahead of you, and I will drive out the Canaanites, Amorites, Hittites, Perizzites, Hivites, and Jebusites.
3 It is a land flowing with milk and honey. However, I will not go with you, since they are a stubborn people, and I may be tempted to destroy them along the way." **4** When the Israelites heard this disastrous news, they began to mourn, and they stripped the jewelry from their clothes.
5 Adonai told Moses to say to the Israelites, "You are a stubborn people. In just one second I can completely destroy you. Now remove your jewelry and I will think about how to punish you."
6 After that warning at Mount Horeb, the people no longer wore their jewelry.
7 Now Moses took his personal tent and set it up outside the camp. He called it the Meeting Tent. Anyone who wanted to consult Adonai would go to the Meeting Tent outside the camp.
8 Whenever Moses went out to his tent, all the people would stand at attention, watching Moses until he entered his tent.
9 Whenever Moses went into his tent, a pillar of cloud would descend and stand guard at the tent's entrance, and there Adonai would speak to Moses. **10** When the people saw the pillar of cloud standing at the entrance of the tent, they would stand and bow toward the entrance of his tent.
11 There Adonai would speak to Moses face to face, just as a person speaks to a close friend. Afterwards Moses would return to the camp. But his assistant, Joshua son of Nun, remained in the tent.

Moses Asks for Guidance
3rd Aliyah

12 Moses said to Adonai, "You told me to lead the Israelites to the Promised Land, but You did not tell me who You would send with me. You also said that You specially chose me because You are pleased with me. **13** Now, if You are really pleased with me, guide me so that I will know how to continue pleasing You. And remember that this nation of Israel is Your people."

---

2. I will drive out the Canaanites, Amorites, Hittites, Perizzites, Hivites, and Jebusites.
As Adonai promised (in Shemot 3:8), He will keep His promise and still drive out these six nations.

4. When the Israelites heard this disastrous news, they began to mourn.
They heard that Adonai had called them a "stubborn people," so they went into mourning.

11. But his assistant, Joshua son of Nun, remained in the tent.
The Rambam says that Moses was 80 years old and Joshua, his assistant, was 42 years old.

13. Guide me so that I will know how to continue pleasing You.
Moses pleads with Adonai to explain His way of dealing with humans. He wants to lead and govern the Israelites in accordance with Adonai's will.

14 Adonai replied, "I will go and lead you." **15** Moses said, "If You are not going to accompany us personally, do not make us leave this place. **16** Unless You accompany us, no one will even know that I and Your people have pleased You. How will anyone know that we are different from any nation on the face of the earth?"

No Human Will Ever See My Face *4th Aliyah*

17 Adonai said to Moses, "You have pleased Me, and I chose you by name. I will fulfill your request." **18** Moses begged, "Please let me see Your Holy Presence." **19** Adonai replied, "I will make My Presence pass before you, and I will reveal the meaning of My Holy Name to you, and I will have mercy and show kindness to anyone I choose." **20** Adonai explained, "You will not see My face. No human can see Me and remain alive." **21** Then Adonai said to Moses, "However, I have a safe place on the rocky mountain where you can stand. **22** When My Presence passes by, I will place you in a crack in a rock and cover you with My hand. This will protect you from My power when I pass by. **23** Then I will remove My protective power, and you will have a vision of My back. My face itself, however, will not be seen."

The Second Ten Commandments *5th Aliyah*

34 Adonai said to Moses, "Carve two tablets of the Ten Commandments, just like the first ones. I will write on those tablets the same commandments that were on the first tablets, the ones you shattered. **2** Be ready to climb Mount Sinai in the morning and stand waiting for Me on the mountaintop.
3 Allow no person to climb up with you, and let no one else on the entire mountain. Even the cattle and sheep must not graze close to the mountain."
4 Moses carved two stone tablets like the first. Early in the morning, as Adonai had commanded him, he climbed Mount Sinai, carrying the two stone tablets.
5 Adonai descended in a cloud, and stood there near Moses.

---

16. Unless you accompany us, no one will even know that I and Your people have pleased You. How will anyone know that we are different from any nation on the face of the earth?
Moses asks Adonai to personally accompany the Israelites in their conquest of Canaan. Moses argues that all nations recognize that the power and strength of the Hebrew people emanates from Adonai.

Otherwise, they are no different from any other nation; they are only an easily erased footprint in the history of mankind.

18. Please let me see Your Holy Presence.
Moses pleads with Adonai and says, "Please give me the wisdom to understand and carry out your orders."

23. Then I will remove my protective power, and you will have a vision of My back. My face itself, however, will not be seen.
Adonai has no material body and therefore cannot possibly be seen. He has no beginning and no end. The commentators all struggle with the meaning of these phrases.

Some interpret the phrases to mean the glow of His radiance.

3. Allow no person to climb up with you.
When Moses went up the mountain for the first time, he was escorted part of the way by others. Now he went alone, and this was proper for, having failed in the first ascent. Moses now preferred to do things quietly and without fanfare.

6 Adonai passed before Moses and proclaimed, "I am Adonai, Adonai. merciful and kind, am I. I am slow to anger, overflowing with love and truth.
7 I show love for thousands of generations, I forgive sin and rebellion, but I do not forgive those who are guilty. I remember the sins of the parents, and I will punish the children and grandchildren up to the third and fourth generation."
8 Moses immediately bowed his head and worshipped.
9 He said, "Adonai, if You are pleased with me, come among us. This nation may be stubborn, but please forgive our sins and errors, and make us Your special people."

Do Not Trust the Inhabitants
6th Aliyah

10 Adonai said, I will make a covenant with the Israelites and will perform miracles that have never been done before among any nation. All the Israelites with you will see the miracles that I, Adonai, will perform.
11 Listen carefully to what I am telling you today. I will drive out the Amorites, Canaanites, Hivites, Perizzites, Hittites, and Jebusites before you. **12** Never make a treaty with the people who live in the land where you are going, because they will trap you. **13** You must destroy their altars, smash their sacred pillars, and cut down their goddess Asherah trees. **14** Do not worship any other gods, because I, Adonai, demand exclusive worship.
15 You must not make a treaty with the people who live in the land. They will invite you to pray and sacrifice to their gods, and you will end up eating their sacrifices. **16** Then you will allow their daughters to marry your sons, and when their daughters worship their gods, they will lead your sons to follow their religion.
17 Do not make idols of any kind. **18** Observe the Festival of Matzot. You must eat matzot for seven days, just as I have commanded, at the designated time in the month of Aviv. It was in the month of standing grain that you left Egypt. **19** The first-born is Mine. You must separate the males of the first-born cattle and sheep from all your livestock.

---

6. Adonai, merciful and kind.
Beginning with this verse and through verse 8, Adonai's thirteen qualities are present:

(1) Adonai is doubly merciful, (2) the Ruler of nature and mankind, (3) sympathetic to sufferers, (4) gracious to the oppressed, (5) slow to anger, (6) generous to humans, (7) truthful, (8) remembers the good deeds of ancestors, (9) forgives the sins which humans commit because of weakness, (10) forgives the sins which humans commit because of rebelliousness, (11) forgives the sins committed by error, (12) punishes only those who deserve punishment.

7. I remember the sins of the parents, and I will punish the children and grandchildren up to the third and fourth generation.
Adonai waits patiently in the hope that the sinner will repent and change his behavior. He will wait until the third and fourth generation for punishment. However, if the descendants continue and add to the wickedness then they will be punished.

10. I will make a covenant with the Israelites.
In answer to Moses' prayer for the forgiveness of Israel, Adonai promised to continue His remarkable deeds for them, to demonstrate His continued interest in their well-being.

13. And cut down their goddess Asherah trees.
Asherah was the name of a Canaanite goddess, the mother of seventy gods. Asherah also refers to a wooden pole or tree which stood in front of Canaanite temples.

Asherah was the goddess of fertility and a tree or pole was her symbol. When the Israelites entered Canaan, many were attracted to the symbol of Asherah. The Canaanites invited the Israelites to pray and sacrifice to their gods.

20 The first-born of a donkey can be redeemed with a sheep, and if it is not redeemed, you must kill it. You must also redeem every first-born of your sons.
Do not appear in My Tabernacle empty-handed.
21 You may work on the six workdays, but on Saturday you must stop working and stop plowing and reaping.
22 Observe the Festival of Shavuot, of the first fruits of your wheat harvest. Also keep the Harvest Festival (Sukkot) at the turn of the year.
23 Three times each year all your males must appear before Adonai.
24 When I drive out the other nations and enlarge your boundaries, no one will attack your land when you appear before Adonai three times each year.
25 Do not slaughter the Passover sacrifice with leaven. Do not allow the meat of the Passover sacrifice to remain until morning.
26 Bring the best of the first fruits of your crops to the Temple of Adonai.
Do not boil a goat in the milk of its mother.

Moses Returns from Mount Sinai *7th Aliyah*

27 Adonai said to Moses, "I want you to write these words down, since it is with these words that I have made a covenant between you and Israel.
 28 Moses stayed on the mountain for forty days and forty nights without eating or drinking. Adonai wrote the words of the Ten Commandments on the two tablets of stone.

---

22. Observe the Festival of Shavuot.
Shavuot is one of the oldest of all Jewish festivals. "Shavuot" means "weeks" and it falls exactly seven weeks after the second day of Passover, on the sixth and seventh days of the month of Sivan. (Reform Jews observe only the first of the two days.) Another, non-Jewish, name for Shavuot is Pentecost, which in Greek means "fiftieth," because it takes place on the fiftieth day after the beginning of Passover.

Shavuot is a triple holiday, a threefold celebration which commemorates the giving of the Torah on Mount Sinai, the harvesting of wheat in Israel, and the ripening of the first fruits in the Holy Land.

22. Keep the Harvest Festival (Sukkot).
Five days after Yom Kippur, the holiest day of the Jewish Year, comes one of the happiest of all festivals. It is called Sukkot, which means "booths" or "tabernacles." One of the nicest things about Sukkot is that it lasts for nine days and contains a variety of celebrations.

(Reform Jews observe only one of the first two days, and combine the last two days.)

In the Torah, Sukkot is called *Hag ha-Sukkot*, the Festival of Booths (or Tabernacles), and *Hag ha-Asif*, the Harvest Festival.

Before the reading of the Torah in the synagogue we recite a blessing, and after the reading of the Torah we recite a blessing. If you count the words of both of these blessings, you will find a total of forty words.

Our sages say that this is to remind us that Moses spent forty days and forty nights on Mount Sinai while receiving the Torah.

28. Moses stayed on the mountain for forty days and forty nights.
There is a story in the Talmud about Rabbi Yochanan, who told Rabbi Hayya bar Abbi that he sold a vineyard and a field of olive trees for a large sum of money. I sold the field for six gold coins and bought something worth forty gold coins. Rabbi Hiyya asked, "Please explain the transaction to me." Rabbi Johanan explained, "I sold vineyard and fields, which were created in six days, and I bought the Torah, which was created in forty days.

Midrash Tanhuma

29 Moses came down from Mount Sinai with the two tablets of the Ten Commandments. As Moses descended from the mountain, he did not realize that his face was glowing because Adonai had spoken to him.
30 When Aaron and all the Israelites saw that the face of Moses was glowing with a brilliant light, they were afraid to approach him.
31 Moses called them, and when Aaron and the community leaders came to him, Moses spoke to them.
32 Afterwards all the Israelites came, and Moses relayed the instructions Adonai had given him on Mount Sinai.

Moses and His Veil *Maftir*

33 When Moses finished speaking with them, he placed a veil over his face.
34 Whenever Moses went to speak with Adonai, he would remove the veil until he was ready to leave. Then he would go out and speak to the Israelites, and tell them what he had been commanded. **35** The Israelites could see that the face of Moses was glowing brilliantly. Moses would then replace the veil over his face until he once again went in to speak to Adonai.

---

29. As Moses descended from the mountain, he did not realize that his face was glowing because Adonai had spoken to him.
Years ago one of the anti-Semitic ways of picturing a Jew was to show him with horns. In fact, people who lived in places where they had never seen a Jew sometimes heard – and believed – stories that a Jew had horns. The origin of this silly but painful accusation may have come through a mistake in understanding the passage that described how Moses looked when he came down from Mount Sinai.

It says that his face glowed with a brilliant light. The Hebrew word *keren*, which is used for a beam of light, basically also means "horn."

At the end of the Middle Ages, during the period of the Renaissance, when non-Jews were rediscovering Hebrew, the secondary meaning of *keren* ("beam") was not always realized. Michelangelo, the great sculptor of those days, made a famous statue of Moses – a statue which shows how much he respected Moses – he actually put horns on his forehead.

32. Afterwards all the Israelites came, and Moses relayed the instructions Adonai had given him on Mount Sinai.
The Israelites were camped around Mount Sinai and accepted the teaching of the Torah. Each generation has passed down the teaching of the Torah to the next generation, and now it is in the hands of the present generation.

The Mishnah (collection of Jewish law) says: "Moses received the Torah at Sinai and handed it to Joshua. Joshua handed it to the elders, and the elders to the prophets, and the prophets to the people of the Great Assembly."

33. When Moses finished speaking with them, he placed a veil over his face.
The glow on the face of Moses was his sign of authority. Moses, the leader, spoke with authority when he relayed Adonai's instructions to the community leaders.

Moses was the consummate teacher who instructed by face-to-face interaction.

34. Whenever Moses went to speak with Adonai, he would remove the veil until he was ready to leave.
Moses was a leader with three different personalities. When Adonai spoke with him, when he transmitted Adonai's message to the Israelites, and when he was engaged in his own personal affairs.

Moses did not use his glow when dealing with his family or personal affairs such as eating, drinking, and conversing with his family. However, when he was engaged in teaching or transmitting a message from Adonai, he did not veil his face, so the people would feel the spirituality and holiness of the message.

וַיַּקְהֵל Vayakhel

MOSES ASSEMBLES THE ISRAELITES

35 Moses assembled the entire Israelite community and said to them, "These are the laws that Adonai has commanded you to observe: **2** You may do work during the six workdays, but Saturday must be kept holy as a Sabbath of rest. Whoever does any work on that day shall be put to death. **3** Wherever you live, do not light a fire on the Sabbath."

4 Moses continued and said, "This is the law that Adonai has commanded: **5** Collect gifts among yourselves as an offering to Adonai. Any person who willingly feels like giving an offering to Adonai can bring any of the following: gold, silver, copper, **6** blue wool, purple wool, wool dyed scarlet, fine linen, goats' wool, **7** tanned rams' skins, dyed blue sealskins, acacia wood, **8** oil for the menorah, aromatic spices for the anointing oil and perfume incense, **9** as well as onyxes and other precious jewels for the ephod and the breastplate.

10 Every skilled person can volunteer and help make everything that Adonai has commanded: **11** The Tabernacle with its tent, roof, clasps, frames, crossbars, and pillars; **12** the ark and its carrying poles, the ark cover, the cloth partition; **13** the table along with its carrying poles, all its utensils and the showbread; **14** the menorah with its utensils, lights, and illuminating oil; **15** the incense altar and its carrying poles; the anointing oil, the perfumed incense, the curtain for the entrance to the Tabernacle; **16** the sacrificial altar with its carrying poles and all its utensils; the washbasin, **17** the curtains for the enclosure, its frames and its bases, the curtain for the entrance to the enclosure, **18** the pegs for the tent, the pegs for the enclosure, the tying ropes; **19** the packing cloths for sacred use, the sacred garments for Aaron the priest, and the garments that his sons will wear during the services in the Tabernacle."

---

1. Moses assembled the entire Israelite community.
Moses assembled the entire community the day after the Day of Atonement, Yom Kippur, and informed them how they could help build the Tabernacle. Because the entire community was present, no one could complain that they did not have the opportunity to contribute to the building of the Tabernacle. *Rashi*

2. You may do work during the six workdays, but Saturday must be kept holy as a Sabbath of rest.
Most of the work of humans involves the use of light or heat. It includes lighting a match, turning on an electric light, and all kinds of work in manufacturing products, driving, flying etc.

3. Wherever you live, do not light a fire on the Sabbath.
This is mitzvah number 114.

The commentator Keli Yakar views "wherever you live" as excluding the Temple, where fires were lit for the purpose of offering Sabbath sacrifices.

5. Collect gifts among yourselves as an offering to Adonai.
Contributing gold and precious gifts for the Tabernacle was the way that the Children of Israel atoned for their sin in having worshipped the golden calf. By accepting the gifts and allowing the Tabernacle to be built, Adonai demonstrated to the Israelites and the entire world that He had forgiven them for the sin of the golden calf.

Gifts for the Tabernacle
2nd Aliyah

20 The entire Israelite community left Moses. **21** And everyone who was willing to volunteer came forward. Each person who wanted brought an offering to Adonai for the construction of the Meeting Tent and all its furnishings, and for the sacred garments.

22 The men and the women, and all who wanted to, brought offerings of bracelets, earrings, rings, and ornaments, all made of gold. They presented their gold offerings as wave offerings to Adonai.

23 Every person who had blue wool, purple wool, scarlet wool, fine linen, goats' wool, tanned rams' skins or blue-dyed sealskins, brought them. **24** Those who offered silver or copper brought it as a divine offering, and everyone who had acacia wood that could be used for the Tabernacle also brought it.

25 Every skilled woman who could sew brought spun yarn of blue wool, purple wool, scarlet wool, and woven linen.

26 Highly skilled women also spun the goats' wool.

27 The tribal leaders brought onyxes and other precious jewels for the ephod and the breastplate. **28** They also brought aromatic spices and olive oil for the menorah, the anointing oil, and the perfumed incense.

29 Every man and woman willingly brought offerings to Adonai to complete all the tasks Adonai had commanded through Moses.

Betzalel the Architect
3rd Aliyah

30 Moses said to the Israelites, "Adonai has chosen Betzalel son of Uri, grandson of Hur, from the tribe of Judah, **31** and has filled him with a divine spirit of wisdom, understanding, knowledge, and a talent for all types of craftsmanship.

32 He will be the architect, and he will also create artistic objects of gold, silver, and copper, **33** cut precious jewels, and do carpentry and other skilled work.

34 Adonai has also given Oholiav son of Achisamakh, of the tribe of Dan, the ability to teach others.

---

27. The tribal leaders brought onyxes and other precious jewels for the ephod and the breastplate.
The Tabernacle was constructed by everyone in the Israelite nation. Only after the general population brought their donation did the leaders bring theirs. They said, "Let the people bring whatever they like; then we will provide whatever is lacking." However, the Israelites brought a surplus and no more was needed. The leaders were distressed because they could not contribute, so they brought jewels for the outer garments of the High Priest.

29. Every man and woman willingly brought offerings to Adonai.
Adonai desires that the offerings come from the heart and be given freely and generously.

He could have taxed the Israelites to contribute each a set amount based on their worth or income. Instead they were asked to give what they could afford.

34. Adonai has also given Oholiav son of Achisamakh, of the tribe of Dan, the ability to teach others.
Dan was one of the lowliest tribes, since they were descended from a maidservant Bilhah. Yet, despite Oholiav's background, Adonai rated him as the equal to Betzalel, who was from the mighty tribe of Judah. The midrash says that the selection of both men was significant. Everyone was equal, the insignificant from Dan and the mighty from Judah.

35 Adonai has granted them a talent for all types of craftsmanship, to weave materials, to embroider patterns with blue, red, and crimson wool, and to weave fine linen. These experts will be able to perform and do all the necessary planning and work.

36

Betzalel, Oholiav, and every other skilled individual to whom Adonai has granted the wisdom and understanding to know how to do all the work necessary for the sacred task shall carry out all that Adonai has commanded."
2 Moses summoned Betzalel, Oholiav, and all the other skilled individuals upon whom Adonai had bestowed a natural talent, and who volunteered to dedicate themselves to completing the task. **3** They took from Moses all the materials that the Israelites had brought to complete the sacred task. Meanwhile, the Israelites continued bringing more gifts.
4 The craftsmen engaged in the sacred work **5** complained to Moses, "The people are bringing much more than is needed to complete the work that Adonai commanded to do."
6 So Moses made an announcement in the camp, "Let no man or woman bring any more contributions for the Tabernacle." The people stopped bringing, **7** because there was more than enough materials for all the work that had to be done.

Erecting the Tabernacle — *4th Aliyah*

8 The most talented craftsmen worked on the Tabernacle itself, which consisted of ten tapestries made of woven linen, with blue, purple, and scarlet wool, embroidered with cherubs.

---

1. Betzalel, Oholiav.
The midrash notes that Betzalel came from the largest tribe of Judah. Oholiav came from one of the smallest tribes.

This selection teaches us that in Israel, both the mighty and the meek must be united to produce a successful and a united nation.

3. They took from Moses all the materials that the Israelites had brought to complete the sacred task.
The Israelites brought their donations to Moses. Then the artisans and the builders came and selected the materials they needed.

4-5. The craftsmen engaged in the sacred work complained to Moses, "The people are bringing much more than is needed to complete the work that Adonai commanded to do."
The people continue to bring materials, and our workshops are overflowing with goods. We have no place to work and we have more than enough to complete our work. Please stop!

7. Because there was more than enough materials for all the work that had to be done.
The artisans did not need to skimp or cut corners, because there were enough materials.

8. The most talented craftsmen worked on the Tabernacle itself.
The building of the Tabernacle required a high quality of workmanship in constructing things out of metal, wood, or cloth. While spinning and weaving on a simple loom was widely known in those days, the Torah's use of different terms applied to the manufacture of cloth suggests that more complicated processes were used, including embroidery with different colors perhaps, or even the weaving of scenes into the cloth. Archaeological evidence of paintings on walls shows that these processes too were known.

Similarly in the construction of the Tabernacle, accurate and skillful craftsmanship was required. Archaeological evidence shows that in those days carpentry was done with such tools as saws, chisels, drills, and hammers.

Finally, the Israelites had learned much about metal work also, creating things not only out of pure (a bar of) gold such as the cherubim and the menorah, but also out of wood overlaid with gold, such as the ark and the table.

9 All the tapestries were the same size: 42 feet long and 6 feet wide. **10** The first five tapestries and the second five tapestries were sewn together. **11** Loops of blue wool were sewn on the edge of the last tapestry of the first group of five, and loops were also sewn on the second group of tapestries.

12 The fifty loops on the first set of tapestries and the fifty loops on the edge of the second set of tapestries were exactly opposite each other. **13** Fifty gold fasteners were made to join the two sets of tapestries together to make the Tabernacle into a single unit.

14 They wove eleven sheets of goats' wool to cover the roof of the Tabernacle. **15** All the sheets were the same size: 45 feet long and 6 feet wide.

16 Five sheets were sewn together to form one group, and six to form the second group.

17 Fifty loops were sewn on the last sheet of the first group, and another fifty loops on the edge of the last sheet of the second group. **18** They also made fifty copper fasteners to join the sheets together and make it into a single unit.

19 They made the roof for the Tabernacle out of tanned rams' skins, and another roof above it out of blue-dyed sealskins.

Making the Frame   5th Aliyah

20 They made the upright frames for the Tabernacle out of acacia wood. **21** Each frame was 15 feet long and 2.25 feet wide, **22** with two matching square pegs on the bottom. All of the Tabernacle's frames were made exactly the same.

23 They made twenty frames for the southern wall of the Tabernacle, **24** with forty silver bases to go under the twenty frames. There were two bases under each frame, one base under each of the two square pegs at the bottom of each frame.

25 They also made twenty frames on the second wall of the Tabernacle to the north, **26** along with forty silver bases, two bases under each frame's two pegs.

27 They made six frames for the western wall of the Tabernacle, **28** and two frames for the corners of the Tabernacle.

29 At the bottom, all the frames were joined next to one another on top, every pair was joined with a square ring. The two frames on the two corners were also joined together with a square ring.

---

20. They made the upright frames for the Tabernacle out of acacia wood.
Several species of the acacia tree grow in Israel, mostly in the Judean desert and in the southern Negev. It is a small tree with a thin trunk. At present, a species of the acacia tall trees with thick trunks are found in the Jordan Valley near the mouth of the Yarmuk River. These trees are regarded as holy and are not cut down by the local inhabitants. This species must have been the trees that provided the wood for the Tabernacle.

The wood from the tall acacia is very hard but light. It does not absorb moisture and is suitable for construction and was used in shipbuilding.

20. They made the upright frames for the Tabernacle out of acacia wood.
There are several versions of the construction details of the beams. This version is by Senash.

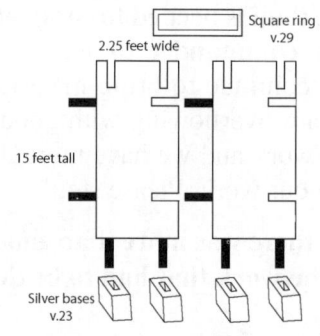

30 On the western side, there was a total of eight frames, along with sixteen bases, two bases for each frame.
31 They made five crossbars of acacia wood for the first wall of the Tabernacle to the south, **32** a second set of five crossbars for the second wall of the Tabernacle to the north, and five similar crossbars for the western wall of the Tabernacle.
33 The middle crossbar was made to go through the center of the frames from one end to the other.
34 They covered the frames with a layer of gold.
They also made the rings that would hold the crossbars out of gold, and they covered the crossbars with a layer of gold.
35 They made the cloth partition out of blue, purple, and scarlet wool and woven linen, embroidered with cherubs.
36 They made four acacia poles to hold it, covering the poles with a layer of gold with gold hooks attached. They also cast four silver bases for these poles.
37 They made an embroidered curtain for the entrance to the tent out of blue, purple, and scarlet wool and woven linen.
38 There were five poles to support it, along with gold hooks, caps, and bands. There were five copper bases for these poles.

37

Betzalel made the ark of acacia wood: 3.5 feet long and 2.25 feet wide, and 2.25 feet high.
2 He covered it with a layer of pure gold on the inside, and made a gold molding for it all around. **3** He cast four gold rings for its four corners, two rings for one side, and two for the other.
4 He made carrying poles of acacia wood and covered them with a layer of gold. **5** Then he fitted the carrying poles into the rings on the sides of the ark, so that it could be carried with them.

---

1. Betzalel made the ark of acacia wood.
In His instructions to Moses about the construction of the Tabernacle, Adonai asked that Moses "Accept the gifts from everyone who wants to give willingly" (Shemot 25:2). No one was to be forced to give for the building of the Tabernacle. The Israelites in the wilderness were completely generous in their response. They gave gold and silver. They gave materials of every kind. They also gave the services of their labor. The Tabernacle proved to be a beautiful House of Worship which accompanied them all the years of their wandering. In the Ark of the Tabernacle were placed the Tablets of the Law.

Wherever Jews have settled throughout the world they have built synagogues.

The oldest standing synagogue in the United States is the Touro Synagogue in Newport, Rhode Island. Begun in 1759, it was completed in 1763. It has been designated a National Historical Site and is visited by large numbers of people annually. Like the Tabernacle of the wilderness, the Touro Synagogue of Newport was also built by freewill gifts of pioneer Jewish colonists.

1. Betzalel made the ark of acacia wood: 3.5 feet long.
Betzalel, the chief and most skilled artisan, made the ark as a labor of love entirely by himself since he was endowed with a "special spirit" (Shemot 31:3). He understood Adonai's design and made the ark exactly as He wanted it.

6 He made a pure golden cover, 3.75 feet long and 2.25 feet wide. **7** He hammered two golden cherubs from the two ends of the cover. **8** The cherubs were made from the same piece of gold as the cover, one cherub on one end, and the second cherub on the other end. **9** The cherubs had their wings stretched outward so as to shield the ark cover with their wings. The cherubs faced each other, with their faces turned downward toward the cover of the ark.
10 He made the table out of acacia wood, 3 feet long, 18 inches wide, and 2.25 feet high.
11 He covered the table with a layer of pure gold. **12** He made a 3-inch-wide gold rim for it and placed the gold rim on the frame.
13 He cast four gold rings for the table, attaching the rings on the corners of its four legs.
14 The rings were close to the frame and were able to hold the poles used to carry the table.
15 He made acacia poles to carry the table, and covered them with a layer of gold.
16 Out of pure gold he made pans to go on the table, bread pans, bowls, ladles, and jars, and side frames to serve as dividers for the bread.

Making the Menorah *6th Aliyah*

17 He made the menorah out of pure gold, hammering the menorah, with its base, stem, decorative cups, buds, and flowers, out of a single piece of gold.
18 Six branches extended from the menorah's sides, three branches on one side, and three branches on the other. **19** There were three embossed cups, a bud, and a flower on each branch. All six branches extending from the menorah were exactly the same.
20 The menorah's stem had four embossed cups, along with its own buds and flowers. **21** There was a bud at the base of each of the six branches extending from the center. **22** The buds and branches were all made from the same golden ingot as the menorah itself. The menorah was hammered from a single ingot of pure gold.
23 He made the menorah with seven lamps. He also made its wicks, the tongs, and the ash shovels out of pure gold. **24** The menorah and all its parts were made from a talent of gold weighing 75 pounds.
25 He constructed the incense altar of acacia wood, 18 inches square and, including its horns, 3 feet high. **26** He covered its top, its walls, and its horns with a layer of pure gold, and made it a gold rim all around.

---

7. He hammered two golden cherubs from the two ends of the cover.
In addition to angels, the Torah also refers to other supernatural beings such as *cherubim* and *seraphim*. They have no human form but are winged creatures that the Torah (Ber. 3:24) refers to as angels with revolving swords at the east of Eden, to guard the path to the Tree of Life.

25. He constructed the incense altar of acacia wood.
He constructed the altar as a hollow structure made out of boards.
   The boards were made of acacia wood.

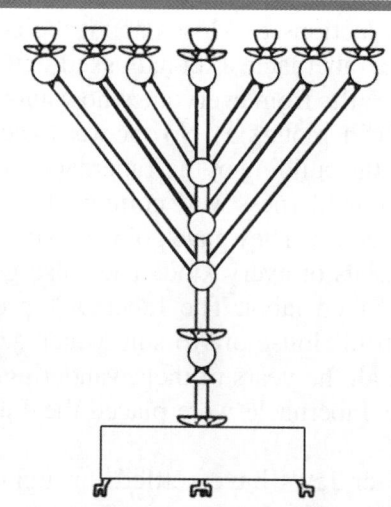

27 He made two rings for the altar below its rim on its two opposite sides, so as to hold the poles with which the altar was carried.
28 He made the carrying poles out of acacia wood and covered them with a layer of gold.
29 Using the skills of a perfumer, he blended the sacred anointing oil and the pure perfume incense.

Making the Altar
7th Aliyah

38 He made the sacrificial altar out of acacia wood, 7.5 feet square and 4.5 feet high. **2** He made horns on all four corners as part of the altar, and then covered the entire altar with a layer of copper.
3 He made all the altar's utensils, pots, shovels, basins, hooks, and fire pans. They were all made out of copper.
4 He made a grating out of copper mesh, and placed it below the altar's border, and extended it downward to the middle of the altar.
5 He cast four rings on the copper screen to hold the carrying poles. **6** He made acacia carrying poles and covered them with a layer of copper.
7 He inserted the carrying poles into the rings on the altar's corners, so that it could be carried. He constructed the altar as a hollow structure made out of boards.

---

29. Using the skills of a perfumer, he blended the sacred anointing oil and the pure perfume incense.
The "sacred anointing oil" was used for anointing the priests as well as the dishes and implements used in the Tabernacle services.

The perfumer used spices such as myrrh, aromatic cinnamon, and cassia which were soaked in boiling water and then kept in olive oil until they became saturated with their odors. The incense which was burnt every day consisted of a variety of herbs which were finely ground.

Perfumers also compounded cosmetics by mixing herbs and spices with oil.

The special incense called *ke- torat ha-sammim* (Vayikrah 4:7) was offered on the incense altar.

This incense offering was known as *ketoret tamid*, meaning "perpetual incense, was always burned day and night bu the high priest."

1. He made the sacrificial altar out of acacia wood.
The literal meaning of the Hebrew term *mizbeach* is "altar." More that four hundred references to altars are in the Torah. The Torah specifies unhewn stones or mounds of earth for altar construction.

The use of iron in the construction of the altar was unlawful; hence the stones had to be of naturally unhewn rock.

"An altar of earth you shall make. If you make an altar of stone for me, do not build it of cut stone (*gazith*), for by putting your tool to it you desecrate it" (Shemot 20:21–22).

This is explained in the Talmud to the effect that iron weapons shorten life while the altar, symbolizing peace between Adonai and man, prolongs it.

In Solomon's Temple, there was an altar of brass for burnt offerings and a golden altar for the burning of incense.

The small gold-plated altar of incense stood in front of the flight of stairs leading to the Holy of Holies (*Devir*), whereas the great altar for the burnt offerings was in the outer court.

Seizing the horns of the altar gave asylum to a person who had committed an act of unintentional homicide. If it was intentional, even a priest officiating at the altar could not escape his punishment. "If a person intentionally plots to kill his neighbor, then you must drag him even from My altar to put him to death" (Shemot 21:14).

8 He made the copper washbasin and its copper base from the mirrors of the women workers at the entrance of the Meeting Tent.

9 He made the enclosure for the Tabernacle. On the southern side, the woven linen hangings were 150 feet long; **10** the hangings were supported by twenty poles, with twenty copper bases and silver pole hooks and bands.

11 On the northern side, it was also 150 feet long, supported by twenty poles, with twenty copper bases and silver pole hooks and bands.

12 On the western side, the curtains were 75 feet long supported by ten poles, with ten bases and silver pole hooks and bands.

13 The eastern side was also 75 feet wide.

14 The hangings on one side of the enclosure were 22.5 feet long, supported by three poles with three bases.

15 The hangings on the other side of the enclosure's entrance were also 22.5 feet wide, supported by three poles with three bases.

16 The enclosure's hangings were all made of woven linen.

17 The bases for the poles were made of copper, while the pole hooks and bands were made of silver. All the enclosure's poles also had silver caps, and the poles themselves were covered with silver.

The Entrance Curtain
Maftir

18 The curtain for the entrance to the enclosure was embroidered out of blue, purple, and scarlet wool, together with woven linen. It was 30 feet long and 7.5 feet high, just like the other hangings of the enclosure.

19 It was supported by four poles, having four copper bases, and silver hooks, caps, and bands.

20 The pegs used for the Tabernacle and the surrounding enclosure were all made of copper.

---

8. He made the copper washbasin and its copper base from the mirrors of the women workers at the entrance of the Meeting Tent.
Abarbanel explains, he made the basin and stand from the mirrors of the women who crowded at the door of the Meeting Tent. Pure copper could not be polished to act as a mirror. Abarbanel said that they were made out of brass, which is an alloy of copper and other metals. Brass can be polished and can reflect an image just like a mirror. The pious women freely gave away their mirrors and found no more need to beautify themselves.

8. He made the copper washbasin and its copper base from the mirrors of the women workers at the entrance of the Meeting Tent.
The dimension of the copper basin is not given. The amount of mirror donations determined the size.

8. He made the copper washbasin and its copper base from the mirrors of the women workers at the entrance of the Meeting Tent.
These skilled women were those who could sew and spin goat's wool (Shemot 35:25–26) into clothes and decorative curtains.

פְּקוּדֵי Pekuday

THE INVENTORY OF THE TABERNACLE

21 This is the inventory of the construction materials used to build the Tabernacle. Moses directed the Levites to assemble the quantities, and Ithamar, the son of Aaron, recorded the numbers. **22** Betzalel son of Uri, grandson of Hur, from the tribe of Judah, used these materials to construct everything that Adonai had commanded Moses. **23** His assistant was Oholiav son of Achisamakh, from the tribe of Dan, who was a skilled carpenter, and also was an expert in embroidering with blue, purple, and scarlet wool, and fine linen. **24** All the gold was used in the work to complete the sacred task. The amount of gold donated as a wave offering weighed 2,200 pounds by the sanctuary weight standard. **25** The silver census money collected from the community weighed 7,545 pounds by the sanctuary weight standard.

26 This total consisted of a third of an ounce of silver for each of the 603,550 men over twenty years old included in the census. **27** The 7,500 pounds of silver were used to cast the bases for the sanctuary and the cloth partition. There were a total of one hundred bases, 75 pounds for each base. **28** The hooks, clasps, and hoops for the pillars were made out of the remaining 45 pounds of silver. **29** The copper donated as a wave offering weighed 5,310 pounds. **30** It was used to make the bases for the entrance to the Meeting Tent and the copper altar along with its copper screen and all the altar's utensils, **31** the bases for the surrounding enclosure, the bases for the enclosure's entrance, the pegs for the Tabernacle, and the pegs for the surrounding enclosure.

39 They made the packing cloths for sacred use from the blue, purple, and scarlet wool. They also made the sacred garments for Aaron, just as Adonai had commanded Moses.

The Ephod and the Breastplate   *2nd Aliyah*

2 He wove the ephod out of gold thread, blue, purple, and scarlet wool, and woven linen.

---

21. This is the inventory of the construction materials used to build the Tabernacle.
The verses following give details and account for the material used for the construction of the Tabernacle.

21. Moses directed the Levites to assemble the quantities, and Ithamar, the son of Aaron, recorded the numbers.
The Israelites not infrequently complained about and were suspicious of the intentions and integrity of their leader.

The sages were very much aware of the problem, so every leader and public servant had to be open and above suspicion. "These are the quantities and the number." The books were open and anyone could inspect them.

29. The copper donated as a wave offering weighed 5,310 pounds.
The copper was used to make the rust-proof sockets, pegs, and the copper grating for the Tabernacle.

We also know that the artisans cast a huge basin and stand (Shemot 30:18) of copper, which is not mentioned in the first collection.

3 They hammered out thin sheets of gold and cut them into threads, which were woven into the blue, purple, and scarlet wool, and the fine linen. The ephod was made as an embroidered brocade.
4 They made shoulder pieces for the ephod and attached them to the two corners. **5** The ephod belt was made in the same way, out of gold thread, blue, purple, and scarlet wool, and woven linen. It was made exactly as Adonai had commanded Moses. **6** They prepared two onyx stones to be placed in gold settings. The stones were engraved with the names of Israel's sons. **7** He set them in the shoulder pieces of the ephod as a remembrance for Israel's sons. It was completed exactly as Adonai had commanded Moses.
8 The breastplate was embroidered, just like the ephod. It was also made from gold thread, blue, purple, and scarlet wool, and woven linen. **9** The breastplate was square when folded over. It was 18 inches long when folded over, and 18 inches wide.
10 The breastplate was decorated with four rows of precious jewels:
The first row: ruby, emerald, topaz.
11 The second row: amber, sapphire, jasper.
12 The third row: jacinth , agate, crystal.
13 The fourth row: beryl, onyx, amethyst.
14 Each of the jewels was engraved with the name of one of Israel's sons. Twelve names were engraved. There was one engraved jewel for each of the tribes.
15 Matched braided chains of pure gold were attached to the breastplate. **16** They made two gold settings and two gold rings, and they placed the two rings on the breastplate's two upper corners. **17** The two gold braids were then attached to the two rings on the breastplate's corners.
18 The two braids on the two corners were attached to the two gold settings on the shoulder pieces of the ephod.
19 They made two gold rings and placed them on the breastplate's two lower corners, on the inside edge of the ephod.
20 They made two gold rings and placed them on the bottoms of the ephod's two shoulder pieces toward the front, near where they were attached, above the ephod's belt.

10–14. The breastplate was decorated with four rows of precious jewels... Each of the jewels was engraved with the name of one of Israel's sons. Twelve names were engraved. There was one engraved jewel for each of the tribes.
The breastplate symbolized the diversity of the Israelite tribes. Each tribe will be allotted its own territory in Canaan. Each tribe was different in its own way of life, habits, and special ways of earning a livelihood, and each had its own special talents.

There are various opinions on the order of the tribal names and the identity of the jewels.

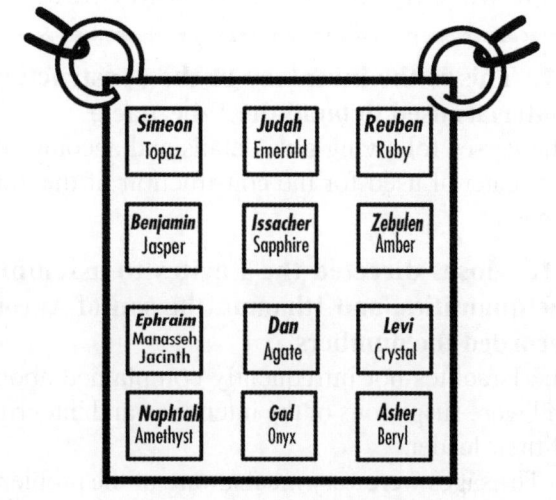

21 The rings on the breastplate were fastened to the rings of the ephod with a cord of blue wool, so that the breastplate would remain above the ephod's belt. Thus the breastplate could not be detached from the ephod.
All this was done exactly as Adonai had commanded Moses.

The Robe and the Ephod *3rd Aliyah*

22 He made the robe for the ephod, weaving it completely out of blue wool.
23 The robe's opening was in the middle, with a border all around so that it would not tear.
24 On the skirt of the robe, they made pomegranates out of blue, purple, and scarlet wool.
25 They made pure gold bells and placed the bells inside the pomegranates. The bells were all around the bottom of the robe between the pomegranates.
26 There was a bell and a pomegranate, a bell and a pomegranate, all around the bottom of the robe. It was specially made for the holy service, just as Adonai had commanded Moses.
27 They made the robes for Aaron and his sons by weaving them out of fine linen.
28 They made the linen headdresses and linen undergarments for Aaron and his sons.
29 They embroidered the belt from woven linen and blue, purple, and scarlet wool.
It was all done exactly as Adonai had commanded Moses.
30 They made a sacred medallion out of pure gold. It was engraved with the words "Holy to Adonai."
31 They put a cord of blue wool on the medallion so that it could be worn at the front of the headdress. Everything was done exactly as Adonai had commanded Moses.
32 All the work on the Meeting Tent was completed. The Israelites did all the work exactly as Adonai had instructed Moses.

Moses Inspects the Tabernacle *4th Aliyah*

33 Moses inspected the entire Tabernacle. He checked the Meeting Tent with its equipment, its fastenings, frames, crossbars, pillars, and bases; **34** the roof of tanned rams' skins and the roof of blue-dyed sealskins, the cloth curtain;
35 the ark and its carrying poles, the ark cover, **36** the table and its equipment, the showbread, **37** the pure gold menorah along with its prescribed lamps, all its utensils, and the illuminating oil;

---

25. They made pure gold bells and placed the bells inside the pomegranates.
They placed the bells inside the pomegranates before they were attached to the hem of the robe.
Maimonides

28. They made the linen headdresses and linen undergarments for Aaron and his sons.
The headdresses and the undergarments were the same for Aaron and his sons.
Maimonides

32. All the work on the Meeting Tent was completed.
The work on the Meeting Tent was completed on the 25th day of Kislev.
Hizkuni

37. The pure gold menorah along with its prescribed lamps.
The menorah was made of pure gold. The gold in every item in the Tabernacle was also pure. The menorah was the only object that did not use any additional material such as wood.
Bekor Shor

38 the golden altar, the anointing oil, the perfumed incense, the curtain for the Meeting Tent; **39** the copper altar with its carrying poles and all its equipment; the washbasin and its base; **40** the hangings for the enclosure, its poles and bases, the curtain for the entrance to the enclosure, its tying ropes and pegs, all the equipment used in the service in the Meeting Tent, **41** the packing cloths for sacred use, the sacred garments for Aaron the priest, and the garments that his sons would wear to serve in the Tabernacle.

42 The Israelites performed all the work exactly as Adonai had instructed Moses.

43 When Moses saw that all the work had been done exactly as Adonai had ordered, he blessed the craftsmen.

Erect the Meeting Tent
5th Aliyah

40 Adonai spoke to Moses, saying:
2 "You shall erect the Meeting Tent on the first day of the first month [Nisan]. **3** Put the ark in it and enclose the ark with the cloth partition. **4** Bring in the table and set the menorah on it and light its lamps.

5 Place the gold incense altar directly in front of the ark, and then set up the curtain at the entrance of the Tabernacle.

6 Place the sacrificial altar in front of the entrance of the Meeting Tent. **7** Then place the washbasin between the Meeting Tent and the altar, and fill it with water.

---

42. The Israelites performed all the work exactly as Adonai had instructed Moses.
Every item was supervised by Moses, and the order in which it was brought into the Tabernacle was exactly as Adonai commanded Moses.

43. When Moses saw that all the work had been done exactly as Adonai had ordered, he blessed the craftsmen.
It had been a huge task, carried out under difficult conditions in the desert, far from material sources. The laborers worked with enthusiasm and dedication and deserved a thank you from a grateful leader, Moses.

43. When Moses saw that all the work had been done exactly as Adonai had ordered, he blessed the craftsmen.
Moses was the consummate executive. He delegated authority to experienced professionals and was astute enough to compliment them on their efficiency.

Aaron was the head of the Religious Department and Joshua was the Chief of the Military. Betzalel headed the Engineering Department.
Shenash

43. When Moses saw that all the work had been done exactly as Adonai had ordered, he blessed the craftsmen.
The Israelites utilized all their skills and enthusiastically cooperated to build the Tabernacle. Work was one of the cohesive forces that united the Israelites into a community and into a nation. One person cannot acquire all the skills necessary for the gratification of all his needs; he therefore must exchange services with his neighbors. The exchange of services brings about interdependence and interaction, which in turn bring about the unity needed to turn individuals into a community and a nation.
Rabbi Joseph B. Soloveitchik

2–3. You shall erect the Meeting Tent on the first day of the first month [Nisan]. Put the ark in it and enclose the ark with the cloth partition.
The work on the Tabernacle took about four months to complete.

Nine months has passed since they had arrived in the wilderness of Sinai. The Tabernacle was erected (40:17) in the last month of the second year of the Exodus. Nine months had elapsed since they arrived in the wilderness of Sinai.

8 Set an enclosure all around it, and hang the curtain over the entrance to the enclosure.
9 Take the holy anointing oil, and anoint the Tabernacle and everything in it. This will sanctify all the equipment.
10 Anoint the sacrificial altar and all its equipment. In this way you will sanctify the altar, and it will become holy.
11 Anoint the washbasin, and make it holy.
12 Bring Aaron and his sons into the Meeting Tent, and have them cleanse themselves.
13 Then have Aaron put on the sacred garment, and anoint him, and ordain him as a priest to serve Me.
14 Clothe Aaron's sons in their robes. **15** Then anoint them, just as you anointed Aaron, their father, so that they will become priests to serve Me. This anointing ceremony will ordain them and their descendants as priests throughout all the generations to come."
16 Moses did everything exactly as Adonai had instructed him.

The Tabernacle Is Erected
6th Aliyah

17 The Tabernacle was erected in the first month of the second year of the Exodus, on the first of the month.
18 Moses supervised the erection of the Tabernacle. He helped by setting up the bases, placing the frames in them, and fastening them together with the crossbars. He helped to set up the pillars.
19 He helped spread the tent over the Tabernacle, and placed the roof of the tent over it. It was all done exactly as Adonai had commanded Moses.
20 He took the tablets of the Ten Commandments and placed them in the ark. He then inserted the carrying poles into the ark, and set the cover on top of the ark.
21 He brought the ark into the Tabernacle, and set up the cloth partition so that it shielded the ark. Everything was done exactly as Adonai had instructed Moses.
22 He also helped place the table in the Meeting Tent outside the cloth curtain, on the northern side of the Tabernacle.
23 Then he placed the showbread on the table before Adonai. It was done exactly as Adonai had commanded Moses.
24 He placed the menorah in the Meeting Tent next to the table, on the southern side of the Tabernacle.
25 Moses then lighted the menorah before Adonai. Everything was done exactly as Adonai had instructed Moses.
26 Moses helped place the golden altar in the Meeting Tent in front of the cloth partition.
27 Then he burned perfumed incense on it. Everything was done exactly as Adonai had commanded Moses.

---

20. He took the tablets of the Ten Commandments and placed them in the ark.
Moses kept the two stone tablets in a box in his own tent. Now he placed them into the ark.

27. Then he burned perfumed incense on it.
Moses burned aromatic incense during the seven-day ordination of the priests.

According to the Torah (Shemot 30:7–8), Aaron is to burn incense every morning when he tends the menorah and at twilight when he lights the menorah.

The Curtain and the Altar
7th Aliyah

28 He hung the curtain over the entrance of the Tabernacle.

29 Then he helped place the sacrificial altar in front of the entrance of the Meeting Tent Tabernacle, and he sacrificed the burnt offerings and the meal offerings on it. It was all done exactly as Adonai had commanded Moses.

30 He set the washbasin between the Meeting Tent and the altar, and he filled it with water for cleansing.

31 Moses, Aaron, and Aaron's sons cleansed their hands and feet in it.

32 They would cleanse themselves in this way whenever they entered the Meeting Tent or offered sacrifice on the altar.
Everything was done exactly as Adonai had instructed Moses.

33 He set up the enclosure surrounding the Tabernacle and altar, and he placed the curtain over the entrance of the enclosure. At last, Moses completed all the work that Adonai had entrusted to him.

The Cloud and the Fire
Maftir

34 The cloud covered the Meeting Tent when Adonai's glory filled the Tabernacle. **35** Moses could not enter the Meeting Tent once the cloud rested on it and Adonai's glory filled the Tabernacle.

36 Whenever the cloud lifted up above the Tabernacle, it signaled that the Israelites could move on.

37 When the cloud did not rise, they would not begin their march until it lifted.

38 Adonai's cloud covered the Tabernacle by day, and the fire by night. The clouds by day and the fire by night led the Israelites in all their journeys.

---

31. Moses, Aaron, and Aaron's sons cleansed their hands and feet in it.
At that time, Moses was also functioning as a priest. *Rashi*

33. At last, Moses completed all the work that Adonai had entrusted to him.
When all the work was done exactly as Adonai had instructed Moses, then Aaron and his sons were anointed for service. Then, Adonai signified his satisfaction by sending a cloud, a visible token of his presence. Now, the Meeting Tent was filled with the dazzling glory of Adonai's divine presence.

34. Adonai's glory filled the Tabernacle.
The "glory" signaled that the building of the Tabernacle had been satisfactorily completed exactly "as Adonai had commanded Moses." Now Adonai had an earthly dwelling place and "His glory filled the Tabernacle."

Rabbi Samson Raphael Hirsch

35. Moses could not enter the Meeting Tent once the cloud rested on it and Adonai's glory filled the Tabernacle.
Once the cloud settled on the Meeting Tent, Moses could not enter. However, when the cloud passed, Moses could enter and communicate with Adonai.

38. The clouds by day and the fire by night led the Israelites in all their journeys.
The miracles were renewed so that the Israelites would follow Adonai's commands. The cloud and the fire set the schedule for the travels in the wilderness on the way to the Promised Land.

Nothing was left to chance. On each of their journeys, the cloud would settle on the exact area on which to set up their camp.

סֵפֶר וַיִּקְרָא

THE BOOK OF VAYIKRA

The Hebrew name for the third book of the Torah is Vayikra. The title is taken from the book's opening word, which means "and Adonai called." The Greek name of the book is Leviticus, meaning "about the Levites."

The book of Vayikra is a manual for living a holy and ethical life. The key phrase is found in (11:45):

Since I am holy, you too must remain holy. Here the people of Israel are commanded by Adonai to observe the commandments and thereby enrich their lives and make the world a better place in which to live.

The first eight chapters (1:1–8:36) deal with the sacrifices, followed by the installation of Aaron and his descendants into the priesthood.

The second section (chapters 9–15) alerts the Israelites to problems of health and hygiene and specifies which foods are permitted and which are forbidden to be eaten.

The third section (chapters 16–20) contains the Holiness Code and sets the rules of conduct that Jews must practice to live a holy life.

The fourth section (chapters 21–27) includes instructions for celebrating Shabbat and the festivals, some of which are tied to seasons, harvests, and historical events. The theme for Rosh Hashanah and Yom Kippur is teshuvah – a time for forgiveness.

Vayikra is the source (25:10) of the quotation inscribed on the Liberty Bell: Proclaim liberty throughout all the land unto all the inhabitants thereof.

For the former slaves, the book of Vayikra was a road map for living a holy life in the midst of an idol-worshipping society. In reality, Adonai was preparing the Israelites for a military and spiritual clash with forces that would test their commitment to ethics and morality.

סֵפֶר וַיִּקְרָא

THE BOOK OF VAYIKRA

Masoretic Torah Notes

Here is a list of some of the Masoretic notes for the Book of Vayikra.

1. The Book of Vayikra contains 859 verses.
2. The Book of Vayikra contains 27 chapters.
3. The Book of Vayikra contains 10 sidrot.

These are the sidrot in the Book of Vayikra.

סֵפֶר וַיִּקְרָא	263	Book of Vayikra
וַיִּקְרָא	265	Vayikra
צַו	274	Tzav
שְׁמִינִי	281	Shemini
תַזְרִיעַ	288	Tazria
מְצֹרָע	294	Metzora
אַחֲרֵי מוֹת	301	Achare Mot
קְדֹשִׁים	308	Kedoshim
אֱמֹר	314	Emor
בְּהַר	324	Behar
בְּחֻקֹּתַי	330	Bechukkotai

וַיִּקְרָא *Vayikra*

ADONAI SPOKE TO MOSES

1 Adonai spoke to Moses from the Meeting Tent and said: **2** Speak to the Israelites, and give them the following instructions:

When a person presents an animal as an offering to Adonai, he must bring it from the bulls, sheep, or goats.

3 If the sacrifice is a burnt offering, a healthy male bull must be taken from the herd. He must bring it to the entrance of the Meeting Tent, so it can be presented before Adonai. **4** He shall place his hands on the head of the offering, and it will be accepted as his substitute and make atonement for him.

5 The young bull should be slaughtered. Then Aaron's sons, the priests, shall present the blood, by sprinkling it on all four sides of the altar that is at the entrance of the Meeting Tent.

6 Then the burnt offering should be skinned and cut into pieces. **7** Aaron's sons shall build a wood fire on the altar, **8** and arrange the body parts on top of the altar fire.

9 First the inner organs and legs must be cleansed with water. Then the priest shall burn the parts of the animal on the altar as a complete burnt fire offering to Adonai. This burnt offering is a thank you gift to Adonai. **10** If the burnt offering is a sheep or a goat, it must be a healthy male animal. **11** It shall be slaughtered on the northern side of the altar, and the priests who are Aaron's descendants shall sprinkle its blood on all sides of the altar.

12 Then the offering shall be cut into pieces, and the priest shall arrange all the body parts on top of the wood on the altar fire.

13 The organs and feet shall first be cleansed with water, and then the priest shall burn them on the altar. This offering is a thank you gift to Adonai.

Procedures for the Grain Offering *2nd Aliyah*

14 Should the burnt offering be a turtle dove or a pigeon, **15** the priest shall bring it to the altar and remove its head and burn it on the altar. Then he shall drain the bird's blood and sprinkle the blood against the wall of the altar.

---

1. Adonai spoke to Moses from the Meeting Tent.
This was the first day after the Mishkan was completed. The cloud of Adonai filled the Meeting Tent and Moses could not enter. So Moses was forced to stand on the outside of the Meeting Tent and spoke to Adonai.

After that first day Moses could enter the Meeting Tent and Adonai would speak to him from the other side of a veil.

Adonai's voice was very powerful, but only Moses could hear it. *Sforno*

2. Speak to the Israelites, and give them the following instructions.
These instructions are composed of laws about sacrifices (Vayikra 1–7), the ritual for the installation of priests (Vayikra 8–10), and the laws of purity (Vayikra 11–16)

All of the enactments, together with the Law of Holiness (Vayikra 17–26), form the Priestly Code.

3. If the sacrifice is a burnt offering.
In Hebrew this offering is called *olah*, meaning an offering that ascends. The entire offering ascends up into the sky. This offering was completely burned and was the first sacrifice mentioned in the Torah. See Bereshit 8:20.

16 Then he shall remove the bird's neck and its feathers and throw them into the ashes, to the east of the altar.
17 The priest shall then burn the bird on the altar. This burnt offering is a thank you gift to Adonai.

2

If anyone presents a grain offering to Adonai, it must consist of the finest flour; he shall mix it with olive oil and place frankincense upon it.
2 Then he shall bring it to the priest, and he shall take a handful of the flour and oil, and all the frankincense. The priest shall burn this small portion on the altar as a fire offering. This fire offering is a thank you gift to Adonai.
3 The remainder of the grain offering shall belong to Aaron and his descendants as their food. This is a holy part of the fire offerings to Adonai.
4 If he brings a grain offering that was baked in an oven, it must be made of unleavened flour mixed with olive oil, or unleavened matzot spread with olive oil.

More Grain Offerings *3rd Aliyah*

5 If the offering is fried, it shall be made of unleavened flour mixed with olive oil.
6 It should be broken into small pieces, and olive oil poured on them. It should be treated like any other grain offering.
7 If the offering is cooked in a pot, it shall be made of flour with olive oil.
8 Any type of grain offering that is brought must be presented to the priest and brought to the altar. **9** Then the priest will remove a token portion from the grain offering and burn it on the altar. This offering is a thank you gift to Adonai. **10** The remainder of the grain offering belongs to Aaron and his descendants as their food. This part is the most holy because it is a portion from Adonai's fire offering.

---

17. This burnt offering is a thank you gift to Adonai.
Most of the book of Vayikra involves *korbonot* or sacrifices which were to be offered in the desert sanctuary. These sacrifices were meant to draw the worshipper closer to Adonai. This was the ancient method of thanking Adonai or asking for forgiveness for sins.

Maimonides explains that the sacrifices were an early form of worship practiced by the Israelites so they could learn how to serve Adonai without feeling different from the population among whom they lived.

In time the Jews developed the idea that prayer and good deeds, *mitzvot*, were a better way of getting closer to Adonai.

1. If anyone presents a grain offering to Adonai, it must consist of the finest flour.
Naturally, a grain offering does not require the slaughter of an animal. However, it is just as important.

The offering consists of flour and oil, which are obtained by hard work and one's commitment to the service of Adonai.

3. The remainder of the grain offering shall belong to Aaron and his descendants as their food.
The meal offerings were eaten by the priests within the area of the sanctuary.

4. If he brings a grain offering that was baked in an oven, it must be made of unleavened flour mixed with olive oil.
The grain offering was similar to the matzot we eat on Passover. The meal offerings called *minhah* consisted of agricultural ingredients. They were offered in a variety of forms: as unleavened cakes or parched grains. The meal offerings were prepared in special utensils such as a griddle.

11 Do not offer any grain offering that is made with leavened dough, because neither yeast nor honey is acceptable as a fire offering to Adonai. **12** Although you may bring them as a first-fruit offering to Adonai, they must not be offered on the altar. **13** Every grain offering must be seasoned with salt. Always add salt to your grain offering because it will remind you of Adonai's covenant. Do not forget to add salt to all your animal sacrifices. **14** When you present an offering from the first grain harvest, bring it from freshly picked roasted kernels of barley. **15** Pour olive oil and frankincense on it, just as for any other grain offering. **16** And offer it as a grain offering to Adonai. The priest shall then burn a token portion taken from the barley grain, olive oil, and frankincense.

Procedures for the Peace Offerings   *4th Aliyah*

3 If the sacrifice is a peace offering taken from the cattle herd, it can be either a healthy male or a healthy female.
2 He shall place his hands on the head of the animal, and have it slaughtered at the entrance of the Meeting Tent. Then a priest, one of Aaron's descendants, shall sprinkle its blood on all four sides of the altar.
3 A peace offering that is presented as a fire offering to Adonai must include the fat around the internal organs. **4** The two kidneys and the liver must also be removed.
5 The priest shall burn all of these parts on the altar, as a burnt offering on the wood fire. This fire offering is a thank you gift to Adonai. **6** If the sacrifice is a peace offering to Adonai, you may present a healthy male or female goat or sheep. **7** If you bring a sheep as a gift, you shall present it before Adonai.

---

11. Do not offer any grain offering that is made with leavened dough, because neither yeast nor honey is acceptable as a fire offering to Adonai.
Yeast is a leavening agent that causes bread to rise. Honey is also a leavening agent. Much of the honey is made from dates.   *Ibn Ezra*

13. Every grain offering must be seasoned with salt.
Salt was necessary for the daily diet. Salt was also used in sacrifices. It was to be used in every cereal offering. Eventually a connection developed between salt and the making of treaties. Among the ancients, eating salt with a person meant sharing his hospitality. Covenants and treaties were usually confirmed by sacrificial meals, and salt was always present.

Every time we have a meal and recite the blessing (*hamotzi*), we are obligated to sprinkle salt on the bread as a symbol of our dedication to the covenant made with Abraham (Bereshit 17:7).

14. When you present an offering from the first grain harvest.
This was the best grade of barley meal.   *Rashi*

2. He shall place his hands on the head of the animal, and have it slaughtered at the entrance of the Meeting Tent.
The individual must bring the animal and place both his hands upon the animal to indicate his complete dedication to the purpose of his sacrifice. It may not be brought by a proxy standing in for the guilty person.

4. The two kidneys and the liver must also be removed.
These organs were burned on the altar.

Today doctors are aware that these two organs are often susceptible to disease. Perhaps the Israelites were aware of a medical expertise that pinpointed that these organs are disease carriers. When a ritual slaughterer (*shochet*) examines the organs of a kosher animal, these are the organs that he specifically checks for abnormalities.

8 He shall place his hands on the head of the animal and have it slaughtered at the entrance of the Meeting Tent. The priests, Aaron's descendants, shall then sprinkle its blood on all four sides of the altar. **9** Parts of the peace offering shall be presented as a fire offering to Adonai. The peace offering shall not include the fat. **10** The kidneys and the liver must also be removed. **11** The priest shall burn the parts on the altar, to be consumed as a fire offering to Adonai. This offering is a thank you gift to Adonai. **12** If the sacrifice is a goat, **13** he shall place his hands on its head and have it slaughtered at the entrance of the Meeting Tent. The priests, Aaron's descendants, shall then sprinkle its blood on all four sides of the altar. **14** As part of his fire offering to Adonai, he shall present the fat that covers the internal organs. **15** The kidneys and the liver shall also be removed. **16** The priests shall burn these parts on the altar as a fire offering to Adonai. This offering is a thank you gift to Adonai. Remember that all the fat belongs to Adonai. **17** No matter where you may live, it shall be a law for all your generations that you must not eat any fat or blood that is usually sacrificed.

When a High Priest Sins
5th Aliyah

4 Adonai told Moses **2** to speak to the Israelites and tell them the following: This is the law when a person accidentally commits a sin by violating one of Adonai's commandments. **3** If a High Priest accidentally commits a sin and brings guilt on the whole community, he shall bring a healthy young bull as a sin offering to Adonai.
4 He shall bring the bull to the entrance of the Meeting Tent and place his hands on the bull's head. Then he shall slaughter the bull before Adonai. **5** Then the priest on duty shall take some of the bull's blood and bring it into the Meeting Tent. **6** The priest shall dip his finger into the blood and sprinkle it seven times toward the Holy Ark that is behind the cloth partition in the sanctuary.

---

17. No matter where you may live, it shall be a law for all your generations.
The prohibition against eating fat and drinking blood was enforced during the forty years of wandering in the desert. It is both a religious as well as a health issue. The prohibition was also observed to those living in foreign lands where sacrifices could not be offered.

2. This is the law when a person accidentally commits a sin by violating one of Adonai's commandments.
If a native–born person or convert mistakenly does something that is prohibited, the individual is punished either by *karet* (exile from the community) or by flogging. *Ibn Ezra*

3. If the High Priest accidentally commits a sin and brings guilt on the whole community.
The High Priest, because as the religious leader of the Israelites, can accidentally commit unintentional violations. The biblical standards of behavior were high, and when the High Priest sinned, his sin brought guilt on all the people.

3. He shall bring a healthy young bull as a sin offering to Adonai.
The High Priest can obtain acceptability in the eyes of Adonai by bringing a sin offering.

A person who recognizes his error and publicly admits to a sin by bringing a sin offering is an individual who has cleansed his conscience.

If Adonai accepts the sin offering of the High Priest, then he will surely accept the atonement sacrifice of an ordinary Israelite.

6. And sprinkle it seven times toward the Holy Ark that is behind the cloth partition in the sanctuary.
Toward the Holy Ark, making sure that the blood does not touch the cloth partition. *Rashi*

7 The priest shall smear some of the blood on the horns of the incense altar, which is in the Meeting Tent. He shall then sprinkle some of the blood at the base of the sacrificial altar, which is at the entrance of the Meeting Tent.

8 The priest shall remove all the fat from the sin offering.

9 The two kidneys and the liver shall also be removed.

10 All these are the same as the parts removed from the peace offering. The priest shall burn them on the sacrificial altar.

11 He shall take the bull's skin and all its flesh **12** and remove them to a clean place outside the camp, where the altar's ashes are thrown. They shall be burned on a wood fire in the place where the ashes are thrown.

13 If the entire community of Israel accidentally commits an error, even though the people were unaware that they had violated one of Adonai's commandments, they are still guilty.

14 When the sin they have committed becomes known, the congregation must bring a young bull as a sin offering and present it at the entrance of the Meeting Tent.

15 The elders of the community shall place their hands on the bull's head, and it shall be slaughtered before Adonai.

16 Then a priest shall bring some of the bull's blood into the Meeting Tent. **17** He shall dip his finger into the blood and sprinkle it seven times toward the Holy Ark, which is behind the cloth partition.

18 He shall then smear some of the blood on the horns of the incense altar, which stands before Adonai in the Meeting Tent. The remainder of the blood must be poured at the base of the sacrificial altar, which is in front of the entrance of the Meeting Tent.

19 The priest shall then remove all of the fat and burn it on the altar, **20** and do exactly the same with this bull as he did with the bull that was sacrificed as a sin offering for the anointed priest. In this way the priest will make atonement for the community, and they will be forgiven.

21 The priest shall take the bull outside the camp and burn it just as he burned the first bull. This is the sin offering for the entire community of Israel.

---

7. The horns of the incense altar.
The four horns that were at each corner of the altar. The horns pointed toward the sky, toward Adonai.

11–12. He shall take the bull's skin and all its flesh and remove them to a clean place outside the camp, where the altar's ashes are thrown. They shall be burned on a wood fire in the place where the ashes are thrown.
He shall take the bull's skin and flesh to a special pure area beyond the three encampments, or later the Temple (in Jerusalem), where the ashes from the altar are to be thrown and parts of the bull shall be burned on a wood fire. *Rashi*

15. The elders of the community shall place their hands on the bull's head.

The elders were the leaders of the tribes.

They represented their community in making political, military, and some religious decisions. Now the elders are called upon to act as representatives of their tribes and ask for forgiveness for their sins which were accidentally committed.

The leaders are a part of the nation. They represent the eyes, ears, and conscience of the community. When they deliberately or accidentally make an error, then both the leaders and the community whom they represent are guilty of sin.

Ibn Ezra

22 If a leader accidentally commits a sin and violates one of Adonai's commandments, then he is guilty. **23** When he becomes aware of the sin he has committed, he must bring a healthy male goat as his sacrifice. **24** He shall place his hands on the goat's head and have it slaughtered as a sin offering in the same place where the burnt offering is slaughtered. **25** Then the priest, with his finger, shall smear some of the blood of the sin offering on the horn of the sacrificial altar. The rest of the blood shall be poured out at the base of the sacrificial altar.
26 All the animal's fat shall be burned on the altar, just like the fat of the peace offerings. In this way the priest will make atonement for the leader, and he will be forgiven.

Sin Offerings for Israelites   6th Aliyah

27 If an ordinary Israelite accidentally commits a sin by violating one of Adonai's commandments, he is guilty.
28 When he is made aware of the sin he has committed, he must bring a healthy female goat as a sacrifice for the sin he has committed. **29** He shall place his hands on the head of the sin offering, and the goat shall be sacrificed in the same place as the burnt offerings.
30 The priest, with his finger, shall smear some of the goat's blood on the horns of the sacrificial altar and spill the rest of the blood at the base of the altar.
31 He shall remove all the fat, just as he did with the fat of the peace offering, and the priest shall burn it on the altar.
This offering is a thank you gift to Adonai. In this way the priest will make atonement for the individual, and he will be forgiven.
32 If anyone brings a sheep as a sin offering, he shall bring a healthy female animal. **33** He shall place his hands on the head of the sin offering and have it slaughtered in the same place that the burnt offerings were slaughtered.
34 The priest, with his fingers, shall take some of the blood of the sin offering and smear it on the horns of the sacrificial altar, and spill the rest of the blood at the altar's base.

---

22. If a leader accidentally commits a sin and violates one of Adonai's commandments, then he is guilty.
All types of people commit sins and must repent. A true leader will protect his reputation and acknowledge his own sin. If for some reason he is unaware of his error, then someone should inform him of his transgression. He will atone for his offense by bringing a male goat as a sin offering. In this way he will be forgiven for his transgression.
Sforno

22. If a leader accidentally commits a sin and violates one of Adonai's commandments, then he is guilty.
The Torah recognizes the fallibility of humanity and now sets up disciplines for rehabilitation. He must first acknowledge his guilt and follow the procedure for atonement.

26. In this way the priest will make atonement for the leader, and he will be forgiven.
The priest shall perform the sacrifice of atonement on behalf of the leader, and the leader will be forgiven.

27. If an ordinary Israelite accidentally commits a sin by violating one of Adonai's commandments, he is guilty.
An ordinary Israelite means all Israelites, including priests, and Levites.
Ibn Ezra

35 He shall remove all the fat parts, just as he removed all the fat parts from the sheep offering brought as a peace offering, and shall burn them on the altar along with the fire offerings. In this way the priest will make atonement for the sin the person committed and he will be forgiven.

5 If a person has sworn an oath to give evidence in court about something that he witnessed or something that he knew, and then refuses to testify, he has committed a sin and should be punished.
2 A person is guilty if he touches anything unclean, whether it is a dead animal, either wild or domestic, or a dead creeping animal. He has, without realizing it, committed a sin.
3 If he comes in contact with any unclean waste from a human being, and accidentally forgets about it, he may later discover that he has committed a violation.
4 This is also true if a person makes a promise to do something good or bad and then forgets about the promise. In all of these cases, the person is considered guilty as soon as he becomes aware of what he has done.
5 In all of these cases he is guilty, and he must confess the sin he has committed.
6 He must also bring a guilt offering to Adonai for the sin he has committed. It must be a female sheep or goat, brought as a sin offering. The priest will then make atonement for the person's sin.
7 If he cannot afford a sheep, the guilt offering he presents to Adonai for his sin shall be two doves or two pigeons. One of them shall be a sin offering, and one of them shall be a burnt offering.

---

1. If a person has sworn an oath to give evidence in court about something that he witnessed or something that he knew, and then refuses to testify, he has committed a sin and should be punished.
It is a mitzvah (122) to testify in court in civil or capital cases. Testimony of a witness can prevent a miscarriage of justice.

    The Torah system of justice has no prosecutor, executioner, or police official who has the responsibility to find criminals and bring them to justice. The Torah chose not to appoint an enforcer who could possibly be power hungry. On the other hand, the Torah visualizes that every citizen becomes a prosecutor.

    Every Israelite becomes responsible and is obliged to help others in need. There is a saying: "All Israelites have responsibility for each other."

5. In all of these cases he is guilty, and he must confess the sin he has committed.
The sinner must admit to himself that he has sinned. Confession is an important step to acknowledging shortcomings and resolving to repent (do *teshuvah*). The offering is the outward sign, and the confession is the inward resolve not to commit the offense.

7. If he cannot afford a sheep, the guilt offering he presents to Adonai shall be two doves or two pigeons.
Birds as well as animals were used in sacrifices. The only birds domesticated by the Israelites were pigeons and doves, and both were permitted for sacrificial use. The birds were usually offered by the poor in place of expensive animals.

7. One of them shall be a sin offering, and one of them shall be a burnt offering.
The sin offering comes before the burnt offering. First the sinner must obtain pardon from Adonai. Once he has been pardoned, his gift is now acceptable.

8 He shall bring them to the priest, who shall first offer a dove as the sin offering. He shall wring its neck without separating the head from the body. **9** He shall then spill some of the blood on the side of the altar, and the rest of the blood at the base of the altar. The dove is the sin offering.

10 As the law requires, he shall also sacrifice a pigeon as a burnt offering.

In this way the priest will make atonement for the sin the person committed, and he will be forgiven.

Sin Offerings *7th Aliyah*

11 However, if the sinner is poor and cannot afford the two doves or two pigeons for the sacrifice, he can bring two quarts of fine flour as a sin offering. Since it is a sin offering, he shall not mix it with olive oil or frankincense.

12 He shall bring the flour to the priest, and the priest shall take a handful of flour as a token portion. He shall burn this token portion as a sin offering on the altar just like any other fire offering.

13 In this way the priest will make atonement for the person's sin, and he will be forgiven. Just as in the case of the grain offering, the unburned portions of these sacrifices shall belong to the priest.

14 Adonai spoke to Moses, saying: **15** If a person accidentally sins by taking something that is sacred to Adonai for his own personal use, he shall bring a healthy ram as his guilt offering to Adonai or pay the price for a ram having the same value in silver according to the sanctuary weight standard.

16 For taking something that was sacred, he must make full restitution, and add twenty percent of its value, and give the payment to the priest.

In this way the priest will atone for him with the guilt offering of a ram, and he will be forgiven.

17 If a person, without knowing it, sins by violating one of Adonai's commandments, he is still responsible for his error.

---

13. In this way the priest will make atonement for the person's sin.

Humans sin in three different ways: by thought, by speech, and by deeds. To receive atonement, a person must orally confess his sins that he committed by thought or by speech. The individual must also confess his sins committed by his hands.

The sacrifices, atonements, and confessions were early attempts to alleviate behavioral problems. Today individuals with problems discuss them with rabbis, psychologists, social workers, or psychiatrists.

The father of modern psychiatry, Sigmund Freud, may have gotten some of his ideas from his study of the Torah.

15. If a person accidentally sins by taking something that is sacred to Adonai for his own personal use.

This refers to gifts that are donated to the Meeting Tent, and food portions that are for the priests.

17. If a person, without knowing it, sins by violating one of Adonai's commandments, he is still responsible for his error.

This is mitzvah number 128.

If an individual is in doubt on whether or not he committed a sin, then he is obligated to bring a *korban asham*, or a sin offering. This *asham* completes the atonement for the sin. The *asham* is mandatory for six types of offenses, and its purpose is to protect the transgressor from his own guilty conscience.

18 He must bring a healthy ram to the priest as a guilt offering or pay the price for a ram in silver according to the sanctuary weight standard. The priest shall then make atonement for the accidental sin the person committed, and he shall be forgiven for the oversight.
19 It is a guilt offering that he has committed against Adonai.
20 Adonai said to Moses:
21 This is the law when a person sins and commits an offense against Adonai by lying to his neighbor about an article that was entrusted to him for safekeeping, or cheats on a business deal, or by robbery, or by withholding money, **22** or by finding a lost object and denying it.
A person who swears falsely in any of these cases is considered to have sinned. **23** When he is judged guilty of such a sin, he must return the stolen article or money, the withheld funds, the article left for safekeeping, or the found article.

Offerings for Dishonesty   *Maftir*

24 For these or for anything else about which he swore falsely, he must repay the full amount plus twenty percent. On the day that he seeks atonement for his crime, he must repay the total amount to its rightful owner.
25 He must bring to the priest his sin offering of a healthy ram as a guilt offering or pay the price for a ram according to the sanctuary weight standard.
26 The priest shall make atonement for him before Adonai, and he will then be forgiven for any crime he has committed.

---

23. When he is judged guilty of such a sin, he must return the stolen article or money, the withheld funds, the article left for safekeeping, or the found article.
This is Mitzvah number 130

A thief must return the object or money he stole. If the object is damaged or altered, he must repay its monetary value. Should the victim die, the robber must return the object to his inheritors.

The Nazis robbed their victims of valuable paintings, antiques, property, and jewels. The courts have ruled that these valuable items which are in museums and private collections must be returned to the owner or family.

25. He must bring to the priest his sin offering of a healthy ram as a guilt offering.
Even though the thief has returned all the stolen materials, he must bring a guilt offering, because embezzlement and burglary are very serious criminal acts.

26. The priest shall make atonement for him before Adonai, and he will then be forgiven for any crime he committed.
The individual will not be forgiven by Adonai for the sin committed against Him until he has returned the stolen material and compensated the victim.

The Torah is very much aware that humans are subject to moments of weakness, which they ordinarily do not practice. Its system of guilt offerings is a rehabilitation process, which washes away the sin and restores their moral standing in the community.

When a sinner has confessed openly his crime and has returned the stolen item or repaid the cost plus 20 percent, then he must bring a guilt offering. Only then is the stain removed and can he be at peace with his conscience and be forgiven by Adonai.

צַו *Tzav*

INSTRUCT AARON AND HIS SONS

6 Adonai spoke to Moses, telling him **2** to instruct Aaron and his sons. The burnt offering must remain on the altar until morning, and the altar's fires must continue to burn all night.

3 Then the priest shall dress in his priestly garments and linen undergarments. He shall remove the ashes of the burnt offering, and pile them near the altar.

4 He shall then remove his garments and put on his everyday garments, and then move the ashes to a ritually clean place outside the camp.

5 The fire of the altar shall be kept burning, and each morning the priest shall add more wood to the fire. He shall arrange the burnt offerings on the wood and burn parts of the peace offerings. **6** In this way, the fire under the altar will never go out.

7 These are the rules of the grain offering that one of Aaron's descendants shall offer before Adonai, on the altar. **8** The priest shall take a handful of the flour and oil offering and all the frankincense that is on the offering. He shall burn this on the altar. This grain offering is a thank you gift to Adonai. **9** Aaron and his descendants shall then eat whatever remains of the grain offering. It must he eaten as unleavened bread in a holy place; therefore they must eat it in the courtyard. **10** It must not be baked as leavened bread. I have given them their portion of My grain offerings, and it is holy, just like the sin and the guilt offerings. **11** Only the males among Aaron's descendants are entitled to eat it. It is a law for all the generations that it be taken from Adonai's fire offerings. Anyone who touches it becomes holy.

The Offering of the High Priest *2nd Aliyah*

12 Adonai spoke to Moses, saying: **13** This is the offering that Aaron and his descendants must bring when one of them is anointed as High Priest. It shall consist of two quarts of fine flour, and it shall be a daily grain offering, with one quart in the morning and one quart in the evening.

1–2. Adonai spoke to Moses, telling him to instruct Aaron and his sons.
The next two chapters of *Sidrah Tzav* is addressed to Aaron and his sons. These two chapters contain instructions for sacrifices by the priests.

2. The burnt offering must remain on the altar until morning, and the altar's fires must continue to burn all night.
The burnt offering that was for sinful thoughts was the most important of the sacrifices and was totally burned. The Kohen who conducted the sacrifice received no part of the offering. It burned all night, until it was totally consumed. Our sages reasoned that since sinful thoughts usually occur at night, the offering should burn all night so as to totally destroy the sinful thoughts. The Hebrew word *olah* means "to ascend." In Hebrew the burnt offering is called *olah*, meaning "ascends." It is so called because it is completely consumed as the smoke rises.

4. He shall then remove his garments and put on his everyday garments, and then remove the ashes to a ritually clean place outside the camp.
The priest must change his priestly attire for everyday clothing, since removing the ashes is not a holy duty. The priest must make sure that the ashes are deposited in a clean place.

14 It shall be prepared in a frying pan with olive oil and then baked. It is to be presented as a grain offering of broken pieces of bread. This offering is a thank you gift to Adonai.
15 For all time it is a law that the newly appointed priest chosen from Aaron's descendants shall offer it completely burned.
16 Every grain offering brought by a priest must be completely burned and must not be eaten. **17** Adonai spoke to Moses, saying: **18** Instruct Aaron and his descendants about the laws of the sin offering: The holy sin offering must be slaughtered before Adonai in the place where the burnt offering is slaughtered.
19 The priest who offers the sin offering may eat it. It must be eaten in a holy place, in the courtyard near the Meeting Tent.
20 Whatever touches the sin offering will become holy, and any blood that is sprinkled on a garment must be washed in a holy area.
21 The clay pot in which the offering is cooked must be broken, but if the offering is cooked in a copper pot, it must be scrubbed and rinsed with water.
22 Any priest may eat it, although it is holy.
23 But a sin offering whose blood is brought into the Meeting Tent for an atonement must not be eaten. It must be burned in fire.

7 This is the holy law of the guilt offering:
2 The guilt offering must be slaughtered in the same place that the burnt offering is slaughtered, and its blood must be sprinkled around the altar. **3** All the fat, **4** and the two kidneys, and the liver must be removed. **5** The priests must burn all these parts as a guilt offering on the altar, as a fire offering to Adonai.
6 Only the priests may eat the offering. It must be eaten in a holy place, because it is sacred.
7 The same law applies to the priest who makes the sin offering and the guilt offering. It shall belong to the priest who makes atonement with it.
8 The priest who offers a person's burnt offering can keep the skin of the burnt offering for himself. **9** Any of the leftover grain offering which is baked in an oven, pan fried, or deep fried shall also be given to the priest who offered it.
10 Every grain offering, whether mixed with olive oil or dry, shall be shared by Aaron's descendants.

---

18. Instruct Aaron and his descendants about the laws of the sin offering: The holy sin offering must be slaughtered before Adonai in the place where the burnt offering is slaughtered. These instructions refer to the sin offerings which were to be brought when the Israelites had their own country. The offerings were to be brought by the High Priest or the members of the Sanhedrin when they erroneously sinned.

Sforno

22. Any priest may eat it, although it is holy. Only an unblemished person is fit to eat the sin offering, which has been brought to secure atonement.

Ibn Ezra

1. This is the holy law of the guilt offering. A guilt offering is a means of getting relief from guilty feeling and asking Adonai for forgiveness.

Nachmanides explains that normally humans harbor all kinds of secret and evil thoughts, and these evil inclinations can lead to wrongdoing. The guilt offering is a means of admitting and confessing a person's sinful thoughts.

The Peace Offerings
3rd Aliyah

11 These are laws of the kinds of peace offerings that are to be presented to Adonai. **12** A peace offering must be presented along with a variety of unleavened loaves mixed with olive oil, flat matzot with oil, and loaves made of fine flour mixed with oil. **13** The peace offering shall be presented with loaves of leavened bread. **14** One of each of the four breads shall be presented as an elevated gift to Adonai. The bread will then belong to the priest who sprinkles the blood of the sacrificed offering.

15 The flesh of the peace offering must be eaten on the same day that it is sacrificed. None of it may be saved until morning. **16** But if the offering is meant to fulfill a vow or a pledge, it can be eaten on the same day that it is sacrificed, and whatever is left over can be eaten the next day.

17 But any meat that is left over from the sacrifice on the third day must be burned in fire. **18** The sacrifice will not be acceptable if the person bringing the peace offering plans to eat it on the third day. It will have no holy value as a sacrifice. The person who eats it will be guilty of a sin.

19 Any sacrificial meat that comes in contact with something unclean must not be eaten; it must be burned in fire. As for the other meat, any ritually clean person may eat it. **20** But if a person who is in an unclean state eats the meat of a peace sacrifice that was presented to Adonai, he will no longer belong to the community of Israel. **21** Any person who comes in contact with something unclean, such as human waste, or with an unclean animal or any other unclean creature, and then eats the meat of Adonai's peace offering, that person will no longer belong to the community of Israel.

---

11. These are laws of the kinds of peace offerings that are to be presented to Adonai.
There are three types of peace offering.
  1. Thanksgiving offering for deliverance from danger or sickness.
  2. Completion of a vow or promise made in time of trouble.
  3. Offerings made in times of happiness and joy.
  Today it is customary for an individual who has survived a physical or medical danger to recite the *gomel*, a thanksgiving blessing, during the Torah reading.

13. The peace offering shall be presented with loaves of leavened bread.
The peace offerings could not be offered on the altar, since the loaves of bread were leavened. Ordinary leavened bread was eaten during a regular or a sacrificial meal.

15. The flesh of the peace offering must be eaten on the same day that it is sacrificed.
It must be eaten by the person who brought it and his family. Only those who are ritually pure may eat it.
Ibn Ezra

15. The flesh of the peace offering must be eaten on the same day that it is sacrificed.
There was no refrigeration, so all meat had to be eaten promptly. Because of the hot climate in the desert, meat spoiled quickly and thus became ceremonially impure and also dangerous to eat.

17. But any meat that is left over from the sacrifice on the third day must be burned in fire.
Moses told Aaron to approach the altar and present the sin offering and the burnt offering, to make atonement first for himself and then for the people. Before an individual can rebuke others, he or she must be blameless. Now Moses tells Aaron to atone and make himself virtuous; only then can he find fault with others.
Tzenah Urenah

22 Adonai spoke to Moses, saying, **23** Tell the Israelites the following: Do not eat any of the fat of an ox, sheep, or goat. **24** The fat of an animal that is not properly slaughtered or is found dead may be used for any purpose you see fit, as long as you do not eat it. **25** Anyone who eats the fat of any animal that has been offered to Adonai will no longer belong to the community of Israel.
26 No matter where you may live, you must not eat any blood from an animal or a bird.
27 Any person who eats blood will no longer belong to the community of Israel.
28 Adonai spoke to Moses, saying: **29** Speak to the children of Israel and tell them that anyone who brings a peace offering to Adonai must also bring a special offering to Adonai. **30** He must bring the fat as well as the breast, and he shall present the breast before Adonai.
31 The priest shall burn the fat on the altar, but the breast shall belong to Aaron and his descendants.
32 You shall give the right hind leg of your peace offerings as a gift to the priest. **33** Any descendant of Aaron who is permitted to sprinkle the blood and offer the fat of the peace offerings shall be given the right leg as his portion.
34 Because I have chosen the breast and the hind leg of the peace sacrifices as an elevated gift from the Israelite sacrifices to be forever set aside for the priests, I have given these parts to Aaron the priest and his descendants. It is the law for all time that these parts taken from the Israelites are to be given to the priests forever.

22-23. Adonai spoke to Moses saying, Tell the Israelites the following: Do not eat any of the fat of an ox, sheep, or goat.
This is prohibitive mitzvah number 147.
The Torah teaches the Israelites a cardiovascular lesson. Cholesterol and fatty substances block the arteries with cholesterol, which shortens a person's life span. *Shenash*

24. The fat of an animal that is not properly slaughtered or is found dead may be used for any purpose you see fit, as long as you do not eat it.
The animal that is not properly slaughtered or that has died of other causes is called a *nevelah*. Its meat can be eaten by animals and the fat can be used to make candles, to grease wheels, or for other usages.

26. No matter where you may live, you must not eat any blood from an animal or a bird.
This is prohibitive mitzvah number 148.
Dietary laws are surrounded by regulations that cause us to develop a reverence for life.

In the process we are forbidden to eat blood, which is the source of life. All meat must be drained of blood at its source, and during preparation.
Kosher meat must be salted to remove the blood before it is cooked. However, since birds and fish are not mentioned, they do not have to be salted.

30. He must bring the fat as well as the breast, and he shall present the breast before Adonai.
Anyone who brings a peace offering must with his own hands wave the offering. This indicates that he is willingly presenting the total offering to Adonai.

31. The priest shall burn the fat on the altar, but the breast shall belong to Aaron and his descendants.
After the fat was burned, the priest was entitled to the breast and the right hind leg.

32. You shall give the right hind leg of your peace offering as a gift to the priest.
The right hind leg was considered one of the most desirable parts of the animal. This part was usually reserved for a special guest.

35 This is the portion of the fire offerings made to Adonai that shall be given to Aaron and his sons from the day they are ordained as priests to Adonai.
36 On the day they were ordained, Adonai commanded that the Israelites are to give them as their share the breast and the right leg. This is an eternal law for every generation to come.
37 These are the laws of the burnt offering, the meal offering, the sin offering, the guilt offering, the ordination offering, and the peace offering. **38** Adonai gave these instructions to Moses on Mount Sinai, so that they would know how to present the sacrifices to Adonai in the wilderness of Sinai.

The Ordination of Aaron and His Sons *4th Aliyah*

8 Adonai spoke to Moses, saying: **2** Gather Aaron and his sons, and their garments, the anointing oil, the bull for the sin offering, the two rams, and the basket of unleavened bread. **3** Then assemble the entire community to meet at the entrance of the Meeting Tent.
4 Moses did as Adonai commanded, and the entire community gathered at the entrance of the Meeting Tent.
5 Moses said to the Israelites, "This is what Adonai has instructed me to do."
6 Moses presented Aaron and his sons, and cleansed them with water.
7 He clothed Aaron with the embroidered robe and the sash, and he put the robe of the ephod on him and fastened the ephod with its straps.
8 Then Moses strapped the breastplate to the ephod on Aaron and inserted the Urim and Thumim in the breastplate. **9** He put the headdress on Aaron's head and tied the sacred golden medallion on the front of the headdress. Moses clothed Aaron just as Adonai had commanded him. **10** Then Moses took the anointing oil and sanctified the Tabernacle and everything in it. **11** He sanctified the altar and sprinkled some of the oil on the altar seven times. He then sanctified the altar, all its utensils, as well as the washbasin and its base.

---

3. Then assemble the entire community to meet at the entrance of the Meeting Tent.
This was a community of half a million people, who would have to stand outside along the slopes of Mount Sinai. Ibn Ezra and other commentators suggest that only the heads of the tribes and clans were invited to the inauguration of the sanctuary service.

5. Moses said to the Israelites, "This is what Adonai has instructed me to do."
Some elements in the Israelite camp were jealous of the privileged position of Moses and Aaron. So Moses assured the Israelites that he was not playing favorites, since the ordination was ordered by Adonai.

7. He clothed Aaron with the embroidered robe and the sash, and he put the robe of the ephod on him and fastened the ephod with its straps.
The specially designed garments and regalia conferred upon them were the visible emblems of their holy functions.

8. Then Moses strapped the breastplate to the ephod on Aaron and inserted the Urim and Thumim in the breastplate.
The meaning and structure of the Urim and Thumim are obscure. They may have had the twenty-two pieces of the Hebrew alefbet on twenty-two separate pieces of wood and metal; the priest would lift various letters randomly and combine them by divine inspiration to form an answer to his questions.
Targum Onkeles

11. He sanctified the altar and sprinkled some of the oil on the altar seven times.
The sanctification ceremony was seven days long. Moses sanctified the altar on each of the seven days.

12 He poured anointing oil on Aaron's head, and he sanctified him.

13 Next Moses presented Aaron's sons, and he clothed them in robes, and tied them with sashes, and placed headdresses on them, just as Adonai had commanded Moses.

The First Ram of Ordination   *5th Aliyah*

14 Moses then presented a bull for the sin offering, and Aaron and his sons placed their hands on its head.

15 Moses slaughtered the bull and took some of the blood, and with his finger he smeared the blood on the horns of the altar to purify it. He poured the rest of the blood at the base of the altar to sanctify it so that atonement could be offered on it.

16 Moses took the fat, the liver, and the two kidneys, and burned them on the altar.

17 The rest of the bull its skin, the meat, and the internal organs he burned outside the camp. It was all done just exactly as Adonai had commanded Moses.

18 Next Moses presented a ram for the burnt offering, and Aaron and his sons placed their hands on its head. **19** Moses slaughtered it and sprinkled its blood on all sides of the altar.

20 He cut the ram into pieces, and Moses burned the fat, the head, and some of the cut pieces on the altar.

21 After that he washed the internal organs and legs with water. Then Moses burned the entire ram on the altar as a whole burnt offering. The fire offering was a thank you gift to Adonai. It was all done exactly as Adonai had commanded Moses.

The Second Ram of Ordination   *6th Aliyah*

22 Now Moses presented the second ram, which was the ordination ram. Aaron and his sons placed their hands on the head of the ram. **23** Then Moses slaughtered the ram and took some of its blood and smeared it on Aaron's right ear, and on his right thumb, and on his right big toe.

---

13. Next Moses presented Aaron's sons, and he clothed them in robes, and tied them with sashes, and placed headdresses on them, just as Adonai had commanded Moses.
First Aaron's sons had to be dressed in their official priestly garments. Only then were they officially permitted to participate in the ordination ceremonies.

14. Moses then presented a bull for the sin offering, and Aaron and his sons placed their hands on its head.
Moses told Aaron to approach the altar and present the sin offering and the burnt offering, to make atonement first for himself and then for the people. Before an individual can rebuke others, he or she must be blameless. Now Moses tells Aaron to atone and make himself virtuous; only then can he find fault with others.   *Tzenah Urenah*

18. Next Moses presented a ram for the burnt offering.
Two rams were sacrificed during the induction ceremony of Aaron and his sons. The first ram was a burnt offering to atone for the sins committed by Aaron and his sons. The second ram was the ordination ram.

23. Then Moses slaughtered the ram and took some of its blood and smeared it on Aaron's right ear, and on his right thumb, and on his right toe.
The sages say that the right ear is to listen to the problems of the people, the thumb is to try to help the Israelites with their problems, and the toe is to hurry to help Israelites who needed medical care or religious advice.

24 Next, Moses presented Aaron's sons, and he smeared some of the blood on their right ears, their right thumbs, and their right big toes. Moses also sprinkled some of the blood on all sides of the altar.

25 Moses took the fat, the liver, the two kidneys, and the right hind leg, **26** and on top of these, from the basket of unleavened breads, before Adonai, he placed a loaf of unleavened bread, a loaf of unleavened oil bread, and one thin loaf with olive oil.

27 Moses gave all these to Aaron and his sons, and he waved them as an offering before Adonai.

28 Then Moses took all the offerings from their hands, and he burned them on the altar. This ordination offering was a thank you gift to Adonai.

29 Now Moses took the breast of the ram and waved the offering before Adonai. This was Moses' own portion of the ordination ram. It was all done exactly as Adonai had commanded Moses.

Moses Sanctifies the Priestly Garments *7th Aliyah*

30 Next Moses took the anointing oil, and some of the blood from the altar, and he sprinkled it on the garments of Aaron and his sons. This is how he sanctified the garments of Aaron and his sons.

31 Then Moses said to Aaron and his sons, "Cook the meat at the entrance of the Meeting Tent, and eat it there with the bread from the ordination basket, just as I commanded you.

32 Any of the meat or bread that is left over must be burned.

The Seven Days of Ordination *Maftir*

33 "You must remain at the entrance of the Meeting Tent for seven days until the ordination ceremony is finished.

34 Adonai has commanded that the ceremony will take seven days to make atonement for you.

35 You must remain at the entrance of the Meeting Tent for seven days and nights, and do everything that Adonai demands of you. In this way you will remain alive." **36** Aaron and his sons obeyed everything exactly as Adonai had instructed Moses.

---

31. Cook the meat at the entrance of the Meeting Tent, and eat it there.
It was customary to seal agreements and treaties by eating a meal. The meal sealed the covenant between the priests and Adonai.

33. You must remain at the entrance of the Meeting Tent for seven days.
The Torah means that they should not concern themselves with any family problems or any other type of distractions. *Ibn Ezra*

34. Adonai has commanded that the ceremony will take seven days to make atonement for you.
The same ceremony that was performed on the first day was repeated on each of the next six days.

35. You must remain at the entrance of the Meeting Tent for seven days and nights.
They could leave whenever they needed to.
Ibn Ezra

36. Aaron and his sons obeyed everything exactly as Adonai had instructed Moses.
Without hesitation Aaron and his sons underwent ordination. The public ceremony testified their willingness to serve Adonai.

שְׁמִינִי *Shemini*

ON THE EIGHTH DAY

9 On the eighth day, Moses assembled Aaron, his sons, and the leaders of Israel. **2** He said to Aaron, "Choose a healthy young calf for a sin offering and a healthy ram for a burnt offering, and sacrifice them before Adonai. **3** Then speak to the Israelites, and tell them to choose five healthy animals: a goat for a sin offering, a young calf and a lamb for a burnt offering, **4** and a bull and a ram for peace offerings, and sacrifice them before Adonai along with a grain offering mixed with oil, because today Adonai Himself will appear to you."

5 The Israelites brought everything Moses requested to the entrance of the Meeting Tent, and the entire community gathered and stood before Adonai.

6 Then Moses said, "This is what Adonai has commanded. Do it exactly, and Adonai in His glory will appear to you."

7 Moses then told Aaron to approach the altar and present the sin offering and the burnt offering, to make atonement first for himself and for the people. He presented the people's offering to atone for them, just as Adonai had commanded.

8 Aaron once again approached the altar, and slaughtered the calf for the sin offering for himself. **9** Then Aaron's sons brought him some of the blood, and he dipped his finger in it. Aaron sprinkled some of the blood on the horns of the altar. He spilled the rest of the blood at the base of the altar.

10 He burned the fat, the kidneys, and the liver as a sin offering. It was all done exactly as Adonai had commanded Moses.

11 He then burned the meat and skin of the sin offering in fire outside the camp.

12 Aaron slaughtered the burnt offering, and Aaron's sons brought him some of the blood, and he sprinkled the blood on all sides of the altar.

---

1. On the eighth day, Moses assembled Aaron, his sons, and the leaders of Israel.
The seven days of ordination were finished, and on the eighth day Moses assembled his cabinet. Rashi says that the leaders came to be informed that Adonai had appointed Aaron as the High Priest. Obviously some leaders felt that Moses was favoring his brother Aaron. Now they knew that Adonai had appointed Aaron.

6. Then Moses said, "This is what Adonai has commanded."
Do it exactly, and Adonai in his glory will appear to you.

Adonai's presence will not appear in the sanctuary until the *Kohanim* (priests) and the Israelites have been atoned.

7. Moses then told Aaron to approach the altar and present the sin offering and the burnt offering to make atonement first for himself and for the people.
Before an individual can rebuke others, he or she must be blameless. Now Moses tells Aaron to atone and make himself virtuous, and only then can he find fault with others.

Tzenah Urenah

12. Aaron's sons brought him some of the blood, and he sprinkled the blood on all sides of the altar.
Aaron's sons the priests would at some time in the future be performing the same rite. They were being trained by participating in the service.

Sforno

13 Piece by piece they handed him the cut-up parts and the head for the burnt offering, and he burned them on the altar.
14 He washed the internal organs and the feet, and he burned them, too, on the altar as a burnt offering.
15 Next Aaron presented the offering of the Israelites. He took the goat that was the sin offering of the people and slaughtered it, and he prepared it as a sin offering, just like the first offering. **16** Then he brought the burnt offering and prepared it according to the law.

Adonai's Glory Is Revealed *2nd Aliyah*

17 Then he brought the grain offering. He took a handful of fine flour and burned it on the altar. This was in addition to the regular morning grain offering
18 Next, he slaughtered the bull and the ram that were the people's peace sacrifice. Aaron's sons brought some of the blood to him, and he sprinkled it on all sides of the altar.
19 They also brought him the parts of the bull and ram: the fat, the kidneys, and the liver.
20 He placed the fat on top of the breasts of the animals, and burned the fat, kidneys, and liver on the altar. **21** Aaron waved the breasts and the right hind legs as an offering before Adonai. It was done exactly as Adonai had commanded Moses.
22 Then Aaron raised his hands over the people and blessed them. He stepped down from the altar where he had presented the sin offering, the burnt offering, and the peace offerings.
23 Moses and Aaron went into the Meeting Tent, and when they came out they blessed the people. And then the glory of Adonai was seen by all the Israelites.

Nadav and Avihu *3rd Aliyah*

Fire blazed from Adonai and vaporized the burnt offering and the parts on the altar. When the people saw this, they raised their voices in prayer and bowed down.

10 Aaron's sons, Nadav and Avihu, each took his fire pan, placed burning coals in it, and sprinkled incense on the flames. They presented this before Adonai, but it was not an authorized fire that Adonai had commanded.

---

22. Then Aaron raised his hands over the people and blessed them.
Aaron, as the newly appointed High Priest, gave the Israelites his first official blessing.

22. He stepped down from the altar where he had presented the sin offering.
The altar was 54 inches high, so Aaron had to go down the steps.

1. Aaron's sons, Nadav and Avihu, each took his fire pan and placed burning coals in it, and sprinkled incense on the flames. They presented this before Adonai, but it was not an authorized fire that Adonai had commanded.

Nadav and Avihu were Aaron's oldest sons.
For some reason they decided to bring their fire pans, with fire that had not been taken from the holy altar, and dared to enter the sanctuary with this unauthorized fire.
To compound the sin, it was the day of the consecration of the sanctuary. Performing sacrifices in the correct way showed respect for Adonai. Nadav and Avihu were disrespectful and ignored Adonai's law for sacrifices. Some of the commentators says that the two were jealous and in this way challenged the authority of Aaron and Moses.

2 Flames of fire blazed down from Adonai and burned them up, and they died before Adonai.
3 Moses said to Aaron, "This is exactly what Adonai meant when he said,
> 'I will be holy to those who worship Me; to them I will show My glory.'"

Aaron remained speechless. **4** Then Moses summoned Mishael and Elzafan, the sons of Aaron's uncle Uzziel, and said to them, "Come and remove your cousins from inside the sanctuary and take their bodies outside the camp."
5 They came and dragged Nadav and Avihu by their robes outside the camp, as Moses had ordered.
6 Moses said to Aaron and his two remaining sons, Elezar and Ithamar, "Do not mourn them by tearing your hair or your clothes; or Adonai will get angry and will also strike you, and you too will die. As far as your brothers are concerned, the entire community of Israel can mourn for them.
7 You are a priest, and you must not leave the entrance of the Meeting Tent, because Adonai's anointing oil is still on you, or else you will die."

They did as Moses commanded.
8 Adonai said to Aaron, **9** "Neither you nor your descendants may drink wine or any other alcoholic liquor when you enter the Meeting Tent, or you will die. This law must be observed for all coming generations.
10 If you are sober you will be able to tell the difference between the holy and the ordinary, and between honesty and dishonesty. **11** You will, moreover, be able to make correct legal decisions for the Israelites on all the laws that Adonai has taught Moses."

---

2. Flames of fire blazed down from Adonai and burned them up, and they died before Adonai.
Jewish interpreters have wrestled with the harshness of this punishment. Were they challenging the authority of their father Aaron? Were they drunk? Whatever the explanation, the story was a warning to the priests that they must follow the rules and exactly carry out their duties in the Temple.

3. Aaron remained speechless.
His heart stopped beating and he did not act like a father who had just lost two children. He accepted their fate like a leader, with resignation and composure. A good example of this behavior is the army, navy, and marines who, especially in wartime, must carry out the orders of their superiors. Another example is workers in a nuclear power plant. They must obey the rules and carry out their responsibility to the letter. Even a tiny slipup can cause a nuclear disaster.

8. Adonai said to Aaron.
Aaron was also a prophet. Some say that Adonai spoke to Aaron only through Moses.

9. Neither you or your descendants may drink wine or any other alcoholic liquor when you enter the Meeting Tent.
Adonai warns Aaron to be careful and not die like his two eldest sons. Alcoholic beverages destroy the sense of reality. Aaron is the High Priest and the Israelites look up to him for advice and holiness. Drunkenness will destroy his image and his reputation, and Adonai's holiness will be judged by his behavior.

10. If you are sober you will be able to tell the difference between the holy and the ordinary, and between honesty and dishonesty.
The plague of drunkenness has adversely infected humanity since Noah planted grapevines. Drunkenness has ruined reputations, families, governments, and caused untold health problems.

The Holy Service Is Finished
4th Aliyah

12 Then Moses spoke to Aaron and his surviving sons, Eleazar and Ithamar: "Take the remainder of the holy grain offering that has been presented to Adonai, and eat it unleavened near the altar. **13** Adonai has commanded that you must eat it in a holy place because it is the portion that has been given to you and your descendants.

14 Remember, the breast taken as a wave offering and the hind leg taken as an elevated gift are yours, and your sons and daughters may eat them. They are the portion from the peace sacrifices that has been given to you and your descendants.

15 The hind leg for the elevated gift, and the breast for the wave offering, shall be placed on top of the fat as a fire offering and are to be presented as a wave offering. The legs and the breast are designated as a gift for you and your descendants for all time, as Adonai has commanded."

Moses Forgives Aaron
5th Aliyah

16 When Moses asked about the goat for the sin offering, he was told that it had already been burned. Moses became angry at Aaron's sons, Elezar and Ithamar. He said to them, **17** "Why didn't you eat the holy sin offering in a holy place? It was specially given you to remove the community's guilt and to atone before Adonai.

18 Since its blood was not brought into the inner sanctuary, you should have eaten it in a holy place, as I instructed you."

19 Their father Aaron answered Moses, "Today a tragedy happened and I lost my sons when they sacrificed their sin offering and burnt offering before Adonai. If I had eaten the sin offering today, would Adonai have been pleased with me?"

20 Moses sadly forgave Aaron when he heard his explanation.

---

13. Because it is the portion that has been given to you and your descendants.
The priests were not given land in Canaan and had no way of earning a living. They subsisted on the portions of animal and grain sacrifices. Even as they wandered through the deserts they ate portions of the sacrifices.

14. Remember, the breast taken as a wave offering and the hind leg taken as an elevated gift are yours, and your sons and daughters may eat them.
The peace offerings could be eaten in any clean place within the Israelite camp. Thus the peace offering could be eaten by the whole family, which included the wife and children.

16. Moses became angry at Aaron's sons, Elazar and Ithamar.
This was a tragic event in Aaron's life. Now Moses becomes angry at Aaron's two remaining sons, Elazar and Ithamar. Moses was angry at them because they had not eaten the offering of a goat in a holy place. The two sons were saved from the flames that killed their two brothers. They should have been aware and not repeat the mistakes of their brother's deliberate stupidity.

19. If I had eaten the sin offering today, would Adonai have been pleased with me?
Aaron explained to Moses that his children were in mourning and thought that they should not eat the holy sacrifice.

20. Moses sadly forgave Aaron when he heard his explanation.
Moses initially reacted out of anger, and then he reconsidered and forgave his brother Aaron. He realized that Aaron had just lost two children. He also realized that Elazar and Ithamar were also affected by the loss of their two brothers and were confused by the event. Moses admitted that he was wrong and asked Aaron to forgive him.

The Dietary Laws

6th Aliyah

11 Adonai spoke to Moses and Aaron and told them: **2** Speak to the Israelites and instruct them: These are the only land animals that you may eat: **3** You may eat any animal that has split hoofs and chews its cud. **4** However, you must not eat the following cud-chewing, hoofed animals. You must not eat the camel, although it chews its cud, because it does not have a real hoof. **5** You must not eat the hare, even though it brings up its cud, because it too does not have a real hoof. **6** You must not eat the rabbit, even though it brings up its cud, because it does not have a true hoof. **7** You must not eat the pig, even though it has a true hoof, because it does not chew its cud. **8** You must not eat the flesh of any of these animals. And at no time shall you touch their carcasses, because they are unclean. **9** These are the creatures that live in the water that you may eat. You may eat any creature that lives in the water, in the seas or in the rivers, as long as it has fins and scales. **10** But all marine creatures that live in the seas and rivers and do not have fins and scales, whether they are small or large creatures which crawl in the water, must not be eaten. **11** They are forbidden to you. You must not eat their flesh. **12** Every creature in the water that has no fins and scales must not be eaten.

---

1. Adonai spoke to Moses and Aaron.
Aaron was the High Priest and he had to instruct the others how to distinguish between the animals that were fit to eat and those that were forbidden.

2. These are the only land animals you may eat.
This is mitzvah number 153.
 An animal must have two signs to make it permissible (kosher) to eat.
  1. It must chew its cud.
  2. It must have split hooves.

Types	Allowed (Kosher)	Disallowed (non-Kosher)
Land	Cud chewers, Split hoofs	Non–cud chewers, Non–split hoofs
Birds	Chickens, ducks, pigeons, doves	Birds of prey
Fish	Fins and scales	No fins and scales
Insects	Grasshoppers	Non–jointed legs
Reptiles	Forbidden	Forbidden

There are nine species of animals with these two requirements: ox, sheep, goat, deer, gazelle, wild goat, ibex, antelope, mountain sheep.

4 You must not eat the camel, although it chews its cud, because it does not have a real hoof.
The camel is known as "the ship of the desert." Its hoof has a cushion which helps it walk on sand. This cushioned hoof is not split which makes it unkosher.

8. At no time shall you touch their carcasses, because they are unclean.
Anyone who touches their bodies is virtually impure until evening. *Ibn Ezra*

9. These are the creatures that live in the water that you may eat.
This is mitzvah number 155.
 A fish must have scales and fins.

12. Every creature in the water that has no fins and scales must not be eaten.
In general this prohibition refers to crabs, lobsters, clams, and shellfish.
 These marine creatures were and are today subject to outbreaks of a variety of dangerous marine diseases which frequently occur in hot climates. Today these types of marine creatures are subject to invasions of the red tide and diseases.

13 The following birds must not be eaten. These are the flying animals that you must avoid: the eagle, the vulture, the buzzard, **14** the kite and birds of the falcon family, **15** ravens of every kind, **16** the ostrich, the owl, the sea gull, and hawks of every kind, **17** the falcon, the cormorant, the ibis, **18** the marsh hen, the pelican, the magpie, **19** the stork and herons of every kind, the hoopoe, and the bat.

20 Every flying insect that uses four legs for walking shall not be eaten. **21** The only flying insects that you may eat are those with jointed legs extending above their feet, which they use to hop on the ground.

22 Among these are the various kinds of locusts, grasshoppers, and the cricket family.

23 All other flying insects with four feet must not be eaten.

24 Anyone who touches the bodies of dead animals will be unclean until evening. **25** Anyone dealing with their bodies must wash his clothes and remain unclean until evening. **26** Every animal that does not have cloven hoofs and does not chew its cud must not be eaten, and anyone touching its flesh shall become unclean.

27 Every four-footed animal that walks on its paws must not be eaten, and anyone touching their bodies shall be unclean until evening. **28** Anyone that carries their bodies must wash his clothing and then remains unclean until evening.

29 The following small animals that live on land must not be eaten: the weasel, the mouse, the rat, **30** the hedgehog, the chameleon, the lizard, the snail, and the mole.

31 These small animals must not be eaten; whoever touches them when they are dead shall remain unclean until evening.

32 When any of these dead animals falls on wooden dishes, clothing, leather goods, sackcloth, or any other article with which work is done, each item must be washed; it remains unclean until evening, and then becomes clean and usable.

Laws About Dead Animals *7th Aliyah*

33 If a dead animal falls on the inside of a clay pot, anything inside it becomes unclean, and the pot shall be broken.

13–19. The following birds must not be eaten. These are the flying animals that you must avoid: the eagle, the vulture, the buzzard, the kite and birds of the falcon family, ravens of every kind, the ostrich, the owl, the sea gull, and hawks of every kind, the falcon, the cormorant, the ibis, the marsh hen, the pelican, the magpie, the stork and herons of every kind, the hoopoe, and the bat.

Most of the enumerated are birds of prey.

The birds that are permitted must have a crop to receive its food from the beak and a gizzard which grinds the food. When these birds are slaughtered ritually, the crop is thrown away and the inner lining of the gizzard is peeled away and discarded.

25. Anyone dealing with their bodies must wash his clothes and remain unclean until evening.

The authorities were aware that animals, just like humans, can die because of diseases or infestation which can be contracted by contact with a dead body. Washing the clothing was a precaution against contamination.

31. These small animals must not be eaten.

It is forbidden (mitzvah 159) to eat the following eight small rodents: weasel, mice, toads, hedgehogs, chameleons, lizards, snails, and moles. The Torah warns that these creatures are a dangerous source of contamination. In Bible times anyone who had contact with any of these eight species was forbidden to enter the Holy Temple.

34 Any food soaked with water from the clay pot must not be eaten. Any liquid in the clay pot is also unclean.

35 Anything upon which a dead body falls is unclean; even an oven or a range becomes unclean, and must be destroyed.

36 The only thing that is always ritually clean is a body of water, either a well or a natural spring of water. Any other water that is touched by the dead body of any of these animals shall become unclean.

37 If a dead body falls on any planted seeds, they are still ritually clean. **38** But if the dead body falls on seeds that have been soaked in water, the seeds become unclean. **39** If any animal that you are permitted to eat dies naturally, then anyone touching its carcass shall be unclean until evening.

40 Anyone eating anything from a dead animal must wash his clothing, and then remains unclean until evening. Anyone who moves a dead animal must wash himself and his clothing, and also remains unclean until evening.

41 Every creature that crawls on the ground must not be eaten. **42** You must not eat any creature that crawls on its belly, or any animal with four or more feet that lives on land. All of these animals must not be eaten.

43 Do not make yourselves unclean by eating any of these creatures, or you will become unclean as they are.

44 I am Adonai; I am holy, and therefore you must make yourselves holy. Do not make yourself unclean by eating any of the small creatures that crawl on the earth.

The Israelites Must Be Holy　　　　　　　　　　　　　　　*Maftir*

45 I am Adonai,
I brought you out of Egypt
to be your Elohim. Since I am holy,
you too must remain holy.

46 These are the laws about animals, birds, marine creatures, and creatures that creep on the ground.

47 I have given you these laws so that you can tell the difference between the unclean and clean animals, and between the animals that you may eat and those that you must not eat.

---

39. If any animal that you are permitted to eat dies naturally, then anyone touching its carcass shall be unclean until evening.

This is mitzvah number 161.

The animals are permitted to be eaten as food. However, if they die of natural causes they are considered in the category of *nevelah*, meaning unclean animal carcasses.

The *nevelah* may be a source of contamination. Today we are aware of the dangers of bird flu and mad cow disease. Obviously the Torah was aware of the danger of eating diseased animals.

41. Every creature that crawls on the ground must not be eaten.

Mitzvah 162 prohibits the eating of any creeping animals such as snails and rodents, found on land or in any body of water.

44. I am Adonai: I am holy, and therefore you must make yourselves holy.

Holiness is not something reserved for elite human beings. It is not a state of being. It is a way of looking at the world, of reacting to it, of living in it. It is the term the Torah uses when it wants to say that humans should strive to be more like Adonai.

תַזְרִיעַ *Tazria*

WHEN A WOMAN GIVES BIRTH

12 Adonai spoke to Moses, and told him to **2** inform the Israelites of the following laws: When a woman becomes pregnant and gives birth to a boy, she is ritually unclean for seven days, just as she is unclean during the time when she has her period. **3** On the eighth day, the boy must be circumcised. **4** The woman must wait another thirty-three days until her blood is ritually clean. Until this cleansing period is complete, she must not touch anything holy and must not enter the sanctuary.

5 Every woman who gives birth to a girl is unclean for fourteen days, just as she is during her menstrual period. After that she shall have a waiting period of sixty-six days until her blood is ritually clean. **6** When her cleansing period either for a son or a daughter is completed, she shall bring to the priest, at the entrance of the Meeting Tent, a lamb for a burnt offering and a pigeon or a dove for a sin offering.

7 The priest shall offer the sacrifice before Adonai and atone for the woman, cleansing her of the blood coming from her womb. This law applies to a woman whether she gives birth to a boy or to a girl.

8 If the woman cannot afford a lamb, she can bring two doves or two pigeons, one for a burnt offering and one for a sin offering. Then the priest shall make atonement for her, and she shall be clean.

13 Adonai spoke to Moses and Aaron, saying:
2 If a person has a white sore or a rash, and it spreads on the skin of his body, and it is suspected of being leprosy, he must be brought to Aaron, or to one of Aaron's descendants. **3** A priest shall then examine the sores on the person's skin, and if the hairs on the sores have turned white, and the infection has penetrated under the skin, then it is a sign of leprosy. The priest who examines the infected area must declare the person unclean.

---

6. When her cleansing period either for a son or daughter is completed, she shall bring to the priest, at the entrance of the Meeting Tent, a lamb for a burnt offering and a pigeon or a dove for a sin offering.
The burnt offering was a thank you gift for an easy childbirth and for rewarding her with a beautiful, healthy child.

8. Then the priest shall make atonement for her, and she shall be clean.
The waiting period before the woman can bring her sacrifices are geared to her peace of mind. Although she is physically and ritually clean, she is not yet in the holy and spiritual frame of mind. After the thirty-third day the birth mother can now pray with *kavanah* (intent) and concentrate on the holiness of the sacred offering. *Sforno*

3. And the infection has penetrated under the skin, then it is a sign of leprosy.
The Hebrew word *zara'at* is conveniently translated as "leprosy." The word "leprosy" is used for a variety of skin infections and dermatological diseases such as psoriasis, especially infectious ones which can spread through a community, such as chicken pox.

The diagnosis and cure were the responsibility of the priests. Biblical law prescribed the rigid exclusion of "unclean" persons afflicted with leprosy until they were cleared by the priest after a period of isolation.

4 However, if there are white spots on the skin but they are only on the surface of the skin, and the hairs in the infected area have not turned white, then the priest shall quarantine the infected person for seven days. **5** On the seventh day the priest shall reexamine the person. If the sores have remained the same size, the priest shall quarantine the patient for another seven days.

Skin Diseases
2nd Aliyah

6 On the seventh day the priest shall reexamine him, and if the sores have healed and the infection has not spread, the priest shall announce that the person is healed, since it is just a plain white sore. The person must wash his clothing, and he is then clean.
7 However, if the white sores on the skin continue to spread and increase in size after they were examined by the priest, then the person must be reexamined by the priest.
8 If the priest determines that the rash on the skin has increased in size, he must pronounce him a leper.
9 When a person has a skin condition, he must be brought to a priest. **10** If the priest sees that there are large white sores on the skin, and some of the hairs have turned white, **11** the priest must declare leprosy. He must quarantine the person for further examination because he is obviously unclean.
12 These are the laws if the rash spreads and covers all of the skin of the infected person from head to foot, so that the priest can easily see it.
13 When the priest sees that the rash has covered all of the person's skin, he shall declare the infected person clean. As long as the skin has turned completely white, he is clean.

---

4. The priest shall quarantine the infected person for seven days.
Many illnesses and infections change for the better after seven days. The purpose of the quarantine was a precaution to prevent the spread of infectious disease. *Ibn Ezra*

5. On the seventh day the priest shall re-examine the person.
The priest was the expert who determined whether the afflicted person was cured or not. He was given the responsibility because he was highly experienced and could distinguish between different types of infections.

Also, there was a belief that the infection was caused by the person's sinful practices. The Kohen could council the individual to change his attitude, redirect his behavior, and become a respectable citizen.

6. The person must wash his clothing, and he is then clean.
If the sores are healed, then the individual is not infectious. However, as an extra precaution he must wash his clothing. The laws were especially strict with diseases that are infectious, which could initiate an epidemic.

9. When a person has a skin condition, he must be brought to a priest.
When a person discovers a skin abnormality such as a sore, scab, or swelling, he must bring it to the attention of a priest.

To confirm the diagnosis of the priest and to minimize the spread of the infection, the patient is placed in isolation. If the condition subsides, the patient is discharged. However, if the condition spreads or fails to respond to treatment, the patient is then isolated for another seven days. If there is no improvement, then the patient is isolated outside the camp until the individual shows a sign of responding to a cure.

14 But if the sores came back and are filled with pus, the priest must rule that the person is unclean. **15** When the priest sees the discolored skin, he shall declare the person unclean. The healthy skin is a sign of uncleanness, because it is leprosy.

16 But if the skin again turns white, the person must return to the priest. **17** When the priest determines that the infected area has healed completely and is white, the priest shall say to him, "You are cured."

Leprosy Disease
3rd Aliyah

18 These are the laws when an infection develops on a person's body and then heals. **19** If a white or red sore develops where the infection was, it must be shown to the priest.

20 The priest shall examine it, and if it appears to have penetrated under the skin and the hair has turned white, the priest must declare that the person has leprosy.

21 But if the priest examines the infection and does not see any white hair, and the infection has not penetrated the skin and it is a dull white, then the priest shall quarantine the person for seven days.

22 If the infection on the skin spreads during this time, the priest shall declare the person unclean, because it is leprosy.

23 However, if the infection does not spread and remains in the same place, it is scar tissue from the infection, and the priest shall declare the person clean.

Burns and Leprosy
4th Aliyah

24 These are the laws when a person has a burn on the body, and the burned area develops a red or white sore.

25 The priest shall examine it, and if the hair in the burned area has turned white, and the infection has penetrated under the skin, it is leprosy that is breaking out in the burned area. Since it is leprosy, the priest shall declare the person unclean.

26 But if the priest examines the area, and the burned area does not have white hair, and the infection has not penetrated under the skin, the priest shall quarantine the person for seven days.

27 At the end of seven days, the priest shall reexamine the skin. If the infection has increased in size, the priest shall declare the person unclean, since it is leprosy.

28 But if the burned area has not increased in size and the redness has faded, then it is just a scar because of the burn.

Since it is scar tissue from the burn, the priest shall declare the person clean.

18–19. These are the laws when an infection develops on a person's body and then heals. If a white or red sore develops where the infection was, it must be shown to the priest.
This refers to a situation where an infection seems to be healed but now a different and secondary infection has appeared in the same area or close to it.

20. The priest shall examine it, and if it appears to have penetrated under the skin and the hair has turned white, the priest must declare that the person has leprosy.
Some researchers believe that the described medical condition does not fit the diagnosis for modern leprosy, called Hansen's disease. Hansen's disease causes numbness, but the Torah never mentions this effect.

Leprosy and Baldness
5th Aliyah

29 These are the laws if a man or a woman has an infection on the head or chin. **30** The priest shall examine the infection, and if it has penetrated the skin and blond hairs are found in the infected area, the priest shall declare the person unclean. Such an infection is a sign of leprosy on the head or chin.

31 If the priest examines the area, and the infection has not penetrated under the skin and does not have black hairs in it, the priest must quarantine the person with the infection for seven days. **32** On the seventh day, the priest shall again examine the area, and if the infection has not increased in size, and there is no blond hair in it, the infection has not penetrated under the skin. **33** In this case the person shall shave, but without shaving off the hair in the infected area. The priest shall then quarantine the person with the infection for a second seven-day period.

34 The priest shall reexamine the infection on the seventh day, and if the infected area with the fallen hair has not increased in size, or if the infection has not penetrated under the skin, the priest shall declare the person clean. The person must then wash his clothing, and he is clean.

35 But if the infection with the fallen hair continues to spread after he has cleansed himself, **36** the priest must reexamine the person again. If the bald patch has increased in size, the priest need not check for blond hairs, since the person is unclean.

37 However, if the infected bald patch remains the same size and the black hairs are growing back, then the infection has healed and the person is clean. The priest shall declare the person clean.

38 If a man's or woman's body breaks out with white spots, **39** the priest shall carefully examine the infected area. If the skin is just covered with dull white spots, it is a simple skin rash and the person is clean.

---

29. These are the laws if a man or a woman has an infection on the head or chin.
The area that appears to be healthy is shaved without disturbing the infected area. Then the patient is isolated for seven days until the priest determines that is healing. Anyone who is cleared by the priest remains under continuous observation until the infected area is cleared.

It is the responsibility of the priest to protect the health and welfare of the community. The Torah emphasizes the importance of preventing a person from becoming a carrier of disease or infection and endangering the whole community.

30. The priest shall examine the infection.
In ancient Israel the priests were the physicians and lived in special cities scattered throughout the kingdom so that they could treat the Israelites wherever they lived. Their descendants provided half of the physicians in Medieval Europe. Even anti-Semitic kings and clergy invariably had Jewish personal physicians, and when entire Jewish communities were exiled, the Jewish physician was forced to remain.

In modern times, Jews have garnered more than forty Nobel prizes in medicine. Jewish doctors have provided medical miracles and breakthroughs that have saved many millions of lives.

32. On the seventh day, the priest shall again examine the area, and if the infection has not increased in size, and there is no blond hair in it, the infection has not penetrated under the skin.
The priest must check for three visual signs of infection: (1.) yellow hair; (2.) growth of the lesion; (3.) lesions under the skin.

Then to make doubly sure, the patient must remain quarantined for another seven days.

Unclean and Contagious
6th Aliyah

40 When a man loses the hair on his head and simply becomes bald, he is clean. **41** If he loses the hair near his face, it is just a sign of a receding hairline and he is clean.

42 But if he has a red infection on the bald spots and finds sores and swelling in the front or back of his head, it may be a sign of a skin disease. **43** The priest shall examine the reddish sores on his bald spots, and if he finds swelling around the sores it is leprosy.

44 The person is considered infected with leprosy, and he is unclean. Since he is unclean because of the infection on his head, the priest must declare him unclean.

45 A person who is a leper must tear his clothing and leave his hair uncut, and wherever he goes he must cover his head and must call out, "Unclean! Contagious! Unclean! Contagious!"

46 He shall be unclean as long as the disease lasts. Since he is unclean, he must be isolated and live outside the camp.

47 These are the laws when a garment contains a mildew infection. It can be woolen clothing, linen clothing, **48** wool yarn, or anything made of leather. **49** If a green or red discoloration appears in the cloth, leather, yarn, or any leather article, it may be a fungus infection, and it must be shown to the priest.

50 The priest shall examine the mildewed area and quarantine the infected article for seven days. **51** On the seventh day, he shall examine the affected area, and if the mold in the mildewed area has increased in size on the cloth, the yarn, or the article made from leather, then it is a fungus infection, and it is unclean.

---

43. "Leprosy."
A more appropiate word here would be "psoriasis," denoting a variety of skin disease.

45. A person who is a leper must tear his clothing and leave his hair uncut, and wherever he goes he must cover his head and must call out, "Unclean! Contagious!"
The people must be aware that he is infected and can possibly infect others and cause an epidemic.
Ibn Ezra

45. A person who is a leper must tear his clothing and leave his hair uncut, and wherever he goes he must cover his head and must call out, "Unclean! Contagious!"
This is mitzvah number 171. The sages say that a person who is infected with leprosy is an individual who has spoken evil, *lashon hara*. For such an individual, isolation is the appropriate punishment.

Slanderous remarks have caused quarrels and separations between people and families so he or she deserves to be separated from the company of other people.

47–49. These are the laws when a garment contains a mildew infection. It can be woolen clothing, linen clothing, wool, yarn, or anything made of leather. If a green or red discoloration appears in the cloth, leather, yarn or any leather article it may be a fungus infection, and it must be shown to the priest.
Fungi parasites depend on living animals and plants. The parasites are responsible for many serious human and plant diseases. Some of these fungi form furry growths on food, leather, textiles, and other materials in hot moist environments. These molds obtain their food by assisting in the decay of organic material in which they grow.

Mold structures are black, blue, green, orange, and red.

Sforno says: "The green and red discoloration may be a warning that the owner of the garment or domicile must examine his personal business and family affairs, to alert his senses to deviations in his behavior and to repent for his sins.

52 The cloth, the yarn, whether wool or linen, or the leather article containing the fungus must be burned. Since it is a fungus infection, it must be burned in fire.

53 However, if, when the priest examines it, the mildew in the garment, the yarn, or the leather article has not spread, **54** the priest shall order that the mildewed article be scrubbed and quarantined for a second seven-day period.

Mildew Infections *7th Aliyah*

55 After the mildew has been scrubbed and quarantined, the priest shall examine the article, and if the mildew has not changed in appearance or spread, then it is still unclean and must be burned.

56 If the priest examines the item after it has been scrubbed and quarantined, and the mold from the mildew has faded from the cloth, then he shall cut off the mildewed spot from the cloth, the leather, or the yarn.

Clean and Unclean *Maftir*

57 But if the mildew reappears on the same cloth, yarn, or leather item, then it is infected, and the article having the mildew must be burned.

58 If the fungus mold is completely removed from the cloth, yarn, or leather article, and is then scrubbed and washed a second time, it is considered clean.

59 These are the laws for deciding whether cloth, leather items, or yarn are clean or unclean from fungus infections.

---

52. The cloth, the yarn, whether wool or linen, or the leather article containing the fungus must be burned.
The type of fungus rarely attacks anything other than wool or linen. *Ibn Ezra*

59. These are the laws for deciding whether cloth, leather items, or yarn are clean or unclean from fungus infections.
The purpose of all these laws is to prevent the spread of disease among the general population.

מְצֹרָע *Metzora*

THE LAWS OF LEPROSY

14 Adonai spoke to Moses, saying:
2 These are the instructions which must be followed when you think that the leper under the care of a priest has been cured.
3 The priest shall go outside the camp to examine the leper and check whether the leprosy has healed.
4 The priest shall conduct a cleansing ceremony for the person by taking two live clean birds, a piece of cedar wood, some red wool, and a hyssop branch.
5 The priest shall delegate another priest to slaughter a bird over a clay bowl filled with fresh spring water.
6 Then he shall take the second live bird and the piece of cedar wood, the red crimson wool, and the hyssop branch, and along with the live bird he shall dip the cedar, the wool, and the hyssop into the spring water mixed with the blood of the slaughtered bird.
7 The priest shall then sprinkle this mixture seven times on the person undergoing the cleansing from leprosy, thereby making him clean. When the ceremony is over, the priest shall release the living bird and let it fly away.
8 The person undergoing cleansing shall wash his clothing and shave off all the hair on his body. He shall then wash himself and in this way complete the first part of the cleansing. He may return to the camp, but he must remain outside his tent for seven days.
9 On the seventh day, the person shall once again shave off all the hair on his head, beard, eyebrows, and other body hair. He shall then wash his clothing and body, and then he is completely clean.
10 On the eighth day, he shall take two healthy rams, one healthy lamb, and three-fifths of a pint of fine flour mixed with olive oil as a meal offering, and three-fifths of a pint of olive oil.

---

3. The priest shall go outside the camp to examine the leper and check whether the leprosy has healed.
Although the *kohen* has declared that the leper is ritually cured, he still may not enter the camp until he has offered his ritual purity sacrifice. *Ibn Ezra*

4. The priest shall conduct a cleansing ceremony for the person by taking two live clean birds, a piece of cedar wood, some red wool, and a hyssop branch.
After a person has recovered from leprosy, he was required to purify himself by sacrificing birds (pigeons) and undergoing an atonement ritual performed by a priest. The priest was to sprinkle the person seven times with the mixture of cedar wood and red wool dipped in the blood of a bird.

The hyssop plant is an aromatic plant and is used as a seasoning by many people.

Before the exodus from Egypt, "a bunch of hyssop" (Shemot 12:22–23) was used to smear blood on the doorposts of the Israelites to save them from the slaying of the first-born.

7. When the ceremony is over, the priest shall release the living bird and let it fly away.
After the ceremony, the live bird is released as a symbol of the release of the person being returned to his freedom, his family, and his home.

11 The priest will then present the offering and the person undergoing cleansing before Adonai at the entrance of the Meeting Tent.

12 The priest shall take one ram with the olive oil and present it as a guilt offering. He shall offer them as a wave offering before Adonai.

Healed of Leprosy
2nd Aliyah

13 Then he shall slaughter the lamb in the same place where burnt offerings and sin offerings are slaughtered.

This guilt offering is holy and is just like a sin offering to the priest.

14 The priest shall take some blood from the guilt offering and smear it on the right earlobe, right thumb, and right big toe of the person who is being cleansed.

15 The priest shall pour some of the olive oil into the palm of his own left hand. **16** Then he shall dip his right forefinger into the oil in his left hand, and with his finger sprinkle some oil seven times before Adonai.

17 The priest shall then smear some of the oil from his hand on the right earlobe, right thumb, and right big toe of the person undergoing cleansing, over the guilt offering's blood.

18 The priest shall pour the rest of the oil in his hand onto the head of the person that is being cleansed. In this way, the priest shall make atonement before Adonai for the healed person.

19 Then the priest shall sacrifice the sin offering and make atonement for the person being cleansed. After that, he shall slaughter the burnt offering,

20 and the priest shall present the burnt offering and the grain offering on the altar. In this way the priest shall make atonement for the person who is cured and is now ceremonially clean.

---

14 The priest shall take some blood from the guilt offering and smear it on the right earlobe, right thumb, and right big toe of the person who is being cleansed.
The ear, thumb, and toe ceremony is exactly the same as in the consecration of the priests (8:23).

17. The priest shall then smear some of the oil from his hand on the right earlobe, right thumb, and right big toe of the person undergoing cleansing, over the guilt offering's blood.
The cleansing ceremony is symbolic. The healed person is cleaned from his head – the earlobe – down to his hand – the thumb – and to the end of his body – the toe. *Shenash*

18. In this way, the priest shall make atonement before Adonai for the healed person.
The sidrah *Metzora* deals with laws of leprosy. These laws are both hygienic and religious. Medicines in ancient times were primitive, and the Israelites depended upon the quarantine to stop the spread of infection and disease. The rite of purification does not involve any prayer.

The atonement sacrifice which takes place after the determination of a cure is the official price or ticket to readmission to camp.

Only after all the offerings are completed is the leper considered ritually pure like everyone else.

20. In this way the priest shall make atonement for the person who is cured and is now ceremonially clean.
The leper is returned to camp in stages. First there is complete isolation. Then the priest conducts a cleansing ceremony, which includes sacrifices, washing, and shaving. Then the leper has to remain outside of his tent for seven days. Now the person is medically and ceremonially clean. The various stages permitted the priests to continue monitoring the symptoms of the leper.

A Poor Person's Offering
3rd Aliyah

21 If the leper is poor, however, and cannot afford the two lambs, he can bring one lamb as a guilt offering this shall be the wave offering to atone for him and two quarts of the best flour mixed with olive oil as a grain offering, and three-fifths of a pint of olive oil.

22 In addition, he shall bring two doves or two pigeons, whichever he can afford, one for a sin offering and the other for a burnt offering.

23 On the eighth day, the person being cleansed shall bring the offering to the priest, at the entrance of the Meeting Tent, before Adonai. **24** The priest shall take the lamb for the guilt offering and the olive oil, and offer them as a wave offering before Adonai.

25 He shall slaughter the lamb as a guilt offering. The priest shall take the blood of the guilt offering and place it on the right earlobe, the right thumb, and the right big toe of the person undergoing purification.

26 The priest shall then pour some of the oil into the palm of his left hand. **27** Then he shall dip his right finger and sprinkle some of the oil from his left hand seven times before Adonai.

28 The priest shall place some of the oil from his hand on the right earlobe, right thumb, and right big toe of the person undergoing cleansing, right over the place where the blood of the guilt offering was put. **29** The priest shall pour the rest of the oil from his hand onto the head of the person undergoing cleansing. With all this he shall make atonement for the person before Adonai.

30 He shall then prepare one of the doves or pigeons, whichever the person was able to afford.

31 With this offering, the priest shall sacrifice one bird as a sin offering and one as a burnt offering, and then present it with the grain offering.

In this way the priest shall make atonement before Adonai for the person undergoing cleansing.

32 These are the instructions for cleansing the person who has a skin disease and cannot afford to bring the usual sacrifice for his cleansing.

Mildewed Houses
4th Aliyah

33 Adonai spoke to Moses and Aaron, saying:

---

21. If the leper is poor, however, and cannot afford the two lambs.
Ibn Ezra says that the word "poor" has two connotations: (1) poverty, (2) poor in health. If he is poor, then he can substitute pigeons or doves, which are much cheaper.

24. The priest shall take the blood of the guilt offering and place it on the right earlobe, the right thumb, and the right big toe of the person undergoing purification.
The entire procedure – the sprinkling of blood, the oil on the body and head – is symbolic and the priest must be prepared to use all of his senses to become a more dedicated individual: (1) to absorb the words of the Torah by his ear; (2) to accomplish good deeds as symbolized by his thumb; and (3) to climb the ladder of success as symbolized by his big toe. *Rabbi Samson Raphael Hirsch*

34 When you come to the land of Canaan, which I am giving you as a permanent possession, and I for some reason contaminate houses in the land you inherit, **35** the owner of such a house must go and tell the priest, "It looks to me as if there is mildew growing in my house."

36 The priest shall order that the house be completely emptied so that everything in the house will not become unclean. Only then shall a priest inspect the house.

37 The priest shall examine the mildew to see whether the streaks of the green or red fungus have penetrated into the wall.

38 If the fungus mold has grown into the wall, then the priest shall leave and stand outside the entrance of the house. The priest shall quarantine the house for seven days. **39** On the seventh day the priest shall return and check whether the mold on the wall of the house has spread.

40 If the fungus has grown, the priest shall order the owner to dump the infected stones in an isolated place outside the city.

41 Afterwards the owner shall scrape the inside of the house, especially around the mildewed area. The workmen doing the scraping shall dump the plaster and stones outside the city in an isolated place. **42** Then the owner shall replace the stones and replaster the entire house with new clay.

43 But if the stones have been removed and the house has been scraped and plastered, and the mildew comes back, **44** the priest shall return and reexamine the house. If the fungus mold has grown again in the house, then the whole house is unclean. **45** The priest must order the house completely torn down, and all the wood and stones and plaster from the house shall be moved outside the city to an isolated dump.

34–35. When you come to the land of Canaan, which I am giving you as a permanent possession, and I for some reason contaminate the houses in the land you inherit, the owner of such a house must go and tell the priest, "It looks to me as if there is mildew growing in my house."
Some of the sages say that the mildew in the house is a warning to the owner to repent.

If the owner repents, then the mildew will disappear. If not, then the stones are removed and if this warning is ignored the house will be disassembled. If none of these warnings causes repentance, then the fungus will attack the individual.

34. When you come to the land of Canaan, which I am giving you as a permanent possession, and I for some reason contaminate houses in the land you inherit.
Rashi says that the Amorites hid their valuables in the stone walls of their houses so the invading Israelites would not find them.

Adonai struck those houses with mildew, forcing the new owners, the Israelites, to tear down their homes and thereby find the valuables.

36. The priest shall order that the house be completely emptied so that everything in the house will not become unclean.
The priests were very much concerned about the properties within the house, so they ordered the residents to remove their personal property before the priests condemned the physical structure of the domicile.

45. The priest must order the house completely torn down, and all the wood and stones and plaster from the house shall be moved outside the city to an isolated dump.
The discarded, material should be removed to an isolated, ritually impure place so that no one will take and reuse them. Mildew is a severe problem in hot, moist climates.
Ibn Ezra

46 As long as the house is in quarantine, anyone entering the house will be unclean until evening. **47** If someone eats or sleeps in the house, he must wash both his body and his clothing. However, he must wash his clothing only if he has remained in the house long enough to eat a small meal.

48 When the priest returns at the end of the seven days, after the house has been replastered, and he sees that the mold has not reappeared in the house, then the fungus has gone away and the priest shall declare the house clean. **49** To cleanse the house, he shall take two birds, a piece of cedar wood, some red wool, and a hyssop branch. **50** He shall slaughter one bird over a clay bowl filled with fresh spring water. **51** And then he shall take the cedar wood, the hyssop, the red wool, and the live bird, dip them in the blood of the slaughtered bird and the fresh spring water, and sprinkle it on the house seven times.

52 He shall cleanse the house with the bird's blood and spring water, along with the live bird, cedar wood, hyssop, and crimson wool. **53** He shall then release the live bird in a field outside the city. This is how he shall make atonement for the house, and it is then clean.

Skin and Mildew Infections   *5th Aliyah*

54 These are the laws for dealing with skin diseases and mildew infections, **55** if mildew streaks appear on a garment or in a house, **56** and white sores or discolorations appear on the skin. **57** These instructions must be followed when dealing with skin diseases and mildew, and to tell when someone or something is clean or unclean. These are the laws dealing with skin infections.

15 Adonai spoke to Moses and Aaron, and told them **2** to speak to the Israelites and tell them the following: When a man has a pus discharge from his penis, this discharge can make him unclean. **3** He becomes unclean if his penis drips pus or if some of the pus is stuck to his body. These discharges make him unclean, so that **4** any bed the man with the dischargelies in becomes unclean, and any object he sits upon also becomes unclean.

---

49. To cleanse the house, he shall take two birds, a piece of cedar wood, some red wool, and a hyssop branch.
Cedar wood contains a substance used in medicine for skin diseases. Hyssop, perhaps the herb marjoram, contains a mild antiseptic. Today we have the same type of inspection and treatment for dry rot and mildew.

57. These are the laws dealing with skin infections.
Today skin diseases are a highly technical medical specialty called dermatology. The ancient priests who were the doctors and diagnosticians were responsible for treating diseases. They had to differentiate between the various symptoms and decide how to treat the patient.

Here the Torah describes skin diseases, discharges, and sores for humans and mildew for houses and garments. The Torah also warns the Israelites how to prevent infections from spreading. Most of these warnings and precautions are applicable today. Unfortunately, the priests did not have the medicines that are now available for their patients.

2. When a man has a pus discharge from his penis, this discharge can make him unclean.
This type of discharge can be a bacterial infection or it can be a sign of a venereal disease such as syphilis, herpes, or gonorrhea. These diseases are infectious, so precautions should be taken to prevent the individual from infecting others.

5 Any person who lies in the man's bed must wash his clothing and his body, and then remains unclean until evening. **6** Anyone who sits on an object upon which the man with a discharge has been sitting must also cleanse his clothing and his body, and then remains unclean until evening.
7 If anyone touches the body of a person with a pus discharge, he must wash his clothing and his body, and then remains unclean until evening.
8 If the saliva of someone with a discharge is spat on a ritually clean person, that person must wash his clothing and his body, and remains unclean until evening.
9 Any saddle or seat upon which the person with the discharge sits is unclean. **10** Anyone who touches something that has been under a person with a discharge shall be unclean until evening. Anyone who carries such an object must cleanse his clothing and his body, and then remains unclean until evening.
11 If anyone touches a man with a discharge who has not immersed even his hands in water, that person must immerse his clothing and his body in water, and then remains unclean until evening. **12** Any clay pot touched by a man with a discharge must be broken. Every wooden utensil must be washed.
13 Seven days after a person with a pus discharge gets well, he is to be considered clean if he washes himself and his clothing in a stream of spring water.
14 On the eighth day, he shall take two doves or two pigeons, and present them before Adonai at the entrance of the Meeting Tent, and he shall give the birds to the priest.
15 The priest shall present one bird as a sin offering and one as a burnt offering. In this way the priest will make atonement for the person before Adonai, cleansing him of his discharge.

Bodily Discharges   6th Aliyah

16 When a man has a discharge of semen, he must wash his entire body and remains unclean until evening.
17 If any semen comes in contact with an article of clothing or a leather item, it must be washed and remains unclean until evening.
18 If a woman has sexual intercourse with a man, both of them must wash and then remain unclean until evening.

---

6. Anyone who sits on an object upon which the man with a discharge has been sitting must clean his clothing and his body, and then remains unclean until evening.
This type of discharge could indicate diarrhea or a gonorrhea infection.

8. If the saliva of someone with a discharge is spat on a ritually clean person, that person must wash his clothing and his body, and remain unclean until evening.
The level of medicinal healing was on a very primitive level. However, the ancients were very much aware of how infections could spread and progress into a full-blown epidemic.

They understood the value of washing as a way of stopping the spread of infection. They also were aware of quarantines and isolation as a methodology for stopping the spread of diseases.

The same precautions are practiced today.

Shenash

12. Any clay pot touched by a man with a discharge must be broken.
Clay is a porous material and can absorb harmful bacteria and pathogens, which can proliferate and spread disease.   *Shenash*

19 Whenever a woman has her menstruation, she shall remain ritually unclean for seven days, and anyone touching her shall be unclean until evening.
20 When a woman is in her menstrual state, anything upon which she sits or lies becomes unclean, and anyone sitting or lying on it also becomes unclean.
21 Whoever lies on her bed must wash his clothing and his body, and then remains unclean until evening. **22** The same applies to anyone who touches anything upon which she has rested. He must wash his clothing and his body and remains unclean until evening. **23** If he touches anything that is on her bed or any other article upon which she rested, he is unclean until evening.
24 If a man has sexual intercourse with her and her menstrual discharge touches him, he shall be unclean for seven days, and any bed upon which he lies shall be unclean.
25 If a woman has a discharge of blood for a long time when it is not time for her monthly menstrual period, or if she has a discharge beyond the usual time of her period, then she is unclean, just as when she has her period.
26 Anything upon which she sits or rests during the time of her discharge shall be unclean just as it would be during her normal period. **27** Anyone touching these articles must wash his clothing and his body, and remains unclean until evening.
28 Seven days after the woman is rid of her discharge, she must undergo cleansing.

Atonement for an Unclean Discharge   *7th Aliyah*

29 On the eighth day, she shall take two doves or two pigeons and bring them to the priest at the entrance of the Meeting Tent.
30 The priest shall prepare one bird as a sin offering and the other bird as a burnt offering, and the priest shall make atonement for her before Adonai, cleansing her from her discharge.

Separate the Clean from the Unclean   *Maftir*

31 Now Moses and Aaron must separate the Israelites from things that make them impure so that they will not die by corrupting My Tabernacle that I have placed among them.
32 These are the laws for a man who is unclean because of a discharge of semen, **33** and for a woman who has her monthly period, and for a man who has a genital discharge or who has sex with a ritually unclean woman.

---

28. Seven days after the woman is rid of her discharge, she must undergo cleansing.
This is mitzvah number 183.

The cleansing consists of bringing two offerings, a sin offering and a burnt offering.

28. Seven days after the woman is rid of her discharge, she must undergo cleansing.
Today the cleansing consists of going to the *mikvah*. A *mikvah* is a pool of water for ritual immersion and cleansing.

According to the rabbis, a *mikvah* must contain about 190 gallons of water so a person can immerse herself completely. The water in the *mikvah* should come from a natural source such as rainwater, springs, or snow.

After the cessation of the menstrual flow and after seven clean days she is to immerse herself in a *mikvah*.

These laws are based on Vayikra 15:19–33, 18:19, and 20:18. *Niddah* is the term applied to menstruating women.

אַחֲרֵי מוֹת *Achare Mot*

THE DEATH OF AARON'S SONS

16 Adonai spoke to Moses right after the death of the two sons of Aaron who had disobeyed Adonai and brought an unauthorized offering. **2** Adonai said to Moses: Tell your brother Aaron not to enter the Holy of Holies that is behind the curtain concealing the ark or else he will die, because I appear there in a cloud over the ark.

3 Before Aaron enters the inner sanctuary, he must bring a young bull for a sin offering and a ram for a burnt offering. **4** He must clothe himself in the white linen robe, his linen undergarments, his linen belt, and his headdress. These are sacred garments, and before putting them on he must cleanse himself. **5** The Israelite community shall bring him two goats for sin offerings, and one ram for a burnt offering. **6** First he shall ask forgiveness for himself and his family by presenting a bull for his own sin offering. **7** Then he shall take the two goats, and lead them before Adonai at the entrance of the Meeting Tent. **8** Aaron shall cast two lots for the two goats: one lot marked "For Adonai," and the other lot marked "For Azazel."

---

4. He must clothe himself in the white linen robe, his linen undergarments, his linen belt, and his headdress.

These are sacred garments, and before putting them on he must cleanse himself. Throughout the year Aaron officiated wearing his golden garments with special decorations. But the holiday of Yom Kippur was entirely different. The High Priest dressed in simple white linen garments – as symbols of purity of the body, mind, and spirit. Today on Yom Kippur it is a custom for the rabbi and cantor to wear white robes. In Orthodox synagogues many of the worshippers wear a white robe, called a *kittel*.

6. First he shall ask forgiveness for himself and his family by presenting a bull for his own sin offering.

The basic connotation of *kaparah* is the burial of the past so that the sins of the past should not in any way harm the individual's future life. The stipulation for *kaparah* (atonement) is a pledge to fulfill the intention and to resolve to behave differently. The first instance of *kaparah* is found in the story of Cain and Abel. Adonai says to Abel, "If you do good, your future will be special, but if you do not do right, then only sin will be at your door" (Ber. 4:7).

8. Aaron shall cast two lots for the two goats: one lot marked "For Adonai," and the other marked "For Azazel."

The Day of Atonement, Yom Kippur, which was and is observed on the tenth of the month of Tishri, is the most solemn holiday of the Jewish year. There was a special ritual for the Temple sacrifices. There was a sin offering for Aaron's own transgression and that of the priesthood. During these ceremonies he dressed in white, and made his entry into the Holy of Holies. Next came the ritual of the two goats. One was sacrificed to atone for the sins of the people and the priests. The second goat, the scapegoat, was offered by the community and destined for the devil Azazel. The High Priest placed his hands on the head of this scapegoat and annulled all the sins of the people. Then the goat was taken to a wilderness area and released. The goat for Azazel was not sacrificed to Adonai, because it had been charged with the sins of the people and was impure for sacrifice.

8. Aaron shall cast two lots for the two goats: one lot marked "For Adonai," and the other lot marked "For Azazel."

On the holiday of Yom Kippur today every Jew has the opportunity to make a choice "for Adonai" or "for Azazel." You can choose Adonai and resolve to resist all temptations and strengthen the influence of Adonai in your life. Or you can choose Azazel and wander through the desert of sin and evil.

9 Aaron shall present the goat that was chosen by lot for Adonai so that it can be offered as a sin offering.

10 But the goat that was chosen by lot for the demon Azazel must remain alive, so that it will be able to remove the sins of the Israelites and send the sins to Azazel in the desert.

11 Aaron shall present his bull as a sin offering and ask forgiveness for himself and for his fellow priests. Then he shall slaughter his bull as a sin offering.

12 Next he shall take a fire pan filled with burning coals from the side of the altar that is before Adonai, along with two handfuls of perfume incense, and bring them both into the inner sanctuary behind the cloth partition.

13 There he shall sprinkle the incense on the coals, so that the smoke from the incense covers the ark and the Ten Commandments. If he follows My instructions, he will not die.

14 Aaron shall then take some of the bull's blood, and with his forefinger sprinkle drops of the blood seven times toward the ark.

15 Then he shall slaughter the goat as the people's sin offering, and bring its blood into the inner sanctuary behind the cloth curtain. Aaron shall do the same with this blood as he did with the bull's blood, and sprinkle it both above and below the ark.

16 With this offering, he will take away the sins of the Israelites for their rebellious acts and all their uncleanness. He shall then perform exactly the same ritual in the Meeting Tent, which remains among the Israelites despite their misdeeds.

17 No one must be in the Meeting Tent from the moment that Aaron enters the sanctuary to make atonement until he leaves. In this way Aaron will remove the sins from himself, from his family, and from the entire Israelite community.

The Azazel Goat *2nd Aliyah*

18 After leaving the tent, Aaron shall make atonement by smearing some of the blood from the bull and the goat on the horns of the altar.

19 With his finger he shall sprinkle the blood on the altar seven times, and it will completely cleanse the sins of the Israelites.

20 When he has finished making atonement in the inner sanctuary, in the Meeting Tent, and on the altar, he shall present the live goat.

---

11. Aaron shall present his bull as a sin offering and ask forgiveness for himself and for his fellow priests.
The steps leading to human forgiveness are somewhat different from those preceding divine forgiveness. In place of penitence, a term that has theological connotations, it is preferable to demand an expression of regret and remorse. The sequence preceding human forgiveness is as follows: an admission of guilt, an expression of regret, an apology, and a request for forgiveness. There must also be an offer to make restitution for any damage to as well as mental suffering of the injured party.

16. With this offering, he will take away the sins of the Israelites for their rebellious acts and all the uncleanness.

The Hebrew word *kaparah* means atonement – taking away the sins. The custom of *kaparot*, or atonement, originated in Geonic times and became widespread in Eastern Europe. It consists of swinging a chicken around one's head and praying that the life of the chicken will substitute for the punishment due to oneself. In very Orthodox homes this ritual is performed the morning of the day before Yom Kippur.

21 Aaron shall place both of his hands on the head of the goat and confess all the sins of the Israelites, their rebellious acts and their sins. Then Aaron will select someone to lead the Azazel goat into the wilderness.
22 When the person frees the goat in the wilderness, all of the sins of the Israelites will be transferred to Azazel. **23** Next Aaron shall enter the Meeting Tent and remove the priestly garments that he wore when he entered the Holy of Holies and leave his sacred garments there.
24 Aaron shall then bathe in a sacred place, and dress in his regular clothing. Then he shall complete his own and the people's burnt offerings, thus atoning for himself and the people.

The Sabbath of Sabbaths *3rd Aliyah*

25 Aaron shall also burn the fat of the sin offering on the altar.
26 The person who leads the goat to Azazel in the wilderness shall wash his clothing and body, and only then can he reenter the camp. **27** The remains of the bull and the goat presented as sin offerings, whose blood was brought into the inner sanctuary to make atonement, must be taken outside the camp, where their skin, flesh, and organs shall be burned. **28** The person who does the burning shall wash his clothing and body, and only then can he return to the camp. **29** This shall be a permanent law for all time. Every year, on the tenth day of the seventh month [Tishri], you must spend the day fasting and not doing any work. This law is the same for Israelites and for the foreigner who lives among you.
30 On this day you will be cleansed of all your sins before Adonai.

---

21. Aaron shall place both of his hands on the head of the goat and confess all the sins of the Israelites.
During the services in the temple on Yom Kippur, the Day of Atonement, fifteen sacrifices were brought. During the services, the High Priest made three confessions. The third was a plea for forgiveness made on behalf of the entire people of Israel. Two goats were chosen and one was sacrificed. The other, the "scapegoat," was sent into the wilderness to Azazel to die.

The pair of goats were to remind the Jew of the twins Jacob and Esau; Jacob lived a holy life while Esau lived in the wilderness far from his family. The goat for Azazel was chosen by lots – reminding the Jews that Yom Kippur is the time to make a choice, to live like Jacob or like Esau – and the goat was not sacrificed to Adonai, because it had been charged with the sins of the people and therefore was impure for sacrifice.

Abarbanel

22. When the person frees the goat in the wilderness, all of the sins of the Israelites will be transferred to Azazel.
The goat was transported to a far place so it would not find its way back to camp.

This custom has led to a similar custom called *tashlich*. During the afternoon of the first of Rosh Hashanah it is customary to go to any body of moving water and recite prayers and symbolically "cast one's sins into depths of the sea." Crumbs of bread, symbols of sins and of broken promises, are thrown into the moving waters.

30. On this day you will be cleansed of all your sins before Adonai.
The tenth day of the month of Tishri is Yom Kippur, a day for fasting and for the cleansing of sins.

The name of the holiday comes from the Hebrew word *kaparah*, which means forgiveness. This is a legal term borrowed from the laws of property. Just as a person may release his fellow man from a debt owed to him, so may Adonai forgive a person of a penalty due to sin. *Kaparah* means to remove the need for punishment.

31 From now on the Sabbath of Sabbaths will be, for Israelites, a day of fasting and resting. This is a law, and it must be observed each year.

32 A priest who is anointed and ordained as the new High Priest shall make atonement by wearing the sacred garments of white linen. **33** He shall make his atonement in the Holy of Holies, in the Meeting Tent, and on the altar. The atonement that he makes shall be for the priests and for the Israelites.

34 This shall be a law for all time for you, so that the Israelites once each year will be able to gain forgiveness for their sins. Moses later did exactly as Adonai had commanded him.

Official Sacrifices   4th Aliyah

17 Adonai spoke to Moses, and told him: **2** Speak to Aaron, his sons, and the other Israelites, and tell them that this is what Adonai has commanded:

3 If any Israelite sacrifices an ox, sheep, or goat to Adonai whether in or outside the camp, **4** but does not bring the sacrifice in person to the Meeting Tent, he is treated as a murderer. He shall be considered guilty of murder, and he must be driven out of the community.

5 The Israelites must take the sacrifices that they are now offering in the fields and bring them to Adonai, to the entrance to the Meeting Tent, and present them to the priest. They will be offered as peace offerings to Adonai. **6** The priest will sprinkle the blood against the altar at the entrance of the Meeting Tent and burn the fat as a thank you gift to Adonai.

7 The Israelites must no longer sacrifice to the goat demons who tempt them to worship. This shall be a law for all the generations to come.

Do Not Eat Blood   5th Aliyah

8 Any person, whether an Israelite or a foreigner who lives among you, who wishes to offer a burnt offering or any of the sacrifices, **9** must bring it to the Meeting Tent to present it to Adonai. If he does not, he must be driven out of the community of Israel.

---

31. Sabbath of Sabbaths.
The commentators call it the holiest of all Sabbaths.

3–4. If any Israelite sacrifices an ox, sheep, or goat to Adonai whether in or outside the camp, but does not bring the sacrifice in person to the Meeting Tent, he is treated as a murderer.
This is prohibitive mitzvah number 186.

The Torah specifically prohibits the sacrifice of holy offerings outside the sanctuary. Even if the slaughter takes place in the sanctuary area but is sacrificed somewhere else, it is considered a violation.

Before the erection of the sanctuary, the Israelites could sacrifice on their own private altars. However, now all sacrifices had a fixed place to which to bring their offerings.

5. The Israelites must take the sacrifices that they are now offering in the fields and bring them to Adonai, to the entrance to the Meeting Tent, and present them to the priest.
All the prophets preached against the idolatrous practice of the Israelites. Centralizing the sacrifices in the mishkan was an attempt to deter the idol worshippers.

7. The Israelites must no longer sacrifice to the goat demons.
The ancient Israelites believed in demons called *shaydim*, and some tried to contact them so they could foretell future events. Maimonides called the demons *jinns*, who drank blood and assumed the form of a goat.

However, the Torah treats the belief in demons as a form of idol worship and forbids any attempt to contact them.

10 If any person, whether of the family of Israel or a foreigner who lives among you, eats blood, it will make Me angry, and that person must be outlawed from among his people.
11 Because the life-force of a living thing is in its flesh and blood, and that is why I have given you the blood of animals to sacrifice instead of your own lives.
12 Therefore I say to the Israelites, "Do not eat blood." A foreigner who lives among you must also not eat blood. **13** If any person, whether of the family of Israel or a foreigner who lives among you, hunts and kills an animal or a bird which one is permitted to eat, he must drain its blood and must bury the blood in the earth.
14 The existence of every living creature is in its blood. That is why I have warned the Israelites not to eat any blood, because the life-force of every creature is in its blood. That is why anyone who eats blood must be driven out of the community of Israel. **15** Any Israelite or foreigner who eats a creature that is permitted to be eaten but has died a natural death or was killed by beasts must wash his clothing and body. He shall remain unclean until evening.
16 If he does not wash his clothing and body, he will be held responsible for his sin.

18

Adonai spoke to Moses and told him: **2** Speak to the Israelites, and say to them: I am Adonai.
3 You must not follow the customs of the Egyptians, among whom you once lived, and also do not follow the customs of the people of Canaan, where I will be bringing you. You must not imitate their way of life.

---

10. If any person, whether of the family of Israel or a foreigner who lives among you, eats blood, it will make Me angry, and that person must be outlawed from among his people.
A group called Chaldeans drank blood in order to contact the demons who would give them the power to predict future events. The Torah tried to stop this pagan custom by forbidding the eating of blood.

The Torah countered the idea of eating blood by using the blood for sprinkling and also for atonement on the altar. The Torah's explanation cites the reason for the prohibition in Vayikra 17:14: "not to eat any blood because the life-force of any creature is in its blood."   *Maimonides*

11. Because the life-force of a living thing is in its flesh and blood, and that is why I have given you the blood of animals to sacrifice instead of your own lives.
Blood means life. No human can exist without blood. Blood also represents a person's wild angry animal impulses. It is this unthinking, wild and angry tendency that causes humans to commit unethical and immoral acts.

The blood of the sacrificed animals is accepted by Adonai in atonement for sins. The sacrifice and the animal blood remind the sinner that his anger brought his or her blood to a boil, which had disastrous consequences.   *Shenash*

3. You must not follow the customs of the Egyptians, among whom you once lived, and also do not follow the customs of the people of Canaan, where I will be bringing you. You must not imitate their way of life.
The Israelites escaped from the land of Egypt, where people prayed to idols, and went to Canaan, another idol-infested country. Adonai was aware that idol worship with its pagan ceremonies was very attractive. He did not want the Israelites to conform to the Canaanite way of life, culture, and religion. The Torah warns the Israelites not to imitate the religious practices of the Egyptians and the Canaanites. The Torah also forewarns the Israelites that the land of Canaan, which they will soon enter, is a cesspool of evil. The corruption refers to their sexual activities and their social activities.

4 Obey My laws and carefully observe My commandments. I am Adonai. I demand it.

5 If you observe My commandments and laws, then you will surely live a good life. I am Adonai. I demand it

Unlawful Sexual Acts *6th Aliyah*

6 You must not proposition a relative to commit a sexual act. I am Adonai. I forbid it.

7 You must not commit a sexual act with your close relatives especially your mother.

8 You must not commit a sexual act with your father's wife.

9 You must not commit a sexual act with your sister. It makes no difference if she is your sister or your stepsister.

10 You must not commit a sexual act with the daughter of your son or daughter.

11 You must not commit a sexual act with the daughter of your father's wife. She is your sister, and you must not commit a sexual act with her.

12 You must not commit a sexual act with your father's sister. She is your father's relative. **13** You must not commit a sexual act with your mother's sister. She is your mother's relative.

14 You must not commit a sexual act against your father's brother by having sexual contact with his wife. She is your aunt.

15 You must not commit a sexual act with your daughter-in-law. She is your son's wife.

16 You must not commit a sexual act with your brother's wife.

---

4. Obey My laws and carefully observe My commandments. I am Adonai. I demand it.
The Mosaic Code was intended to "build a fence" around the Israelites and separate them from the secular conduct and religious practices of the Egyptians and Canaanites.

The Israelites were being held to higher moral and ethical standards than their soon to be neighbors. They were to become "a holy nation." The Torah specifically warns the Israelites against the rituals of idolatry. You must not follow the customs of the Egyptians, among whom you once lived and also do not follow the customs of the people of Canaan, where I will be bringing you. You must not imitate their way of life.

7. You must not commit a sexual act with your close relatives especially your mother.
Science 4,000 years ago had not yet learned about DNA and genetic structures. However, intuitively they were aware that mating of close relatives could became a genetic problem and produce progeny with mental defects.

It is a scientific and statistical fact that closely related families whose children marry each other have high incidents of problem offspring.
Shenash

10. You must not commit a sexual act with the daughter of your son or daughter.
This is prohibitive mitzvah number 102.

The Torah warns the Israelites not to follow the customs of the Egyptians and specifically refers to their sexual conduct.

This mitzvah pinpoints the problem of incest. In ancient times, and also today, some children were abused by fathers, stepfathers, brothers, and uncles. The Torah highlights the problem and tries to educate the Israelites to the evils of incest and rape and the ruined lives of molested children.

16. You must not commit a sexual act with your brother's wife.
Aside from the ethical and moral implications of aberrant sexual activities, the Torah was very much aware of the medical implications of such conduct. Behind the religious restriction was the realization that wild sexual activities could lead to medical problems such as syphilis, gonorrhea, yaws, and herpes.

15. You must not commit a sexual act with your daughter-in-law. She is your son's wife.
The rule forbids marriage between a man and his daughter-in-law after her husband's death or a divorce.

17 You must not commit a sexual act by marrying a woman and her daughter. Do not even marry her son's daughter or her daughter's daughter. They are your relatives, and it is a sin.
18 You must not marry a woman and also marry her sister as long as the first wife is alive.
19 You must not sleep with a woman who is ritually unclean because of her menstruation.
20 You must not have sex with your neighbor's wife.
21 You must not allow any of your children to be sacrificed to the idol Molech. I am Adonai. I demand it.

You Must Observe My Laws   *7th Aliyah*
22 You must not practice homosexuality. It is a sin.
23 You must not perform any sexual act with animals, because it is unclean. Nor shall a woman have sexual contact with an animal. It is a sin.
24 You must not lower yourself into the gutter by imitating any of these sexual acts. It is because they engage in these evil practices that I am driving away the nations who stand in your way.
25 The land has become unclean, and so I must punish the people who live there. Soon the land will vomit them out.
26 Every Israelite and every foreigner who settles among you must observe My rules and commandments and not perform any of these disgusting acts.
27 The nations who inhabited the land before you practice all these disgusting acts and have made the land unclean.

You Must Not Imitate Their Customs   *Maftir*
28 Do not imitate them, or I will throw you out of the land just as I will throw out the people who lived there before you.
29 Anyone who performs any of these degrading acts will be outlawed from his people.
30 Follow My commandments; do not imitate any of the disgusting customs that were practiced before you arrived, lest you be defiled by them. I am Adonai. I forbid it.

---

18. You must not marry a woman and also marry her sister as long as the first wife is alive.
As long as his wife is alive, the husband must not marry his wife's sister. However, if she dies, then he is permitted to marry the sister. The Rabbis encouraged such marriages, since a sister would likely be familiar with the children and family customs.

21. You must not allow any of your children to be sacrificed to the idol Molekh.
Molekh was worshipped by the Ammonites. An idol was heated and the bodies of newly sacrificed children were placed in its arms.

Molekh was known to the Israelites before they entered Canaan, and Moses prohibited its worship. Nevertheless, some of the kings of Israel permitted its worship.

Our sages say that Adonai gave the land of Israel to its enemies because of such idol worship.

23. You must not perform any sexual act with animals.
The Torah warns the Israelites not to sink to the carnal and incestuous acts of the Canaanite environment. Vayikra Chapter 18 is read in the synagogue every Yom Kippur.

קְדוֹשִׁים *Kedoshim*

YOU MUST BE HOLY

19 Adonai spoke to Moses, and told him: **2** Speak to the Israelite community and say to them:
You must be holy, because I am Adonai and I am holy.
3 Every person must respect his mother and his father. You must observe the Sabbath as a day of rest. I am Adonai. I demand it.
4 You must not worship false gods, and you must not make idols of any kind. I am Adonai. I forbid it.
5 When you bring a peace offering to Adonai, you must do it willingly. **6** And you must eat it on the same day you sacrifice it or on the next day, but anything that is left over on the third day must be burned.
7 If any of the offering is eaten on the third day, it will be considered impure and I will reject it.
8 Whoever eats it will be punished, because he has desecrated that which is holy to Adonai. Such a person must be exiled from the community of Israel.
9 When you reap your grain harvest, leave some of the wheat at the edges of your fields, and do not pick up the loose stalks that have fallen to the ground.

---

3. Every person must respect his mother and his father.
The Torah mentions the mother before the father. Children are usually more fearful of their father than of their mother. By placing the mother first, the Torah emphasizes that a child should have as much respect for the mother as for the father.

3. Every person must respect his mother and his father.
This is mitzvah number 212

It is a mitzvah for a child to be respectful of his or her parents. In biblical times there were numerous signs of respect.

1. A child must not sit or stand where his parents usually sit and stand.

2. A child is forbidden to disagree with parents in the presence of others.

3. A child must not call the parents by their first name.

9. When you reap your grain harvest, leave some of the wheat at the edges of your fields.
No people of old showed as much concern for the livelihood of those in want as in Israel.

In the ancient Hebrew state, the poor were assured of a living by five rights in the harvest which the Bible gave them.

1. The poor had the right to any crops that grew in the corners of the field ("corner").

2. The poor had the right to crops dropped on the ground when the corn was being picked ("gathering").

3. The poor had the right to grapes that were dropped in the vineyard ("dropping").

4. The poor had the right to grapes that were not perfect ("young clusters").

5. The poor had the right to crops that were forgotten by the farmer ("forgetfulness").

All these parts of the harvest belonged to the poor. The farmer was not allowed to gather them, and all needy people – the poor, the widow, the orphan, and the stranger (whether Jew or non-Jew) – were entitled to them.

There was also a special poor tax, known as "poor tithe." Every third year, the Jewish farmer had to set aside one-tenth of his harvest and take it to a special storehouse in his district where the poor tithe was kept for distributing to the needy. Even today many Jews continue to give one tenth of their earnings *ma'aser* (ten percent) to charities.

10 You must not pick up the fallen bunches of grapes in your vineyards. And you must not pick up the loose grapes that have fallen to the ground in your vineyards. Leave it all for the poor and the stranger who lives in your midst. I am Adonai. I demand it.
11 You must not steal. You must not cheat. You must not lie to one another.
12 You must not swear falsely and use My name. If you do, you will bring shame to My name. I am Adonai. I forbid it. **13** You must pay your worker on time. You must not withhold the daily wages of your workers until morning.
14 You must not curse a deaf person. You must not trip a blind (handicapped) person. You must fear Adonai. I am Adonai. I demand it.

You Must Not
2nd Aliyah

15 You must not interfere with justice. Do not favor the poor or show favoritism to the rich. You must judge people fairly. **16** You must not spread gossip.
You must not stand still if your neighbor's life is in danger. You must try to help. I am Adonai. I demand it.
17 You must not be jealous of your neighbor.
You must warn your neighbor if he does something wrong. You must not close your eyes to wrongdoing.

---

10. You must not pick up the loose grapes that have fallen to the ground in your vineyards. Leave it all for the poor and the stranger who lives in your midst.
Do not pick up the *olelot*, the young, immature grapes. Leave them for the poor and the strangers. This mitzvah was a reminder that Adonai owned the land and that the people were only the caretaker.

11. You must not steal. You must not cheat. You must not lie to one another.
Mitzvah 224 warns us not to steal, cheat, or lie. These three basic prohibitions cover a huge area from stealing in business, cheating in exams, lying on applications to school, and purchasing merchandise that has been stolen.

14. You must not trip a blind (handicapped) person.
Rashi says, "You must not trip a handicapped person" is meant not only physically but also mentally. Do not deliberately give a "handicapped" person wrong monetary or medical or even religious advice. A realtor must not deliberately persuade someone to purchase poor property for which he gets an extra commission. A stockbroker must not advise you to buy or sell stock so that he can earn more commissions.

15. You must not interfere with justice. Do not favor the poor or show favoritism to the rich. You must judge people fairly.
This is mitzvah number 233.

Judges must be aware that they are to be neutral when judging a trial. They are forbidden to take sides and must provide justice based upon honest witnesses and pure evidence.

Judges must recuse themselves from a trial if they have familial, economic, or political ties to any of the claimants.

16. You must not spread gossip.
This is mitzvah number 236. *Re-chee-lut* means gossip. It is forbidden to spread *re-chee-lut* about a person even if the news is true. Nachmanides says that slander begins when a person deliberately searches into a person's private life with the express purpose of finding information which can harm a person financially, politically and personally.

Today there are newspapers, magazines, television programs, and computer blogs that spread *re-chee-lut*.

In many ways a slanderer can be classified as a murderer. He murders reputations, kills businesses, and can destroy families.

18 You must not hold a grudge against people. You must love your neighbors as much as you love yourself. I am Adonai. I demand it **19** You must faithfully observe My commandments. You must not mate your cattle with other species. You must not plant your fields with different kinds of seeds. You must not wear clothing that contains a forbidden mixture of wool and linen (*shatnez*).

20 If a man sleeps with a slave woman who is engaged to another man, and she has not been given her freedom, she must be tried in court, but neither of them shall be put to death, because she was not free.

21 The man must bring a ram as his guilt offering to Adonai at the entrance of the Meeting Tent. **22** The priest shall make atonement for him before Adonai with the guilt ram for the sin that he committed. In this way he will gain forgiveness.

---

18. You must love your neighbors as much as you love yourself.
This is mitzvah number 243.

It is known as the "Golden Rule."

The observance of this mitzvah includes good deeds such as visiting the sick, arranging for the burial of the dead, comforting the bereaved, and protecting the property and possessions of another as if they were your own.

Ibn Ezra says there should be no difference between what a person wishes for himself and his family and the good that he wishes for his fellow man, for we were all created by Adonai.

The basic biblical injunction against hate is found in Leviticus: "You shall not hate your brother in your heart." The phrase "your brother" appears significant. It seems to imply that individuals who normally act in a brotherly fashion and pose no threat to society do not merit the hate of their fellow men, even in the event that they commit an occasional wrong. Such people are generally amenable to correction, and they are entitled to be given a chance to make amends.

18. You must love your neighbors as much as you love yourself.
Hillel was once asked by a non-Jew to distill the Torah into a simple sentence. He said, "Respect your neighbor as much as you respect yourself."

18. You must love your neighbors as much as you love yourself.
This command is supposed to apply to all nations as well as individuals. Small and big, rich and poor, black, yellow, or white, we're all Adonai's children. We're always in His sight.

18. You must love your neighbors as much as you love yourself.
The book *Pirke Avot*, "Sayings of the Fathers," quotes Rabbi Simeon ben Azzai, who says, "The reward for doing a mitzvah is the opportunity to do another mitzvah."

19. You must not mate your cattle with other species. You must not plant your fields with different kinds of seeds. You must not wear clothing that contains a forbidden mixture of wool and linen (*shatnez*).
The Rabbis declared that there are six types of mixed species, called *kilayim*, that are forbidden:
   1. Planting different seeds in the same plot.
   2. Grafting different tree species together.
   3. Mixing seeds in the vineyard.
   4. Cross–breeding two different animals.
   5. Plowing with two different animals.
   6. Weaving wool and linen (*shatnez*) in the same fabric.

The sages differ on the reasons for the restrictions. Nachmanides says that it is forbidden to change the order of creation and that inbreeding changes the rules of nature.

19. You must not mate your cattle with other species.
You must not do anything to an animal, which alters Adonai's creation.

Today, gene alteration to animals and plants may be creating species, which may be harmful to the environment. Genetically altered seeds may upset the fragile ecological balance.

Genetically altered animals made turn into monsters.

Forbidden Fruit

3rd Aliyah

23 When you enter into the Promised Land and plant new fruit trees, you must not eat the fruit for the first three years. Avoid the fruit as a forbidden growth. **24** In the fourth year, all of the fruits shall be holy and must be given to Adonai as a tithe. **25** In the fifth year, you may eat its fruit and in this way your crops will increase. I am Adonai. **26** You must not eat blood.

You must not consult witches or fortune-tellers. You must not practice magic.

27 You must not cut off the hair on the sides of your head. You must not clip off the edges of your beard. **28** You must not cut yourself when you are in mourning.

You must not make any tattoo marks on your body. I am Adonai. I forbid it.

29 You must not degrade your daughter and make her into a prostitute, because you will make the land immoral, and the land will be filled with evil.

30 You must observe the Sabbath and respect My sanctuary. I am Adonai. I demand it.

31 You must not consult fortune-tellers or oracles who falsely claim to talk to the dead. I am Adonai. I forbid it.

32 Respect elderly people. I am Adonai. This I expect.

---

26. You must not consult witches or fortune-tellers. You must not practice magic.
Mitzvah 249 prohibits consulting palm readers and astrologists who claim that the movement of stars and planets can predict the future. Voodoo doctors and those who claim to have secret medical formulas that can cure disease or prolong life also fall into the forbidden category. The prohibition is valuable. In today's business climate promoters who sell fake gold certificates, peddle stock tips, and sell underwater acreage are all magic practitioners.

28. You must not make any tattoo marks on your body.
This is prohibitive mitzvah number 253.

It is forbidden to desecrate your body with tattoos. In ancient days and even today idol worshippers marked their bodies with symbols of pagan worship or gang membership. Tattoos are also a health hazard.

28. You must not cut yourself when you are in mourning.
It was the custom of the Amorites, as a sign of mourning, to cut themselves when there was a death in the family.

30. You must observe the Sabbath and respect My sanctuary.
This is mitzvah number 254.

It is a mitzvah to observe the proper decorum and respect in the synagogue. The synagogue is a temporary substitute for the ancient Temple in Jerusalem. It is the place where Jews have a conversation with Adonai through prayer. Maimonides says that whether a person is moved by the holiness of the synagogue or not, he will become spiritually conditioned to fulfill the mitzvot of the Torah.

31. You must not consult fortune- tellers or oracles who falsely claim to talk to the dead.
This is mitzvah number 256.

It is forbidden to consult wizards who claim to talk to the dead. The wizards conduct séances and hoodwink the participants with tricky sounds and fake voices of the departed.

32. Respect elderly people.
This is mitzvah number 257.

It is a mitzvah to show respect for elderly people. Remember their wisdom and experience can save you from many mistakes. You can show respect by simply holding doors open, giving them the right of way, and simply helping them cross streets or even carrying grocery bags for them. Remember, some day you will be old and will expect respect from others.

Honest Weights and Measures
4th Aliyah

33 When a foreigner comes to live in your land, do not insult or discriminate against him. **34** The foreigner who becomes a citizen must be treated exactly the same as a native-born person. You must love him just as much as you love yourself. You must remember that you were once foreigners in Egypt. I am Adonai.

35 You must not use dishonest standards when measuring length, weight, or volume.

36 You must use an accurate scale, correct weights, and honest dry and liquid measuring cups.

I am Adonai, who took you out of Egypt. **37** Observe My rules and My commandments. I am Adonai. I demand it.

Penalties for Disobeying Adonai
5th Aliyah

20 Adonai spoke to Moses, and told him: **2** Say the following to the Israelites: Any person, whether an Israelite or a foreigner, who lives among you and sacrifices his children to the idol Molekh must be executed.

3 I will be angry at that person because he has sacrificed his children to Molekh. He has disregarded everything that is holy to Me and degraded My holy name. **4** If the people allow him to sacrifice his children and do not put him to death, **5** then I will act against that person and his family.

I will outlaw him from among his people, together with everyone who follows him to worship Molekh.

6 I will be an enemy to any person who consults fortune-tellers or psychics and follows their advice. I will be angry at them and cut them off from the community.

7 You must sanctify yourselves and be holy, for I, Adonai, am holy.

You Must Obey My Commandments
6th Aliyah

8 You must observe all of My commandments, for I, Adonai, have made you holy.

9 Any person who curses his father or mother must be put to death. **10** If a man has sex with a married woman, and she is the wife of a fellow Israelite, both the man and the woman shall be sentenced to death. **11** If a man has sexual relations with his father's wife, he has committed a sin against his father. Both of them shall be sentenced to death.

---

33. When a foreigner comes to live in your land, do not insult or discriminate against him.
You must treat the foreigner with respect. You must remember that you were once strangers in Egypt and you were not treated with respect.

36. You must use an accurate scale, correct weights, and honest dry and liquid measuring cups.
This is mitzvah number 259.

It is forbidden to use dishonest weights and measures. This prohibition also covers mislabeling of goods or old food. A person or a company that commits this type of crime is considered a thief. Drug companies must provide accurate information about the effects of the medication they sell.

37. Observe My rules and My commandments.
The commandments are divided into two categories. There are rules, *mishpatim*, between people, which are logical commandments. There are also commandments, *chukim*, which are laws between Adonai and man.

12 If a man has sexual relations with his daughter-in-law, both of them must be sentenced to death, because they have committed a vulgar sin.
13 If a man has homosexual relations with another man, both of them have committed a vulgar sin. And both of them shall be sentenced to death.
14 It is a sin if a man marries both a mother and a daughter; all of them shall be punished.
15 If a man has sex with an animal, he must be put to death, and the animal must also be put to death.
16 If a woman has sex with an animal, both the woman and the animal shall be sentenced to death.
17 It is a disgrace if a man has sex with his sister or his step-sister, and both of them must be exiled from their people, because he has committed incest with his sister and must be held responsible.
18 If a man has intercourse with a woman during her menstrual period, he has committed a sexual offense with her. He has violated her body, and both of them shall be driven out of the community.
19 You must not have sex with your mother's sister, since this disgraces a blood relative, and both of them are guilty of a sin.
20 If a man has sexual relations with his aunt, he has dishonored his uncle. Both of them are guilty, and they will die childless.
21 If a man marries his brother's wife, he has committed a sin against his brother, and both the man and the woman will die childless.
22 You must observe all My commandments and laws and obey them, to ensure that the land you are going to inherit does not throw you out.

Do Not Follow Their Customs *7th Aliyah*

23 You must not follow the customs of the nations that I am driving out before you, because they are completely immoral and I detest their customs.
24 As I have already said to you, "Conquer the land that I have promised to give you as an inheritance. It is a land flowing with milk and honey." I, Adonai, have chosen you from among all the other nations.

You Must Be Holy *Maftir*

25 You must make a distinction between the clean animals and birds and the unclean animals and birds. Do not degrade yourselves by eating animals, birds, or other creatures that I have set apart for you as unclean. **26** You shall be holy to Me, for I, Adonai, am holy, and I have chosen you from among the nations to be My own.
27 Any man or woman who practices witchcraft or talks to the dead shall be put to death.

---

24. It is a land flowing with milk and honey.
The Torah describes Canaan as a land of milk and honey. The country was divided into five distinct areas.
  1. The coastal plain has fertile soil with rich vineyards and citrus plantations.
  2. The central mountain area is ideal for growing fruits, vegetables, and grains.
  3. The Jezreel Valley is ideal for farmers and for raising poultry.
  4. The Jordan Rift was a vast swamp.
  5. The Negev is a hot, dry desert with few people. The area contained copper mines, and the Dead Sea provided salt.

אֱמֹר *Emor*

SPEAK TO THE LEVITES

21 Adonai told Moses to speak to Aaron's descendants, the priests: You must not make yourselves ritually unclean by contact with the dead, **2** unless it is a blood relative, such as a mother, father, son, daughter, or brother, **3** or an unmarried sister.

4 But you must not defile yourself even for a close married relative.

5 No priest shall shave off hair from his head, nor may they shave off their beards or mutilate themselves while in mourning.

6 They must be holy to Adonai, and not shame the name of Adonai. They must remain holy, because they present fire offerings to Adonai.

7 They must not marry an immoral woman. And they must not marry a woman who has been divorced.

A priest must be holy to Adonai.

8 They must be treated with respect, because they present food offerings to Adonai. Priests must be holy because I am Adonai I am holy, and I have made them holy. **9** The daughter of a priest who prostitutes herself has disgraced her father's position, and she must be put to death.

10 The High Priest who wears the special priestly garments must not go bareheaded or tear his garments in mourning.

11 The High Priest must never go near a dead body even if it is his father or his mother.

12 A High Priest must not leave the sanctuary to participate in a funeral, because he has been ordained and he will defile Adonai's sanctuary. I am God. I command it.

13 A High Priest must marry a virgin. **14** He must not marry a widow, a divorcee, or an immoral woman.

He may marry only a virgin from among the tribe of the Levites.

15 A High Priest must not dishonor his children because of the reputation of his wife. He must do all this because I am Adonai, and I make him holy.

---

1. Adonai told Moses to speak to Aaron's descendants, the priests: You must not make yourselves ritually unclean by contact with the dead.
After commanding the children of Israel to be holy, the Torah now commands Aaron's descendants, the priests, to observe additional restrictions because they are dedicated to the service of Adonai.

5. No priest shall shave off hair from his head.
The Mosaic law insists upon the complete elimination of foreign religious practices. In Vayikra 19:27, the Israelites were forbidden to shave the head and the edges of the beard, which was a regular religious practice in the ancient world.

Now the prohibition is repeated in order to emphasize that priests were also included.

12. A High Priest must not leave the sanctuary to participate in a funeral.
A High Priest occupies a special holy position and must demonstrate to the public that the holiness and honor of the sanctuary supersedes the honor of the dead.

Priests with Defects
2nd Aliyah

16 Adonai spoke to Moses, and said to him:

17 Instruct Aaron as follows:

Any of your descendants who has a physical defect must not approach the altar to present a food offering to Adonai.

18 A priest with a physical defect must not offer sacrifices. Nor a priest who is blind, deformed, or disfigured. **19** Nor any priest with any other physical defect. **20** Nor a priest who has a skin disease and running sores.

21 A descendant of Aaron the priest who has a defect is not permitted to offer fire offerings to Adonai.

22 He may still, however, eat the food offerings from the holy and from the most holy. **23** A priest with a defect must not go behind the cloth partition in the sanctuary, and he must not approach the altar. He must not defile My holy sanctuary. I am Adonai, and I make it holy.

24 Moses instructed Aaron and his sons and all the Israelites.

22

Adonai spoke to Moses, and said:

2 Instruct Aaron and his sons to be careful how they handle the sacred offerings that the Israelites present to Me, to ensure that they do not desecrate My holy name. I am Adonai.

3 Remind them that if any of their descendants is in an unclean state when he presents the sacred offerings to Adonai, he shall be cut off spiritually from Me. I am Adonai. **4** A priest who is a leper or who has a discharge from his penis must not eat any sacred offerings until he has cleansed himself.

Any priest who touches a dead person or who has an emission of semen **5** or who has touched an unclean animal or an unclean person **6** a priest who touches any of the above shall be unclean until evening, and he shall not eat any sacred offering until he has cleansed himself.

7 Then at sunset when he becomes ritually clean, he can eat the sacred offerings.

8 The priest must not eat any clean creature that has died from natural causes or has been killed by wild animals. It is forbidden because it will make him unclean. I am Adonai. I demand it.

9 The priests shall observe all My rules and not profane the sacred offering or they will die. Remember: I am Adonai, and I make them holy.

---

18. A priest with a physical defect must not offer sacrifices. Nor a priest who is blind, deformed, or disfigured.
There are three categories of physical defects that prevent a priest from participating in ceremonies connected with sacrifices.

The first is congenital, the second is the result of an accident, and the third is physical deformity resulting from sickness.

Priests with physical defects are entitled to share in the gratuities, since it is not their fault that they have a physical defects.   *Sforno*

8. The priest must not eat any clean creature that has died from natural causes or has been killed by wild animals.
The exact same prohibitions apply to every Israelite. These prohibitions are intended to protect the health of the Israelites, since the animals may have died as a result of a disease.

10 A non-priest is never allowed to eat sacred offerings. Even if he lives with a priest or is hired by him, he is still not allowed to eat the sacred offering.

11 However, if a priest purchases a slave, then the slave may eat the sacred offering. A slave born in the house of a priest may also eat his food.

12 If a priest's daughter marries a non-priest, she can no longer eat the sacred food.

13 But if the priest's daughter has no children, or is widowed or divorced, she may return to her father's house with the same status as when she was a girl, and then she is permitted to eat her father's food. No unauthorized person may eat the food offering. **14** If a person by mistake eats a sacred offering, he must pay the price of the food plus twenty percent and give it to the priest. **15** The priests shall not profane the sacred offerings which the Israelites give as gifts to Adonai by allowing non-priests to eat the sacred offerings.

16 If they eat the sacred offerings, they will be guilty of sin. I am Adonai, and it is I who make these offerings holy.

No Sacrifices with Defects *3rd Aliyah*

17 Adonai spoke to Moses, and said to him: **18** Instruct Aaron and his sons and all the Israelites, and say to them:

These are the laws for any person, whether an Israelite or a foreigner who resides among you, who brings an animal to present as a burnt offering to Adonai to fulfill a promise or as a voluntary gift. **19** It must be a healthy male animal taken from the cattle, sheep, or goats.

20 An animal with a defect will not be acceptable.

21 When a person presents a peace offering of cattle or sheep to fulfill a promise or as a voluntary gift, it must be healthy to be acceptable. It shall not have any defect.

22 You must not offer Adonai an animal that has any physical defects or sores or skin diseases. You must not offer such an animal as a fire offering to Adonai. **23** An ox or a sheep that has an extra or a missing limb can be brought as an offering to the sanctuary. But no such animal is acceptable as a sacrifice on the altar. **24** You must not offer an animal that has a genital injury to Adonai. **25** You must not offer such animal even if it is presented by a gentile. Animals that have physical defects are not acceptable for sacrifice.

26 Adonai instructed Moses, and said: **27** When a bull, sheep, or goat is born, it must remain with its mother for seven days, but after the eighth day it is acceptable as a fire offering to Adonai. **28** You must not slaughter a female animal and its child on the same day, whether it is a bull, a sheep, or a goat.

---

18. These are the laws for any person, whether an Israelite or a foreigner who resides among you, who brings an animal to present as a burnt offering to Adonai to fulfill a promise or as a voluntary gift.
The law concerning promises or voluntary gifts applies equally to Israelites and to foreigners.
Ibn Ezra

28. You must not slaughter a female animal and its child on the same day, whether it is a bull, a sheep or a goat.

The food for humans consists of vegetables, grains, and the flesh of animals, fish, and birds. The need for food necessitates the killing of animals. Jewish laws insist that animals must be slaughtered in a humane way. The reason for prohibiting the slaughter of the mother and the young on the same day is to teach us the quality of mercy.

People must not become hardened to suffering. In following the rules of *shechitah* (ritual slaughter), humans are helped to develop a sense of compassion for Adonai's creations.

29 When you bring a thanksgiving offering to Adonai, it must be properly sacrificed. **30** It must be sacrificed and eaten on the same day; leave nothing until the next morning. I am Adonai. I command it.
31 You must observe My commandments and faithfully keep them; I am Adonai.
32 Do not profane My holy name. I must be respected among the Israelites.
I am Adonai, and I am making you holy. **33** Remember: I, Adonai, brought you out of Egypt. Remember: I am Adonai.

The Festivals
4th Aliyah

23 Adonai spoke to Moses, and said to him: **2** Instruct the Israelites and say to them:
These are the special times that you must celebrate as sacred holidays to Adonai. These are My special festivals:
3 During the six weekdays you may do your work, but the seventh day is the Sabbath, a day of rest. It is a sacred time to Adonai, and you shall do no work, no matter where you live; it is Adonai's Sabbath.
4 These are the festivals that you must celebrate as sacred holidays at their appointed times:
5 In the first month [Nisan], on the afternoon of the fourteenth day, you must sacrifice a Passover offering to Adonai.
6 Then, on the fifteenth of the month [of Nisan] you shall celebrate the Festival of Unleavened Bread, and you must eat matzot for seven days.
7 The first day shall be a sacred holiday, and you must not do any work.
8 Then for seven days you shall bring sacrifices to Adonai. The seventh day shall be a sacred holiday, and once again you must not do any work.

---

30. It must be sacrificed and eaten on the same day.
The Torah sets time limits on sacrifices. Sacrifices were intended for a special purpose and had to be eaten on the day of the offering.

31. You must observe My commandments and faithfully keep them.
"Observe" means to study the commandments, "keep them" means to do them. *Rashi*.

32. Do not profane my holy name. I must be respected among all the Israelites.
This is prohibitive mitzvah number 295.
We are forbidden to commit a sin that may cause people to lose respect for the Torah, for the Jewish religion, or for a Torah scholar. This type of sin is called *chilul hashem*, meaning desecrating the name of *Hashem* (Adonai).

2. These are the special times that you must celebrate as sacred holidays to Adonai.
The Israelites were assembled by the blowing of two silver trumpets (Bamidbar 10:1–10).
The trumpets signaled the Israelites to appear at the sanctuary on the sacred holidays of the Three Pilgrimage Festivals: Sukkot, Passover, and Shavuot.

7. The first day shall be a sacred holiday, and you must not do any work.
This is mitzvah number 297.
On the first and last days of Passover, no work is to be done. The preparation of food is permitted except if the festival coincides with the Sabbath.

8. The seventh day shall be a sacred holiday, and once again you must not do any work.
This is mitzvah number 354.
The Sabbath is not a festival of a special season of the year. It is a day set by Adonai for observance throughout the entire year. It is included here to emphasize that if the Sabbath coincides with a festival, it must be observed in its completeness.

9 Adonai spoke to Moses, and told him to **10** instruct the Israelites and say to them: When you enter the land that I am going to give you, and gather your harvest, you must bring an omer (two quarts) of barley grain from your first harvest to the priest. **11** He shall present it as a wave offering to Adonai. The priest shall present a wave offering from you on the day after the first Sabbath of the Passover holiday.

12 On the day you present the wave offering of an omer of barley grain you shall also present a healthy lamb as a burnt offering to Adonai.

13 The grain offering to Adonai shall consist of four quarts of barley grain mixed with olive oil. The liquid offering shall consist of one quart of wine.

14 Until the day that you bring this sacrifice to Adonai, you must not eat leavened bread or roasted grain or fresh grain. No matter where you live, this shall be a permanent law for all generations.

15 From the day following the Passover holiday, when you brought the omer as a wave offering, you shall count seven complete weeks

---

10. Bring an omer (two quarts) of barley grain from your first harvest to the priest.
This is mitzvah number 302.

An *omer* has two meanings: (1) a measure; (2) the first of the harvest of sheaves of barley or ears of grain.

This omer was taken to the altar and offered as a wave offering. It is an expression of gratitude and thanksgiving to Adonai for His goodness. The omer was brought on the second day of Passover.

11. He shall present it as a wave offering to Adonai.
The individual bringing the omer shall wave it in four directions. First he moves the omer away from himself, and then he moves it back to himself. This is to prevent harmful winds. Then he moves the omer upward and then downward. This movement is to prevent destructive dews.

Today during the Sukkot holiday we recite blessings over the *etrog* and *lulav*. At this time we wave the *lulav* exactly the same way our ancestors waved the barley offering.   *Rashi*

14. Roasted grain.
Grain that has been dried in an oven.

14. Until the day that you bring this sacrifice to Adonai, you must not eat leavened bread or roasted grain or fresh grain. No matter where you live, this shall be a permanent law for all generations.
This is prohibitive mitzvah number 189.

The law of *chadash* (new) forbids eating the new grain until after the second day of Passover. This means that any grain that has not yet been planted is forbidden to be eaten until the next Passover. Today, this law does not apply ouside the Holy Land.

15. From the day following the Passover holiday, when you brought the omer as a wave offering, you shall count seven complete weeks.
It is a mitzvah (306) to count the omer.

Starting from the second day of Passover, a special counting of the omer prayer is recited each day. The Torah tells us to count the omer for seven complete weeks, starting from the sixteenth day of the month of Nisan.

The Rabbis deduced that the words of "You shall count" obligates every Israelite personally to count the omer.

After leaving Egypt, the Israelites waited for forty-nine days to rid themselves of their slave mentality. On the fiftieth day they were spiritually ready to receive the Torah on the holiday of Shavuot.

16 until the day after the seventh week; there shall be a total of fifty days. Then, on the fiftieth day (Shavuot), you shall present an offering of new grain to Adonai. **17** From wherever you live, you must bring two loaves of bread as a wave offering.

The loaves shall be made of four pounds of flour and shall be baked as leavened bread. This will be your first-harvest offering to Adonai. **18** With this bread, you shall present seven healthy lambs, one young bull, and two rams as a burnt offering. These, together with the grain and liquid offering, shall be presented as a thank you gift to Adonai. **19** You shall also present one goat as a sin offering, and two lambs as peace sacrifices. **20** The priest shall present them as wave offerings before Adonai with the loaves of bread which are baked with grain from the first-harvest offering. These offerings are sacred to Adonai and are a gift to the priest.

21 That same day shall be celebrated as a sacred holiday (Shavuot) on which no work shall be done. This is a permanent law and must be observed wherever you may live.

22 When you gather your harvest, you must not completely harvest the ends of your fields. Also, do not pick up the stalks of grain that have fallen to the ground. You must leave all of it for the poor and the stranger.

I am Adonai. I command it.

---

16. Then on the fiftieth day (Shavuot) you shall present an offering of new grain to Adonai.
At about this time of year the new grain (wheat) was harvested. The first fruits also began to ripen on the trees and vines in Israel. The Torah commanded the farmers to bring their first fruits (*bikkurim*) as an offer of thanks to Adonai. At the Temple in Jerusalem, the Israelites expressed their thanks by bringing gifts of "seven kinds" as offerings. The seven kinds were wheat, barley, grapes, figs, pomegranates, dates, and olives. This is why Shavuot is also called the Festival of the First Fruits.

21. That same day shall be celebrated as a sacred holiday (Shavuot) on which no work shall be done.
This is mitzvah number 308.

Shavuot is the third of the three pilgrimage festivals on which Jews from all parts of Israel used to make pilgrimages to the Holy Temple in Jerusalem. Shavuot means "weeks." This festival falls exactly seven weeks after the second day of Passover.

As a Torah festival Shavuot is known as "the time of the giving of our Torah." It was on Shavuot that Adonai spoke to Moses on top of Mount Sinai and gave him the Ten Commandments.

In addition to being a Torah festival, Shavuot is also a harvest festival. In ancient days the grain harvest was begun on the second day of Passover with the ripening of the barley. On this day an omer (measure) of grain was brought to the Temple as a thank you gift to Adonai. Because the Jewish people received the Torah on Shavuot, it is also the holiday for a special ceremony in which young adults in Reform and Conservative synagogues are confirmed. Youngsters who have completed the course of study in a religious school become confirmed and are initiated into the fellowship of the Jewish people.

In the synagogue, besides the regular Shavuot service, the Book of Ruth is read. The reason is that this beautiful story of faith and devotion took place during the harvest season. King David was descendant from Ruth, and it is believed that he was born and died on Shavuot.

22. When you gather your harvest, you must not completely harvest the ends of your fields. Also, do not pick up the stalks of grain that have fallen on the ground. You must leave all of it for the poor and the stranger.
This was a reminder to the Israelites to share their harvest with the less fortunate. Sharing the harvest with the hungry is comparable to bringing an offering to Adonai.

Rosh Hashanah and Yom Kippur
5th Aliyah

23 Adonai spoke to Moses and said: **24** Instruct the Israelites and say: The first day of the seventh month [Tishri] shall be a day of complete rest. It is a sacred holiday of remembrance and shall be welcomed by sounding the shofar. **25** On this day (Rosh Hashanah) you must not do any work, and you must bring a fire offering to Adonai. **26** Adonai spoke to Moses, and said: **27** The tenth of the seventh month [Tishri] shall be celebrated as a Day of Atonement (Yom Kippur).

It is a sacred holiday, and you must fast and bring an offering to Adonai. **28** Do not do any work on this day; it is a Day of Atonement, when you ask Adonai to forgive your sins. **29** Anyone who does not fast on this day shall be cut off from his people. **30** And no one is to work on this day; I will punish any Israelite who works.

31 No matter where you may live, you must not do any work on Yom Kippur. This is a permanent law for all generations. **32** For you it is a Sabbath, a day of rest and of fasting. You must observe this holiday from the ninth day of the month of Tishri in the evening until the evening of the tenth.

---

24. The first day of the seventh month (Tishri) shall be a day of complete rest. It is a sacred holiday of remembrance and shall be welcomed by sounding the shofar.
The Jewish year ends on the 29th day of the month of Elul, the last month in the Hebrew calendar. This is the day before the Jewish New Year, which begins on the first of the month of Tishri.

The Jewish New Year begins with a period called the Ten Days of Repentance, also known as the High Holy Days and the Fearful Days (*Yamim Noraim*).

The first of these days is Rosh Hashanah. The Bible calls Rosh Hashanah the "day of the sounding of the ram's horn."

The whole spirit of Rosh Hashanah and the Ten Days of Repentance is one of seriousness and solemnity.

The ram's horn, or shofar, has been so long associated with Jewish tradition that it has become a Jewish symbol. It recalls that Adonai sent a ram as a substitute for his son as a sacrifice on the altar.

The month of Tishri is filled with holidays. In that one month we observe Rosh Hashanah, Yom Kippur, Sukkot, and Simchat Torah.

27. The tenth of the seventh month (Tishri) shall be celebrated as a Day of Atonement (Yom Kippur).
This is mitzvah number 313.

The Torah tells us that it is a mitzvah to fast on the tenth day of the month of Tishri, which is Yom Kippur. Our sages tell us to begin the fast just before twilight of the preceding evening and fast all of the next day, until it is night, twenty-five hours later. The ten-day period between Rosh Hashanah and Yom Kippur is called the Ten Days of Repentance. Our sages suggest that we should personally and sincerely ask our friends, family, and business associates for forgiveness for any insult or anything we have wrongfully done to them.

28. Do not do any work on this day; it is a Day of Atonement, when you ask Adonai to forgive your sins.
Repentance on the Day of Atonement atones only for those sins that are between man and the Adonai. But sins between man and his fellow men, such as injuring, cursing, or robbing him, are never pardoned until one makes restitution and appeases his fellow man. Even if he returns money that is owed, he must ask for pardon. Even if he has only provoked his neighbor in words, he must make peace and entreat him until he forgives.

The Festival of Sukkot
6th Aliyah

33 Adonai spoke to Moses and instructed him: **34** Speak to the Israelites, and say: Beginning on the fifteenth of the seventh month [Tishri] you shall celebrate the Festival of Sukkot to Adonai for seven days.

35 On the first day of this sacred holiday you must not do any work.

36 For seven days, you must present offerings to Adonai. The eighth day shall be a sacred holiday, and you shall bring an offering to Adonai. It is a time of complete rest, and you shall not do any work.

37 These are Adonai's special times, and they must be observed as sacred holidays. On these special festivals you must present burnt offerings, grain offerings, and liquid offerings, **38** in addition to Adonai's Sabbath offerings, and the pledges and the voluntary gifts that you offer to Adonai. **39** Remember: on the fifteenth of the seventh month [Tishri], when you begin to harvest the grain, you shall celebrate the Festival of Sukkot for seven days. The first day of Sukkot shall be a day of complete rest, and the eighth day shall also be a day of complete rest.

40 On the first day of Sukkot you must take a fruit of the citron tree (an *etrog*), a palm branch, myrtle branches, and willows that grow near the brook. You shall celebrate the Festival of Sukkot before Adonai for seven days.

41 During these seven days of each year, you shall observe the Festival of Sukkot.

42 All Israelites must live in thatched huts (*sukkot*) during these seven days.

---

40. On the first day of Sukkot you must take a fruit of the citron tree (an *etrog*), a palm branch, myrtle branches, and willows that grow near the brook

Why do we use these, the "four kinds"? Our Rabbis of old thought of several reasons. One explanation is that the *etrog* is like the heart, without which one cannot live. The palm branch (*lulav*) is the spine, the myrtle is the eye, and the willow leaves are lips. Together they declare that a human being ought to serve Adonai with all his soul and body.

40. On the first day of Sukkot you must take a fruit of the citron tree (an *etrog*), a palm branch, myrtle branches and willows.

It is a mitzvah (324) to recite blessings over the four kinds. Maimonides writes that the proper way to perform this mitzvah is to wave in six directions – front, back, left side, right side, upward, and downward – and to shake the *lulav* three times in each direction. These wavings are called *na-nu-eem*.

40. You shall celebrate the Festival of Sukkot before Adonai for seven days.

This phrase gave rise to the processions with *lulavim* and *etrogim* around the Temple. The seventh day of Sukkot is called *Hoshanah Rabbah* (the great hoshanah) because of the seven processions (*hakafot*) around the synagogue with *lulav* and *etrog* while reciting prayers for deliverance.

In Temple times, the people formed a procession around the altar on each of the six days of Sukkot while chanting "Adonai, we beg you, save us." On the seventh day of Sukkot, they made seven processions, after which they would beat willow branches against the ground, symbolically casting off sins, as the leaves fell off the branches.

42. All the Israelites must live in thatched huts (*sukkot*) during these seven days.

The Torah tells us that it is a mitzvah to live in a sukkah for seven days from the fifteenth to the twenty-second day of the month of Tishri.

When we sit in a sukkah and see the stars through the leafy roof, we are reminded of the great miracles that Adonai performed for our ancestors and is still performing for us.

43 In this way future generations will know that I made their ancestors live in huts when I brought them out of Egypt. I am Adonai.

44 This is how Moses instructed the Israelites to celebrate the festivals to Adonai.

The Golden Menorah *7th Aliyah*

24 Adonai spoke to Moses, and told him to **2** instruct the Israelites to bring pure olive oil made from hand-crushed olives, to keep the golden menorah constantly burning.

3 Aaron and the priests shall keep the menorah continually lighted with the oil, before Adonai, from evening to morning, outside the cloth curtain in the Meeting Tent. This must be a permanent law for all your generations.

4 The priest must keep the lamps on the pure gold menorah burning before Adonai from morning to night.

5 You shall take the finest grade of flour and bake it into twelve loaves. Each loaf shall weigh about four pounds.

1–2. Adonai spoke to Moses, and told him to instruct the Israelites to bring pure olive oil made from hand-crushed olives, to keep the golden menorah constantly burning.
When the sanctuary was first completed, the Israelites contributed oil for the menorah. Now the original amount of oil was exhausted and new contributions of oil were needed to keep the menorah alight.

Adonai showed Moses the prototype of the menorah when he handed down the Ten Commandments on Mount Sinai. It was a sacred object to be used only in the Tabernacle and later in the Temple. The original menorah was made of a solid slab of gold and was brought into the Tabernacle. When Solomon built the Temple in Jerusalem, he placed ten golden menorot inside, in addition to the menorah of Moses. All of these were destroyed when the first Temple was destroyed in 586 B.C.E. The returning Babylonia exiles rebuilt the Temple in 516 B.C.E. and made a new menorah according to the descriptions in Shemot (25:31–40 and 37:17–24).

In 169 B.C.E. King Antiochus of the Hanukah story removed it. Judah Maccabee replaced it.

During the final destruction of the Temple by Titus in 70 C.E., the menorah was seized and carried in triumphal procession through Rome. The Arch of Titus in Rome, in one relief, shows the Roman soldiers carrying the menorah in the triumphal procession.

Some commentators say that six branches remind us of the six days of creation and the seventh branch reminds us of the Sabbath. The special candleholder used on Hanukah has eight branches and is called a *hanukiah*.

Today the menorah is the emblem of the modern State of Israel.

2. Instruct the Israelites to bring pure olive oil made from hand-crushed olives, to keep the golden menorah constantly burning.
Three types of oil are pressed from fresh olives. The first pressing is called "pure." It burns cleanly and has very few impurities.

5. You shall take the finest grade of flour and bake it into twelve loaves.
The twelve loaves were symbolic of the twelve tribes Israel. The loaves of bread were called *lechem ha-panim* meaning "the bread of display."

6 Arrange the loaves in two rows, six loaves to each row, and place them on a special table before Adonai.
7 Alongside each row place pure frankincense as a memorial portion that will be presented to Adonai.
8 Every Sabbath, fresh loaves shall be arranged before Adonai. Priests in every generation must continue to do this for the Israelites.
9 The bread shall be given to Aaron and his descendants, but since it is one of Adonai's fire offerings, it must be eaten in a sacred area. This is a permanent law.
10 An Israelite woman married an Egyptian man. Their son quarreled with an Israelite man **11** and cursed Adonai.
The people angrily brought him to Moses. His mother's name was Shelomith daughter of Divri, of the tribe of Dan. **12** They imprisoned him until Adonai would tell them what to do. **13** Finally Adonai spoke to Moses, and said:
14 "Take the man who cursed me out of the camp, and let witnesses who heard him curse Me place their hands on his head. Then the entire community shall put him to death.
15 Warn the Israelites and say:
Anyone who curses Adonai will bear his sin. **16** However, if someone deliberately curses the Holy Name YHVH, he shall be put to death.
It makes no difference whether he is a foreigner or an Israelite, he shall be put to death.
17 Anyone who murders someone must be put to death.
18 If someone kills an animal that belongs to someone else, he must pay the cost of the animal.
19 If someone deliberately injures his neighbor, whatever he has done to his neighbor must be done to him. **20** Full compensation must be paid for a fracture or the loss of an eye or a tooth. If someone causes an injury to another person, then the same injury shall be inflicted on him.

Equality Under the Law *Maftir*

21 If someone kills an animal, he must pay for it, but if he kills a human being, he must be put to death. **22** There shall be equality under the law for both the foreigner and the native born. I am Adonai. I command it."
23 After Moses explained all this to the Israelites, they took the man who had cursed Adonai out of the camp and executed him. Thus the Israelites did as Adonai had commanded Moses.

---

8. Every Sabbath, fresh loaves shall be arranged before Adonai. Priests in every generation must continue to do this for the Israelites.
The twelve loaves of bread remained on the table which was overlaid with pure gold for one whole week. The loaves were replaced each Sabbath with new bread.

10–11. An Israelite woman married an Egyptian man. Their son quarreled with an Israelite man and cursed Adonai.

The Torah does not inform us of the cause of the fight. In Shemot 20:7 the third commandment states: "Do not misuse the name of Adonai. He will not allow anyone who misuses His name to go unpunished." In v.16 of this chapter the Torah states: "If someone deliberately curses the Holy Name YHWH, he shall be put to death."

Offenses committed by non-Israelites are punishable according to the same rules as the Israelites. So the blasphemer was taken outside of the camp. They carried out the sentence imposed by Adonai.

בְּהַר Behar

ON MOUNT SINAI

25 When Moses was on Mount Sinai, Adonai spoke to him and said: **2** Speak to the Israelites and say to them: When you enter the land that I am giving you, you must allow the land to remain unused for a period of rest, a Sabbath to Adonai. **3** You may plant your fields, prune your vineyards, and harvest your crops for six years **4** but the seventh year shall be a Sabbath for the land. It is Adonai's Sabbath, during which you must not plant your fields, or prune your vineyards, **5** or harvest crops that grow by themselves, or gather the grapes on your vines, because it is a year of rest for the land.
6 While the land is resting, anything that continues to grow naturally may be eaten by you, by your slaves, and by your employees and hired workers who live with you. **7** The crops may also be eaten by your domestic cattle or by wild animals.

---

2. You must allow the land to remain unused for a period of rest, a Sabbath to Adonai.
The sabbatical year resembles the Sabbath day. Just as an Israelite must not allow a resident alien to work on the Sabbath as long as he or she is under his control, an Israelite must not allow a resident alien to plant his field during the sabbatical year.
Ibn Ezra

3–4. You may plant your fields, prune your vineyards, and harvest your crops for six years but the seventh year shall be a Sabbath for the land. It is Adonai's Sabbath, during which you must not plant your fields, or prune your vineyards.
This is a prohibitive (326) mitzvah. The law states that fields, vineyards, and olive groves must be left untended (*shmittah*) every seventh year. During the *shmittah* year their produce is reserved for the poor.

Adonai pledged (Vayikra 25:21) that the sixth year would produce enough for the farmers to live through the *shmittah* year until the harvest of the following year. Adonai depends upon every Jew to be His partner in the task of *tikkun olam*, "improving the world."

Adonai, who created the world in six days, now depends upon humanity to continue to preserve and improve the world. When we conserve the land and allow it to rest we are participating in the task of *tikkun olam* and keeping the world healthier and preserving the environment.

4. But the seventh year shall be a Sabbath for the land.
The land, just like humans, is Adonai's creation. Humans are alive and can think for themselves, protect themselves, and make their own decisions. Land can breathe, give birth, become sick, and even die. Land has a life but it is inanimate and cannot protect itself from exploitation and destruction. Adonai is the protector of the land. The Sabbath is Adonai's way of resting the land and allowing it to regenerate and regain its health.
Shenash

5. Harvest crops, that grow by themselves.
This refers to crops not planted by the farmer. These crops grow from seeds, that accidentally fall to the ground from a growing plant. These types of crops are also not to be harvested by the farmers.

5. It is a year of complete rest.
During the sabbatical year, it is as if the farmer does not own the land.
Ibn Ezra

9. Then, in the forty-ninth year, on the tenth day of the seventh month (Yom Kippur), you shall blow a shofar.
The seventh month is Tishri.

8 You must count seven Sabbath years seven times for a period of forty-nine years.
9 Then, in the forty-ninth year, on the tenth day of the seventh month [Yom Kippur], you shall blow a shofar. **10** You shall consecrate the fiftieth year, and proclaim liberty for the slaves in your land in the Jubilee Year. This is your Jubilee Year. This is the time when all family hereditary lands sold to others must be returned to the original families. **11** The fiftieth year shall also be a restful time for you. You must not plant or harvest crops that grow on their own, or gather grapes from unpruned vines during that year. **12** Since it is a holy Jubilee Year, you must eat only crops from fields that grow naturally by themselves.
13 In the Jubilee Year, every man shall return to his ancestral property.

The Jubilee Year
2nd Aliyah

14 When you buy or sell land to your neighbor, do not cheat each other. **15** Remember that you are buying the land only for the number of crops it will produce until the Jubilee Year.

---

10. You shall consecrate the fiftieth year, and proclaim liberty.
The Liberty Bell, which is an important symbol of American democracy, has engraved on it a verse from the Bible (Vayikra 25:10): "You shall consecrate the fiftieth year, and proclaim liberty for the slaves in your land in the Jubilee Year."

This was the phrase used in the Bible to proclaim the Jubilee year. The Liberty Bell is located in Philadelphia. It was in Philadelphia, in 1776, that the Declaration of Independence was signed. After it was signed, the bell was rung to announce to the new nation that "liberty" had been "proclaimed throughout the land." To this day the Liberty Bell remains a national historic treasure. Visitors from all over the world visit Independence Hall to see the Liberty Bell and read the inscription from the Bible.

12. Since it is a holy Jubilee Year, you must eat only crops from fields that grow naturally by themselves.
Farmers may not store any produce that grows in their fields. However, whenever they need produce for themselves, they are permitted to go out and harvest what they need.

13. In the Jubilee Year, every man shall return to his ancestral property.
Adonai had given the land to the people of Israel. At each Jubilee Year, the land had to revert to its original owners. In this way rich and poor become equals, since both recovered their original land.

The Torah was very much aware that money and power corrupt and that wealth concentrated in the hands of a few would result in the oppression of the masses. The purpose of the *taryag mitzvot* was to redress the balance and provide help for those in need. Judaism teaches that all wealth belongs to Adonai, the Parent. Everyone should have a fair share of it, as children would share the inheritance of their parents. Everything belongs to Adonai and will return to Him. Knowing that all lands will be restored to their original owners and all slaves released ensured security, justice, and liberty in Israel.

14. When you buy or sell land to your neighbor, do not cheat each other.
This is prohibitive mitzvah number 205.

It is forbidden to overcharge a buyer. It is also forbidden for a buyer who is an expert in, for example, jewelry or art, to deliberately purchase an object whose seller is ignorant of the item's true value. Ideally, complete trust should prevail between buyer and seller.

15. Remember that you are buying the land only for the number of crops it will produce until the Jubilee Year.
The law of the Jubilee Year was observed as long as the entire territory of the Holy Land was inhabited by Israelites. When a portion of the children of Israel went into exile, the laws of the Jubilee Year no longer applied.

The occupying countries refused to accept and honor Torah rules and customs.

16 He is selling you the land for a specified number of harvests. You can increase the price if it will be for many years, and lower it if only for a few years.
17 You must be fair and not take advantage and cheat one another. You must fear Adonai. **18** Observe My commandments and My laws. If you obey them, you will live securely in your land.

The World Belongs to Me *3rd Aliyah*

19 The land will produce its crops, and you will eat your fill, and you will live in peace.
20 In the seventh year you may ask, "What will we eat during the Jubilee Year, since we are not allowed to plant or harvest crops?"
21 The answer is: I will send My blessings to your land in the sixth year, and the land will produce enough food to last for three years. **22** You will be eating your old crops, and when you plant after the eighth year, you will still be eating your old crops until the ninth year, when the new crops are ripe and ready to be harvested.
23 The world belongs to Me, and no land must be sold permanently, because as far as I am concerned, you are just My guests and tenants, **24** and therefore you must allow the redemption of all hereditary lands.

Redemption of All Hereditary Lands *4th Aliyah*

25 If your relative becomes poor and sells some of his hereditary land, a close relative can redeem the land that has been sold. **26** If a man does not have anyone to help him redeem his land but later earns enough money to be able to buy it back, **27** the price for the land shall be based on the number of years until the next Jubilee Year. Then the original owner can return to his land.
28 However, if he does not have the money to redeem the land, then it shall remain with the buyer until the next Jubilee Year. Then the land will be released in that year, so that the original owner can return to his hereditary land.

---

22. You will be eating your old crops, and when you plant after the eighth year, you will be eating your old crops until the ninth year, when the new crops are ripe and ready to be harvested.
In the eighth year, on Sukkot, the new crop was planted, and the produce was available at the beginning of the ninth year.

23–24. The world belongs to Me, and no land must be sold permanently, because as far as I am concerned, you are just My guests and tenants, and therefore you must allow the redemption of all hereditary lands.
This is mitzvah 339.
 This tells us that the buyer must not refuse to return the land to its original owners during the Jubilee Year. The purchaser was buying only the crops that the land produced, since the land itself belonged to Adonai.

25. If your relative becomes poor and sells some of his hereditary land, a close relative can redeem the land that has been sold.
The close relative, the redeemer, is called a *go'el*. only The calculation of the redemption price was based on the Jubilee law, which assumed that land was sold only for the number of years until the next Jubilee. To redeem the sale, the original owner or the *go'el* had to pay only for the value of the land for the remaining years.
 With the establishment of the monarchy, these rules came into conflict with economic realities and created a conflict with the farmers and the wealthy merchants. Large estates that used hired workers and slaves began to replace the small farms.
 Today, the plight of the small farms mirrors the same problems of the ancient Israelite peasant farmers.

Houses in Walled Cities

5th Aliyah

29 When a man sells a house in a walled city, he has only one full year to redeem it.
30 If the house in the walled city is not redeemed by the end of this year, it shall become the permanent property of the buyer and can be passed down to his descendants, and it is not released in the Jubilee Year.
31 But houses in unwalled villages shall be considered the same as open land. They must be returned to the original owner in the Jubilee Year.
32 The Levites shall always have the right to redeem the houses in the cities belonging to them.
33 If someone buys a house in one of their cities from a Levite, it must be released in the Jubilee Year, for the houses in the Levite cities are their hereditary property. **34** The open fields surrounding the Levite cities cannot be sold permanently, because it is their hereditary property.

29–31. When a man sells a home in a walled city, he has one full year to redeem it. If the house in the walled city is not redeemed by the end of the year, it shall become the permanent property of the buyer and can be passed down to his descendants, and it is not released in the Jubilee Year. But houses in unwalled villages shall be considered the same as open land. They must be returned to the original owner in the Jubilee Year.

Why the difference between walled cities and unwalled villages? Although the Israelites had not yet entered the Promised Land, the Torah has already set rules and regulations for land use and retention of framlands.

It was mitzvah number 341 to repurchase the ancestral property in a walled city during the first year.

The Torah was aware that there would be two separate economic engines in Israel, agricultural and commercial, and each depended upon the other.

The inhabitants in walled cities consisted of merchants, artisans, and professionals who owned their businesses and could not give up their establishments, which consisted of stores, workshops, and offices. They were allowed to own land permanently.

Israel was primarily an agrarian country and dependant upon its farms and herders to produce food for internal consumption and export.

The agricultural lands had to be preserved so that the property would remain within the clan.

The laws of the Jubilee Year guaranteed that the land would remain within the clan and would be used for either agriculture or cattle raising.

Today, with the spread of housing into the suburbs, agricultural land is also slowly being eaten up and special incentives have been established to preserve farmlands.

It is mitzvah number 341 to repurchase the ancestral property in a walled city during the first year.
Shenash

31. But houses in unwalled villages shall be considered the same as open land. They must be returned to the original owner in the Jubilee Year.

The cities were to be prevented from expansion into metropolises at the expense of arable soil. If the cities became over-crowded, new cities could be built, but only on land that was unsuitable for agricultural purposes.

32. The Levites shall always have the right to redeem the houses in the cities belonging to them.

The tribe of Levi, consecrated to the service of Adonai, received no special residential area in Canaan. However, they were allotted forty-eight cities in the territories belonging to the other tribes. The purpose of scattering the Levitical cities among the tribes was to enable them to act as Torah teachers. The Levites were dependent on the tithes donated to them by the Israelites.

35 When your neighbor becomes poor and is unable to support himself, you must help him to survive, whether he is a foreigner or an Israelite.
36 Do not take any interest from him. Fear Adonai, and allow him to live alongside you as your brother.
37 Do not take advantage of him and do not make him pay interest for your money, and do not sell him food at high prices. **38** I am Adonai, who brought you out of Egypt to give you the land of Canaan.

Redemption of the Poor   6th Aliyah

39 If your fellow Israelite becomes poor and sells himself to you, you must not treat him like a slave.
40 Treat him as an employee or a hired worker. He shall serve you only until the Jubilee Year. **41** Then he and his children shall be free to leave you and return to his family and his hereditary land.
42 Always remember that you are My servants whom I freed out of Egypt. Your fellow Israelites must not be sold in the market as slaves.

---

35. When your neighbor becomes poor and is unable to support himself, you must help him to survive.
The Rabbis say that charity in its noblest form consists of keeping a person from falling into poverty. The position of such a person must be stabilized and his dignity preserved by either gifting him, extending an interest-free loan, creating a meaningful job for him, or providing professional help to save his business. According to Maimonides, preventing a man from falling into poverty is the most meaningful of his eight categories of charity giving.

36. Do not take any interest from him. Fear Adonai, and allow him to live alongside you as your brother.
Napoleon's Sanhedrin (1806) declared that the Talmud understood that the prohibition of intrest among brothers, refers only to benevolent loans, but not to commercial ones, that can entail risks.

In a mixed economy, people refused to lend money for business or investment purposes, thus limiting the prosperity of the kingdom.

37. Do not take advantage of him and do not make him pay interest for your money.
This is prohibitive mitzvah number 343.

It is more of a mitzvah to provide interest-free loans to a Jew than to give him or her charity.

An interest-free loan adds dignity, and the recipient will not feel humiliated by accepting charity. Some synagogues have committees which distribute interest-free loans.

36. Fear Adonai, and allow him to live alongside you as your brother.
The Rabbis say, "Your welfare takes precedence over the welfare of your friend." This means you shall help your friend (brother) when you have sufficient means so that you and your family can live in dignity. Do not deprive your family to the point that you yourself are in need. (*Bava Metziah 62a*)

38. I am Adonai, who brought you out of Egypt to give you the land of Canaan.
Keep in mind that you were once slaves in the land of Egypt and Adonai freed you from bondage. Now, it is your turn to help your fellow citizen, and free him from poverty and bondage.

42. Always remember that you are My servants whom I freed out of Egypt. Your fellow Israelites must not be sold in the market as slaves.
No Israelite is allowed to sell himself permanently, since he is the servant of Adonai; in the Jubilee Year his servitude is finished and he is allowed to return home.   *Sforno*

43 Do not mistreat or brutalize them, because you must show your respect for Adonai. **44** You can purchase male or female slaves from the nations around you. **45** You can also buy slaves from the foreigners who live among you, and from their families that are born in your land. These shall become your property. **46** They are property that you can pass down to your children, and they can be your slaves forever.

But as far as your fellow Israelites are concerned, you must not be cruel to them.

Israelite Slaves
7th Aliyah

47 If a foreigner becomes wealthy while your Israelite brother becomes poor and is sold to a foreigner who worships idols, he must be saved. **48** After he is sold, he must be redeemed by one of his close relatives **49** his uncle or cousin, or the closest relative in his family. If he manages to earn enough money, he can redeem himself.

50 The price for his freedom shall be based on the number of years that remain until the Jubilee. **51** If there are still many years until the Jubilee, the freedom money he pays his purchaser shall be based on the amount of money for which he was sold and when he sold himself.

52 If only a few years remain until the Jubilee Year, he shall repay only a small amount. In all cases he shall repay a sum of freedom money based on the number of years until the Jubilee Year.

53 Such a slave must be treated the same as an employee hired on a yearly basis. You must not allow his master to treat him cruelly.

54 If the slave is not freed by any of the above means, then he and his children shall be freed in the Jubilee Year.

Do Not Pray to Idols
Maftir

55 All this is because the Israelites are actually My slaves. They are My slaves because I brought them out of Egypt and saved them. I am Adonai.

26 You must not make idols. Do not carve stone idols or erect sacred pillars. Do not erect idols in your land and worship them. I am Adonai. I forbid it. **2** Observe My Sabbaths and respect My sanctuary. I am Adonai. I demand it.

---

43. Do not mistrust or brutalize them, because you must show your respect for Adonai.
Although the Torah mentions only that the Israelite slave is to be treated with kindness, we are to understand from this that all slaves, Jewish or gentile, are to treated by their Jewish owners with kindness. *Maimonides*

47–48. If a foreigner becomes wealthy while your Israelite brother becomes poor and is sold to a foreigner who worships idols, he must be saved. After he is sold, he must be redeemed by one of his close relatives.

In ancient Israel, the members of the family had an obligation to help and protect each other. This obligation calling for action was called *go'el*, from the root meaning "to buy back "or to redeem."

The *go'el* was a redeemer, a defender of the individual and the clan. When an Israelite was forced to sell himself into slavery to repay a debt, he would be redeemed by a relation. Jews who were captured during war or by raiders or pirates were often sold into slavery. Jewish communities or wealthy Jews frequently ransomed and redeemed their co-religionists. The act of redeeming prisoners is called *pidyon shevuyim*.

בְּחֻקֹּתַי *Bechukkotai*

OBSERVE MY COMMANDMENTS

3 If you follow My laws and faithfully observe My commandments, **4** I will provide you with rain in season, so that your land will grow your crops and the trees will produce fruit.
5 Your harvest will be so plentiful that your threshing season will continue until your grape harvest, and your grape harvest will continue until planting time. You will have more than enough food, and you will live in safety in the land.

I Will Bless the Land
2nd Aliyah

6 I will bless the land with peace, so that you will be able to sleep without fear. I will remove the dangerous animals and protect your land from your enemies.
7 You will defeat your enemies and destroy them.
8 Only five of you will be able to defeat a hundred, and only a hundred of you will defeat ten thousand.

---

2. They left Rephidim and entered the wilderness of Sinai, camping in the wilderness at the base of the mountain.
The specific purpose of the journey was to reach Mount Sinai where they would receive the Torah. The Midrash says that Adonai gave the Israelites the Torah on Saturday. The prayer *Yismach Moshe* (Moses was overjoyed) is recited on the Sabbath because the Torah was given to Moses who immediately transmitted it to the Israelites on the Sabbath.

3–4. If you follow My laws and faithfully observe My commandments, I will provide you with rain in season, so that your land will grow your crops and the trees will produce fruit.
A covenant is a two-way relationship. You are required to study the laws, to teach them to your children, and also to observe them. If you do not, punishment will follow. If you will do as I say, then I will respond positively. Adonai promises that if you abide by My commandments and protect the ecology of the land, then I will reward you with peace and tranquility and you will enjoy the fruits of labor.

3. If you follow My laws.
The name of the sidrah *Bechukkotai*, meaning "my commandments," is also known as *tochacha*, meaning scolding or criticism. The sidrah contains thirty verses of criticism against thirteen blessings.

The curses are given in detail to discourage the readers. The blessings are more subdued and are stated in a general fashion.

Notice that the sidrah starts with blessings for obedience, immediately followed with curses for disobedience. During the Torah reading the Torah reader (*Baal Koreh*) recites the prescribed blessings before and after the terrifying passages.

Notice that the blessings and curses are phrased in the second person.

4. And the trees will produce fruit.
Your non-bearing trees which you planted will now begin to produce an abundance of fruit. *Rashi*

5. Your harvest will be so plentiful that your threshing season will continue until your grape harvest.
The amount of your harvest will be so great that you will be busy until the grape season.

6. I will bless the land with peace so that you will be able to sleep without fear.
Adonai promises the nation that they will be blessed with peace and contentment if they obey the commandments.

6. I will remove the dangerous animals and protect your land from your enemies.
Your enemies will not come to make war against you. They will avoid and not even pass through your land to reach their enemies. *Rashi*

9 I will be kind to you, and your nation will grow and become numerous, and I will keep My promises to you.

You Will Be My People
3rd Aliyah

10 Each year your barns will overflow with crops, and you will be forced to clear out the old crops because of the new.
11 I will establish My sanctuary among you, and I will never grow tired of you.
12 I will always dwell among you. I, Elohim, will be with you, and you will always be My people, dedicated to Me.
13 I am Elohim. I rescued you from slavery in Egypt. I broke your chains and now you can live in dignity. **14** But if you do not listen to Me, and do not keep My commandments, **15** if you reject My laws, and do not observe My commandments, you will have broken My covenant with you. **16** Then I will turn around and do the same to you. I will punish you with terror and disease, and I will make your lives miserable. You will plant your crops in vain, because your enemies will eat them.
17 I will be angry at you and your enemies will defeat and rule over you. You will be frightened of your own shadows.
18 If you still disobey Me, I will increase the punishment for your sins seven times as much.
19 I will break your pride, and the skies will not produce rain, and your land will not yield any crops.
20 You will exhaust your strength in vain, since your land will not yield its crops, and the trees of the land will not produce fruit.
21 If you still do not listen to Me, I will again increase the punishment for your sins seven times over.
22 I will send wild beasts to kill your children and destroy your cattle, and I will decimate your population, so that the roads will be deserted.
23 If this punishment does not reform you, and you continue to ignore Me, **24** then I will ignore you, and I will again punish you for your sins seven times over.

---

9. I will be kind to you, and your nation will grow and become numerous, and I will keep My promises to you.
The original promise that Adonai made to Abraham is still operative. The promise, *brit* (covenant), will most certainly be fulfilled. The Israelites will grow into a large and successful nation.

10. You will be forced to clear out the old crops because of the new.
The wonder will be that the farmers, because of their successful harvest, will have to remove the old crops to make room for the new crops.

13. I am Elohim. I rescued you from slavery in Egypt. I broke your chains and now you can live in dignity.
Adonai freed the Israelites out of slavery and gave them freedom. He also lifted the spirits of the fallen and gave them dignity and a feeling of self-worth.

14–15. But if you do not listen to Me, and do not keep My commandments, if you reject My laws, and do not observe My commandments, you will have broken My covenant with you.
The next fifteen sentences are warnings dealing with the punishments that the Israelites will suffer if they sin and break the covenant. The consequences will be sickness, defeat, famine, wild animals, siege, and exile.

25 I will send enemies against you because you broke My covenant, and you will hide in your cities. Then I will punish you with the plague, and your enemies will take you captive.
26 I will deprive you of your food supply so that ten women will have only enough flour to bake bread in one oven, and they will bring back only a few crumbs. There will not be enough to satisfy your hunger.
27 If you still do not listen to Me but remain hostile to Me, **28** then I will be hostile to you and will punish you seven times over for your sins. **29** You will be so hungry that you will eat the flesh of your sons and your daughters.
30 I will destroy your altars and smash your gods. I will pile your dead bodies around your broken idols.
I will despise you. **31** I will let your cities become desolate and ruin your sanctuaries. I will not accept your sacrifices.
32 I will devastate the land so that even your enemies who live there will be shocked at the devastation.
33 I will scatter you among the nations, and I will use my sword against you. Your land will be devastated, and your cities will be in ruins.
34 As long as the land remains desolate and you are in exile, the land will at last enjoy its missed Sabbaths. Then the land will finally rest and enjoy its sabbatical years.
35 As long as the land remains desolate, it will enjoy the sabbatical rest that you would not give it every seven years while you lived there.
36 In exile you will tremble at the sound of a rustling leaf, and you will run with fear and panic when no one is chasing you.
37 You will have no power to resist your enemies.
38 You will die among the foreign nations, and your enemies will destroy you.

---

26. I will deprive you of your food supply so that ten women will have only enough flour to bake bread in one oven, and they will bring back only a few crumbs.
In ancient Israel, each household had its own oven and each had enough flour to bake bread for a whole week. Now there will be only enough flour for one simple stove for ten families.

31. I will let your cities become desolate and ruin your sanctuaries.
The punishments of wars – swords, famine, wild animals, and epidemics – have all been listed. Now the Torah describes the desolation and destruction of the population center, the cities. A sage comments, "even your enemies who will occupy your land will suffer by lack of food, disease, and plagues."

Rashi says "that is good news for Israel, for the enemies will not find any joy in Israel's defeat."

33. I will scatter you among the nations, and I will use my sword against you. Your land will be devastated, and your cities will be in ruins.
The commentator Abarbanel, who lived during the period of the expulsion from Spain, provides the text with a historical meaning.

After the destruction of the Second Temple in 70 C.E., the Jews were scattered through the world and many emigrated to Spain, France, England, and many other countries. There, in their new countries they experienced persecution and death. Adonai says that even there He will not have compassion on them. "I will use my sword against you."

39 Those who survive will rot away in enemy lands because of their sins. The survivors will realize that their existence is threatened because of their own sins and those of their ancestors. **40** Then they will finally confess their sins and the sins of their ancestors against Me. **41** Because of their sins I remained indifferent to them and exiled them into the land of their enemies. But when they ask for forgiveness, **42** I will keep my covenant with Abraham, Isaac, and Jacob and I will remember the land. **43** Now, the land will enjoy its rest while you are in exile. They will pay for their sins because they rebelled against Me and My laws.
44 Even when they are in exile in the land of their enemies, I will never completely reject them or destroy them and break My covenant with them, because I am Adonai, their protector. **45** I will remember My covenant with their ancestors when I, Adonai, brought them out of Egypt while the nations watched. I am Adonai.
46 These are the commandments and laws that Adonai gave to the Israelites at Mount Sinai by the hand of Moses.

Donations
4th Aliyah

27 Adonai spoke to Moses, and told him to **2** instruct the Israelites and say to them:
This is the law when an Israelite decides to honor a person by donating a sum of money to Adonai.
3 The donation for a male aged twenty to sixty years shall be fifty shekels according to the sanctuary weight. **4** For a woman, the donation shall be thirty shekels.
5 For a person between five and twenty, the donation shall be twenty shekels for a male and ten shekels for a female.
6 For a person between one month and five years old, the donation shall be five shekels for a male and three shekels for a female.
7 For a person over sixty years old, the donation shall be fifteen shekels for a man and ten shekels for a woman.
8 In the case of a person too poor to give the statutory donation, the priest will decide the amount.
The priest shall make his decision on the basis of how much the person wishing to make the donation can afford.
9 If the donation is a healthy animal and it can be presented as a sacrifice to Adonai, then the gift to Adonai becomes holy.
10 The animal cannot be exchanged or replaced by a better animal or a worse animal. If the animal, nonetheless, is replaced, then both the substituted animal and the original animal shall become holy.

---

44. Even when they are in exile in the land of their enemies, I will never completely reject them or destroy them and break My covenant with them.
Ibn Ezra interprets the statement to mean "In exile I will not destroy them. I will discipline them until they change their behavior."

Other commentators see an agreement of mutuality – a tradeoff. If you the Israelites observe the laws of the Torah, then Adonai's relationship with Israel will never be broken.

11 But if the donation is an unclean animal, it cannot be presented as a sacrifice to Adonai. In such cases the owner shall present the animal to the priest, **12** and the priest will determine its value.

13 If the owner wishes to redeem the animal, its value shall be set by the priest, and he shall add twenty percent to the donation.

14 If a person donates a house to Adonai, the priest shall set its value according to its condition. The value shall be determined by the priest. **15** If the person who donated his house wishes to buy it back, he must add twenty percent to its value, and then the house becomes his again.

Donations of Farmlands *5th Aliyah*

16 If a man donates a field from his ancestral property to Adonai, its value shall be determined by the amount of seed required to plant it fifty shekels for every ten bushels (*chomer*) of barley seed.

17 If this donation is made just after the Jubilee Year, the land is valued at its full price. **18** But if someone donates his field after the Jubilee Year, the priest shall determine its value on the basis of the number of years remaining until the next Jubilee Year.

19 If the person who donates his field wishes to buy it back, he must pay the full price plus twenty percent. **20** But if he does not buy back the field, or if the land is sold to someone else, it can no longer be bought back.

21 When the field is released in the Jubilee Year, it becomes holy and special to Adonai, and then becomes the hereditary property of the priest.

Forbidden Animals and Farmland *6th Aliyah*

22 If someone donates a field to Adonai that he bought, and thus it is not his ancestral property, **23** the priest shall determine its value depending on the number of years remaining until the next Jubilee Year. On that day, he can buy back the land by donating the purchase price to Adonai. **24** In the Jubilee Year, the field shall return to its original owner.

25 Every monetary donation shall be set according to the sanctuary standard.

26 You cannot present first-born animals to Adonai, whether an ox, sheep, or goat, because these animals already belong to Adonai.

---

20. But if he does not buy back the field, or if the land is sold to someone else, it can no longer be bought back.
The field can be redeemed by the original owner. However, if the owner refuses or is not financially able to redeem the field, then the sanctuary at the next Jubilee becomes the owner of the property.

22. If someone donates a field to Adonai that he bought, and thus it is not His ancestral property.
The individual is aware that he purchased the piece of property only until the Jubilee, at which time it must be returned to its original owner. The gift to the sanctuary is only temporary.

26. You cannot present first-born animals to Adonai, whether an ox, sheep, or goat, because these animals already belong to Adonai.
In Shemot 13:2 we are told "Dedicate to Me every first-born among the Israelites. Both man and beast are Mine." The first-born animal already belongs to Adonai. A person cannot present an animal that does not belong to him as a gift to the sanctuary. The animal has already been gifted.

27 But if the first-born of a nonkosher animal is presented, it can be redeemed by paying its value plus twenty percent. If it is not redeemed, the priest can sell it.

28 However, anything a person owns, whether it is a slave, an animal, or his hereditary field, that has been forbidden (placed in *cherem*) shall be specially set apart for Adonai and must never be sold or redeemed. This is true of everything he owns. Everything that is specifically donated is holy to Adonai.

Tithes for Crops and Fruits *7th Aliyah*

29 A person who has been condemned to death (placed in *cherem*) cannot be saved. He must be put to death.

30 One-tenth of the crops of the soil or the fruit of trees is set apart for Adonai. **31** If a person wishes to redeem his tithe, he must pay its market value plus twenty percent.

Tithes for Animals *Maftir*

32 When you count your herds and flocks, you shall give every tenth animal to Adonai.

33 It makes no difference whether the animal is healthy or not. You must not substitute one animal for another. But if a substitution is made, then both the original animal and its replacement shall be holy and cannot be redeemed.

34 These are the commandments that Adonai gave Moses for the Israelites on Mount Sinai.

---

28. However, anything a person owns, whether it is a slave, an animal, or his hereditary field, that has been forbidden (placed in *cherem*) shall be specially set apart for Adonai and must never be sold or redeemed.
The term *cherem* is property that has been set apart for Temple use or things consecrated by an extreme vow or curse requiring their destruction. For example, property of an idolater is considered *cherem* and no enjoyment is to be derived from it. Goods taken from an enemy and placed in *cherem* were brought into the Temple treasury. During the Middle Ages the *cherem* was a powerful weapon in the hands of the Jewish communities.

It was also used to discipline congregants who did not pay their fair share of community taxes. The *cherem* was also used against Jews who strayed from the community and became irreligious or who were criminals.

Cherem also means excommunication, excluding an individual or group from the community and severing social relations.

The *cherem* was a weapon used by religious groups to enforce discipline on their members. During the Middle Ages the Rabbis drew up a list of reasons for the *cherem*. The ban was used mostly in cases against religious apostates. However, because it was frequently abused, it gradually disappeared as a form of punishment or coercion.

32. When you count your herds and flocks, you shall give every tenth animal to Adonai.
This is the "second tithe," one-tenth of the farmer's produce. The rationale is that the whole world belongs to Adonai, and the people are His tenants. The ten percent, the tithe that the farmer and herder dedicated to Adonai, is rent for the use of His land.

סֵפֶר בַּמִדְבָּר

THE BOOK OF BAMIDBAR

Bamidbar *is the fourth of the Five Books of Moses. The Hebrew word* bamidbar *means "in the wilderness," and this name was given to the book because it chronicles some of the things that happened to the Israelites during their forty years in the wilderness after leaving Egypt. The English name of the book, translated from the Greek, is Numbers. The book was given this name because it reports the details of a census in which Moses counted all the able-bodied men.*

The book of Bamidbar can be divided into five sections.

In the first section (chapters 1–10), Adonai tells Moses to take a census to determine the number of men aged twenty and above who are available for military service. The census shows that there are 603,550 able-bodied men. Adonai also tells Moses how to organize the tribal camps. The section ends with the celebration of the first Passover in the wilderness.

The second section (11–21) describes the hardships of life in the wilderness, the difficulties Moses faced as leader of the Israelites, and a series of rebellions against him and Adonai. The Israelites still have a slave mentality and are afraid to confront the inhabitants of Canaan even though Adonai has promised that they will be victorious. So Adonai punishes them and makes them wander in the wilderness for forty years until the generation of slaves dies out and a determined, desert-hardened new generation arises. The section ends with the Israelites camped near Pisgah.

The third section (22–25) starts with the conquest of the land east of the Jordan River. Balak, the king of Midian, realizes that he is too weak to defeat the Israelites, so he hires the prophet Balaam to curse them and weaken them. Adonai intervenes, and instead Balaam blesses the Israelites.

In the fourth section (26–34), the generation born in Egypt has passed away, and the new generation of tough, fearless Israelite warriors is confidently prepared to cross the Jordan and claim their heritage. Moses once again counts the Israelites, and he appoints Joshua ben Nun as his successor.

The book concludes (35–36) with a series of new laws.

Bamidbar *describes a people with a slave mentality searching for strength and stability in the shifting sands of the desert. Adonai is aware of their fears and, like a loving father, He encourages and protects them until they have the ability to stand on their own feet. He knows that in time the Israelites will mature into a strong and powerful nation.*

סֵפֶר בַּמִדְבָּר
THE BOOK OF BAMIDBAR

Masoretic Torah Notes

Here is a list of some of the Masoretic notes
for the Book of Bamidbar.

1. The Book of Bamidbar contains 1,288 verses.
2. The Book of Bamidbar contains 36 chapters.
3. The Book of Bamidbar contains 10 sidrot.

These are the sidrot in the Book of Bamidbar.

סֵפֶר בַּמִדְבָּר	336	Book of Bamidbar
בַּמִדְבָּר	338	Bamidbar
נָשֹׂא	348	Naso
בְּהַעֲלוֹתְךָ	358	Beha'alotecha
שְׁלַח לְךָ	370	Shelach Lecha
קֹרַח	380	Korach
חֻקַּת	388	Chukkat
בָּלָק	397	Balak
פִּנְחָס	406	Pinchas
מַטּוֹת	417	Mattot
מַסְעֵי	424	Massay

בַּמִּדְבָּר *Bamidbar*

IN THE WILDERNESS

1 On the first day of the second month [Iyar], in the second year of the Exodus, Adonai spoke to Moses in the Wilderness of Sinai, in the Meeting Tent, saying: **2** Take a census of the entire Israelite community. Do it by their clans and families, and record the names of every male. **3** You and Aaron shall record every male over twenty years old who is fit for military service. **4** Choose one leader from each tribe to assist you.

---

1. On the first day of the second month (Iyar), in the second year of the Exodus, Adonai spoke to Moses in the Wilderness of Sinai, in the Meeting Tent.
Bamidbar, meaning "In the Wilderness," is the fourth book of the Five Books of Moses. It continues to record the forty years of travels after the Israelites left Mount Sinai.

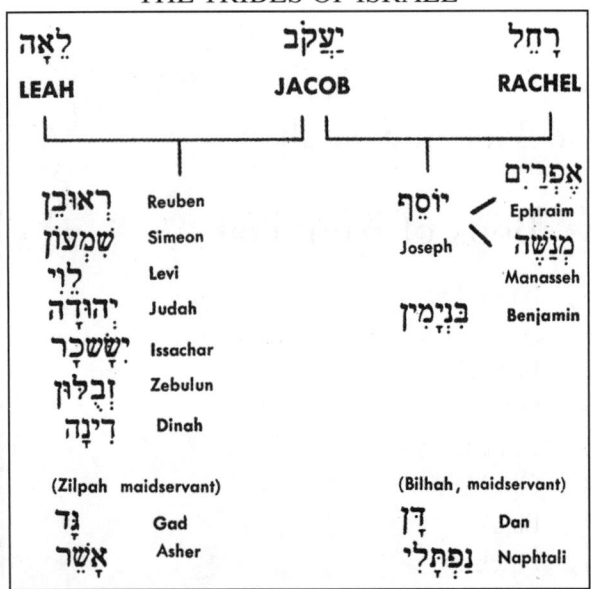

THE TRIBES OF ISRAEL

The sages taught that the Torah was given through three things: through fire, through water, and through the desert.

Why was it given through these three things? Simply because these are free for all who come into the world, So is the Torah; its laws, commandments, and mitzvot are all free and available for those who are thirsty for Adonai's blessings.

Midrash Tanhuma

2. Take a census of the entire Israelite community. Do it by their clans and families, and record the names of every male.
The census was preliminary to conscription and organization of an army to invade Canaan. Adonai directed that the army be organized by family units. In this way the family would fight as one cohesive unit and would defend and care for each other.

The Torah informs us, in detail, about the first census taken by Moses and Aaron. The numbering was to be "clan by clan, family by family," each tribe being composed of clans, and each clan being composed of families.

Every ten years the U.S. government conducts a census. Questionnaires are sent to every family and eventually the answers given are tabulated by giant computers. Finally we get a picture of Americans – how they live, what work they do, how large their families are, etc. This is very important information for government planning.

3. You and Aaron shall record every male over twenty years old who is fit for military service.
Moses and Aaron were planning to conquer Canaan. They had to know the number of available soldiers.

4. Choose one leader from each tribe to assist you.
All the Israelite teens wanted to join the army and they deliberately falsified their ages. The leaders from each of the tribes knew the families and reluctantly refused to enlist them.

Shenash

5 These are the names of the leaders who will assist you: For Reuben, Elitzur son of Shedeur.
6 For Simeon, Shelumiel son of Zurishaddai.
7 For Judah, Nachshon son of Aminadab.
8 For Issachar, Nethanel son of Zuar. **9** For Zebulun, Eliav son of Helon.
10 For Joseph's two sons: For Ephraim, Elishama son of Amihud. For Manasseh, Gamliel son of Pedahzur. **11** For Benjamin, Avidan son of Gidoni.
12 For Dan, Achiezer son of Amishaddai.
13 For Asher, Pagiel son of Okhran. **14** For Gad, Eliassaf son of Deuel.
15 For Naphtali, Achira son of Eynan.
16 These are the leaders, the heads of their tribes and the leaders of the thousands of Israelites.
17 Moses and Aaron assembled the tribal leaders.
18 The leaders summoned the entire Israelite community on the first day of the second month [Iyar], and all the people registered according to their tribal families. All males over twenty years of age were registered by name.
19 Moses counted the Israelites in the Wilderness of Sinai just as Adonai had commanded him.

The Tribal Census
2nd Aliyah

20 According to the records of the tribe, the number of males over twenty years of age fit for military service **21** from the tribe of Reuben was 46,500 soldiers.
22 According to the records of the tribe, the number of males over twenty years of age fit for military service **23** from the tribe of Simeon was 59,300 soldiers.
24 According to the records of the tribe, the number of males over twenty years of age fit for military service **25** from the tribe of Gad was 45,650 soldiers.
26 According to the records of the tribe, the number of males over twenty years of age fit for military service **27** from the tribe of Judah was 74,600 soldiers.
28 According to the records of the tribe, the number of males over twenty years of age fit for military service **29** from the tribe of Issachar was 54,400 soldiers.
30 According to the records of the tribe, the number of males over twenty years of age fit for military service **31** from the tribe of Zebulun was 57,400 soldiers.
32 Among the two sons of Joseph, Ephraim and Manasseh: According to the records of the tribe, the number of males over twenty years of age fit for military service **33** from the tribe of Ephraim was 40,500 soldiers.
34 According to the records of the tribe, the number of males over twenty years of age fit for military service **35** from the tribe of Manasseh was 32,200 soldiers.
36 According to the records of the tribe, the number of males over twenty years of age fit for military service **37** from the tribe of Benjamin was 35,400 soldiers.
38 According to the records of the tribe, the number of males over twenty years of age fit for military service **39** from the tribe of Dan was 62,700 soldiers.
40 According to the records of the tribe, the number of males over twenty years of age fit for military service **41** from the tribe of Asher was 41,500 soldiers.

---

18. All the people registered according to their tribal families. All the people registered because each individual was important. Each and every one, high and low, was equally valuable in the eyes of Adonai.

42 According to the records of the tribe, the number of males over twenty years of age fit for military service **43** from the tribe of Naphtali was 53,400 soldiers.

44 The following is the official count tabulated by Moses, Aaron, and the twelve tribal leaders of Israel:

45 The number of Israelite males according to their tribes, over twenty years old and all fit for military service **46** officially counted was 603,550 soldiers. **47** However, the men from the tribe of Levi were not counted together with the other Israelites.

48 Adonai explained to Moses, saying: **49** Do not count the Levites together with the other Israelites. **50** Put the Levites in charge of the Tabernacle and all its furniture and equipment. They will carry the Tabernacle and all its furniture, and they will take care of it, and they will camp around the Tabernacle.

51 Whenever the Tabernacle is moved, the Levites shall take it down, and whenever it is to be erected they will assemble it. Any non-Levite who touches anything belonging to the Tabernacle shall die. **52** Whenever the Israelites halt, each tribe shall camp under its own tribal banner. **53** The Levites, however, must camp around the Tabernacle, to protect the Israelites from Adonai's anger. The responsibility of safeguarding the Tabernacle shall belong to the Levites.

54 The Israelites did everything exactly as Adonai commanded Moses.

The Order of the March   *3rd Aliyah*

2 Adonai spoke to Moses and Aaron and instructed them, saying: **2** Each Israelite tribe shall camp around its own tribal banner. Each of the tribal encampments shall be erected in a specified area around the Meeting Tent.

3 Three tribes shall camp to the east, in the direction of the sunrise, under the marching banner of Judah. The leader of the tribe of Judah was Nachshon son of Aminadab. **4** His tribe enrolled 74,600 soldiers.

---

49. Do not count the Levites together with the other Israelites.
The Levites differed from the Israelites in three ways.
   1. They were in charge of the sanctuary.
   2. They camped around the sanctuary while the Israelites camped in specific tribal areas.
   3. The Israelites were counted from the age of twenty while the Levites were counted from the age of thirty days.   *Sforno*

52. Whenever the Israelites halt, each tribe shall camp under its own tribal banner.
Each tribe had a flag of a different color. The colors corresponded to the colors of the precious stones on Aaron's breastplate.

2. Each Israelite tribe shall camp around its own tribal banner.

The tribes marched toward the Promised Land in a military formation. Each tribe had its own flag so that people would know exactly where to camp. The flags, which flew high above the marchers, could also be used as a means of communication, like a semaphore code. The proudly flying flags helped turn a group of freed slaves into a disciplined, orderly group of marchers. Rabbi Judah Halevi compares the camp and the tribes camped around it to a living body and its limbs. The Tabernacle – the central feature – was the heart and soul of the Israelites.

2. Each of the tribal encampments shall be erected in a specified area around the Meeting Tent.
The tribes of Israel were divided into four divisions. The tribes of Judah, Reuben, Ephraim, and Dan each headed a division.

5 The tribe of Issachar shall camp near the tribe of Judah. The leader of the tribe of Issachar was Nethanel son of Zuar. **6** His tribe enrolled 54,400 soldiers.
7 The tribe of Zebulun camped near the tribe of Judah. The leader of the tribe of Zebulun was Eliav son of Helon. **8** His tribe enrolled 57,400 soldiers.
9 The total number of troops in Judah's part of camp was 186,400 soldiers. On the march, these three tribes will lead the way.
10 The three tribes under the marching banner of Reuben shall camp to the south. The leader of the tribe of Reuben was Elitzur son of Shedeur. **11** His tribe enrolled 46,500 soldiers.
12 The tribe of Simeon shall camp near the tribe of Reuben. The leader of the tribe of Simeon was Shelumiel son of Zurishaddai. **13** The tribe of Simeon enrolled 59,300 soldiers.
14 The tribe of Gad shall camp near the tribe of Reuben. The leader of the tribe of Gad was Eliassaf son of Reuel.
15 The tribe of Gad enrolled 45,650 soldiers.
16 The total number of troops in Reuben's part of the camp was 151,450 soldiers. On the march, these three tribes will be second in the line of march.
17 On the march, the Meeting Tent and the camp of the Levites shall march in the middle of the four groups. The people shall travel in the same order that they camp. Each person shall be in his place, under his own tribal banner.
18 The three tribes under the banner of Ephraim shall camp to the west. The leader of Ephraim was Elishama son of Amihud. **19** The tribe of Ephraim enrolled 40,500 soldiers **20** The leader of the tribe of Manasseh shall camp near the tribe of Ephraim. The leader of Manasseh's descendants was Gamliel son of Pedahzur.
21 The tribe of Manasseh enrolled 32,200 soldiers.
22 The tribe of Benjamin camped near the tribe of Ephraim. The leader of Benjamin's descendants was Avidan son of Gidoni. **23** The tribe of Benjamin enrolled 35,400 soldiers
24 The total number of troops in Ephraim's part of the camp totaled 108,100 soldiers. On the march, these three tribes shall be third in line.
25 The three tribes under the marching banner of Dan shall camp to the north. The leader of the tribe of Dan was Achiezer son of Amishaddai. **26** The tribe of Dan enrolled 62,700 soldiers.

17. On the march, the Meeting Tent and the camp of the Levites shall march in the middle of the four groups.
The mishkan (Tabernacle) occupied a central position in the Israelite camp. Levites camped to the north, west, and south of the Tabernacle. Moses, Aaron, and his family, the priests, occupied the eastern section of the square.

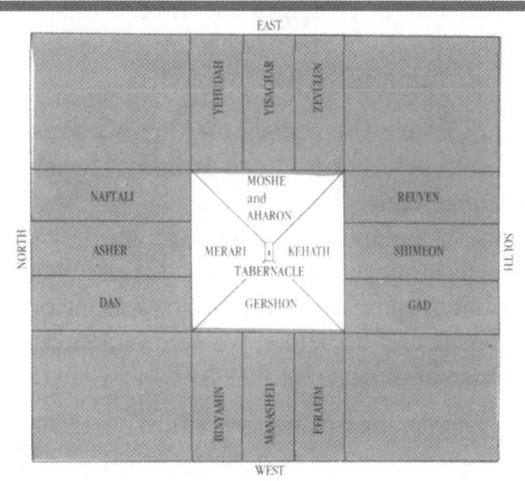

27 The tribe of Asher camped near the tribe of Dan. The leader of the tribe of Asher was Pagiel son of Okhran.
28 The tribe of Asher enrolled 41,500 soldiers.
29 The tribe of Naphtali camped near the camp of Dan. The leader of the tribe of Naphtali was Achira son of Eynan.
30 The tribe of Naphtali enrolled 53,400 soldiers.
31 The total number of troops in the camp of Dan was 157,600 soldiers.
On the march, their column shall be the last of the tribes.
32 This is the number of Israelite soldiers counted according to their tribes: the Israelite troops in all the tribal camps totaled 603,550 soldiers.
33 The Levites were not counted with the rest of the Israelites, just as Adonai had commanded Moses.
34 The Israelites did everything that Adonai had commanded Moses. They camped around their banners, in family groups and tribes.

Aaron's Family Tree   *4th Aliyah*

3 This is the family tree of Aaron and Moses on the day that Adonai spoke to Moses at Mount Sinai:
These are the names of Aaron's sons: Nadav the first-born, Avihu, Elazar, and Ithamar.
3 These are the names of Aaron's sons, the anointed priests who were ordained to serve in the Tabernacle.
4 Nadav and Avihu died before Adonai when they presented an offering with unauthorized fire to Adonai in the Wilderness of Sinai. They had no children.
During the lifetime of their father, Aaron, only Elazar and Ithamar served as priests. **5** Adonai spoke to Moses, saying:

---

2. These are the names of Aaron's sons: Nadav the first-born, Avihu, Elazar, and Ithamar.
Nadav and Avihu died when they offered strange fire. Elazar became High Priest when Aaron died. Ithamar was in charge of the Tabernacle and supervised the Kehothites, who carried the ark and the holy furniture on their shoulders.

3. These are the names of Aaron's sons, the anointed priests who were ordained to serve in the Tabernacle.
All priests and Levites are descendants of the tribe of Levi. Aaron and his descendants were given the honor of the priesthood because he was the brother of Moses, and he helped free the Israelites from Egyptian slavery.

The anointing and the ordination of Aaron's sons as priests were previously performed. The priests had authority over the Levites. The Levites were given to Aaron for service in connection with the Tabernacle and its functions. Levites were forbidden to trespass into areas dedicated for the priesthood.

Levites served as assistants to the priests. They were the Temple musicians, judges, scribes, and also the teachers of Torah. One tenth of the total tithe was set aside for the Levites.

All of the tribes were given a territory in Canaan except the priests and the Levites. They were to earn their living by performing sacrifices and teaching Torah.

6 Assemble the tribe of Levi, and assign them to Aaron the priest, so that they can help him. **7** They will work for him and the entire Israelite community in the Meeting Tent, performing the sacred services. **8** They shall care for the furniture in the Meeting Tent on behalf of the Israelites, doing the holy work during the Tabernacle service. **9** Assign the Levites to Aaron and his descendants. And they will be their assistants.

10 Make Aaron and his descendants responsible for observing the priestly duties. Any non-priest who tries to perform priestly duties shall die.

11 Adonai spoke to Moses, saying: **12** I have chosen the Levites from the other Israelites as substitutes for all the first-born among the Israelites; the Levites shall be Mine. **13** This is so because every first-born became Mine on the day I killed all the first-born in Egypt. I set apart for Myself every first-born in Israel, man and beast alike, and they shall remain Mine. I am Adonai.

The Census of the Levites
5th Aliyah

14 Adonai spoke to Moses in the Wilderness of Sinai and instructed him: **15** Count the Levites, family by family. Count every male over the age of one month.

16 At Adonai's command Moses counted them, just as he had been instructed.

---

6. Assemble the tribe of Levi, and assign them to Aaron the priest.
There were 22,000 Levites involved in religious responsibilities. They were made up of three divisions: the Gershonites, Kehothites, and Merarites, named for the sons of Levi.

8. They shall care for the furniture in the Meeting Tent.
These included the curtains and tapestries, the ark, the table, the menorah, the altars, and the entire framework of the Tabernacle. The Levites had to set them up and take them down when the Israelites moved from encampment to encampment.

9. Assign the Levites to Aaron and his descendants. And they will be their assistants.
The Levites were assigned to work outside the Meeting Tent. They were to transport the furniture and guard the Tabernacle. They had no access to the Meeting Tent.

10. Make Aaron and his descendants responsible for observing the priestly duties.
The priests (Kohanim) had sole access to the Tabernacle.

13. This is so because every first-born became Mine on the day I killed all the first-born in Egypt. I set apart for Myself every first-born in Israel, man and beast alike, and they shall remain Mine. I am Adonai.
Rashi says that the first-born were initially to be given the honor of serving Adonai. However, because many of them participated in the worship of the golden calf, they lost that privilege. The Levites were chosen because they were the only tribe (Shemot 32:28) who responded to Moses, call to kill the worshippers of the golden calf.

15. Count the Levites, family by family. Count every male over the age of one month.
The fact that the Levites were counted at a very young age indicates that the children had to be educated and trained to perform a variety of functions which required much skill. The Levites were the physicians, the teachers of the Torah, the religious leaders, and the judges. Their education had to start at an early age because there was much to learn.

Moses complained, "How can I go around from tent to tent into the midst of the houses to count each and every one of them?" Then Adonai said to Moses, "You do your part and I will do Mine." So Moses would go from tent to tent and the Divine Presence would say to him, "There are so many souls in this tent and so many souls in the next tent." We arrived at this conclusion since the sages say, "At Adonai's command, Moses counted them just as he had been instructed."

Shenash

17 Levi had three sons: Gershon, Kehoth, and Merari.
18 Gershon had two sons, Livni and Shimi, who were the heads of their families.
19 The four sons of Kehoth were Amram, Yitzhar, Hebron, and Uzziel, and they were the heads of their families.
20 Merari had two sons, Machli and Mushi, who were the heads of their families.
These are the three Levite families. **21** The Gershonites included the Livnite family and the Shimite family. **22** There were 7,500 Gershonites one month of age and older. **23** The Gershonite family shall camp to the west, behind the Tabernacle.
24 The leader of the Gershonites was Eliassaf son of Lael.
25 The descendants of Gershon shall be responsible for the Meeting Tent, the Tabernacle tapestries, the two roofs, the curtains in the entrance of the Meeting Tent, **26** the hangings at the entrance of the enclosure surrounding the Tabernacle, the altar, the ropes, as well as all the equipment used in the ceremonies.
27 The descendants of Kehoth comprised four families: the Amramite family, the Yitzharite family, the Hebronite family, and the Uzzielite family.
28 There were 8,600 males one month of age and older in the four Kehoth families.
They were responsible for all the holy articles in the sanctuary.
29 The family of Kehoth's descendants shall camp on the southern side of the Tabernacle.
30 The leader of the Kehothite family was Elzafan son of Uzziel.
31 They shall be responsible for the ark, the table, the golden menorah, the two altars, the holy utensils, the partition curtain, and all the equipment involving these items. **32** Eleazar son of Aaron the priest shall be the one in charge of the Levites' leaders. He shall be responsible for safeguarding the holy articles.
33 The descendants of Merari were the Machli family and the Mushi family.
34 There were 6,200 males one month of age and older in the Merari families.
35 The leader of the families of Merari was Zuriel son of Avichail. The family of the Merari shall camp on the northern side of the Tabernacle.
36 The responsibility of the descendants of Merari shall include the frames, crossbars, pillars, and bases of the Tabernacle, all its utensils, and the equipment for their use, **37** as well as the pillars, bases, pegs, and ropes of the surrounding enclosure.

---

18. Gershon had two sons, Livni and Shimi.
The Levinites and the Shimites were assigned a camping area west of the Tabernacle during the wilderness wanderings. The Gershonites were assigned specific tasks in the care of the Meeting Tent and were later involved in King David's musical organization.

27. The descendants of Kehoth comprised four families: the Amramite family, the Yitzharite family, the Hebronite family, and the Uzzielite family.
The Kehothite family was situated to the south of the Tabernacle. The family was in charge of moving the holy furniture after it was packed by the Levites.

28. There were 8,600 males one month of age and older in the four Kehoth families.
The Kehothites were assigned to move and carry the parts of the sanctuary when they moved from camping ground to camping ground.

34. There were 6,200 males one month of age or older in the Merari family.
Merari was the third and youngest son of Levi. His descendants were divided into two groups: Machlites and Mushites.

During the wanderings, the Merarites were assigned duties connected with transporting the less sacred parts of the Tabernacle.

Members of the Merarite family played a prominent role in the Temple music.

38 Moses and Aaron and his sons shall camp to the east, in front of the Tabernacle, and they shall be responsible for the sanctuary on behalf of the Israelites. Any unauthorized person who interferes or performs the duties of Moses and Aaron shall be put to death. **39** All the families of the tribe of Levi were counted, and there were 22,000 males more than one month old.

Census of the First-born
6th Aliyah

40 Moses and Aaron counted all the first-born male Levites who were over one month old and registered their names.
41 Adonai said, "The Levites are reserved for Me in place of all the first-born Israelite males. I will also accept the Levites' first–born animals in place of the Israelites' first-born animals."
42 Moses recorded all the first–born Israelite males, just as Adonai had commanded him.

---

38. Moses and Aaron and his sons shall camp to the east, in front of the Tabernacle.
The *mizrach* (east) was where the sun rose in the morning. The text is prophesying that in the future the Tabernacle will be established in the holy city of Jerusalem.
Today in many homes in the western hemisphere, a mizrach, a picture or a special decoration, is hung on the east wall of a home to indicate the geographical position of Jerusalem as the correct direction for prayer. *Shenash*

38. Moses and Aaron and his sons shall camp to the east, in front of the Tabernacle, and they shall be responsible for the sanctuary on behalf of the Israelites.
Moses and Aaron and his sons were responsible for the care of the Tabernacle. The only entrance into the Tabernacle was on the east side, and from this point they could see and supervise the Temple activities. Only the priests and Levites could enter the Tabernacle, and only the High Priest could enter the Holy of Holies, once a year on Yom Kippur, the Day of Atonement.

41. I will also accept the Levites' first-born animals in place of the Israelites' first-born animals.
Just as the first-born Israelites must be redeemed, so must their cattle be redeemed. The first of the animals are dedicated to Adonai. They must not be sacrificed on the altar.

42 Moses recorded all the first-born Israelite males, just as Adonai had commanded him.
The Hebrew word *bechor* is used to refer to first-born males and first-born animals. During the biblical era, the first-born received the right to inherit a double portion of his father's estate as well as the family leadership. One of the reasons for this distinction was the fact that Adonai, when liberating the Israelites from Egyptian slavery, had preserved the first-born of the Israelites from the tenth and last plague, during which all the Egyptian first-born died. The ceremony of the redemption of the first-born (*pidyon ha-Ben*) occurs on the thirty-first day after the son's birth. If he is the first-born (*b'chor*) of the mother, he is redeemed by the payment of five shekels.

42. Moses recorded all the first-born Israelite males, just as Adonai had commanded him.
The reason for this custom is that in olden days first-born males were dedicated to the service of Adonai, to act as priests, musicians, and servants in the Temple. Later, the tribe of Levi was appointed to officiate in the Temple. From then on, every first-born male child was freed or redeemed from service by paying the *kohen* or Levite who served in his place. Today a *kohen*, or descendant of the priestly tribe, is invited to the *Pidyon ha-Ben* ceremony. After receiving the five *shekalim*, he usually turns the money over to a charitable Jewish cause.

43 All of the first-born males listed by name added up to 22,273.
44 Adonai spoke to Moses, and said, **45** "Take the Levites in place of all the first-born male Israelites. Also take the first-born livestock of the Levites in place of the first-born Israelite animals. The Levites shall be Mine. I am Adonai."
46 There were 22,273 first-born Israelites and 22,000 first-born Levites.
47 You must collect five pieces of silver from each of the 273 extra first-born Israelites.
48 Give the silver to Aaron and his sons as the redemption price for the extra 273 first-born Israelites.
49 Moses collected the redemption money for the extra first-born Israelites who had not been redeemed by the Levites.
50 The silver that he collected from the first-born Israelites weighed 34 pounds.
51 With Adonai's permission, Moses gave the silver for those who were redeemed to Aaron and his sons.
It was all done exactly as Adonai had commanded Moses.

Duties of the Kehoth Family *7th Aliyah*

4 Adonai instructed Moses and Aaron, saying:
2 Take a census of the Kehoth families of the tribe of Levi. **3** Count all the males from thirty to fifty years old who are able to work in the Meeting Tent.
4 The following will be the duties of the descendants of Kehoth in the Meeting Tent:
5 When the Israelites are ready to travel, Aaron and his sons shall take down the partition drape and use it to cover the ark, **6** and wrap a cover of blue-tanned sealskins over it, and on top of that a cloth of blue wool. They shall then insert its carrying poles into the rings.
7 Next they shall wrap blue cloth over the inner table. Then they shall set in place on it the bread forms, incense bowls, and covering side frames, so that the bread can constantly remain on the table.
8 Over it all, they shall place a red wool cloth, and cover it with a box made of blue-tanned sealskins. They shall then insert its carrying poles into the rings.
9 They shall take a cloth of blue wool and wrap the golden menorah lamp and its oil cups, wick tongs, and ash shovels and the oil containers for it.
10 The menorah and all its utensils shall be placed in a box made of blue-tanned sealskins, and placed on a carrying frame.
11 They shall wrap a blue wool cloth around the golden altar and cover it with a box made of blue-tanned sealskins. Then they shall insert its carrying poles in the rings.
12 They shall take all the sanctuary's service utensils and wrap them in blue wool cloths. Then they shall cover them with a box made of blue-tanned sealskins and place it on a carrying frame.

---

47. You must collect five pieces of silver from each of the 273 extra first-born Israelites.
Coinage was not invented until the seventh century B.C.E. The amount of silver was a fixed unit of weight.

3. Take a census of the Kehoth families of the tribe of Levi.
The Kehothites were descendants of the family of Moses and Aaron. They were counted first because they were of the lineage of Moses and Aaron.

13 They shall remove all the ashes from the altar and cover the altar with a purple cloth. **14** They shall place on the altar all the utensils used for its service, such as the fire pans, hooks, shovels, and sacrificial basins. Then they shall put them in a box made of blue-tanned sealskins, and insert carrying poles in the rings.
15 Afterward Aaron and his sons shall finish covering the holy furniture and all the sanctuary utensils, and only then can the camp begin its journey. The Kehothites are permitted to carry these holy items only after the priests finish packing them, because they will die if they touch the sacred objects.
All these are the articles the Kehothites must carry from the Meeting Tent.
16 Elazar son of Aaron the priest shall be in charge of the oil for the golden menorah, the perfume incense, the grain offerings for the daily sacrifice, and the anointing oil. He shall also be in charge of the entire Tabernacle and all its holy furniture and utensils.

Do Not Destroy the Kehothites *Maftir*

17 Adonai instructed Moses and Aaron, saying:
18 Make sure that the Kehothites do not destroy themselves, **19** so that they live, and do not die, when they enter the Holy of Holies. Aaron and his sons must enter first and assign each load so that every Kehothite can do his job and carry his assigned load. **20** The Kehothites are not permitted to enter and see the holy furniture being packed. If they do, they will destroy themselves.

---

15. All these are the articles the Kehothites must carry from the Meeting Tent.
Only after the priests have packed the holy sanctuary items are the Kehothites permitted to carry these holy items.

16. He shall also be in charge of the entire Tabernacle and all its holy furniture and utensils.
Elazar was to be in complete charge of dismantling and erecting the Tabernacle. His responsibility was to make sure that all the furniture was properly packed and unpacked.

18. Make sure that the Kehothites do not destroy themselves.
The assembly and disassembly of the Tabernacle was a difficult and complicated task. The priests assigned specific tasks of carrying in a prearranged order to avoid mixups and the desecration of the holy objects. The Kehothites were assigned to carry the ark only after Aaron and his sons had covered it up. The prohibition of touching the holy vessels was designed to deflate their pride and save their lives.

The sages explain that humans are naturally inquisitive and yearn to see behind the forbidden curtain. Therefore, you must conceal and cover up, so that they shall not die as a result of breaching the forbidden barrier. Sforno explained that the text is simply telling the priest to delegate the tasks of carrying the holy object in a prearranged order to avoid desecrating the holy Tabernacle objects.

20. The Kehothites are not permitted to enter and see the holy furniture being packed. If they do, they will destroy themselves.
The Kehothites were aware of the importance and sanctity of the ark. All of them might scramble to carry the ark and reap a greater reward in the world to come. There would be quarrels and each one would claim the right to carry the ark and ignore the less important objects. So Adonai instructed Moses to institute a system whereby the Kehothites would not fight and destroy themselves. Aaron and his sons designated each object to a specific carrier.

Bamidbar Rabbah

נָשׂא *Naso*

TAKE A CENSUS

21 Adonai instructed Moses, saying:
22 Take a census of Gershon's two Levite families, the Gershonites and the Meraris. **23** Count everyone from thirty to fifty years old who is able to work in the service of the Meeting Tent.
24 The Gershonites shall be responsible for maintaining and carrying the following:
25 They shall carry the tapestries for the Meeting Tent, the tanned ram skins for the roof and the blue-tanned sealskins for the over-roof, the drape at the entrance of the Meeting Tent, **26** the enclosure's hangings, the curtain at the entrance to the enclosure around the Tabernacle and altar, the ropes, and all the tools necessary for their maintenance.
27 Aaron and his sons shall supervise all the carrying and maintenance work of the Gershonites. The Gershonites shall be assigned to carry specific loads.
28 Ithamar son of Aaron the priest shall supervise the duties of the Gershonites at the Meeting Tent.
29 Take a census of the family of Merari.
30 Count the Meraris from thirty to fifty years old who are fit for service in the Meeting Tent. **31** The Meraris shall be responsible for carrying and maintaining these items in the Meeting Tent: the frames, crossbars, pillars, and bases of the Tabernacle, **32** the pillars of the surrounding enclosure, their bases, pegs, and ropes, all their tools, and all their maintenance equipment. The Meraris shall be specifically assigned by name to carry all the loads with which they are entrusted.
33 All the duties of the Meraris in the Meeting Tent shall be under the direction of Ithamar son of Aaron the priest.
34 Moses, Aaron, and the communal leaders counted the descendants of the Kehothites by families, **35** including everyone from thirty to fifty years old who was fit for service in the Meeting Tent **36** and the total number added up to 2,750.
37 This was the complete count of the Kehothite family who served in the Meeting Tent, as tabulated by Moses and Aaron. It was done as Adonai had directed Moses.

---

22. Take a census of Gershon's two Levite families.
The Hebrew term *aliyah* denotes the honor given to a worshipper to ascend the *bimah* (platform) in the synagogue for the public Torah reading. The first *aliyah* is given to a *Kohen* or a person of priestly descent, the second to a descendant of the tribe of Levi, and the third to an Israelite.

32. The Meraris shall be specifically assigned by name to carry all the loads with which they are entrusted.
Each of the Meraris was assigned a very specific task and burden. The Meraris had to carry heavy loads for long distances. By being assigned items to be carried, they were prevented from refusing to carry heavy burdens.

Assigning the articles to specific people was a method of inventory control.

34. Moses, Aaron, and the communal leaders counted the descendants of the Kehothites by families.
The Kehothites were very important, so they were counted by Moses, Aaron, and the communal leaders. They were counted first because they carried the holy vessels – the ark, the table, the menorah, and the altar.

Hizkuni

Gershon's Descendants
2nd Aliyah

38 This was the count of Gershon's descendants, **39** which included all males from thirty to fifty years old who were fit for service in the Meeting Tent. **40** The total added up to 2,630 Gershonites.
41 This was the complete count of the Gershonites who served in the Meeting Tent. The census was taken by Moses and Aaron as Adonai had directed.
42 The count of Merari's descendants **43** included everyone from thirty to fifty years old who was fit for service in the Meeting Tent. **44** The count of the Merari family added up to 3,200 males. **45** This was the complete count of the families of Merari's descendants. The census was taken by Moses and Aaron as Adonai had directed Moses.
46 The entire census that Moses, Aaron, and the communal leaders took of the Levites **47** included everyone from thirty to fifty years old who was fit for service in the Meeting Tent. **48** The total added up to 8,580 males. **49** At Adonai's request, each individual was given a special responsibility for what he would carry.

Do Not Contaminate the Camp
3rd Aliyah

5 Adonai spoke to Moses, and said:
2 Command the Israelites to send away anyone in the camp who has a skin disease or an infection, and anyone who is ritually unclean from touching a dead person.
3 You must remove all sick persons, male or female, from the camp so that they will not contaminate the camp where I live among you.
4 The Israelites did this, and removed all infected people from the camp. The Israelites did exactly as Adonai had instructed Moses.
5 Adonai instructed Moses, and told him to **6** speak to the Israelites:
If a man or a woman has committed a sin against his fellow man, thereby being unfaithful to Adonai and becoming guilty of a crime,

---

38. This was the count of Gershon's descendants.
The Kehothites were the first Levite family to be counted. Next came the descendants of Gershon. They used wagons and oxen to transport the Tabernacle materials. They were counted right after the Kehothites because Gershon was the eldest son of Levi. *Hizkuni*

43. Included everyone from thirty to fifty years old who was fit for service in the Meeting Tent.
It was extremely important to have an accurate count, since any service performed by a Levite younger or older than thirty would have been invalid.

3. You must remove all sick persons, male or female, from the camp so that they will not contaminate the camp where I live among you.
The campsite consisted of three separate areas. The first was the area within the curtains where the Tabernacle and the Meeting Tent were located. The second area was where the Levites camped. The third camping area was by far the largest and consisted of the camps of the tribes of Israel. The infected individuals were to be removed from all the camping areas. *Rashi*

6. If a man or a woman has committed a sin against his fellow man, thereby being unfaithful to Adonai and becoming guilty of a crime.
Any human committing a wrong or crime against another person is considered to have committed a wrong or a crime against Adonai.

7 that person must confess the crime that he has committed and must repay what he has stolen. He must also pay one-fifth extra to the victim of his crime.
8 But if there is no relative to whom the money can be repaid, then the money belongs to Adonai and must be given to the priest. This payment is in addition to the ram of the atonement, and only then is the sin forgiven.
9 All the offerings that the Israelites present as elevated gifts shall belong to the priest. **10** The offerings are given to the priest and belong to him.

Adultery and Unfaithfulness   4th Aliyah

11 Adonai spoke to Moses and told him: **12** Speak to the Israelites and say to them: This is the law if any man's wife is suspected of committing adultery and being unfaithful to her husband. **13** If she willingly slept with a man and kept it hidden from her husband, and there was proof against the woman, **14** and the husband became suspicious of his wife, and even if she was innocent: **15** the law is that the husband must bring his wife to the priest and bring an offering of two quarts of barley flour without oil or frankincense on it, since it is a suspicion offering to determine the truth. **16** The priest shall confront the woman and have her stand before Adonai. **17** He shall pour holy water into a clay bowl and add some earth from the Tabernacle floor and mix it into the water. **18** Then the priest shall stand the woman before Adonai and loosen her hair. The priest shall put in her hands the suspicion offering to determine whether the husband's complaints are justified. The priest shall stand next to the woman and hold the curse-bearing bitter water in his hands. **19** Then the priest shall ask the woman to take an oath. He will say, "If a man has not slept with you, and you have not committed adultery, the curse-bearing bitter water will have no effect on you. **20** But if you have committed adultery against your husband and have slept with a man other than your husband –"

---

7. That person must confess the crime that he has committed and must repay what he has stolen. He must also pay one-fifth extra to the victim of his crime.
This is mitzvah number 364.

The text speaks of a person who has committed a crime, confesses his guilt, and wishes to make amends for his robbery.

He has to bring restitution and add one-fifth of the value as a fine. In addition he must bring an offering of a ram for atonement.

He must orally confess his guilt to the court. Maimonides says, "When a person commits a sin, then he shall confess orally and make a firm commitment not to become a repeat offender."

8. But if there is no relative to whom the money can be repaid, then the money belongs to Adonai and must be given to the priests.
This statement puzzled the sages, who asked, "Is there anyone in Israel who does not have a brother, sister, uncle, nephew, or a third cousin?"

After much analysis they decided that the statement referred to a *ger* (convert) who died and left no apparent heirs.

12. This is the law if any man's wife is suspected of committing adultery and being unfaithful to her husband.
This is mitzvah number 365.

It is a mitzvah for a husband who suspects his wife of infidelity to bring her to a priest who will question her to determine if she is guilty. A *sotah* was a woman whose husband became suspicious of her behavior and in the presence of ten witnesses warned her to stop the meetings.

21 Then the priest shall continue and say to the woman, "Now Adonai will ruin your reputation and make it into a curse among your people, and you will become infertile and your belly will swell. **22** This curse-bearing water will enter your body and cause your belly to swell and make you infertile." The woman shall be required to respond, "Amen. Amen."
23 Then the priest will write curses on a piece of parchment, and wash the writing off into the bitter water.
24 Then he shall make the woman drink the curse-bearing bitter water, and it will make the woman sick with guilt feelings.
25 Next the priest shall take the suspicion offering from the woman, and wave the offering before Adonai, and carry it to the altar.
26 After he makes the woman drink the water, the priest shall take some of the grain offering and burn it on the altar.
27 If the woman has been untrue to her husband, the curse-bearing water will enter her body and make her sick and cause her belly to swell and she will become infertile, and she will lose her reputation and will become a curse among her people.
28 However, if the woman is innocent and has not been unfaithful to her husband, she will remain healthy and she will be able to give birth to children.
29 This is the law for dealing with jealousy if a woman commits adultery and becomes unfaithful, **30** or when a man becomes suspicious of his wife's actions. The priest shall stand the woman before Adonai and follow this entire ritual.
31 Then the husband will be clear of sin, but the woman will be held accountable for her behavior.

6 Adonai spoke to Moses and told him to **2** speak to the Israelites and say to them: This is the law when a man or a woman wishes to take a Nazirite vow to Adonai.
3 He must not drink wine and liquor. He must not even use vinegar made from wine. He must not drink any grape juice or eat any grapes or raisins.
4 As long as he is a Nazirite, he must not eat anything made from grapes, including their seeds and skin.

---

22. The woman shall be required to respond, "Amen, Amen."
The word *Amen* occurs fourteen times in the Torah and was recited at the end of a prayer or agreement. By pronouncing *Amen*, the listeners associate themselves with what has been said. The Israelites said *Amen* to the commandments that Moses gave them. The word *Amen* is also used when one person agrees with the word(s) of another. The ceremony of the bitter water was a type of psychological warfare. Maimonides says the fear of the bitter water will cause the *sotah* to admit guilt or refuse to drink. The midrash speaks of women who say, "I will not drink."

2. This is the law when a man or a woman wishes to take a Nazirite vow to Adonai.
Both men and women took Nazirite pledges. A single girl needed the permission of her father. A married woman needed the acquiescence of her husband.

3. He must not drink wine or liquor.
The Nazirite in the Torah abstains from wine and grape products just for a limited time. He does not abstain from any other bodily pleasures. This type of abstinence could readily describe an individual with a drinking problem who is trying to dry out.
Shenash

5 As long as he is a Nazirite, he must never cut the hair on his head. During the entire Nazirite period he is holy to Adonai and he must let the hair on his head grow long.
6 As long as he is a Nazirite to Adonai, he must not have any contact with the dead. **7** As long as he is a Nazirite and the uncut hair is still on his head, he must not make himself unclean even when his father, mother, brother, or sister dies.
8 As long as he is a Nazirite, he is dedicated to Adonai.
9 If a person suddenly dies in the presence of a Nazirite, rendering the long hair of his Nazirite "crown" ritually unclean, then when he purifies himself on the seventh day, he must shave off the hair on his head.
10 On the eighth day, he must bring two doves or two pigeons to the priest at the entrance of the Meeting Tent. **11** The priest shall prepare one bird as a sin offering and one as a burnt offering to atone for his defilement by the dead. On that day, he shall resanctify his head **12** and again begin counting his Nazirite days to Adonai, and he shall bring a lamb as a guilt offering; since his Nazirite crown was made unclean, the days of his vow preceding this incident no longer count.
13 The following is the law of what the Nazirite must do when the term of his Nazirite vow is complete, and what he must bring to the entrance of the Meeting Tent: **14** The offering that he must present shall be one healthy male lamb for a burnt offering, one healthy female lamb for a sin offering, one healthy ram for a peace offering, **15** and a basket of unleavened bread mixed with olive oil and matzot spread with olive oil as well as a grain offering and a liquid offering.
16 The priest shall appear before Adonai and present the Nazirite's sin offering and burnt offering. **17** He shall then sacrifice the ram as a peace offering to Adonai, to go with the basket of unleavened bread.
The priest shall also present the meal offering and libation.

---

5. As long as he is a Nazirite, he must never cut the hair on his head.
This is mitzvah number 373
A Nazir is forbidden three activities:
1. Contact with a dead body.
2. Cutting the hair on his head.
3. Eating or drinking grape products.

This last one includes wine, grape juice, grape skins, and raisins.

Both Samson (Judges 13:4) and Samuel (1 Samuel 1:10) were Nazirites.

8. As long as he is a Nazirite, he is dedicated to Adonai.
A Nazirite was generally motivated by a religious impulse "to dedicate himself to Adonai."

Does the Torah consider the Nazirite a saint or a sinner? Nowhere does it praise naziritic restraints as a virtuous practice.

14. One healthy female lamb for a sin offering.
The sin offering refers to actions that preceded the Nazirite pledge. Obviously the Nazirite has realized his shortcomings in his inability to control his actions as imposed by the Torah and has vowed to change his persona. The Nazirite was a self-imposed restriction for spiritual problems.

16. The priest shall appear before Adonai and present the Nazirite's sin offering and burnt offering.
The prescribed guilt offering which a Nazirite was required to bring upon the expiration of his naziritic term has an ambivalent implication. Rabbis of the strict school attributed the Nazirite's guilt to the termination of his abstinence. Others, on the other hand, regarded the guilt offering as displeasure with the naziritic vows.

18 After the service at the entrance of the Meeting Tent, the Nazirite shall shave off the hair on his head and place the hair from his head on the fire that is under the peace sacrifice.
19 After the Nazirite has been shaved, the priest shall take the cooked shoulder of the ram and one unleavened loaf and one flat matzah from the basket and place them on the Nazirite's hands. **20** The priest shall wave them before Adonai. These holy gifts belong to the priest, in addition to the animal's breast and right thigh. After all this, the Nazirite may drink wine.
21 This is the entire law concerning the Nazirite who takes a vow to bring his Nazirite sacrifice to Adonai. This is in addition to anything else that he may wish to present to fulfill his special vow, which must be brought above and beyond what the law requires for his Nazirite vow.
22 Adonai said to Moses, telling him to **23** instruct Aaron and his sons: "You will bless the Israelites with this special blessing:

> **24** 'May Adonai bless you
> and keep watch over you.
> **25** May Adonai bless you and protect you.
> May Adonai smile on you and be kind to you.
> **26** May Adonai be good to you
> and give you peace.'

---

18. After the service at the entrance of the Meeting Tent, the Nazirite shall shave off the hair on his head and place the hair from his head on the fire that is under the peace sacrifice.
One of the requirements of a Nazirite was not to cut his hair during the consecration to Adonai. When the time was completed, the Nazir would have his hair cut in a special room in the Temple.

22–23. Adonai said to Moses, telling him to instruct Aaron and his sons: "You will bless the Israelites with this special blessing"
The chanting of the Priestly Blessing was one of the highlights of the service in the Jerusalem Temple. It was pronounced from a special platform, the *duchan*, after the sacrifice of the daily offering each morning and evening. The Priestly Benediction consists of three blessings. The first blessing has three words, the second has five words, and the third has seven words. This teaches us that the three patriarchs, the five books of the Torah, and the seven heavens are the basis of all blessings.
The Priestly Blessing is continued today in the synagogue prayers.

23. Instruct Aaron and his sons: "You will bless the Israelites with this special blessing."
This is mitzvah number 378.

It is a mitzvah for the priests to bless the congregation every day. During the blessing the priests raised their hands and spread out their fingers in the traditional priestly manner. In Temple times the priests pronounced the blessing every day. Today the priestly blessing is recited only on Rosh Hashanah, Yom Kippur, Passover, Shavuot, and Sukkot.

In Israel the priestly blessings are recited every day.

24. Bless you and keep watch over you.
With life, health, and protection from trouble.

26. May Adonai be good to you and give you peace.
When there is *shalom* for the individual and in society, there is peace all over the world.

27 With this special blessing I link My name with the people of Israel. And I Myself bless them."

Offerings of the Tribal Leaders *5th Aliyah*

7 On the day that Moses finished erecting the Tabernacle, he anointed all its furniture and made each item holy. He also anointed the altar and all its utensils and made them holy.
2 The leaders of Israel, all of them the heads of their tribes, then came forward. They were the leaders of the tribes and the ones who had organized the census.
3 The offerings they presented to Adonai consisted of six covered wagons and twelve oxen. There was one wagon for each two leaders, and one ox for each one. They presented the gifts in front of the Tabernacle.
4 Adonai said to Moses, **5** "Take the offering from them, and let the wagons and oxen be used for service in the Meeting Tent. Give them to the Levites, to be used for carrying the sacred furniture." **6** So Moses took the wagons and oxen and presented them to the Levites. **7** He gave two wagons and four oxen to the descendants of Gershon, as gift for their work.
8 To the descendants of Merari, he gave four wagons and eight oxen. All their work was done under the direction of Ithamar son of Aaron the priest.
9 However he did not give any wagons to the descendants of Kehoth, because they had responsibility for the most sacred articles, which they were required to carry on their shoulders.
10 The leaders presented their dedication offerings for the altar. They placed their offerings before the altar on the day that it was anointed. **11** Adonai said to Moses, "Let each leader present his offerings on a different day."
12 Nachshon son of Aminadav, leader of the tribe of Judah, brought his offering on the first day. **13** His offering consisted of one silver bowl weighing 3.5 pounds, and one silver basin weighing 1.75 pounds, both filled with fine flour mixed with olive oil for a meal offering;

---

3. There was one wagon for each two leaders, and one ox for each one. They presented the gifts in front of the Tabernacle.
Each of the leaders could easily have provided his own wagon. The sharing demonstrated that the tribes were united into one complete unit-the nation of Israel.

9. However he did not give any wagons to the descendants of Kehoth.
The Kehotites were provided with carrying poles with which to carry the holy objects. The holy vessels could not be transported by wagons, which were unwieldy and subject to breakdowns and accidents.

11. Let each leader present his offerings on a different day.
There are twelve tribes, and for each of twelve days a different leader presented offerings of his tribe. The exact same ceremony was repeated for twelve days. There was complete harmony, and none of the leaders tried to outdo each other.

14 one gold bowl weighing 4 ounces filled with incense; **15** one young bull, one lamb for a burnt offering;
16 one goat for a sin offering; **17** and two oxen, five rams, five male goats, and five lambs for the peace offering. This was the offering of Nachshon son of Aminadav.
18 Nethanel son of Tzuar, leader of the tribe of Issachar, brought his offering on the second day.
19 His offering consisted of one silver bowl weighing 3.5 pounds, and one silver basin weighing 1.75 pounds, both filled with fine flour mixed with olive oil for a meal offering;
20 one gold bowl weighing 4 ounces filled with incense;
21 one young bull, one lamb for a burnt offering; **22** one goat for a sin offering; **23** and two oxen, five rams, five male goats, and five lambs for the peace offering. This was the offering of Nethanel son of Tzuar.
24 Eliav son of Helon, leader of the tribe of Zebulun, brought his offering on the third day.
25 His offering consisted of one silver bowl weighing 3.5 pounds, and one silver basin weighing 1.75 pounds, both filled with fine flour mixed with olive oil for a meal offering;
26 one gold bowl weighing 4 ounces filled with incense; **27** one young bull, one lamb for a burnt offering;
28 one goat for a sin offering; **29** and two oxen, five rams, five male goats, and five lambs for the peace offering. This was the offering of Eliav son of Helon.
30 Elitzur son of Shedeur, leader of the tribe of Reuben, brought his offering on the fourth day.
31 His offering consisted of one silver bowl weighing 3.5 pounds, and one silver basin weighing 1.75 pounds, both filled with fine flour mixed with olive oil for a meal offering;
32 one gold bowl weighing 4 ounces filled with incense;
33 one young bull, one lamb for a burnt offering;
34 one goat for a sin offering; **35** and two oxen, five rams, five male goats, and five lambs for the peace offering.
This was the offering of Elitzur son of Shedeur.
36 Shelumiel son of Zurishaddai, leader of the tribe of Simeon, brought his offerings on the fifth day.
37 His offering consisted of one silver bowl weighing 3.5 pounds, and one silver basin weighing 1.75 pounds, both filled with fine flour mixed with olive oil for a meal offering;
38 one gold bowl weighing 4 ounces filled with incense;
39 one young bull, one lamb for a burnt offering; **40** one goat for a sin offering; **41** and two oxen, five rams, five male goats, and five lambs for the peace offering. This was the offering of Shelumiel son of Zurishaddai.

The Leaders Continue Their Offerings *6th Aliyah*

42 Eliassaf son of Deuel, leader of the tribe of Gad, brought his offering on the sixth day.
43 His offering consisted of one silver bowl weighing 3.5 pounds, and one silver basin weighing 1.75 pounds, both filled with fine flour mixed with olive oil for a meal offering; **44** one gold bowl weighing 4 ounces filled with incense; **45** one young bull, one lamb for a burnt offering;

46 one goat for a sin offering; **47** and two oxen, five rams, five male goats, and five lambs for the peace offering.
This was the offering of Eliassaf son of Deuel.
48 Elishama son of Amihud, leader of the tribe of Ephraim, brought his offering on the seventh day.
49 His offering consisted of one silver bowl weighing 3.5 pounds, and one silver basin weighing 1.75 pounds, both filled with fine flour mixed with olive oil for a meal offering;
50 one gold bowl weighing 4 ounces filled with incense;
51 one young bull, one lamb for a burnt offering;
52 one goat for a sin offering; **53** and two oxen, five rams, five male goats, and five lambs for the peace offering.
That was the offering of Elishama son of Amihud.
54 Gamliel son of Pedahzur, leader of the tribe of Manasseh, brought his offering on the eighth day.
55 His offering consisted of one silver bowl weighing 3.5 pounds, and one silver basin weighing 1.75 pounds, both filled with fine flour mixed with olive oil for a meal offering;
56 one gold bowl weighing 4 ounces filled with incense;
57 one young bull, one lamb for a burnt offering;
58 one goat for a sin offering; **59** and two oxen, five rams, five male goats, and five lambs for the peace offering. This was the offering of Gamliel son of Pedahzur.
60 Avidan son of Gidoni, leader of the tribe of Benjamin, brought his offering on the ninth day.
61 His offering consisted of one silver bowl weighing 3.5 pounds, and one silver basin weighing 1.75 pounds, both filled with fine flour mixed with olive oil for a meal offering;
62 one gold bowl weighing 4 ounces filled with incense;
63 one young bull, one lamb for a burnt offering;
64 one goat for a sin offering; **65** and two oxen, five rams, five male goats, and five lambs for the peace offering. That was the offering of Avidan son of Gidoni.
66 Achiezer son of Amishaddai, leader of the tribe of Dan, brought his offering on the tenth day.
67 His offering consisted of one silver bowl weighing 3.5 pounds, and one silver basin weighing 1.75 pounds, both filled with fine flour mixed with olive oil for a meal offering;
68 one gold bowl weighing 4 ounces filled with incense; **69** one young bull, one lamb for a burnt offering; **70** one goat for a sin offering; **71** and two oxen, five rams, five male goats, and five lambs for the peace offering.
That was the offering of Achiezer son of Amishaddai.

Asher and Naphtali Bring Offerings *7th Aliyah*

72 Pagiel son of Okhran, leader of the tribe of Asher, brought his offering on the eleventh day.
73 His offering consisted of one silver bowl weighing 3.5 pounds, and one silver basin weighing 1.75 pounds, both filled with fine flour mixed with olive oil for a meal offering;

74 one gold bowl weighing 4 ounces filled with incense;

75 one young bull, one lamb for a burnt offering;

76 one goat for a sin offering;

77 and two oxen, five rams, five male goats, and five lambs for the peace offering. This was the offering of Pagien son of Okhran.

78 Achira son of Eynan, leader of tribe of Naphtali, brought his offering on the twelfth day.

79 His offering consisted of one silver bowl weighing 3.5 pounds, and one silver basin weighing 1.75 pounds, both filled with fine flour mixed with olive oil for a meal offering;

80 one gold bowl weighing 4 ounces filled with incense;

81 one young bull, one lamb for a burnt offering;

82 one goat for a sin offering;

83 and two oxen, five rams, five male goats, and five lambs for the peace offering. That was the offering of Achira son of Eynan.

84 These are the totals of the dedication offerings brought by the tribal leaders on the day that the altar was anointed. There were twelve silver bowls, twelve silver basins, and twelve gold incense bowls.

85 Each silver bowl weighed 3.5 pounds, and each silver basin weighed 1.75 pounds. All together the silver in the two bowls weighed 60 pounds.

86 There were twelve golden bowls filled with incense; each golden bowl weighed 4 ounces. All the gold in the incense bowls weighed 3 pounds.

Adonai Speaks to Moses   *Maftir*

87 For burnt offerings there were twelve oxen, twelve rams, and twelve lambs, along with their grain offerings. There were also twelve male goats for sin offerings.

88 For the peace offerings there were twenty-four bulls, sixty rams, sixty male goats, and sixty lambs. These were the dedication offerings after the altar was anointed.

89 Whenever Moses went into the Meeting Tent to speak with Adonai, he heard the Voice speaking to him from between the two cherubs on the cover of the ark with the Ten Commandments. That was how Adonai communicated with Moses.

---

84. These are the totals of the dedication offerings brought by the tribal leaders on the day that the altar was anointed.
There were twelve silver bowls, twelve silver basins, and twelve gold incense bowls.

There was peace and harmony between each of the twelve tribal leaders. All of their gifts were exactly the same shape, size, and weight.

85. Each silver bowl weighed 3.5 pounds, and each silver basin weighed 1.75 pounds.
Each of the bowls and basins was made by master craftsmen and each weighed exactly the same. There was absolutely no difference in the weights of the bowls and basins.   *Rashi*

89. Whenever Moses went into the Meeting Tent to speak with Adonai, he heard the Voice speaking to him from between the two cherubs on the cover of the ark with the Ten Commandments.
Moses heard the voice of Adonai speaking to him. Now that the Tabernacle was finished, Adonai had another important task for Moses. Now Adonai was to reveal the laws and teachings which were to be Israel's constitution.

בְּהַעֲלֹתְךָ *Beha'alotecha*

WHEN YOU LIGHT THE MENORAH

8 Adonai spoke to Moses and said to him: **2** Speak to Aaron and tell him: When you light the menorah, position the seven lamps and place them to illuminate the front of the menorah.
3 So Aaron did so, and positioned the lamps to illuminate the area in front of the menorah, just as Adonai had commanded Moses.
4 The menorah was hammered out of a single gold ingot. Everything extending from its base to its blossom consisted of a single piece of hammered gold. The menorah was made exactly to the design that Adonai showed Moses.
5 Adonai spoke to Moses, and said:
6 Remove the Levites from among the Israelites and make them ritually clean. **7** To make them acceptable to Me, you must sprinkle them with the water of purifica- tion, and have them shave their entire bodies with a razor, and wash their clothes and their bodies to make themselves ritually clean.
8 Then have them bring a young bull and a grain offering consisting of the finest flour mixed with olive oil. You shall also present a second bull as a sin offering.
9 Bring the Levites to the front of the Meeting Tent, and assemble the entire Israelite community.
10 Present the Levites before the Meeting Tent, and have the Israelites place their hands on the Levites.
11 Aaron is to present the Levites as a wave offering to Adonai from the Israelites, and thus the Levites will become the ones to perform Adonai's service. **12** Afterwards the Levites shall place their hands on the heads of the bulls, and you shall present one bull as a sin offering and one as a burnt offering to Adonai, to make an atonement for the Levites.

---

7. To make them acceptable to Me, you must sprinkle them with the water of purification, and have them shave their entire bodies with a razor, and wash their clothes and their bodies to make themselves ritually clean.
The Levites' role as bearers and guardians of the Tabernacle was one of great holiness; great care had to be taken to ensure their absolute ritual cleanliness. This was the purpose of the special ceremony described here, which included sprinkling them with water of purification and shaving off all their hair. The sprinkling of water was apparently intended to cleanse a man of any possible impurity contracted by contact with the dead. We find the sprinkling water both in the rites for cleansing a leper and in some biblical passages dealing with ritual purity.

7. And wash their clothes and their bodies to make themselves ritually clean.
The washing of clothes was customary to prevent it becoming ritually unclean. As a sign of respect, the Levites were commanded to wash their clothes before they started to officiate in their special functions in the sanctuary.

10. Have the Israelites place their hands on the Levites.
The act of placing of hands on a rabbinical student is an act of ordination into the rabbinate. In this case it was to ordain the Levites as (*kohanim*) priests.

The ordination of a rabbinical student is called *semichah*.

13 Next, assemble the Levites in front of Aaron and his sons, and present them as a wave offering dedicated to Adonai. **14** With this ceremony you will separate the Levites from the other Israelites, and the Levites shall become exclusively Mine.

The Levites and Aaron
2nd Aliyah

15 After you have purified them and dedicated them with a wave offering, the Levites shall come to perform the service in the Meeting Tent.

16 From among the Israelites the Levites are given to serve Me in place of the first–born of all the Israelites.
I have chosen the Levites for Myself.

17 All first–borns of the Israelites are Mine, man and beast alike. I sanctified them for Myself on the day that I killed all the firstborns in Egypt. **18** Now I have chosen the Levites in place of all the firstborn sons of the Israelites.

19 I have given the Levites as assistants to Aaron and his descendants. From now on they will perform the service for the Israelites in the Meeting Tent and make atonement for the Israelites, so that no plague will strike them when they approach the sanctuary.

20 Moses, Aaron, and the entire Israelite community dedicated the Levites and followed all the instructions that Adonai had given Moses. The Israelites followed all the instructions exactly.

21 The Levites purified themselves with a sin offering and washed their bodies and their clothing. Aaron presented them as a wave offering before Adonai and made atonement for them to purify them. **22** From then on, the Levites performed the service in the Meeting Tent under the direction of Aaron and his sons. The Levites did everything exactly as Adonai had commanded Moses.

23 Adonai spoke to Moses and said:

24 These are the rules for the Levites: They must begin serving in the Tabernacle at the age of twenty-five, and become a part of the workforce in the service of the Meeting Tent.

25 When they are fifty years old they must retire from the active workforce. **26** After retirement they can assist the priests in the Meeting Tent, but they must not officiate in the divine service. This is how you shall designate the responsibilities.

---

16. From among the Israelites the Levites are given to serve Me in place of the first-born of all the Israelites.
The duties of the Levites are to carry the Tabernacle and the holy furniture and to sing the psalms in the sanctuary. *Rashi*

17–18. All the first-borns of the Israelites are Mine, man and beast alike. I sanctified them for myself on the day I killed all the first-borns in Egypt. Now I have chosen the Levites in place of all the first-born sons of the Israelites.
I protected them when the Egyptian first-borns were stricken, so they were Mine. They were Mine until they worshipped the golden calf. Now I have replaced them with the Levites. *Rashi*

24. These are the rules for the Levites. They must begin serving in the Tabernacle at the age of twenty-five, and become a part of the workforce in the service of the Meeting Tent.
At twenty-five he is to take his place in the formal structure of the holy community and be eligible for communal office. At thirty he may take part in litigation and in rendering judgments and may occupy a position on the staff of the militia.

Passover in the Wilderness

3rd Aliyah

9 Adonai spoke to Moses in the Wilderness of Sinai, in the second year of the Exodus from Egypt, in the first month [Nisan], saying: **2** Tell the Israelites to prepare the Passover offering at the proper time. **3** The proper time to celebrate Passover shall be the fourteenth day of this month [Nisan] in the evening. They must prepare the Passover offering in accordance with all its regulations and laws. **4** So Moses spoke to the Israelites and told them to prepare the Passover offering. **5** They prepared the Passover offering in the Wilderness of Sinai, on the fourteenth of the first month in the evening. The Israelites did everything exactly as Adonai had instructed Moses. **6** But there were some men who had come in contact with the dead, and they could not prepare the Passover offering on that day because they were ritually unclean. During the day, they came to Moses and Aaron. **7** The men said to Moses, "We are ritually unclean because we came into contact with the dead. Why should we lose out and not be able to present Adonai's offering at the appointed time, along with the other Israelites?" **8** Moses answered, "Wait until I ask and receive instructions from Adonai about your problem." **9** Adonai answered Moses and said: **10** Speak to the Israelites, saying: If any Israelite becomes ritually unclean because of contact with the dead, or is on a long trip, he may still celebrate Passover. **11** They too are to celebrate Passover on the evening of the fourteenth of the second month, and they shall eat the Passover offering with matzot and bitter herbs.

---

3. The proper time to celebrate Passover shall be the fourteenth day of this month (Nisan) in the evening.
A year had passed since the Israelites had escaped from the torment of Egypt. Now Adonai establishes Passover as a historical commemoration to be forever observed at a specific time.

4. So Moses spoke to the Israelites and told them to prepare the Passover offering.
This was the only Passover offering celebrated in the desert.
Passover is the most famous and festive of our holiday. It begins on the eve of the 15th day of the hebrew month of Nisan and lasts for eight days. On Passover we remember how Moses freed the Israelites who were slaves in Egypt. The holiday received its name from the hebrew word pasach. When all the firstborn sons of the Egyptians were killed in the tenth plague, the angel of death passed over (pasach) the homes of the Jews and their lives were saved. Passover is also called the Feast of Matzot, because the Jews left Egypt in such a hurry they did not have time to let the dough for bread rise. This bread was flat and hard. The flat unleavened bread is called matzah.

7. Why should we lose out and not be able to present Adonai's offering at the appointed time, along with the other Israelites?
The people complained to Moses and said, "We are ritually observant Israelites who have suffered an accidental loss through no fault of our own. Why should we not be able to participate in the Passover celebration?"

11. They too are to celebrate Passover on the evening of the fourteenth of the second month, and they shall eat the Passover offering with matzot and bitter herbs.
This is mitzvah number 380.
Moses consulted Adonai, who provided a second Passover for those who were unable to celebrate the festival at its appointed time.

11. They shall eat the Passover offering with matzot and bitter herbs.
Bitter herbs are called *maror*. Today at the seder the participants also eat matzah before the *maror*.
The sequence teaches that only after the Israelites tasted freedom did they feel and understand the bitterness and the deprecation of slavery. Only when people become free do they begin to understand the value of freedom.

12 They shall not leave over any of the offering until morning, and not break any bone in it. They shall prepare the offering according to all the Passover rules.

13 However, if a man is ritually clean, and not on a jour- ney, and he refuses to prepare the Passover offering, then that person shall be cut off from the community.
He shall suffer the consequences of his sin for not offering Adonai's sacrifice at the proper time.

14 Any foreigner who lives among you may also prepare Adonai's Passover offering and present it according to the regulations and laws of the Passover offering. The same law shall apply to you and the foreigner in your midst.

The Cloud and the Fiery Glow   *4th Aliyah*

15 On the day that the Tabernacle was erected, a cloud covered the Tabernacle and the Meeting Tent. Then, in the evening, a glow like a fire covered the Tabernacle, and remained there until morning. **16** From then on it was a regular occurrence. A cloud covered the Tabernacle by day, and a fiery glow covered it by night.

17 Whenever the cloud rose up above the Meeting Tent, the Israelites would set out on the march, and they would camp wherever the cloud settled.

18 In this way the Israelites moved forward at Adonai's command. They remained in one place as long as the cloud remained over the Tabernacle.

19 If the cloud remained over the Tabernacle for a long time, the Israelites kept their trust in Adonai and did not resume their journey.

20 Sometimes the cloud would settle on the Tabernacle for just a few days, and so they remained camped for only a few days. They would move on only at Adonai's command.

21 Sometimes the cloud remained only overnight, and in the morning, when the cloud lifted, they would journey on. By day or by night, whenever the cloud lifted, they would break camp and move on.

22 Whether the cloud remained at rest over the Tabernacle for two days or a month or a full year, no matter how long, the Israelites would remain and not move on. But as soon as the cloud lifted they resumed their journey.

---

17. Whenever the cloud rose up above the Meeting Tent, the Israelites would set out on the march, and they would camp wherever the cloud settled.
The Israelites placed their complete trust in Adonai. They camped in the exact place the cloud settled even if the spot was a wilderness.

17. Whenever the cloud rose up above the Meeting Tent, the Israelites would set out on the march, and they would camp wherever the cloud settled.
Whenever the Israelites were told by Adonai to move, the cloud would lift and shift to cover the tribe of Judah. Then shofars would sound three *tekiah* notes; at that moment Moses said, "Rise up O' Adonai…" then the banners of the tribe of Judah were raised and the march would begin.
Sifri

20. Sometimes the cloud would settle on the Tabernacle for just a few days, and so they remained camped for only a few days.
At times the cloud rested on a green oasis with fresh water for themselves and their cattle and the cloud rested for just a few days. Then when the cloud lifted, the Israelites without hesitation packed their belongings and continued their journey.

23 They placed their trust in Adonai and moved at Adonai's command. The Israelites obeyed Adonai's commands as delivered through Moses.

10

Adonai spoke to Moses, saying:
2 Make two silver bugles. Hammer them out of silver, and blow the bugles to assemble the community and to break camp.
3 When both of the bugles are blown with a long blast, the entire community shall assemble at the entrance of the Meeting Tent.
4 But if only one long blast is sounded on just one of the bugles, then the leaders of tribes shall assemble to meet with you.
5 When you blow a series of short blasts, the camps to the east of the Tabernacle shall begin the march.
6 And when you sound a second series of short notes, the camps to the south of the Tabernacle shall begin the march, following the other tribes.
When the Israelites are to move on, you are to signal with a series of short bugle notes.
7 When the whole community is to be assembled, the bugles shall be blown with a long note. **8** Aaron's descendants, the priests, shall be the ones to blow the bugles. This shall be a permanent law to be followed in every generation.
9 When you go to war in your land against an enemy who attacks you, you shall blow a long blast on the bugles.
Then Adonai will come to your aid, and you will defeat your enemies.

---

5. When you blow a series of short blasts (*t'kiot*), the camps to the east of the Tabernacle shall begin the march.
The camp to the east consisted of the tribes of Judah, Issacher, and Zebulun.

6. And when you sound a second series of short notes, the camp to the south of the Tabernacle shall begin to march.
The bugler blew two kinds of notes. The *tekiah* was a simple straight sound. The second note was the *teruah*, the alarm note.

When the camp was ready to march, both the *tekiah* and the *teruah* were sounded.

6. And when you sound a second series of short notes, the camps to the south of the Tabernacle shall begin the march, following the other tribes.
The Gershonites and Merarites, who carried the board, curtains, etc. of the sanctuary traveled with this group. The Gershonites camped in the west, and the Merarites in the north. The tribes to the south consisted of Reuben, Simeon, and Gad. The Kehothites, who carried the holy vessels and furnishings, traveled with this group.

7. When the whole community is to be assembled, the bugles shall be blown with a long note.
The eastern and western camps did not merit a special shorter blast since they did not have any part of the sanctuary in their midst.

9. When you go to war in your land against an enemy who attacks you, you shall blow a long blast on the bugles.
Bugles, which were made of hammered silver, served for various purposes in war and in peace. In peacetime they were used to summon communities for special meetings.

Bugles were used in orchestras for joyous ceremonial occasions, for festivals and for new moon celebrations. In wartime, bugles were used to summon the soldiers from the countryside and were essential for signaling. Their sharp penetrating notes could travel far and could clearly be heard over the noise of battle.

10 During your times of rejoicing, your festivals and your new moon celebrations, you shall sound the bugles for your burnt offerings and your peace offerings. The sounds will remind you of Adonai. I am Adonai. I will surely remember you.

From Sinai to Paran
5th Aliyah

11 In the second year of the Exodus, on the twentieth of the second month [Iyar], the cloud lifted from the Tabernacle. **12** So the Israelites resumed their journey, departing from the Wilderness of Sinai, until the cloud stopped in the Wilderness of Paran. **13** This was the first time that Adonai told Moses to order the Israelites to move forward.
14 The tribes under the marching banner of Judah set out first, led by Nachshon son of Aminadav. **15** Nethanel son of Zuar headed the tribe of Issachar, **16** Eliav son of Helon headed the tribe of Zebulun. **17** The Tabernacle was taken down, and the descendants of Gershon and Merari from the tribe of Levi, who carried the Tabernacle, began the march.
18 The tribes under the marching banner of Reuben then began to march, under the leadership of Elitzur son of Shedeur.
19 Shelumiel son of Zurishaddai headed the tribe of Simeon.
20 Eliassaf son of Deuel headed the tribe of Gad.
21 The Kehothites from the tribe of Levi, who carried the sacred furniture, then began their march. The Tabernacle would already be set up when they arrived at the new destination.

---

10 During your times of rejoicing, your festivals and your new moon celebrations, you shall sound the bugles for your burnt offerings and your peace offering.
The festivals included Sukkot, Passover, Shavuot, Rosh Hashanah, and Yom Kippur. These festivals were celebrated by special sacrifices.

11. In the second year of the Exodus, on the twentieth of the second month (Iyar) the cloud lifted from the Tabernacle.
The journey toward Canaan began ten months and ten days after they arrived at Mount Sinai. The cloud acted as their guide as they journeyed to the Wilderness of Paran.

12. So the Israelites resumed their journey, departing from the Wilderness of Sinai, until the cloud stopped in the Wilderness of Paran.
Paran is located in the Sinai Peninsula and was the area in which Ishmael lived. Later on, twelve spies left from the Wilderness of Paran to search the land of Canaan and then returned to it with their report.

13. This was the first time that Adonai told Moses to order the Israelites to move forward.
The cloud lifted but Moses had to give the command to continue the journey. Adonai wanted the Israelites to respect and obey Moses, so Adonai purposely gave Moses the final decision. *Shenash*

17. The Tabernacle was taken down, and the descendants of Gershon and Merari from the tribe of Levi, who carried the Tabernacle, began the march.
The Tabernacle was dismantled by the Gershonites, and the Merarites packed the boards, fabrics, curtains, etc. upon six wagons. When they came to their new encampment, the Kehothites would find the Tabernacle already assembled.

The task of the Kehothites was to carry the packed sacred objects on their shoulders and bring them into the assembled Tabernacle.

21. The Kehothites from the tribe of Levi, who carried the sacred furniture, then began their march. The Tabernacle would be set up when they arrived at the new destination.
The Kehothites, who were the carriers, would deposit their burdens in their appointed places in the Tabernacle.

22 The tribes under the marching banner of Ephraim then began the march, under the leadership of Elishama son of Amihud.
23 Gamliel son of Pedahzur headed the tribe of Manasseh, **24** and Avidan son of Gidoni headed the tribe of Benjamin.
25 Then the tribes under the marching banner of Dan, the last of the camps, began their march, under the leadership of Achiezer son of Amishaddai.
26 Pagiel son of Okhran headed the tribe of Asher, **27** and Achira son of Eynan headed the tribe of Naphtali.
28 This was the marching order of the Israelites, in which the tribes marched group by group and banner by banner when they began to travel.
29 Moses said to his father-in-law, Hovev son of Reuel the Midianite, "We are now on our way to the land that Adonai promised to give us. Come with us and share the benefit of all the good things that Adonai has promised Israel."
30 Hovev replied, "No, I would rather not go. I wish to return to my land and my birthplace."
31 Moses said, "Please do not leave us. You can be our guide, because you know the good camping places in the desert.
32 If you come with us, we will share with you whatever good Adonai grants us."
33 The Israelites began their journey from Mount Sinai. They marched for three days, and the ark traveled three days ahead of them to scout out a suitable place to camp.
34 As they began the march, Adonai's cloud was continually with them.

Adonai, Stay with Us *6th Aliyah*

35 When the ark traveled, Moses would say,
"Adonai, rise up, and scatter your enemies!
Let your foes flee before You!"
36 When the ark came to rest, Moses would say,
"O Adonai, stay with us;
remain with the people of Israel."

---

25. Then the tribes under the marching banner of Dan, the last of the camps, began their march, under the leadership of Achiezer.
The job of the tribe of Dan was to collect the stragglers and find lost children and return them to their parents. In addition, they acted as a lost and found group and retrieved items accidentally lost during the march.

30. Hovev replied, "No, I would rather not go. I wish to return to my land and my birthplace."
Hovev pleaded, I am an old man, and I wish to return to my homeland.

Sforno

31. Moses said, "Please do not leave us. You can be our guide, because you know the good camping places in the desert."
Moses complimented Hovev and let him know that he was important and was needed because of his special skills. Compliments are appreciated and can often build special relationships.

33. They marched for three days, and the ark traveled three days ahead of them to scout out a suitable place to camp.
There are very few oases in the Wilderness of Sinai, and only experienced desert travelers could find the locations. So Moses asked his father-in-law, Hovev, to be their guide because he knew the good camping places in the desert.

11 The Israelites began to complain. When Adonai heard them, He became angry, and a fire from Adonai blazed out and destroyed those at the edge of the camp. **2** The people begged Moses to save them, so Moses prayed to Adonai and the fire died down. **3** They named the place Taberah (Burning), because Adonai's fire had burned them.

4 Now the foreign rabble among the Israelites became homesick and had a strong yearning for the food of Egypt. The Israelites again began to complain, saying, "We are hungry for meat. **5** We remember the delicious fish and the cucumbers, melons, leeks, onions, and garlic that we ate in Egypt. **6** But now our appetites are gone, and day after day all we get is manna for breakfast, lunch, and supper." **7** The manna was shiny yellow in color and looked like coriander seed. **8** The people just gathered it up from the ground and ground it or crushed it into flour and cooked it in a pan or baked it into flat cakes. It tasted like a pancake fried in oil. **9** At night, manna would fall on the camp like dew.

10 Moses heard the people and their families complaining near the entrances of their tents. Adonai became very angry, and Moses was also upset. **11** Moses asked Adonai, "Why are You testing me so strongly, and why are You treating me like this? Why did You place so heavy a burden upon me? **12** The Israelites are not my children. I did not give birth to them. You made them a promise, and You told me that I would have to nurse them in my bosom, just as a nurse carries a newborn baby, until we conquer the land that You promised their ancestors. **13** Where in the middle of this forsaken wilderness can I find enough meat to feed all these people? They are always complaining and asking me to give them some meat to eat. **14** I cannot be responsible for this entire nation of whining cry-babies all by myself.

---

1. The Israelites began to complain. When Adonai heard them, He became angry, and a fire from Adonai blazed out and destroyed those at the edge of the camp.
Marching through the hot desert sand without rest and a scarcity of water made the Israelites a discontented people. After they received the Ten Commandments at Mount Sinai and built the sanctuary, the Israelites once again complained about their living conditions. They had completely forgotten the pain of slavery and their thoughts turned to the food in Egypt. Adonai was upset at the heat of the Israelite complaints, so he punished them with fire. The frightened people begged Moses to save them. Moses then prayed to Adonai and the fire died down.

4. Now the foreign rabble among the Israelites became homesick and had a strong yearning for the food of Egypt.
When the Israelites left Egypt, some of the other slaves joined the Exodus. These ex-slaves had no religious commitment and no political future. They were interested primarily in a more comfortable life.

4. The Israelites again began to complain, saying, "We are hungry for meat."
It was not true that the Israelites did not have meat to eat. We are told in other parts of the text that they had flocks of birds and herds of cattle. The truth was that the rebels were just looking for an excuse to complain.

5. We remember the delicious fish and the cucumbers, melons, leeks, onions, and garlic that we ate in Egypt.
The Nile was the lifeblood of Egypt. It provided water for farmers and lots of fresh fish.

8. The people just gathered it up from the ground and ground it or crushed it into flour.
In Bible times there were two methods of converting grain into flour. The grain was milled by being ground between two millstones until it became a fine powder. The grain could also be pounded into flour with a mortar and pestle.

15 It would be much better if You did me a favor and just killed me! I just don't have the strength to carry this great responsibility."

16 Adonai said to Moses, "Gather seventy of Israel's elders and leaders. Bring them to the Meeting Tent, and I will meet you there. **17** I will come down and speak to you there. I will take some of the spirit that is in you and put it in them. Then you will not have to bear the responsibility all by yourself.

18 By the way, tell the people to be prepared, because tomorrow they will have meat to eat. Say to them, 'You have been whining in Adonai's ears, saying,

"Who will give us some meat to eat? Life in Egypt was much better for us." Now Adonai is going to send you meat, and you will have to eat it. **19** You will eat it not just for one day, not just for two days, not just for five days, not just for ten days, and not just for twenty days. **20** You will eat meat until it is coming out of your nose and you are sick of it.'

I will do this because you have lost faith in Adonai, because even though He is right here among you, you continually ask, 'Why did we ever leave Egypt?'"

21 Moses said, "Here I am alone among 600,000 men, and You promise to give them enough meat to eat for a full month! **22** Even if we butchered all of our cattle and sheep, there could never be enough meat for all of them. Even if all the fish in the sea were caught, it still would not be enough for them."

23 Adonai said to Moses, "Is there any limit to My power? Now you will see whether My power is limited."

24 Moses went out of the Tabernacle and told the people what Adonai had said. He assembled seventy of the elders and stationed them around the Meeting Tent.

---

16. Adonai said to Moses, "Gather seventy of Israel's elders and leaders. Bring them to the Meeting Tent, and I will meet you there."
Adonai was preparing the Israelites for the change of the leadership. Moses had grown old and tired and it was time to spread the responsibility among all the tribal leaders.

17. I will come down and speak to you there. I will take some of the spirit that is in you and put it in them. Then you will not have to bear the responsibility all by yourself.
Adonai promises to endow the elders with some of your prophetic power. The elders and leaders of the tribes were trusted by the Israelites. Now your decisions will be approved by the elders and leaders and the people will follow the decisions without hesitation.

23. Adonai said to Moses, "Is there any limit to My power. Now you will see whether My power is limited."
Adonai assures Moses that the Israelites will overeat to the point that many will become sick and die. Adonai sent a strong wind which brought so many quail that they were piled all around the camp.

24–25. He assembled seventy of the elders and stationed them around the Meeting Tent. Adonai descended in a cloud and spoke to Moses. He took some of the spirit (responsibility) from Moses and placed it upon the seventy elders. When the spirit rested on them, they gained the gift of prophecy.
Adonai said: "Choose seventy elders who enjoy the confidence and respect of the people and install them as a cabinet. They will assist you in governing the people. I will give the elders special powers and authority to teach and instruct the people. However they will not have the power in the future."

24. He assembled seventy of the elders.
There were supposed to be seventy-two elders, six from each of the twelve tribes.

25 Adonai descended in a cloud and spoke to Moses. He took some of the spirit (responsibility) from Moses and placed it upon the seventy elders. When the spirit rested on them, they gained the gift of prophecy.
26 Two of the seventy elders, Eldad and Medad, remained in the camp, and the spirit also rested on them. Although they were among the seventy elders, they had not gone to the Meeting Tent, yet the spirit rested on them and they prophesied in the camp. **27** A young man ran to tell Moses, "Eldad and Medad are prophesying in the camp!" **28** Joshua son of Nun, the assistant of Moses, protested, "My lord Moses, make them stop!"
29 Moses replied, "Are you jealous for my sake? I wish that all of Adonai's people were holy enough to have the gift of prophecy! Let Adonai grant His spirit to everyone who deserves it."

The Hail of Quail *7th Aliyah*

30 Then Moses along with the elders of Israel returned to the camp.
31 Adonai sent a strong wind, and it started to blow and swept the quail up from the sea. They ran out of strength over the camp, and the quail were scattered in piles three feet deep throughout the camp and for miles in every direction. **32** All that day, all night, and the entire next day the people gathered quail. Even the slowest person gathered ten chomer (60 bushels). The people spread them out to dry in the sun around the camp.
33 While still eating the meat, the people began to die because they ate too much. Adonai was angry at the Israelites, and He struck them with a plague.
34 Moses named the place Kivroth HaTaavah (Graves of Craving) because it was there that they buried the people who had greedy cravings for meat and died from overeating.
35 From Kivroth HaTaavah, the people traveled to Hatzeroth.

---

26. Two of the seventy elders, Eldad and Medad, remained in the camp, and the spirit also rested on them.
Initially there were supposed to be 72 elders, six from each tribe. However, these two elders arrogantly decided not to present themselves to Moses at the Meeting Tent. Eldad and Medad were testing to see whether the spirit could rest upon them without the presence of Moses. In the spirit of *shalom bayit*, peace in the family, they were also inspired with Adonai's spirit.

28. Joshua son of Nun, the assistant of Moses, protested, "My lord Moses, make them stop."
Joshua felt that Eldad and Medad had insulted and denied the leadership of Moses. Rashi interprets "Make them stop" to mean destroy them.
Joshua was concerned that Eldad and Medad were spreading dissension among the Israelites. He was worried that the two pseudeo-prophets would reduce the authority of Moses and could split the nation into two separate camps.

31. Adonai sent a strong wind, and it started to blow and swept the quail up from the sea.
Sforno says that the quail were blown in from the Red Sea.

33. While still eating the meat, the people began to die because they ate too much.
Quail are considered a delicacy, but the meat contained disease-carrying germs which, when too much of it is eaten, can cause severe illness.
    In addition to the manna, the Israelites supplemented their diet probably with wild dates, meat, and milk from their flocks and from permitted animals such as gazelles, chickens, and antelope. The forty years of wandering in the desert helped to toughen the new generation for the struggles which lay ahead.

12 Miriam and Aaron began to criticize Moses because he had married a Cushite woman, a dark-skinned woman. **2** They complained, "Adonai speaks only to Moses. Why doesn't he speak to us?" But Adonai heard it.
3 However, Moses was very humble. He was more humble than any man on the face of the earth.
4 Suddenly Adonai ordered Moses, Aaron, and Miriam, "All three of you, come to the Meeting Tent!" When the three of them got there, **5** Adonai descended in a pillar of cloud and stood at the entrance of the Meeting Tent. He called Aaron and Miriam, and they both stepped forward.
6 Adonai said, "Listen carefully to My words. With anyone else who experiences divine prophecy, I make Myself known to him in a vision, and speak to him in a dream. **7** But with My trusted servant Moses, **8** I speak to him face-to-face, and not in riddles. You have no reason to criticize My servant Moses."

---

1. Miriam and Aaron began to criticize Moses because he had married a Cushite woman, a dark-skinned woman.
Aaron and his sister Miriam criticized Moses' marriage to a Cushite woman. Some commentators believe that the real basis of their protest seems to have been their resentment at his authority and his unique position as Adonai's spokesman.

Both Miriam and Aaron argued that they too wished to receive divine revelations. They complained (v. 2), "Adonai speaks only to Moses. Why doesn't he speak to us?"

Adonai heard their complaints, (12:5) so He appeared in a cloud and expressed his confidence in Moses.

As punishment (12:10), Miriam was stricken with leprosy. She was pardoned when Aaron and Moses interceded on her behalf with Adonai.

1. Miriam and Aaron began to criticize Moses because he had married a Cushite woman, a dark-skinned woman.
Others believe Aaron and Miriam did not like having a black woman marry into the family. Adonai's reaction was swift and unequivocal: Miriam had offended a woman because she was black, so Adonai punished her and made her as white as snow. Had Moses not interfered on her behalf, Adonai's anger would have resulted in further enduring punishment.

2. They complained, "Adonai speaks only to Moses. Why doesn't he speak to us?"
Both Aaron and Miriam were jealous because Adonai spoke only to Moses and excluded them. Sometimes the dreams of power overwhelm normal family relationships. Miriam and Aaron felt that they as brother and sister of Moses should have been included in the special relationship with Adonai.

4. Suddenly Adonai ordered Moses, Aaron, and Miriam, "All three of you, come to the Meeting Tent."
Like a concerned parent, Adonai called His children into the Meeting Tent and laid down the law. He said, "Moses is the leader that I have personally chosen. You two, Aaron and Miriam, are my beloved children. But Moses is my chosen one. You have no reason to criticize him. That is the law."
Shenash

8. I speak to him face-to-face, and not in riddles.
Moses our teacher was the greatest of them all. The difference between the prophecy of Moses and that of the others was that the others prophesied by means of dreams and visions but Moses prophesied when he was awake and standing up, as was said: "Whenever Moses went into the Meeting Tent to speak with Adonai, he heard the Voice speaking to him" (Bamidbar 7:89). All the others received it from a messenger in the form of a parable or allegory.
Maimonides

9 Adonai was angry at them and left.
10 Suddenly the cloud over the Meeting Tent lifted. Miriam became leprous, and as white as snow. When Aaron saw what had happened to Miriam, **11** he said to Moses, "My lord, please do not punish us for acting foolishly and sinning. **12** Do not let your sister Miriam be like a stillborn child, born with its flesh rotting away."
13 Moses prayed to Adonai, "O Adonai, please heal her!"

Miriam Is Cured *Maftir*

14 Adonai answered Moses, "Wouldn't Miriam be disgraced for seven days if her father had punished her by spitting in her face? So I will punish her by banishing her for seven days outside the camp, and then I will let her return home."
15 Miriam remained outside the camp for seven days, and the people did not move on until Miriam was cured and returned home. **16** Then the Israelites left Hatzeroth, and they made their camp in the Wilderness of Paran.

---

10. Miriam became leprous, and as white as snow.
One should not mistake the disease known in the Torah as *tza-ra-at*, which afflicts Miriam here and others later, with the modern disease known as leprosy, even though they have the same name and are similar in some respects. First, leprosy is almost incurable. Second, one of its most horrible and obvious symptoms, the withering away of the part of the body afflicted, is never mentioned in the Torah. Third, it takes a long times to develop. Most important, however, leprosy is not contagious. It cannot be "caught."

We must conclude therefore that when people such as Miriam were afflicted with *tza-ra-at* and sent out of the camp, it was not leprosy as we know it today. It is also possible, of course, that the reason "lepers" such as Miriam were quarantined was that it was believed that their sinfulness was catching, for most often when this disease is mentioned in the Torah, it is seen as a punishment from Adonai. *Shenash*

13. Moses prayed to Adonai, "O Adonai, please heal her!"
Notice that Moses does not mention the name of Miriam.

The Talmud (Ber.34a) concludes that it is not required to mention a person's name when offering a prayer on behalf of an individual.

A sage noted, "Words need thought but thought has no need of speech."

13. Please heal her.
I do not want to shame my sister by sending her, like a common leper, outside the camp.

15. Miriam remained outside the camp for seven days, and the people did not move on until Miriam was cured and returned home.
The cloud had lifted (v.10), which meant that the camp was to be moved, but the people did not move. Out of their love and respect for Miriam they remained for seven days. The moment Miriam returned, the Israelites packed and moved to the Wilderness of Paran.

16. Then the Israelites left Hatzeroth, and they made their camp in the Wilderness of Paran.
Hatzeroth was a camping ground on Israel's journey in the wilderness, 40 miles from Mount Sinai near the gulf of Aqaba. The Israelites stayed there after the plague at Kibroth HaTaavah (Bamidbar 11:35). Miriam and Aaron also made their rebellion against Moses (Bamidbar 12) in Hatzeroth.

שְׁלַח־לְךָ *Shelach Lecha*

SEND SCOUTS TO CANAAN

13 Adonai instructed Moses and said, **2** "Send out scouts as spies to explore the Canaanite territory that I am about to give the Israelites. Choose one scout from each tribe. Make sure that each scout is a leader of his tribe." **3** At Adonai's command, Moses sent them from the Wilderness of Paran. All the men were leaders of the tribes. **4** Their names were as follows:

From the tribe of Reuben, Shamua son of Zakur.
5 From the tribe of Simeon, Shaphat son of Chori.
6 From the tribe of Judah, Caleb son of Yefuneh.
7 From the tribe of Issachar, Yig'al son of Joseph.
8 From the tribe of Ephraim, Hoshea son of Nun.
9 From the tribe of Benjamin, Palti son of Raphu.
10 From the tribe of Zebulun, Gadiel son of Sodi.
11 From the tribe of Manasseh from Joseph, Gaddi son of Susi.
12 From the tribe of Dan, Amiel son of Gemalli.
13 From the tribe of Asher, Sethur son of Michael.
14 From the tribe of Naphtali, Nachbi son of Vafsi.
15 From the tribe of Gad, Geuel son of Makhi.
16 These are the names of the men Moses sent to explore the land. However, Moses gave Hoshea son of Nun a new name, Joshua.
17 When Moses sent the scouts to explore the Canaanite territory, he said to them, "Head north to the Negev, and then continue to the hill country. **18** See what kind of land it is. Are the people who live there strong or weak, few or many?
19 Is the inhabited area good or bad? Are the cities where they live open or fortified?

---

2. Send out scouts as spies to explore the Canaanite territory.
The Rabbis tell us that Adonai did not suggest sending an expedition to observe the land. It was the people who kept asking Moses to allow them to send an expedition to go first, for they were not fully convinced that it was a good land. So Adonai, in speaking to Moses, says, "If you wish, send out scouts"; I am not commanding you to do so."

19. Is the inhabited area good or bad?
Are the cities where they live open or fortified?
   Apart from military intelligence, the spies were instructed to collect information about the nature and economic resources of Canaan.
   The various parts of the country differ in economic importance. The coastal plain has abundant water resources and fertile soils; the hills of the lowlands are well suited for vineyards and olive groves. The central mountains were covered by forests in antiquity, and some of the wide valleys intersecting them from east to west are among the most fertile parts of the country. Against this "rich land" there is the "poor": the Negev, the Judean desert, and parts of the Jordan valley. The spies, who traveled along the mountains, saw before their eyes the typical landscape of Canaan: on the one hand, fields of corn, orchards, and woods; and on the other – east of the water-shed – barren gray hills, dry and desolate, the few green spots between them only serving to emphasize their desert character.

20 Is the soil rich or weak? Does the land have trees or not? Make a special effort to bring back samples of the fruits."

It was the season when the first grapes were beginning to ripen.

The Cluster of Grapes *2nd Aliyah*

21 The scouts headed north and explored the land, from the Wilderness of Zin all the way to Rechov on the road to Hamath. **22** On the way they passed through the Negev, until they came to Hebron. There they saw the Achiman, Sheshai, and Talmi, descendants of the Anakim (giants). Hebron was founded seven years before the Egyptian city of Zoan. **23** When they came to Nahal Eshkol (Cluster Valley), they cut a branch with a cluster of grapes. It was so large that it needed two men to carry it on a pole. They also took some pomegranates and figs. **24** Because of the grape-cluster that the Israelites cut there, the place was named Cluster Valley. **25** At the end of forty days they came back from exploring the land. **26** When they arrived, they went directly to Moses, Aaron, and the entire Israelite community, who were waiting for them in the Wilderness of the Paran near Kadesh. They brought their report to Moses, Aaron, and the entire community, and showed them fruit from the land. **27** They gave the following report: "We went to the land where you sent us, and as you can see from its fruit, it is really flowing with milk and honey. **28** However, the people living in the land are powerful, and the cities are large and well fortified. We also saw the descendants of the Anakim (giants). **29** Amalek lives in the Negev; the Hittites, Jebusites, and Amorites live in the hills; and the Canaanites live near the Mediterranean Sea and on the banks of the Jordan."

---

20. Make a special effort to bring back samples of the fruits.
Moses knew that specimens of the fruit would show the people how fertile the country was. It took courage, however, to obtain the fruit without arousing the suspicion of the inhabitants.

22. Hebron was founded seven years before the Egyptian city of Zoan.
The founding of Zoan served as the starting point of an era. Rameses II built his capital at Zoan and renamed it "The House of Rameses." The pharaoh then set up a monument to commemorate the four hundredth anniversary of the rule of the Egyptian god Seth.

This quote tells that Zoan and Hebron were founded at the end of the eighteenth century B.C.E.

26. When they arrived, they went directly to Moses, Aaron, and the entire Israelite community, who were waiting for them in the Wilderness of Paran near Kadesh.
Kadesh means holy and was an area with a good water supply where the Israelites had established a temporary station. It was located about fifty miles south of Hebron in the Sinai Peninsula.

26. Wilderness of Paran near Kadesh.
Today the quantity of water produced by the Kadesh springs is small, but the springs in an adjacent oasis yield about fifty times as much water. There can be no doubt that the Israelites' prolonged sojourn in Kadesh was made possible by its water and its good soil. Moses' purpose for the long stay, however, was to wait for the next generation to come of age, the young people who knew neither slavery nor the pleasures of the villages and towns of the Nile Delta. Here, under the cloudless skies of Kadesh Barnea, the Jewish nation was born.

30 Caleb tried to encourage the people. Caleb said "We must advance and occupy the land. We can do it!"
31 The other scouts disagreed with Caleb. "We cannot conquer them! They are much too powerful for us!" **32** Then they began to spread discouraging reports about the land they had explored. They told the Israelites, "The land we scouted is a land that will defeat invaders. All the men we saw there were huge!
33 While we were there, we saw Anakim (giants). Compared with them we looked and felt like tiny grasshoppers!"

14

That night, after the report of the scouts, the entire community began to shout and cry. **2** The Israelites complained to Moses and Aaron. The entire community grumbled, "It would have been better if we had died in Egypt or in this desert! **3** Did Adonai bring us to this land so that we, our wives, and our children could die by the sword or spend our lives as slaves? It would be best for us to return to Egypt!"
4 The people began to plot among themselves. "Let's choose a new leader and return to Egypt."
5 Moses and Aaron bowed down and prayed before the assembled Israelite community.
6 Two of the scouts, Joshua son of Nun and Caleb son of Yefuneh, tore their clothes in shame. **7** They said to the whole Israelite community, "The land that we explored is a very good and fertile land!

The Israelites Rebel   *3rd Aliyah*

8 "If Adonai is pleased with us, He will bring us to this land flowing with milk and honey. **9** Only don't rebel against Adonai!
Don't be afraid of the people in the land! Because they have lost their protection and Adonai is on our side."

---

30. Caleb tried to encourage the people. Caleb said, "We must advance and occupy the land." Caleb was able to silence them because they were under the impression that he was going to berate Moses, but once he gained their attention, he reminded them of all of Moses' accomplishments.

32. Then they began to spread discouraging reports about the land.
The spies' tactics had been to present facts about the Holy Land which, though true, were calculated to discourage the people. However, since Caleb had made an impression on many of the Israelites, they were encouraged to go on. Now the other ten spies began to spread false information.

33. While we were there, we saw Anakim (giants). Compared to them we looked and felt like tiny grasshoppers!
The Israelites were desert dwellers. Walled cities were amazing structures. Warriors dressed in armor, perhaps mounted on horses or camels, looked like giants to the spies. Looking up at the guards on the towers magnified the size of the soldiers.

2. It would have been better if we had died in Egypt or in this desert!
The spies returned from their scouting mission to Canaan and publicly announced that the land was filled with giants and was unconquerable. Spies are sent to gather intelligence and report their observations quietly to their commanders; then he and his experts combine their reports with other data and reach a conclusion based on a variety of facts. The exaggerated reports of the spies panicked the Israelites.

9. Because they have lost their protection and Adonai is on our side.
Don't be afraid of the enemy. They are doomed, because Adonai is on our side.

10 The rebellious mob threatened to stone Moses and Aaron to death. Suddenly Adonai appeared in a cloud over the Meeting Tent.
11 Adonai said to Moses, "How long will this people continue to anger Me? How long will they refuse to believe in Me despite all the miracles that I have done for them? **12** I will kill them with a plague. Then I will make you and your descen- dants into a greater, more powerful nation."
13 Moses replied to Adonai, "Just imagine what the Egyptians would think when they hear about it. Remember that with Your great power You rescued this nation from out of Egypt.
14 Just imagine what they will tell the people who live in this land. They are aware that You, Adonai, have been with this nation Israel. They know that You, Adonai, have revealed Yourself to them face-to-face, and that Your cloud leads them. You lead them in a pillar of cloud by day, and a pillar of fire at night.
15 And now you want to slaughter this entire nation! The nations that have heard about You will say that **16** Adonai is weak and unable to lead this nation into the land that He swore to give them, and so He just killed them in the desert.
17 Now, O Adonai, prove to the world that Your power is great and exercise restraint. You once said,
18 'Adonai is slow to anger, rich in love, and forgiving of sin and rebellion. But He does not forgive those who do not repent. He does not leave the guilty unpunished, He punishes the children for the sins of their parents to the third and fourth generation.' **19** Please, with Your great love, forgive the sins of this nation, just as You have forgiven them from the time they left Egypt until now."
20 Adonai answered, "I will pardon them as you have requested. **21** But as surely as I live, and as surely as My glory fills all the world, **22** I will punish all the people who have witnessed My glory and the miracles I performed in Egypt and the wilderness but who still test Me and refuse to obey Me.

---

17. Now, O Adonai, prove to the world that Your power is great and exercise restraint.
Adonai, should you decide to destroy this nation, then the nations of the world would conclude that You were unable to fulfill your promises, and that is why You destroyed them in the desert.

18. He punishes the children for the sins of their parents to the third and fourth generation.
The mishnah of Rabbi Eliezer explains that Adonai suspends judgment for four generations in the hope that someone in these generations will become righteous and thus suspend the punishment. The Rambam explains that if the sin of the parents cannot be completely erased, then let the punishment be eased bit by bit over four generations.

19. Please, with Your great love, forgive the sins of this nation, just as You have forgiven them from the time they left Egypt until now.
Moses was the first biblical leader to assert the crucial importance of forgiveness in Adonai's relationship with man. The doctrine that emerged out of the dialogue between Adonai and Moses established the principle that forgiveness is a conditional privilege which only those who are worthy of divine compassion may expect. Shemot 34:6 says, "I am Adonai, Adonai, merciful and kind, am I." In order to deserve forgiveness, a wrongdoer must admit wrongdoing and express penitence.

23 They will never see the land that I swore to give to their ancestors. None of those who doubted Me will ever enter the land.
24 Only my servant Caleb will enter the land, because he was loyal and showed a different spirit and followed Me wholeheartedly. I will bring him into the land that he explored, and his descendants will receive their share. **25** Beware the Amalekites and the Canaanites who are living in the valley. Tomorrow leave the place and march into the desert toward the Sea of Reeds."

You Will Wander for Forty Years
4th Aliyah

26 Adonai spoke to Moses and Aaron, saying, **27** "How long will you allow this evil mob to exist, and to complain against Me? I have heard the complaints of the Israelites about Me. **28** Tell them as follows: 'As surely as I live, I will do to them the things that they accuse Me of doing. **29** Because they complained about Me, they will all die in this desert.
Everyone over twenty years old who was counted will die **30** and will not enter the land which I swore to give to you. The only two exceptions will be Caleb son of Yefuneh and Joshua son of Nun.
31 The rebels predicted that their children would be taken captive; their children are the ones who will enjoy the land that they rejected.
32 Your bodies will rot in the desert. **33** Your children will wander from place to place in the desert for forty years, and suffer for your lack of faith until the last of your corpses drop here in the desert. **34** Your punishment of forty years will equal the number of days the scouts spent exploring the land. I will punish you for forty years, one year for each day, a total of forty years until your sin is forgiven. You will discover that I am very angry.
35 I, Adonai, have spoken! I will do this only to every member of the community that complained against Me.
They will end their lives in this desert, and here is where they will die.'"

---

23. They will never see the land that I swore to give to their ancestors.
It was not only the anger of Adonai that caused Him to send Israel into the desert for forty years. It was His concern that the land be developed by a strong and capable people.

Adonai had offered the land of milk and honey as a reward to the people who had come out of Egypt. However, they were not able to see that Adonai would help them to achieve it if they persevered and had faith in Him. They did not possess an important quality of a pioneer people – a strong, dedicated people worthy of the land of Israel.

The Israelites of the next generation, led by Joshua and Caleb, were able to achieve it. The Israelis of today have demonstrated the same hope, faith, and courage that is needed to develop Israel.

29–30. Everyone over twenty years old who was counted will die and will not enter the land I swore to give to you.
The people had sinned repeatedly and had doubted that Adonai would bring them safely into the possession of the Promised Land. Their punishment was forty years of wandering in the desert so that none but Joshua and Caleb might survive to reach Canaan. It was only the older generation that was doomed, and Adonai would fulfill His promise to Israel through their children and grandchildren. While this was a very severe punishment, the people as a nation could go on, for though they sinned, they had raised their children according to Moses' teaching. While the older generation may not receive the rewards, Jews have always been able to look forward to their children benefiting from them.

36 The scouts whom Moses had sent to explore the land, and who had circulated false rumors about the land, **37** who had brought discouraging reports about the land, died in a plague. **38** Among the twelve scouts who explored the land only Joshua son of Nun and Caleb son of Yefuneh remained alive.
39 When Moses reported Adonai's decision to the Israelites, there was great sorrow.
40 They got up early in the morning, and began to march toward Canaan, saying, "Now we are ready!
We are ready to enter the land that Adonai has promised us. We know now that we were wrong."
41 Moses said, "Once again you are disobeying Adonai. **42** Do not go forward. Adonai is not with you. You will be defeated by your enemies!
43 The Amalekites and Canaanites will attack you, and you will fall by their swords. You have disregarded Adonai, and He will not be with you."
44 But the people refused to listen and climbed toward the hill country of Canaan. The ark of Adonai's covenant and Moses remained in the camp.
45 The Amalekites and Canaanites who lived in the hills ambushed the Israelites, and routed them, and chased them all the way back to Hormah.

15 Adonai spoke to Moses, and instructed him to **2** speak to the Israelites and say to them: When you finally come to your homeland that I am giving you, **3** you will wish to present fire offerings to please Adonai.
They may be burnt offerings for a vow or a free-will offering for your festivals. The sacrifices must be taken from the cattle or sheep or goats as a thank you gift to Adonai.

---

40. We are ready to enter the land that Adonai has promised us. We know now that we were wrong.
The Israelites were sorry for their rebellious nature and for their belief in the negative reports of the ten scouts and their desire to return to Egypt.

42. Do not go forward. Adonai is not with you. You will be defeated by your enemies!
Adonai was very angry at the Israelites for their constant complaints and their desire to return to Egypt. Adonai declared that everyone over twenty years old would die in the desert except for Joshua and Caleb.

Some of the more militant Israelites organized an expedition to penetrate the hill country through the Negev. Moses was against this attempt, but his objections were ignored. The attack was repulsed by the Amalekites and the Canaanites. The Israelites suffered a severe defeat and incurred heavy losses.

44. The ark of Adonai's covenant and Moses remained in the camp.
The attack was not sanctioned by Adonai and was against His wishes. So the ark and Moses remained in the camp.

The people's self-confidence could not be contained by Moses so they attacked and were severely defeated.

45. And chased them all the way back to Hormah.
Hormah, meaning "destruction," was a town in the hill country of Judea near the border of Edom. Its exact site is unknown but it is believed to have been near Beer-sheba. In the early phase of the conquest, the Israelites were defeated there by the Canaanites and Amalekites. Later Hormah was captured and destroyed by Israel.

4 The person presenting the sacrifice to Adonai must bring a grain offering of two quarts of the best grade of flour mixed with one quart of olive oil. **5** For each lamb presented as burnt or peace sacrifice you shall also present one quart of wine for the libation.
6 For a ram, you shall also present a grain offering of three quarts of flour mixed with 2.5 pints of olive oil.
7 You shall also present a libation of 2.5 pints of wine as a thank you gift to Adonai.

Grain Offerings
5th Aliyah

8 When you present an animal as a burnt offering to fulfill a special vow or a peace offering to Adonai, **9** you must bring with each animal five quarts of choice flour as a grain offering, mixed with two quarts of olive oil.
10 Also, as a libation, bring two quarts of wine as a thank you gift to Adonai.
11 You must do the same for each bull, ram, sheep, or goat.
12 You must present the same meal offering for each of your sacrifices.
13 Every Israelite who presents a fire offering as a thank you offering to Adonai must present his gift with the grain offering in the same way.
14 The foreigner who lives among you and presents a fire offering as a thank you gift to Adonai, he must follow the exact same procedure.
15 The same rule shall apply both to you and to the foreigner who lives among you. It is a law for all generations that the foreigner and you are the same before Adonai.
16 You and the foreigner who lives among you shall be judged by the exact same law.

The Dough Offering
6th Aliyah

17 Adonai spoke to Moses, and told him to **18** speak to the Israelites and say to them: When you arrive in the land to which I am bringing you, **19** and you eat the crops of the land, you must remember **20** to set aside a gift from the first portion of your baking dough as an offering to Adonai; it must be separated just like the elevated gift that is taken from the threshing floor.

---

4. The person presenting the sacrifice to Adonai must bring a grain offering of two quarts of the best grade of flour mixed with one quart of olive oil.
Minchah is the term used for the fine flour offering attached to a burnt or peace offering. The meal offering could be in the form of either flour, in which case oil and frankincense would be put on it, or sometimes wine and salt. In no case should leaven or honey be added. A similar meal offering was made for the first fruits.

14. The foreigner who lives among you and presents a fire-offering as a thank you gift to Adonai, he must follow the exact same procedure.
The foreigner can be a guest worker, a visitor, or person who enjoys living among Israelites. He also can offer sacrifices as the Israelites as long as he follows the same rules and regulations as the Israelites.

20. Set aside a gift from the first portion of your baking dough as an offering to Adonai.
This is mitzvah number 385.
It was a mitzvah to separate a portion of the dough which was given to the *kohanim*. This mitzvah is called separating the *challah*. This separation was applicable only for dough suitable for making bread from the five species of grain.
The Rabbis instituted the mitzvah of *challah* outside *Eretz Yisrael* so that the laws of *challah* would not be forgotten. Today when baking *challah* it is customary to pinch off a piece of dough the size of an olive and burn it.

21 In future generations, you must set aside a gift to Adonai from your first batch of baking as a gift to Adonai.

22 This is the law if you mistakenly violate any of the commandments that Adonai has given to Moses:

23 If your descendants fail to obey a law that Adonai has commanded through Moses, **24** or if the community, because of its leader, has committed a sin by mistake, then the community must present a bull for a burnt offering as a thank you gift to Adonai, with a grain offering and a liquid offering as a libation. The community must also present one goat for a sin offering. **25** In this way the priest will make atonement for the entire Israelite community, and they will be forgiven. It was a mistake, and they presented a fire offering and a sin offering before Adonai to atone for their mistake.

26 The entire Israelite community as well as the foreigner who lives among you shall be forgiven for the mistake.

Individual Sin Offering *7th Aliyah*

27 If a person unintentionally commits a sin, he must bring a young female goat for a sin offering.

---

21. In future generations, you must set aside a gift to Adonai from your first batch of baking as a gift to Adonai.
The first baking refers to *challah*. Since challah can no longer be observed as a priestly offering and in order that this mitzvah not be invalidated, Jewish housewives who bake challah are told to throw a small portion of the dough into the fire. This act is accompanied by a blessing "Praised are you, Adonai, who commanded us to set aside challah." It is also customary to place a coin into a charity box when the challah is removed.

21. In future generations, you must set aside a gift to Adonai from your first batch of baking as a gift to Adonai.
Rashi says that the first batch means the first loaf, meaning the first challahs.

22. This is the law if you mistakenly violate any of the commandments that Adonai has given to Moses.
The Torah predicts that Jews will live in many different countries and will be influenced by foreign lifestyles and religions of their host country. Our sages say that the act of idolatry, even if mistaken, is the denial of the belief in Adonai. The Jewish relationship to Adonai consists of observing all of the commandments. A defection from any of the laws of the Torah is a defection from Adonai.

24. If the community, because of its leader, has committed a sin by mistake.
Leaders have a great variety of responsibilities and unfortunately are liable to make mistakes in judgment. The Torah calls this type of mistake *bish-ga-gah*. This type of mistake is in contrast to a deliberate, willful defiance of one or several of Adonai's commandments.

26. The entire Israelite community as well as the foreigner who lives among you shall be forgiven for the mistake.
During the opening service on Kol Nidre night verse 26 is repeated three times.

Man appears before Adonai to plead forgiveness for his sins. Tradition teaches that only the sins that man has committed against Adonai are forgiven on the Day of Atonement. For sins committed against fellow men, one must seek forgiveness from them and if necessary make restitution.

27. If a person unintentionally commits a sin.
Rashi says by worshipping idols.

28 In this way the priest will make atonement for the guilty person before Adonai, and the person will be forgiven for his sin.

29 The exact same law applies to Israelites and to the foreigners who live among you.

30 But if a person deliberately commits a sin, then it makes no difference whether he is an Israelite or a foreigner, he has willfully disobeyed Adonai and shall be cut off from the community.

31 He has violated Adonai's commandments, and therefore he shall be cut off from the community, and his sin will not be forgiven.

32 While the Israelites were in the desert, they found a man gathering firewood for the Sabbath.

33 He was brought before Moses, Aaron, and the entire community. **34** And they held him under guard because no one knew how to deal with the problem. **35** Adonai instructed Moses, "Tell the people to take him outside the camp and execute him." **36** So the entire community took him outside the camp, and they executed him, just as Adonai commanded.

Sew Fringes on Your Garments *Maftir*

37 Adonai spoke to Moses, and told him: **38** Tell the Israelites to sew fringes (*tzitzit*) on the corners of their garments and insert a blue cord in each corner of the fringe.

---

30. But if a person deliberately commits a sin, then it makes no difference whether he is an Israelite or a foreigner, he has willfully disobeyed Adonai and shall be cut off from the community.
A person who deliberately and knowingly goes out of his way to commit a sin and challenges the authority of Adonai deserves a severe punishment.

38. Tell the Israelites to sew fringes (*tzitzit*) on the corners of their garments and insert a blue cord in each corner of the fringe.
The blue thread was dyed with the blood of a rare mollusk *hillazon*, which was found along the shore of the Mediterraneon Sea. This mollusk disappeared and the rabbis decreed that white *tzitzit* were to be used. The sages tell us that the blue reminds us of the sea and the blue sky, which reminds us of Adonai in heaven which further reminds the Jews of mitzvot in their daily life. Israeli divers have discovered the *hillazon* mollusk in the Red Sea, and *tzitzit* with blue threads are now available.

38. Tell the Israelites to sew fringes (*tzitzit*) on the corners of their garments and insert a blue cord in each corner of the fringe.
This is mitzvah number 386.

The *tzitzit* are tied in a special way. Four threads are used, doubled over, making eight. One thread, the *shamash*, longer than the others, is wound around them seven times, then eight, then eleven, then thirteen times. These windings are separated by double knots. The numerical value of the word *tzitzit*, that is, the sum you get when you count *aleph* as 1, *bet* as 2, *gimel* as 3, and so on, plus the numerical value of the windings and the knots, totals 613. This number represents the sum of the 248 positive and 365 negative commandments in the Torah. This great preoccupation of our sages with devices and symbols arranged to help the Jew recall his responsibilities of Adonai indicates the seriousness with which they looked upon these responsibilities.

38. And insert a blue cord in each corner of the fringe.
The blue cord is called the *p'seel tchelet*. Originally the blue dye came from a shell-fish found along the shores of the Mediterranean. After the disappearance of the shell-fish the method of dying became a forgotten skill and the use of the blue thread was discontinued.

39 When they see the fringes, they will be reminded to obey Adonai's commandments and not follow the evil in their hearts and be blinded by the degrading sight of their eyes.
40 When they see the fringes, they will remember and observe all My commandments and be faithful to Adonai.
41 I am Adonai, who brought you out of Egypt. Remember: I am Adonai.

39. When they see the fringes, they will be reminded to obey Adonai's commandments.
When people wear the *tallit* with *tzitzit* during the daily and Sabbath prayers, they are, reminded that they are the servants of the Almighty. Ibn Ezra states that it is more important to wear *tzitzit* all day, during business dealings, and during one's daily, routine so as to remember not to sin.

39. When they see the fringes, they will be reminded to obey Adonai's commandments and not follow the evil in their hearts and be blinded by the degrading sight of their eyes.
The text is concerned with the tendency of humans to go astray with evil thoughts that may lead to disregarding the laws of the Torah.

The commentator Rashi says: the heart and the eyes of the body are the instigators for sins. The eyes see, the heart desires, and the body commits the sin.

39. When they see the fringes, they will be reminded to obey Adonai's commandments.
The method of making the *tzitzit* helps in achieving this purpose. Thus, according to Rashi, the eight threads correspond to the eight days that elapsed between the day that the children of Israel began their journeys from Egypt and the day they sang the Song of the Reed Sea. The five double knots correspond to the Five Books of Moses. The number of rings wound around the *tzitzit* equals thirty-nine, corresponding to the numerical value of the Hebrew letters in "Adonai is One." The four corners ensure that one will see this reminder in whichever direction one looks.

Orthodox men wear a *tallit katan*, a small tallit under their shirts as they go about their daily routine.

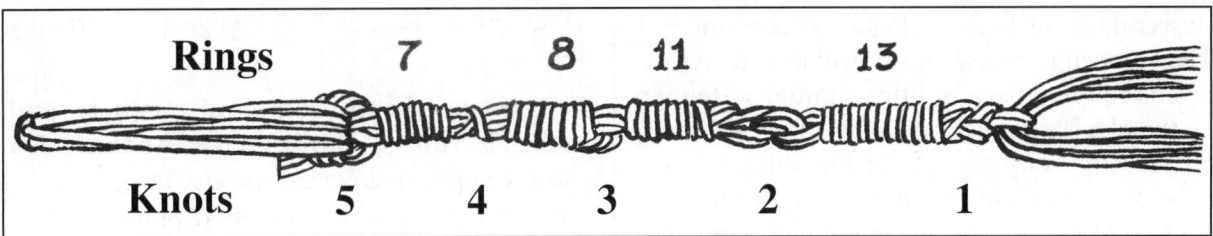

קֹרַח *Korach*

KORACH THE REBEL

16 Korach son of Yitzhar, a grandson of Kehoth and great-grandson of Levi, together with Dathan and Aviram, both of them sons of Eliav, and On son of Peleth, all three of whom were descendants of Reuben, began a rebellion. **2** They and 250 Israelite leaders challenged the authority of Moses.

3 They confronted Moses and Aaron with the accusation, "You have gone too far! Everyone in the community is holy, and Adonai is with us. So why do you two think that you are superior to everyone else?"

4 When Moses heard this, he began to pray. **5** Then he spoke to Korach and his followers and said, "Tomorrow morning, Adonai will show us the person He has designated as His holy spokesman. Adonai will choose those who shall be privileged to present offerings to Him.

6 Tomorrow this is what you must do: Korach, you and your associates must take your fire pans **7** and burn incense in them before Adonai. Then we will find out who Adonai has chosen to be the holy one.

You Levites have overstepped and gone too far!" **8** Then Moses said to Korach, "Levites, listen to me.

---

1. Korach son of Yitzhar, a grandson of Kehoth and great-grandson of Levi, together with Dathan and Aviram, both of them sons of Eliav, and On son of Peleth, all three of whom were descendants of Reuben, began a rebellion.
The Reubenite rebellion of Dathan and Aviram seems to have been political. Initially Reuben, as the eldest son, held the leadership. After the Exodus the religious leadership shifted to the tribe of Levi (Moses and Aaron) and the military leadership to the tribe of Ephraim (Joshua). The rebellion may have been an attempt to recover the leadership.

2. They and 250 Israelite leaders challenged the authority of Moses.
The Israelites had previously rebelled against Moses for a variety of reasons. They wanted water. They were dissatisfied with the food. They were unhappy over the report of spies. Now another uprising took place. This one must have troubled Moses very deeply because it was brought on by his cousin, Korach, who wanted a bigger share in the leadership of the people. Korach suffered a bad case of envy, and he stirred up a small group of petty people like himself to challenge Moses' leadership. Moses was stunned. He had certainly shared the leadership responsibility by spreading it among seventy elders, many judges, and the tribal chiefs. Korach's challenge was certainly unfair.

3. Everyone in the community is holy, and Adonai is with us. So why do you two think that you are superior to everyone else?
The rebels accused Moses of stripping the first-born of their right to serve in the Tabernacle, and keeping the honor for his brother Aaron and his sons. This obviously was an excuse, since the rebels were aware that the Levites were chosen to replace the first-born after the sin of the golden calf. They were also aware that the Levites were chosen openly in broad daylight before the congregation.

8. Levites, listen to me.
Moses now spoke to the tribe of Levi so that they would not be influenced by Korach. The Levites were in the service of Adonai, and their participation in this revolt would be considered a greater sin than those of other tribes.

9 Adonai has honored you and has separated you from the rest of the community of Israel and has brought you close to Him, allowing you to serve in the Tabernacle and help the community to worship with reverence.
10 He gave this honor to you and all your fellow Levites, and now you are also demanding the priesthood! **11** You and your followers are really rebelling against Adonai and not against Aaron. After all, who is Aaron that you should have grievances against him?" **12** Now Moses sent for Dathan and Aviram, the sons of Eliav, but they sent back this message: "We won't come! **13** It's bad enough that you brought us out of Egypt, a land flowing with milk and honey, just to kill us in the wilderness! You have no right to tell us what to do.

The Rebellion of Korach
2nd Aliyah

14 "Look around, you didn't bring us to a land flowing with milk and honey, or give us fertile fields and vineyards. Do you think that you can keep fooling us? We will definitely not come to meet with you!" **15** Moses became very angry, and he said to Adonai, "Do not listen to them or accept their offerings. I did not even take a single donkey from them! I did not harm any of them!" **16** Then Moses said to Korach, "Tomorrow you and your associates must come and present yourselves before Adonai. You and your associates and Aaron must appear tomorrow. **17** Make sure that each man brings his fire pan and fills it with incense, so that your 250 followers can present them before Adonai." **18** So the rebels all brought their burning fire pans filled with incense and stood at the entrance of the Meeting Tent with Moses and Aaron. **19** Meanwhile, Korach brought more of his followers to the entrance of the Meeting Tent. Suddenly Adonai's glory appeared to the entire community.

Moses Pleads with Adonai
3rd Aliyah

20 Adonai spoke to Moses and Aaron, and said, **21** "Separate yourselves from this band of rebels because I am going to destroy them."

---

11. You and your followers are really rebelling against Adonai and not against Aaron.
Moses angrily accuses Korach of instigating a revolt against Adonai's leadership. Moses says to Korach: "Look at Aaron's record! Did he attack you personally? Did he in any way sin against you or the nation of Israel? Accusing Aaron is a very transparent excuse. You are just looking for power."

12. Now Moses sent for Dathan and Aviram, the sons of Eliav, but they sent back this message: "We won't come!"
Moses teaches us an important lesson here: It is necessary in all disputes to make a sincere effort to arrive at a peaceful settlement. Moses called to them and tried to win them over by talking to them. However, they refused to appear before Moses and to settle the problem.

Korach's rebellion was against Aaron's position as a priest. He wanted himself and his relatives included in the priesthood. On the other hand, Dathan and Aviram rebelled, against the authority of Moses. They wanted to topple Moses from his position as a political leader. Moses decided to deal with Dathan and Aviram first, but they refused to talk and negotiate with Moses.

19. Meanwhile, Korach brought more of his followers to the entrance of the Meeting Tent.
On hearing Korach's challenge to his and Aaron's leadership, Moses tried to reason with the small band of complainers. Korach's group was certainly among Israel's decision-makers. But Moses was unable to defuse their envy. It had reached explosive proportions and a showdown had to follow.

22 But Moses and Aaron bowed and pleaded, "Adonai, Creator of all living souls. If one man sins, must you punish the entire community?"
23 Adonai spoke to Moses and directed him to **24** warn the entire community to move away from the tents of Korach, Dathan, and Aviram.
25 So Moses and the elders of Israel rushed to the tent of Dathan and Aviram.
26 Moses warned the community, "Hurry, run away from the tents of these wicked men. Do not touch anything that belongs to them or you too will be punished because of all their sins." **27** The people retreated from around the tents of Korach, Dathan, and Aviram. Dathan and Aviram, along with their sons, daughters, and infants, stood defiantly at the entrance of their tents. **28** Moses announced, "Now you will know that Adonai sent me to do all these deeds, and it was not my own doing. **29** If the rebels die like ordinary men, then you will know that Adonai did not send me. **30** But if Adonai performs a miracle and makes the earth open its mouth and swallow them and all their belongings, so that they descend to the depths alive, then you will know that these men were provoking Adonai." **31** As Moses finished speaking, the ground under Dathan and Aviram split open. **32** The earth opened its mouth and swallowed them and all the men who were with Korach and all their property. **33** They all fell alive into the earth, along with all their property. Then the earth closed over them, and they disappeared from the community. **34** The Israelites around them all heard their cries, and ran away as the earth swallowed them up. **35** Then streaks of fire came down from Adonai and burned up the 250 men who were offering incense.

17

Adonai spoke to Moses, saying, **2** "Tell Elazar son of Aaron the priest to gather up all the fire pans because they have been sanctified, and scatter the burning coals.

22. If one man sins, must you punish the entire community?
Moses pleads with Adonai and tells him that, since He is the Creator not only of man's body but also of his spirit, it is in His power to know all the thoughts of man; He therefore should punish the guilty only and spare the innocent.

25. So Moses and the elders of Israel rushed to the tent of Dathan and Aviram.
The seventy elders (v 11:16) were the tribal leaders who were spiritually endowed to assist Moses. The seventy elders remained one hundred percent loyal during the rebellion.

26. Hurry, run away from the tents of these wicked men.
A dangerous challenge to the leadership of Moses and to Adonai's authority was swiftly suppressed. Moses told everyone in the vicinity to move away from the tents of the three ringleaders, Dathan, Aviram, and On.
They were about to be punished.

32. The earth opened its mouth and swallowed them.
Once again as in Egypt, Adonai uses supernatural forces to punish the rebels. The phenomenon may be the fracture of the hard crusty surface which covered deep lakes of liquid mud in the Aravah, where this incident occurs.
In Bamidbar 26:11, the Torah points out that despite the destruction of Korach and his group, the sons of Korach didn't die. They repented and survived and became the musicians of the Holy Temple in Jerusalem.

2. Gather up all the fire pans because they have been sanctified, and scatter the burning coals.
The fire pans with incense and the burning coals had acquired holiness because the rebels had brought them to the entrance of the Meeting Tent. Now Adonai tells Moses to scatter the coals because they are not to be used for ordinary purposes.

3 The fire pans belonging to the rebels who sinned are holy. Save the copper pans and hammer the metal into sheets to cover the altar. The metal covering will be a warning to Israel that Adonai is in their midst."
4 So Elazar gathered the copper fire pans of the rebels and hammered them into metal sheets as a covering for the altar.
5 The copper altar covering was intended to be a visual reminder to the Israelites that only descendants of Aaron are authorized to burn incense before Adonai. Any others would be punished just like Korach and his followers.
6 The next day the entire Israelite community began to complain against Moses. Now they grumbled, "You have killed Adonai's people!"
7 The people, still complaining against Moses and Aaron, turned and faced the Meeting Tent. Suddenly the tent was covered with a cloud, and Adonai's glory appeared. **8** Moses and Aaron went to the front of the Meeting Tent.

Atonement for the Israelites   *4th Aliyah*

9 Adonai spoke to Moses, saying, **10** "Get away from this congregation because in one moment I will destroy all of them." Moses and Aaron threw themselves on their faces.
11 Moses said to Aaron, "Hurry! Take your fire pan and put some hot coals from the altar in it. Quickly, offer incense to make atonement for the community, because Adonai is angry and the plague has already begun!"
12 So Aaron took his fire pan, as Moses had ordered him, and bravely ran into the midst of the community. He offered the incense to atone for the people.
13 He stood among the dead and the living, until the plague stopped.
14 But 14,700 people died in the plague, in addition to those who died because of Korach's rebellion. **15** When the plague stopped, Aaron returned to Moses at the entrance of the Meeting Tent.

Aaron's Staff Blossoms   *5th Aliyah*

16 Adonai spoke to Moses, telling him to **17** speak to the Israelites and to take twelve staffs, one from each tribe, and let each leader write his name on his own staff.
18 "Write Aaron's name on Levi's staff because there must be only one staff for each tribe.

---

6. You have killed Adonai's people.
The commentators indicate here that the people were not angry at the death of the chiefs of the rebellion, but they did not feel that the others should have been killed since it was Moses and Aaron who had told them to offer incense. The people refused to recognize that by entering the "contest," the others had in effect defiantly joined the rebellion.

11. Moses said to Aaron, "Hurry! Take your fire pan and put some hot coals from the altar in it. Quickly, offer incense to make atonement for the community, because Adonai is angry and the plague has already begun!"
Adonai has told Moses how to remove the sins of the Israelites for their rebellious acts. Now, Moses urges Aaron to use his fire pan to make atonement and stop the plague.

13. He stood among the dead and the living, until the plague stopped.
Why was the plague stopped by means of the incense? The Israelites spoke ill of the incense and alleged that it was poison – it had caused the death of 250 men. Adonai therefore used the incense to stop the plague, thereby teaching the people that they had nothing to blame except their own sins for any calamity that befell them.

19 Place the staffs in the Meeting Tent in front of the ark where I meet with you. **20** The staff of the man whom I choose will blossom. Then I will once and for all put an end to the Israelites' complaints against you."

21 Moses spoke to the Israelites, and each leader gave him a staff to represent his tribe. There were twelve staffs, with Aaron's staff among them. **22** Moses set the staffs before Adonai in the Meeting Tent.

23 The following day Moses entered the Meeting Tent, and Aaron's staff, representing the house of Levi, had blossomed and almonds were ripening on it.

24 Then Moses brought out all the staffs from before Adonai and let the Israelites see them. Each leader took his own staff.

The Symbol
6th Aliyah

25 Adonai said to Moses, "Put Aaron's staff in front of the ark as a symbol. Let it be a warning to anyone who wants to rebel and challenge Me. This should put an end to complaints against Me, and prevent any more deaths."

26 Moses did exactly as Adonai had instructed him.

27 The Israelites said to Moses, "We are as good as dead! We will all be destroyed! We are all lost!

28 Anyone who approaches the Tabernacle is as good as dead! We are all doomed to die!"

18 Adonai said to Aaron: You, your sons, and the members of your tribe will be responsible for the sanctuary. You and your descendants will also be responsible for any sins connected with the priesthood.

2 Enlist your relatives, the members of the tribe of Levi. Let them assist you and help you perform your sacred duties in the Meeting Tent.

3 The Levites shall perform their duties in the Meeting Tent under your supervision, but under no circumstances may they handle any of the sacred objects or the altar utensils or they will die.

4 The Levites shall be your assistants and they will be responsible for the care and maintenance of the Meeting Tent, and no unauthorized person is permitted to join them.

---

23. Aaron's staff, representing the house of Levi, had blossomed and almonds were ripening on it.

There was a constant battle for the reins of leadership. Korach and his group of rebels rebelled against the authority of Moses and Aaron. Adonai used the staffs of the tribes in this way to solidify and confirm the leadership of Moses.

When Aaron's staff, representing the tribe of Levi, blossomed, the tribal leaders accepted the omen of the preeminence of the house of Aaron and the tribe of Levi. According to Jewish tradition, the staff of the Messiah will also be an almond branch.

1. Adonai said to Aaron: "You, your sons, and the members of your tribe will be responsible for the sanctuary."

You and the members shall guard the sanctuary so that no stranger shall enter. It is your responsibility to prevent a stranger from interfering or participating in the priestly service.

2. Enlist your relatives, the members of the tribe of Levi. Let them assist you and help you perform your sacred duties in the Meeting Tent.

Adonai instructs Aaron that he and his sons have the primary responsibility for caring for the sanctuary. He also instructs Aaron to use his relatives the Levi families, the Gershonites and the Merarites, as their assistants.

5 Let them be entrusted with responsibility for the sanctuary and the altar, so that I will not become angry and punish the Israelites.

6 I have chosen your relatives the Levites from among the Israelites as a gift to you. They are dedicated to help and assist you to perform the service in the Meeting Tent.

7 Aaron, you and your sons shall perform all the priestly duties. These include conducting all the sacred services associated with the altar and all the services inside the cloth partition. The work of the priesthood is the gift of service that I have given you. Any unauthorized person who comes near the sanctuary shall die.

8 Adonai announced to Aaron: I have set you in charge of the sacred gifts and sacrifices brought by the Israelites. From now on you and your descendants will receive a regular share of the offerings.

9 This is what shall be yours: all the Israelites' sacrifices, and all their grain offerings, and all their sin and guilt offerings shall belong to you and your descendants.

10 All male priests may eat these offerings, but they must be eaten in a most holy area and must remain holy to you.

11 Remember, these sacred offerings are dedicated to you and can be eaten by your sons and daughters. Any person in your household who is ritually clean may eat them.

12 The best of the olive oil, wine, and grain that are presented to Adonai is given to you. **13** The first fruit of everything that grows in your land, which is presented to Adonai, shall be yours. Everyone in your household who is ritually clean may eat it.

---

5. Let them be entrusted with responsibility for the sanctuary and the altar.
This is mitzvah number 391.

It was the responsibility of the priests and the Levites to continuously guard the Tabernacle against intruders.

7. These include conducting all the sacred services associated with the altar and all the services inside the cloth partition.
Only active priests were permitted to officiate at the altar. All but the High Priest were prohibited from entering the Holy of Holies inside the cloth partition.

8. Adonai announced to Aaron: I have set you in charge of the sacred gifts and sacrifices brought by the Israelites. From now on you and your descendants will receive a regular share of the offerings.
From now on you will be in charge of all the holy rules and regulations which I command. For your service you will receive the priestly gifts enumerated in this section.

10. All male priests may eat these offerings, but they must be eaten in a most holy area and must remain holy to you.
Refers to the courtyard of the Meeting Tent.

11. Remember, these sacred offerings are dedicated to you and can be eaten by your sons and daughters. Any person in your household who is ritually clean may eat them.
Verses 11–15 contain a list of holy gifts which were to be donated to the priests. The gifts of food could be eaten at home by the members of the priestly family.

12. The best of the olive oil, wine, and grain that are presented to Adonai is given to you.
The staples of the Israelite diet were olive oil, wine, and grain. Everyone in the household who was ritually clean was permitted to eat the food presented to Adonai.

14 Everything that the Israelites pledge to Adonai shall also be yours.

15 The first-born that is offered to Adonai, whether man or beast, shall belong to you. But you must redeem the first-born sons and the first-born unclean animals on the payment of five pieces of silver.

16 They must be redeemed when they are one month old by the payment of five silver coins.

17 However, the first-born of oxen, sheep, or goats cannot be redeemed, because they are sacred to Me.

You must slaughter them and sprinkle their blood on the altar and burn their fat as a thank you gift to Adonai.

18 You are permitted to eat the meat of these animals just as you can eat the breast and right hind leg of a wave offering.

19 From now on, whatever is presented as a holy offering I give to you and your descendants as a regular share. This shall be a permanent covenant sealed with salt between Adonai and your descendants.

20 Then Adonai said to Aaron, You and your descendants will not own any property in the land of the Israelites.

I Myself shall be your share and your inheritance among the Israelites.

Tithes for Tithes   *7th Aliyah*

21 To the descendants of the Levites I am now giving all the tithes in Israel as their inheritance. This is in return for the services and work that they perform in the Meeting Tent.

22 From now on no other Israelites shall enter into the Meeting Tent or they will become guilty of sin and die.

---

15. The first-born that is offered to Adonai, whether man or beast, shall belong to you.
Pidyon ha-Ben, the redemption of the first-born son, is a ceremony that takes place 30 days after the birth of the first son. Since a first son belongs traditionally to the service of Adonai, he is symbolically redeemed by his father by an offering of money (5 shekels) to a Kohen or a Levite, since they were dedicated to the service of Adonai in place of the first-born.

19. This shall be a permanent covenant sealed with salt between Adonai and your descendants.
Salt was always used in sacrifices and was a necessary part of the daily diet. In time "eating salt" with a person became a symbol of hospitality.

When special purchases, agreements, and covenants were ratified, they were sealed via sacrificial meals in which both of the parties "ate salt," which meant that the agreement was certified.

20. You and your descendants will not own any property in the land of the Israelites.
Aaron and his descendants were not given any territory when the land of Canaan was divided among the tribes.

21. To the descendants of the Levites I am now giving all the tithes in Israel as their inheritance. This is in return for the service and work that they perform in the Meeting Tent.
The tithe was 10 percent of the agricultural harvest and 10 percent of the herds. It was to be donated every third year.

This was the first of three tithes. The second tithe (Devarim 15:23) was to be eaten in the sanctuary. The third tithe was the "poor tithe." The Torah tells us that "the foreigners, orphans, and widows who live in your community will have enough food to eat." The third tithe was to come from the first tithe.

23 Only the Levites shall conduct the necessary services in the Meeting Tent, and they will make an atonement for the Israelites.

It is a law for all future generations that the Levites do not have any inheritance of land. **24** The inheritance I am giving the Levites shall instead consist of all the tithes that the Israelites present as wave offerings. I have told the Levites that these gifts belong to them, and they have no need for an inheritance of land among the Israelites. **25** Adonai spoke to Moses and said to him: **26** Speak to the Levites and say to them: When an Israelite presents his tithe that I have given you as your inheritance from them, you must separate a tithe from their tithes as a gift to Me, a tithe of the tithe. **27** The tithe given to you by the Israelites is your own gift from the threshing floor or wine from the winepress.

28 Now you must take a tithe from all the tithes that you have collected from the Israelites and must present it as Adonai's gift to Aaron the priest. **29** From the tithe of all the tithes you shall pick the choicest parts as Adonai's portion, to be given to Aaron the priest and his descendants.

A Tithe of the Tithes
Maftir

30 Say to the Levites: After you have separated out the dedicated tithe for the priest, the remainder of the tithes shall be for all the Levites exactly as if it came from your own threshing floor and your own winepress. **31** You and your family can eat it anywhere because it is payment for your service in the Meeting Tent.

32 Once you have set aside the best of all your tithes, you will not be guilty of sinning, because you have not defiled the sacred offerings of the Israelites, and you will not die.

---

23. Only the Levites shall conduct the necessary services in the Meeting Tent.
This is mitzvah number 394.

It was the duty of the Levites to sing prayers and play musical instruments. The duty of the kohanim was to tend to the communal burnt offerings.

23. It is a law for all future generations that the Levites do not have any inheritance of the land.
Each of the tribes of Israel was allotted a portion of land in Canaan, except for the Levites. Instead, the Levites were to live from tithes, sacrifices, and the gifts brought to the Tabernacle.

The Levites were the teachers and the doctors. They had no land of their own but were scattered throughout the population so they could serve all of the Israelites.

24. The inheritance I am giving the Levites shall instead consist of all the tithes that the Israelites present as wave offerings. I have told the Levites that these gifts belong to them.
The Levites, in exchange for their dedication and their labor as partners with the priests, were to receive all the wave offerings.

The Levites, were to guard the sanctuary against illegal trespass and desecration. The person who presented the wave offering could designate the recipient of the heave offering.

32. Once you have set aside the best of your tithes, you will not be guilty of sinning, because you have not defiled the sacred offerings of the Israelites, and you will not die.
The farmers in Israel had to tithe all the crops of oil, wine, and grain that were personally consumed. Crops that were grown for commercial purposes were not subject to tithes.

חֻקַּת *Chukkat*

THIS IS THE LAW OF THE TORAH

19 Adonai spoke to Moses and Aaron, and told them: **2** This is the law of the Torah that Adonai has commanded the Israelites. Speak to the Israelites and have them bring a completely healthy red cow, one that has never done any farm work.

3 Give it to Elazar the priest, and he shall take it outside the camp, where it shall be slaughtered in his presence.

4 Then Elazar the priest shall dip his finger in its blood and sprinkle it seven times toward the Meeting Tent.

5 The whole cow shall be burned; its skin, flesh, blood, and organs must be burned in the presence of Elazar.

6 The priest shall then take a piece of cedar wood, some hyssop, and some red wool, and throw it into the fire.

7 After the ceremony the priest shall wash his garments and his body. He remains unclean until evening, and then he may return to the camp. **8** The person who burns the cow must also wash his clothing and body and will also remain unclean until evening. **9** A ritually clean person shall gather up the ashes of the cow and place them outside the camp in a clean place. The ashes of the cow are to be mixed in water by the Israelites for the ceremony of purification for the removal of sin. **10** The person who gathers up the ashes of the cow must wash his body and his clothing, and remains unclean until evening.

This shall be a permanent law for the Israelites and for any foreigner who lives among you. Those who have any contact with a dead human being shall become ritually unclean for seven days.

12 They must purify themselves on the third and seventh days by sprinkling themselves with the purification water. Anyone who does not undergo purification on the third and seventh days will remain ritually unclean even after the seventh day. **13** Any person who touches a dead human being and does not have himself sprinkled shall be cut off from the community of Israel if he desecrates Adonai's Tabernacle by entering it. Since the purification water was not sprinkled on him, he remains unclean.

---

2. Speak to the Israelites and have them bring a completely healthy red cow, one that has never done any farm work.
This is mitzvah number 397.

The ritual of the red cow is a mysterious rite which has puzzled the sages, and no one has yet determined its meaning and purpose.

In short, the cow was to be sacrificed and burnt into ashes, which were to be divided into three parts, mixed with fresh water, and sprinkled on a ritually impure person.

In the ritual a piece of cedar wood and a bunch of hyssop tied with a red cord were burnt with the red cow.

The symbolism was that scholarly Jews are compared to tall cedars and ordinary ones to the lowly hyssop. The ritual is aimed at both categories of Jews.

According to some interpretations, the ritual of the red cow is one of the four laws in the Torah for which there is no rational explanation.

14 This is the law when a man dies in a tent: Anyone who enters the tent and everyone who lived in the tent shall remain unclean for seven days. **15** Every open container that was not sealed shall be declared unclean.

16 Anyone who touches the body of someone who was killed or of a person who died naturally, and so too a person who touches a human bone or an open grave that person shall be unclean for seven days.

17 To remove defilement, mix some of the ashes from the burnt purification offering in a vessel that has been filled with water from a running spring.

The Purification Process
2nd Aliyah

18 A ritually clean person shall then dip a hyssop branch into the water and sprinkle the water on all the containers and people who were in the tent and on anyone who touched a bone, a murder victim, or any other dead body, or a grave.

19 On the third and seventh days, the ritually clean person shall sprinkle some of the purification water on the unclean person. The purification process is completed on the seventh day, when the person undergoing cleansing washes his clothing and body, and then becomes ritually clean in the evening.

20 If a person is unclean and refuses to purify himself, and desecrates Adonai's sanctuary by entering it, he shall no longer be a part of the Israelite community. As long as the purification water has not been sprinkled on him, he shall remain unclean.

21 This is a permanent law. Anyone who sprinkles the purification water must bathe his body and wash his clothing. If he merely touches the purification water, however, he shall be unclean until evening.

22 Anything that an unclean person comes in contact with shall become unclean, and anyone who touches him shall be unclean until evening.

20 In the first month, the entire Israelite community reached the Wilderness of Sin, and the people camped in Kadesh. It was there that Miriam died and was buried. **2** There was no water to drink, and the Israelites blamed Moses and Aaron.

---

15. Every open container that was not sealed shall be declared unclean.
Ancient populations were very much aware of plagues and took precautions to prevent them. Deadly illnesses can be caused by a variety of factors, including bacteria and body fluids, and can be spread by contact.

Earthenware are made of clay, which is porous and can absorb dangerous solids and liquids. Therefore tightly closing or sealing clay vessels could prevent possible contamination.

21. Anyone who sprinkles the purification water must bathe his body and wash his clothing.
The Torah is very much aware of contamination. Even the individual who performs the ceremonial sprinkling must bathe and wash his clothing.

1. The Wilderness of Sin, and the people camped in Kadesh.
Kadesh is located in the Negev, about fifty miles south of Beersheva.

1. Miriam died.
Miriam died in the first month of the fortieth year after the departure from Egypt. Aaron died four months later (Vayikra 20: 23–29).

2. There was no water to drink.
This verse immediately follows the words in the Torah that tell us of Miriam's death. The Rabbis suggest that it was through Miriam's merit that they had had water during the forty years in the wilderness.

3 The people quarreled with Moses. They complained, "We wish that we had died together with our brothers! **4** Did you bring us into this desert so that we and our livestock should die here? **5** Why have you led us out of Egypt and brought us to this miserable place? There are no plants, no figs, no grapes, no pomegranates. And now there is not even a drop of water to drink!" **6** Moses and Aaron turned away from the angry crowd toward the entrance of the Meeting Tent and prayed.

Suddenly Adonai's presence appeared to them.

Water from the Rock *3rd Aliyah*

7 Adonai spoke to Moses, **8** "Take your miracle staff, and you and Aaron assemble the community. Speak to the rock before their eyes, and it will gush out water. You will bring water from the rock, so that the Israelites and their cattle can drink."

9 So Moses took his staff from before Adonai. **10** Then Moses and Aaron assembled the Israelites in front of the rock. Moses shouted, "You rebels, listen to me now! Now you will see water flow from this rock." **11** With that, Moses raised his hand, and struck the rock twice with his staff. A river of water gushed out, and the community and their cattle had plenty of water to drink.

---

4. Did you bring us into this desert so that we and our livestock should die here?
The Israelites were shepherds and were concerned about the welfare of their flocks.

7. Adonai spoke to Moses, Take your miracle staff and you and Aaron assemble the community. Speak to the rock before their eyes, and it will gush out water.
The staff of Moses was used to perform the miracles which liberated the Israelites.

8. Take your miracle staff, and you and Aaron assemble the community.
The staff was used by Moses to perform miracles in Egypt. Its was also used at Rephidim when the community, because of a lack of water, complained to Moses. At that time Moses struck the rock at Horeb (Shemot 17:6) and water gushed out.

11. Moses raised his hand, and struck the rock twice with his staff.
Life was very difficult for the Hebrews in the desert. The hot sun baked them during the day and the cold desert froze them at night. There was a constant lack of food and water for them and their animals. Canaanite and Amorite tribes attacked and stole their property and flocks. Many Hebrews died of disease, hunger, and thirst. Slavery had weakened them.

They regretted leaving Egypt. They began to lose faith in Adonai's promises and in the leadership of Moses. The Hebrews relapsed and worshipped the golden calf.

Initially Moses wisely accepted their complaints and reassured them that Adonai's promises would be fulfilled. But after a while he lost patience with their whining and complaints. In a moment of weakness, Moses disregarded Adonai's command to speak to the rock and instead he angrily struck it. Momentarily losing his faith, Moses behaved like an ordinary human being. In disobeying Adonai's direct command, he dishonored Adonai in the presence of the Israelites.

11. With that, Moses raised his hand, and struck the rock twice with his staff.
Adonai performed the miracle but Moses took the credit for it. Moses was the leader of the Israelites. Because of his great responsibility to the nation, he had to be punished.

Leaders are not immune from obedience to Adonai's laws.

11. A river of water gushed out, and the community and their cattle had plenty of water to drink.
Once again the Torah shows its concern not only for the Israelites but also for their cattle.

12 But Adonai angrily said to Moses and Aaron, "I told you to speak to the rock. But neither of you trusted Me, and instead you struck the rock in the presence of the Israelites! Therefore, you shall not lead the Israelites into the land that I have given you." **13** That is why the place was called Mai Meribah (Waters of Dispute), because there the Israelites disputed with Adonai, and there He demonstrated His power and gave them water to drink.

Edom Refuses Israel
4th Aliyah

14 Moses sent ambassadors from Kadesh to the king of Edom with the following message: "This is what your brother Israel says:
You are aware of all the troubles that we have encountered.
15 Our ancestors lived in Egypt for a long time. The Egyptians were cruel to our ancestors and to us. **16** So we cried out to Adonai. He heard our voice and sent a messenger to lead us out of Egypt. Now we are camped around the city of Kadesh, on the border of your land. **17** Please let us pass through your land. We will be careful not to trespass on any of your fields or vineyards, and we will not drink any water from your wells. We will only travel along the King's Highway, not turning right or left until we have passed through your lands."
18 The king of Edom answered, "No! you must not pass through my land. If you do, I will destroy you with my army!" **19** The Israelites answered, "We will stay on the main road. If we or our cattle drink any of your water, we will pay the full price. We only want to pass through your country on foot." **20** The king of Edom answered, "Keep out! Do not come into our country!" The king of Edom mobilized his army and opposed the Israelites with a large force of heavily armed soldiers. **21** Edom refused to allow Israel to pass through its territories, and Israel was forced to go around the area.

---

12. I told you to speak to the rock. But neither of you trusted Me, and instead you struck the rock in the presence of the Israelites!
Nearly four decades had passed since Moses had taken over the leadership of his people. He was beginning to tire as a result of the heavy responsibility which he carried. If only the Israelites would let him have some peace in his old age!

But they would not. Again, there was a water shortage in the wilderness. Again, Israel cried in complaint. Adonai assures Moses and Aaron and that water is available nearby at a spot marked by a large boulder.

Moses and Aaron and the Israelites moved toward the rock. But here the impatience of the two old leaders showed itself. They hammered away impatiently at the boulder. There was water, but Moses and Aaron had shown their weakness. It was time for younger men to take over the leadership.

13. That is why the place was called Mai Meribah (Waters of Dispute).
Mai means "waters of." *Ribah* means "strife" or "conflict."

14. This is what your brother Israel says.
The expression "your brother" indicates that Israel is appealing to the fact that Edom and the Israelites had common ancestors – Abraham and Isaac. Edom, otherwise known as Esau, was Jacob's brother.

17. "We will only travel along the King's Highway, not turning right or left until we have passed through your lands."
We will travel only the road, that you the king of Edom will permit us to use. We will not deviate from the designated road until we have passed through your land.

Aaron Dies
5th Aliyah

22 The Israelites proceeded from Kadesh to Mount Hor.
23 When they got there, Adonai said to Moses and Aaron,
24 "The time has come for Aaron to die and join his ancestors. He will not enter the land that I am giving the Israelites because you both disobeyed me at Mai Meribah.
25 Moses, take Aaron and his son Elazar up to the top of Mount Hor.
26 Remove Aaron's priestly garments and put them on his son Elazar. There Aaron will die and be gathered to his ancestors."
27 Moses did everything that Adonai had commanded him. The three of them climbed Mount Hor as the entire community watched.
28 Moses removed Aaron's priestly garments and put them on Aaron's son Elazar. Aaron died on the top of the mountain. When Moses and Elazar came down from the mountain,
29 the people knew that Aaron had died, and the entire community of Israel mourned for Aaron for thirty days.

---

22. The Israelites proceeded from Kadesh to Mount Hor.
The united, invigorated community was ready to invade Canaan and take over their heritage. The older generation, those of the desert, had already passed away. *Rashi*

25. Moses, take Aaron and his son Elazar up to the top of Mount Hor.
Now that Aaron has to meet death, you, Moses, speak consoling words to him; show him how fortunate he is to have a son to whom he may give over the priesthood.

26. Remove Aaron's priestly garments and put them on his son Elazar.
Aaron was the High Priest and he wore a specially designed uniform. Now Elazar will inherit the office of High Priest as well as the garments.
The individual changes but the office, its duties, and its responsibilities remain the same.

27. Moses did everything that Adonai had commanded him.
This was no easy task for Moses to do since he loved his brother, but nevertheless he did not delay in obeying God's command.

28. Moses removed Aaron's priestly garments and put then on Aaron's son Elazar.
When he died, Aaron was 123 years old.
Moses was jealous of his brother Aaron. Aaron lived to see his son Elazar assume the office of the High Priest. Moses realized that he would not be succeeded by one of his children.

29. The people knew that Aaron had died, and the entire community of Israel mourned for Aaron for thirty days.
Earlier, the whole community of Israel had accused Moses and Aaron of leading them into the desert to die of thirst. Now the entire community mourned the death of Aaron. In times of stress, nations as well as individuals look for someone to blame. The revolt at Kadesh was a temporary incident brought about by life in a harsh environment.
  In reality, the Israelites admired Moses and Aaron. They appreciated their bravery with Pharaoh. They also knew that the brothers were chosen by Adonai to free them and give their descendants a country of their own.
Rabbi Raphael Samson Hirsch

29. The entire community of Israel mourned for Aaron for thirty days.
It was not only the men that mourned Aaron's death, but the women too. Aaron was known as the peace-maker among the people and specialized in bringing about many a reconciliation between husbands and wives estranged from each other. Therefore he was greatly loved by the Israelites. The Torah teaches us that the period of mourning for a beloved one is thirty days.

21

When the Canaanite king of Arad, who lived in the Negev, heard that the Israelites were moving along the Atharim highway, he mobilized his army and attacked them and took some captives. **2** The Israelites prayed to Adonai and said, "If You help us to defeat the Canaanites, we will destroy their cities and everything in them." **3** Adonai answered their prayers and helped them to defeat the Canaanites. The Israelites completely destroyed the Canaanite cities. Therefore the place was called Harmah (Destroyed Place).
4 The Israelites marched from Kadesh toward the Sea of Reeds so as to go around the territory of Edom. The people became impatient and complained.
5 The people spoke out against Adonai and Moses: "Did you take us out of Egypt to die in the desert? We have no bread to eat and no water to drink! We hate our tasteless food."

---

1. When the Canaanite king of Arad, who lived in the Negev heard that the Israelites were moving along the Atharim highway, he mobilized his army and attacked them and took some captives.
Arad is located in the Negev about 17 miles south of Hebron. The ancient city is situated on a hill called Tel Arad. The territory of Arad included the desert of Sin.
Arad was a Canaanite town on the plateau west of the Dead Sea. The Canaanite king of Arad barred the advance of the Israelites into Canaan. According to the Torah (Devarim 1:44), he repulsed the Israelites with heavy losses and chased them back to the base camp.

Some of the more militant Israelites organized an expedition that tried to penetrate the hill country through the northern Neper. Moses was against the attempt but his objections were ignored.

1. When the Canaanite king of Arad, who lived in the Negev, heard that the Israelites were moving along the Atharim highway, he mobilized his army and attacked them and took some captives.
The Israelites were attacked without reason or provocation. Israel realized that the neighboring kings had to be taught a lesson. The situation demanded a message to all the surrounding nations. Do not mess with us! It totally destroyed the Canaanites.

2. The Israelites prayed to Adonai and said, "If You help us defeat the Canaanites, we will destroy their cities and everything in them."
Israel realized that it was necessary to teach them as well as the other tribes who were attacking and taking hostages that these actions could not be tolerated. Nations should be aware of the consequences of attacking Israel.

3. Adonai answered their prayers and helped them to defeat the Canaanites.
Instead of making statements, the Israelites took action to protect their vulnerable population. From this verse we learn that Israel was successful and totally destroyed the Canaanite towns. After the victory they called the town Harmah, meaning complete destruction. Unfortunately, the state of Israel finds itself in the same situation today.

4. The Israelites marched from Kadesh toward the Sea of Reeds so as to go around the territory of Edom.
The Edomites refused to allow the Israelites to pass through their territory. The Israelite military commander avoided a battle with the Edomites. The strategists were saving their energy and military resources for the invasion of Canaan. *Shenash*

5. The people spoke out against Adonai and Moses.
When the Israelites left Egypt, they enthusiastically praised Moses for his strength and his leadership. Now they turned against Adonai and Moses and complained.

They bit the hand that fed them.

6 So Adonai punished them and sent poisonous snakes that bit the people, and many of the Israelites died. **7** The people rushed to Moses and said, "We admit that we have sinned by insulting Adonai and you. Please pray to Adonai, and ask Him to remove the snakes from among us." So Moses prayed for the people.

8 Adonai answered Moses, "Make a metal image of a poisonous snake and mount it on a tall pole. Anyone who has been bitten can just look at it and live."

9 Moses made a copper snake and mounted it on top of a tall pole. Whenever a snake bit somebody, he or she would look at the copper snake and live.

Israel Defeats the Amorites 6th Aliyah

10 From there the Israelites moved on and camped in Oboth.

11 Then they proceeded from Oboth and camped at Iye-Abarim in the wilderness along the Moab border toward the east. **12** From there they continued their journey and camped along the Brook of Zered. **13** Then they went on and camped in the desert near the border of the Amorites, on the opposite side of the Arnon River. The Arnon was the border separating the Moabites from the Amorites.

14 This is a song in the Book of Adonai's Wars:

"The town of Waheb near Suphah and the valleys of the Arnon River

---

6. So Adonai punished them and sent poisonous snakes that bit the people, and many of the Israelites died.
The area around Pethor had numerous snakes and perhaps some Israelites died of snake bites. However, this event can easily be transformed into an allegory. The snake in Jewish and general literature is considered to be evil. The snake in the Garden of Eden convinced Adam and Eve to sin. Now the Israelites were beginning to act like sinful snakes. The desert heat, the endless treeless piles of sand, and the lack of water and food had weakened the physical and moral character of the former slaves. They began to act like snakes: hissing at each other, lying like snakes in the grass, hitting and biting each other, and sneaking into tents and stealing. These older former slaves felt hopeless and were dying in large numbers as if in a plague.

8. Make metal image of a poisonous snake and mount it on a tall pole. Anyone who has been bitten can just look at it and live.
When the Israelites fled from Egypt through the wilderness, they complained about the lengthy journey, the long detour around Edom, and the monotony of the manna.

Moses and Aaron were concerned about the psychological breakdown of the moral and morality of the Israelites so they set up the bronze serpent on a tall pole. The Israelites could see the bright bronze snake from all four corners of the encampment. Now, the moment they felt like committing a sin, the serpent would remind them not to act like a snake but to retool their morality.

9. Moses made a copper snake and mounted it on top of a tall pole. Whenever a snake bit somebody, he or she would look at the copper snake and live.
The bites of the snakes injected poison, which produced inflammations, fevers, and sometimes death. The Hebrew word for inflammation and fever is *ka-da-chas*. The symbol of the medical profession is a stick with two snakes wound around it. This symbol is called a *caduceus*.

The medical profession adopted the snakes as their symbol and the name *ka-da-chas* from this biblical event.   *Shenash*

15 with its valleys stretched as far as the city of Ar on the border of Moab."
16 From there the Israelites traveled to the well of Beer. This is the well where Adonai said to Moses, "Gather the people, and I will give them water."
17 It was here that Israel sang this song:
"O well, rise up, sing this song.
18 This well was dug by princes,
Sunk by the people's leaders,
Carved out with their scepters."
From the desert, the Israelites proceeded to Matanah, **19** from Matanah to Nachaliel, and from Nachaliel to Bamoth. **20** From Bamoth they went to the plain of Moab, situated near the top of Mount Pisgah, which overlooks the desolated area of Yeshimon.

Israel Defeats King Sichon
7th Aliyah

21 Israel sent ambassadors to Sichon, king of the Amorites, with the following message:
22 "Allow us to pass through your land. We promise to keep away from your fields and vineyards, and we will not drink any of your well water. We will stay on the King's Highway until we have passed through your territories."
23 But Sichon refused to allow Israel to pass through his territories. Instead, he mobilized his army and marched out to attack Israel in the desert.
Sichon's army attacked the Israelites near the town of Yahaz.
24 But Israel defeated the Amorites and occupied their land from the Arnon River to the Jabbok River, but only as far as the fortified borders of the Ammonites.

---

17. O well, rise up, sing this song.
Finding a well in the desert is like finding a needle in a haystack. Wells are difficult to find, and finding water in the desert is an occasion to celebrate. This song describes the digging of the well and is a song of thanksgiving.

22. Allow us to pass through your land.
Moses put out "peace feelers" to Sichon, the Amorite king. Israel wanted only the privilege to move quickly through Amorite territory on their way to Canaan. The message from Moses to Sichon is as honorable and as peaceful as can be: "Allow us to pass through your land. We promise to keep away from your fields and vineyards, and we will not drink any of your well water." When Sichon refused, Israel defeated the Amorites and occupied their land.

It is a mitzvah (527) to first try to come to an agreement, but if it becomes necessary, you must do battle. The same principle holds true in everyday life – in school, at home, or in business.

First talk and try to settle. If the person or the company or a government agency refuses to discuss the problem, then take off your gloves and fight.

22. We will stay on the King's Highway until we have passed through your territories.
The King's Highway ran the entire length of Transjordan from south to north. The southern section of the road was known as the Road of Edom. This road and the coastal road of "Via Maris" formed the main arteries of Palestine east and west of the Jordan.

24. But only as far as the fortified borders of the Ammonites.
The Ammonites were considered to be descendants of Abraham's nephew Lot. Their country, part of which is now in Jordan, was located east of the Jordan River and the Dead Sea. The Ammonites were enemies of the Israelites and a force for spiritual corruption that delighted in spreading idol worship.

25 Israel captured all the Amorite cities. They settled in Heshbon and its surrounding towns.
26 Heshbon was the capital of Sichon, king of the Amorites. He had defeated the first king of Moab and taken over all of his land as far as the Arnon River.
27 That is why the minstrels used to sing:
"Come to Heshbon, Sichon's capital city.
28 A fire has come out of Heshbon; a flame from Sichon's capital has consumed Ar of Moab, the rulers of Arnon's heights.
29 Moab, woe to you;
Nation of Chemosh, you are destroyed, your sons have become refugees, your daughters are captives to Sichon, king of the Amorites. **30** Moab's kingdom was wiped out from Heshbon as far as Dibon, and was laid waste as far as Nopheh and Medeba."
31 So Israel settled in the land of the Amorites.
32 Now Moses sent out scouts to explore the town of Yaazer, and later the Israelites captured the villages in its vicinity, driving out the Amorites who lived there.
33 From there the Israelites marched northward toward the land of Bashan. Og, king of Bashan, deployed his entire army at the town of Edrei to battle the Israelites.

Israel Defeats Og King of Bashan
Maftir

34 Adonai said to Moses, "Do not be afraid of King Og. I will help you defeat him and his army. I will give you his territory and all its inhabitants. I will do the same to him as I did to Sichon, king of the Amorites, who ruled in Heshbon."
35 The Israelites killed Og along with his sons and all his people, leaving no survivors, and they took possession of his territory.

22 From there the Israelites moved on, and they traveled to the western plains of Moab, and camped along the Jordan across from Jericho.

---

25. Israel captured all the Amorite cities. They settled in Heshbon and its surrounding towns.
Forty years after the Exodus, Moses, now an old man, decided that the time had come to resume the suspended invasion. He and his military advisers decided to skirt around the Dead Sea and invade Canaan from the east across the Jordan River. The country of the Amorite king Sichon was the first region east of the Jordan to be conquered by the Israelites.

The name of Heshbon, the capital city of Sichon, is still preserved in the Arab village of Heshbon, which is about twenty miles east of Jericho.

35. The Israelites killed Og along with his sons and all his people.
Once Israel was victorious over the strong Amorites, the other nations of the Middle East became frightened. Directly beyond the Amorite kingdom was the territory of Bashan, known as a powerful military people. No doubt Moses worried a great deal about Israel's ability to move through that land.

Og, king of Bashan, certainly had great confidence in his army's strength. No sooner did he hear that Israel was approaching than he marched against them.

At Edrei, thirty miles east of Lake Tiberias, the two armies clashed. After a fierce battle the Israelites again won. This time the mighty Og suffered defeat.

בָּלָק *Balak*

THE STORY OF KING BALAK

2 When Balak son of Tzippor heard how Israel had defeated the Amorites, **3** he was terrified because of the great victory won by the Israelite soldiers.
4 So Moab sent a message to the leaders of Midian: "The Israelite army will eat up everything around us, just as a bull eats up all the vegetables in the field."
Balak son of Tzippor, king of Moab, **5** sent messengers to Balaam son of Beor, who lived in Pethor near the Euphrates River. They brought him the following message:
"I desperately need your help. This nation is too powerful for us to defeat alone.

2–3. When Balak son of Tzippor heard how Israel had defeated the Ammorites, he was terrified because of the great victory won by the Israelite soldiers.
After the victories over Sichon, king of the Amorites, and Og, king of Bashan, the Israelites were close by the border of Moab. Now it was Moab's ruler, King Balak, who was frightened by Israel.

The Moabites and the Israelites were related. Lot, the nephew of Abraham, was the forefather of the Moabites. They were aware that the Israelites would not attack their own kinsmen but they feared and distrusted the desert wanderers. Instead of seeking a peaceful solution, they opted for a military response.

4. So Moab sent a message to the leaders of Midian: "The Israelite army will eat up everything around us just as a bull eats up all the vegetables in the field."
Midian and Moab were enemies, but in time of mutual danger they formed an alliance.

4. So Moab sent a message to the leaders of Midian.
The midrash says that the king of Moab was frightened by the military power of the Israelites. He sent a message to the leaders of Midian asking them to explain the power of Moses to achieve military victories. He asked the leaders, "Moses grew up in Midian. Can you explain the source of his military powers?"

Little did the king of Moab realize that Moses had acquired "Adonic" power.

4–5. Balak son of Tzippor, king of Moab, sent messengers to Balaam son of Beor, who lived in Pethor near the Euphrates River.
Pethor is situated in a section of Babylon near the Euphrates that was very famous in its day for its magicians, sorcerers, and seers.

These men were used by the local kings to advise them and even by the common people who came to worship and to have these men invoke curses and blessings. The seers would resort to all manner of hocus-pocus as they pretended to have super-human power to bring about people's wishes or to heal the sick.

Balaam was believed to be such a "diviner." Instead of negotiating peacefully, Balak quickly invited Balaam to curse the oncoming Israelites, offering him a large reward.

King Balak was terrified of the Israelites. He saw how the Amorites were defeated and he was in a state of panic. Balak compares the Israelites to a strong bull devouring everything in its path.

4–5. Balak son of Tzippor, king of Moab, sent messengers to Balaam son of Beor, who lived in Pelthor near the Euphrates River. They brought him the following message: "I desperately need your help."
The Israelites defeated Balak the Amorite after they were suddenly attacked by him. Now Balak tells Balaam to curse the Israelites. Instead, the curses of Balaam became blessings.

6 Please come and curse this nation for me.
Then, perhaps, we will be able to defeat them and drive them from the area.
I know that anyone you bless is successful, and whoever you curse is doomed." **7** The leaders of Moab and Midian, who were expert magicians, went to Balaam and brought him Balak's message. **8** Balaam replied, "Spend the night here, and when Adonai speaks to me, I will be able to give you an answer." So the Moabite leaders stayed with Balaam. **9** That night Adonai appeared to Balaam and asked, "Who are these men, and what do they want from you?" **10** Balaam replied to Adonai, "Balak son of Tzippor, king of Moab, has sent them to me with this message: **11** 'A mighty nation that covers the face of the earth has come here from Egypt. Come and curse them for me. If you do, I will be able to defeat them and drive them away.' "
12 Adonai warned Balaam, "Do not go with Balak's messengers. Do not curse the nation, because I have blessed them."

Balaam Refuses to Curse Israel *2nd Aliyah*

13 In the morning, when Balaam got up he said to the leaders, "Go back home! Adonai will not allow me to go with you."
14 The Moabite leaders returned to king Balak and said, "Balaam refused to come with us."
15 So Balak sent another delegation, this time with many more important leaders. **16** They came to Balaam and, in the name of Balak, gave him the following message: "Do not refuse to come to me. **17** I will honor you greatly and give you anything you want. Please come and curse this nation for me."
18 But Balaam replied to Balak's servants and said, "Even if Balak gave me his whole palace full of gold and silver, I am powerless to do anything against the wishes of Adonai. **19** But stay here overnight, and then I will know what Adonai wants me to do." **20** That night, Adonai appeared to Balaam and said to him,
"Since the leaders have come for you, go with them. But be sure to do only what I tell you to do."

Adonai Sends an Angel *3rd Aliyah*

21 In the morning Balaam got up, saddled his donkey, and went with the Moabite leaders. **22** Adonai was angry because Balaam was so eager to go with them. An angel of Adonai stood in the middle of the road to stop Balaam, who was riding his donkey. **23** When the donkey saw Adonai's angel standing in the road with a sword in his hand, it ran from the road into the field. Balaam beat the donkey to get it back on the road.

---

6. Please come and curse this nation for me.
For maximum effectiveness, curses must be pronounced close to the person. Distance weakens the strength of the incantation.

18. But Balaam replied to Balak's servants and said, "Even if Balak gave me his whole palace full of gold and silver, I am powerless to do anything against the wishes of Adonai.
Balaam was really interested in a rich monetary reward but he sadly says, "I am powerless to do anything against the wishes of Adonai."

23. Balaam beat the donkey to put it back on the road.
Maimonides says that there was really no talking donkey.
  The talking donkey happened in Balaam's dream. Psychologically, Balaam was unhappy with his mission, and the symbolic dream donkey warned him that he would be unable to fulfill it because he had no faith in what he was going to do.

24 Then the angel of Adonai stood in the middle of a narrow path between two vineyards, where there was a fence on either side.
25 When the donkey saw the angel of Adonai, it moved against one of the fences, crushing Balaam's foot, and Balaam beat it even more.
26 The angel of Adonai moved again and stood in a narrow spot where there was no room to turn around.
27 When the donkey saw Adonai's angel, it lay down and refused to move. Once again Balaam lost his temper and beat the donkey with a stick.
28 When this happened Adonai gave the donkey the power of speech, and it asked Balaam, "What did I do to you, to make you beat me three times?"
29 Balaam shouted, "You made me look like a fool. If I had a sword, I would kill you!"
30 The donkey answered Balaam, "But I am the same donkey that you always ride. Have I ever done this to you before?" And Balaam answered, "No!"
31 Now Adonai gave Balaam the power to see, and he saw the angel with a sword in his hand standing in the road. Balaam kneeled and bowed down.
32 The angel of Adonai said to him, "Why did you beat your donkey three times? I have come out to stop you, because your mission is against my wishes. **33** When the donkey saw me, it turned aside three times. If it had not turned aside, I would have killed you and let the donkey live."
34 Balaam said to Adonai's angel, "I was wrong! I didn't know that you were standing on the road to stop me. If you are angry with me, I will return home."
35 Adonai's angel said to Balaam, "I want you to go with the leaders. But say only exactly what I tell you." So Balaam went with Balak's messengers.
36 When Balak heard that Balaam had arrived, he went to meet him in the capital city of Moab, which is near the Arnon River.
37 Balak said to Balaam, " Why didn't you come to me the first time. Did you think I wouldn't pay you?"
38 Balaam replied to Balak, "Do you think I can prophesy any time I want to? I can only repeat the words that Adonai tells me to say."

---

28. When this happened Adonai gave the donkey the power of speech and it asked Balaam, "What did I do to you, to make you beat me three times?"
The commentator S. D. Luzzato explains that the donkey did not really speak but protested by braying, "Why are you beating me?" The donkey really protested and hee-hawed in anger. When this happened Adonai gave the donkey the power of speech. Some say that the donkey really didn't speak. It was a prophetic dream.

30. Have I ever done this to you before?
Here the animal indicates to Balaam that he should realize that, since his behavior is so peculiar, Balaam should not continue on his mission; it will only prove to be a failure.

34. I was wrong! I did not know that you were standing on the road to stop me. If you are angry with me, I will return home.
Now Balaam is finally convinced that it is useless to defy Adonai's resolve. He now realizes that he wanted nothing to do with Balak.

Now he is forced to become Adonai's messenger and bless the nation of Israel instead of cursing them.

Israel Is a Peaceful Nation

4th Aliyah

39 Balaam went with Balak to the town of Kiryat Huzoth.

40 There Balak sacrificed cattle and sheep, and sent the meat to Balaam and the leaders who were with him.

41 In the morning, Balak took Balaam to the town of Bamoth Baal (Altars of Baal), a place from which he could see the Israelite camp.

23 Balaam said to Balak, "Build seven altars here, and bring me seven bulls and seven rams."

2 Balak did as Balaam asked. Then Balak and Balaam sacrificed a bull and a ram as a burnt offering on each of the seven altars.

3 Balaam said to Balak, "Wait here with your burnt offerings, and I will see if Adonai wishes to meet me and tell me what to say." So Balaam went to a quiet place to meet with Adonai.

4 Balaam said to Adonai, "I have set up seven altars, and I have sacrificed a bull and a ram as a burnt offering on each of the altars."

5 Then Adonai gave Balaam a message and said, "Return to Balak, and say exactly what I tell you."

6 When Balaam returned, Balak and the Moabite dignitaries were still standing near the burnt offerings.

7 This was Balaam's prophecy:

"Balak, king of Moab, has brought me from Aram,
from the hills of the east, and told me to come and curse Jacob
and bring divine anger against Israel.
8 But how can I curse
if Adonai will not allow me to curse?
How can I curse
If Adonai is not angry?

---

41. In the morning, Balak took Balaam to the town of Bamoth Baal (Altars of Baal).
The idol Baal was their most important god. Baal was usually worshipped on (*bamoth*) high places.

1. Build seven altars here, and bring me seven bulls and seven rams.
Balaam felt that the number seven had a special, mystical significance in Adonai's eyes.

7. Balak, king of Moab, has brought me from Aram from the hills of the east.
Aram is in Mesopotamia. It is the shortened name for Aram Naharaim, meaning Aram of the two rivers. It included the present country of Syria and parts of Iraq.

7. And told me to come and curse Jacob and bring divine anger against Israel.
For the benefit of his audience, Balak emphasized the curse and two names, Jacob and Israel. If one curse didn't work, two would surely be better.

8. But how can I curse if Adonai will not allow me to curse?
Balaam does not have the power to curse Israel. What he has seen makes it impossible for him to curse them.

Balak now furiously attacks Balaam and shouts, "I brought you to curse my enemies, but you have made every effort to bless them."

9 From mountaintops I see this nation,
and watch them from the heights.
It is a nation at peace,
far away from other nations.
10 Jacob is numerous like the dust;
who can count his people?
Who can count the Children of Israel?
When I die a righteous death,
let my death be like theirs!"

11 Balak said to Balaam, "What have you done to me? I brought you to curse my enemies, but you have made every effort to bless them!"

12 Balaam interrupted and said, "Didn't I warn you that I must be very careful to say only what Adonai tells me?"

Balaam's Second Prophecy   *5th Aliyah*

13 Balak replied, "Please, come with me to a place where you will be able to see just a small part of the Israelite camp. Perhaps from there you will be able to curse just a few of them for me. **14** So Balak took Balaam to the field of Zophim at the top of Mount Pisgah. There Balak built another seven altars and offered a bull and a ram on each altar.

15 Balaam said to Balak, "Wait here with your burnt offerings, and I will go to meet Adonai."

16 Adonai appeared to Balaam and gave him a message. He said, "Go back to Balak, and prophesy exactly what I tell you."

17 So Balaam returned and found Balak and the Moabite leaders standing near the burnt offerings. Balak asked, "What has Adonai said to you?"

18 Balaam prophesied,

"Balak son of Tzippor,
rise, and pay attention to my words.

---

9. It is a nation at peace, far away from other nations.
Standing on the mountain, Balaam is hypnotized by the rows of tents, with children happily playing and men and women peacefully tending to their chores. As hard as he tries, Balaam cannot curse the Israelites, yet he is afraid to bless them since Balak and his guards are observing every one of his actions.

So he prophesies that the Israelites are just a small, distant nation who wants to live in peace with its neighbors. They are a holy people who wish to live by the commandments.

10. When I die a righteous death, let my death be like theirs.
Let my death be that of a righteous person and not like that of a wicked man who defied the will of Adonai by cursing his chosen people. Balaam did not die a righteous death. The Israelites mounted a surprise attack against Midian (v. 31:8), and the five kings of Midian as well as Balaam son of Beor were killed.

14. So Balak took Balaam to the field of Zophim at the top of Mount Pisgah.
The Hebrew word *zofeh* means "watchmen." The field of Zophim (watchmen) was a high place where watchmen stood guard to watch out for raiders and enemies.

17. Balak asked, "What has Adonai said to you?"
Balaam is an absolute king and demands results. He is tired of being run around by Balaam. The king is used to getting results from his underlings. Now, Balak impatiently asks, "What has Adonai said to you?"

19 Adonai is not human, and He does not lie.
Adonai is not mortal
and does not change His mind.
He speaks and does it.
What He says, He fulfills.
20 I have been given a command to bless,
and I cannot reverse it.
21 Adonai does not see evil in Jacob,
and He sees no misery in Israel.
Adonai is with them,
they have His admiration.
22 Adonai brought them out of Egypt.
He supports them with his strength.
23 No curse can harm Jacob,
and no sorcery can overpower Israel.
Adonai has performed wonders for Israel.
24 It is a nation as powerful as the king of beasts, majestic like a lion.
It does not rest until it defeats the enemy and wins the victory."
25 Balak said to Balaam, "If you cannot curse them, at least don't bless them!"
26 Balaam replied, "I warned you before. I can only prophesy what Adonai puts in my mind and my mouth."

---

19. Adonai is not human, and He does not lie. Adonai is not mortal and does not change His mind. He speaks and does it. What He says, He fulfills.
Balak, listen to me. You just cannot grasp the concept of a spiritual power versus the worship of Baal. Adonai's power does not come from a wooden idol. Adonai has blessed Israel and I am powerless to reverse His decision.

21. Adonai does not see evil in Jacob, and he sees no misery in Israel. Adonai is with them, and they have His admiration.
Balaam tries to convince hardheaded Balak that his curses are useless. Adonai has no complaints about Israel. In fact, Adonai has commanded Balaam to bless them. He cannot in any way refuse Adonai's commands.

21. He sees no misery in Israel.
The Israelites are brave and they are determined to settle in Canaan. Neither you nor your allies will ever be able to frighten them. They are tireless and with Adonai's help will achieve their goal.

23. No curse can harm Jacob, and no sorcery can overpower Israel. Adonai has performed wonders for Israel.
Israel has no need for believers in sorcery. Adonai, Master of the world, has and will perform wonders for His people Israel.

24. It is a nation as powerful as the king of beasts, majestic like a lion.
The lion, king of the beasts, the most ferocious of the animals, is used to symbolize the military strength of the Israelites.

25. If you cannot curse them, at least don't bless them.
After two defeats, Balak has arrived at the conclusion that he had been defeated by the unseen adversary, Adonai. He tries to cut his losses by begging Balaam to at least not bless Israel.

26. Balaam replied, "I warned you before. I can only prophesy what Adonai puts in my mind and my mouth."
Balak had to admit that he was not free to do what he wanted. He was like a ventriloquist's dummy who spoke whatever Adonai put into his mouth.

Shenash

Balaam's Third Prophecy

6th Aliyah

27 Then Balak said to Balaam, "I will take you someplace else. Perhaps Adonai will allow you to curse them for me from there." **28** Balak took Balaam to the top of Mount Peor. **29** Then Balaam said to Balak, "Build seven altars here, and prepare seven bulls and seven rams." **30** Balak did as Balaam said, and he sacrificed a bull and a ram as a burnt offering on each of the seven altars.

24 By now Balaam realized that Adonai planned to bless Israel, so he no longer tried to use magic to find out what to do. Instead, he looked toward the desert. **2** Then Balaam clearly saw the tribes of Israel living in peace. Adonai's spirit enveloped him. **3** And he began to prophesy:

"These are the words of Balaam son of Beor,
 the words of a man with a clear vision.
4 The words of a man who listens to Adonai,
 who sees a vision of the Almighty
 and falls into a trance with open eyes.
5 Jacob, how beautiful are your tents; Israel,
 your tabernacles are very peaceful.
6 They stretch out like palm trees in gardens by the river,
 like aloe trees planted by Adonai,
 like cedars near the water.
7 Israel's water shall overflow,
 and their crops shall have abundant water.
When their kingdom is established, their king will be mightier than King Agag.
8 With power Adonai brought them out of Egypt, they are His strength. They will defeat many enemy nations, crushing their fortresses and wounding them with arrows.
9 Israel crouches like a mighty lion, who will dare challenge him?
Those who bless you will be blessed, and those who curse you will be cursed."

---

27. Perhaps Adonai will allow you to curse them for me from there.
Three times Balak and Balaam went through the same ritual and three times Balaam blessed Israel, making Balak angrier and angrier. The fourth prophecy became a blessing predicting a remarkable future for the Israelites.

5. How beautiful are your tents; Israel, your tabernacles are very peaceful.
When Balaam arrived at Balak's palace, he was given a grand reception. Balak believed that Balaam's technique would surely spell the doom of Israel. Balaam's curse would spare Moab a defeat. Such a man must be honored.

After the warm welcome, King Balak took Balaam to three different mountaintops from which would be seen the Israelite encampment. But Balak was disappointed.

At each of the three points Balaam looked down and blessed Israel. In his third tribute, Balaam spoke the great words: "How beautiful are your tents, Israel."

No curse was uttered by Balaam. In terrible anger, Balak sent Balaam away.

5. Tabernacles.
According to the sages, the "tents" are the schools which teach Torah and the tabernacles are the synagogues, the spiritual home of the Jews wherever they have lived.

10 When Balak heard Balaam's prophecy, he became angry and shouted, "I brought you here to curse my enemies, but instead you blessed them three times! **11** Now run home as fast as you can! I promised to pay you, but now, thanks to Adonai, you will not be paid!" **12** Balaam answered Balak, "Right at the outset I told your messengers, when you sent for me, that **13** even if King Balak were to give me his whole palace full of gold and silver, I could not promise to do anything good or bad, because I must obey Adonai. I can only prophesy whatever Adonai tells me to say.

Balaam's Final Prophecy *7th Aliyah*

14 "So now I am returning to my people, but first I must warn you about what the Israelites will eventually do to your people." **15** Balaam then prophesied:

"I am Balaam son of Beor,
The words of a man who sees clearly, **16** and hears Adonai's words.
I saw a vision of the Almighty, and my mind and eyes were opened.
17 I see Israel's distant future.
A star will shoot out from Jacob, and a ruler will arise in Israel
and crush the leaders of Moab,
and rule over the descendants of Seth. **18** Edom will be destroyed.
His enemy, Seir, will be decimated, And Israel shall be triumphant.
19 A ruler shall rise out of Jacob who will destroy the survivors."

20 When Balaam saw Amalek, he continued to prophesy,
"Amalek is a leader among nations but in the end he will forever be destroyed."
21 When he saw the Kenites, he again prophesied,
"Though you live in a fortress, and have built your homes among the rocks,
22 in the end the Kenites will be destroyed, when Assyria conquers them."
23 Balaam ended his prophecy:
"No one can survive Adonai's devastation. **24** Warships shall sail from the ports of the Kittim, and they will destroy Assyria and Eber. But in the end they too will be destroyed."
25 When Balaam finished, he returned home. Balak left and also went on his way.

25

While Israel was camped in Shittim, some of the young men became involved with Moabite girls.

---

17. I see Israel's distant future. A star will shoot out from Jacob, and a ruler will arise in Israel and crush the leaders of Moab.
Rashi explains that the star out from Jacob refers to the Messiah. Other commentators interpret the phrases to refer to King David, who defeated the Moabites.

The flag of Israel contains a *Magen David*, a star of David.

1. While Israel was camped in Shittim, some of the young men became involved with Moabite girls.
Shittim was located at the end of the Dead Sea opposite the city of Jericho. It was the last camping place before the Israelites crossed the Jordan. Joshua sent spies to reconnoiter the invasion route before the Israelites entered the Promised Land.

It was at Shittim that the Israelite young men became sexually and religiously involved with the Moabite girls.

2 The girls invited the boys to sacrifice and to worship the Moabite idols. **3** Some of the Israelites began to worship the idol Baal Peor, thereby angering Adonai.
4 Adonai said to Moses, "Take the leaders who are responsible for this behavior and have the idolaters publicly executed before Adonai. Then I will not be angry with Israel."
5 Moses said to Israel's tribal judges, "Each of you must put to death any of your tribesmen who have worshipped the idol Baal Peor."
6 The judges at the entrance of the Meeting Tent began to weep about this decision. At that very moment, an Israelite brought a Midianite woman into the Israelite community in front of Moses and all the people.

Pinchas Stops the Plague
Maftir

7 When Pinchas son of Elazar, a grandson of Aaron the priest, saw this, he jumped up and took a spear in his hand.
8 He rushed into the tent of the Israelite man, and drove his spear through the Israelite man and the Midianite woman. Seeing this, Adonai stopped the plague against the Israelites. **9** In that plague, 24,000 Israelites died.

---

6. The judges at the entrance of the Meeting Tent began to weep about this decision.
The judges realized that they would have to kill their own clan and family members. This was a horrific command, and they wept at the thought of carrying out their responsibility.

7. When Pinchas son of Elazar, a grandson of Aaron the priest, saw this, he jumped up and took a spear in his hand…and drove his spear through the Israelite man and the Midianite woman.
Life in the desert had not prepared the people for the temptations which arose from close contact with erotic alien people. In the land of Moab, Israelite men were seduced into cohabitation by female erotic fertility rites which were an important part of Canaanite cults.

The problem is highlighted by an Israelite who brazenly brought a Midianite woman into his tent. Pinchas, a grandson of Aaron, plunged a spear through both their bodies during intercourse.

9. In that plague 24,000 Israelites died.
Because of the idol worshipping of the Israelites, Adonai sent a plague, which killed 24,000 Israelites. The plagues, according to medical experts, was a venereal disease which was caused by contact with diseased Moabite women.

9. In that plague 24,000 Israelites died.
The Moabite sex scandal resulted in the death of 24,000 Israelites whereas the affair of the golden calf caused only 3,000 deaths. Why the disparity in punishments? Rabbi Hirsch postulated that at this point in time, sexual immorality was a greater danger than idol worship. The nation of Israel was in its early formative stage and the Moabite women were a sexual fifth column, which could destroy the formation of a holy and moral Israelite nation. It was imperative to issue a severe warning to the Israelites that they were in danger of losing Adonai's protection.

The plague which befell the Israelites when they commited sexual acts with the daughters of Moab (25:1) is referred to as a *magefah*, a term meaning "epidemic." It is thought that this particular *magefah* was a venereal disease.

פִּנְחָס *Pinchas*

THE REWARD OF PINCHAS

10 Then Adonai spoke to Moses, and said, **11** "Pinchas son of Elazar and grandson of Aaron the priest was faithful to Me and turned My anger away from the Israelites, so that I did not destroy them.
12 Therefore, tell him that I have made a covenant of peace with him.
13 In this covenant I promise that he and his descendants shall always be My priests. It is given to him because he was loyal to Me and made atonement for the Israelites."
14 The name of the man who was killed was Zimri son of Salu, a leader of the tribe of Simeon. **15** The name of the Midianite woman who was killed was Kazbi daughter of Tzur; her father was the leader of a Midianite family.
16 Adonai spoke to Moses, saying, **17** "Attack the Midianites and destroy them **18** because they tricked some Israelites into worshipping the idol Peor, and because of their sister, Kazbi, daughter of the Midianite leader, who was killed on the day of the plague at Peor.

26 After the plague had ended, Adonai spoke to Moses and Elazar son of Aaron the priest, and said, **2** "Take a census of the men in the Israelite community, and count every male over twenty years old who is fit for military service."
3 Moses and Elazar the priest spoke to the Israelites in their camp on the Plains of Moab near the Jordan River, just across from Jericho, saying, **4** "Count all the men over twenty years of age, just as Adonai commanded Moses when they left Egypt."

The Census of the Tribe
2nd Aliyah

5 Reuben was Israel's first-born. The descendants of Reuben were the Enochite family from Enoch, the Paluite family from Palu, **6** The Hetzronite family from Hetzron, and the Karmite family from Karmi.

---

13. In this covenant I promise that he and his descendants shall always be My priests. It is given to him because he was loyal to Me and made atonement for the Israelites.
Pinchas, a son of Elazar, son of Aaron, succeeded his father to the High Priesthood. He killed an Israelite who brought a Midianite woman into his tent. Zimri, the Israelite was responsible for tempting the Israelites to follow her idol worship.

14. The name of the man who was killed was Zimri son of Salu, a leader of the tribe of Simeon.
Zimri's grandfather, Simeon, helped wipe out the city of Shechem because Hamor, who committed an immoral act, raped Simeon's sister Dinah. Now his grandson, Zimri, committed an immoral act by having illicit relations with a Midianite woman. Pinchas of the tribe of Levi killed Zimri, who was a leader in the tribe of Simeon.

The family of Zimri was very powerful. In his anger Pinchas was not concerned about any danger or revenge by Zimri's relatives, because he was inspired with a holy passion. Adonai's reputation had to be protected, so Pinchas reacted spontaneously.

2. Count every male over twenty years old.
Twenty was the age at which they were considered ready for military service.

7 There were 43,730 qualified men fit for military service in the tribe of Reuben.
8 The sons of Pallu were Eliav. **9** The sons of Eliav were Nemuel, Dathan, and Aviram. Dathan and Aviram were the leaders who led Korach's rebellion against Moses and Aaron and Adonai. **10** But the earth opened its mouth and swal- lowed them and Korach. At the same time a streak of fire from Adonai destroyed the 250 followers of Korach. This was a divine miracle. **11** The sons of Korach, however, were not killed.
12 By families, the descendants of Simeon were the Nemuelite family from Nemuel, the Yaminite family from Yamin, the Yakhinite family from Yakhin, **13** the Zarchite family from Zerach, and the Saulite family from Saul.
14 There were 22,200 men fit for military service in the tribe of Simeon.
15 By families, the descendants of Gad were the Tzefonite family from Tzefon, the Haggite family from Haggi, the Shunite family from Shuni, **16** the Aznite family from Aznil, the Erite family from Eri, **17** the Arodite family from Arod, and the Arelite family from Areli.
18 There were 40,500 men fit for military service in the tribe of Gad.
19 The sons of Judah were Er and Onan, but Er and Onan died in the land of Canaan.
20 By families, the descendants of Judah were the Shelanite family from Shelah, the Partzite family from Peretz, and the Zarchite family from Zerach.
21 The descendants of Peretz were the Chetzronite family from Chetzron, and the Chamulite family from Chamul.
22 There were 76,500 men fit for military service in the tribe of Judah.
23 By families, the descendants of Issachar were the Tolaite family from Tola, the Punite family from Puvah.
24 the Yashuvite family from Yashuv, and the Shimronite family from Shimron.
25 There were 64,300 men fit for military service in the tribe of Issachar.
26 By families, the descendants of Zebulun were the Sardite family from Sered, the Elonite family from Elon, and the Yachlielite family from Yachliel.
27 There were 60,500 men fit for military service in the tribe of Zebulun.
28 By families, the descendants of Joseph were Manasseh and Ephraim.
29 The descendants of Manasseh were the Makhirite family from Makhir. Makhir's son was Gilead, and from Gilead came the family of the Gileadites.
30 These were the descendants of Gilead: the Iyezerite family from Iyezer, the Helekite family from Helek, **31** the Azrielite family from Azriel, the Shikhmite family from Shekhem, **32** the Shemidaite family from Shemida, and the Hefrite family from Hefer.
33 Chefer's son, Tzelafechad, did not have any sons, only daughters. The names of Tzelafechad's daughters were Machla, Noah, Chaglah, Milkah, and Tirtzah.
34 There were 52,700 men fit for military service in the tribe of Manasseh.
35 By families, the descendants of Ephraim were the Shuthalchite family from Shuthelach, the Bakhrite family from Bekher, and the Tachanite family from Tachan.

36 The descendants of Shuthelach were the Eranite family from Eran.
37 There were 32,500 men fit for military service in the tribe of Ephraim. These are the descendants of Joseph by their families.
38 By families, the descendants of Benjamin were the Bal'ite family from Bela, the Ashbelite family from Ashbel, the Achiramite family from Achiram,
39 the Shefufamite family from Shefufam, and the Hufamite family from Hufam.
40 The sons of Bela were Ard and Naaman. These gave rise to the Ardite family, and the Naamite family from Naaman.
41 There were 45,600 men fit for military service in the tribe of Benjamin.
42 By families, the descendants of Dan were the Shuchamite family from Shucham. This was the only family of Dan.
43 There were 64,400 men fit for military service in the tribe of Dan.
44 By families, the descendants of Asher were the Yimnah family from Yimnah, the Yishvite family from Yishvi, and the Berite family from Beriah.
45 The descendants of Beriah were the Hevrite family from Hever and the Malkielite family from Malkiel. **46** The name of Asher's daughter was Serach.
47 There were 53,400 men fit for military service in the tribe of Asher.
48 By families, the descendants of Naphtali were the Yachtzielite family from Yachtziel, the Gunite family from Guni, **49** the Yitzrite family from Yetzer, and the Shilemite family from Shilem.
50 There were 45,400 men fit for military service in the tribe of Naphtali.
51 There was a total of 601,730 Israelite men fit for military service.

Dividing the Land
3rd Aliyah

52 Adonai spoke to Moses, saying: **53** "You shall divide the land as an inheritance among the people, based on the number of recorded names.
54 To a larger group you shall give a larger inheritance, whereas to a smaller group you shall give a smaller inheritance. Each group shall receive its inheritance according to the number of people in it. **55** Make sure to allot the land to the tribes through a lottery system. **56** The large tribal family will be assigned more land, and the smaller tribal family will be assigned less land.
Whether a group is large or small, its hereditary property shall be divided by a lottery system."

---

54. To a larger group you shall give a larger inheritance, whereas to a smaller group you shall give a smaller inheritance. Each group shall receive its inheritance according to the number of people in it.
The land was allotted on the basis of the second census. There had been large changes due to the Israelites who died in the wilderness, so a second census was necessary.

Each of the tribes was given an equal share of the land by Moses and Aaron.

Then the leaders of the individual tribes were responsible for subdividing the land and allocating the portions to the families according to their number of people.

55. Make sure to allot the land to the tribes through a lottery system.
Moses, Aaron, and the other leaders, bent over backwards to prevent the Israelites from accusing them of favoritism. They allotted the land by a lottery so that they would not be accused of favoring one group over another.

57 These are the families of the Levites: the Gershonite family from Gershon, the Kehothite family from Kehoth, and the Merarite family from Merari.
58 These are the subfamilies of Levi:
the Libnite family, the Hevonite family, the Machlite family, the Mushite family, and the Korchite family. Kehoth had a son named Amram. **59** While in Egypt, Amram married Yoheved, a daughter of Levi. She gave birth to Aaron and Moses, and their sister Miriam.
60 Aaron had four sons: Nadav, Avihu, Elazar, and Ithamar.
61 But Nadav and Avihu died when they offered unauthorized fire before Adonai.
62 There were 23,000 Levite males over one month of age.
They were not counted with the other Israelites because they were not allotted any land when it was divided among the Israelite tribes.
63 The above is the census that Moses and Elazar the priest took of the Israelites on the Plains of Moab, across from Jericho, near the Jordan River. **64** Not a single person who was counted by Moses and Aaron forty years earlier in the Wilderness of Zin was still alive. **65** Adonai had told the Israelites that they would all die in the desert, and that not a single person would remain alive except for Caleb son of Yefuneh, and Joshua son of Nun.

27

One day a petition was presented by the daughters of Tzelafechad son of Hefer, son of Gilead, son of Makhir, son of' Manasseh, of the family of Joseph's son Manasseh. The names of his daughters were Machlah, Noah, Haglah, Milkah, and Tirtzah. **2** They stood before Moses, Elazar the priest, the tribal leaders, and the entire community at the entrance of the Meeting Tent with the following petition:
3 "Our father died in the wilderness. He was not one of the members of Korach's party who rebelled against Adonai, but he died because of his own sin without leaving any sons.
4 Why should our father's family be penalized because he did not have a son? Give us an inheritance of land just like our father's brothers."
5 Moses brought their petition before Adonai.

---

57. These are the families of the Levites: the Gershonite family from Gershon, the Kehothite family from Kehoth, and the Merarite family from Merari.
The Israelites and the Levites were counted separately. The tribes counted only males over 20 years of age. The census of the Levites counted only the males from the age of one month.

3. 'Our father died in the wilderness. He was not one of the members of Korach's party who rebelled against Adonai, but he died because of his own sin without leaving any sons.'
Tzelafechad was one of the 600,000 Israelites who were freed by Moses. His was the generation of the desert, who because of their sin of cowardice were destined to die before crossing the Jordan into Canaan.

4. Why should our father's family be penalized because he did not have a son? Give us an inheritance of land just like our father's brothers.

The law stated that only sons had the right to inherit and the first-born was to receive a double share of the family estate. The girls did not need to inherit property for their own survival, since they would be supported by their husbands when they married.

The daughters of Tzelafechad complained to Moses and Elazar the High Priest that their fathers had died without leaving any sons. According to the laws of inheritance, they were counted in the census and they were legally entitled to a portion of their father's land.

Inheritance for the Daughters
4th Aliyah

6 Adonai answered Moses, saying: **7** "The daughters of Tzelafechad are right. Give them a portion of land alongside their uncles. Give them their father's inheritance of land. **8** Now speak to the Israelites and tell them that if a man dies and has no sons, his hereditary property shall pass over to his daughters. **9** If he has no daughters, then his hereditary land shall be given to his brothers. **10** If he has no brothers, you shall give his land to his father's brothers.

11 However, if his father had no brothers, then you shall give his land to the nearest relative in his family. This shall be the law for the Israelites, as Adonai has commanded Moses."

12 Adonai said to Moses, "Climb up to the top of Mount Avarim, where you will be able to see the land that I am giving to the Israelites. **13** After you see it, you will die and be gathered to your people, just as your brother Aaron was.

14 When the community rebelled against My instructions in the Wilderness of Zin, you disobeyed My commandment and did not believe in my holy power." Adonai was speaking about Mai Meribah (Waters of Dispute) at Kadesh in the Wilderness of Zin.

15 Moses spoke to Adonai, saying, "Adonai, source of all living beings, appoint a new leader over the community. **16** Your people need a strong leader to lead them in battle. **17** Do not let Adonai's community wander like sheep without a shepherd."

18 Adonai said to Moses, "Choose Joshua son of Nun, for he is a man of spirit. Place your hand on him. **19** Present him to Elazar the priest, and let the entire community watch as he appoints him.

---

7. The daughters of Tzelafechad are right. Give them a portion of land.
According to law, a family inheritance was to remain in the family, thereby continuing the family name. The request of the women was unusual, since according to ancient law, women normally did not inherit property. Adonai rewarded the daughters for their faith and their knowledge of the law. Now the law was changed and the daughters could inherit the property and would remain within the clan. Elazar the High Priest and the tribal leader recognized the merit of their pleas. Moses agreed with their pleas and passed a law that if a man dies and has no sons, his hereditary property (land) shall revert to his daughters. The rights given to the daughters served as a precedent for the laws of inheritance by family members.

12. Climb up to the top of Mount Avarim.
In Devarim 32:49, Avarim is described as Mount Nebo. It is identified today as a peak twelve miles east of the northern end of the Dead Sea.

13. After you see it, you will die and be gathered to your people, just as your brother Aaron was.
Moses wished to die in the same manner as did his brother, through the kiss of Adonai.

16. Your people need a strong leader to lead them in battle.
When Moses is told by Adonai that he is to die, he shows the greatness of his character by not pleading for his life; his chief concern was his people and their needs.

18–19. Choose Joshua son of Nun, for he is a man of spirit. Place your hands on him. Present him to Elazar the priest, and let the entire community watch as he appoints him.
Moses wisely presents the political and spiritual leaders to the community and confirms their authority. He sets the stage for close cooperation between the two centers. Moses transferred the leadership to his assistant, Joshua, by ordaining him and giving him *semichah* (ordination). Joshua had to lower his head in submission to his master. This was to teach Joshua that he must always think what Moses would have done and make his decisions accordingly.

20 Publicly hand him your authority so that the entire Israelite community will obey him. **21** Let him stand before Elazar the priest, who will ask on his behalf the decision of the Urim before Adonai. At Joshua's command, the Israelite community shall go out, and at his command they will return."

22 Moses did as Adonai had ordered him. He took Joshua and had him stand before Elazar the priest and before the entire community. **23** He placed his hands on him and publicly passed his authority to Joshua. It was all done exactly as Adonai had commanded Moses.

The Daily Sacrifices
5th Aliyah

28 Adonai spoke to Moses, telling him to **2** give the following instructions to the Israelites and tell them: Make sure to present My fire-offering food sacrifices, because they please Me.

3 The fire offering to be presented each day to Adonai shall consist of two healthy lambs without blemish each day as a regular daily burnt offering.

4 Present one lamb in the morning, and the second lamb in the late afternoon. **5** Also present two quarts of flour for the grain offering, mixed with three pints of pure hand-pressed olive oil. **6** This is the regular daily burnt offering, the same as was presented at Mount Sinai as a thank you fire offering to Adonai. **7** The accompanying libation shall consist of three pints of wine for each lamb, a drink offering to Adonai.

---

21. Let him stand before Elazar the priest, who will ask on his behalf the decision of the Urim before Adonai.
The leadership of the Israelites was split between Joshua, who was in the day-to-day command, and Elazar the priest, who inherited the religious leadership.

Thus, there was a separation of powers, the executive branch was led by Joshua, and the religious branch was under the authority of Elazar.

23. He placed his hands on him and publicly passed his authority to Joshua. It was all done exactly as Adonai had commanded Moses.
In verse 18 Adonai tells Moses to place his (one) hand on Joshua. Now, Moses, as a sign of respect and confidence, goes beyond Adonai's command, and places his two hands on Joshua, as he passes on his authority.

Midrash

23. He placed his hands on him and publicly passed his authority to Joshua.
Placing hands on the shoulders or head is a traditional form whereby a leader grants authority to a disciple.

Rabbis who graduate from a rabbinical seminary receive *semichah*, meaning the official degree of rabbi. All rabbis are ordained by their teachers in this manner.

In England it is a custom for the king to knight a person by placing a sword on the person's shoulder.

6. This is the regular daily burnt offering, the same as was presented at Mount Sinai as a thank you fire offering to Adonai.
The daily *korban tamid* sacrifice consisted of one animal brought on behalf of the entire *tzibur*, community. It had no individual ownership and was the sacrifice that covered every member of the Jewish nation. According to Rabbi Soloveitchik, every Jew has two obligations, first as an individual Jew and then as a member of the *tzibur*, or community.

In Pirke Avot (Sayings of the Fathers) 2:5 Hillel teaches us that one should not separate himself from the community: *Al tifrosh min ha-tzibur*.

8 In the late afternoon you shall present the second lamb. Present it with the same meal offering and libation as the morning sacrifice; it is a thank you offering to Adonai. **9** On the Sabbath, you shall present two additional healthy lambs with six quarts of flour mixed with olive oil as a grain offering, and the usual libation. **10** This is the burnt offering for each Sabbath in addition to the regular daily burnt offering and its libation.

11 On the first of every month, on the new moon (Rosh Hodesh) festival, you shall present as a burnt offering to Adonai two young bulls, one ram, and seven lambs, all without defects.

12 There shall be a grain offering of six quarts of flour mixed with olive oil for each bull, a grain offering of six quarts of flour mixed with olive oil for the ram, **13** and a grain offering of three quarts of flour mixed with olive oil for each lamb. This shall be the burnt offering presented as a thank you gift to Adonai.

14 The wine libations shall consist of six quarts of wine with each bull, four quarts of wine for the ram, and three pints for each lamb. This is the new moon burnt offering, to be made every month of the year.

15 Besides these offerings you shall present one goat sin offering to Adonai. This is in addition to the regular daily burnt offering and its libation.

The Passover Festival
6th Aliyah

16 You must celebrate Adonai's Passover on the fourteenth day of the first month [Nisan].

---

11. On the first of every month, on the new moon (Rosh Hodesh) festival, you shall present as a burnt offering to Adonai two young bulls...
The Jewish holidays are tied to the cycle of the moon, which takes 29½ days to complete its cycle. The beginning of a new month, a new moon, symbolizes to the Jew the up and down of his fortunes in life. It is a time to reflect and reorder his priorities in life.

In ancient days, before there was no written calendar, observers were placed on mountain tops to report the appearance of the new moon to the Sanhedrin, who officially announced the new moon. Fires were lit on mountaintops to notify all the towns of the new moon.

11. On the first of every month, on the new moon (Rosh Hodesh) festival, you shall present as a burnt offering to Adonai two young bulls...
At the time of the First Temple (*Bet ha-Mikdash*), the beginning of the new month was celebrated with great festivity. The shofar was blown. People did not go to work.

They came to Jerusalem and they sacrificed a special new-month offering. Afterwards, a family feast was held. A special feature of the day was that women were released from all their chores as a reward, because after leaving Egypt, when the Jews were wandering in the desert, the women had refused to contribute their jewelry to help build an idol.

After the First Temple was destroyed, many of these customs were no longer practiced, but other customs developed. Special prayers were said in honor of the new moon. One of the prayers was *Hallel*, a special prayer of praise to Adonai that is recited only on holidays; for the new moon, only half–*Hallel* is recited.

15. Besides these offerings you shall present one goat sin offering to Adonai.
A sin offering was brought on all the feasts to atone for any religious deviations unintentionally committed by the Levites.

16. You must celebrate Adonai's Passover on the fourteenth day of the first month [Nisan].
Verses 16–25 provide the sacrificial order for the Festival of Passover, the holiday of freedom.

17 Then, on the fifteenth day of the month, the Passover festival shall begin, and you shall eat matzot for seven days.
18 The first day shall be a sacred holiday when you do no regular work. **19** You shall offer two young bulls, one ram, and seven lambs, all without defects, as a burnt fire offering to Adonai. **20** These shall be accompanied by a grain offering of flour mixed with five quarts of olive oil for each bull **21** and three quarts for each of the seven lambs.
22 To make atonement for yourselves you shall also offer a male goat as a sin offering. **23** You shall present all of these in addition to the regular morning burnt offering.
24 On each of the seven days of the Passover festival, you shall prepare a similar sacrifice as a fire offering that is a thank you gift to Adonai. This shall be offered in addition to the regular daily burnt offering and its libation.
25 The seventh day of the festival shall be a sacred holiday to you, when you shall not do any regular work. **26** The day of first fruits is when you bring Adonai a new grain offering as part of your Shavuot festival. You shall observe it as a sacred holiday, and you must not do any regular work.

---

17. Then, on the fifteenth day of the month, the Passover festival shall begin, and you shall eat matzot for seven days.
Today the Passover festival begins with a ceremonial meal called the seder. The essence of the seder is not just to retell the story of the Exodus but to turn back the clock and to act and feel the misery of slavery–and then to sing with joy and thanksgiving at the redemption from Egypt. At this point in the seder we will shortly begin the recitation of the thanksgiving prayer, the Hallel.

26. The day of the first fruits is when you bring Adonai a new grain offering as a part of your Shavuot festival.
The name *Shavuot* means "weeks"; the holiday falls exactly seven weeks after the second day of Passover, on the sixth and seventh day of the month of Sivan. Reform Jews observe only the first of the two days.

Shavuot is a triple holiday. It commemorates the giving of the Torah on Mount Sinai, the harvesting of wheat in Israel, and the ripening of the first fruits in the Holy Land.

Shavuot is one of the three pilgrimage holidays, the *Shalosh Regalim*, when Jews from all parts of historic Israel and surrounding countries used to make pilgrimages to the Holy Temple in Jerusalem. The other two pilgrimage holidays were Passover and Sukkot.

Pilgrims were called *olei regel*, meaning "those who go up by foot." They were so called because Jerusalem is located high in the hills of Judea and the pilgrims had to climb by foot to reach the Temple. Ancient sources state that thousands made their way to the Temple during the three holidays. The Talmud describes Jews from as far as Babylon, Persia, Egypt, Ethiopia, and Rome coming to worship.

They traveled in large groups. They marched with flying banners announcing the name of their clan, town, or village. Many were accompanied by musicians who played marching songs. Psalms 42, 82, and 122 are designated as Psalms of Ascent and were sung as the pilgrims ascended to Jerusalem.

The object of the pilgrimage was to bring *bikkurim* (first fruits) and offer a sacrifice at the Temple. The Torah also commands: "None shall appear empty-handed. Every person shall give as they are able." The sages decided that the minimum offering was to be three pieces of silver. The proceeds were to be used for the upkeep of the Temple and to care for the sick, aged, and infirm.

26. The day of the first fruits is when you bring Adonai a new grain offering as part of your Shavuot festival.
Shavuot is the holiday of a "new" beginning. When the Israelites received the Torah, they became a "new" people with a "new" enthusiasm who had acquired a "new" and holy mitzvah-filled lifestyle.
Abarbanel

27 As a thank you gift to Adonai you shall present a burnt offering consisting of two young bulls, one ram, and seven lambs.
28 These shall be accompanied by a grain offering consisting of flour mixed with five quarts of olive oil for each bull, three quarts for the ram, **29** and two quarts for each of the seven lambs.
30 Also offer one male goat to atone for yourselves.
31 You must present all of these offerings in addition to the regular daily burnt offering and its meal offering. Be sure that the animals you present are without defects.

29

The day of sounding the ram's horn (*shofar*), on the first day of the seventh month [Tishri], shall be a sacred holiday [Rosh Hashanah] to you, and you must not do any regular work.
2 As a thank you gift to Adonai, you must present a burnt offering consisting of one young bull, one ram, and seven lambs, all without defects. **3** The grain offering of flour mixed with olive oil shall consist of five quarts for the bull and three quarts for the ram,
4 and two quarts for each of the seven lambs.
5 In addition you shall sacrifice one goat as a sin offering to make atonement for yourselves.
6 All these sacrifices shall be in addition to the new moon (Rosh Hodesh) offering and the regular required daily offerings which are a thank you gift to Adonai.

---

27. As a thank you gift to Adonai you shall present a burnt offering consisting of two young bulls, one ram, and seven lambs.
The following verses anticipate Israel's occupation of the Holy Land. The sacrificial order and its gratitude to Adonai are expressed even before the occupation of Canaan.

1. The day of sounding the ram's horn (shofar), on the first day of the seventh month (Tishri), shall be a sacred holiday.
In biblical times the shofar was used to herald great moments. It proclaimed the ascent of a new king upon the throne; it announced the Jubilee every fiftieth year and the beginning of Sabbaths and festivals. In wartime it signaled the army to battle.

The shofar has so long been associated with Jewish tradition that it has become a holy symbol.

It recalls the offering of Isaac by Abraham, for on that occasion Adonai, recognized Abraham's devotion, and ordered him to substitute a ram for his son as a sacrifice on the altar. It reminds us of the giving of the Ten Commandments to the accompaniment of shofar blasts on Mount Sinai.

It is a mitzvah (405) to listen to the sound of the shofar on Rosh Hashanah.

The *bal tokeah* (shofar blower) sounds a total of 100 notes. The sounds of the shofar are: *tekiah*, a long single note; *shevarim*, three short notes; and *teruah*, nine very short notes.

1. The day of sounding the ram's horn (shofar).
The Rabbis say that the sounds of the shofar are meant to remind us that Rosh Hashanah is no ordinary holiday. It is the day of judgment and the time for us to awaken from our spiritual slumber. Rosh Hashanah is the time of the year to ask forgiveness from your teachers, friends, and family.

1. The day of sounding the ram's horn (shofar).
The Torah calls Rosh Hashanah a day of the sounding of the ram's horn. Legends have centered on Rosh Hashanah. It was said that this was the day on which Adam was created out of clay; it was also the birthday of Abraham and Isaac and Jacob; it was the day on which Joseph was released from prison in Egypt; and it was the day Moses appeared before Pharaoh, demanding that the Egyptian king let our people go.

7 Ten days later, the tenth of the month [of Tishri] shall be a sacred holiday when you must fast and not do any work [Yom Kippur].
8 As a burnt offering and a thank you gift to Adonai, you shall present one young bull, one ram, and seven lambs, all without defects.
9 The grain offerings of flour shall be accompanied by olive oil: five quarts for the bull, three quarts for the ram, **10** and two quarts for each of the seven lambs.
11 You shall also sacrifice one goat as a sin offering, in addition to the atonement sin offering. All these sacrifices and their libations are in addition to the regular daily burnt and grain offerings.

The Holiday of Sukkot *7th Aliyah*

12 On the fifteenth day of the seventh month you shall celebrate a sacred holiday when no regular work shall be done [Sukkot]. For seven days you shall celebrate this festival to Adonai.
13 As a thank you gift to Adonai, you shall present a burnt offering of healthy animals consisting of thirteen young bulls, two rams, and fourteen lambs, all without defects.
14 The grain offering of flour mixed with olive oil shall be six quarts for each of the thirteen bulls, three quarts for each of the two rams, **15** and two quarts for each of the fourteen lambs.
16 You shall also present one goat as a sin offering. This is in addition to the regular daily burnt offering, its grain offering, and its libation.
17 On the second day you shall present twelve young bulls, two rams, and fourteen lambs, all without defects, **18** in addition to the grain offerings and libations appropriate for the number of bulls, rams, and sheep. **19** You shall also present one goat as a sin offering. These offerings and their libations shall be in addition to the regular daily burnt offering and its grain offering.
20 On the third day you shall present eleven young bulls, two rams, and fourteen lambs, all without defects, **21** along with the grain offerings and libations appropriate for the number of bulls, rams, and lambs.
22 You shall also present one goat as a sin offering, in addition to the regular daily burnt offering, its grain offering, and its libation.
23 On the fourth day you shall present ten young bulls, two rams, and fourteen lambs, all without defects, **24** along with the grain offerings and libations according to the number of bulls, rams, and lambs.

---

7. Ten days later, the tenth of the month (of Tishri) shall be a sacred holiday when you must fast and not do any work (Yom Kippur).
The holiday of Yom Kippur is the end of the Ten Days of Repentance. The Shabbat between Rosh Hashanah and Yom Kippur is called *Shabbat Shuvah*, the Shabbath of Penitence or Repentance.

13. As a thank you gift to Adonai, you shall present a burnt offering of healthy animals consisting of thirteen young bulls, two rams, and fourteen lambs, all without defects.
During the Sukkot holiday, the Israelites are instructed to sacrifice a huge number of animals, including seventy bulls. The seventy bulls symbolically represent the seventy nations of the earth. These are thanksgiving offerings for each of the nations.

25 You shall also present one goat as a sin offering, in addition to the regular daily burnt offering, its grain offering, and its libation.
26 On the fifth day, you shall present nine young bulls, two rams, and fourteen lambs, all without defects, **27** along with the grain offerings and libations according to the number of bulls, rams, and lambs. **28** You shall also present one goat as a sin offering. All this is in addition to the regular daily burnt offering, its grain offering, and its libation. **29** On the sixth day, you shall present eight young bulls, two rams, and fourteen lambs, all without defects, **30** along with the grain offerings and libations according to the number of bulls, rams, and lambs.
31 You shall also present one goat as a sin offering. All this is in addition to the regular daily burnt offering, its grain offering, and its libation.
32 On the seventh day, you shall present seven young bulls, two rams, and fourteen lambs, all without defects, **33** along with the grain offerings and libations for the number of bulls, rams, and lambs. **34** You shall also present one goat as a sin offering. All of this is in addition to the regular daily burnt offering, its grain offering, and its libation.

The Shemini Atzeret Offering
Maftir

35 The eighth day shall be a time of rest for you (Shemini Atzeret), and you shall do no regular work.
36 As a burnt fire offering and as a thank you gift to Adonai, you shall present one bull, one ram, and seven lambs, all without defects, **37** along with the prescribed number of meal offerings and libations.
38 You shall also present one goat as a sin offering, in addition to the regular daily burnt offering, its grain offering, and its libation.
39 On your festivals you must present all of these offerings to Adonai, in addition to your burnt offerings, grain offerings, libations, and peace offerings, together with the free-will offerings and pledges.

30
Moses spoke to the Israelites and told them everything that Adonai had commanded him.

---

35. The eighth day shall be a time of rest for you (Shemini Atzeret), and you shall do no regular work.

The *etrog* is a citron fruit and the *lulav* is a palm branch. They represent the harvests in Israel. On Sukkot, blessings are recited over them.

On the eighth day of Sukkot, the *etrog* and the *lulav* are laid aside to celebrate the festival of Shemini Atzeret, the eighth day of solemn assembly. On this holiday memorial prayers called *Yizkor* are recited. A prayer called *Geshem* (rain) is also recited. In the Holy Land, summer is the dry season; since it rains only during the winter, the crops of the spring depend on the rains of October.

35. The eighth day shall be a time of rest for you (Shemini Atzeret), and you shall do no regular work.

The one-day holiday of Shemini Atzeret falls into the category of two other one-day holidays: Rosh Hashanah (in Israel) and Yom Kippur. These three holidays do not commemorate a historical event nor an agricultural happening; they are theological holidays.

The ancient calendar of Jewish holidays was equally divided by the three agricultural and historical holidays of Sukkot, Passover, and Shavuot.

מַטּוֹת *Mattot*

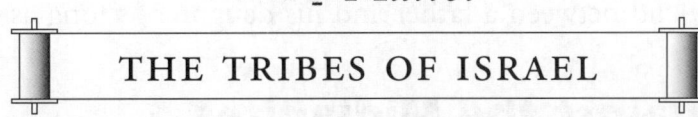

THE TRIBES OF ISRAEL

2 Moses spoke to the Israelite leaders, saying: This is what Adonai has commanded: **3** If a man makes a promise to Adonai, or promises to do something, he must not break his promise. He must do exactly what he promised. **4** If a woman makes a promise to Adonai while living with her parents, **5** and her father hears about her promise but says nothing, she must keep the promise.

6 However, if he learns about it and objects, then she is no longer obligated to keep her promise, because her father has forbidden her to fulfill the promise. Since her father has forbidden her, Adonai will forgive her.

7 If she marries and her promise is still in force, she is still obligated by her promise.

8 If her husband learns about it and remains silent and does not object, then her promise must be kept. **9** However, if her husband refuses to accept her promise, he can cancel all her promises and Adonai will forgive her.

10 Any promise made by a widow or a divorcee must be fulfilled, no matter what obligation she takes upon herself.

11 This is the law if a woman makes a promise while in her husband's house: **12** If her husband learns about the promise and remains silent without stopping her, then all her promises and obligations must be kept. **13** However, if her husband voids them when he hears about them, then all her promises and obligations need not be kept. Since her husband voided the promises, Adonai will forgive her.

14 Every promise of self-denial by a woman can be upheld or voided by her husband.

15 However, if the entire day goes by and her husband does not object, then he has automatically agreed to the promise she has assumed. He has agreed to the promised obligations by remaining silent on the day he heard them. **16** However, if he voids them after learning about them, he removes any guilt that she may have for violating them.

---

3. If a man makes a promise to Adonai, or promises to do something, he must not break his promise.
This is prohibitive mitzvah number 407.

A *nader* is a holy promise. It is forbidden to make a *nader* such as pledging money to a synagogue and not carrying it through.

3. If a man makes a promise to Adonai, or promises to do something...
The Torah is aware of human frailty. People, sometimes in a fit of anger, remorse, or sorrow, will make vows that they will regret. So Moses instructs the tribal leaders how to absolve any person who makes a vow and cannot fulfill it because of circumstances.

7. If she marries and her promise is still in force, she is still obligated by her promise.
A woman who has made a vow before marriage is obligated to fulfill her promise.

However, now that she is married, her husband has the power to declare the vow null and void.

15. However, if the entire day goes by and her husband does not object, then he has automatically agreed to the promise she has assumed.
If the husband, who has the power to protest and negate the vow, remains silent, then it means that he has consented and agrees with her and intends for her to fulfill her vow.

17 These are the laws that Adonai commanded Moses concerning the relationship between a man and his wife, and between a father and his daughter as long as she is living in her father's house.

Revenge Against the Midianites
2nd Aliyah

31 Adonai spoke to Moses, saying, **2** "Take revenge for the Israelites who were tempted by the Midianites, who tempted them into idol worship. After that, Moses, you will die and be gathered to your ancestors."
3 Moses spoke to the people, saying, "Choose men for armed conflict against Midian, so that Adonai's revenge can be taken against the Midianites. **4** Select one thousand soldiers from each of Israel's tribes for armed service."
5 One thousand men volunteered from each tribe, for a total of twelve thousand troops.
6 Moses sent an army of one thousand men from each tribe under the command of Pinchas son of Elazar the priest, who was in charge of the sacred articles and the trumpets for sounding the battle signal.
7 Just as Adonai had instructed Moses, they mounted a surprise attack against Midian, and killed all the adult males.
8 And they also killed the five kings of Midian: Evi, Rekem, Tzur, Hur, and Reba. They also killed Balaam son of Beor.
9 The Israelites captured all of Midian and their women and children. They seized all their animals, and everything that belonged to them. **10** Then the Israelites burned down all the Midianite cities and forts **11** and assembled everything they had captured, both humans and beasts. **12** They brought the captives and everything they had captured to Moses, Elazar the priest, and the entire Israelite community, who were camped in the hills of Moab, across from the city of Jericho.

---

1. Adonai spoke to Moses, saying, "Take revenge for the Israelites who were tempted by the Midianites, who tempted them into idol worship.

Balaam was well acquainted with Israel's laws and commandments, because he failed to defeat Israel with his incantations and sacrifices. He devised another scheme to defeat the Israelites religiously and morally. Balaam organized a "honey trap" of the beautiful Moabite women who invited the Israelite men to worship their god Baal-Peor. Many Israelites accepted their invitations. Now Adonai tells Moses to rid the area of the Midianites and their idols. The Israelites killed all the males as well as the mastermind Balaam.

3. Choose men for armed conflict against Midian, so that Adonai's revenge can be taken against the Midianites.

The Israelites will carry out Adonai's revenge.
Rashi

6. Moses sent an army of one thousand men from each tribe under the command of Pinchas son of Elazar the priest.

Elazar was the High Priest and he was forbidden to contaminate his holiness by a shedding of blood and corpses. Pinchas was to serve as a symbol that the war was sanctioned by Adonai.

7. Just as Adonai had instructed Moses, they mounted a surprise attack against Midian, and killed all the adult males.

The Israelite treatment of the captured enemies depended upon whether the war was by Adonai's command or was an optional war. The attack of the Midianites was a "holy war" and the male adults, the fighters, were killed.

The plunder was divided equally between the soldiers and the community. Special portions were set aside for the priests and the Levites.

Purification After the War
3rd Aliyah

13 Moses, Elazar, and the communal leaders went outside the camp to greet the victorious troops.
14 However, Moses was angry at the army's commanders.
15 Moses angrily asked, "Why are the women still alive? **16** They are the ones who at Balaam's urging caused the Israelites to be unfaithful to Adonai at Mount Peor and brought a plague on Adonai's community. **17** Now kill every male child, as well as every woman who has had sexual relations with a man.
18 All the young girls who have not had sexual relations with a man, however, you may keep alive for yourselves.
19 You must all remain outside the camp for seven days. All those who killed anyone or touched a dead body must purify themselves on the third and seventh days.
20 You must also purify every garment, every leather article, anything made of goat hair, and every wooden article."
21 Then Elazar the priest explained to the soldiers returning from the campaign: "This is the law that Adonai commanded Moses:
22 Anything that can withstand heat, such as gold, silver, copper, iron, tin, and lead, **23** must be put through fire and cleansed and then purified with the waters of purification. But everything that burns can be purified by immersion in water.
24 Remember, you must also cleanse your bodies and wash your clothing on the seventh day, and then you will be purified and entitled to return to the camp."

Dividing the Captured Property
4th Aliyah

25 Adonai spoke to Moses, saying, **26** "You and Elazar the priest and the tribal leaders must count all the captives and animals. **27** Divide everything into two equal parts, giving half to the soldiers who went into battle and the other half to the community.
28 Levy a tax for Adonai on the soldiers who participated in the campaign, consisting of one of every five hundred of the captives, cattle, donkeys, and sheep.

---

15. Moses angrily asked, "Why are the women still alive?"
The Torah in Devarim 20:14 allows the Israelites to keep the spoils in a captured city. Spoils included women, children, animals, and property. However, Moses was angry with the commanders who allowed the women to live whom Balaam organized to entice the Israelites to commit immoral sexual acts.

17. Now kill every male child.
This was to prevent revenge seekers from growing up and causing blood feuds. Blood feuds even in the time of Moses were common among the nations in the Middle East. Nothing much has changed. Holy wars and bloody religious feuds which now consist of suicide bombers, ambushes, and wholesale slaughter are common, causing thousands of innocent deaths.

19. You must remain outside the camp for seven days. All those who killed anyone or touched a dead body must purify themselves on the third and seventh day.
Combat in biblical times was mostly violent, close, hand-to-hand combat with swords and hammers and axes. The blood and gore of the corpses often spilled on the combatants, who were themselves wounded and were liable to infection.

By isolating and quarantining the soldiers, they avoided the possibility of diseases, which could spread. Today medical personnel wear rubber gloves when treating the sick or accident victims to avoid infectious diseases.
Shenash

29 Take this quota from their half, and give it to Elazar the priest as a gift to Adonai.
30 From the half-share that is going to the other Israelites, take one of every fifty captives, cattle, donkeys, sheep, and other animals, and give it to the Levites, who are in charge of Adonai's Tabernacle." **31** Moses and Elazar the priest did exactly as Adonai had commanded Moses.
32 In addition to everything else the troops had captured, there were 675,000 sheep, **33** 72,000 head of cattle, **34** 61,000 donkeys, **35** and 32,000 females who had never had sexual relations with a man.
36 The half-share for the soldiers who fought the Midianites was 337,500 sheep, **37** and Adonai's share came to 675 sheep.
38 There were 36,000 cattle, and Adonai's share was 72 animals.
39 There were 30,500 donkeys, and Adonai's share was 61 donkeys.
40 There were 16,000 captives, and Adonai's share was 32 individuals.
41 Just as Adonai had commanded, Moses gave the tax to Elazar the priest as a gift to Adonai.

A Gift to Adonai *5th Aliyah*

42 The half-share that Moses took from the soldiers for the other Israelites as **43** the community's portion consisted of 337,500 sheep, **44** 36,000 cattle, **45** 30,500 donkeys, **46** and 16,000 captives.
47 From the Israelite half, Moses selected one of every fifty and gave them to the Levites, who were in charge of Adonai's Tabernacle. It was all done exactly as Adonai had commanded Moses.
48 Then the commanders, generals, and captains of the army approached Moses.
49 They said to Moses, "We have counted the warriors under our command, and not a single soldier has been lost.
50 Therefore we want to bring a gift to Adonai. Every soldier who found a gold article, such as an anklet, a bracelet, a finger ring, an earring, or a body ornament wishes to bring it to atone for ourselves before Adonai."

---

30. From the half-share that is going to the other Israelites, take one of every fifty captives, cattle, donkeys, sheep, and other animals, and give it to the Levites.
The Levites were given one-fiftieth of all the spoils that were captured. The priests (*kohanim*) were given one-tenth what the Levites were given. The Levites were given ten times as much as the priests, because there were ten times as many Levites.

49–50. They said to Moses, "We have counted the warriors under our command, and not a single soldier has been lost. Therefore we want to bring a gift to Adonai. Every soldier who found a gold article, such as an anklet, a bracelet, a finger ring, an earring, or a body ornament wishes to bring it to atone for ourselves before Adonai."
Army commanders are often faced with difficult decisions as a result of which their troops will surely suffer casualties. A famous military commander once said, "War is hell." War is death, and when an attack succeeds without losses, it becomes an occasion to say, "Thank you." The Israelite commanders and soldiers said "Thank you" by donating their booty to Adonai. Before the invention of coinage, gold jewelry was a portable form of personal possessions which could serve as a valuable resource in times of emergency.

Shenash

51 Moses and Elazar the priest took all the gold jewelry from them. **52** The entire gift of gold that was offered to Adonai by the officers of the army weighed 400 pounds. **53** But the ordinary soldiers kept their plunder for themselves.

54 So Moses and Elazar the priest accepted the gold from the officers and brought it to the Meeting Tent to remind the Israelites of their battle against the Midianites.

Reuben and Gad Petition Moses   *6th Aliyah*

32 The descendants of Reuben and Gad had large herds and flocks, and they saw that the area of Jazer and Gilead had good grass for their livestock. **2** So the descendants of Gad and Reuben came and petitioned Moses, Elazar the priest, and the tribal leaders, saying, **3** "The cities of Ataroth, Dibon, Jazer, Nimrah, Heshbon, Elaleh, Sebam, Nebo, and Beor **4** have a lot of grass, and the land is ideal for our livestock."

5 They continued, "Do us a favor, and give this land to us as our permanent possession, and do not make us cross the Jordan." **6** Moses answered the descendants of Gad and Reuben, "Why should your brothers go out and fight while you remain here? **7** Why are you discouraging the Israelites from crossing over to the land that Adonai has given them? **8** That is just what your fathers did when I sent them from Kadesh Barnea to explore the land. **9** They explored as far as the Valley of Eshkol, but then they discouraged the Israelites from entering the land that Adonai had given them.

10 That day Adonai became angry and said, **11** 'None of the men over twenty years old who left Egypt will ever see the land that I swore to give to their ancestors Abraham, Isaac, and Jacob, because they did not believe in My power. **12** The only exceptions shall be Caleb son of Yefuneh the Kenizite and Joshua son of Nun, because they totally believe in My power.' **13** Adonai was very angry at the Israelites, and He made them wander in the desert for forty years until the generation who did not believe in Adonai's power had died out.

---

51. Moses and Elazar the priest took all the gold jewelry from them.
The commanders were ecstatic, since they had won a tremendous victory without the loss of a single soldier. They were aware that they owed their victory to the protection and influence of Adonai. In appreciation, they donated 400 pounds of the women's gold jewelry, which they had confiscated. The removal of the jewelry also symbolically erased the memory of the Midianite women who tempted them into idol worship.

54. So Moses and Elazar the priest accepted the gold from the officers and brought it to the Meeting Tent to remind the Israelites of their battle against the Midianites.
The golden jewelry was placed on display so that the Israelites could take pride in the bravery of their soldiers and their great victory.

6. Why should your brothers go out and fight while you remain here?
Your brothers helped you conquer Jazer and Gilesh and now you have the audacity to abandon them and let them conquer their land by themselves? Do you think it's fair and do you for one moment think that Adonai would allow it to happen?

8. That is just what your fathers did when I sent them from Kadesh Barnea to explore the land.
This is the same sort of cowardice that your ancestors exhibited almost forty years ago. Your actions are discouraging other tribes, who will have to battle and conquer the west side of the Jordan without you.

14 Now you are following the model of your sinful fathers, and you are making Adonai even more angry.
15 If you again refuse to follow him, He will again leave you in the desert, and you sinners will be completely destroyed."
16 The Reubenites and Gaddites drew near to Moses and said, "First let us build sheepfolds for our flocks and fortified cities for our families. **17** Then we will arm ourselves and go ahead and fight side by side with the other Israelites until we have brought them to their homeland. Let our children stay in the fortified cities because of the danger from the inhabitants,
18 but we will not return home until every Israelite has taken possession of his inheritance.
19 Nonetheless, we will not take possession with them on the far side of the Jordan, since our inheritance shall come to us on the Jordan's eastern bank."

The Advance Force
7th Aliyah

20 Moses said to them, "If you do that and go forth as an advance force ahead of your brothers, your petition will be granted. **21** Your entire force must cross the Jordan before Adonai, and fight until He has driven away His enemies. **22** When the land is conquered for Adonai, you may return home, and you will be free of any obligation in the eyes of Adonai and Israel. This land will then be yours as your permanent property before Adonai. **23** But if you do not do so, you will have sinned before Adonai, and your sin will be your undoing.

---

16. The Reubenites and the Gaddites drew near to Moses and said, "First let us build sheepfolds for our flocks and fortified cities for our families."
Sheepfolds were fortified shelters to protect the shepherds and the flock from desert raiders.

The tribes of Reuben and Gad were experienced cattle raisers and chose the territories of Gilead and Jazer on the eastern banks of the Jordan River. They also promised to fight side-by-side with their Israelite brothers until the invasion was completed.

16. The Reubenites and the Gaddites drew near to Moses and said, "First let us build sheepfolds for our flocks and fortified cities for our families."
Moses was angry at the priorities of the tribes, and he corrects them. He tells them that their first priority is the protection for their families and then the sheepfold for the animals. Families are more important than animals. The reprimand struck home and the two and a half tribes offered to help the other tribes.

The final resolution made everyone happy. The two and a half tribes fortified their own cities and did not compromise their involvement with the invasion.

18. We will not return home until every Israelite has taken possession of his inheritance.
This reflects a change in the tone of the people. Their fathers, who had been slaves, whined and complained when they did not have their way. Their children, educated in the ways of freedom, responsibility, and dignity, made the request for the land east of the Jordan. When they learned the terms whereby they might have that land, they did not complain. Instead they agreed to Adonai's order, left their families and flocks, and went over the Jordan to help their brothers. This was the behavior of a mature and free people, not of slaves. Thus Moses was rewarded by knowing, even before the Jordan was crossed, that he had done his job well. A new Israel was born.

22. When the land is conquered for Adonai, you may return home and you will be free of any obligation in the eyes of Adonai and Israel. We are one nation.
One for all and all for one. You must help your brothers fight the battle for their homeland just as they helped you acquire your territory.

24 Now go, build cities for your children and sheepfolds for your sheep." **25** The descendants of Gad and Reuben said to Moses, "We will do as you have ordered. **26** Our children, wives, property, and livestock will remain here in the cities of Gilead. **27** Meanwhile, our entire armed army will cross the Jordan, as you have said." **28** Then Moses instructed Elazar the priest, Joshua son of Nun, and the tribal leaders. **29** Moses said to them, "If the entire Gaddite and Reubenite army crosses the Jordan to fight at your side, then when the land is conquered, you shall give them the land of Gilead as their permanent property. **30** But if they do not fight at your side, then they must accept property with you in the land of Canaan." **31** The descendants of Gad and Reuben responded, "We promise to do whatever Adonai has told us to do. **32** Our soldiers will cross into the land of Canaan, and then we will inherit our permanent hereditary property on this side of the Jordan."
33 Moses then gave the descendants of Gad and Reuben, and the half-tribe of Manasseh son of Joseph, the kingdom of Sichon, king of the Amorites, and the kingdom of Og, king of Bashan. He gave them the entire country, along with the cities and the territories around them.
34 The descendants of Gad built the cities of Dibon, Ataroth, Aroer, **35** Atroth Shofan, Jazer, Jagbehah, **36** Beth-nimrah, and Beth-haran. They built walls around the cities and sheepfolds for their flocks.
37 The Reubenites built Heshbon, Elaleh, Kiryathaim, **38** Nebo, Baal–meon, and Sibmah. They renamed the cities that they rebuilt.

Machir, Jair, and Novah *Maftir*

39 The sons of Machir son of Manasseh went to Gilead and conquered it, and drove out the Amorites who were living there.
40 Moses gave Gilead to Machir son of Manasseh, and he settled there.
41 Jair, a grandson of Manasseh, conquered the villages in this district, and he named them Havoth Jair (Villages of Jair). **42** Then Novah went and captured Kenath and its surrounding towns and renamed them Novah after himself.

29–30. Moses said to them, "If the entire Gaddite and Reubenite army crosses the Jordan to fight at your side, then when the land is conquered, you shall give them the land of Gilead as their permanent property. But if they do not fight at your side, then they must accept property with you in the land of Canaan."
Obviously Moses did not trust the promises of the two tribes, so he specified that the tribes should not receive the land on the east side of the Jordan until they had finished helping the other tribes conquer the land. However, they refused to accept this provision. They were willing to join the battle and then demanded immediate possession of the land.

33. The half-tribe of Manasseh.
The Torah in Bamidbar 26:29–32 tells that the tribe of Manasseh consisted of eight clans (subtribes). Six of the subtribes were given territory on the west of the Jordan River.

39. The sons of Machir son of Manasseh went to Gilead and conquered it, and drove out the Amorites who were living there.
Inspired by the sight of Gad and Reuben building settlements for their families and fortifying their communities, the families of Machir, Jair and Novah, struck out to conquer their own territory. They defeated the Amorites and drove them out and renamed the villages. Now the tribes of Gad, Reuben, and half of Manasseh occupied the eastern side of the Jordan.

מַסְעֵי *Massay*

THE JOURNEYS OF ISRAEL

33 These are the places where the Israelites who left Egypt camped under the leadership of Moses and Aaron. **2** At Adonai's command, Moses kept a written record of their stopping places along the way. These are the places where they camped: **3** The Israelites left the Egyptian city of Rameses on the fifteenth day of the first month [Nisan]. On the day after the Passover sacrifice the Israelites marched out in full view of the Egyptians, **4** who were still burying all their first-born, who had been killed by Adonai. Adonai had also defeated their idols.
5 The Israelites left Rameses and camped in Sukkoth.
6 Then they left Sukkoth and camped in Etham on the edge of the wilderness.
7 They left Etham and returned to Pi-haviroth (Freedom Valley) opposite Baal-zephon and camped near Migdal (Tower).
8 They left Freedom Valley and crossed the Sea of Reeds into the wilderness. Then they journeyed for three days into the wilderness of Etham and camped in Marah. **9** They left Marah and camped in Elim, where there were twelve water springs and seventy palms.
10 They left Elim and camped near the Sea of Reeds.

The Travels of the Israelites
2nd Aliyah

11 They left the Sea of Reeds and camped in the Wilderness of Sin.
12 They left the Wilderness of Sin and camped in Dofkah.
13 They left Dofkah and camped in Alush. **14** They left Alush and camped in Rephidim, where there was no water for the Israelites to drink. **15** They left Rephidim and camped in the Wilderness of Sinai. **16** They left the Wilderness of Sinai and camped in Kivroth HaTaavah (Graves of Craving).
17 They left Kivroth HaTaavah and camped in Hatzeroth.
18 They left Hatzeroth and camped in Rithmah.

---

1. These are the places where the Israelites who left Egypt camped.
The Torah lists the camping sites of the Israelites during their long march from Egypt to the plains of Moab. Today it is impossible to identify most of these camping sites. However the limited number of water places provide a possible route through the desert.

2. At Adonai's command, Moses kept a written record of their stopping places along the way
During their forty years in travel through the desert, the Israelites made forty-two stops. Each of these stops was made "at Adonai's command."

They made fourteen stops the first year, eight stops the last year, and twenty stops in the middle thirty-eight years.

3. The Israelites left the Egyptian city of Rameses on the fifteenth day of the first month (Nisan). On the day after the Passover sacrifice, the Israelites marched out in full view of the Egyptians.
Moses reminded the Israelites of their victorious march in full view of the Egyptians. They had won the battle for freedom. The Egyptian populace was probably happy to see the pesky, plague-bringing Israelites leave.

19 They left Rithmah and camped in Rimmon-peretz.
20 They left Rimmon-peretz and camped in Livnah.
21 They left Livnah and camped in Rissah.
22 They left Rissah and camped in Kehelathah.
23 They left Kehelathah and camped at Mount Shefer.
24 They left Mount Shefer and camped in Haradah.
25 They left Haradah and camped in Macheloth.
26 They left Macheloth and camped in Tachath.
27 They left Tachath and camped in Terach.
28 They left Terach and camped in Mitkah.
29 They left Mitkah and camped in Hashmonah.
30 They left Hashmonah and camped in Moseroth.
31 They left Moseroth and camped in Bene-jaakan.
32 They left Bene-jaakan and camped in Hor-HaGidgad.
33 They left Hor-ha Gidgad and camped in Jatvatah.
34 They left Jatvatah and camped in Avronah.
35 They left Avronah and camped in Etzyon-gever.
36 They left Etzyongever and camped in Kadesh in the Wilderness of Zin, also called Kadesh.
37 They left Kadesh and camped at Mount Hor, on the border of the land of Edom.
38 At Adonai's command, Aaron the priest climbed to the top of Mount Hor, and he died there on the first day of the fifth month [Av] in the fortieth year of the Israelites' exodus from Egypt. **39** Aaron was 123 years old when he died on Mount Hor.
40 It was there that the Canaanite king of Arad, who lived in the Negev in the land of Canaan, heard that the Israelites were approaching his land.
41 The Israelites left Mount Hor and camped in Zalmonah.
42 They left Zalmonah and camped in Punon. **43** They left Punon and camped in Oboth.
44 They left Oboth and camped in Iye-avarim (Desolate Borders) in the land of Moab.

---

19. They left Rithmah and camped in Rimmon-peretz.
Rimmon-peretz means "Spreading Pomegranate Tree." In modern Hebrew *rimmon* also means "grenade."

33. They left Hor-ha Gidgad and camped at Jatvatah.
The wandering Israelites camped at the oasis of Jatvatah, which the Torah describes as an "area filled with flowing brooks" (Dev. 10:7). This oasis is identified with an oasis 22 miles from Eilat named Ain Ghadyan. This is the most plentiful source of water in the area. Potsherds and the remains of a fort dating from the time of the king of Judah have been found. Nearby the road from the Dead Sea meets the road from the Mediterranean to the Gulf of Eilat.

38–39. At Adonai's command, Aaron the priest climbed to the top of Mount Hor, and he died there on the first day of the fifth month (Av) in the fortieth year of the Israelites' exodus from Egypt. Aaron was 123 years old when he died on Mount Hor.
Aaron, brother of Moses, acted as Moses' spokesman before the Israelites. He also took part in the miracles and signs which helped free the Israelites from Egypt. A Levite, Aaron was the first High Priest of Israel. All lawful priests were descended from him, while other members of the tribe of Levi acted in subordinate roles.

45 They left Iye-avarim and camped in Dibon-gad. **46** They left Dibon Gad and camped in Almon-diblathayim. **47** They left Almon-diblathayim and camped in the mountains of Avarim close to Mount Nebo. **48** They left the mountains of Avarim and camped on the plains of Moab beside the Jordan River, opposite the city of Jericho. **49** They camped along the Jordan River from Beth Hajeshimoth as far as Abel Shittim in the plains of Moab.

Drive Out the Inhabitants *3rd Aliyah*

50 Adonai spoke to Moses while the Israelites were camped on the plains of Moab along the Jordan River opposite Jericho, and told him: **51** Speak to the Israelites and say to them: "When you cross the Jordan into the land of Canaan, **52** you must drive out the land's inhabitants. You must destroy all their carved images and destroy all their metal idols and altars. **53** Settle the land and live in the land I have given you. **54** You shall divide the land among your families. Give a large portion of land to a large family, give a small portion of land to a small family. Distribute the land to the tribes, and give each tribe what the sacred lottery indicates. **55** If you do not drive out the land's inhabitants, those who remain shall be splinters in your eyes and thorns in your sides. They will cause you troubles in the land where you will live. **56** Then I will treat you cruelly, as I originally planned to treat them."

34 Adonai spoke to Moses, telling him to **2** give the Israelites these instructions: I am giving you the land of Canaan as your inheritance, and these will be the boundaries of the land.

3 Your southern boundary shall begin in the Wilderness of Sin adjacent to Edom. Your southern border to the east shall be the edge of the Dead Sea.

---

47. They left Almon-diblathayim and camped in the mountains of Avarim close to Mount Nebo.
The Torah, Devarim 32:49, tells us that Moses died on Mount Nebo.

50. Adonai spoke to Moses while the Israelites were camped on the plains of Moab along the Jordan River opposite Jericho.
This was Israel's last camping site before beginning the invasion of Canaan.

52. You must drive out the land's inhabitants. You must destroy all their carved images and destroy all their metal idols and altars.
Idol worship was a constant attraction to the Israelites. Adonai warns the Israelites to rid the land of their idols and places of worship. If you don't, says Adonai, idol worship will spread through your towns and cities. If you do not take steps to drive out the inhabitants, then you will be in danger and then I will treat you cruelly.

53. Settle the land and live in the land I have given you.
I, Adonai created the world. This land is My land. I have the right to give My land to whomever I choose. I have chosen you, the Israelites, to live in My land.

54. You shall divide the land among your families. Give a large portion of land to a large family, give a small portion of land to a small family.
Each tribe's land area was decided by a lottery. The division of the tribal land was by family within the tribe's boundary.

2. I am giving you the land of Canaan as your inheritance.
Rashi says: "If you drive out the inhabitants, only then will you inherit the land and live in it in peace."

4 Your border shall turn to the south of the Scorpion Pass (Akrabim) and then shall extend toward Zin. Its southernmost point will be at Kadesh Barnea, and then extend to Hatzar-adar and reach as far as Atzmon.
5 From Atzmon the border shall turn north and follow the Wadi of Egypt and end at the Mediterranean Sea.
6 Your western boundary shall be the coast of the Mediterranean Sea. This shall be your western border.
7 Your northern boundary will begin at the Mediterranean Sea and run east to Mount Hor. **8** From Mount Hor your boundary will run to Lebo-hamath, and on, through Zedad **9** and Zephron, to Hatzar-eynan. This will be your northern border. **10** For your eastern boundary, you shall draw a line from Hatzar-eynan to Shefam. **11** The boundary shall then descend southward from Shefam to Rivlah to the east of Ain. From there the boundary shall continue to the south, along the eastern shore of the Sea of Galilee. **12** The boundary shall then continue southward along the Jordan River, until the Dead Sea. All these shall be the boundaries of your country.
13 Then Moses gave the Israelites the following instructions:
This is the land that Adonai has commanded you to divide by lottery and distribute to the nine and a half tribes.
14 The descendants of Reuben and Gad and the half-tribe of Manasseh have already taken possession of their hereditary land.
15 These two and a half tribes have already been given their land east of the Jordan River opposite Jericho.

Divide the Land   *4th Aliyah*

16 Adonai spoke to Moses, saying:
17 These are the names of the men who shall divide the land. First, there shall be Elazar the priest and Joshua son of Nun.

---

11. From there the boundary shall continue to the south, along the eastern shore of the Sea of Galilee.
The Sea of Galilee is also known as the Sea of Kinneret and Lake of Tiberias.

13–14. This is the land that Adonai has commanded you to divide by lottery and distribute to the nine and one half tribes.
The descendants of Reuben and Gad and the half-tribe of Manasseh have already taken possession of their hereditary land.

The traditional number of the "twelve" tribes was sacrosanct, but the numbers for religious and historical purposes could fluctuate. The tribe of Levi occupied no territory.

The number "twelve" was adhered to by splitting the tribes of Joseph into the tribes of Manasseh and Ephraim.

The tribe of Reuben lost significance, and Simeon became a part of Judah.

Although Manasseh occupied territory on both the eastern and western sides of the Jordan, it was counted as one. The traditional number of "twelve" remained inviolable.

17. These are the names of the men who shall divide the land.
Dividing the land of western Canaan fairly was an extremely difficult political enterprise. Ten leaders, one from each tribe, were given the honor. Caleb, who played an important role in Israel's history and who was from the tribe of Judah, was the first leader chosen.

18 You shall also appoint one leader from each tribe to help them divide the land. **19** These are the names of the leaders: Caleb son of Yefuneh for the tribe of Judah. **20** Shemuel son of Amihud for the tribe of Simeon. **21** Elidad son of Kislon for the tribe of Benjamin. **22** Bukki son of Yagli for the tribe of Dan. **23** Haniel son of Ephod for the tribe of Manasseh. **24** Kemuel son of Shiftan for the tribe of Ephraim. **25** Elitzafan son of Parnach for the tribe of Zebulun. **26** Paltiel son of Azzan for the tribe of Issachar. **27** Achihud son of Shelomi for the tribe of Asher. **28** Pedahel son of Amihud for the tribe of Naphtali. **29** These are the leaders whom Adonai has chosen to distribute the land to the Israelites in the land of Canaan.

Assign Cities for the Levites
5th Aliyah

35 Adonai spoke to Moses on the plains of Moab along the Jordan River across from Jericho. **2** Instruct the Israelites and have them assign cities for the Levites from their hereditary lands. Also, provide pasture lands for the Levites around their cities. **3** The cities shall be their residence, while the pasture lands shall be for their flocks and herds.
4 The pasture land that you shall assign to the Levites shall extend outward 1,500 feet from the city walls in every direction. **5** Measure 3,000 feet outside the city on the eastern side, 3,000 feet on the southern side, 3,000 feet on the western side, and 3,000 feet on the northern side. This shall be their pasture land, with the city in the exact center.

---

18. You shall appoint one leader from each of the tribes to help them divide the land.
Ten leaders were appointed to oversee the distribution of the land on the western side of Jordan. Two tribes had already chosen land on the eastern side, so only ten portions of land were to be distributed.

2. Instruct the Israelites and have them assign cities for the Levites from their hereditary lands.
This is mitzvah number 408.

It was a mitzvah for the Israelites to provide forty-eight cities for the Levites in which to live.

The tribes in which the Levitical cities were located owned the land. However the Levites had the right to live in those cities.

2. Instruct the Israelites and have them assign cities for the Levites from their hereditary lands.
The tribe of Levi did not receive any territory in Israel as did the other tribes. They therefore were allocated cities in which to settle and raise their families.

Six of the Levitical cities were designated as cities of refuge for those committing accidental murders, three on the western side of the Jordan and three on the eastern side.

4. The pasture land that you shall assign to the Levites shall extend outward 1,500 feet from the city walls in every direction. Measure 3,000 feet outside the city on the eastern side, 3,000 feet on the southern side, 3,000 feet on the western side, and 3,000 feet on the northern side. This shall be their pasture land, with the city in the exact center.
The plans for the Levitical cities were symbols of the consecration and utility. Rashi says that "the first fifteen hundred feet were to be open land with the intent of beautifying the area. The second fifteen hundred were to be used for farming and the raising of cattle."

6 You shall also provide the Levites with six safe refuge cities, where a person who has accidentally killed someone can find refuge. In addition to these six cities you shall also provide them with forty-two additional cities.
7 In total you shall give the Levites forty-eight cities along with the surrounding pasture lands.
8 These cities shall be assigned from the lands of the Israelites, more from a larger tribe, and less from a smaller tribe. Each tribe shall give the Levites cities in proportion to the hereditary land that it has been given.

Cities of Safe Refuge
6th Aliyah

9 Adonai spoke to Moses and told him: **10** Speak to the Israelites and say to them: Now that you are crossing the Jordan into the land of Canaan, **11** you must designate towns which shall serve as safe refuge cities where a murderer who has accidentally killed a person can find safe refuge. **12** These cities shall serve you as a safe refuge from an avenger. A murderer must not be judged until he has had a fair trial before a court. **13** You shall provide six safe refuge cities.
14 You shall provide three safe cities on this side of the Jordan River, and three safe cities in the land of Canaan.
15 These cities shall be safe havens for both foreigners and Israelites, so that anyone who accidentally kills a person will find safety there. **16** However, if someone deliberately strikes another person with an iron weapon and kills him, then he is a murderer, and he must be executed. **17** Or if he strikes someone with a large stone, and the person dies, then he is a murderer and must be executed. **18** Or if he strikes someone with a deadly wooden weapon, and the person dies, then he is a murderer and must be executed.
19 In such cases, after the trial, a relative of the victim is allowed to kill the murderer wherever he finds him.

---

8. These cities shall be assigned from the land of the Israelites, more from a larger tribe, and less from a smaller tribe.
The assignment of the cities was in proportion not to the size of the tribe but to the importance of that city and the value and fertility of the open space. Here again Moses tries to treat each of the tribes equally to avoid the problem of favoritism.

11. You must designate towns which shall serve as safe refuge cities where a murderer who has accidentally killed a person can find safe refuge.
Every murderer who deliberately or accidentally killed someone would escape to a safe refuge city. Then a court would send for him and investigate the crime. If the court determined that he had deliberately murdered someone, he was executed. If the death was accidental, he was safely sent back to the city of refuge.

12. A murderer must not be judged until he has had a fair trial before a court.
This is prohibitive mitzvah number 409.

It is forbidden to execute a person until the court has decided that he is guilty and deserves death. The accused must not be executed until he or she is given a fair trial by an impartial judge and jury.

19. In such cases, after the trial, a relative of the victim is allowed to kill the murderer wherever he finds him.
After a fair trial by a court, if a person is found guilty of premeditated murder and is sentenced to death, the execution is entrusted to a family member.

Such a legal process will ultimately lead to eradication of blood feuds which were and are still practiced in the Middle East.

20 It is murder if a person deliberately knocks his victim down or throws something dangerous at him and causes the victim to die.
21 It is murder if he deliberately strikes someone with his fist and causes the victim to die. The person striking the blow is a murderer and he must be executed. Once he has been judged guilty, a relative of the victim is allowed to kill the murderer wherever he finds him.
22 However, if a person accidentally pushes his victim or throws an object at him without planning to injure anyone, **23** even if it is a large stone that can kill, but he did not see the victim, and it killed him, then he is not a murderer, because he was not an enemy and did not even have a grudge against his victim.
24 In such cases, the community shall follow these laws and judge between the killer and the avenger.
25 The community must protect the accidental murderer from the blood avenger and send him to a safe city. The killer must remain there until the death of the High Priest.
26 If the killer leaves the boundaries of the safe refuge city to which he fled, **27** and the blood avenger meets him outside the borders of his safe refuge city, then the blood avenger may kill him, and it is not considered an act of murder.
28 The killer must continue to live in his safe refuge city until the High Priest dies. After the High Priest dies, the killer is free and can return to his hereditary land.
29 No matter where you live, these shall be the laws in all your cities for every generation.
30 If anyone kills a human being, the murderer shall be put to death only on the basis of eyewitness testimony.
A single eyewitness is not enough testimony against a person when the death penalty is involved.
31 Never accept ransom for the life of a murderer who is under the death penalty, because he must be executed.
32 You must not accept ransom from a murderer in a safe city and allow him to return to his home before the High Priest dies.
33 Do not desecrate the land in which you live, because blood pollutes the land. When blood is spilled on the land, it cannot be cleansed except by the blood of the person who shed it.
34 You must not desecrate the land upon which you live, for I live among you. I, Adonai, live among My people the Israelites.

---

25. The community must protect the accidental murderer from the blood avenger.
In ancient times, the right to avenge a murder belonged to a close relative of the slain. Shame rested upon the family until its representative, called "blood avenger" (*go'el ha-dam*), killed the individual responsible for the death of one of its members.

This system, which prevailed among many nations, was destroyed by the Mosaic legislation assigning the fate of the slayer to an impartial court of justice.

30. A single eyewitness is not enough testimony against a person when the death penalty is involved.

This is mitzvah number 411.

The Torah insists upon several corroboratory witnesses when the death penalty is involved. Human life is sacred and all precautions must be taken to see that justice is done.

A tribunal can sentence a person to death only if the murder is verified by two witnesses.

Women Who Inherit Lands

7th Aliyah

36 The leaders of the family of Gilead son of Machir, son of Manasseh, son of Joseph, petitioned Moses and the elders who were the tribal leaders of the Israelites. **2** They said, "Adonai has commanded you to divide the land among the Israelites as hereditary land by a lottery system. Adonai has also commanded you to give the hereditary land of our relative Tzelafechad to his daughters.

3 But if they marry a member of another Israelite tribe, then the hereditary land belonging to us from our ancestors will became a part of the tribe into which they marry. In this way our hereditary land from the lottery system will became smaller. **4** Then, when the Jubilee Year comes, their hereditary land will be added to the land of the tribe into which they marry, and it will be subtracted from the land of our ancestors."

5 So Moses gave the Israelites instructions from Adonai. "The tribe of Joseph's descendants are right.

6 This is Adonai's decision concerning the daughters of Tzelafechad. You may marry anyone you wish as long as you marry within your ancestral tribe. **7** In this way the hereditary land of the Israelites will not be transferred from one tribe to another, and every Israelite will remain attached to the hereditary land of his father's tribe.

8 Every girl who inherits property must marry a member of her father's tribe. Then each Israelite will inherit his father's hereditary land, **9** and the hereditary land will not be transferred from one tribe to another. Each of the Israelite tribes will remain attached to its own hereditary land."

The Five Daughters Marry

Maftir

10 Tzelafechad's daughters did exactly as Adonai had commanded Moses.
11 Machlah, Tirtzah, Haglah, Milkah, and Noah, the five daughters of Tzelafechad, married their cousins. **12** They married into the families of Manasseh son of Joseph, and their hereditary land remained with their father's family.
13 These are the commandments and laws that Adonai gave the Israelites through Moses in the plains of Moab near Jericho on the Jordan River.

---

3. But if they marry a member of another Israelite tribe, then the hereditary land belonging to us from our ancestors will become a part of the tribe into which they marry.
The son's tribal relationship follows his father, and the land which the daughters own would now belong to the son, who will now be a member of another tribe.

4. When the Jubilee Year comes, their hereditary land will be added to the land of the tribe into which they marry.
The leaders of the family of Gilead complained that if the daughters of Tzelafechad married men from another tribe, then their children, whose father was a member of another tribe, would eventually inherit the land which they inherited from their father. The family of Gilead was concerned that the land of the women would pass out of their tribe.

11. Machlah, Tirtzah, Haglah, Milkah, and Noah, the five daughters of Tzelafechad, married their cousins.
The daughters are enumerated in the order of their birth.

Rashi

סֵפֶר דְּבָרִים

THE BOOK OF DEVARIM

Devarim, meaning "words," is the Hebrew name for the fifth book of the Torah. The Greek-speaking Jews of ancient times called it Deuteronomy, meaning "second law." They gave it this name because it summarizes and reviews the laws given in the preceding books of the Torah.

The old generation who had been slaves in Egypt have died in the desert, and the new generation of freedom-loving Israelites are eager to cross the Jordan River and claim the heritage that Adonai had promised them. Moses, however, will not enter the land of Canaan with them.

Moses led the Israelites from the brickyards of Egypt to a new life of freedom. They emerged from Egypt demoralized, undisciplined, and unorganized. During the forty hard years in the wilderness, Moses molded them into a cohesive nation. Now, at the ripe old age of 120, he hands the leadership over to Joshua.

However, before relinquishing his leadership, Moses delivers four sermons.

In his first sermon (1:6–4:40) Moses recalls the forty years of wandering and the battles against enemies such as Sichon and Og.

In the second sermon (4:44–28:69) Moses tells the Israelites how Adonai wants them to behave, summarizing the laws given earlier.

In the third sermon (29:1–30:20) Moses urges the Israelites to keep their agreement with Adonai, thereby choosing life and success.

The fourth sermon (32:1–33:29) contains the Song of Moses and the blessing of the tribes.

After the final sermon, Moses hands over the leadership to Joshua, and all alone he climbs to the top of Mount Pisgah. From a distance he views the Promised Land which he cannot enter. Then Moses disappears and no one has ever found his grave.

In all of Jewish history since, there has never been a prophet of the same stature and ability as Moses.

There has been much scholarly debate about the authorship of the Torah. Two statements in the Torah point to Moses as the author:

1. "Moses wrote the last scroll of the Torah [Devarim] and gave it to the priests." (31:9)
2. "Take the (fifth) scroll of the Torah and place it in the ark." (31:24–26)

Moses wrote all of the words of the Torah in a scroll to the very end, even including an account of his own death.

סֵפֶר דְּבָרִים

THE BOOK OF DEVARIM

Masoretic Torah Notes

Here is a list of some of the Masoretic notes
for the Book of Devarim.

1. The Book of Devarim contains 955 verses.
2. The Book of Devarim contains 34 chapters.
3. The Book of Devarim contains 11 sidrot.

These are the sidrot in the Book of Devarim.

סֵפֶר דְּבָרִים	432	Book of Devarim
דְּבָרִים	434	Devarim
וָאֶתְחַנַּן	442	Va'etchanan
עֵקֶב	453	Ekev
רְאֵה	462	Re'eh
שׁוֹפְטִים	474	Shoftim
כִּי תֵצֵא	482	Ki Tetze
כִּי תָבוֹא	492	Ki Tavo
נִצָּבִים	502	Nitzavim
וַיֵּלֶךְ	506	Vayelech
הַאֲזִינוּ	510	Ha'azinu
וְזֹאת הַבְּרָכָה	516	Vezot Ha'Berachah

דְּבָרִים *Devarim*

THESE ARE THE WORDS

1 These are the words that Moses spoke to the Israelites when they were camped on the east bank of the Jordan River, in the wilderness, in the Jordan Valley, near Suf, close to the cities of Paran, Tofel, Lavan, Hatzeroth, and Di-zahav. **2** It was an eleven-day journey from Horeb to Kadesh Barnea by way of Mount Seir. **3** Moses spoke to the Israelites in the fortieth year, on the first of the eleventh month [Shevat], and told them everything that Adonai had commanded him. **4** This was after he had defeated King Sichon of the Amorites, who lived in Heshbon, and Og, king of the Bashan, who lived in Ashtaroth, near Edrei.

5 It was on the east bank of the Jordan, in the land of Moab, that Moses reviewed the events of the past, saying:

Moses' First Address

6 Adonai spoke to us at Horeb, saying, "You have remained too long at this mountain. **7** Turn around and head toward the Amorite country and all the neighboring territories in the Jordan Valley, the lowlands, the Negev, the seashore, the Canaanite territory, and Lebanon, all the way to the Euphrates River.
8 Look! I am giving you this land. Go forth and conquer the land that Adonai promised to give to your ancestors, Abraham, Isaac, and Jacob, and to all of their descendants."
9 Then I said to you, "You are a burden, and I cannot lead you all by myself. **10** Adonai has multiplied your numbers, and now you are as many as the stars in the sky. **11** May Adonai increase your numbers a thousand times and bless you, as He has promised.

---

2. It was an eleven-day journey from Horeb to Kadesh Barnea.
In the Torah, places sometimes have several names. Horeb is Sinai.

3. Moses spoke to the Israelites in the fortieth year, on the first of the eleventh month.
By this time the older generation who had been slaves in Egypt had already died.
Now Moses spoke to the new generation of desert-hardened Israelites. Moses reviewed the Torah teachings and informed the people that they were the generation of the future and it was their obligation to observe the laws of the Torah.

6. Adonai spoke to us.
This section (1:6–4:40) is the first of four sermons which Moses delivered before he died.
In this sermon Moses reminds the Israelites of their forty-year journey through the desert. He also reminds them that they are the new generation and they will enter Canaan and conquer it. Moses also recalls the battles against Og and Sichon.

8. Look! I am giving you this land. Go forth and conquer the land that Adonai promised to give to your ancestors Abraham, Isaac, and Jacob.
The phrase, "The land that…and Jacob" appears more than twenty times in the Book of Devarim. Adonai guarantees the Israelites that they will be successful in their military campaign to conquer their future country, Canaan. However, the generation of former slaves had not yet acquired the confidence of conquerors. They still had fear in the back of their minds. So instead of bravely moving forward to claim their promised heritage, they delayed the invasion by sending spies. Instead of trusting Adonai and the pillar of cloud, they stood at the threshold of Canaan and refused to enter. Some even wanted to return to slavery in Egypt.

Appoint Tribal Leaders
2nd Aliyah

12 "How can I carry the burden and responsibility and settle your disputes all by myself? **13** Choose men from among your tribes who are wise and understanding, and I will appoint them as your leaders."

14 And you agreed with me and answered, "Your plan is wise."

15 So I chose wise and experienced men from every tribe and appointed them to lead you as captains of thousands, captains of hundreds, captains of fifties, captains of tens, as leaders for your tribes.

16 I then instructed your judges, saying, "Listen carefully and patiently to every problem that your brethren bring you, and judge fairly between each man and his brother, even when a foreigner is involved. **17** Do not favor any person when mak- ing a decision. Pay attention to great and small alike, and do not be influenced by anyone, since you are judging in place of Adonai. If a case is too complicated, bring it to me, and I will judge it."

---

12. How can I carry the burden and responsibility and settle your disputes all by myself?
Ibn Ezra explains the word "burdens" as providing food and water for the people as well as the flocks. The lack of these necessities caused much of the resentment and hostility toward Moses.

The sidrah Devarim is read on the Sabbath before the fast days of Tisha B'av because this sentence starts with the Hebrew word *eichah*. The word *eichah*, meaning "how," begins the Book of Lamentations (*Eichah*), which we chant on the fast day of Tisha B'av, the day that marks the destruction of the First and Second Temples as well as the 1492 expulsion from Spain. *Eichah* is the third of the Five Megillot. It contains songs of sorrow written by the prophet Jeremiah, who witnessed the destruction of Jerusalem and the destruction of the First Temple in 586 B.C.E.

13. Choose men from among your tribes who are wise and understanding, and I will appoint them as your leaders.
Moses was an experienced executive and wanted the final say in the choice of leaders. Pick your candidates and I will interview them and check whether or not they will make effective leaders.

15. So I chose wise and experienced men from every tribe and appointed them to lead you as captains of thousands, captains of hundreds, captains of fifties, captains of tens, as leaders for your tribes.
The captains were responsible for both judicial and military leadership.

16. I then instructed your judges saying, "Listen carefully and patiently to every problem that your brethren bring you."
The office of the judge was elective. Judges were chosen primarily from the Levites. They were highly respected and often scribes.

16. Judge fairly between each man and his brother, even when a foreigner is involved.
The Talmud explains that the court must not listen to one of the parties before the opponent arrives.

A foreigner is as entitled to justice as is any Israelite. Jews living in foreign countries also wanted their cases judged on its merits.

The law must be impartial to everyone, even to a foreigner. Today most of the democratic countries practice this principle.

17. Do not favor any person when making a decision. Pay attention to great and small alike.
Moses repeats the admonition of mitzvah number 414.

Now Moses instructs the judges that all their decisions must be based on facts and not on friendships or bribes. It doesn't matter if one of the litigants is a noble or an ordinary worker. The same law applies to everyone.

18 And at that time I also gave you other instructions that you must do.

19 As Adonai instructed us, we then left Horeb and made our way all through that terrifying wilderness that you saw, and then we arrived in the hill country of the Amorites. And finally we arrived in Kadesh Barnea.

20 There I said to you, "You have come to the Amorite hills, which Adonai is giving us.

21 Look! Adonai has placed the land before you. March north and occupy it, as Adonai told you. Do not be afraid and do not be discouraged."

The Scouts Explore the Land *3rd Aliyah*

22 At that time some of you approached me and said, "First let us send scouts ahead of us to explore the land.
Let them report the best way to invade and what kind of cities we will encounter."

23 I approved your idea and chose twelve men, one from each tribe. **24** They set out and headed north toward the hill country, going as far as Nahal Eshkol (Cluster Valley), and explored the area. **25** They brought back samples of the fruits. They reported to us and said, "The land that Adonai is giving us is very fertile."

26 However, you decided not to go ahead, and you rebelled against Adonai. **27** In your tents you complained, and said, "Adonai brought us out of Egypt because He hates us! He wants the Amorites to slaughter us!

28 Where are we going? Our scouts have brought back a terrifying report. They say that they saw people who were stronger and taller than we are. Their cities were fortified with high walls, and their children, too, were giants."

29 So I said to you, "Don't be afraid of them! **30** Adonai is going before you. He will fight for you, just as you saw him fight for you in Egypt. **31** You saw, as well, how Adonai took care of you in the desert as you journeyed to this place, just as a father cares for his son.

32 But now you have lost faith in Adonai!. **33** He guides you by fire at night and in a cloud by day to show us where to camp."

34 When Adonai heard your complaints, He became angry and said, **35** "Not one person of this generation will ever see the good land that I have sworn to give your ancestors.

---

21. Look! Adonai had placed the land before you. March north and occupy it, as Adonai told you. Do not be afraid and do not be discouraged.
Why did Adonai decide to delay the entry of the Israelites in Canaan for forty years?

Maimonides explains: People who are brought up as slaves cannot be quickly converted into soldiers who have to make battlefield decisions and fight for their lives. Surviving the hardships of the desert strengthened the body, the resourcefulness, and the courage of the children of the Israel.

24. Going as far as Nahal Eshkol (Cluster Valley), and explored the area.
The area was called Cluster Valley because it was famous for its huge clusters of grapes.

27. In your tents you complained.
You grumbled and complained. You were a nation of complainers who even wanted to return to the slavery of Egypt.

31. You saw, as well, how Adonai took care of you in the desert as you journeyed to this place, just as a father cares for his son.
The Torah uses this symbolism to show the love of Adonai for the nation of Israel. Adonai, the Parent, the Creator of the nation, supports and lovingly carries His child through the perils of the desert.

36 The only exception will be Caleb son of Yefuneh, because he totally believes in Me. Not only will he see it, but I will give him and his descendants the land that he explored."
37 Adonai was also angry at me because of you, and He said, "You will not enter the Promised Land. **38** Joshua son of Nun, who stands at your side, will be the one to enter, and he will lead the Israelites into the Promised Land.

The Amorites Defeat Israel *4th Aliyah*

39 "Your children, who you feared would be taken captive, and your little ones, who do not even know the difference between good and evil, will occupy the land that I will give you. **40** Now you must turn back and march into the desert toward the Sea of Reeds."
41 Then you confessed to me and said, "Yes, we have sinned against Adonai! Now we will march north and fight, just as Adonai has commanded us." Then each of you took his weapons, and marched north into the hill country.
42 Adonai said to me, "Warn them not to go and not to attack, because I will not go with them. If they attack, they will be killed by their enemies."
43 I warned you, but you refused to listen. You ignored Adonai's warnings and headed north to the hill country.
44 The Amorites, who lived in the hills, flew down to attack you, and chased you like bees. They pursued you from Seir as far as Hormah.
45 Then you returned and wept before Adonai, but He refused to listen to you.
46 You camped in Kadesh Barnea for a long time.

2 As Adonai had directed me, we then turned around and headed into the wilderness toward the Sea of Reeds. We wandered in the hills of Seir for a long time.

Israel Begins to Wander *5th Aliyah*

2 Adonai said to me, **3** "You have wandered around these hills long enough. Turn around and march north. **4** Give the people the following instructions:
Soon you will be passing by the borders of your relatives, the descendants of Esau, who live in Seir. They are afraid of you. Be very careful **5** and do not start a fight with them.

---

38. Joshua son of Nun who stands at your side.
Joshua and Caleb were the only two of their generation to enter the land of Canaan. They believed in Adonai and His promise that the Israelites would enter and conquer Canaan.

39. Your children, who you feared would be taken captive, and your little ones, who do not even know the difference between good and evil, will occupy the land that I will give you.
"Your children" refers to individuals under the age of twenty. They were not involved in any of the political, communal, military, or religious decisions of their parents. They will have a more courageous attitude than their parents. They will have the proper attitude and the strength to conquer Canaan.

44. And chased you like bees.
When someone approaches and disturbs their hives, bees emerge and chase the intruder and sting him. Bee stings have been known to be fatal.

4. Soon you will be passing by the borders of your relatives, the descendants of Esau, who live in Seir.
Rashbam explains that the eastern land of Edom was inhabited by Bedouins, who were the descendants of Esau. They were friendly and allowed the Israelites to pass through their land. This was in contrast to the antagonistic Edomites in the western part of the land, who threatened to declare war against the Israelites if they marched through the land.

I will not give you even one thin slice of their land, for I have given Mount Seir to Esau as an inheritance.

6 You must pay for the food you eat and the water you drink."

7 Adonai has blessed every step of your forty-year journey through the wilderness. Adonai was with you, and you lacked for nothing.

8 We passed through the lands of our relatives, the descendants of Esau who live in Seir, and marched through the Jordan Valley from Eilat and Etzion Gever. We turned back and passed through the Wilderness of Moab.

9 Adonai warned me, "Do not attack Moab, and do not start a war with them, because I will not give you their land as an inheritance, since I have already given Ar to Lot's descendants as their heritage.

10 The Emim who used to live there were a powerful and numerous race, as tall as the Anakim (giants). **11** The Moabites called them Emim, and others called them Rephaim.

12 At one time the Horites lived in Seir, but they were driven out by Esau's descendants, who annihilated them and settled in their place, just as Israel must displace the Canaanites in the hereditary land that Adonai gave them.

13 Now get moving and cross the Brook of Zered!"

So you crossed the Brook of Zered. **14** From the time that we left Kadesh Barnea until we crossed the Brook of Zered, thirty-eight years had passed, in which time, as Adonai had decreed, this generation of warriors died.

15 Adonai's hand was directed against them, until all of them died.

16 When all the warriors had died, **17** Adonai said to me, **18** "Soon you will pass through Ar, which is Moabite territory.

19 And you will be coming close to the Ammonites. Do not attack or start a war with them. I will not allow you to occupy the land of the Ammonites, for I have given the land as a heritage to the descendants of Lot.

---

8. And marched through the Jordan Valley from Eilat to Etzion Gever.
Eilat is situated on the northern tip of the Red Sea. It is located about eight miles from Mount Sinai and the hills of Edom.

Eilat was incorporated into the new State of Israel in 1949. The harbor of this port city can handle ocean-going vessels and is an important oil terminal linked to Ashkelon on the Mediterranean Coast. Its dry, hot climate has made Eilat a major tourist destination.

8. Etzion Gever.
Etzion Gever is known at "Solomonport."

Solomon built ships there and manned them with Israelite sailors and with Phoenicians supplied by his friend King Hiram of Tyre. The Book of Kings says that these ships sailed to Ophir and brought back gold to King Solomon. The Queen of Sheba landed at Etzion Gever on her way to visit Solomon in Jerusalem.

19. And you will be coming close to the Ammonites. Do not attack or start a war with them. I will not allow you to occupy the land of the Ammonites.
The new generation of desert-hardened, tough Israelites were anxious to prove their bravery and strength. But Adonai advises them to save their aggressiveness. Adonai warns them not to attack the sons of Esau, the Moabites and the Ammonites. They were to pass through their lands and purchase what they needed from them. However, they had Adonai's permission to attack and annihilate the Amorites.

20 That area was once the territory of the Rephaim (giants), who originally lived there. The Ammonites called them Zamzumim.
21 The Rephaim were once a large and powerful race, as tall as the giants, but Adonai destroyed them so that the Ammonites could drive them out and settle in their place. **22** Adonai destroyed the Horites for Esau's descendants who lived in Seir, and He allowed Esau's descendants to drive them out and settle in their land.
23 This was also true of the Avim, who lived from Hatzerim to Gaza; the Kaftorim came from Crete and defeated them, and settled and occupied their lands.
24 Now get up and cross the Brook of Arnon. Attack! I will help you defeat Sichon, the Amorite king of Heshbon, and I will give you his land. Begin the advance! Attack him!
25 Today I will begin to make all the nations in the area afraid of you. Whoever hears of you will tremble with fear and worry about your presence."
26 I sent ambassadors from the Wilderness of Kedemoth to Sichon, king of Heshbon, with a message of peace, saying, **27** "Allow us to pass through your land. We will travel only along the main highway, and we will not turn to the right or to the left.
28 Sell us food to eat, and water to drink for a price in silver. We only want your permission to pass through, **29** just as we passed by the territory of Esau in Seir and Moab in Ar. We wish only to cross the Jordan River into the land that Adonai is giving us." **30** But Sichon, king of Heshbon, refused to allow us to pass through his land. Adonai had stiffened his will and made him stubborn, so that we could defeat him and occupy his land.

---

23. The Kaftorim came from Crete and defeated them, and settled and occupied their lands.
The Kaftorim were the Philistines who came from Crete. They controlled five major cities along the southern Mediterranean coast: Ashkelon, Ashdod, Ekron, Gaza, and Gath. Each of these cities was ruled by an independent prince. All five cities were strongly united in war and in peace.

24. Now get up and cross the Brook of Arnon. Attack! I will help you defeat Sichon, the Amorite king of Heshbon, and I will give you his land.
The Arnon, which rises in the mountains of Moab and flows into the Dead Sea, is the second largest river in biblical Canaan. It is one of the primary sources of water in Transjordan.

The Arnon served as a political boundary between the kingdoms of Sichon and Moab. Later it became the boundary between Moab and the territories of the tribes of Reuben and Gad. From time to time, Moab expanded past the Arnon.

Now Adonai urges the Israelites to attack the Amorites. The kingdom of the biblical Amorites at one time occupied large areas in Canaan. In the ensuing battle the Israelites defeated the Amorites and killed King Sichon.

26. I sent ambassadors from the Wilderness Kedemoth to Sichon, king of Heshbon, with a message of peace.
I did not want to start a war with King Sichon. I proposed to pass peacefully through his territory and promised to pay for anything that we needed. But Sichon took my offer of peaceful passage as a sign of weakness, and he organized his army and challenged us.

28-29. We only want your permission to pass through, just as we passed by the territory of Esau in Seir and Moab in Ar.
If you don't believe us, just check with the leaders in the territory of Esau. We marched through their land and paid for the food we ate and the water we drank. We want to pass through your land peacefully.

The Defeat of Kings Sichon and Og
6th Aliyah

31 Adonai said to me, "Look! I am giving King Sichon's land to you. Attack and begin to occupy his land."

32 Sichon mobilized his troops and advanced to oppose us in battle at Yahatz. **33** Adonai helped us, and we killed him and his sons and defeated his army. **34** Then we captured all his cities, and destroyed every one, including the men, women, and children, and left no survivors. **35** All that we took as plunder were the animals and the goods in the cities we captured.

36 We conquered the territory from Aroer, the city in the valley on the edge of the Arnon River, as far as Gilead. There was no city that was strong enough to defend itself against us, because Adonai had weakened them.

37 But we did not trespass onto the Ammonite territory, along the Jabbok River, and the cities of the hill country, which Adonai had warned us not to enter.

3 Next we turned and marched toward the Bashan, where Og and his troops came to oppose us in battle at Edrei. **2** Then Adonai said to me, "Do not be afraid of him, because I will help you defeat him and his army, and you will take possession of his land. You will defeat him just as you defeated King Sichon of Heshbon."

3 Adonai helped us defeat Og, king of the Bashan, and his army, and we left no survivors. **4** Then we conquered all his cities. Og's kingdom in the Bashan included the entire Argov region with its sixty cities. **5** They were all fortified with high walls, gates, and bars, but there were also many open towns. **6** We destroyed the cities of Bashan just as we had done to those of Sichon, king of Heshbon, and killed every man, woman, and child. **7** But for ourselves, we kept all the animals and plundered the cities. **8** At that time we also conquered the lands of the two Amorite kings who lived to the east of the Jordan River, in the area between the Brook of Arnon and Mount Hermon. **9** The people of Sidon called Mount Hermon Siryon, while the Amorites call it Senir. **10** The conquered territory included all the cities on the plateau of Gilead, and the entire Bashan as far as the cities of Salhah and Edrei; these cities were part of Og's kingdom in the Bashan.

---

32. Sichon mobilized his troops and advanced to oppose us in battle at Yahatz.
King Sichon was so full of confidence that he did not call his ally to help him battle the Israelites. His ego and self-assurance were his downfall.
Shenash

3. Adonai helped us defeat Og, king of the Bashan, and his army.
Og, the Amorite, was a giant, as were the members of his kingdom. Og's defeat shattered the myth of Amorite invincibility. His kingdom consisted of sixty separate cities and communities east of the Jordan River. In the partition of Canaan, Og's territory was assigned to Reuben, Gad, and the half-tribe of Manasseh.

The Bashan contained the best grazing area in Israel and was renowned for the quality of its cattle.

9. The people of Sidon called Mount Hermon Siryon, while the Amorites call it Senir.
Mount Hermon majestically rises to a height of 9,300 feet and is snow capped most of the year. At the foot of the mountain, the melting snows create springs which form the headwaters of the Jordan River.

11 Of all the Rephaim (giants), only Og, king of Bashan, survived. His iron bed was thirteen feet long and six feet wide. It is now in the Ammonite city of Rabbah.
12 I gave the Reubenites and Gaddites all the captured territory between Aroer on the Arnon River and the southern half of the Mount Gilead area, including all the cities.
13 I gave to half of the tribe of Manasseh the rest of the Gilead and all of Bashan, which had been Og's kingdom. This included the entire Argov region and the entire Bashan, which was known as the land of the Rephaim.
14 Jair, a descendant of Manasseh, acquired the Argov region as far as the borders of the Geshurites and Machathites, and he renamed the area in the Bashan, Harvath Jair (Jair's Villages), a name that is still in use today.

Every Able-Bodied Man Must Fight *7th Aliyah*

15 I gave the Gilead region to Machir.
16 To the Reubenites and Gaddites, I gave the territory between the Gilead and the Armon River, as far as the Jabbok River, the border of the Ammonites. **17** It also included the Jordan Valley and the Jordan River, from the Kinnereth as far as the Dead Sea. **18** At that time I instructed you, saying, "Adonai has given you this land as your heritage. Every able-bodied man among you must join your fellow Israelites as a striking force. **19** I am aware that you have much cattle. Your wives, children, and cattle can remain in the cities I have given you.

Do Not Be Afraid *Maftir*

20 "Only when your brothers finally occupy the land that Adonai is giving them across the Jordan River will each man be able to return to his inheritance that I have given you."
21 I instructed Joshua, saying, "With your own eyes you have seen all that Adonai has done to these two kings. Adonai will do the same to all the kingdoms in the land on the other side of the Jordan River. **22** Do not be afraid of them, because Adonai will be fighting for you."

---

11. Of all the Rephaim (giants) only Og, king of Bashan, survived. His iron bed was thirteen feet long and six feet wide.
The Hebrew word *eres* means both bed and coffin. This bed may have been his coffin. Such coffins have been excavated in Bashan. Og's bed was probably made of wood with iron reinforcements or decorations.

11. It is now in the Ammonite city of Rabbah.
Rabbah was the capital of Ammon; today it is the Jordanian capital and is named Ammon.

Centuries later King David conquered the city and utilized the inhabitants as forced laborers. Archaeologists have found the defensive wall of Rabbah and attribute its destruction to David.

15. I gave the Gilead region to Machir.
Machir was a grandson of Joseph. See Bamidbar 32:39

17. It also included the Jordan Valley and the Jordan River, from the Kinnereth as far as the Dead Sea.
The Kinnereth is today known as Lake Tiberias.

וָאֶתְחַנַּן *Va'etchanan*

I PLEADED WITH ADONAI

23 At that time I pleaded with Adonai, saying, **24** "O Adonai, You have begun to show me Your greatness and power. Is there any power in heaven or on earth who can perform deeds and miracles as You do? **25** Please let me cross the Jordan River. Let me see the wonderful Promised Land, the beautiful hills, and the mountains of Lebanon across the Jordan." **26** But because of you Adonai was angry at me, and He would not listen. Adonai angrily told me, "That is enough! Do not speak to Me any more about My decision. **27** You can climb to the top of Mount Pisgah, and look to the west, north, south, and east. Take a good look, because you will not cross the Jordan River. **28** I want you to encourage Joshua and make him strong, because he will be the one to lead the Israelites across the river and he will distribute the land to them that you will see." **29** At that time we were camped in the valley facing Beth Peor.

4 And now, Israel, if you wish to be successful, listen carefully to the rules and laws that I am teaching you, so that you will remain alive and occupy the land that Adonai is giving you **2** Do not add other laws or subtract from these commandments. You must carefully observe all the commandments of Adonai which I am giving you. **3** With your own eyes you have seen what Adonai did to the idol Baal Peor. Adonai destroyed every person among you who worshipped the idol Baal Peor. **4** Only you, the ones who have remained faithful to Adonai, are all alive today.

---

25. Let me see the wonderful Promised Land.
Moses, the leader of the Israelites, who for forty years led the freed slaves and molded them into a nation, does not discuss his life of service. From the top of Mount Nebo Moses sees the rich fertile land. Adonai says to him, "I have let you see it but you shall not cross into it." Moses appeals to Adonai and begs for permission to cross the Jordan and touch the earth and breathe the air of Canaan. Crossing the Jordan was a new phase in Israel's history, and Joshua would now take over the leadership.
Rashi

28. I want you to encourage Joshua and make him strong, because he will be the one to lead the Israelites across the river.
Joshua was at your side and was aware of all the problems that leadership demands. I want you to encourage him so he does not become overwhelmed with the problems his leadership will face when the Israelites cross the Jordan. I know that Joshua is a strong leader but even he needs encouragement.

1. And now, Israel, if you wish to be successful, listen carefully to the rules and laws that I am teaching you.
The previous three sidrot reviewed the history of Israel. This is now followed by a reminder of the events on Mount Sinai and the importance of total obedience to laws and commandments in the Torah.

2. Do not add other laws or subtract from these commandments.
The commandments were engraved on stone tablets and were not to be changed. The fundamental authority in religious matters has always been the Torah. The Rabbis saw the need for greater clarification to meet new political, humanitarian, or medical realities. The various religious denominations have designated *halachah* (Jewish law) committees who are actively engaged in clarifying the laws to meet the needs of their congregants.

I Have Taught You Rules and Laws
2nd Aliyah

5 I have taught you the rules and laws that Adonai gave me, so that you will be able to observe them in the land where you will be living.

6 Obey and observe these rules, so nations will respect your wisdom and understanding. They will hear all these rules and say, "This great nation is certainly a wise and intelligent people."

7 No other nation is so fortunate as to have Adonai in its midst. Adonai is among us. **8** No other nation possesses such humane rules and laws as are in the Torah that I am giving you today.

9 Beware and be careful not to forget the miracles that you have seen with your own eyes. Do not let these memories escape your minds as long as you live. Teach them to your children and your grandchildren.

10 Recall the day you stood before Adonai at Mount Horeb (Sinai). It was there that Adonai said to me, "Gather the people and I will allow them to hear My words. I will teach them to respect Me as long as they live on earth, so that they can teach My commandments to their children."

11 You came and stood at the foot of the mountain. The mountain was ablaze with a fire reaching up to heaven, surrounded by darkness and clouds.

12 Then Adonai spoke to you out of the fire. You heard the sound of words but saw no image; there was only a voice.

13 He presented His covenant to you, and instructed you to observe the Ten Commandments, which He engraved on two stone tablets.

14 At that time, Adonai commanded me to teach you His rules and laws, so that you will be able to observe them in the land you are soon to occupy.

15 Be very careful! Just remember that you did not see an image in the fire on the day that Adonai spoke to you at Mount Horeb. **16** So do not commit a sin and make an idol to worship. Do not make any male or female idols, **17** or statues of animals or winged creatures that fly through the air, **18** or any form of animal that walks on land or any fish that swims in the ocean.

19 When you raise your eyes to the sky, and see the sun, moon, stars, and other heavenly bodies, do not bow down to them or worship them. Adonai created these heavenly bodies only to provide light for the nations of the world.

20 Remember, Adonai has chosen you, and He brought you out of the fiery furnace of Egypt, to be His special people as you are today.

---

7. No other nation is so fortunate as to have Adonai in its midst. Adonai is among us.
No other nation possesses such humane rules and laws as are in the Torah that I am giving you today.

Israel is Adonai's chosen people. The actions of Israel reflect upon Adonai. If Israel observes the laws and statutes, then there is justice and righteousness, which reflects positively on Adonai.

However, if Israel acts perversely, then its image as a "holy people" is besmirched throughout the world and her reputation is profaned.

9. Beware and be careful not to forget the miracles that you have seen with your own eyes.
Even if you forget everything else, do not forget the miracles you saw when you stood at Mount Sinai.

21 Adonai was angry at me because of you. He punished me and decided that I would not cross the Jordan River, and that I would not enter the Promised Land that He is giving you as an inheritance. **22** I must die on this side of the Jordan River, but you will be the ones to cross over and occupy the Promised Land.

23 Beware, and do not break Adonai's covenant with you. Adonai has forbidden you to worship idols.

24 Remember! Adonai is like a devouring fire, and demands loyalty.

25 After you have fathered children and grandchildren, and have been settled in the land for a long time, perhaps you will anger Him by making a statue of some image and worshipping an idol and committing a sin in the eyes of Adonai. **26** Let heaven and earth be my witnesses that you will then quickly disappear from the land that you are crossing the Jordan to occupy. You will not remain there very long, for you will be totally destroyed.

27 Adonai will scatter you, and you will remain only a handful among the nations to which Adonai will exile you. **28** There you will worship gods of wood and stone, which cannot see, hear, eat, or smell. **29** Then you will once again begin to seek Adonai, and you will pursue Him with all your heart and soul, and you will, in the end, find Him.

30 When you are in distress because of these calamities that will have happened to you, then you will finally return to Adonai and obey Him. **31** Adonai is merciful, and He will not abandon you or destroy you; He will not forget the covenant that He made with your ancestors.

---

22. I must die on this side of the Jordan River, but you will be the ones to cross over and occupy the Promised Land.
Adonai has informed me that I will not cross the Jordan with you.
Rashi says that Moses was aware that even his body would not be buried in the Holy Land.

25. After you have fathered children and grandchildren, and have been settled in the land for a long time, perhaps you will anger Him by making a statue of some image and worshipping an idol and committing a sin in the eyes of Adonai.
Moses the prophet looks into the future and sees the danger enveloping the Israelites. The danger will come from future generations who will intermarry with their neighbors. The prophecy of Moses proved to be true, and the Israelites began to intermarry and worship idols. *Shenash*

28. There you will worship gods of wood and stone.
Abarbanel, who experienced the expulsion from Spain, explains the dilemma of his co-religionists. "Many Jews will under extreme pressure be forced to convert knowing full well that they are worshipping man–made idols just to escape death and burning at the stake. Forced conversion will be the climax of their sufferings. In their hearts they will love their true faith, but under pressure will be forced to pay lip service to a faith that was forced upon them."

29. Then you will once again begin to seek Adonai, and you will pursue him with all your heart and soul, and you will, in the end, find Him.
This was a message for the Jews all over the world who have been discriminated against for their beliefs. Even Jews who have been forcibly coerced into conversion can inwardly worship Adonai and, when the opportunity becomes available return openly to their faith.

Historically, Marranos, German Jews, Russian and Polish Jews, Jews in Arab countries, and even Jews in some Western countries including England and France have at one time practiced forced conversion.

Some of these victims managed to escape to freedom and once again returned to the practice of Judaism. Unfortunately, hundreds of thousands have been lost from the religion of their ancestors.

32 Search from the beginning of time, when Adonai created people on earth, and from one end of the heavens to the other end, and see whether anything as great as this has ever happened, or whether anyone else has ever known anything as great as this. **33** No nation except you has ever heard Adonai speak out of fire, and lived. **34** Has Adonai ever saved another nation with miracles, signs, wonders, and with a mighty hand and outstretched arm, and such great acts of power as Adonai performed for you in Egypt before your very eyes?

35 He has shown this to you so that you will understand that Adonai is the Supreme Being, and there is none like Him.

36 You heard His voice from the heavens instructing you, and here on earth He showed you His pillar of fire, and you heard His words from the midst of the fire.

37 Adonai used His great power and brought you out of Egypt because He loved your ancestors and chose to bless their children. **38** He will help you to defeat nations that are greater and stronger than you, and will give you their lands as an inheritance, just as He is doing today.

39 Remember, treasure it in your heart. Adonai is the Supreme Being in heaven above and on the earth below; there is no other.

40 Observe His laws and commandments that I am giving you today; then He will be good to you and your descendants after you. And you will live to a ripe old age in the land that Adonai is giving you forever and ever.

The Cities of Safe Refuge
3rd Aliyah

41 Then Moses chose three safe refuge cities on the east of the Jordan River, **42** where a person who accidentally kills someone can find a safe refuge.

43 These cities were Betzer in the wilderness belonging to the Reubenites, Ramoth in the Gilead belonging to the Gaddites, and Golan in Bashan belonging to the Manassites.

---

34. Has Adonai ever saved another nation with miracles, signs, wonders, and with a mighty hand and outstretched arm.
"Signs" refers to Moses, who turned his rod into a snake. "Wonders" refers to the plagues with which Adonai punished Egypt.

35. He has shown this to you so that you will understand that Adonai is the Supreme Being, and there is none like Him.
There is only one Supreme Being. If you acknowledge Him and follow His commandments, you will succeed in all your endeavors.

40. Observe His laws and commandments that I am giving you today; then He will be good to you and your descendants after you. And you will live to a ripe old age in the land that Adonai is giving you forever and ever.
Your life in the land of Israel will be long and successful on the condition that you remain true to your spiritual heritage.
Rabbi Samson Raphael Hirsch

41. Then Moses chose three safe refuge cities on the east of the Jordan River.
Now the plan for the invasion and the development of a government begins on the east side of the Jordan River. Moses chooses three safe refuge cities known as *Oray Miklat*.

43. These cities were Betzer in the wilderness belonging to the Reubenites, Ramoth in the Gilead belonging to the Gaddites, and Golan in Bashan belonging to the Manassites.
The city of Betzer was a city of refuge.

When someone accidently killed a person, he took refuge there, and was safe from revenge seekers.

Moses' Second Address

44 These are the words that Moses spoke to the Israelites.
45 These are the rituals, rules, and laws that Moses presented to the Israelites when they left Egypt.
46 They were camped at this time on the east bank of the Jordan River, in the valley near Beth Peor in the land of Sichon, king of Heshbon, whom Moses and the Israelites had defeated when they left Egypt.
47 The Israelites occupied the land of King Sichon, as well as the land of King Og of Bashan. These were the two Amorite kings who ruled the land on the eastern side of the Jordan River.
48 Their territories extended from Aroer on the edge of the Arnon River to Mount Siyon, also known as Mount Hermon, **49** as well as the Jordan Valley on the eastern bank of the Jordan River, as far as the Dead Sea below the slopes of Pisgah.

The Second Ten Commandments   *4th Aliyah*

5 Moses assembled all the Israelites, and said to them:
Hear O, Israel, listen to the rules and laws that I am publicly giving to you today. Learn them and carefully follow them.
2 Adonai made a covenant with you at Mount Horeb.
3 It was not with your ancestors that Adonai made this covenant, but with those of us who are still alive here and now. **4** Adonai spoke to us face-to-face out of the pillar of fire on the mountain. **5** At that time I stood between you and Adonai and repeated Adonai's words to you, because you were afraid of the fire and did not dare to climb the mountain.
Then Adonai gave the Ten Commandments for the second time. This is what he said:

First Commandment
I am Adonai, who brought you out of Egypt, from the land of slavery.

---

44. These are the words that Moses spoke to the Israelites.
The next section (4:44–28:69) is the second of the four final sermons which Moses delivered before he died. This sermon summarizes the laws that were previously given to them. Moses also reminds them of the Ten Commandments and their awesome experience at Mount Sinai.

2. Adonai made a covenant with you at Mount Horeb.
Biblical laws are a treaty between two parties, a relationship between humanity and divine forces. After Sinai, the Israelites and Adonai join into a covenant of mutual obligations. Adonai agrees to reward the Israelites when they uphold their obligations and punish them when they break the covenant. The covenant is given to Israel, but Adonai's justice applies to the entire world.

Adonai will judge all the people of the earth according to their moral behavior. The covenant is optimistic; it believes that people have the ability to improve the world (*tikkun olam*) and to achieve peace throughout the world.

3. It was not with your ancestors that Adonai made this covenant, but with those of us who are still alive here and now.
The covenant, or *brit*, was not made exclusively with those who left Egypt and stood around Mount Sinai. The timeless Torah was given to every generation that followed. The covenant is in force today with every Jew, including the ones that follow.

4. Adonai spoke to us face-to-face.
Adonai spoke to you not in a dream or a vision but while you were very much alive and awake, when you were completely in command of all your senses.

Second Commandment

7 You must not worship any gods but Me.

8 You must not make any idol or statue or image of anything in the heaven above, on the earth below, or in the waters below.

9 You must not bow down to idols and must not worship them. I, Adonai, demand exclusive worship. I will punish the children down to the third and fourth generations because of the sins of the father.

10 But I will show kindness to those who love Me and observe My commandments. To them I will show love for thousands of generations.

Third Commandment

11 You must not swear falsely by using the name of Adonai. I will not allow the person who uses My name falsely to go unpunished.

Fourth Commandment

12 You must observe the Sabbath to keep it holy, just as Adonai has commanded you.

13 You can work on the six weekdays and do all your tasks, **14** but Saturday must be devoted to Adonai, and you must not do any work.

This includes you, your son, your daughter, your male and female servants, your ox, your donkey, all your other animals, and the foreigner who lives in your lands. Your male and female servants must be able to rest just as you do. **15** Remember that you were once slaves in Egypt, and Adonai liberated you with a strong hand and a mighty arm. Therefore Adonai has commanded you to observe the Sabbath.

Fifth Commandment

16 You must honor your father and your mother as Adonai has commanded you. If you do, you will live long and prosper on the land that Adonai is giving you.

Sixth Commandment

17 You must not commit murder.

Seventh Commandment

You must not commit adultery.

Eighth Commandment

You must not steal.

Ninth Commandment

You must not be a false witness against your neighbor.

---

15. Remember that you were once slaves in Egypt, and Adonai liberated you with a strong hand and a mighty arm. Therefore has Adonai commanded you to observe the Sabbath.
You experienced the bitterness and sufferings of slavery, so it is your responsibility to protect the rights and welfare of your slaves. Your slaves must be allowed to rest and enjoy the Sabbath just as you do.

You were freed on the condition that you observe the commandments.

16. You must honor your father and your mother as Adonai has commanded you. If you do, you will live long and prosper on the land that Adonai is giving you.
Future generations owe their success to the fact that their link to the past (parents) is strong and secure. Jewish generations, wherever they live, will be granted continuity only if they accept the tradition of history and religion from their forebears.

Shenash

Tenth Commandment

18 You must not be envious of your neighbor's house, his field, his male or female servants, his ox, his donkey, or anything else that belongs to him.

When We Hear It, We Will Obey *5th Aliyah*

19 From the mountain, out of the fire and mist, Adonai spoke these commandments in a loud voice to the entire assembly. He also wrote these words on two stone tablets and gave them to me.

20 When you heard the voice out of the darkness, the mountain was surrounded by flames. Then your leaders and elders approached me **21** and said, "Yes, Adonai has truly showed us His glory and greatness, and we have heard His voice in the midst of the fire. Today, with our own eyes and ears, we have seen and heard that a human need not die when Adonai speaks to him. **22** But we are still in danger. If we continue to hear the voice of Adonai much longer, this great fire will destroy us, and we will all die. **23** No human has ever heard the voice of the living Adonai speaking out of fire as we have and survived. **24** Moses, approach Adonai, and listen to all He says. And then you can tell us whatever Adonai tells you, and when we hear it, we will obey."

25 Adonai heard what you said, and He said to me, "I have heard what the people have said to you and they are right.

26 I wish that their hearts would always remain the same and be willing to obey Me. Then they would observe My commandments forever, so that they and their children would forever enjoy a life of success.

27 Now, go tell them to return to their tents. **28** You, however, must remain here with Me. And I will give you all the rules and commandments, and you will teach them the laws so that they can understand and obey them in the land I am giving them."

---

18. You must not be envious of your neighbor's house, his field, his male or female servants, his ox, his donkey, or anything else that belongs to him.
Envy can make a person miserable. It is a force that can tear apart families and friends. Instead of thinking about what you don't have, concentrate on what you do have and try to be content.

22. If we continue to hear the voice of Adonai much longer, this great fire will destroy us.
The first two commandments consist of the first ten words that were spoken directly to the Israelites by Adonai. However, the next eight commandments were transmitted by Moses. The Israelites would not listen to the voice of Adonai because it was too awesome and powerful so the remainder of the commandments were given by Moses. The Israelites told Moses: "You can tell us whatever Adonai tells you, and when we hear it, we will obey."

28. You, however, must remain here with Me. And I will give you all the rules and commandments, and you will teach them the laws so that they can understand and obey them in the land I am giving them.
It is a Jew's first duty to learn the rules and commandments of his faith. The pursuit of this knowledge, is a lifelong task. Possessing this knowledge, a Jew can live a disciplined and dedicated life.

Moses, founder of the faith, is not called prophet or savior but "Moses our Teacher." The prophet preaches, the savior promises salvation, and the teacher instructs.

The Hebrew word that encompasses all our religious literature is called *Torah,* which literally means "teaching."

29 Be careful to do what Adonai has commanded you, and do not deviate to the right or to the left. **30** If you follow all of Adonai's commandments, then you will live long and prosper in the land you are about to occupy.

6 These are the commandments and the laws that Adonai commanded me to teach you, so that you can observe them in the land you will soon occupy.
2 Respect Adonai and observe all of His commandments and laws that I am teaching you. In this way you and your children and your grandchildren will obey Adonai as long as they live.
3 Hear, O Israel, and be careful to observe them. If you do, then just as Adonai has promised you, your future will be successful and you will give birth to many children in the land flowing with milk and honey.

Teach Your Children *6th Aliyah*

4 Hear, O Israel, Adonai is supreme, Adonai is one.
5 You shall love Adonai with all your heart, with all your soul, and with all your might.

---

1. These are the commandments and the laws that Adonai commanded me to teach you, so that you can observe them in the land you will soon occupy.
This refers to the Ten Commandments (Chapters 19–20) in the Book of Shemot which Moses brought down from Mount Sinai.

2. Respect Adonai and observe all his commandments and laws that I am teaching you. In this way you and your children and your grandchildren will obey Adonai as long as they live.
You will instruct future generations to observe the commandments. They in turn will pass the commandments to their future generations.

4. Hear, O Israel. Adonai is supreme. Adonai is one.
This phrase summarizes the teachings of the first and second of the Ten Commandments.
This is mitzvah number 417.
The *Shema* consists of three sections of the Torah: Devarim 6:4–9, Devarim 11:13–21, and Bamidbar 15:37–41. The *Shema* is a declaration of the existence and the oneness of Adonai, Israel's loyalty to Adonai and the commandments, the belief in Divine justice, and the remembrance of the liberation from Egypt.

5. You shall love Adonai with all your heart.
One can love Adonai with all one's heart by reciting prayers three times daily. The prayers are *Shacharit*, the morning prayer, *Minhah*, the afternoon prayer, and *Maariv*, the evening prayer.
Loving Adonai implies more than just fulfilling the letter of the law. It means we must go beyond it and also observe the spirit of the law. *Talmud*

5. You shall love Adonai with all your heart, with all your soul, and with all your might.
This is mitzvah number 418.
The Rabbis explained that the phrase "with all your soul" means to love Adonai with your life and with your last drop of blood.
Rabbi Akiba lived in the second century, when the Romans ruled Jerusalem. He was a leader and a great rabbi. Rabbi Akiba joined Bar Kochba in a rebellion against the Romans. When the rebellion failed, Rabbi Akiba, who was arrested while studying the Torah, was tortured to death. As he died he recited the words of the *Shema* with his last breath. Since that time many Jews who are near death recite the *Shema* as their last words.
"Might" means with all your possessions, wealth, power, and status.

5. With all your heart.
A Rabbinic source says, "Love Him in times of joy and love Him in times of distress."

6 These words which I am commanding you today must remain on your heart.
7 Teach them to your children and speak of them when you are at home, when traveling on the road, when you lie down and when you rise up.
8 Tie these words as a sign around your hand, and wear them as a symbol in the center of your forehead.

---

7. Teach them to your children and speak of them when you are at home, when traveling on the road.
This is mitzvah number 419.

This mitzvah is directed to every Jew, old and young, rich and poor, wherever he or she lives. Torah study is an obligation, not a privilege; every Jew is obligated to study it under all circumstances each day.

Nachmanides says, " If the Torah is to remain a permanent possession of Israel, it is important to teach it to the next generation."

Recanti says, "You must teach your children Torah so they can create for themselves a life structure that will have a moral and religious meaning." The children must be taught to have a clear knowledge of the ethics and traditions of their faith.

7. When you lie down and when you rise up.
This is mitzvah number 420.

It is a mitzvah to recite the first paragraph of the *Shema* (Devarim 6: 4–9) twice daily, "When you lie down and when you rise up." This paragraph is a declaration of faith and is to be recited with the right hand covering the eyes. The purpose of covering the eyes is to enhance one's concentration.

8. Tie these words as a sign around your hand and wear them as a symbol in the center of your forehead.
This commandment, number 422, refers to the *tefillin*. The tefillin are two small leather boxes with attached leather straps. The straps are to be wrapped around the head and arm to hold them in place. Inside each of the leather boxes are handwritten parchments with quotations from the Torah. Jews wear the tefillin during the morning prayer service except on the Sabbath and holidays. It is customary to start putting on tefillin when becoming a Bar Mitzvah at the age of thirteen.

8. Tie these words as a sign around your hand and wear them as a symbol in the center of your forehead.
A prayer is recited before putting the tefillin around the arm and head. Adonai has commanded us to wind the *shel yad* on the arm because of His outstretched arms, and opposite the heart to promise that you will do His will with all your heart. You place the *shel rosh* opposite the brain, to make sure that the mind and all your senses are dedicated to the 613 commandments.

The tefillin for the hand. Note the knot tied in the shape of a *yud*.

The tefillin for the head. Note the knot tied in the shape of a *dalet*.

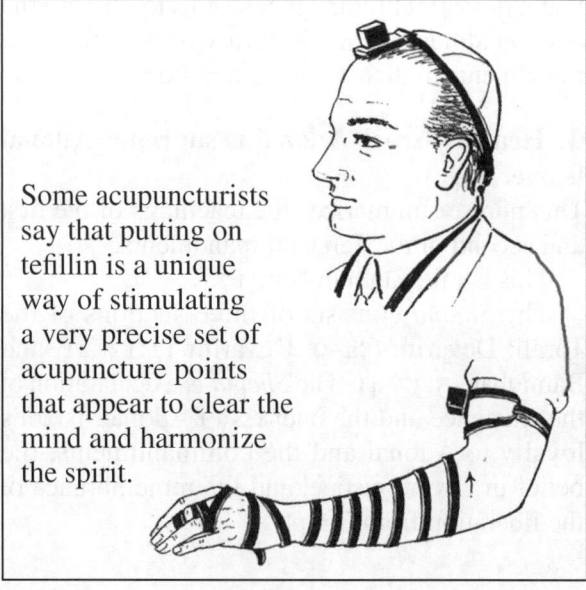

Some acupuncturists say that putting on tefillin is a unique way of stimulating a very precise set of acupuncture points that appear to clear the mind and harmonize the spirit.

9 Write them on parchments attached to the doorposts (*mezzuzot*) of your houses and your gates.
10 When Adonai brings you to the land that He swore to give to your ancestors, Abraham, Isaac, and Jacob, you will find large, busy cities that you did not build. **11** You will also discover houses filled with beautiful furnishings that you did not put there. You will find wells that you did not dig, and vineyards and olive trees that you did not plant.
After you have eaten and are filled, **12** be careful and do not forget that Adonai is the one who brought you as free people out of Egypt, the land of slavery.
13 Respect Adonai, worship Him, and be loyal to His name.
14 Do not worship the idols of the nations around you. **15** Adonai demands loyalty from you. Do not make Adonai angry, because He will destroy you from the face of the earth.
16 Do not anger Adonai as you angered Him in Massah. **17** Make sure to observe the commandments of Adonai, as well as the rituals and decrees that He has commanded you. **18** Do what is upright and good in the eyes of Adonai, so that He will be good to you. Then you will come and occupy the good land that Adonai promised your ancestors. **19** Adonai will defeat all your enemies that surround you, just as He promised.
20 In the future, when your child asks you, "What is the meaning of the rituals, rules, and laws that Adonai has commanded us?"
21 here is how you must answer him: "We were slaves to Pharaoh in Egypt, but Adonai brought us out of Egypt with a mighty hand. **22** Before our very eyes Adonai produced great miracles against Pharaoh and all his household. **23** He brought us out of Egypt to give us the land He promised our ancestors He would give to us. **24** Adonai has commanded us to observe all these commandments and remain faithful to Him for all time, so that we would survive, just as we are now. **25** If we faithfully observe Adonai's instructions, then all will be well with us."

---

9. Write them on parchments attached to the doorposts.
The *mezzuzah* is wooden or metal case in which the *Shema* and another passage from Deuteronomy are handwritten on a tiny scroll. It is placed on the right side of doorposts of homes and synagogues, in accordance with the Biblical commandment.

Maimonides wrote that the *mezzuzah* was a constant reminder of Adonai's presence in the world. He believed that when a person saw the *mezzuzah* when he left or entered his home, he would be reminded of Adonai's commandments and conduct his daily affairs in accordance with the rules and laws of the Torah.

9. And your gates.
Rashi explains that gates refers to the gates of courtyards and the gates of walled cities.

11. You will also discover houses filled with beautiful furnishings that you did not put there. You will find wells that you did not dig, and vineyards and olive trees that you did not plant.
You will win a military victory and you will also find fertile farms with deep wells and well-built houses filled with beautiful furnishings. After you have settled down, do not forget that it was Adonai who freed you from the land of slavery and helped you win the military victory.

18. Do what is upright and good in the eyes of Adonai.
In commanding us to do what is upright and good, Adonai is reminding us that we have a moral obligation to go beyond what is legally required of us – that is, to do what is "good" as well as what is "right."
Rashi

You Are Adonai's Special People
7th Aliyah

7 When Adonai brings you to the land that you are soon to occupy, He will destroy seven nations who are more numerous and powerful than you: the Hittites, the Girgashites, the Amorites, the Canaanites, the Perizzites, the Hivites, and the Jebusites. **2** When Adonai weakens them and you defeat them, then you must completely destroy them, and refuse to sign any treaty with them or show them any mercy. **3** You must not intermarry with them. You must not marry your daughters to their sons, and you must not marry their daughters to your sons. **4** If you do, they will lead your children away from worshipping Me and lead them to worship idols. Then Adonai will be angry at you, and you will quickly be destroyed. **5** This is what you must do to them. Destroy their altars, smash their sacred pillars, cut down their holy Asherah trees, and burn their idols. **6** You are a nation dedicated to Adonai. From among all the nations on the face of the earth, Adonai has chosen you to be His special people. **7** He chose you not because you were more numerous than the other nations. In fact you were one of the smallest. **8** Adonai chose you because He loves you, and because He kept the promise that He made to your ancestors. That is why Adonai brought you out with a mighty hand and rescued you from slavery, and from the power of Pharaoh, king of Egypt.

Study the Rules and Laws
Maftir

9 I want you to know that Adonai is faithful to those who keep His covenant for thousands of generations, for He loves those who love Him and observe His commandments. **10** But He takes revenge against those who hate him. He does not delay their punishments and He punishes them publicly. **11** Therefore study the rules and laws that I am teaching you today, so you will know how to observe them.

---

3. You must not intermarry with them. You must not marry your daughters to their sons, and you must not marry their daughters to your sons.
Judaism does not tolerate marriages that are at variance with the religious standards of the two parties. The best partners for an enduring union is one in which both parties have similar religious loyalties.

However, Judaism is a practical religion and the Rabbis have designed standards and ceremonies to convert individuals who wish to adopt the Jewish faith.

5. This is what you must do to them. Destroy their altars, smash their sacred pillars, cut down their holy Asherah trees, and burn their idols.
You are a holy people to Adonai (Devarim. 7:6) is the reason given to destroy the physical presence of any type of idolatry.

The ruins of Canaanite temples indicate that the Israelite conquerors thoroughly destroyed all evidence of Canaanite idolatry. The chief figure among the Canaanite gods was Baal. His name means lord. The Asherah was a tree which was worshipped. Alongside the asherahs were *matzevot*, or stone pillars.

5. Destroy their altars, smash their sacred pillars, cut down their holy Asherah trees, and burn their idols.
The Torah is very much aware of other religions which try to entice Jews to join their faith, so it advises the Israelites to remove temptations and totally destroy their religious structures.

Historically, idol worship made inroads into the Israelite population during the rules of some of the kings of Israel and Judea.

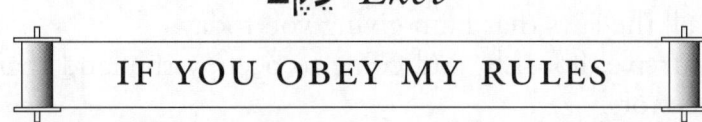

עֵקֶב Ekev

IF YOU OBEY MY RULES

12 If you obey My rules and observe the commandments, then Adonai will remember His covenant which He made with your ancestors.
13 He will love you. He will bless you, He will make you numerous.
He will bless you with many children, He will increase the crops of your land, your grain, your wine, your oil, the calves of your herds, and the lambs of your flocks, in the land that He promised your ancestors to give to you.
14 Adonai will bless you more than any nation. Your families and your livestock will increase, and none of your animals will be barren.
15 Adonai will remove sickness from you. He will not allow you to become ill with any of the Egyptian sicknesses that you suffered from while you were there. He will give them to your enemies.
16 Show no mercy to the nations that Adonai delivers into your hands. Do not worship their idols, because that will be a deadly trap.
17 Perhaps you are thinking, "These nations are more numerous than we are. We will never be able to defeat them."
18 Do not be afraid of them. Just remember what Adonai did to Pharaoh and to all of Egypt.
19 Remember the great miracles that you saw with your own eyes – the signs, the wonders, the mighty hand and the outstretched arm with which Adonai liberated you out of Egypt. Adonai will do the same to all the nations you fear. **20** Adonai will send deadly hornets to attack them, so that the survivors hiding from you will also be destroyed.
21 Do not be afraid of those nations, because Adonai is watching over you.
22 Little by little Adonai will drive out these nations.
Do not drive them out too quickly; otherwise the wild animals will became too numerous.
23 Adonai will put these nations in your power and He will panic them until they are destroyed. **24** He will put their kings at your mercy, and you will destroy them. **25** You must burn their idols. You must not save the gold and silver that cover the idols. It will entrap you because it is hateful to Adonai. **26** Do not bring any idols into your house, because you must not worship them or you too will be destroyed. Totally reject them because they are absolutely forbidden.

---

12. Adonai will remember His covenant which he made with your ancestors.
Adonai made His covenant with the patriarchs Abraham, Isaac, and Jacob. He kept His promises and freed the Israelites from the brickyards of Egypt. Now Adonai will lead you to victory in Canaan.

14. Adonai will bless you more than any nation.
Adonai assures the Israelites that if they obey the laws of the Torah, their crops, their cattle, and their families will increase. The condition for this blessing is very much alive today.

17. Perhaps you are thinking, "These nations are more numerous than we are. We will never be able to defeat them."
Do not have a defeatist attitude. Yes, your enemies are stronger and they are very numerous, but do not fear them! I am Adonai and I am on your side. In the end you will surely triumph.

20. Adonai will send deadly hornets to attack them.
Adonai will send swarms of stinging hornets, which will weaken the resistance of the enemy.

8 You must obey all the laws that I am giving you today. Then you will survive, flourish, and come to occupy the land that Adonai swore to give to your ancestors. **2** Remember how Adonai led you these forty years in the wilderness. He sent hardships to test you, to determine what is in your heart: whether you would keep His commandments or not. **3** He made life difficult for you by letting you go hungry, and then He fed you the manna, which neither you nor your ancestors had ever eaten. This was to teach you that man does not live by bread alone, but by the words that come out of Adonai's mouth.
4 For forty years the clothing you wore did not wear out, and your feet did not become blistered. **5** Beware that just as a parent disciplines his child, so Adonai is disciplining you.
6 Observe Adonai's commandments, walk in His ways, and worship Him.
7 Adonai is bringing you to a fertile land with flowing streams and with springs gushing from valleys and mountains. **8** It is a land overflowing with wheat, barley, grapes, figs, and pomegranates – a land of olive and honey-date trees.

---

1. You must obey all the laws that I am giving you today.

The sages say that if you obey all the laws (mitzvot), then you will achieve longevity.

2. He sent hardships to test you, to determine what is in your heart: whether you would keep His commandments or not.

The test refers to the manna which Adonai daily sent to Israel and a double portion for the Sabbath. Rashi believes that the test was twofold: to refrain from leaving manna until the next day, and not to gather manna on the Sabbath. How the Israelites obeyed these two instructions would be an indication whether they would follow and be loyal to Adonai's commandments and judgments.

3. This was to teach you that man does not live by bread alone, but by the words that came out of Adonai's mouth.

The spiritual needs of people are more important than their physical needs.
Adonai's words are the laws and commandments of the Torah.

7–8. Adonai is bringing you to a fertile land with flowing streams and with springs gushing from valleys and mountains. It is a land overflowing with wheat, barley, grapes, figs, and pomegranates a land of olive and honey-date trees.

Just about the time the wheat was harvested, the first fruits began to ripen on trees and vines in Israel. The Torah commanded the farmers to bring their first fruits of these "seven kinds" to the Temple in Jerusalem as an offering of thanks to Adonai. Our ancestors were grateful to Adonai for a bountiful harvest. That is why one name for Shavuot is *Chag ha-Bikkurim*, the Festival of First Fruits.

The Rabbis tell how the first ripe fruits were selected. Upon visiting his field and seeing a ripe fig or cluster of grapes or pomegranate, the owner would tie a thread around the fruit, saying, "This shall be among the *bikkurim*."

Each of the seven kinds of fruits mentioned in the Bible played an important part in the Torah and in Jewish history.

8. It is a land overflowing with wheat, barley, grapes, figs, and pomegranates-a land of olive and honey-date trees.

Canaan had an ideal climate and soil for grape growing. Almost every book in the Tanak mentions vines, grapes, and wine. Wine was a popular beverage both for religious purposes and also to drink. Wine had a great variety of uses. It was mixed with water as a purifier and swallowed when water was scarce. Wine was a remedy for intestinal ailments and was used like vinegar for pickling vegetables. Fresh juicy grapes in summer and raisins in winter were popular foods.

9 It is a land of plentiful food, where nothing is lacking, a land where iron stones are plentiful, and the mountains are filled with copper.
10 When you eat and are satisfied, you must thank Adonai for the good land He has given you.

Do Not Forget Adonai
2nd Aliyah

11 Be careful not to forget Adonai, and to observe His commandments, decrees, and laws, which I am giving you today. **12** When you have eaten well and built fine houses to live in, **13** and your herds and flocks have grown and you have earned much silver and gold, and everything you own has prospered, **14** then you may become forgetful, and you will no longer remember Adonai, who liberated you from slavery in Egypt.

---

9. A land where iron stones are plentiful, and the mountains are filled with copper.
Today we know that there are extensive copper deposits in the Timna Valley in Israel. In biblical times Solomon's mines provided copper for smelting. Despite the heat and the lack of fuel, the Israelite metallurgists managed to extract copper, which was then exported.

Hiram, king Solomon's metal expert, cast bronze utensils for the Temple (I Kings 7:47). The text says that there were so many bronze utensils in the clay soil between Sukkot and Zarethan, that it was impossible to weigh them.

9. It is a land of plentiful food, where nothing is lacking, a land where iron stones are plentiful, and the mountains are filled with copper.
The midrash says that the verse refers to the Torah, comparing it to food. Just as a person cannot live without food, no one can live without Torah.

9. It is a land of plentiful food, where nothing is lacking.
The pomegranate was an essential food. It was valued for a threefold symbolism – sanctity, fertility, and abundance. The shape of the pomegranate adorned the fringes of the holy vestments and, in the course of time, the silver ornaments of the Torah. The pomegranate had therapeutic value for various ailments such as intestinal worms. In Hebrew the pomegranate is called *rimmon*. The midrash says that the *rimmon* has 613 seeds just like the pellets in a hand grenade and the mitzvot in the Torah. An Israeli hand granade is called *rimmon*. *Shenash*

10. When you eat and are satisfied, you must thank Adonai for the good land He has given you.
This is mitzvah number 430.

The *Birkat ha-Mazon*, grace after meals, consists of four blessings which are recited after a meal.

According to tradition, each of the four blessings was instituted by different persons. The first blessing is credited to Moses. The second blessing was instituted by Joshua. The third blessing was introduced by Kings David and Solomon. The fourth blessing was added by the Rabbis.

Nachmanides says that reciting the *Birkat ha-Mazon* is an easy mitzvah to perform if we think about all the millions of people all over the world who are not as fortunate as we are but are hungry and even starving. When we recite, "who feeds the world with goodness, with grace, with lovingkindness and tender mercy: He gives food to all flesh for his lovingkindness endures forever," we acknowledge that Adonai is the Creator. People cannot create matter or life. The Creator of the universe gives the world its material wealth.

10. When you eat and are satisfied, you must thank Adonai for the good land He has given you.
Our sages say that your meal should be a time for strengthening family ties, for the exchange of news, views, comings and goings, and especially problems. When you hallow your family meal with the *Birkat ha-Mazon*, you are unifying your family and your table becomes the altar blessed by Adonai.

12–13. When you have eaten well and built fine houses to live in, and your herds and flocks have grown…
Moses warns the Israelites not to think that they have made it on their own. Just remember that when you succeed, it is Adonai who has given you the intelligence and the energy to get ahead.

15 He led you through the great, terrifying wilderness, overrun by snakes, vipers, and scorpions, and with no water to drink. When there was no water, it was He who brought you water from a solid rock. **16** In the wilderness He fed you manna, a food that was unknown to your ancestors. He sent you hardships to test your loyalty, so that He could later do more good things for you. **17** Later, when you are successful, take care not to say to yourself, "It was my own strength and my power that made me successful." **18** Always keep in mind that it is Adonai who gives you the ability to be successful. He does this to preserve the covenant that He made with your ancestors, just as He is keeping it today with you. **19** Here and now I warn you, do not forget Adonai and follow idols by worshipping and bowing to them, because then you will be totally destroyed. **20** If you do not obey Adonai, you will be destroyed just like the nations that Adonai is destroying right now for you.

9 Hear, O Israel, today you are about to cross the Jordan River. When you are on the other side, you will have to drive out nations greater and more powerful than you, with great cities whose walls reach to the skies. **2** You will encounter nations as tall as giants, and you have heard the expression, "Who is strong enough to stand up against a giant?" **3** Today be aware that Adonai is the One who will cross ahead of you. He is like a fierce fire, and as Adonai has promised you, He will weaken the nations before you and drive them out and destroy them.

You Made Adonai Angry   *3rd Aliyah*

4 After Adonai chases them out before you, do not say to yourselves, "It was because of my righteousness that Adonai brought me to occupy this land."
No! It was because of the wickedness of these nations that Adonai is driving them out before you.

---

15. When there was no water, it was He who brought you water from a solid rock.
On their travels through the desert the children of Israel were dependent on the limited supplies of water. Most of the water found in the ground originates as rain and is constantly being replenished. The rain water trickles through the soil and bedrock, where it moves through crevices. The downward flow is halted when the water encounters impermeable rocks. Sometimes it continues to flow under the force of gravity. In places where reservoir rock is exposed, one can find springs of fresh water trickling down a slope. In places where the solid reservoir rock is near the surface, water can be drawn by breaking or cracking the rock to release the water.   *Edward Sturm*

1. When you are on the other side, you will have to drive out nations greater and more powerful than you, with great cities whose walls reach to the skies.
The Israelites, the desert wanderers, were amazed at the size of the fortified Canaanite cities. The cities were for strategic reasons built on hills which seemed to touch the sky.

They were encircled with high earthen and stone walls, which were difficult to breach and had to be captured by strategic means.

4. After Adonai chases them out before you, do not say to yourselves, "It was because of my righteousness that Adonai brought me to occupy the land."
Before Moses leaves the scene, he delivers a wake-up call to the Israelite community in which he criticizes their reactions and attitudes.

Moses bluntly tells them that they are being given the land of Israel for two reasons:

1. The nations living there are unworthy.

2. Adonai is fulfilling His absolute promise made to the patriarchs Abraham, Isaac, and Jacob.

5 It is not because of your righteousness and goodness that you are going to occupy their land, but because of the wickedness of these nations that Adonai is driving them out before you. Adonai is also keeping the promise that He made to your ancestors, Abraham, Isaac, and Jacob.

6 I want you to know that you are a very stubborn nation, and it is not because of your righteousness that Adonai is giving you this land to occupy.

7 Remember and never forget how you angered Adonai in the wilderness. From the day you left Egypt, you have been rebelling against Adonai.

8 Even at Horeb you angered Adonai. And He was ready to destroy you.

9 At that time I climbed the mountain to get the tablets of the Ten Commandments, the covenant that Adonai had made with you. For forty days and forty nights I remained on the mountain without food or water. **10** Then Adonai gave me two stone tablets engraved with His finger. On them were written all the words that Adonai had spoken to you out of the fire, on the day of assembly at Mount Horeb.

11 At the end of the forty days and forty nights, Adonai gave me the two stone tablets of the covenant.

12 Then Adonai said to me, "Quick! Get moving and hurry down! The Israelites that you brought out of Egypt are acting wickedly. They have strayed from the commands I gave them and have made themselves an idol."

13 Then Adonai said to me, "I realize that this is a very stubborn nation. **14** Just leave Me alone, so that I can destroy them and blot out their name from under the heavens. Afterwards I will make your descendants into a nation greater and more numerous than they are."

15 So I turned around and started down the mountain. The mountain was still blazing with fire, and the two tablets of the covenant were in my hands.

16 I saw at once that you had sinned against Adonai by making a golden calf and by so quickly abandoning the path that Adonai had made for you.

17 In anger I raised the two tablets, and threw them down and shattered them right before your eyes.

18 Then I bowed down before Adonai, and once again I did not eat or drink for forty days and forty nights. I did this on account of the sin you had committed, by doing evil in the eyes of Adonai.

19 I was afraid that Adonai was angry enough to destroy you. But Adonai listened to my prayer.

---

8. Even at Horeb you angered Adonai. And He was ready to destroy you.
Horeb is thought to be synonymous with Mount Sinai. It was the place where Moses hit the rock. It is also the area where the golden calf was worshipped.

18. Then I bowed down before Adonai, and once again I did not eat or drink for forty days and forty nights.
When Moses received the first set of *luchot* (tablets), he fasted for forty days and forty nights. Now he again fasts for forty days and forty nights. However, this time Moses fasts because the Israelites had committed a major sin in praying to the golden calf.

19. But Adonai listened to my prayer.
Moses was afraid that Adonai would desert the Israelites, but the earnest prayers of Moses saved them from destruction.

20 Adonai was angry at Aaron too, and threatened to destroy him. So I also prayed for Aaron. **21** I took the golden calf that you had made, and I burned it in fire. I ground it up until it was as fine as dust, and I threw the dust into the stream flowing down from the mountain. **22** You also angered Adonai at Taberah, and at Massah, and at Kivroth-HaTaavah (Graves of Craving). **23** Then, at Kadesh Barnea, when Adonai said, "March north and occupy the land that I have given you," you again rebelled against the word of Adonai and did not believe that He would help you.

24 From the very first day that I knew you, you have been rebelling against Adonai. **25** I was so sure that Adonai would destroy you that I threw myself down before Him and lay face-down for forty days and forty nights. **26** I begged Adonai, "Adonai! Please do not destroy your nation which You liberated with miracles and brought out of Egypt with a mighty hand. **27** Think about your servants, Abraham, Isaac, and Jacob. Overlook the stubbornness and wickedness of this nation. **28** Do not let the Egyptians in the land of slavery jeer and sneer, 'Adonai brought them out just to kill them in the wilderness, because He hated them and was powerless to bring them to the land He promised them.'

29 Remember, they are still Your people and Your heritage. You brought them out with Your great power and with Your mighty arm!"

The Second Ten Commandments   *4th Aliyah*

10 At that time, Adonai said to me, "Carve out two stone tablets like the first ones, and return to Me on the mountain and make a wooden ark. **2** I will engrave the tablets with the words that were on the first tablets that you broke, and you shall place them in the ark."

3 I made an ark out of acacia wood and carved two tablets like the first. Then I climbed the mountain with the two tablets in my arms.

4 Once again Adonai engraved the tablets with the original text of the Ten Commandments that He gave you out of the fire on the mountain on the day of assembly. Adonai gave them to me. **5** So I turned and went down from the mountain. I placed the tablets that I had made in the ark, and they remained there just as Adonai had commanded.

---

20. Adonai was angry at Aaron too, and threatened to destroy him.

The position of power does not protect a person from the consequences of his actions. Powerful individuals have a greater responsibility than run-of-the-mill individuals. Aaron, the future High Priest, made a mistake in judgment and helped make the golden calf.

For his cowardice, Adonai decided to destroy Aaron and his four sons, but Moses interceded and saved their lives.

His prayer was partially effective. Aaron and his two sons Elazar and Ithamer were saved, but Nadav and Avihu died.

25. Forty days and forty nights.

Moses reviewed the two times he fasted for forty days and forty nights. The first time was before the giving of the first set (v. 9) of *luchot*; the second time was when he gave the second set of *luchot* after the people sinned with the golden calf.

1. At that time, Adonai said to me, "Carve out two stone tablets like the first ones, and return to Me on the mountain and make a wooden ark."

The first two tablets were given by Adonai (Sh-emot 20:1). The second set of tablets, because of the sin of the golden calf, did not have the same intense holiness as the first set.

6 Later, the Israelites continued their journey, from Beeroth-bene-Jaakan (Wells of Jaakan) to Moserah, where Aaron died and was buried. His son Elazar became the next High Priest.
7 From there, they proceeded to Gudgodah, and from Gudgodah to Yatvathah, an area filled with flowing brooks.
8 After I came down from the mountain, Adonai appointed the tribe of Levi to carry the ark containing the Ten Commandments and to stand before Adonai and serve Him, and to offer blessings in His name.
9 That is why the tribe of Levi was not given any inherited land among the other tribes. As Adonai promised, He is their inheritance.
10 This time I remained on the mountain for forty days and forty nights, just like the first time, and Adonai listened to me and agreed not to destroy you.
11 Then Adonai said to me, "Get up and continue the march at the head of the people. Advance and occupy the land that I swore to their ancestors I would give them."

Observe Adonai's Commandments *5th Aliyah*

12 And now, Israel, what does Adonai demand of you? Only that you revere Adonai and that you follow all His commands and love Him, and serve Adonai with all your heart and with all your soul. **13** You must, for your own good, observe Adonai's commandments and decrees that I am giving you today.
14 The heavens, the earth, and everything in it all belong to Adonai. **15** It was with your ancestors that Adonai entered into a loving relationship. He chose them and their descendants from among all the nations, and today you are still His people.
16 Now is the time to cleanse your heart and stop being so stubborn.
17 Adonai is the Supreme Being. Adonai is powerful, great, mighty, and awesome. Adonai's decisions are fair and He cannot be bribed. **18** He provides justice to orphans and widows, and takes care of foreigners, and gives them food and cloth- ing. **19** You too must show respect toward foreigners, because you were once foreigners in the land of Egypt.
20 Respect Adonai, and worship Him, cling to Him, and revere His name.

---

13. You must, for your own good, observe Adonai's commandments and decrees that I am giving you today.
Moses explained to the Israelites that for your own good you must follow the rules and commandments of the Torah. If you decide to follow a different path and worship Adonai in a different way, then you are looking for trouble. In unity Israel can achieve the highest spiritual level. Religious factions are an evil inclination and can only lead to disaster.

19. You too must show respect toward foreigners, because you were once foreigners in the land of Egypt.
This is mitzvah number 431.
   This mitzvah refers to individuals who do not understand the ideals and laws of Judaism.

It is not easy for converts to leave their family and friends and enter the Jewish faith.
   The Torah tells us that one must extend the hand of friendship to them and make them feel comfortable and welcome. Jews must remember that they were once strangers in the land of Egypt.
   Anyone who observes this mitzvah is also observing the mitzvah of "Love your neighbor" (mitzvah number 243).

20. Respect Adonai and worship him, cling to Him, and revere His name.
This is mitzvah number 432.
   It is a mitzvah to be respectful of Adonai. A person can be respectful of Adonai by praying with *kavanah* (devotion) and observing decorum in the synagogue.

21 Adonai is worthy of your praise. He is the One who performed miracles and great and awesome deeds that you saw with your very own eyes.
22 Your ancestors went down to Egypt with only seventy individuals, but now Adonai has made you as numerous as the stars in the sky.

11

You must love Adonai, and obey His decrees, laws, and commandments.
2 Remember, I am not speaking of your children, who never knew and never experienced the lessons that Adonai taught by His greatness, His mighty hand, and the strength of His outstretched arm.
3 They never saw the signs and miracles that He performed in Egypt against Pharaoh, king of Egypt, and all his land. **4** They never saw how He drowned the army of Egypt – their horses and chariots, in the waters of the Sea of Reeds. Adonai destroyed them, and to this very day they have not recovered.
5 They did not see how He took care of you in the wilderness until you came to this place.
6 They did not see what He did to Dathan and Aviram, the sons of Reuben's son Eliav, when the earth opened its mouth and swallowed them, along with their houses, their tents, and all their families. **7** But you, with your own eyes, have seen all the miracles and great deeds that Adonai has done.
8 Observe all the commandments that I am giving you today so that you will have the strength to occupy the land you are soon to conquer. **9** Then you will enjoy long life on the land that Adonai swore to your ancestors and their descendants, a land flowing with milk and honey.

The Blessings of Obedience 6th Aliyah

10 The land you are soon to possess is not like Egypt, the place you escaped from. There you could plant your seed and could easily water it by yourself, just like a vegetable garden.

---

21. He is the One who performed miracles and great and awesome deeds that you saw with your very own eyes.
With your own eyes you saw the ten plagues, the splitting of the Sea of Reeds, and the drowning of the mighty Egyptian army. You also experienced and felt the prescence of Adonai at Mount Sinai when you received the Ten Commandments.

4. Adonai destroyed them, and to this very day they have not recovered.
Forty long years have passed and the Egyptian army has still not recovered from the disaster in the Sea of Reeds.

10. The land you are soon to possess is not like Egypt, the place you escaped from.
The verse highlights the difference in geographical conditions between Egypt and Canaan. Egypt was supplied with plentiful water by the Nile River. The farmers had dug miles and miles of irrigation canals which watered the inland farms. Canaan, on the other hand, depended primarily on seasonal rains. When the rains did not appear, the drought brought famine, and those who had the means journeyed down to Egypt, which, because of the Nile, had abundant food to sell.

10. There you could plant your seed and could easily water it by yourself.
The Nile River in Egypt easily supplied as much water as the farmer needed.

The Egyptians had long water channels reaching from the river to the fields. The farmers used water wheels, which were turned by pedals to pump the water onto the vegetables and fruit.

11 But the land you are crossing to occupy is a land of mountains and valleys, watered mostly by the rain.
12 From the beginning of each year until the end of each year, it is a land constantly under Adonai's personal care.
13 If you observe My commandments, which I am giving you today, and if you love Adonai with all your heart and soul, then Adonai has promised **14** to send the fall and spring rains at the proper time so that you can harvest your grain, oil, and wine. **15** He will provide grass for your animals, and you will eat and be satisfied.
16 Take care, however, that your hearts do not turn away and worship other idols.
17 Then Adonai will be angry, and He will shut down the skies so that there will be no rain. The land will not grow crops, and you will soon disappear from the Promised Land that Adonai is giving you.
18 Keep these words of mine in your heart and in your soul.
Wind them as a reminder (*tefillin*) on your arm, and let them be a sign in the center of your forehead.
19 Teach them to your children, and speak of them when you are at home, and when you travel on the road, and when you lie down, and when you rise up.
20 Write them on parchments attached to the doorposts (*mezzuzot*) of your houses and gates.
21 If you do this, you and your children will live long on the land that Adonai swore to give to your ancestors, as long as the heavens are above the earth.

You Will Be Victorious
7th Aliyah/Maftir

22 If you carefully observe and keep all the commandments that I give you today, to love Adonai, and follow all His ways, and stay close to Him, **23** then Adonai will drive out all the nations that stand in your way.
24 You will conquer every piece of land upon which you walk. Your borders will extend from the wilderness to the mountains of Lebanon, from the Euphrates River as far as the Mediterranean Sea. **25** No power will be able to stop you. Just as He promised, Adonai will make you feared and dreaded throughout the region.

---

11. But the land you are crossing to occupy is a land of mountains and valleys, watered mostly by the rain.
Canaan is a land of hills and valleys which topographically can be divided into four sections: the coastal plain, the west hill region, the Jordan Valley, and the trans-Jordan plateau. Each of these geographical areas, with the variations of temperature, water resources, and soil, influenced the forms of settlement and history of Israel.

17. Then Adonai will be angry, and He will shut down the skies so that there will be no rain.
The Torah warns the Israelites that if they listen to Adonai's commandments, He will provide adequate rain for their crops. However, if they fail to observe His laws, there will be a drought.

20. Write them on parchments attached to the doorposts (*mezzuzot*) of your houses and gates.
A *mezzuzah* is a handwritten parchment which is affixed to the doorposts of Jewish homes. The *mezzuzah* scroll contains the two biblical passages from Devarim 6:4–9. The *mezzuzah* holder has a small opening through which is seen the Hebrew word *Shaddai*, meaning "Almighty."

The Hebrew word *mezzuzah* means "doorpost."

רְאֵה *Re'eh*

YOU HAVE A CHOICE

26 You have a choice between a blessing and a curse. **27** You will be blessed if you obey the commandments of Adonai that I am giving you today.
28 You will be cursed if you do not obey the commandments of Adonai, and stray from the path that I have marked out for you, by worshipping the idols of other nations.
29 When Adonai brings you to the land that you will soon occupy, you must pronounce these blessings on Mount Gerizim, and these curses on Mount Ebal.
30 Both mountains are across the Jordan River, on the western road on the way to Gilgal, near the oak trees of Moreh, in the territory of the Canaanites who live in the Jordan Valley.
31 You soon will cross the Jordan River and conquer the land that Adonai is giving you. When you have conquered it and settled down, **32** you must carefully observe all the commandments and laws that I am giving you today.

12 These are the commandments and laws that you must carefully observe in the land that Adonai is giving you, so that you will be able to occupy it as long as you live on earth:
2 Destroy all the places where the nations you are driving out worship their idols, whether they are on mountaintops, on the hills, or under flowering trees.
3 You must destroy their altars, flatten their sacred pillars, burn their Asherah trees, chop down the statues of their idols, and erase their names from their temples.
4 You must not worship Adonai in the same manner as they worship their idols.

---

26. Your have a choice between a blessing and a curse.
I created you with free will. You can follow the commandments and you will succeed in all your efforts. Or you can deviate and choose the path of wickedness and your life will be cursed with problems and punishments.

1. These are the commandments and laws that you must carefully observe.
In the following chapters (12–20) Moses details the laws and commandments between man and Adonai, and between man and man. The legal codes include the previous laws and customs and have now become an official part of the Mosaic covenant between Adonai and the Israelites.

The section, ends in chapter 30, where Adonai blesses the nation and promises that "good things will happen only when you obey Adonai" (30:10).

2. Destroy all the places where the nations you are driving out worship their idols.
This is mitzvah number 436.

When you conquer an area, your first duty is to destroy the idols and the places where the idols are worshipped. The idols and places of worship will lead the people to sin.

3. You must destroy their altars, flatten their sacred pillars, burn their Asherah trees, chop down the statues of their idols, and erase their names from their temples.
Adonai was aware that if the Israelites began to use their altars, they might be tempted to worship their idols. The Israelites were to start a new religious life without the distractions and temptations of the old. Idols and altars must, like cancers, be eradicated before they spread throughout the Israelite community.

5 You must worship Adonai only at a sanctuary that He will choose from among all your tribes. He will choose a sanctuary as a place to establish His name. It is there that you shall go to worship Him.
6 That will be the place to which you must bring your burnt offerings and sacrifices, your tithes, your elevated gifts, your pledges, and the first-born of your cattle and flocks. **7** It is in the sanctuary that you and your families shall eat in the presence of Adonai and rejoice after all your labors, because Adonai has blessed you.
8 You must not continue to act as you now do, whereby everyone does what is right in his own eyes. **9** You have not yet come to the Promised Land that Adonai is giving you. **10** Soon, however, you will cross the Jordan and live in the land Adonai is giving you. The moment you are safe and secure from the enemies around you, and you are living in peace,

Adonai Will Choose His Sanctuary *2nd Aliyah*

11 then you must bring all your burnt offerings, sacrifices, tithes, elevated gifts, and pledges to the sanctuary Adonai shall choose for Himself.
12 There you will celebrate before Adonai, along with your sons, your daughters, your male and female servants, and the Levites from your settlements, who have no hereditary land.
13 Beware not to offer your offerings in any other sanctuary that you may see. **14** You must bring your sacrifices only to the sanctuary that Adonai will choose in the territory of one of your tribes. Only there is it permissible to bring sacrifices, and only there may you present offerings to Me. **15** In all your settlements, whenever you wish you may slaughter cattle and eat the meat that Adonai has given as His blessing. Any Israelite, whether ritually clean or unclean, may eat the meat, just like that of the deer and the gazelle. **16** However, you must not drink the blood; you must pour it on the ground like water.

---

5. You must worship Adonai only at a sanctuary that he will choose from among all your tribes.
As the conquest of Canaan proceeded, Joshua established a sanctuary in Shiloh, where the Holy Ark and the Tabernacle were kept. It was to Shiloh that the Israelites made their pilgrimages, bringing their sacrifices and praying there together. Later, when Solomon built the Temple in Jerusalem, all the religious activities were transferred there.

The purpose of centralization was to mold the separate tribes into one nation and establish a national government.

6. That will be the place to which you must bring your burnt offerings and sacrifices, your tithes, your elevated gifts, your pledges, and the first-born of your cattle and flocks.
When the Israelites had conquered Canaan, they were commanded to establish a central sanctuary. At first King David established a central sanctuary in Shiloh. Later King Solomon built a magnificent Temple in Jerusalem. Three times each year, farmers, shepherds, and merchants joyfully brought their *bikkurim* to Jerusalem.

11. Then you must bring all your burnt offerings, sacrifices, tithes, elevated gifts, and pledges to the sanctuary Adonai shall choose for Himself.
The central sanctuary was eventually established in Jerusalem by King Solomon. The purpose of a central synagogue was to unite the Israelites socially, politically, militarily, and religiously.

Ancient Israel was divided into tribal areas. A central sanctuary would help the people unite under a single government with a common political agenda and a single military command.

Shenash

17 You must not eat the tithes of your wheat, wine, and oil, or the first-born of your cattle and flocks, or any pledges that you make, or elevated gifts in your own settlements.
18 These must be eaten only in the sanctuary that Adonai chooses.
You shall eat the tithes with your son, your daughter, your male and female servants, and the Levites who live in your settlements, and you shall thank Adonai for the blessings He has given you. **19** Make sure not to neglect the Levites when you are settled in the Promised Land.
20 When Adonai enlarges your lands, as He has promised you, and you say to yourself, "I am hungry for meat," you may eat as much meat as you desire. **21** If the sanctuary chosen by Adonai and dedicated to His name is far away, you may slaughter your animals that Adonai will have given you in the manner that I have commanded you. Then you may eat them in your settlements whenever you desire, **22** just as you do with a deer or gazelle. The ritually clean and the ritually unclean alike may eat them. **23** Be extremely careful not to drink the blood, because the blood is the life of the animal, and you must not eat anything that is filled with life. **24** You must not drink the blood; just spill it out on the ground like water. **25** You will be doing what is right in Adonai's eyes if you do not drink it. If you do this, then you and your descendants will have a good life.
26 Your sacred offerings and gifts must be brought to the sanctuary that Adonai will choose.

---

18. You shall eat the tithes with your son, your daughter…
There is no joy, no *simchah*, unless there is a sharing. The matriarch Sarah initiated the principle that *simchah* and sharing are synonymous. When she received the news of Isaac's birth she said: "Adonai has made me laugh. All who hear about it will laugh with me."

Whenever the Torah speaks of *simchah*, *it* never forgets that one has to share his blessings with somebody else.

19. Make sure not to neglect the Levites when you are settled in the Promised Land.
As long as the Levites live in the Promised Land, they are to be supported by the sacrifices and the tithes. The Levites are the spiritual links between sanctuary and the nation. You must always remember the Levites as the nation develops politically, militarlily, and financially. They are your moral compasses and they will help you adhere and follow the laws of the Torah.

21. You may slaughter your animals that Adonai will have given you in the manner that I have commanded you.
Kosher meat must be carefully supervised from the moment the animal is slaughtered to the time it reaches the table. Only a *shochet*, a learned and pious person who is thoroughly trained, is permitted to slaughter a kosher animal.

Shechitah, the act of slaughtering, is a religious rite; the rules must be observed strictly. After *shechitah*, the *shochet* carefully examines the insides of the animal to see that it has no disease or other flaw that would render it unfit to eat. The carcass is inspected by a *mashgiach*, who stamps it with an official seal. Kosher retail meat markets are supervised by a *mashgiach* too, to ensure proper handling and care.

21. You may slaughter your animals that Adonai will have given you the manner that I have commanded you.
Kosher slaughtering was orally handed down to Moses, who transmitted the procedure to the Israelites.

Maimonides comments that the natural diet of humans is a vegetarian one. Man is allowed to slaughter animals and to eat their meat, provided he does so in a compassionate manner.

27 There you shall present your burnt offerings, both the flesh and the blood, on the altar of Adonai. The blood of the sacrifices must be poured on the sides of the altar of Adonai, but the flesh may be eaten. **28** Make sure to obey the commandments that I have given you, so that you and your descendants will always have a good life, because you will be doing that which is good and right in the eyes of Adonai.

You Must Not Worship Idols
3rd Aliyah

29 Adonai will drive away the nations in the land where you will live. **30** When He has destroyed them, you must not follow their example and worship their idols.
Do not wonder about their idols and say, "How did these nations worship their idols? I think that I will worship them and try their practices." **31** You must not worship Adonai in the same way. These nations, when they worshipped, committed all sorts of evils detested by Adonai.
They even worshipped their idols by burning their sons and daughters.

13 You must carefully observe the commandments that I am giving you. Do not add rules and do not subtract rules. **2** Someday, a prophet or a dreamer may arise among you, promising to perform miracles and telling you about the future, **3** and he may say to you, "Come, let us worship the idols of other nations."
4 Do not listen to the appeals of that prophet or dreamer. Adonai is really testing you to know whether you love Him with all your heart and all your soul.

---

28. Make sure to obey the commandments that I have given you, so that you and your descendants will always have a good life, because you will be doing that which is good and right in the eyes of Adonai.
Rashi explains, "What is good" means what is good in the eyes of Adonai. "What is right" means in the eyes of the people.

1. You must carefully observe the commandments that I am giving you. Do not add rules and do not subtract rules.
This is mitzvah number 454.

The Torah in its original form has survived for 4,000 years without any additions or deletions. The Torah that was read then was exactly the same document as that the Jewish people are reading today wherever they are situated.

If liberties were taken with the text, then the Torah would continually become an object of debate and different groups would end up with their own versions of the Torah.

The cohesion of the Jewish people depends on all groups reading one Torah. One nation, one Torah.

2-4. Someday, a prophet or a dreamer may arise among you, promising to perform miracles and telling you about the future, and he may say to you, "Come, let us worship the idols of other nations." Do not listen to the appeals of that prophet or dreamer."
This is mitzvah number 456.

There have been and still are numerous groups who have tried to convert Jews into their own religion. They utilize all types of propaganda and lures to entice converts. In Jewish history, there have been several false messiahs who have caused untold damage to the Jewish people. Mohammed claimed that he was a prophet and forcefully tried to convert Jews to his new religion. In the 1648 Shabbtai Tzvee embarked on his messianic career. His claims damaged the lives of tens of thousands of believing Jews. There were many more false messiahs, and all of them duped and disrupted the lives of thousands of families.

5 Follow Adonai and respect Him, and observe His commandments; obey Him and remain faithful to Him.

6 That prophet or dreamer must be put to death because he wanted you to reject Adonai, who brought you out of Egypt and freed you from the land of slavery. He was trying to lead you from the path that Adonai commanded you to follow. You must erase such evil from your midst.

7 This is what you must do if your brother, your son, your daughter, your wife, or your friend secretly tries to tempt you and says, "Come, let us go worship a new god whom we or our ancestors have never before worshipped." **8** That person is tempting you to worship the idols of some other nation from one end of the world or another.

9 Do not be tempted by him, and do not listen to him. Do not pity him, and do not be merciful to him, and do not find excuses for him, **10** because you must be the one to put him to death. You must be the first to kill him, and then the other people must follow.

11 Stone him to death, because he tried to make you abandon Adonai, who brought you out of the slavery of Egypt.

12 When all Israel hears about it, they will be afraid, and no one else will ever again do such an evil thing among you. **13** This is what you must do when you learn that in one of your cities Adonai is giving you to live in, **14** some worthless people among you have persuaded the inhabitants to stray by saying, "Let us worship an idol and enjoy a new experience."

15 You must carefully investigate, and ask many questions, and find out the facts. If such a hateful thing has really occurred in one of your cities,

16 you must execute all the inhabitants of the city. Destroy it and everything in it, and kill all the animals. **17** Then gather all the property of the city's inhabitants in the central square, and burn the city along with all its goods, as a burnt offering to Adonai. The city must remain a ruin forever and must never be rebuilt.

18 Keep none of the property for yourself. Then Adonai will have mercy on you and no longer be angry, and He will make you successful, just as He promised your ancestors **19** if you do this and obey Adonai and observe all the commandments that I am giving you today, and do what is right in the eyes of Adonai.

---

5. Follow Adonai and respect Him, and observe His commandments; obey Him and remain faithful to Him.
The Israelites learned that religious commitment is the product of painstaking preparation of mind and heart. It took Moses forty years to make his people ready for responsibility which freedom and opportunity demand. 1

5. You must carefully investigate, and ask many questions, and find out the facts.
Before accusing anyone of proselytizing or being a false prophet, you must be absolutely sure of your accusation. Before taking action, you must follow three rules:

1. Investigate.
2. Ask questions.
3. Assemble the facts.

If all three steps are positive, then you can take action to remove the false prophet.

18. Keep none of the property for yourself. Then Adonai will have mercy on you and no longer be angry, and He will make you successful, just as He promised your ancestors.
The purpose of not taking any of the property was to prevent crediting any success to the gold, silver, and idols in the city.

Adonai will make you successful without any of the tainted property.

You Are Children of Adonai

4th Aliyah

14 You are children of Adonai. Do not cut yourselves as a sign of mourning, and do not shave the hair in the middle of your head. **2** You are a nation dedicated to Adonai. He has set you apart from every other nation on the face of the earth to be His own special treasure.

3 You must not eat any forbidden foods. **4** These are the animals that you may eat: the ox, the sheep, the goat, **5** the gazelle, the deer, the antelope, the chamois, the wild goat, and the wild sheep.

6 You may eat every animal that has a true hoof cloven in two parts and brings up its cud.

7 However, among the animals that bring up their cud or have a true cloven hoof, there are some that you may not eat.

These include the camel, the hare, and the rabbit, which bring up their cud but do not have true hooves and are therefore unclean to eat.

8 Also included is the pig, which has a true hoof but does not bring up its cud and is therefore forbidden to eat.

You must not eat the flesh of these animals, and you must not touch their carcasses.

9 This is what you may eat among the fish in the water. You may eat anything that has fins and scales.

10 But you may not eat any fish that has no fins and scales, because it is forbidden to you.

11 You may eat every ritually clean bird.

12 You must not eat the following birds: the eagle, the vulture, the osprey, **13** the white vulture, the falcon, the buzzard,

---

1. You are children of Adonai. Do not cut yourselves as a sign of mourning, and do not shave the hair in the middle of your head.
This is mitzvah number 468.

From this passage the Rabbis derived the mitzvah that a person should not mourn in an extreme manner.

Judaism has set up specific periods for mourners to express their grief: seven days for *shivah*; thirty days, called *shloshim*, for regular mourning; and eleven months for the recitation of *Kaddish*.

2. He has set you apart from every other nation on the face of the earth to be His own special treasure.
Rabbi Samson Raphael Hirsch states that the term "his own special people" means that Adonai has exclusive claim to Israel's service to spread the light of truth, equality, and justice.

3. You must not eat forbidden foods.
After the flood, Noah and his descendants were permitted to eat kosher and non-kosher food.

When Adonai presented the Torah to Israel they were then only allowed to eat the creatures enumerated in verses 14:3-21.

The Torah says that these special restrictions were placed on Israel because (V.26) "They are holy people" and conformed to Adonai's will.

4. These are the animals that you may eat.
The flesh of only those animals that have a completely split hoof and that also chew their cud are permitted. That is, their digestive systems are such that the foliage they eat is stored in the stomach and is rechewed later on when the animal is resting. Animals with both of these characteristics are called *kosher*, clean or permitted animals. Generally these are the domesticated animals, such as the cow, sheep, and goat.

Fowl too have clean and unclean categories. Generally speaking, Jews may eat only the common domestic birds such as chicken, goose, squab, duck, and turkey.

14 the entire raven family, **15** the ostrich, the gull and the hawk, **16** the owl, the white and the great owls, the swan, **17** the pelican, the magpie, the cormorant, **18** the stork, the heron family, the hoopoe, and the bat.

19 You must not eat any unclean flying insect.

20 However, you may eat every kind of ritually clean insect.

21 Because you are a holy nation to Adonai, you must not eat any animal or bird that has not been ritually slaughtered. You may give it to the foreigners who live in your settlements, or you may sell it to a foreigner.

You must not boil a lamb in the milk of its mother.

The Second Tithe
5th Aliyah

22 Each year you must set aside some of the crops that grow in your fields.

23 You may eat this second tithe of Adonai in the place that He will choose as His sanctuary. There you shall eat the second tithe of your grain, wine, and olive oil, as well as the first-born of your cattle and flocks. In this way you will forever learn to respect Adonai.

24 But if the sanctuary that Adonai has chosen is too far away for you to transport the produce you have set aside, then you may sell the second-tithe part of your harvest and bring the money to the sanctuary that Adonai has chosen.

---

19. You must not eat any unclean flying insect.
This includes tiny insects such as flies, hornets, bees, moths, and butterflies.

21. You must not boil a lamb in the milk of its mother.
This is mitzvah number 476.

Mixing meat and dairy foods is strictly forbidden by Jewish religious law. This regulation was applied to all manner of meat and dairy products and was extended to utensils. Every kosher home has two sets of dishes, pots, and other food utensils. In order to make the distinction between meat and dairy clear, observant Jews wait six hours after eating meat before eating dairy food.

21. Because you are a holy nation to Adonai, you must not eat any animal or bird that has not been ritually slaughtered.
Judaism has often been described as a way of life. This means that it embraces all aspects of life. One important area of our religion is that of the dietary laws. The Torah contains the basis of our regulations about food. The laws in the Bible were discussed, explained, and expanded by the sages of the Talmud, by philosophers such as Maimonides, in codes of Jewish law such as the *Shulchan Aruch*, and in other works. Some Jews today argue that dietary laws for the modern world should prohibit meat, or at least meat of animals raised under inhumane conditions, and thus should emphasize vegetarianism.

23. You may eat this second tithe of Adonai in the place that He will choose as His sanctuary.
The purpose of instructing the Israelites to eat this tithe in a holy place set aside by Adonai was to remind them that the produce was the gift of Adonai.

24. But if the sanctuary that Adonai has chosen is too far away for you to transport the produce you have set aside, then you may sell the second-tithe part of your harvest and bring the money to the sanctuary that Adonai has chosen.
Israelites who lived too far from the sanctuary could exchange their tithe of produce for money, purchase the food and drink they choose, and have a feast before Adonai with their families and the Levites.

25 You may convert the tithe into silver money, which you can bring to the place that Adonai has chosen.

26 There you may spend the money on anything you desire, whether it be for cattle, small animals, wine, brandy, or anything else for which you have an urge or need. Eat it there before Adonai, so that you and your family will be able to rejoice. **27** This does not mean, though, that you can forget the Levites in your settlements. Every third year you must give them your first tithe, since they have no hereditary land among you.

28 At the end of each three-year period, you must bring out all the tithes of that year's crop and store them in your settlements. **29** In this way the Levites, who do not have a land share of their own, and the foreigners, orphans, and widows who live in your communities, will have enough food to eat and be satisfied. If you do this, Adonai will bless you in all your undertakings.

The Year of Shmittah
6th Aliyah

15 Every seven years, you shall practice the forgiveness of debts (*shmittah*). **2** During the *shmittah* year, every creditor shall cancel any debt owed to him by his fellow Israelites.

3 You may demand payment from the alien, but you must cancel all monetary claims against your brethren.

4 If you do this, there will no longer be any poor among you, because Adonai will make you prosper in the land that you will soon occupy.

5 However, you will be successful only if you obey Adonai and carefully observe all the commandments that I am giving you today. **6** Then Adonai will bless you, as He has promised. You will extend loans to many nations, but you will not need to borrow. Thus you will rule many nations, but none will rule over you.

7 When you settle the land that Adonai is giving you, you must not harden your heart against the needy.

---

3. You may demand payment from the alien, but you must cancel all monetary claims against your brethren.
The aliens were called *gerim*. From the social point of view, these aliens were free men but did not possess full civil rights as Israelite citizens. In Canaan all lands were in the hands of the Israelites and the aliens were reduced to hiring out their services. They were poor and, like the widows and orphans, depended upon Israelite charity. The fallen fruits, the gleaning after the harvest, were left for them. They were entitled to justice just like the Israelites and were liable to the same penalties. Many of the *gerim* shows to become Israelites.

4. If you do this, there will no longer be any poor among you, because Adonai will make you prosper in the land that you will soon occupy.
Hebrew law sets out standards of justice, fairness, humanness, and honesty because these are Adonai's traits. Adonai wants the Israelites to be like Him, in refusing bribes, practicing justice, caring for orphans and widows, and supporting the poor and downtrodden.

7–8. You must not harden your heart against the needy. Be generous, open your hands, and extend him any credit he needs to take care of his wants.
Maimonides states that *tzedakah* is not something to give out of the goodness of your heart. It is a debt you owe. *Tzedakah* is not a free choice but rather an absolute obligation. It must be given with gladness, compassion, dignity, and respect for the recipient, and you must not complain about giving.

8 Be generous, open your hands, and extend him any credit he needs to take care of his wants. **9** Be very careful not to act selfishly and say to yourself, "Soon the seventh year is coming, and it will be the year of debt forgiveness." Because then you will look unkindly at your needy brother and refuse to lend him any money. If he complains about you to Adonai, you will have committed a sin.

10 You must make every effort to freely give him what he needs and you must not complain about giving; then Adonai will bless you in everything you do.

11 Unfortunately, there will always be poor people in the land. That is why this commandment insists that you behave generously to your poor and to the unfortunate Israelites in your land.

12 If you purchase an Israelite man or woman, he or she may serve for six years, but you must free them in the seventh year. **13** When you free them, you must not send them away empty-handed. **14** You must give them generous gifts from your flocks, from your granary, and from your winepress, so that they will also have a share of all the good things with which Adonai has blessed you. **15** This is how you will remember that you were a slave in Egypt until Adonai freed you. That is why I am giving you this commandment. **16** But suppose the slave is happy to serve you and your family and is pleased with you, and he says, "I do not want to leave you." **17** Then you must take an awl and push it through his earlobe and into the door.

Then he will become your slave forever. Do the same with your female slaves.

18 Of course you may be reluctant to free your slave, because for six years he has done double the work of a hired worker. But if you free him, Adonai will bless you in all your undertakings.

---

8. Be generous, open your hands, and extend him any credit he needs to take care of his wants.
The Hebrew word for charity, *tzedakah*, is derived from the root word *tzedek*, meaning righteousness. Judaism provides numerous opportunities for doing *tzedakah*.

All synagogues have a *tzedakah* box in which worshippers can deposit a contribution. This is not an official way of raising funds, but an opportunity for us to show concern for a fellow human before we offer prayers for ourselves.

8. Be generous, open your hands, and extend him any credit he needs.
Our sages said that the proper way to fulfill the mitzvah of *tzedakah* is to give one-tenth of one's earnings or profits. The Torah refers to the ten percent as *ma'aser*, which comes from the Hebrew word *eser*, meaning "ten." In biblical times, the farmer would bring one-tenth of his produce to the Temple in Jerusalem to be divided among the *Kohanim* (priests), the Levites, and the poor.

Today we give *ma'aser* in the form of money. Our sages say that *tzedakah* should always be given in a friendly manner. The most worthy way to give charity is to give it anonymously so that both the donor and the recipient are unaware of each other.

Even better than giving charity is helping an individual become self-supporting. Some communities have Hebrew Free Loan Societies which help needy people. Some synagogues have groups of people who will help businesspeople with free loans and technical assistance.

18. Of course you may be reluctant to free your slave, because for six years he has done double the work of a hired worker.
But if you free him, Adonai will bless you in all your undertakings. Your slave has faithfully worked for six years. Now you must release him and compensate him for his service. If you treat your slave fairly, Adonai will assuredly treat you fairly.

Dedicate the First-born Animals
7th Aliyah

19 You must dedicate to Adonai every male first-born among your cattle and flocks. You must not work your fields with a first-born ox, and you must not shear your first-born sheep. **20** Every year you and your family must eat in the presence of Adonai in the sanctuary that Adonai will choose. **21** If the animal has a defect or is crippled or blind or has another type of blemish, you may not sacrifice it to Adonai. **22** Both the ritually clean and the ritually unclean may eat such animals in their homes, as you would eat the deer and the gazelle. **23** You must not drink the blood; just spill it on the ground like water.

16 Observe the month of Aviv [Nisan] and present a Passover sacrifice to Adonai, because it was during the month of standing grain that Adonai brought you out of Egypt at night. **2** You shall sacrifice the Passover offering with sheep and cattle in the sanctuary that Adonai will choose. **3** You must not eat any leaven with the sacrifice during the Passover holiday. During the Passover holiday you shall eat matzah for seven days. This is the bread of affliction, symbolizing how you left Egypt in a great hurry, and it will enable you to remember your escape from Egypt all the days of your life. **4** For seven days no leavening shall be found in all your territory. You must not eat the flesh that you sacrificed in the evening of the first day of Passover.

---

20. Every year you and your family must eat in the presence of Adonai in the sanctuary that Adonai will choose.
You and your family means the family of the Kohen.
Rashi

1. Observe the month of Aviv (Nisan).
In biblical times the month of Nisan was called Aviv. However, during the Babylonian exile the Israelites adopted the Babylonian names for the months. Now all the months are called by their Babylonian names. Today the month of Aviv is called Nisan. The month of Nisan contains five religious celebrations.
1. Rosh Chodesh
15. First day of Passover
16. Second day of Passover. First day of the fifty-day counting of the omer
21. Seventh day of Passover
22. Eighth and last day of Passover

3. This is the bread of afliction, symbolizing how you left Egypt in a great hurry.
In the Torah, Egypt is called *Mitzrayim*. This name contains the two-letter Hebrew word *tzar*, meaning both narrow and enemy. Geographically, Egypt is a long, narrow (*tzar*) country concentrated along the banks of the Nile River. Politically, *Mitzrayim* was the *tzar* (enemy) of the Israelites. The plural of *tzar* is *tzarot*, meaning troubles.

3. This is the bread of affliction, symbolizing how you left Egypt in a great hurry.
There is a basic difference between bread and matzah. Bread requires much baking time, while matzah is baked quickly. The symbolism of the time to bake matzah indicates the speed with which the Israelites left Egypt.

6. The only place where you may sacrifice the Passover offering is in the sanctuary that Adonai will choose.
Passover is many things. It is a festival of freedom, when we recall how the Almighty released our ancestors from slavery in Egypt and helped a free people come into existence. Passover is an agricultural festival, reminding us of the Land of Israel in ancient times. Our ancestors were farmers, and Passover marked the beginning of the grain harvest.
Passover is also a pilgrimage festival. Three times a year the Israelites marched in joyous processions to Jerusalem, there to celebrate the festivals of Passover, Shavuot, and Sukkot.

5 It is forbidden to slaughter the Passover offering in any of your settlements that Adonai is giving you. **6** The only place where you may sacrifice the Passover offering is in the sanctuary that Adonai will choose.

There, in the evening, you shall sacrifice the Passover offering just as the sun is going down, the same time of day that you left Egypt. **7** You shall roast it and eat it in the sanctuary chosen by Adonai, and then in the morning you may return to your homes. **8** For six days you shall eat matzah. On the seventh day you shall hold an assembly to Adonai, and you must not do any work. **9** Then count seven weeks from the time you first begin to harvest the standing grain. **10** Then you shall celebrate the Festival of Shavuot to Adonai by presenting an offering in proportion to the blessings Adonai has given you. **11** You shall celebrate in the sanctuary that Adonai has chosen. You shall celebrate together with your sons, your daughters, your male and female servants, the Levites in your cities, and the strangers, the orphans, and the widows living among you.

---

6. There, in the evening, you shall sacrifice the Passover offering just as the sun is going down, the same time of day that you left Egypt.
This sentence provided three separate steps in performing the Passover sacrifice. Toward evening sacrifice, the lamb, eat the sacrifice at sunset, and burn whatever is left at the time you left Egypt.

Symbolically burning the remainder of the sacrifice means that you have burnt and removed the vestiges of slavery and you are now free.

9. Then count seven weeks from the time you first begin to harvest the standing grain.
The grain that was cut on the second day of Passover was to be used for the omer offering. In ancient days the omer offering consisted of an omer of the first barley harvest to the Temple as a thank you offering to Adonai for His goodness. Only after bringing the omer to the Temple in Jerusalem was an individual allowed to enjoy eating of the new harvest.

10. Then you shall celebrate the Festival of Shavuot to Adonai by presenting an offering.
Besides being a Torah festival, Shavuot is a harvest holiday. In ancient times, the grain harvest was begun on the second day of Passover with the ripening of barley. On this day, an omer of grain was brought to the Temple as thanksgiving to Adonai.

The forty-nine days from Passover to Shavuot were counted publicly, and this period is called *Sefirat ha-Omer* (counting the omer).

A special prayer is recited each day at the end of the evening service. This prayer counts the days in a distinctive way, referring to them as the first day of the omer, the second day of the omer, and so on, so that an accurate count of the days elapsed can be kept.

After seven weeks of counting came the harvesting of wheat the last cereal grain to ripen.

Thus Shavuot is also known as *Chag ha-Katzir*, the Festival of the Harvest. A successful harvest meant prosperity for the coming year–one more reason why Shavuot was a happy festival in ancient Palestine. Today we continue to count the omer and translate this ritual into a means of strengthening our resolve to reclaim the soil of the Holy Land and to work for the rebuilding of Zion as a homeland for the exiled and as a center of spiritual life for the Jewish people.

In the synagogues, in addition to the regular holiday service, the Book of Ruth is read on Shavuot. The reason is that this beautiful story of faith and devotion took place during the harvest season. Moreover, King David was descended from Ruth, and it is believed that he was born and that he died on Shavuot.

The Book of Ruth is one of the *Five Megillot*. It is recited in the synagogue on Shavuot because its story is set in the harvest field and its leading character embraces Judaism.

12 You must remember that you were a slave in Egypt, and carefully observe all these rules.

The Festival of Sukkot
Maftir

13 You shall celebrate the Festival of Sukkot for seven days after you bring in the grain from your threshing floor and the wine from your winepress.

14 During the Festival of Sukkot you shall rejoice with your son and daughter, your male and female servants, and the Levite, strangers, orphans, and widows in your cities.

15 You shall celebrate the Festival of Sukkot for seven days in the sanctuary that Adonai will choose. Then Adonai will bless all your harvests and all the work of your hands, and you will be happy.

16 Three times each year, all your males must appear before Adonai in the sanctuary that He will choose: on the Festival of Matzot, on the Festival of Shavuot, and on the Festival of Sukkot. During these three festivals you must not appear before Adonai with empty hands.

17 Everyone shall bring an offering in proportion to the blessings that Adonai has given him.

---

14. During the Festival of Sukkot you shall rejoice.
Judaism teaches us that life is to be taken seriously, but at the same time our ancient faith also teaches that we must rejoice in life. The mitzvah (number 488) of joy is particularly emphasized by the Torah concerning the celebration of Sukkot (Devarim 16:13–16).

It was on the Sukkot Festival that our farm ancestors would take a vacation from their work and each would make his way happily up to Jerusalem and there, with thousands of his fellow Israelites, express gratitude to Adonai in the Temple.

16. Three times each year, all your males must appear before Adonai in the sanctuary that He will choose.
The laws concerning the three Pilgrimage Festivals to the Jerusalem Temple are repeated in the Torah five times: twice in Shemot (23:14–19 and 34:18–26), once in Vayikra, (23:4–43), once in Bamidbar (28:16–38), and once in Devarim (16:1–15).

The repetition of these laws by Moses to Israel was intended to prepare the people for a central sanctuary once they entered the Promised Land, because there was the danger that they might establish shrines and altars all over the land, as the Canaanites did. Since these were centers of idol worship. Israel had to remove themselves from this pagan worship, of various deities in different places. Their faith was in Adonai, and sacrifices were to be brought to the one Temple in Jerusalem. That central sanctuary would help to unite the twelve tribes into one people serving Adonai.

17. Everyone shall bring an offering in proportion to the blessings that Adonai has given him.
This was the honor system.

The offerings shall depend on the success of the harvest. Those who had successful harvests are obligated to bring more, and those with a poor harvest can bring less.

17. Everyone shall bring an offering in proportion to the blessing that Adonai has given him.
A charitable individual should not deprive him or herself by giving too much to charity. The Talmud suggests that charity begins at home and one should not give more than 20 percent of his salary; 10 percent is the right amount of charity.

שׁוֹפְטִים *Shoftim*

JUDGES AND JUSTICE

18 Appoint judges and officials for your tribes in the towns that Adonai has given you, and make sure that they judge the people fairly.
19 Do not distort justice and do not give special consideration to anyone. You must not take bribes, because bribery blinds the wise and ruins the words of the righteous. **20** Only pursue justice and honesty, so that you may live and occupy the land that Adonai is giving you.
21 Do not plant an Asherah tree or plant any other tree near the altar that you make for Adonai. **22** Do not build a sacred stone pillar, because this is something that Adonai detests.

17 You must not sacrifice to Adonai any ox, sheep, or goat that has a serious defect, because Adonai considers this an insult.
2 If you discover a man or a woman in one of your communities doing evil, dishonoring Adonai's covenant **3** by bowing down to the sun, the moon, or other heavenly bodies whose worship I have strictly prohibited, **4** when you learn about it, you must listen and carefully question the witnesses.
If the accusation is true, and this revolting practice has taken place in Israel, **5** then you must take the man or the woman who did the wicked act out to the gates of the town, and you shall stone the man or the woman to death.
6 The accused must be put to death only by the testimony of two or three witnesses.

---

18. Appoint judges and officials for your tribes in the towns that Adonai has given you.
This is mitzvah number 491.

Every Jewish community should have judges to serve the people and settle disputes in accordance with Jewish law (*halachah*). In Temple days there were three types of courts.
1. Sanhedrin, the Supreme Court.
2. Small Sanhedrin, a lower major court.
3. Regular court, called a *bet din*.

19. Do not distort justice and do not give special consideration to anyone.
It is important for a judge to be impartial in judging a case. Even when both parties are first submitting their cases, the judge may not be lenient with one and strict with the other.

He should not ask one to stand and the other to be seated, because the one who sees the judge show honor to the other will be so upset that he will not be able to state his case clearly.

21. Do not plant an Asherah tree or plant any other tree near the altar that you make for Adonai.
The Canaanite neighbors had a great influence on the religious life, beliefs, and worship rites of the Israelites. The local inhabitants worshipped wood, stone, and metal images. Their idols were called *ba'alim*, *elilim*, and *asherahs*.

In the Torah, *asherah* had two meanings: a sacred tree or the goddess Asherah. It was a Canaanite custom to plant sacred trees beside places of worship.

The prohibition against trees was even extended to include the planting of trees on the Temple court.

6. The accused must be put to death only by the testimony of two or three witnesses.
The testimony of the witnesses must be positive and agree with each other. The accused must in no way be pressured or tortured to confess.

7 The witnesses shall be the ones to throw the first stones, and only then shall the other people continue the stoning. In this way you will eliminate evil from your midst.

8 If it is difficult to reach a decision in your tribal courts in a case involving capital punishment, legal disputes, or assaults, then you must send the case to the sanctuary that Adonai has chosen.

9 The Levitical priests and judges who are on duty will render a legal decision.

10 You must accept their judgment, because this decision comes from the place that Adonai has chosen.

11 You must follow the laws as they interpret them; you must not wander to the right or the left from the verdict they declare.

12 If anyone disobeys and refuses to accept the decision of the priest or the judge who represents Adonai as the head of the court, then that person must be put to death. In so doing you will rid Israel of an evil influence.

13 When the Israelites hear about it, they will be afraid to challenge the decisions of the court.

If You Appoint a King
2nd Aliyah

14 When you have conquered the land that Adonai is giving you, and you have occupied it and settled down, you will start to think, "We must appoint a king, just like the other nations around us." **15** Then you must appoint the king whom Adonai will choose. You must appoint an Israelite as your king. Do not appoint a foreigner who is not one of your brethren.

16 The king must not build up great herds of horses for himself and send buyers to Egypt to purchase more horses. Adonai has warned you that you must never again return to Egypt.

17 The king must not marry many wives, for they will divert his attention from his governmental duties. The king must not spend his time accumulating silver and gold.

---

8. If it is difficult to reach a decision…
The text *Sefer Ha-Chinuch* states that rabbis are fallible, but the ability to make a decision must rest with an informed authority or a tribunal. Without a central authority, everyone would claim to be right.

The United States has a series of lower courts, and the final authority is the Supreme Court. Israel also has a Supreme Court which exercises authority. Religious denominations also have law committees which set religious standards.

11. You must follow the laws as they interpret them; you must not wander to the right or the left from the verdict they declare.
When an individual is involved in a lawsuit, a judge hands down a judgment based on the laws of the times.

Justice requires that a judge on a panel of judges form his own opinion independently and not just go along with the view of his colleagues. This was especially crucial in criminal cases.

14. We must appoint a king just like the other nations around us.
When the Israelites first entered the land of Canaan, they were led by leaders called *shoftim*, "judges." Both men and women served as judges, and among them were warriors, priests, and seers. After about two hundred years of ceaseless warfare, the elders felt the need for a strong, unified authority. Under Adonai's guidance, the prophet Samuel in 1020 B.C.E. selected Saul as the first king of Israel.

18 When the king is chosen for the royal throne, he must have a copy of the Torah scroll written for him by the Levitical priests.

19 This scroll must always be in his possession, and he must read from it every day of his life. By doing so he will learn to respect Adonai and faithfully observe every commandment in the Torah.

20 He will not feel that he is better than everyone else, and it will prevent him from turning away to the right or to the left. In this way he and his descendants will have a long and successful reign on the throne.

The Levitical Priests
3rd Aliyah

18 **1** The Levitical priests and the entire tribe of Levi will not own any property in the land of Israel. Therefore they shall live only from Adonai's offerings and gifts.

2 Adonai promised them that He will be their heritage among the tribes, and therefore they will not own any land in Israel.

3 The Israelites must give the priests the foreleg, the jaw, and the cheeks when any ox, sheep, or goat is slaughtered as food.

4 You must also give the priests the first fruits of your grain, wine, and oil and the first wool from the shearing of your sheep.

5 This is to be done because Adonai has chosen Levi and his descendants from all your tribes to stand and serve in the name of Adonai for all time.

You Must Remain Faithful
4th Aliyah

6 The Levitical priests, no matter where they live, can move to any town they choose and go to the sanctuary that Adonai has chosen.

7 There he can officiate before Adonai just the same as any of his fellow Levitical priests who regularly officiate there.

8 During the festivals, he shall receive an equal share of the food and gifts from sacrifices, even though he may have an income from an inheritance.

9 When you settle in the Promised Land that Adonai is giving you, you must not imitate the revolting practices of its present inhabitants.

---

18. When the king is chosen for the royal throne, he must have a copy of the Torah scroll written for him by the Levitical priests.
A leader in Israel was a shaper of judicial, moral, religious, and political policy. He must always be aware of his unique responsibilities and shape his decisions with the knowledge gained from the precepts of the Torah.

The Talmud says that the king had to possess two Torahs. One was to be kept in the king's judgement room where he settled judicial and moral problems. The second Torah would travel with the king.

6. The Levitical priests, no matter where they live, can move to any town they choose and go to the sanctuary that Adonai has chosen.
Most of the Levites were scattered among the tribes throughout the kingdom of Israel. When the Levites come to a central tabernacle, they must be allowed to participate in the ceremonies and share in the priestly dispensations.

4. The first wool from the shearing of your sheep.
Each year when they sheared their sheep, a portion of the wool had to be given to the Kohanim. Since no specific amount was indicated, the Rabbis established a set amount of one-sixtieth.

10 No Israelite shall sacrifice his son or his daughter by fire, or practice magic, or try to communicate with evil spirits, or tell fortunes or practice witchcraft,
11 or use mumbo-jumbo incantations, or consult wizards or hold séances or try to talk to the dead. **12** Anyone who does these things is detested by Adonai. It is because of these repugnant practices that Adonai is driving out these nations before you. **13** You must remain totally faithful to Adonai.

Beware of False Prophets   *5th Aliyah*

14 The nations that you are driving out believe in astrology and practice magic. Adonai forbids you to do such things and insists that you are to be different.
15 Instead Adonai will choose one of you from among your brethren to be a prophet like me, and you must listen to him.
16 This is what you asked from Adonai at Horeb on the day of assembly, when you said, "If we hear the voice of Adonai any longer, if we look at this great fire any longer, we will die!"
17 Then Adonai said to me, "The people are right.
18 I will choose a prophet from among them, just like you. I will teach him what to say, and he will speak in My name whatever I tell him.
19 I will punish anyone who does not listen to what he says.
20 Any prophet who speaks in My name when I have not told him to do so, or who speaks in the name of idols, shall die."
21 You have a right to ask, "How can we tell that a prophecy does not come from Adonai?"
22 When a prophet speaks in Adonai's name, and what he says does not happen or come true, then the message was not spoken by Adonai. The prophet was a fake; do not believe his phony prophecies. You must not allow yourself to be impressed by a false prophet.

19 When Adonai removes the nations from the land that He is giving you, and you occupy it and live in their cities and houses,

---

10. No Israelite shall sacrifice his son or his daughter by fire, or practice magic, or try to communicate with evil spirits, or tell fortunes or practice witchcraft.
The residents in the ancient East believed in and practiced all kinds of sorcery and magic. The Egyptians worshipped the sun, the Babylonians worshipped the moon, and the Canaanites worshipped the Asherah, the sacred tree. Some cults had seers who could predict the future and witches who could communicate with the dead.

There were also religions that practiced human sacrifice. Unfortunately, there were periods when the Israelites in Canaan copied these forbidden religious rites and engaged in the idolatrous practices of their neighbors.

18. I will choose a prophet from among them, just like you. I will teach him what to say, and he will speak in My name whatever I tell him.
Adonai promises to send prophets who will tell Israel what to do and how He wants them to act. The prophet will be Adonai's spokesman.

1. When Adonai removes the nations from the land that He is giving you, and you occupy it and live in their cities and houses.
Rabbi Hirsch explains this statement. He says what is important is not what happens in the country or in the cities, but what happens in the homes. It is the morality in the individual homes that determines the spiritual and political well-being of the country. The future of Israel lies in what is thought and transpires in the "houses."

Rabbi Samson Raphael Hirsch

2 then you must set aside three cities in the land that Adonai is giving you.

3 Build roads, and divide the land that Adonai is giving you into three districts. One city in each of these districts shall be a place where a murderer can find safe refuge.

4 The safe cities shall be places where a murderer who has accidentally killed someone can live.

5 Here is an example of why the safe cities are needed. A man and his neighbor are in a forest chopping wood, and the ax head slips off the handle and kills his friend. If an accident of this kind occurs, the man can escape to a safe refuge city and live.

6 If the safe refuge city is too far, the angry blood avenger would be able to catch the killer and kill him, but the slayer had no intent to harm his victim, and therefore cannot legally be put to death.

7 That is why I am commanding you to build three separate safe cities.

8 Adonai will enlarge your borders, as He promised your ancestors, and He will give you all the territory that He promised them.

9 He will do this if you carefully observe all the commandments that I have given you today, loving Adonai, and always walking in His path. When your borders are enlarged, then you will have to add three extra safe refuge cities.

10 This will ensure that innocent blood is not spilled in the land that Adonai is giving you as your heritage.

If you do not do this, then you yourselves will be guilty of murder.

11 But if a person hates his neighbor, and ambushes him and deliberately attacks him, and the victim dies, and the killer finds refuge in one of the safe cities,

12 then the leaders of the killer's city must bring him back from the safe refuge city and hand him over to the blood avenger to be killed. **13** You must not have pity on the murderer. Your life will be safer if you rid Israel of those who have murdered innocent people.

---

2. You must set aside three cities in the land that Adonai is giving you.

Mitzvah number 520 deals with cities of refuge. An accidental slayer must suffer the punishment of exile in one of the cities of refuge. The exile is the slayer's punishment.

The roads to the cities of exile must be clearly marked so the fugitive can safely find his way there.

As long as the slayer remains within the city of refuge, he is protected from revenge by the relatives of the deceased.

There were six such cities, three on the eastern side of the Jordan and three in Canaan proper.

12. Then the leaders of the killer's city must bring him back from the safe refuge city and hand him over to the blood avenger to be killed.

The Torah opposes private revenge and emphasizes that the execution of justice is reserved for the judges. Why does the Torah command the judges to deliver the murderer into the hands of the blood avenger? The sage Luzzato says that it is impossible to change a person's upbringing and attitude from one extreme to another.

Justice is administered by the court, but the execution is transferred to the blood avenger.

In this way the blood avenger becomes the executioner for the community.

Safety in the city of refuge is only for the accidental murderer.

False Witnesses

6th Aliyah

14 You must not move your neighbor's boundary marker, which was set in place by your ancestors to mark their property.

15 One witness is not enough to convict a person for a crime that he may have committed. Guilt must be established by the testimony of at least two or three witnesses. **16** If a false witness testifies against someone, **17** both the accused and the accuser must appear before the priests and judges who are involved in the case.

18 The judges shall carefully question both of them, and if the accuser is found to have lied, **19** he must receive the same punishment as was intended for the accused. This is how you must remove such evil from your midst.

20 In this way other people will learn and will be afraid and will never again commit such a crime.

21 You must have no pity for crimes of this kind. You must take a life for a life, a tooth for a tooth, a hand for a hand, and a foot for a foot.

20

Do not be afraid when you go to war against your enemies and you see horses, armored chariots, and an army larger than yours, because Adonai, who brought you safely out of Egypt, is on your side.

2 Before you approach the battlefield, the priest will speak to the soldiers.

3 He will say, "Soldiers of Israel, today you are about to do battle against your enemies. Do not be fearful, do not be afraid, do not panic, and do not run away from the enemy.

---

14. You must not remove your neighbor's boundary marker, which was set in place by your ancestors to mark their property.
This is mitzvah number 522, prohibiting removal of landmarks consisting of heaps of stones which defined a person's property. Their removal for purposes of enlarging one's own property was equal to theft. Moving of landmarks was an ancient crime which was extremely difficult to stop. Today real estate ownership is determined by official registration and land measurements.

Any unfair and illegal method used to deny another person's legal ownership is strictly forbidden as *hasagat gevul*, the removal of landmarks.

16–19. If a false witness testifies against someone, both the accused and the accuser must appear before the priests and judges who are involved in the case. The judges shall carefully question both of them, and if the accuser is found to have lied, he must receive the same punishment as was intended for the accused. This is how you must remove such evil from your midst.

This is mitzvah number 524.

In this case the law makes the punishment fit the crime. The verdict intended for the accused is imposed on the false witness. Corrupt witnesses must be punished.

21. You must have no pity for crimes of this kind. You must take a life for a life, a tooth for a tooth, a hand for a hand, and a foot for a foot.
Rashi says that the oral tradition interprets this commandment to mean that the victim is entitled to monetary compensation for his injury, which includes medical expenses and loss of earning power.

2. Before you approach the battlefield, the priest will speak to the soldiers.
Modern armies have chaplains attached to their armed forces. The American army has chaplains from a variety of religions. The Jewish chaplains (rabbis) can be identified by the Ten Commandments on the lapels of their uniforms.

4 Adonai is the One who is going into battle with you. He will fight with you against your enemies, and He will make you victorious."

5 Then the tribal leaders shall speak to the troops and say, "Has any man among you just built a new house and not yet moved into it? You can return home, because you may die in battle and then another man will live in it.

6 Are there any soldiers among you who have just planted a vineyard and have not tasted the first grapes? You can go home, because you may die in battle and someone else will enjoy your grapes.

7 Is there any soldier among you who is engaged to be married? You may go home and get married, because it is not right for you to die in battle and for someone else to marry her."

8 The leaders shall then continue speaking to the soldiers and say, "Is there any man among you who is fearful and afraid? You must go home, because your cowardice will demoralize the other troops." **9** When the leaders have finished speaking to the soldiers, they will appoint experienced battle commanders to lead the troops.

War Regulations *7th Aliyah*

10 When you attack a city, you must first propose a peaceful settlement. **11** If the city surrenders peacefully and opens its gates to you, then all the people inside shall become your subjects and serve you as laborers.

12 However, if they refuse your peace offer and decide to resist, you shall besiege the city. **13** When Adonai hands it over to you, kill all the males. **14** However, you may keep the women, children, animals, and all the goods in the city. You may use all the plunder from your enemies for yourself.

15 That is what you must do to the cities that are very far away from you and do not belong to the nations in the area.

16 You must not allow anyone to remain alive in the cities of the nations that Adonai is giving you as your possession.

---

8. You must go home, because your cowardice will demoralize the other troops.
People come in all shapes and forms. Wars are very dangerous and there is always the chance of being wounded or killed. Some people have the inner strength to be a soldier and fight in a battle. However, there are always men who by their psychological and physical makeup should not be exposed to dangerous military activities. These types of personalities can generate a panic and demoralize the troops. Ideally such personalities should not be sent into battle, since they are a danger to themselves and their fellow soldiers.
Shenash

10. When you attack a city, you must first propose a peaceful settlement.
A peaceful settlement can save lives.

Attacking fortified cities with strong fortifications was a very difficult military operation and could result in many deaths.

The city wall had to be breached by climbing tall ladders or tunneling under the walls. All of these military strategies involved a large cost of life.

14. However, you may keep the women, children, animals, and all the goods in the city.
When you attack a city, you must first ask the inhabitants to surrender peacefully, but if they refuse, you must besiege and capture it. Then you kill all the males (v.13). However, the Torah prescribes a more humane conduct toward the women and children, who, with the animals and the goods, become the property of the victors.

17 Adonai has commanded that you must completely wipe out the Hittites, the Amorites, the Canaanites, the Perizzites, the Hivites, and the Jebusites. **18** Otherwise they will infect you with all the revolting practices with which they worship their idols, and tempt you to sin against Adonai.
19 Even if your siege of a city takes a long time, do not cut down any of its food-producing trees. Do not cut down any tree, unless it is being used against you by the enemy forces.
20 But if you know that a tree does not produce food, then you may cut it down to make wooden devices to help you capture the city.

21

When you are living in the Promised Land and you find a murder victim and the killer's identity is unknown, **2** the leaders and judges in the surrounding area must measure the distance to the cities around the corpse.
3 The leaders of the city nearest to the body must then bring a female calf that has never plowed a field or pulled a wagon.
4 The leaders of that city shall bring the calf to a swiftly flowing stream, in a place that has never been plowed or planted, and there at the stream they shall break the calf's neck.
5 Then the priests from the tribe of Levi, whom Adonai has chosen to serve Him and to pronounce blessings in His name, shall come forward. They are empowered to decide lawsuits and criminal cases.
6 The leaders of the city nearest to where the victim was found shall wash their hands over the dead calf beside the stream of running water.

Cleanse Yourself of Guilt   *Maftir*

7 The leaders shall say, "Our hands have not spilled this blood, and our eyes have not witnessed it."
8 The priests shall then say, "Adonai, forgive your people, whom you have liberated. Do not accuse your people of Israel of murdering an innocent person." If you do this, you will be free of guilt. **9** This is how you will cleanse yourself of the guilt of spilling innocent blood, because you will have done what is right in the eyes of Adonai.

---

19. Do not cut down any food producing trees… unless it is being used against you by the enemy forces.
This precept, referred to as *bal tashcheet*, meaning "do not destroy," is a prohibition of purposeless destruction. It prohibits the willful destruction of natural resources or any kind of vandalism.
   According to the Talmud (Sabbath 105B), "Just as one must be careful not to injure or destroy his own body…so he must be careful not to destroy or damage his property needlessly."

5. Then the priests from the tribe of Levi, whom Adonai has chosen to serve Him and to pronounce blessings in His name, shall come forward. They are empowered to decide lawsuits and criminal cases.
The text is explaining that the priests, who come into close contact with many people and are aware of the strengths and deficiencies and conduct of all elements in Israelite society, may be able to detect the murderer.   *Sforno*

7. The leaders shall say, "Our hands have not spilled this blood, and our eyes have not witnessed it."
We did not allow any known murderers to remain in the land.   *Sforno*

כִּי תֵצֵא *Ki Tetze*

WHEN YOU GO TO WAR

10 When you go to war against your enemies, Adonai will help you defeat them, and you will take many prisoners. **11** If you find a beautiful woman among the captives and are attracted to her, you may marry her. **12** When you bring her home, she must shave off the hair on her head and cut her fingernails. **13** Then she must change her foreign clothing and remain in your home, mourning for her father and mother for a full month. After that you may marry her and make her your wife.

14 However, if you do not marry her, you must send her away free, because you have slept with her as your wife. You may not sell her or keep her as a servant.

15 This is the law when a man has two wives, one whom he loves and one whom he dislikes, and both wives, the loved one and the unloved one, have given birth to sons, but the first-born is the son of the unloved wife. **16** When the man divides his property, he must not give the son of the beloved wife more than the first-born son of the unloved wife. **17** He must give the son of the hated wife a double portion of all his property because he is the first-born and it is his legal right.

18 When parents have a difficult son who does not obey his father and mother, they shall discipline him. If he continues to disobey them,

---

10. When you go to war.
This sidrah contains 73 commandments, the largest number of any sidrah. The sidrah starts with mitzvah number 532, which discusses the return of stolen property, and ends with mitzvah number 605, which warns us not to forget the wickedness of Amalek.

11. If you find a beautiful woman among the captives and are attracted to her, you may marry her.
When an Israelite marries a foreign female captured (Dev. 20:10–15) from Canaan, she would, after a month of acclimation, accustom herself to her new surroundings. After the month the couple would be subject to the Israelites' marriage regulations, including cleansing rites. After the cleansing rites she would enjoy the rights and duties of an Israelite wife.

12. When you bring her home, she must shave off the hair on her head and cut her fingernails.
Onkeles explained that the procedure was designed to make her unattractive and to discourage her captor from marrying her.

14. You may not sell her or keep her as a servant.
This is prohibitive mitzvah number 533.

When a woman has been captured during a war and she has spent a long time in his home and he has decided not to marry her, then he must release her. He may not keep her as a slave or sell her into slavery

17. He must give the son of the hated wife a double portion of all his property.
The Talmud prohibits the treatment of a son of a beloved wife as a first-born in this case. When the time comes to divide the property, the first-born of the hated wife is to receive twice as much as every other brother.

18. When parents have a difficult son who does not obey his father and mother, they shall discipline him.
Some things are beyond the control of the parents. A wayward child is a tragedy for both parents as well as the child. The Torah teaches parents to be realistic about their children. Give them the best education, and direction, within your means. What parents cannot do is abandon their children. The philosopher Philo says, "What Adonai is to the world, parents are to their children."

19 his parents must bring him to the elders of the community at the city gate.
20 The parents shall say to the elders of his city, "Our son is dangerous and out of control. He refuses to listen to us, and he eats like a pig and is a drunkard." **21** If the elders all agree that the youngster is dangerous and cannot be controlled, the men of the community shall stone him to death. In this way you will remove an evil influence from your midst. When Israel's young people hear about the punishment, they will be afraid, and they will be respectful and obey their parents.

Regulations of Lost Property *2nd Aliyah*

22 If a person is legally sentenced to death, you must hang him from a tree. **23** You must not allow his body to hang on the tree overnight, but you must bury him on the same day. A person who has been hanged is an insult to Adonai, and you must not let it desecrate the land Adonai is giving you as a heritage.

22 If you see an ox or a sheep wandering around lost, you must not ignore it. You must return it to the owner. **2** If the owner is not nearby, or if you do not know who the owner is, you must take the animal to your own farm. You must care for it until the owner claims it, and then you must return it to him.
3 You must do the same in the case of any animal, or an article of clothing, or anything else that someone loses and you find. You must hold it for the owner.
4 If you see that your neighbor's donkey or ox has fallen on the road, you must not ignore it. You must help it get up. **5** No woman shall dress in men's clothing, and no man shall dress in women's clothing. Adonai hates cross-dressing behavior.
6 If you find a bird's nest in a tree or on the ground, and it contains baby birds or eggs, and the mother is sitting on the chicks or eggs, you must not take the mother away from her chicks.

---

20. He eats like a pig and is a drunkard.
Gluttons and drunks have no way of earning a livelihood. Eventually they will have to commit crimes to satisfy their hunger for food and drink.
Sforno

1. If you see an ox or a sheep wandering around lost, you must not ignore it. You must return it to the owner.
This law requiring return of other's property is also given in Shemot 23:45. Here the law is extended to include other lost articles that should be returned to their owners.

3. You must do the same in the case of any animal, or an article of clothing, or anything else that someone loses and you find. You must hold it for the owner.
This is mitzvah number 539 You must not leave a lost object. You are required to take it and try to return it to its owner.

6. You must not take the mother away from her chicks.
This is mitzvah number 544.

Consideration for animals is called *tzar baaley chayim*. Judaism has always manifested a humane attitude toward animals. In the account of the creation of living creatures, "Elohim made all kinds of wild beasts and tame animals. And Elohim saw that it was good" (Bereshit 1:25).

Animals were placed in "subjugation" to man. This gave man the right to use them in a way that would benefit him. However, man's sovereign power did not give him the right to abuse them.

Kindness to animals was considered the ultimate test of a noble character.

7 You must release the mother, and only then is it permissible to take the chicks. If you do this, you will be successful and live long.

Safety and Agriculture
3rd Aliyah

8 When you build a new house, you must build a railing around your roof. You must make your house safe so that no one can fall from the roof.

9 You must not plant two types of crops in your vineyard. If you do, it is forbidden to eat the yield of the grapes you planted and the fruit from the second crop.

10 You must not plow with an ox and a donkey in the same team. **11** You must not wear clothing in which wool and linen are woven together in the same garment (*shatnez*).

---

7. You must release the mother, and only then is it permissible to take the chicks. If you do this, you will be successful and live long.
This is mitzvah number 545.
The mitzvah applies only to kosher birds and wild kosher birds, that do not belong to anyone. The idea is to spare the mother bird so she does not see and feel the pain of losing her chicks. The Rambam says that this mitzvah also teaches us to be careful not to cause pain and sorrow to a fellow human being.

8. When you build a new house, you must build a railing around your roof.
Mitzvah 546 mandates that a landlord or homeowner surround the roof of his building with a fence.

Israel is a hot country, and the residents frequently sleep on the roof for some relief from the heat. Adults, and especially children, often fell off the roofs in their sleep and were injured.

This mitzvah also requires owners to fence in holes and ditches to prevent injury.

The Rabbis also argued that the Torah warns us to clear the property of any object that can cause injury. Following this line, people in an automobile must wear seat belts, which act as fences.

Another modern application is the sale of untested or dangerous drugs. Dumping dangerous chemicals pollutes the water and is linked to genetic diseases. These acts constitute placing a dangerous object in the public domain. *Shenash*

9. You must not plant two types of crops in your vineyard.
This is prohibitive mitzvah number 548.

It forbids the planting of two types of grain or vegetables in the same garden. The purpose of this prohibition is to protect the purity of growth.

Today with the help of gene technology, seed companies have created designer grains, fruits, and vegetables. There is much opposition to tampering with the gene structure of grains and vegetables.

Despite the opposition, these designer seeds have created disease-resistant varieties of cotton, corn, and wheat.

10. You must not plow with an ox and a donkey in the same team.
This is mitzvah number 550.

Animals of different strengths and species can suffer pain and discomfort when yoked together. The same prohibition can apply to humans. People should not be placed in situations, classrooms, or teams in which they are outclassed either physically or intellectually. *Shenash*

11. You must not wear clothing in which wool and linen are woven together in the same garment (shatnez).
This is prohibitive mitzvah number 55.

You are forbidden to wear any garment made of wool and linen sewn together. This prohibition extends even to towels.

Maimonides explains that Jews are forbidden to wear clothing of mixed wool and linen because ancient priests serving idols used to wear such clothing.

The Zohar says that combining wool and linen creates a spirit of *tumah* (source of evil).

12 You must sew fringes (*tzitzit*) on the four corners of the garments that you wear.
13 This is the law when a man marries a woman, and lives with her, and then decides that he hates her **14** and makes up lies against her by saying, "I married this woman and I found that she was not a virgin when I married her. I have evidence that she has not been faithful to me." **15** The parents of the girl shall bring evidence of their daughter's virginity from the marriage bed and present it to the judges in court. **16** Then the parents of the girl shall say to the judges, "I gave my daughter to this man in marriage, but he despises her. **17** He has invented lies against her and claims that she was not a virgin. But here is evidence of my daughter's virginity." With that, the parents of the girl shall present the bloody sheet from the marriage bed as evidence before the judges.
18 The judges shall then sentence the liar to be whipped.
19 As a penalty they shall fine him one hundred silver shekels for slandering an Israelite virgin. The payment must be given to the parents of the girl. The slanderer must then keep the girl as his wife and is forbidden to divorce her as long as he lives. **20** If the charge is true, however, and there is no evidence of the girl's virginity, **21** they shall take the girl out to the door of her father's house, and the people of her city shall stone her, because she has brought shame upon her parents' family and upon Israel by prostituting herself. You must cleanse immorality from your midst. **22** If a man is found sleeping with someone else's wife, both the woman and the man lying with her shall be put to death. You must rid Israel of evil.
23 This is the law where a virgin girl is betrothed to one man, and another man meets her in the city and has intercourse with her. **24** Both of them shall be brought to the gates of the city, and both of them shall be put to death by stoning. The penalty shall be imposed on the girl because she did not cry out even though she was in the city, and on the man because he had sex with his neighbor's betrothed wife. You must rid yourselves of immorality in your communities.
25 However, if the man met the engaged girl in the fields and raped her, then only the rapist shall be put to death.
26 You must not punish the girl, because she has not committed a sin deserving the death penalty. The crime is like murder where a man sneaks up on his neighbor and kills him.

---

12. You must sew fringes (*tzitzit*) on the four corners of the garments that you wear.
In ancient times all four-cornered garments worn during the day had *tzitzit* on the four corners. The *tzitzit* served as a reminder of Adonai's commandments. "When they see fringes, they will be reminded to obey Adonai's commandments" (Bamidbar 15:39)

The garment with the fringes is the *tallit*. The *tallit* is the prayer shawl worn by congregants during the morning prayer on weekdays, Shabbats, and festivals. It is usually made of wool, silk, or rayon. A person called to the reading of the Torah places a corner of the *tallit* on the word where the portion begins and then kisses the corner of the prayer shawl. After the portion is read, he does the some thing with the last word of the reading. The *tzitzit* have sometimes been called "the badge of holiness." They are a constant reminder of a Jew's responsibility to Adonai.

26. You must not punish the girl, because she has not committed a sin.
This is prohibitive mitzvah number 556.

It is forbidden to punish anyone who has been forced to commit a sin. The girl that was forced to commit sexual intercourse and was the victim of a rape is not liable for punishment. The general principle is that a person who is forced to commit an offense is not to be punished.

27 The man attacked her in the field, and even if the engaged girl had screamed, there would have been no one to help her. **28** If a man meets a virgin girl who is not engaged, and he is caught raping her, **29** the rapist must give the girl's father fifty silver shekels. He must marry the girl that he raped, and he cannot divorce her as long as he lives.

23
A son must not marry his father's wife. This would shame his father. **2** A man who has diseased testicles or an injured penis must not enter the sanctuary. **3** A man born illegitimately is forbidden to marry an Israelite woman. Even in the tenth generation his descendants may not enter the sanctuary.
4 An Ammonite or Moabite man may not marry an Israelite woman even after the tenth generation.
5 The reason for this law is that they did not welcome the Israelites with bread and water when they escaped from Egypt, and also because they hired Balaam son of Beor, from Pethor in Aram Naharaim, to curse you. **6** But Adonai refused to listen to Balaam, and Adonai changed his curse against you into a blessing, because He loves you.
7 Never, as long as you exist, seek peace or make a treaty with these nations.

Do Not Hate the Edomites or the Egyptians 4th Aliyah
8 You must not hate the Edomite, because he is your relative. You must not hate the Egyptian, because you were once a stranger in his land.

28.–29. If a man meets a virgin girl who is not engaged, and he is caught raping her, the rapist must give the girl's father fifty silver shekels. He must marry the girl that he raped, and he cannot divorce her as long as he lives.
He did the deed and he must face the consequences. The man must pay the bride price of fifty shekels, marry her, and lose the right to divorce her.

1. A son must not marry his father's wife.
In biblical times wives were handled just like a commodity. Children inherited the possessions of their fathers, which included his wives.

4. An Ammonite or Moabite man may not marry an Israelite woman even after the tenth generation.
This is mitzvah number 561.
These laws were in effect during the First and Second Temple periods. Since then, these nations have lost the national identities and no one knows whether or not they exist. Today any gentile or a member of another religious sect who wishes to convert is welcomed and is extended the religious rights and privileges of a Jew.

7. Never, as long as you exist, seek peace or make a treaty with these nations.
This is mitzvah number 562.
The nations referred to here are Ammon and Moab.
According to the sages, the Israelites were forbidden from offering them peace proposals. However, we are permitted to accept peace proposals from them. This mitzvah has a current political application to other contemporary conflicts.

8. You must not hate the Egyptian, because you were once a stranger in his land.
This is prohibitive mitzvah number 564.
The Israelites, starting with Abraham, were saved from starving by the Egyptians. Joseph rose to a high position in the Egyptian hierarchy. For hundreds of years the Israelites lived peacefully among the Egyptians before a new pharaoh with a different political philosophy enslaved the Israelites.
It is important to remember the good as well as the bad.

9 Therefore, the grandchildren of the Egyptians who left Egypt with you may convert in the third generation and marry Israelites.
10 When you go to war against your enemies, you must stay away from anything evil. **11** A soldier who becomes unclean because of an emission while he is sleeping must leave the camp and remain outside **12** until evening; then he must cleanse himself and can return to camp at sunset.
13 You must set up a special place outside the camp to use as a latrine. **14** You must also keep a shovel to dig a hole to cover your feces when you go to the latrine.
15 Your camp must be clean and holy, so that Adonai can help you become victorious over your enemy. Your camp must be holy because Adonai is among you.
16 If a slave escapes from his master, you must not force him to return.
17 You must allow him to live alongside you in your cities wherever he chooses, and you must not discriminate against him. You must do nothing to hurt his feelings.
18 There must not be any male or female Israelite prostitutes among you.
19 You must not bring an offering to the temple of Adonai that is paid for by the earnings of a prostitute, because it would be shameful to Adonai. **20** You must not deduct advance interest from loans made to an Israelite, whether for money or for food or for anything else for which interest is normally taken.
21 You may take interest from a foreigner, but you must not do so from an Israelite. If you observe this rule, Adonai will bless you in all your undertakings in the Promised Land that you are going to occupy.
22 When you make a sacred pledge to Adonai, pay it on time, because Adonai demands that you honor all your promises. **23** It is not a sin to avoid making pledges. **24** But if you make a sacred pledge, be sure to keep your promise to Adonai.

Eating Someone Else's Produce *5th Aliyah*

25 If you enter your neighbor's vineyard and you are hungry, you may eat as many grapes as you desire, but you are not permitted to take bunches of grapes home with you.

---

15. Your camp must be clean and holy…because Adonai is among you.
One of the characteristics identified with holiness among the Israelites was hygiene. Only a totally pure individual could approach Adonai to worship.

24. But if you make a sacred pledge, be sure to keep your promise to Adonai.
This is prohibitive mitzvah number 574.

It is forbidden to make a pledge of money, goods, or services and to delay payment or delivery of the goods or services.

25. If you enter your neighbor's vineyard and you are hungry, you may eat as many grapes as you desire, but you are not permitted to take bunches of grapes home with you.
The Mishnah explains that the text does not refer to a passerby who is hungry and helps himself to a bunch of grapes. It refers to a worker, a fruit picker, a harvester, or a supervisor.

Maimonides says that hired laborers should be allowed to eat that on which they are working. The prohibition of taking home bunches of grapes is to restrict the eater and not to exploit the owner.

The principle can be applied to a restaurant. The cook, waiters, and other employees can eat the food on the premises but are not allowed to take food home. The owner may allow perishable food to be taken home, however.

26 It is the same when you are in your neighbor's field of grain. You may pick and eat the grain with your hand, but you are not allowed to cut the stalks with a sickle and take them with you.

24

When a man marries a woman and she displeases him, or if he has evidence of disgraceful conduct on her part, he can hand her divorce papers and send her away from his house. **2** Then she can leave his house and marry another man. **3** However, if her second husband also rejects her and also divorces her, and sends her away from his house, or if her second husband dies, **4** her first husband, who divorced her, cannot remarry her, because she has slept with another man. To do so would be detestable to Adonai, and you must not bring immorality to the land Adonai is giving you as an inheritance.

Newlyweds and Loans
6th Aliyah

5 A newly married man must not be drafted for military service or forced into any other type of service. He must be allowed to remain with his bride for one year, so that he can be happy with his bride.
6 You must not take an upper or lower millstone as a pledge for a loan because the owner makes his living by grinding grain into flour.
7 If a man kidnaps a fellow Israelite, and forces him into slavery and then sells him, the kidnapper shall be put to death. You must rid yourself of such evildoers in your community.
8 You must take care about the signs of contagious leprosy and observe all My health rules. You must take care to do everything I have commanded the priest to do. **9** Keep in mind what Adonai did to Miriam after you left Egypt. **10** When you make a loan of any kind to your neighbor, you must not go into his house to take something as security.
11 You must stand outside, and the man who owes you the money will bring the security item outside to you. **12** If the man is poor and has only a coat to pledge, you must not keep the poor person's warm coat overnight as security.
13 You must return his coat to him at sundown, so that he will be able to sleep in his warm garment, and he will bless you for it. Then you will have performed a righteous deed (*mitzvah*).

---

1. When a man marries a woman and she displeases him, or if he has evidence of disgraceful conduct on her part, he can hand her divorce papers and send her away from his house.
This is mitzvah number 579

When a couple for whatever reason agrees to divorce, it is a mitzvah to do so by means of a document called a *get* which is a rabbinic divorce agreement. The husband must willingly give the *get* in the presence of two witnesses.

6. You must not take an upper or lower millstone as a pledge for a loan because the owner makes his living by grinding grain into flour. The millstone which the housewife uses every morning grinds the grain for bread. The upper millstone, called *rekheb*, is moved with a grinding motion over the *shekheb*, the lower millstone.

This prohibitive mitzvah (number 583) is to protect the debtor from the demands of the lender. The lender is prohibited from entering the debtor's house to take a pledge that is used in the preparation of food.

Today there are specific laws that protect the borrower from unscrupulous debt collectors who threaten their clients.

A Poor Man's Wages
7th Aliyah

14 You must not withhold the wages that are due your poor laborer, whether he is an Israelite or a foreigner living in your land. **15** You must pay him on the same day, before the sun goes down. He is a poor man, and he needs his daily wages because his family depends on the money.

Do not give him a reason to complain to Adonai, because you will be guilty of a sin.

16 Parents shall not be convicted on the testimony of their children, and children shall not be convicted on the testimony of their parents. A person shall be convicted only for his own crime. **17** You must not deny justice to the foreigner or the orphan. You must not take a widow's clothing as a pledge for a loan.

18 Always remember that you were a poor slave in Egypt, and Adonai freed you. That is why I am commanding you to observe these rules.

19 When you harvest your grain and forget a sheaf of wheat in your field, you must not go back to pick it up. Leave it for the foreigners, orphans, and widows. If you do this, Adonai will bless you in everything you do.

20 When you harvest the olives from your trees, do not try to gather every last remaining olive. These olives must be left for the foreigners, orphans, and widows.

21 When you harvest the grapes in your vineyard, you must not harvest them a second time. You must leave the last remaining grapes for the foreigners, orphans, and widows.

22 I am ordering you to do this so that you will always remember that you were a poor slave in Egypt.

25 When there is a problem between people, the judges will decide who is guilty and who is innocent. **2** If the guilty person is to be punished by whipping, the judges will order the person to lie down and be whipped with the number of strokes the crime deserves.

---

15. You must pay him on the same day, before the sun goes down.
This is mitzvah number 580.

It is a mitzvah to pay a hired day worker on the exact same day that he earned it. Of course if the hired worker is to be paid by the week or the month, then he or she must be paid on time. The sages insist that the employer must pay his workers even if he is forced to borrow money.

16. Parents shall not be convicted on the testimony of their children, and children shall not be convicted on the testimony of their parents. A person shall be convicted only for his own crime.
An accused individual must not be convicted on the evidence of relatives. A person should be convicted only on authentic, irrefutable evidence that is above suspicion.

Relatives–including children, step children, divorced wives, feuding family members-frequently for many reasons are in conflict with each other, and their testimony can be biased.

17. You must not deny justice to the foreigner or the orphan.
This is mitzvah number 590.

The Torah is concerned about the weak and helpless, the orphan and the widow and the foreigners who need help and protection. The *ger* (foreign resident) is often referred to as an underprivileged of Israelite society.

Modern Jewish society is also concerned about the weak and helpless. There are numerous Jewish institutions, such as old age homes, hospitals, and welfare groups, that try to help the sick, the aged, and the unfortunate.

3 Forty lashes is the most punishment you can inflict on him, because more strokes will injure and humiliate him in the eyes of the community.

4 You must not muzzle your ox while it is threshing grain.

5 When brothers live in the same area, and one of them dies childless, the widow must not be allowed to marry someone outside the family. It is the brother-in-law's responsibility to marry her.

6 The first-born son she bears will then assume the name of the dead brother, so that his name will not disappear from Israel.

7 If the brother does not wish to marry his dead brother's wife, the widow is to approach the judges in court and say, "My brother-in-law refuses to marry me so that I can bear a son who carries my late husband's name."

8 Then the judges in the city shall send for the brother and try to persuade him to marry the widow. If he continues to refuse to marry her, he must say, "I refuse to marry her." **9** Then his sister-in-law shall approach her brother-in-law and take a shoe off his foot and spit in his face. Then she must say, "This is what must be done to the brother who refuses to create a family for his dead brother."

10 From then on the house of the brother shall be known as "House of the man without a shoe." **11** If two men are fighting and the wife of one of them helps her husband by grabbing the attacker by his testicles,

---

3 Forty lashes is the most punishment you can inflict upon him.
Whipping was a common punishment in the Ancient Middle East. However, the Torah, as a sign of respect for the culprit, limited the number of lashes to forty.

4 You must not muzzle your ox while it is threshing grain.
Threshing removes the kernel of wheat from the chaff. In ancient times, the wheat was spread on the threshing room floor and the ox would trample it, thereby releasing the kernel of wheat. Sometimes the animal was tied to a central post and left to walk in a circle and thresh the wheat.

Allowing the ox to eat helped preserve its strength and allow it to continue working.

5. When brothers live in the same area, and one of them dies childless, the widow must not be allowed to marry someone outside the family. It is the brother-in-law's responsibility to marry her.
This is mitzvah number 597.

A childless widow is forbidden to marry anyone other than her husband's brother so as to perpetuate the name of the deceased. This is called a leverite (*yivum*) marriage.

9. Then his sister-in-law shall approach her brother-in-law and take a shoe off his foot and spit in his face.
This is mitzvah number 599.

If the brother refuses to marry the childless widow, then it is a mitzvah to perform the procedure of *chalitzah*–the unbinding of the shoe. Since the sister-in-law was ready to be her brother-in-law's wife and perform services for him, the Torah commanded her to remove his shoe and spit in front of him to indicate that she no longer had any respect for him.

11–12. If two men are fighting and the wife of one of them helps her husband by grabbing the attacker by his testicles, you must cut off her hand and not have any pity on her.
This is the only instance where the Torah recommends the punishment of mutilation.

The punishment "cut off her hand" was not to be literally applied, though. The Rabbis decided to substitute a monetary penalty depending on the severity of the crime.

The rabbinical tradition substitutes fines for all *talion* measures that advocate punishment equal to the offense: an eye for an eye, a tooth for a tooth, and so on.

12 you must cut off her hand and not have any pity on her.
13 You must not cheat by using two different weights, one heavy and one light.
14 You must not cheat by using two different measures, one long and one short.
15 You must have accurate weights and accurate measures. If you do this, you will enjoy a long life in the land that Adonai is giving you. **16** Using dishonest weights and measures is repugnant to Adonai.

Remember Amalek
Maftir

17 It is important to remember how Amalek treated you when you were leaving Egypt. **18** They watched you as you marched on your way out of Egypt, and when you were tired and exhausted, they killed those who were too weak to keep up with the march. They had no pity and no respect for Adonai.
19 Once Adonai has given you peace from all the enemies surrounding you in the land that He is giving you as a heritage, you must completely wipe out the memory of Amalek. Do not forget: you must avenge yourself against Amalek.

---

14. You must not cheat by using two different measures, one long and one short.
This is mitzvah number 602.

The Torah warns against two different kinds of measures or weights. This refers to dishonest merchants who use long measures or weights for selling and short measures or weights for purchasing. False weights and measures are a recurring problem in the twenty-first century. The problem also applies to financial reports by corporations who falsify sales, profits and losses. Gas stations too have been apprehended for adjusting their computers to pump a short gallon.

17. It is important to remember how Amalek treated you when you were leaving Egypt.
It is a mitzvah (number 603) to remember the evil that Amalek committed against the Jews after their Exodus from Egypt. They ambushed and attacked the unarmed Israelites as they peacefully marched through the hot desert sands.

The forces of history have eliminated the nation of Amalek, but sadly there are no lack of anti-Semites to take their place. In modern times, the Communists in Russia killed millions of Jews and outlawed the practice of Judaism.

The catastrophe of the Holocaust witnessed the murder of six million Jews. Some of your friends and their families may have been impacted by this horrible event. On Tisha B'Av (ninth day of Av), we remember all of our fellow Jews and innocent civilians who throughout history have been murdered by the Amalekites, and we renew our vigilance never again to become victims of anti-Semitism.

כִּי תָבוֹא *Ki Tavo*

WHEN YOU ENTER THE PROMISED LAND

26 When you enter the Promised Land that Adonai is giving you as an inheritance, and you are living there, **2** you must gather the first crops of your harvest in a basket, and you must bring the first and best of your crops (*bikkurim*) to the sanctuary where Adonai has chosen to be worshipped.

3 There you shall give the basket to the priest on duty, and say to him, "This is my gift to Adonai for bringing me to the land that He swore to our ancestors He would give us."

4 The priest will then take the *bikkurim* basket from you and place it in front of the altar of Adonai. **5** Then you shall make the following declaration before Adonai:

"My ancestor was a wandering Aramaean. He went down to Egypt with a small number of people and lived there as a foreigner, and it was there that my ancestors became a great, powerful, and numerous nation. **6** The Egyptians were cruel to us, making us suffer, and they forced us into slavery.

7 So we cried out for help, and Adonai heard our cries and saw our suffering, our hard labor, and our pain.

8 Then Adonai brought us out of Egypt with a strong hand and an outstretched arm, with shattering events and with signs and great miracles.

9 He brought us to this land, and gave us this Promised Land flowing with milk and honey.

---

1. When you enter the Promised Land that Adonai is giving you as an inheritance and you are living there, you must gather the first crops of your harvest in a basket, and you must bring the first and best of your crops (*bikkurim*) to the sanctuary.
The Israelites were not obligated to bring *bikkurim* until they had conquered Canaan and divided the land among the tribes. *Rashi*

2. You must bring the first and best of your crops (*bikkurim*) to the sanctuary.
These crops include wheat, barley, grapes, figs, pomegranates, olives, and dates.

The ceremony of *bikkurim* was a beautiful demonstration of thanksgiving to Adonai for the blessings that come out of nature. These gifts were never to be taken for granted. In the modern period of technology, humans have forgotten Adonai's precious universe, and only recently have they become more ecology minded, realizing that we cannot take nature for granted. It is no less than Adonai's gift to us, and all of it must be treasured.

3. There you shall give the basket to the priest on duty, and say to him, "This is my gift to Adonai for bringing me to the land that He swore to our ancestors He would give us."
The first fruits are not a gift to the priest but are a symbolic offering, a thank you gift to Adonai for bringing us to and giving us the land that He promised to give to our ancestors.

3. This is my gift to Adonai for bringing me to the land that He swore to our ancestors He would give us.
The farmer who brings his *bikkurim* to the priest gives thanks to Adonai for his ancestors in every generation.

During the Passover seder we recite "In every generation every Jew is obligated to see himself as if he personally had gone out of Egypt." It is the duty of everyone at the seder to feel the joy of his or her own ancestors liberation from slavery.

10 In thanks I am now bringing the first crops of the land that Adonai has generously given me." After that, you shall place the basket before Adonai, and bow down. **11** Then you and your family and the Levites and the foreigners shall enjoy a festive meal and thank Adonai for all the good things He has granted you and your family.

The Special Third-Year Tithe *2nd Aliyah*

12 In the third year you must set aside a special tithe to be given to the Levites, the foreigners, and the orphans and widows in your cities, so that they will not go hungry. **13** Then you must make the following declaration before Adonai:
"I have taken the sacred tithe from my house. I have given it to the Levites and to the orphans and widows, and I have followed all the commandments You have given to us. I have not neglected or forgotten any of Your commandments.
14 I did not touch or eat any of the tithe while I was in mourning. Adonai, I have obeyed You, and I have done everything You commanded me.
15 Adonai, look down from Your heavenly dwelling and bless Your people Israel, and the land that You have given us – the land flowing with milk and honey that You promised to our ancestors."

Obey My Commandments *3rd Aliyah*

16 Adonai commands you today to obey all the commandments and laws. You must carefully observe these laws with all your heart and with all your soul.
17 You have agreed today to obey Adonai and have declared allegiance to Adonai, and have pledged to walk in His ways and observe His decrees, commandments, and laws.

---

10. In thanks I am now bringing the first crops of the land that Adonai has generously given me.
In the Mishnah (Bikkurim, chapter 3) there is a full description of the procession of the first fruits to the Temple. This is a small part of that beautiful drama: "The flute was played before them when they reached the Temple Mount, Agrippa the king would take his basket on his shoulder and enter as far as the Temple Court. When they reached the Temple Court the Levites sang the song, 'Adonai I will exalt, for You have raised me up and not made my enemies to be victorious over me.'"

12. In the third year you must set aside a special tithe to be given to the Levites, the foreigners, and the orphans and widows in your cities, so that they will not go hungry.
Every year the Israelite farmer was to set aside ten percent of his harvested crops for the Levites. In addition, ten percent was to be put aside for himself and his family to share in the three Pilgrimage Festivals at the central sanctuary. Every third year ten percent of the harvest was to be distributed among the poor, the widows, and the orphans.

14. I did not touch or eat any of the tithe while I was in mourning.
It was a widespread ancient custom to prepare a feast for the dead and place it on their graves for their journey into the after life. The pyramids, which were the burial sites for the pharaohs, were filled with meals for the deceased.

14. Adonai, I have obeyed You, and I have done everything You commanded me.
The reason for all these declarations is that it is forbidden to bring out one's produce for any purpose whatever before first giving away the tithe which is holy. It would be disrespectful to use the remainder of the produce first, even if it were for a ritual purpose.

18 Today, as He promised you, Adonai has declared that you are His treasured nation. If you observe all His commandments,

19 He will make you greater than all the other nations, so that you will receive praise, fame, and glory.

And just as He promised, you will remain a holy nation consecrated to Adonai.

Write the Laws on the Stones

4th Aliyah

27 Then Moses and the leaders of Israel gave the following instructions to the Israelites:

Observe all the commandments that I am giving you today.

2 As soon as you cross the Jordan to the land that Adonai is giving you, you must set up large stones and coat them with plaster. **3** Once you have crossed over, you shall write these laws on them. This is how you shall enter the land that Adonai is giving you, the land flowing with milk and honey that Adonai promised to give to your ancestors.

4 When you have crossed the Jordan River, you shall set up the stones that I am now describing to you on Mount Ebal, and you shall coat them with plaster.

5 Then you shall build an altar to Adonai from stones that have never been touched by iron tools.

6 Build the altar with whole uncut stones. On this altar you shall offer burnt offerings. **7** You shall also bring peace offerings and feast there, and rejoice before Adonai.

8 You shall write all the words of this law in a clear script on the stones. **9** Then Moses and the priests spoke to the Israelites, saying:

"People of Israel, pay attention and listen. Today you have become a treasured nation to Adonai. **10** Therefore you must obey Adonai and observe His commandments and decrees that I am giving you today."

---

1. Then Moses and the leaders of Israel gave the following instructions to the Israelites.
Moses was the totally dedicated leader until the end of his life. He knew that he would not cross the Jordan River into Canaan, so he involved his cabinet leaders in all his decisions. In this way, the invasion could continue without their missing a single beat.

2. You must set up large stones and coat them with plaster.
The custom of inscribing events and laws on memorial stones was universal in the ancient Near East. Hammurabi, king of Babylonia, had his entire code engraved on a stele about 7 feet high. Whitewashing the stone before the inscription was an Egyptian practice. The whitewashed stone was then written on or painted on in black ink or other contrasting color. Not only is it easier to write on a stone than to engrave it, but it is also easier to read a written script than to decipher letters cut into stone. To ensure the preservation of the inscriptions, the writing was renewed from time to time. If the Lawgiver intended the numerous laws contained in the Book of Devarim to be inscribed in stone, we can well understand why it was specified that the stones erected were to be large ones.

4. When you have crossed the Jordan River, you shall set up the stones that I am now describing to you on Mount Ebal, and you shall coat them with plaster.
Moses involved the civilian and religious authorities in crossing the Jordan River. He had the civilian leaders of Israel help with setting up the stones and the altar.

In verse 9 Moses included the priests and urged the Israelites to observe the commandments. The leaders were involved in the building and engineering while the priests were to teach Torah laws.

Blessings and Curses

5th Aliyah

11 That very same day, Moses gave the Israelites the following instructions:

12 When you cross the Jordan, the tribal leaders of Simeon, Levi, Judah, Issachar, Joseph, and Benjamin shall stand on Mount Gerizim and bless the people.

13 The tribal leaders of Reuben, Gad, Asher, Zebulun, Dan, and Naphtali shall stand on Mount Ebal to curse the people. **14** Then the Levites shall speak in a loud voice and say the following to the assembled Israelites:

15 Cursed is anyone who makes an idol. It is repugnant to Adonai even if it is a beautiful piece of sculpture and is hidden in a secret place.
Let us all say Amen.

16 Cursed is anyone who disrespects his father and mother.
Let us all say Amen.

17 Cursed is anyone who moves his neighbor's boundary marker.
Let us all say Amen.

18 Cursed is anyone who leads a blind person astray.
Let us all say Amen.

19 Cursed is anyone who denies justice to the foreigner, the orphan, and the widow.
Let us all say Amen.

20 Cursed is anyone who sleeps with his father's wife, because he insults his father.
Let us all say Amen.

21 Cursed is anyone who has sex with an animal.
Let us all say Amen.

22 Cursed is anyone who has sex with his sister or with the daughter of his father or of his mother.
Let us all say Amen.

23 Cursed is anyone who has sex with his mother-in-law.
Let us all say Amen.

---

13. The tribal leaders of Reuben, Gad, Asher, Zebulun, Dan, and Naphtali shall stand on Mount Ebal to curse the people.
The denunciations recorded in verses 13–26 are for conduct that only self-discipline can eliminate. The Levites, who stood midway between the slopes of Mount Gerizim and Mount Ebal, made these pronouncements. As the Levites pronounced the curses, they turned to Mount Ebal, and all the people on both mountain slopes replied "Amen."

Then they turned to Mount Gerizim as they pronounced the blessings in 28:1–6 of those who obeyed the commandments. Then all the people upon the slopes of both mountains pronounced their support by replying "Amen."

15. Cursed is anyone who makes an idol. It is repugnant to Adonai even if it is a beautiful piece of sculpture and is hidden in a secret place.
Praying to idols and statues was strictly forbidden by the Torah.

The history of Israel during the First and Second Temple periods records numerous instances of and battles against the inroads of idol worship.

15. Cursed is anyone who makes an idol.
It is repugnant to Adonai even if it is a beautiful piece of sculpture and is hidden in a secret place. This sentence alludes to a Doctor Jeckyll and Mr. Hyde personality.

On the outside he is a popular community leader who participates in numerous charitable events. Secretly he is a slumlord.

24 Cursed is anyone who kills his neighbor.
Let us all say Amen.
25 Cursed is anyone who takes a bribe to put an innocent person to death.
Let us all say Amen.
26 Cursed is anyone who does not obey the laws of the Torah.
Let us all say Amen.

28

If you obey Adonai, and carefully observe all His commandments that I am giving to you today, then Adonai will raise you above all the nations on earth. **2** As long as you obey Adonai, you will be blessed in many ways.
3 You will be blessed in your cities and blessed on your farm.
4 You will be blessed with many children and large crops.
You will be blessed with fertile herds and flocks.
5 You will be blessed with an overflowing food basket.
You will be blessed with kneading bowls filled with bread.
6 You will be blessed when you come in. You will be blessed when you go out.

Blessing for Obedience
6th Aliyah

7 Adonai will make your enemies flee from you in panic. They will attack you from one direction, and they will flee from you in seven directions.
8 Adonai will bless your storehouses and give you success in all your business. Adonai will bless you in the land that He is giving you.
9 If you observe the commandments and walk in His ways, Adonai will make you His holy nation, just as He promised.
10 Then all the nations of the world will know that Adonai favors you, and they will respect you. **11** Adonai will give you many healthy children. Your livestock and the crops of your farms will increase on the fertile land that Adonai promised your ancestors to give you.
12 Adonai will open up the rivers in the sky to water your land just at the right time, and will give you success in everything you do. You will help many nations, but you will not need their help. **13** Adonai will make you into a leader of nations and never a follower. You will be a winner and never a loser. You must observe the commandments of Adonai exactly as I am giving them to you today.

---

6. You will be blessed when you come in. You will be blessed when you go out.
You were born blameless without sin. Your departure from the world, like your birth, will be without sin. *Rashi*

7. Adonai will make your enemies flee from you in panic.
Verses 7–13 list the blessings which you will receive if you obey and observe the commandments. You will defeat your enemies, you will have plentiful harvests, and all your commercial enterprises will succeed.

You will be blessed with numerous healthy children. Because of your strength and wisdom, you will become a leader among the nations.

9. If you observe the commandments and walk in His ways.
This is mitzvah number 611.

This mitzvah is called *imitalo Dei*, meaning "imitation of Adonai." We imitate Adonai, who is compassionate, by showing concern and helping people who need assistance.

Just as Adonai is righteous we can imitate Adonai by living a life of morality.

14 You must not wander to the right or the left from the laws that I am giving you today. I especially forbid you to worship and pray to idols.

15 However, if you do not obey Adonai and do not observe His commandments and laws as I am giving them to you today, then all these curses will afflict you.

16 You will be cursed in the city.
You will be cursed on your farm.
17 You will be cursed in your food basket.
You will be cursed in your kneading bowl.
18 You will be cursed with no children.
You will be cursed with no crops.
You will be cursed with no fertile herds.
You will be cursed with no lambs in your flocks.
19 You will be cursed when you enter.
You will be cursed when you leave.

20 Adonai will send misfortune and failure on everything you do until you are destroyed and have disappeared because you continued your evil ways and forgot My teachings.

21 Adonai will send diseases to infect you until you disappear from the land you are about to occupy. **22** Adonai will strike you with tuberculosis, fevers, rashes, war, heat, and cancer and fungus. These calamities will overpower and destroy you.

23 The skies above you will be as dry as brass, and the earth below will be as hard as iron.

24 Adonai will change your rain into powder, and it will gush down from the skies and bury you.

25 Adonai will make you flee before your enemies.
You will attack in one column, and flee from your enemies in seven columns. You will become an example to be pitied by the whole world.

---

15. However, if you do not obey Adonai and do not observe His commandments and laws as I am giving them to you today, then all these curses will afflict you.
Verses 15 to 68 are warnings. In Hebrew these warnings are called *tochechot*. The warnings can also be perceived as threats. "You will be cursed…." There are more curses (*tochechot*) than (*b'rachot*) blessings. The blessings, *brachot* are found in 28:3.
The curses in this section are almost the same as those found in the Book of Vayikra 26:14-46.
Rashi says that the curses in Vayikra come directly from Adonai, while the curses in this section were pronounced by Moses in his own name.
The curses in Vayikra are expressed in the plural, while the curses in this portion have been moderated by Moses, and appear in the singular mode.

22. Adonai will strike you with tuberculosis, fevers, rashes, war, heat, and cancer and fungus.
The Hebrew word for fungus or mildew is *yerakon*, derived from the word *yerek*, meaning "green."
Rashi considers *yerakon* to refer to diseases that afflict grain in the field in which the surface of the grain becomes first pale and then yellowish green. Other Bible commentators interpret *yerakon* as jaundice, an illness that affects humans. The Talmud says that the illness turns a person's face a greenish color.
Rosner

24. Adonai will change your rain into powder, and it will gush down from the skies and bury you.
Sandstorms called siroccos are common occurrences in desert areas. The dry spell produces powdery sandstorms, which suffocate the herds and bury everything in sight.

26 Your bodies will be food for the birds of the sky and the animals of the earth, and no one will drive them away.

27 Adonai will afflict you with Egyptian boils, and with incurable ulcers, open sores, and itching that can never be cured.

28 Adonai will strike you with insanity, blindness, and dementia. **29** In broad daylight you will wander aimlessly like a blind man in the darkness, and you will not succeed in any of your enterprises. Everyone will cheat and rob you, and no one will try to help you. **30** When you marry, another man will sleep with your wife. When you build a house, you will not live to enjoy it. When you plant a vineyard, you will not get to eat the grapes.

31 Your ox will be slaughtered before your eyes, and you will not eat any of it. Your donkey will be stolen from you, and you will never get it back. Your sheep will be given to your enemies, and no one will help you reclaim them.

32 Your sons and daughters will be sold as slaves to a foreign nation. You will see it happen before your own eyes, but you will be powerless to prevent it. **33** A foreigner will eat the crops of your land, and you will constantly be cheated and oppressed. **34** The sights you will see will drive you insane.

35 Then Adonai will strike you with a cancerous skin disease from head to toe, and there will be no cure for it.

36 Adonai will exile you and your king to a nation unknown to you and your ancestors. In exile you will be slaves to a nation that worships idols of wood and stone. **37** You will became a symbol of horror, a mockery, and a proverb among the nations to where Adonai will exile you.

38 You will plant much seed in your fields, but the locusts will devour your crops and you will gather a tiny harvest.

39 You will plant vineyards and tend them, but the worms will eat the grapes, so you will not even drink wine or have a harvest.

40 In all your territories you will have many olive trees, but the olives will drop off and you will not have enough oil for medicines.

---

32. Your sons and daughters will be sold as slaves.

The kingdom of Israel (in 721 B.C.E.) was defeated by the Assyrian king Sargon II. He deported 27,290 Israelites to distant countries, and they are now referred to as the Ten Lost Tribes.

In 536 B.C.E. on the ninth of Av, Tisha B'Av, Jerusalem was conquered and tens of thousands of Judeans were deported to Babylonia.

In 70 C.E. the Romans destroyed Solomon's Temple. When Roman Emperor Titus returned to Rome, Jewish captives paraded in front of the populace carrying the treasure that Titus had plundered from the Temple.

38. You will plant much seed in your fields, but the locusts will devour your crops.

The plague of locusts is devastating to growing things. They move in huge swarms and quickly defoliate large tracts of farms and forests.

Adonai sent the eighth plague of locusts over the land of Egypt, helping to secure the freedom of the Israelite slaves.

40. And you will not have enough oil for medicines.

Olive oil was widely used to treat skin rashes, burns, and intestinal problems. Today cardiologists advise the use of olives to lower the cholesterol and prevent heart attacks.

41 Your sons and daughters will be taken into captivity.
42 The trees and crops of your farm will be destroyed by locusts.
43 The foreigners among you shall become richer and more powerful than you, while you will become poorer and weaker.
44 They will lend you money, but you will not have any money to lend them. They will become your master, and you will be their followers.
45 All these curses will pursue and catch you and destroy you, because you did not obey Adonai and did not observe the commandments and laws that He gave you.
46 These punishments will be a warning to you and your children forever.
47 When you had an abundance of everything, you refused to serve Adonai willingly and with a glad heart.
48 Therefore you will serve the enemies that Adonai sends against you, and you will suffer hunger, thirst, nakedness, and poverty. Your enemy will place the iron yoke of slavery on your neck until it destroys you.
49 Adonai will bring a far-off nation from the end of the earth, swooping down like an eagle, a nation whose language you do not understand, **50** a cruel, sadistic nation, that will have no mercy on old and on young.
51 That foreign nation will devour all your livestock and the crops of your land, and you will starve.
All of your grain, wine, and oil, the calves in your herds and the lambs in your flocks will disappear.
52 They will surround all your cities, and break down the high fortified walls that you trust to protect you.
That nation will attack every city in the land that Adonai has given you.
53 Then you will even eat your own children.
54 The hunger will degrade the most kind-hearted and gentle person among you, and he will refuse to share with his brother, his wife, and his other children **55** the flesh of the child he is eating, because he has nothing left for himself, and because of the desperate suffering your enemies will cause when they besiege your settlements.

---

43. The foreigners among you shall become richer and more powerful than you, while you will become poorer and weaker.
The tables will now be turned. The foreigners who were workers will become richer, and you will now work for them.

48. Your enemy will place the iron yoke of slavery on your neck until it destroys you.
A yoke is a crossbar that circles the necks of a pair of oxen or other draft animals working as a team. You will slave for your captors like an ox, with a yoke around your neck until you drop dead from overwork.

49. Adonai will bring a far-off nation from the end of the earth, swooping down like an eagle, a nation whose language you do not understand.
The two nations were first the Assyrians and then the Babylonians.

Unfortunately, in the cycle of Jewish history there have been many sadistic nations, in and out of Israel, who have humiliated, degraded, and made Israel suffer.

53. Then you will even eat your own children.
The enemy will besiege your cities, and you will feel the agony of starvation, and you will even eat what is forbidden.

56 The most gentle, delicate woman, who has been brought up in such luxury that she does not let her foot touch the ground, so great will be her lack of food and her desperation when your enemies besiege your cities that she will not share with her husband, her son, and her daughter **57** the flesh of her newborn baby.

58 If you do not observe all the laws that are written in this book, and respect the glorious name of Adonai, **59** then Adonai will punish you and your descendants with great plagues. The punishments will be terrible, and the diseases will be incurable.

60 Adonai will infect you with the diseases you feared in Egypt.

61 Adonai will also bring upon you diseases that are not mentioned in this book of laws until they have destroyed you.

62 Once upon a time you were as numerous as the stars in the sky, and now you will become just a handful of survivors because you refused to obey Adonai. **63** Once Adonai was happy to be good to you and to see you multiply and grow, but now He will be happy to exile and destroy you. You will be uprooted from the land that you are soon to occupy.

64 Adonai will scatter you among the nations, from one end of the earth to the other. There you will be slaves to idolaters who worship idols that your ancestors never knew. **65** You will be aliens among the nations and will find no peace there. Adonai will give you cowardly hearts, and your future will be hopeless.

66 Your life will hang in danger. Day and night, you will live in fear, and you will be so terrified that you will not believe you will ever again see the rising sun. **67** In the morning, you will say, "I wish it were night," and in the evening you will say, "I wish it were morning." You will say this because of the horrors you will experience and the sights your eyes will see. **68** Adonai will send you back to Egypt in ships, something I promised you would never happen. You will offer to sell yourselves as slaves to your enemies, but no one will want to buy you. **69** These are the terms of the covenant that Adonai commanded Moses to make with the Israelites in addition to the covenant that Adonai made with them on Mount Horeb (Sinai).

---

65. You will be aliens among the nations and will find no peace there.
The nations will imprison you in walled ghettos with guarded gates. You will be forced to wear special clothing which will mark you for shame, ridicule, and attacks, as was the case in Germany. You will try to make a living in a variety of businesses and trades, but no one will admit you into their guilds, unions, or places of business.

In the Middle Ages you will be forced into areas of business which were considered shameful, such as money lending and dealing in rags. *Shenash*

68. Adonai will send you back to Egypt in ships, something I promised you would never happen.
These threatening verses list the punishments which are in store for Israel if they disobey the commandments of Adonai; siege, defeat, plague, exile, capture, and imprisonment. The worst punishment will be a return to slavery in the land of Egypt.

68. You will offer to sell yourselves as slaves to your enemies, but no one will want to buy you.

58. If you do not observe all the laws that are written in this book, and respect the glorious name of Adonai.
Respecting the rules and regulations of the Torah must be observed every moment of every day.

Adonai, the Creator, ordained the laws of nature, which gave order and harmony to the cosmos. Adonai presented humans with a moral code. By adhering to these laws, man becomes a partner in creation. The world is now finished and humans are partners in Tikkun Olam, repairing the world.

Moses' Third Address

Moses Spoke to the Israelites *7th Aliyah*

29 Moses summoned all Israel and said to them: With your own eyes you have witnessed everything that Adonai did to Pharaoh and to all his servants, and to all the people in the land of Egypt. **2** You saw the great miracles, the signs and the wonders.

3 But until now Adonai did not give you a mind to understand and eyes to see and ears to hear.

4 Now Adonai says to you: For forty years I led you through the desert, during which time your clothes did not wear out and the shoes on your feet did not tear.

5 I gave you no bread to eat and no wine to drink, so that you would realize that I, Adonai, was taking care of you.

Obey My Covenant *Maftir*

6 When you first came to this area, Sichon, king of Heshbon, and Og, king of the Bashan, attacked you, but you defeated them.

7 Then you took their land and gave their territories to the Reubenites, the Gaddites, and half the tribe of the Manassites.

8 If you obey the terms of our covenant, then you will prosper in everything you do.

---

1. Moses summoned all Israel and said to them.
This is the third address (29:1–30:20) and the shortest, which Moses delivered before he died. Moses urged the Israelites to observe their covenant with Adonai and promised that if they did they would prosper. He assured them that they are His chosen people. Good things will happen when you observe the commandments.

2. You saw the great miracle, the signs and the wonders.
Both the present and the next generation witnessed the wonder of eating only manna. The younger generation witnessed how Adonai helped them defeat the two kings Sichon and Og. *Ibn Ezra*

3. But until now, Adonai did not give you a mind to understand and eyes to see and ears to hear.
You were completely unaware and oblivious to the miracles that Adonai performed for you. All of your faculties and your mind were closed, your eyes were blind, and your ears were deaf to what was happening to you.

4. For forty years I led you through the desert.
During the forty years, two generations witnessed the wonders of the Exodus from Egypt, the miracle of the manna and the quail, and the defeat of Kings Sichon and Og.

8. If you obey the terms of our covenant, then you will prosper in everything you do.
Adonai said to the children of Israel, "My children, if the words of the Torah are dear to you, then you will be dear to me." *Midrash*

8. If you obey the terms of our covenant, then you will prosper in everything you do.
Maimonides says, every person should regard himself as balanced between guilty and innocent. If one commits a sin, he tips the scales for himself to the side of guilt. If he performs a good deed, he tips the scales to the side of merit, and brings for himself blessing and prosperity.

נִצָּבִים *Nitzavim*

YOU ARE STANDING BEFORE ADONAI

9 Today your leaders, your tribal chiefs, your elders, your judges, every Israelite man, **10** your children, your wives, and the foreigner in your camp, even your woodcutters and water drawers – you are all standing before Adonai.

11 Today you are about to be brought into the covenant with Adonai, sealed with the promise that He is making to you today.

Israel Is Adonai's Nation
2nd Aliyah

12 He is confirming that you are His nation, and that He will be your God, just as He promised you, and as He swore to your ancestors, Abraham, Isaac, and Jacob.

13 I am not making this covenant with you alone. **14** I am making this covenant with everyone who is standing here with us today before Adonai and with all the future generations of Israel.

Adonai Will Not Forgive
3rd Aliyah

15 You remember that we lived in Egypt, and that we journeyed through the territories of enemy nations.

16 You saw their stupid idols made of wood and stone, gold and silver.

17 Surely no man, woman, family, or tribe is unfaithful to Adonai by worshipping the idols of those other nations. Make certain that none of you are poisoned by their ideas.

18 When such a traitor hears the warning of this terrible oath, he may say to himself, "I am safe even if I do my own thing." This attitude will lead to his downfall and ruination.

19 Adonai demands exclusive worship and will not forgive such a person. Adonai's anger will be directed like angry flames against that person. All the terrible curses written in this book will bury him, and Adonai will erase his name from under the heavens. **20** Adonai will separate him from all the Israelite tribes, and he will suffer all the dread curses of the covenant that are recorded in this teaching scroll.

21 Then future generations of your descendants, and foreigners from far away, will see the punishment against the land, and the diseases with which Adonai has struck it, and they will say, **22** "Sulphur and salt have burned the soil.

---

10. You are all standing before Adonai.
All the Israelites were assembled around the ark.

12. Your ancestors, Abraham, Isaac, and Jacob.
Chai, which means "life," has a numerical value of eighteen. The phrase "Abraham, Isaac, and Jacob" is mentioned in the Bible *chai* (eighteen) times.

17. Surely no man, woman, family, or tribe is unfaithful to Adonai by worshipping the idols of those other nations.
Make sure that none of you are poisoned by their ideas.

Jews living in foreign lands will find themselves under economic, social, political, and religious pressure to convert and embrace alien faiths. Against their wills they will be forced to pray to gods in which they do not believe.

The soil is burned dry and has become a desert of salt, and not even grass can grow on it, just like the destruction of Sodom, Gomorrah, Adma, and Zevoyim, the cities that Adonai destroyed when He became angry." **23** Nations will ask, "Why did Adonai punish this land? Why was He so angry?"

24 They will be told, "It is because they abandoned the covenant that Adonai made with their ancestors when He freed them from slavery in Egypt. **25** They turned around and bowed down to idols and worshipped them – idols they did not know, that were forbidden to them.

26 Adonai was angry and devastated them with the curses written in this book. **27** With anger and great fury Adonai drove them from their land. He exiled them to another land, where they live today."

28 There are many secrets that Adonai has not told us.
However, the rules and laws that have been revealed are meant for us and our children forever. They must be forever obeyed.

Adonai Will Rescue You　　　　　　　　　　　　　　　　　　　4th Aliyah

30 The time will come when you will experience the blessing and the curses that I have set before you. You will be scattered among many nations and then you will realize that He is punishing you.

2 Then you will return to Adonai, and you will obey Him, and do everything that I am commanding you today. Then you and your children will repent with all your heart and with all your soul.

3 Adonai will have mercy and rescue your remnants. Adonai will once again bring you back from among the nations where He scattered you.

---

28. There are many secrets that Adonai has not told us.
There are numerous secrets that Adonai has not revealed to us because our minds are limited and will not be able to grasp the meaning of these secrets. Humanity must not use the limitations of their intellect as an excuse not to obey the laws and commandments of the Torah.

2. Then you will return to Adonai, and you will obey Him, and do everything that I am commanding you today.
The Hebrew word for "return" is *shuvah*.

Because this Hebrew word in various grammatical forms appears in verses 1–10, this section is read during the High Holy Days-Rosh Hashanah (New Year's) and Yom Kippur (Day of Atonement).

T'shuvah denotes a return to holiness. Repentance on Yom Kippur secures forgiveness only for transgressions committed against Adonai.

However, transgression against an individual is not forgiven until the injured party is compensated in deed and word. If it is a matter of words, an apology will clear up the misunderstanding and is acceptable as an act of *t'shuvah* (repentance).

3–4 Adonai will have mercy and rescue your remnants. Adonai will once again bring you back from among the nations where he scattered you. Even though you are living at the ends of the earth, Adonai will gather you up from there and will bring you back.
Jews have lived in Yemen since biblical times. They were so poor that a whole class had to study Torah from one book, reading upside down and sideways. When the State of Israel was established in 1948, special planes were organized to bring them to their homeland, Israel.

They boarded planes because they remembered that Adonai had promised to bring this people back to Israel "on the wings of eagles." (Shemot 19:4)

4 Even though you are living at the ends of the earth, Adonai will gather you up from there and will bring you back.

5 Then Adonai will bring you to the land that belonged to your ancestors, and now you will possess it once more. Adonai will do good for you, and He will make you even more successful than your ancestors.

6 Adonai will cleanse your minds and hearts, and the minds and hearts of your descendants, so that you will love Adonai with all your heart and soul, so that Israel will once again flourish.

You Must Return and Obey *5th Aliyah*

7 Adonai will turn all these curses against your enemies and against those who pursue you.
8 But you must return and obey Adonai, and observe all His commandments which I am giving you today.
9 Then Adonai will prosper all the work of your hands, and give you many children, and increase your livestock and the crops of your land.
Once again Adonai will be happy to do good for you just as He did good for your ancestors.
10 These good things will happen only when you obey Adonai, and observe all His commandments and laws, just as they are written in this book of laws, and if you return to Adonai with all your heart and soul.

The Commandments Are Close to You *6th Aliyah*

11 These commandments that I am giving you today are not impossible to obey. 12 These laws are not far away in heaven, so that you might say, "These rules are far away in heaven; bring them down to us so that we can hear them and obey them." 13 They are not far away across the ocean so that one can say, "Who can sail across the ocean and bring them to us so that we can hear them and obey them?"
14 No! The commandments are very close to you. They are on your lips and in your heart, so that you can easily obey them.

---

7. Adonai will turn all these curses against your enemies and against those who pursue you. Modern Israel has two types of enemies. The first is those who pretend to be friends yet in their heart hate her; they secretly support her enemies with monies and with arms. The second type hates Israel and openly tries to wipe her off the map.
Shenash

12. These laws are not far away in heaven. Shavuot and the giving of the Torah mark the end of Adonai's responsibility and the beginning of Israel's takeover. Now it is Israel's responsibility whether the Torah remains out of reach in heaven or is brought down to earth and becomes a vehicle in their daily lives.

14. The commandments are very close to you. Adonai's teachings are all around you. Rabbi Jose, the son of Kisma, interpreted the words of the Torah in this way: When you walk, it will show you the way in this world. When you lie down, it will watch over you in your grave. And when you rise up, it will help you in the world to come.

14. They are on your lips and in your heart. When the commandments are in your heart and continually on your lips, they produce good deeds and mitzvot.

Choose Life or Death
7th Aliyah

15 Look! Today I have set before you a free choice: Choose between life and goodness on one side, and death and evil on the other side.
16 I have commanded you today to love Adonai, to walk in His footsteps and observe His commandments, decrees, and laws. If you do this you will live and be successful, and Adonai will bless you in the land that you are about to occupy. **17** But if your heart turns away and you refuse to listen, and if you decide to bow down and worship idols,

Heaven and Earth Are Witnesses
Maftir

18 then I warn you: If you do this you will be completely destroyed. You will not live a long and prosperous life in the land you are crossing the Jordan to occupy.
19 As witnesses I call heaven and earth. I have given you the choice of life or death, blessing or curse. Choose life, so that you and your descendants will live.
20 You must make the choice to love Adonai, and to obey Him, and to commit yourself to Him, for He is your life and the length of your days. Then you will be able to live peacefully in the land that Adonai swore to give to Abraham, Isaac, and Jacob.

---

15. Look! Today I have set before you a free choice. Choose between life and goodness on one side, and death and evil on the other side.
The choice is yours. One depends on the other. If you choose goodness, then you will enjoy a happy and successful life. However, if you choose evil, then you will only suffer defeat and death.

19. As witnesses I call heaven and earth. I have given you the choice of life or death, blessing or curse.
I, Adonai, have given mankind free will. Humans can choose their own ethical and moral environment. If you commit yourself to Adonai, then you and your descendants will live happy and productive lives. The choice is yours to make.

19. Choose life, so that you and your descendants will live.
Today this verse is applicable to many modern-day destructive lifestyles. Choose life and stay away from alcohol and drugs. Choose life and control your eating habits and an urge to gamble. Choose life and wear a seat belt. Choose life and study Torah.
Shenash

20. Then you will be able to live peacefully in the land that Adonai swore to give to Abraham, Isaac, and Jacob.
Adonai promised the patriarchs that if their descendants became worthy, they would achieve their historic goal and occupy the Promised Land and live in peace.

20. You must make the choice to love Adonai, and to obey Him, and to commit yourself to Him, for He is your life and the length of your days. Then you will be able to live peacefully in the land that Adonai swore to give to Abraham, Isaac, and Jacob.
The Torah warns the Israelites that if they want to live peacefully in their land, they must do three things:
1. love Adonai
2. obey Him
3. commit themselves to Him

The text refers to the Land of Israel. However, "in the land" can also refer to wherever you live. The Torah, the commandments, and the love of Adonai can be obeyed wherever you live–"in your land."

וַיֵּלֶךְ *Vayelech*

MOSES WENT AND SPOKE TO THE ISRAELITES

31 Once again Moses spoke to the Israelites and said to them: **2** Today I am 120 years old and I can no longer lead you. Adonai has told me that I shall not cross the Jordan River. **3** But Adonai Himself will go across before you. He will destroy the nations living there, and you will defeat them as Adonai has promised. Joshua is the one who will lead you across.

Be Strong and Courageous *2nd Aliyah*

4 Adonai will destroy the nations just as He destroyed the Amorite kings Sichon and Og, and their lands. **5** When Adonai makes you victorious over them, you must do everything that I have commanded you. **6** Be strong and courageous. Do not be afraid of the other nations. Adonai is going with you, and He will never fail you.

Joshua Becomes the Leader of Israel *3rd Aliyah*

7 Moses summoned Joshua and, in the presence of all Israel, said to him, "You must be strong and courageous, because you are the one who will bring this nation to the land that Adonai promised their ancestors He would give them. You are the one who will divide up the land among them.

---

1. Once again Moses spoke to the Israelites. This is the fourth sermon (31:1–33:29) which Moses delivered to the Israelites before he died. In this farewell address Moses blesses the tribes. He also delivers the famous song of Moses, in which he praises Adonai for His goodness to the Israelites. He tells them, "You are a nation sheltered by Adonai." With that Moses steps off the stage of history and climbs Mount Nebo to disappear.

1. Moses spoke to the Israelites. Great leaders prepare for death by training a successor that they can trust. Moses went to each tribe and personally informed them that he was about to die. He assured the tribal leaders that Joshua, whom he had trained, was an extremely capable leader. He urged them to obey Joshua, just as they had obeyed him.

1. Today I am 120 years old and I can no longer lead you. In rough computation, ancient Israel considered a generation to be approximately forty years. Moses' age as given here is three times forty years, which may mean that he was an old man who had lived to see his grandchildren grow to adulthood.

6. Be strong and courageous. Do not be afraid of the other nations. Adonai is going with you, and He will never fail you. This is the example Moses set for his people. Many times when Israel had sinned, Moses pleaded for them and the punishment was averted. Now he must die before entering the Promised Land in punishment for his sin of pride and disobedience. He does not plead for himself, but first he worries about who will care for his people. This is a true leader, a model for later chiefs of Israel to follow. We may all learn from Moses' devotion to duty, ever cautious not to abuse his relationship with Adonai to obtain an advantage.

7. Moses summoned Joshua, and in the presence of all Israel, said to him, "You must be strong and courageous, because you are the one who will bring this nation to the land that Adonai promised their ancestors He would give them." The midrash says that when Adonai appointed Joshua to succeed Moses, both of them went into the Tabernacle. A cloud separated the two leaders and Adonai spoke only to Joshua. Moses had lost the ability to hear Adonai's voice. Now Moses was aware that his leadership was officially ended and the new leader was his protégé, Joshua.

8 But Adonai is the One who will go before you. He will never fail you or abandon you, so do not ever be afraid of your enemies."
9 Then Moses wrote the last scroll [Devarim] of the Torah and gave it to Levi's descendants, the priests who carried the ark of Adonai's covenant, and to the elders of Israel.

You Must Read the Torah   4th Aliyah

10 Then Moses gave them the following commandments: At the end of every seven years, at the time of the forgiveness of debts (*shmittah*) during the Festival of Sukkot, **11** when all Israel come to present themselves before Adonai in the sanctuary that He will choose, you must read the Torah before all Israel, so that everyone will be able to hear it. **12** You must assemble all the Israelites, the men, women, children, and all the foreigners who live in your cities, and let them hear it, so that they will learn to respect Adonai and to obey carefully all the commandments. **13** Do this so that your children, who have not yet learned the laws, will listen and learn to respect Adonai. If you do this, you will live a long time in the land you are crossing the Jordan to occupy.

Teach This Poem to the Israelites   5th Aliyah

14 Adonai said to Moses, "The time is approaching for you to die. Call Joshua to come to the Meeting Tent, where I shall give him instructions." So Moses and Joshua went into the Meeting Tent. **15** Then Adonai appeared at the entrance of the Tent in a pillar of cloud.

---

9. Then Moses wrote the last scroll (Devarim) of the Torah and gave it to Levi's descendants.
Moses gave the complete Torah, from Bereshit, the first book, to Devarim, the last and fifth book, to the Levites, who were the teachers of the Torah. They in turn presented the Torah to the elders, who then presented the entire Torah to the Israelites.

The Torah was physically transferred three times: from Moses to the Levites, from the Levites to the elders, and from the elders to the Israelites.

Each generation has continued passing the Torah to the next generation. The Torah has been passed down into your hands. You are now studying the Torah which was recorded by Moses four thousand years ago.

11. When all Israel come to present themselves before Adonai in the sanctuary that He will choose, you must read the Torah before all Israel, so that everyone will be able to hear it.
The systematic reading of the Torah has had an extraordinary educational and spiritual impact on the life of Jews throughout their history. The Torah is not just read, it is studied and explained; and its ethical lessons are applied to the daily life of Jews no matter where they reside. The Torah is the cornerstone of the Jewish religion and has had a profound effect on Jewish survival. Judaism is a religion centered on this sacred document.

12. You must assemble all the Israelites, the men, women, children, and all the foreigners who live in your cities, and let them hear it, so that they will learn to respect Adonai and to obey carefully all the commandments.
Mitzvah number 612 is known as *hakhel*, "gathering together." On the intermediate days of Sukkot, trumpets were blown to assemble everyone to listen to the reading of the Torah.

14. So Moses and Joshua went into the Meeting Tent.
Joshua (Hoshea) son of Nun, of the tribe of Ephraim, Moses' assistant and general, after Moses' death led the Israelites into Canaan.

He conquered Jericho and nearly the entire land of Canaan and helped the Israelites settle in their new land.

Joshua defeated six enemy tribes in six years. He staunchly upheld the Israelites' religion against the new influences of Canaan. With the high priest Pinchas, he established the sanctuary of the ark in Shiloh. Joshua died at the age of 110.

16 Adonai said to Moses, "When you die and join your ancestors, this nation will begin to worship idols in the Promised Land which they are about to enter. They will forget Me and reject the covenant I have made with them. **17** Then I will be angry and abandon them. I will ignore them and they will be destroyed.

They will be surrounded by many troubles, and they will say, 'Adonai has abandoned us because we have sinned. That is why these evils have befallen us.' **18** When that time comes, I will completely abandon them because they have sinned and worshipped idols.

19 Now write down the words of this poem and teach it to the Israelites. Make them memorize this poem so that it will serve as a warning for the Israelites.

I Will Tolerate No Excuses *6th Aliyah*

20 "I am bringing them to a land flowing with milk and honey – the land I promised to give to their ancestors – where they can eat and live in luxury. Then they will begin to worship idols and reject My covenant. **21** Then, when they are surrounded by disasters and troubles, this poem will be like a witness and will remind them that they have no excuse for their disobedience. Even before I brought them into the Promised Land I knew exactly what they were thinking and what they were going to do."

22 On that day, Moses wrote down the words of this poem, and he taught it to the Israelites.

23 Adonai also gave Joshua instructions and said, "Be strong and brave, and I will help you bring the Israelites into the land I have promised them."

24 Moses, at the very end of his life, finished writing the [fifth] scroll of the Torah [and he called it Devarim].

---

19. Now write down the words of this poem and teach it to the Israelites.
This is mitzvah number 613 and is the last mitzvah of the Torah. It is a mitzvah for every Jew to write a Torah for himself. Unfortunately, this mitzvah is impossible for most Jews. The writing of a Torah must be done by a skilled *sofer* (scrive) in accordance with specific rules and regulations. Fortunately this mitzvah can be accomplished by participating financially in the purchase of a Torah. The primary purpose of this mitzvah is to involve everyone in the study of Torah and to encourage every Jewish home to have a Jewish library.

19. Now write down the words of this poem and teach it to the Israelites.
Our sages say that this poem (Devarim 32:1–43) was dictated to Moses by Adonai, who said "Now write down the words…"

The words of this poem were the result of Adonai's inspiration.

23. Adonai also gave Joshua instructions and said, "Be strong and be brave, and I will help you bring the Israelites into the land I have promised them.
Authority is respect, and it must be earned, just as Joshua earned his leadership. He was a successful military leader, a brave spy, and a wise assistant upon whom Moses depended for advice. It was a natural transfer because Moses had preplanned it.

24. Moses, at the very end of his life, finished writing the (fifth) scroll of the Torah.
Adonai transmitted all of the Torah to Moses by speaking to him. Then Moses recorded everything exactly as a stenographer takes word-by-word dictation. The Torah is called *Torah min ha-Shamayim* (Torah from heaven), meaning that the Torah is a written message from Adonai.

Place the Scroll in the Ark
7th Aliyah

25 Moses then instructed the Levites who carried the ark of Adonai's covenant, saying,

26 "Take this [fifth] Torah scroll and place it inside Adonai's holy ark so it will serve as a witness for the Israelites.

27 I am well aware that you are rebellious and stubborn. Even now, while I am here with you, you are rebelling against Adonai. How much more rebellious will you be when I am dead.

Assemble the Israelites
Maftir

28 "Assemble all the leaders of your tribes and your judges, and I will teach them the words of this poem. I will call upon heaven and earth as witnesses against them.

29 I know that after I die you will become corrupt and turn away from the path that I have commanded you to follow. In days to come, disasters will surround you because you will do evil in the eyes of Adonai, and anger Him by making idols."

30 Then Moses recited all the words of this poem to the entire assembly of Israel from beginning to end.

---

26. Take this (fifth) Torah and place it inside Adonai's holy ark so it will serve as a witness for the Israelites.
The fifth Torah scroll was placed inside the ark with the Ten Commandments.

26. Take this fifth Torah scroll and place it inside Adonai's holy ark.
The fifth scroll was Devarim. The Torah that is read in your synagogue is an exact duplicate of the Torah which Moses gave to the children of Israel. Today every synagogue has an *Aron Kodesh* (holy ark) facing east toward Jerusalem. The *Aron Kodesh* contains the congregational Torah scrolls. A Torah scroll must be written by someone who is specially trained. That person is called a *sofer* (scribe). The Torah is handwritten in a special script on parchment made from a kosher animal skin. An ancient writing instrument, a feather pen, is used to write the Torah. It is written with no punctuation marks and no vowels. The Torah reading is chanted in special musical notes called *trope*.

Each week a different section of the Torah is read in the synagogue. Each section is called a sidrah. There are fifty-four sidrot in the Torah, just enough for one complete year. At the end of the year, after the Torah is completely read, there is a special celebration called Simhat Torah.

As soon as the reading of all the sidrot is completed, the cycle is begun all over again.

27. I am well aware that you are rebellious and stubborn. Even now, while I am here with you, you are rebelling against Adonai. How much more rebellious will you be when I am dead?
How did Moses know what the Israelites would do after he was gone? He knew because Adonai in verse 16 specifically told him. Why didn't Moses just say, "Adonai told me"?

The Israelites were already aware that Moses, their beloved leader, was about to die, Moses hoped that his forty years of dedicated service to their welfare would be an effective deterrent against rebellion.

הַאֲזִינוּ *Ha'azinu*

O HEAVENS, GIVE EAR

The Poem of Moses and His Blessings

32

O heavens, give ear
And I will speak;
O earth, hear the words
Of my mouth.
2 My truths shall fall like gentle rain, My commandments like dew, Like water on growing plants, like showers on tender grass.
3 I will shout the name of Adonai, I will give glory to His name.
4 He is the Rock, His decisions are just;
Adonai is faithful, never false; He is true and upright.
5 Those who are unfaithful to Him, that crooked and unworthy generation have not obeyed Him.
6 Is this how they repay Adonai? You foolish, stupid people.
Is He not your Creator? He formed you, He gave you life.

Remember the Past
2nd Aliyah

7 Remember the generations gone by,
Think about times that have passed;
Ask your parents, and they will tell you.
Ask your graybeards, and they will explain.
8 When Adonai gave nations their territories
And created different races, He set up boundaries for the people
According to the number of beings.
9 The people of Israel belong to Adonai, the Children of Jacob are in His care.
10 He found Israel in the wilderness
Filled with howling wind; He strengthened and protected them
Just like His own eyes.

---

1. O heavens, give ear and I will speak; O earth, hear the words of my mouth.
In this sidrah, the poem of Moses is the final review of Israel's history.

2. My truths shall fall like gentle rain. My commandments like dew, like water on growing plants, like showers on tender grass.
Dew and rainwater fall on the earth and help trees, flowers, and other growing things spring to life and beautify and feed the people.

Moses wants his words to enter the hearts and minds of Israelites and implant holiness into their lives.

6. Is this how they repay Adonai?
Adonai has freed you from slavery. How easily you have forgotten the one who has given you a new life. Is this how you repay your Creator?

6. He formed you, He gave you life.
You were a bunch of slaves and He made you into a nation among the nations of the world.

8. When Adonai gave nations their territories and created different races.
Rashi says that this refers to the generation after the flood. They were punished by being scattered across the earth for building the tower of Babel (Bereshit 11:1–9).

11 Adonai was like an eagle
Teaching its newborn to fly;
So He spread His wings to protect them
And carried them aloft between His feathers.
12 Only Adonai guided them,
All alone with no foreign helpers.

They Turned Away from Adonai
3rd Aliyah

13 He brought them to high mountaintops,
And they feasted on the crops of the land;
He fed them honey from the rocks
And olive oil from stony soil.
14 He fed them yogurt from the flocks
And milk from the herds.
He fed them fat lambs and male goats,
And rams pastured in Bashan
With the best of grain.
They drank fine wine from bloodred grapes.
15 But soon Jeshurun [Israel] grew fat and rebelled,
They became bloated and crude;
They abandoned Adonai, who made them,
And rejected the help of the Rock.
16 They made Him jealous by worshipping idols,
They angered Him with revolting ceremonies.
17 They sacrificed to demons,
To useless foreign idols
Whom your ancestors never worshipped.

---

11. Adonai was like an eagle teaching its newborn to fly.
The slaves of Egypt were reborn and became a new and free nation. He gave them the Torah, the book of laws and commandments, and the wisdom to live a good and holy life.

13. He fed them honey from the rocks and olive oil from stony soil.

The song of Moses enumerates the blessings that Adonai bestowed on Israel, in the land of Canaan. Even the rocks of the country produced honey and oil. The honey flowed from the bee hives between the rocks and caves. The olive trees grew among the rocks in the Galilee. The olive and its oil played an important role in the economy of Israel. In ancient times Israel was called "the land of olive trees."

15. But soon Jeshurun (Israel) grew fat and rebelled.

Jeshurun is another name for Israel. The name "Jeshurun" comes from the Hebrew word *yashar*, meaning, "to be righteous." Here the name Jeshurun is used with contempt.

The "righteous ones," meaning the leaders and the teachers, have become more enamored of power and money and have abandoned the commandments and forsaken Adonai. They rebelled against Adonai because of food, drink, and luxuries.

They turned their back on the laws of Torah and began to mimic and participate in idol worship of the Canaanite inhabitants. Too much of the good life fattened them and they rebelled against the Torah.
Targum Onkeles

> 18 You turned away from the Rock
> That gave birth to you,
> You forgot the One who gave you life.

Adonai's Anger
4th Aliyah

> 19 Adonai saw this and was angry, so He abandoned His children.
> 20 He said, "I will hide My face from them, and then they shall see
> what will happen to them,
> For they are a disloyal generation, unfaithful children.
> 21 They have made Me very bitter
> And angered Me with their idol worship;
> Now I will make them jealous with a nation of fools.
> 22 Now, My anger is blazing, and it will flame down
> Into the bowels of the underworld.
> It will consume the earth and its crops,
> And it will ignite the foundations of mountains.
> 23 I will bury them with calamities; I will shoot arrows at them.
> 24 I will send famines and plagues; epidemics and wild beasts
> And poisonous snakes will engulf them.
> 25 In the streets they will die by the sword, and in their homes terror will reign.
> Against young and old alike,
> Against nursing children and against oldsters.
> 26 I said, 'I will reduce them to nothing';
> I will erase the memory of their existence.
> 27 But I was afraid that their enemies might boast,
> 'We have achieved a victory,
> And we won without the help of their Adonai.'"
> 28 People of Israel! You have no sense,
> You cannot tell right from wrong.

---

18. You turned away from the Rock that gave birth to you.
The prophet is incredulous: "How could you reject the one that gave birth to you?" Can a person reject his father or mother? You, to your shame, did.

19. Adonai saw this and was angry, so he abandoned His children.
Adonai loved His children, the nation of Israel, but they did not return His love. He gave them the Torah and brought them into their own land, the Land of Israel, but both of the precious inducements failed to cleanse them of their sins.

So now in anger He chose to punish them through Exile. During the time of the First Temple, the Israelites were also exiled.

20 He said, "I will hide My face from them, and then they shall see what will happen to them, for they are a disloyal generation, unfaithful children."
This disloyal generation abandoned Me and worshipped idols.

20. He said, I will hide My face from them, and then they shall see what will happen to them.
I will stop trying to improve their lives and stop protecting them from their enemies.

27. But I was afraid that their enemies might boast, "We have achieved a victory."
Rashi says that the enemy will claim victory because of their power and strength.

The End Results
5th Aliyah

29 If you were smart, you would stop and think;
You would see the end result.
30 Is it possible for one soldier to defeat thousands,
Or for two to rout ten thousand?
Yes! If the Rock stopped protecting them,
And Adonai allowed it to happen.
31 Remember! Their pebble is nothing compared to our Rock.
Even our enemies know this.
32 Their wine is from evil Sodom,
From the vineyards of Gomorrah;
Their grapes are filled with bitterness,
Their clusters are poisoned.
33 Their wine is snake venom and the poison of cobras.
34 I have secreted that poisonous wine, safely secured it in My vaults.
35 Vengeance is mine, I will repay them when their feet slip.
Then their time of doom nears, and fate will finish them.
36 Adonai will save His people and have pity on His servants when He sees
the weakness of their leaders and their people.
37 He will say: Where are their idols? The rock that they depend on,
The idols who ate the best of their offerings,
38 And drank their wine offerings?
Can these idols now help you, can they now protect you?

---

30. Yes! If the Rock stopped protecting them.
Adonai stopped protecting the Israelites because of their sins. Just a few of the enemy defeated thousands of Israelites. This could never have happened if the Rock had not stopped protecting Israel.

32. Their wine is from evil Sodom, from the vineyards of Gomorrah.
Those nations who oppose the children of Israel are drunk on the poisonous wines of Sodom and Gomorrah. Those wicked nations who oppress Israel are also Adonai's enemies. In time they will surely receive their just desserts.

32. Their grapes are filled with bitterness, their clusters are poisoned.
The clusters of grapes glisten in the sun and are beautiful to look at. However, their beauty is a mockery because their juice is bitter and filled with poison.

33. Their wine is snake venom and the poison of cobras.
In ancient times, rulers and kings were frequently assassinated by drinking poisoned wine or eating poisoned food. The enemies of Israel will drink the poisoned wine of doom, defeat, and death.

35. Vengeance is mine, I will repay them.
Adonai promises that He will take revenge against the enemies of Israel. History has proved Adonai right. The ancient enemies of Israel–Babylonia and others–are footnotes in history books, while the modern state of Israel is alive and well.

36. Adonai will save His people and have pity on His servants when He sees the weakness of their leaders and their people.
Adonai will come to the aid of His people because of the righteous ones in their midst. He has seen His people lost and at the end of endurance, close to being wiped away, their leaders weak and helpless. It is now time for Adonai's intervention.
Sforno

39 Don't you realize
There is only one Elohim,
Who sends death and gives life,
Who sickens and heals?
None of your idols
Can save you from My decrees.

Vengence on Adonai's Enemies *6th Aliyah*

40 I will raise My hands and promise and swear:
As surely as I live forever,
41 When I sharpen My gleaming sword,
I will heap vengeance on My enemies,
On my enemies who hate Me.
42 I will drench My arrows in their blood,
And My sword will devour the flesh
Of corpses and prisoners
From the long-haired enemy chieftains.
43 Many nations will praise Israel.
He will heap vengeance on His enemies,
And He will purify the land of Israel.

Teach Your Children *7th Aliyah*

44 Moses came with Hoshea son of Nun and recited all the words of this poem to the people. **45** When Moses had finished reciting the poem to the Israelites, **46** he said to them, "Pay close attention to every word of my warning to you today, so that you will be able to instruct your children to observe carefully all the words of this Torah.

---

40. I will raise My hands and promise and swear: as surely as I live forever.
Today when someone takes an oath in court, he or she raises a hand and swears to tell the truth.

43. He will heap vengeance on His enemies.
The vengeance will be selective and only the enemies of Israel will suffer and be destroyed.

44. Moses came with Hoshea son of Nun.
Notice that Joshua is now called Hoshea. Hoshea was his original name. Rashi says, "To teach us that he was not conceited even though he was now the confirmed leader."

Moses is now securing and consolidating the powerful new leader of the Israelites. Moses in trying to confer his charisma on his successor.

44. Moses came with Hoshea son of Nun and recited all the words of this poem to the people.
Before the curtain falls on the life of Israel's great leader, Moses, he speaks to his successor, Joshua, before all the people: "You must be strong and courageous, because you are the one who will bring this nation to the land that Adonai promised their ancestors He would give them" (Devarim 31:7).

Moses also assures Joshua that Adonai will be with him and he has nothing to fear. Then in another dramatic scene he speaks his farewell words to his beloved people. Moses' farewell address contains nothing of the many difficulties which he has had with them, no criticism. Rather, like a loving father, he blesses them and wishes them happiness.

46. Pay close attention.
I want you to concentrate all of your faculties on the words of the Torah.

47 It is not an empty teaching. It is your life, and with it you will long endure on the land which you are crossing the Jordan to occupy."

Moses Views the Promised Land *Maftir*

48 On that very day, Adonai spoke to Moses, saying:

49 "Climb Mount Avarim to Mount Nebo, in the land of Moab facing Jericho, and see the land of Canaan that I am giving the Israelites as an inheritance.

50 You will die on the mountain that you are climbing, and be gathered up to your people, just as your brother Aaron died on Mount Hor and was gathered to his people.

51 This is because you broke faith with me in full view of the Israelites at Mai Meribah (Waters of Dispute) at Kadesh in the wilderness of Zin, and because you did not sanctify Me among the Israelites.

52 Therefore you will see the land from afar, but you will not enter the land I am giving the Israelites."

---

47. It is not an empty teaching.
Just remember my warning and pass it on to your children. Your Torah is not just a lot of words. If you follow the rules and commandments, you will successfully conquer the land of Canaan.

47. It is your life, and with it you will long endure on the land which you are crossing the Jordan to occupy.
The study of Torah is considered the noblest pursuit of man. Education was esteemed above all other pursuits, and the *Talmud haham* (scholar) was the ornament of the community. The Torah makes the education of the young a religious duty. For almost two thousand years, universal elementary education has been a Jewish communal responsibility.

The Talmud records: Joshua b. Gamala instituted that teachers should be appointed in every province and in every city, and children above the age of six or seven were placed in their charge.

A medieval Jewish authority, Israel Al-Nakawa, wrote: The education of the young is a communal obligation. Every community must provide teachers for the children. A city without pupils is doomed.

Today every congregation has a religious school for its children. So prominent was study in the Jewish scale of values that Judah the Prince stated: The studies of schoolchildren may not be interrupted even for the building of the Holy Temple.

49. Climb Mount Avarim to Mount Nebo, in the land of Moab facing Jericho, and see the land of Canaan that I am giving the Israelites as an inheritance.
Moses, who freed and led a group of slaves out of Egypt, is now at the end of his tumultuous and historic career. He is now old and tired. Adonai permits Moses to view the Promised Land from afar. Now he has to transfer the reins of leadership to his faithful protégé.

There never was, or will be, another charismatic, holy leader like Moses.

49. And see the land of Canaan that I'm giving the Israelites as an inheritance.
To be effective, an individual must see the object he or she is blessing. Adonai ordered Moses to ascend Mount Nebo and see the land of Canaan from afar, and to view and bestow a blessing on the land.

Vezot Ha'berachah וְזֹאת הַבְּרָכָה

THIS IS THE BLESSING

33 This is the blessing that Moses, man of Adonai, gave to the Israelites just before his death. **2** Moses said:

Adonai came down from Mount Sinai and shone on us from Mount Seir; He appeared from Mount Paran and came with numerous angels. He brought a fire with His right Hand.

3 You love all the nations, but Your holy ones grasp You by the hand. They step in Your footsteps, and cherish Your words.

4 Moses brought us the Torah; it is Israel's eternal heritage.

5 He was Israel's king when the people's leaders gathered and the tribes of Israel were united into one. **6** Let Reuben live and not perish, though the tribe is few in number.

7 Moses said to Judah:

May Adonai listen to Judah's voice and return him to his people. Although he is powerful, help him against his enemies.

---

1. *Vezot haberachah*–this is the blessing.
Chapters 33–34 complete the Torah cycle and are read only on Simhat Torah. The Torah reading cycle is completed with this last sidrah and now starts all over again. The study of the Torah is never ending. The Talmud tells us *hafoch bah, v'hafoch bah*. Keep studying the Torah and you will always find new interpretations and new ideas.

1. This is the blessing that Moses, man of Adonai, gave to the Israelites just before his death.
The poem is called "This is the Blessing" because it consists of a series of blessings upon the tribes of Israel (Simeon excepted). Each blessing mentions some distinctive feature of each of the tribes.

1. This is the blessing that Moses, man of Adonai, gave to the Israelites just before his death.
Moses' farewell song had both words of warning and words of consolation, so that the Israelites would know that if they turned against Adonai they would face calamity, but if they obeyed Adonai and His commandments Adonai would console and comfort them.

Moses is called "man of Adonai" because he observed all of Adonai's commandments.

2. Adonai came down from Mount Sinai and shone on us from Mount Seir.
The giving of the Ten Commandments is pictured as a sunrise and the Torah as Israel's eternal heritage.

2. Adonai came down from Mount Sinai and shone on us from Mount Seir, He appeared from Mount Paran and came with numerous angels. He brought a fire with His right hand.
Adonai made an overture to the children of Ishmael who lived around Mount Paran to accept the Torah, but they refused.
Rashi

4. Moses brought us the Torah.
The sages said that when Moses left to climb Mount Nebo, those watching him climb to his death praised him, saying, "Moses brought us the Torah."

5. He was Israel king when the people's leaders gathered and the tribes of Israel were united into one.
When the leaders and the tribes of Israel are united into one single state of religious, social and political unity, only then will Adonai be their king.
Sforno

6. Let Reuben live and not perish, though the tribe is few in number.
At that time the small tribe of Reuben was under attack by the Moabites.

The Blessings of Levi and Benjamin   *2nd Aliyah*

8 To Levi Moses said:
Your Urim and Thumim belong to you. You tested Adonai at Massah, and disputed him at the waters of Meribah.

9 He said of his parents, "I do not consider them."
He disagreed with his family.
But he kept teaching and guarded Your covenant.
10 They shall teach Your law to Jacob,
and Your Torah to Israel.
They shall place incense before You and sacrifices on Your altar.
11 I pray that Adonai will bless his effort and
prosper the work of his hands.
May He smash the bodies
Of those who rebel against him,
so that his enemies will never rise.
12 To Benjamin he said:
You are Adonai's beloved.
You shall safely dwell beside Him.
Adonai constantly protects him
and dwells among their hills.

The Blessings of Joseph   *3rd Aliyah*

13 To Joseph Moses said:
His land is blessed by Adonai,
with precious dew from heaven,
and running waters that lie below,
14 Your crops will ripen in the sun,
and sweeten in the light of the moon,
15 The best crops from the mountains
and abundance from the ancient hills.
16 The gifts of the land and its riches
and the blessing of the One
who dwells in the thornbush.
May blessings encircle Joseph's head,
Crowning the prince among his brothers.

---

8. To Levi Moses said.
Moses blessed the tribe of Levi because they killed all of those who worshipped the golden calf.

10. They shall teach your laws to Jacob, and your Torah to Israel.
The Levites will be in charge of teaching the Israelites the laws and customs of the Torah. In addition they will also be in charge of the sanctuary and the sacrifices.

12. To Benjamin he said: You are Adonai's beloved.
Moses called the tribe of Benjamin "Adonai's beloved" because in the future the Holy City of Jerusalem would be located in its territory.

17 Joseph has the strength of a bull, and his horns are as powerful as a wild ox.
With his horns he shall wound nations at the far ends of the earth.
They are the tens of thousands of the tribe of Ephraim and the thousands of the tribe of Manasseh.

The Blessings of Zebulun, Issachar, and Gad *4th Aliyah*

18 To Zebulun Moses said:
Zebulun! Be happy when you travel. Issachar! Rejoice in your homes.
19 They invite nations to the mountain, to offer righteous sacrifices.
They will be fed by the bounty of the sea and by the secret treasures of the sands.
20 To Gad Moses said:
Blessed is the One who helps the territory of Gad expand.
He is like a fierce lion, waiting to bite the arm and the head.
21 Gad chose the best land for himself,
He received a special leader's share.
When the leaders came together, they followed Adonai's decrees
and judgments about Israel.

Blessings of Dan, Naphtali, and Asher *5th Aliyah*

22 To Dan Moses said:
Dan is a young lion, leaping out from the hills of Bashan.
23 To Naphtali Moses said:
Naphtali will be completely happy
And filled with Adonai's blessings.
He shall possess the land to the south and west of Lake Kinneret.

---

17. Joseph has the strength of a bull.
By "Joseph," Moses is referring to his sons, the tribes of Ephraim and Manasseh.

18. Issachar! Rejoice in your homes.
The territory of Issachar was the fertile eastern section of the *Emek Jezreel* and the northern hills, near the tribe of Zebulun. Issachar's emblem was a donkey; its black banner depicted the sun and the moon. The stone representing Issachar in the High Priest's breastplate was probably a sapphire.

19. They will be fed by the bounty of the sea and by the secret treasures of the sands.
Zebulun was the sixth and last son of Leah. Its assigned territory was between the Sea of Galilee and the Mediterranean and was a haven for ships. The tribe was also involved in maritime shipping. The sands on the beach will provide the material with which to manufacture glass.

20. Blessed is the One who helps the territory of Gad expand. He is like a fierce lion, waiting to bite the arm and the head.
Gad was given a larger portion in Trans-Jordan, since the territory of Kings Sichon and Og was very large. Gad deserved the larger portion because his tribe was like a lion capable of defending itself against enemies.

21. Gad chose the best land for himself.
Gad was Jacob's seventh son; the first-born of Zilpah, Leah's handmaid. Gad's territory was the rich pasture land on the eastern side of the Jordan. Moses granted their request for this land on the condition that they first accompany the rest of the tribes to conquer the territory of Canaan.

23. Naphtali will be completely happy.
According to tradition, the tribe of Naphtali was so successful that they usually were the first to bring their *bikkurim* to the Holy Temple in Jerusalem.

24 To Asher Moses said:
Asher is the most blessed among the sons.
He shall be accepted as the favorite by his brothers,
and may his land produce much olive oil.
25 Your defenses are stronger than iron and copper,
and you will became more powerful each day.
26 Israel! Remember, there is none like Adonai, He speeds through the heavens to save you, He is majestic in the skies.

Sheltered by Adonai
6th Aliyah

27 Adonai is my refuge above, and underneath are His everlasting arms.
He will shatter the enemy before you, and shall shout "Destroy!"
28 As prophesied by Jacob, Israel will dwell in safety in a land bursting with grain and wine, Your heavens will also drip with dew.
29 Happy are you, Israel! Who is like you?
You are a nation sheltered by Adonai, He is the Shield who helps you,
He is your magnificent Sword.
Your enemies will bow down to you, And you shall trample upon their backs.

Moses Dies
7th Aliyah

34 From the plains of Moab Moses climbed up to Mount Nebo, to the top of Mount Pisgah, facing Jericho. Adonai showed him all the land of the Gilead as far as Dan,

---

24. And may his land produce much olive oil.
The territory of the tribe of Asher was famous for its olive trees and the oil they produced.

25. Your defenses are stronger than iron and copper.
You have fortified your lands against attacks by enemy forces.

27. Adonai is my refuge above, and underneath are His everlasting arms.
This is the first sentence of the 6th aliyah in the sidrah. On the holiday of Simhat Torah we read the last and the first sidrah of the Torah. We conclude the one-year cycle and start a new cycle by reading the first sidrah in the Book of Bereshit.

The person who is honored by reading the last section is called the *Hatan Torah*, the Bridegroom of Torah.

The honoree who restarts the cycle by reading from the first sidrah is called *Hatan Bereshit*, Bridegroom of Bereshit.

28. Israel will dwell in safety.
Rashi says that every Israelite will enjoy freedom and dwell in safety. Every Israelite will enjoy life sitting peacefully under his grapevine and under his fig tree, and Israel and the world will know no war.

1. From the plains of Moab Moses climbed up to Mount Nebo, to the top of Mount Pisgah, facing Jericho.
Before he died at the age of 120, Moses climbed up to Mount Nebo to the top of Mount Pisgah and from there Adonai allowed him to look out over the Promised Land before he died. His gaze traveled across the Dead Sea as far as the Mediterranean to the west, the Negev to the south, and the Galilee to the north. Canaan was his destination from the moment Adonai spoke to him from the burning bush. Moses died alone on the mountain top. Adonai buried him somewhere facing the beloved land and no one ever knew his burial place (Dev. 34:6).

The children of Israel mourned the beloved leader for thirty days.

2 all of the land of Naphtali, all of the land of Ephraim and Manasseh, all of the land of Judah as far as the Mediterranean Sea, **3** as far as the Negev, the Jordan Valley and Jericho, the city of palm dates, as far as Zoar.

4 Then Adonai said to him, "This is the land that I swore to give to Abraham, Isaac, and Jacob, saying, 'I will give it to your descendants.' Now I have let you see it with your own eyes, but I will not allow you to cross the river and enter it."

5 So Moses, Adonai's servant, at His command, died in the land of Moab. **6** Adonai buried him in the valley in the land of Moab, near Beth Peor. No one, even to this day, knows the place where he was buried. **7** Moses was 120 years old when he died, but his eyes were sharp and he was still strong and healthy. **8** For thirty days the Israelites mourned Moses on the plains of Moab. When the mourning period for Moses came to an end, **9** Joshua son of Nun acquired the spirit of wisdom, because Moses had laid his hands on him. The Israelites listened to him and obeyed him exactly as they had obeyed Moses. **10** There never was another prophet in Israel like Moses, whom Adonai knew face-to-face. **11** No one else could have performed all the wonders and miracles that Adonai allowed Moses to perform before Pharaoh in the land of Egypt, **12** or any of the powerful miracles and awesome deeds that Moses performed before the eyes of all the Israelites.

---

2. All of the land of Naphtali, all of the land of Ephraim and Manasseh, all of the land of Judah as far as the Mediterranean Sea.
The Mediterranean Sea is mentioned as the natural border of the Promised Land on the west. In the Torah, the Mediterranean is called the "Crest Sea" or the Sea of the Philistines.

The Euphrates River is mentioned as the northeast boundary.

4. This is the land that I swore to give to Abraham, Isaac, and Jacob.
Adonai did not allow Moses to enter, but He allowed him to view the land from the mountain.

The Midrash tells us that Moses as a prophet was able to see the entire history of the Israelites unfold before his eyes.

And so he saw their times of joy and their times of sadness, their moments of victory and their moments of defeat.

5. So Moses, Adonai's servant, at His command, died in the land of Moab.
Even in his death, he acted as Adonai's servant, performing exactly as commanded.

6. Adonai buried him in the valley in the land of Moab, near Beth Peor. No one, even to this day, knows the place where he was buried.
His gravesite was specifically hidden to prevent the Israelites from turning his grave into a shrine and worshipping Moses as a cult figure.

7. Moses was 120 years old when he died, but his eyes were sharp and he was still strong and healthy.
Most of Moses' life was spent in the service of Adonai. Life was not easy for the greatest leader the Hebrews ever had. Despite the dangers and the problems of leadership, his mind and his spirit were still sharp. His eyes could still see the Promised Land in the distance.

Each year the entire Torah is read aloud in the synagogue. When it is completed, the members of the congregation stand up and recite:

חֲזַק חֲזַק וְנִתְחַזֵּק

"Be strong and have courage."

This means, "be strong and live according to the rules and teachings of the Torah."

SPIRITUAL LEADERS and TORAH COMMENTATORS

Page

522 Yohanan ben Zakkai, 1st Century B.C.E.

524 Hillel, 1st. Century B.C.E.

526 Rabbi Akiba, 40-135 C.E.

528 Abba Arikha, 3rd Century C.E.

530 Ezra and Nehemiah, 5th Century B.C.E.

532 Judah HaNasi, 2nd Century C.E.

534 Saadia Gaon, 882-942

536 Rabbi Shlomo ben Itzhak (Rashi), 1040-1105

538 Maimonides (Rambam), 1135-1204

540 Rabbi Moses ben Nachman (Nachmanides), 1194-1270

542 Gersonides, Levi ben Gerson, (Ralbag) 1288-1345

544 Obadiah Sforno 1475-1550

546 Joseph Karo, 1488-1575

548 Isaac Abrabanel, 1437-1508

550 Rabbi Isaac Luria, 1534-1572

552 Israel ben Eliezer (Baal Shem Tov), 1698-1760

554 The Gaon of Vilna, 1720-1797

YOHANAN BEN ZAKKAI, 1st CENTURY B.C.E.

The early Romans were peasants farming the seven small hills beside the Tiber River in central Italy. They were continually attacked by powerful enemies. At first it was a case of poorly armed farmers fighting professional soldiers. But the Roman army soon became well organized. In time the Romans defeated their enemies and took control of the whole Mediterranean world. After many battles, Rome carved out provinces in Spain, France, Sicily, Greece, Tunisia, and part of England. The Rhine and the Danube Rivers were its northern boundary, and much of the Middle East was its eastern boundary.

The Romans Defeat Judea

In 63 B.C.E. the Romans overran Judea and made it part of their far-flung empire. They appointed governors called procurators, who ruled the country with an iron hand. The procurators imposed high taxes and stole the gold from the Temple treasury.

The people of Judea hated the Roman yoke. In 66 C.E., led by the Zealots, they rebelled against the Romans and drove them out of Jerusalem. The Jews were elated, even though they knew that Rome would not give up easily.

Unable to accept defeat, the Romans sent a powerful army, under the command of Vespasian, to stamp out the revolt. Vespasian conquered Galilee and most of Judea, then returned home to become Rome's new emperor.

The Siege and Fall of Jerusalem

Vespasian's son Titus took command of the army and in 70 C.E. began the siege of Jerusalem. It went on for several months. Despite hunger and hardship, the people of the city held out courageously. Day and night they heard the heavy thud of Roman battering rams and the noise of ballistas, which shot 100 pound boulders into the city. The outer walls of Jerusalem crumbled.

Portrait coin of Vespasian, 69-79 C.E.

On the ninth of Av, Roman troops stormed the Temple area. They climbed the walls and hurled burning torches into the city. In moments the Temple was aflame. Some of the Jewish fighters tried to escape to make a stand in another Judean fortress. A few succeeded, but most were killed or captured.

During the revolt against Rome, the rebels minted bronze and silver coins. The inscriptions read: "Freedom of Jerusalem" or "For the Redemption of Zion." Coins such as this one were found in Masada.

When Titus returned to Rome, the Jewish captives were paraded through the streets. They were forced to carry the golden menorah and other loot from the Temple. The Romans erected the Arch of Titus to commemorate the defeat of Judea. It can still be seen in Rome. One of the reliefs on the arch shows the Jewish captives marching in Titus's triumphal procession.

Judea was destroyed and more than a million people died in the war. Thousands were carried off into exile and slavery. Their dreams of independence were drowned in a sea of blood. The land of Israel, now called Palestine, was again ruled by a Roman governor. Jewish communities throughout the world mourned for Judea, for Jerusalem, and above all for the Temple, which had been the spiritual center of their lives. Despite the loss of their land and their Temple, Jews continued to live in accordance with the laws of the Torah. It gave them hope and courage to face the future.

The Jewish defenders who faced the might of Rome were poorly armed. On the other hand, the Romans were equipped with the most modern armaments of the period. Roman catapults could hurl heavy boulders with great force. The Romans also employed battering rams, which destroyed defense walls and paved the way for the Roman infantry.

A copy of the carving on the Arch of Titus, showing the menorah and other furniture of the Temple being carried in triumph through the streets of Rome.

Rabbi Yohanan ben Zakkai

In the days before the siege of Jerusalem, many Jews felt that Rome was sure to win. They feared that Judaism would not survive if the Romans were victorious.

But there were others who believed that the Torah itself was enough: even if land and Temple were lost, the Torah would provide a bond to unite the world's Jews and give meaning to their lives. Among those who held this view was Rabban Yohanan ben Zakkai, a scholar who had been a member of the Great Sanhedrin.

Yohanan ben Zakkai felt that Judaism would survive if the Torah lived in the hearts of the people. He taught that dignity would come not from rebellion but from observance of Jewish law.

As the Roman army neared Jerusalem, Yohanan thought of a way to preserve the Torah. He decided to start a school–an academy of Jewish learning where the Torah could be studied and halachic questions discussed. It would be located at a distance from Jerusalem so as to be safe from the fighting.

In those days it was impossible to leave Jerusalem. With the city busily preparing for the Roman attack, the Zealots were on the lookout for traitors. Anyone who tried to leave was accused of treason.

Determined to start his school, Yohanan put himself into a coffin. His students, pretending he was dead, carried him out of Jerusalem under the watchful eye of the Zealots, supposedly to bury him.

As soon as they exited the city, Yohanan jumped out of the coffin and approached the Roman general. Vespasian was willing to meet with him, for he knew that Yohanan opposed the revolt. When Yohanan predicted that Vespasian would soon become emperor of Rome, the general was pleased and promised to grant anything he requested. This was exactly what Yohanan ben Zakkai had hoped for. He asked for permission to open a school in Yavneh, a small town on the seacoast. Vespasian agreed.

At the Academy in Yavneh

At the academy in Yavneh, the scholars continued their studies. Eventually, Yohanan formed a Sanhedrin modeled after the Great Sanhedrin of Jerusalem. Beloved and respected by everyone, he was its first *nasi* (leader). When the news came that Jerusalem had fallen and the Temple had been destroyed, Yohanan wept and tore his clothes in mourning. Yet he did not allow his disciples to despair.

In the aftermath of the destruction, Yohanan realized that new judges, teachers, and scholars had to be trained and ordained as in the days of the Great Sanhedrin. The scholars would have the title of rabbi, which means "master." Once ordained, each rabbi would himself become a teacher. The rabbis educated at Yavneh would be links in the great unbroken chain of teachers of the Torah.

Yohanan and those who followed him were called *tannaim,* meaning "repeaters" or "teachers." The period in which they were active is known as the tannaitic era. It began around the time of Hillel and ended about 200 C.E.

The interior of the Yohanan ben Zakkai Sephardic synagogue in the Jewish Quarter of Old Jerusalem. It is one of the oldest synagogues in the Meah Shearim section of Jerusalem. In 1948 the synagogue was destroyed by the Arab Legion. It was rebuilt in 1972.

HILLEL, 1st CENTURY B.C.E.

In 40 B.C.E., Herod, whose family had converted to Judaism, was crowned king of Judea by the Roman Senate. He was a brilliant administrator but was very cruel to those he ruled.

Herod the Builder

While the people of Judea hated and feared Herod, the Romans valued him as an ally. During his reign Judea's prosperity increased.

Herod delighted in massive building projects. He founded two new cities in honor of his Roman friends: Tiberias, named for Tiberius, Rome's second emperor, and the coastal city of Caesarea, named for Augustus Caesar, its first emperor. He also built many fortresses, including Masada, near the Dead Sea.

Herod's Temple

Herod's most ambitious project was the reconstruction of the Temple. This was a huge task that took many years to complete. His workmen and architects renovated and completely rebuilt the Second Temple, which dated from the time of Ezra and Nehemiah. They began in 20 B.C.E. and did not finish until several years after Herod's death in 4 B.C.E.

Herod's Temple was a magnificent structure and people marveled at its splendor. He built a strong wall around the Temple, and above the main gate he placed an eagle, the golden emblem of Rome. This deeply disturbed the Jews. How could such an emblem be allowed to disgrace God's peaceful sanctuary? Didn't the Torah forbid the making of graven images? While the beauty of Herod's Temple gave him prestige abroad, it did not win him the confidence and love of his people.

An engraving in a Hebrew-Latin edition of the Mishnah (1744). It illustrates a session of the Sanhedrin.

The Sanhedrin

Distrusting Herod and the high priests, the people of Judea turned for leadership to the religious teachers who made up the Sanhedrin. The Sanhedrin was the institution where the laws of the Torah were interpreted in accordance with the Oral Tradition. Students and scholars from the Jewish communities of Egypt, Babylonia, Syria, Persia, North Africa, and Rome came to Jerusalem, the center of Jewish learning, to learn Torah. When they returned home, they would teach what they had learned. In this way, they became part of the chain of scholars and sages who kept the Oral Tradition alive.

A Roman soldier with his combat equipment. The short sword was called a gladium and the shield was called a scutum.

Herod's family tomb in Jerusalem. Here the monarch buried his wife Marianne and his two sons after murdering them in a maniacal rage.

Mishnah–The Chain of Tradition

According to the Mishnah, the chain of tradition started with Moses. At Sinai, along with the Written Torah, he received an Unwritten Torah that explained and supplemented it. Moses handed the Unwritten Torah–the Oral Tradition-down to Joshua, who in turn passed it on to the elders. From them it came down to the prophets, who handed it over to the members of the Sanhedrin. Sometimes referred to as scribes, the members of the Sanhedrin were the spiritual leaders of Judea and world Jewry.

The Great Sanhedrin, which had 71 members, met in the Temple in Jerusalem. It was presided over by two leaders. One of them was the *nasi* ("literally, prince"); the other was the *av bet din* ("presiding judge"). The two leaders in each generation are collectively referred to as the *zugot* ("pairs").

Hillel and Shammai

The most famous of these pairs of scholars were Hillel and Shammai. Hillel was a brilliant young man who came to Judea from Babylonia. Although very poor, he loved Torah learning. He earned the money to pay for admission to the lectures at the academy by cutting wood.

One cold winter's night, when he did not have the admission fee, Hillel went up to the roof of the schoolhouse and listened to the lectures through the skylight until he fell asleep. The next morning, when the academy assembled, the scholars found the hall exceptionally dark. Looking up at the skylight they saw Hillel's body blocking the sun. Touched by the young man's great devotion to learning, the teachers provided him with a scholarship.

Hillel the Sage

Hillel became a famous sage. He returned to Babylonia to teach, but was invited back to Jerusalem to join the Great Sanhedrin. Hillel said that the way to Torah and to God was to love peace and love one's fellow human beings. He valued the unity of Israel above all, and warned his students never to set themselves apart from the community of Israel.

So greatly respected was Hillel that the office of nasi of the Sanhedrin became hereditary in his family. He founded a school of Torah interpretation known as Bet Hillel ("House of Hillel").

Hillel's colleague, Shammai, the *av bet din*, was a brilliant scholar who came from one of Jerusalem's wealthy noble families. He had his own ideas, and often differed with Hillel on halachic questions. While Hillel usually took the more lenient and flexible view, Shammai interpreted the law strictly. He was a pious scholar devoted to preserving the Torah and the Jewish way of life.

Love Your Neighbor as Yourself

The difference between Hillel and Shammai is illustrated in the famous story of a pagan who tried to make fun of Judaism. He asked Shammai to explain the whole Torah within the time he could stand on one leg. Shammai became angry and chased the pagan out of his house.

Now the pagan approached Hillel and asked the same question. With a smile, Hillel calmly replied, "All of Judaism is contained in the verse in the Torah, You shall love your neighbor as yourself." The pagan was impressed and, according to the story, decided to become a Jew.

Wherever Jews studied and prayed, the teachings of Hillel and Shammai were discussed.

Despite Shammai's reputation for strictness, he believed in treating all people with friendliness.

Hillel teaching the heathen the whole of the Torah while he stands on one leg. Detail from the menorah by Benno Elkan at the Knesset in Jerusalem.

RABBI AKIBA, 40-135 C.E.

After the destruction of Jerusalem in 70 C.E., the Romans allowed Judea a period of peace and reconstruction.

Bust of Hadrian.

However, conditions changed when Emperor Hadrian decided to rebuild Jerusalem. Hadrian visited the city and personally supervised the building projects. On the site of the Holy Temple he built an altar dedicated to the god Jupiter. He also issued laws which made it difficult to practice Judaism.

Many Jews wanted to rebel against Rome and once more fight for freedom. The spirit of revolt even spread to the academy, where the scholars usually favored peace. Rabbi Akiba was one of the leaders who wanted to rebel against Rome.

Simon Bar Kozeba

By the time Hadrian became emperor, Akiba was very old. When he heard about Simon Bar Kozeba, a young man who was organizing a guerilla force to fight the Romans, Akiba felt that the time was at hand. He gave Bar Kozeba his support and renamed him Simon Bar Kochba, meaning "Son of a Star." Akiba believed that Bar Kochba might actually be the Messiah, sent by God to restore the freedom of the Jewish people.

In 1960, Yigal Yadin, professor of archaeology at the Hebrew University in Jerusalem, launched an expedition to explore the caves in the mountains near the Dead Sea. A member of the expedition, exploring one of the narrow tunnels of a cave, discovered a basket filled with objects. Further inspection revealed a treasure trove of artifacts which included sandals, knives, mirrors, jugs, bowls, and the greatest treasure of all–papyrus rolls containing about 40 letters from Bar Kochba.

The Insurrection Begins

The insurrection began in 132 C.E. and lasted for three and one-half years. Roman patrols were ambushed and Roman supplies were captured. Hadrian sent an army to support the Palestine garrison, but his troops were defeated. Bar Kochba marched and lived with his men, sharing all their hardships. He insisted on leading them himself. As a result, his men were devoted to him and would do almost anything he commanded.

Bar Kochba went from victory to victory, and the Roman army retreated into Syria. The victorious Jewish army entered Jerusalem. Under Bar Kochba's leadership, Judea enjoyed two years of independence. Then Hadrian came to Judea in person, bringing reinforcements.

A silver coin issued by the revolutionary government of Bar Kochba. He and his followers set up a Jewish state in 132-135 B.C.E. which was soon crushed by the Romans.

The Defeat of Bar Kochba

Bar Kochba and his brave fighters made a final stand in the mountain fortress of Betar, near Jerusalem. The Jewish soldiers fought desperately, but in the end Betar fell.

Judea was laid waste and completely destroyed. Hundreds of thousands of Jews were killed, and just as many were sold into slavery.

In Jerusalem, as was their custom, the Romans cleared away the rubble and plowed up the ground. On the site they built the new city Hadrian had planned, a heathen city with temples for the worship of Roman gods. It was called Aelia Capitolina.

The Romans knew that Judaism was the source of the Jewish people's strength. They concluded that if the religious leaders were eliminated, the ordinary people would yield to Roman authority. Accordingly, soldiers hunted down the most important leaders.

Rabbi Simeon Bar Yochai a member of the Sanhedrin who had been openly critical of the Romans, had to go into hiding. Rabbi Akiba was arrested and condemned to be skinned alive. With his last breath, the saintly hero proclaimed the words of the Shema, "Hear, Israel, the Lord is our God, the Lord is One."

Rabbi Akiba

Rabbi Akiba was the most outstanding of the many scholars and rabbis who taught at Yavneh. As a young man he had been an uneducated shepherd. Then he married Rachel, the daughter of his wealthy master. Over the years she made many sacrifices to enable him to fulfill his ambition of learning Torah.

When Akiba gave up being a shepherd and left home to attend the academy, Rachel cut off her hair and sold it to a wig merchant in order to pay for his tuition. Thanks to Rachel's sacrifices, Akiba was able to attend the academy of Eliezer and Joshua, who were carrying on the work of Yohanan Ben Zakkai. Akiba was not only a great scholar but a great teacher. Students flocked to the lectures at his academy at B'nei Brak.

Rabbi Akiba instructing his pupils. From the Sarajevo Haggadah.

The Mishnah of Rabbi Akiba

Rabbi Akiba initiated one of the most important projects in the history of Jewish law. With the aid of his colleagues, he set about organizing the vast body of halachot, discussions, and legal cases comprising the Oral Tradition. Akiba did not put all of this down in writing, for it was not yet the custom to do so. However, he originated the idea of classifying the material by subject.

Thanks to this system, which is known as the Mishnah of Rabbi Akiba, scholars found it much easier to locate important information.

Akiba and Rachel

Akiba was away studying for twenty-four years. When he finally returned, he was recognized as a great scholar, and was respected by thousands of students. The people crowded around to see him. Among them was an old man dressed in fine clothing but with a sorrowful face.

"Many years ago," he said to Akiba, "I made a vow. Now I am old, and do not have many years left. I regret my vow and would like to know if I can be released from it."

"What was the vow?" asked Rabbi Akiba.
"When my daughter angered me by marrying a poor shepherd," said the man, "I swore I would never speak to her or help her in any way."
"Why did you make the vow?" asked Rabbi Akiba.
"Because he was an ignorant man, who could not even read or write," said the old man.
"Vows can easily be nullified," said Akiba.
"But this one was made because of a certain condition," said the old man.
"If the condition has changed, the vow need no longer be kept," said Akiba. "You may consider your vow null and void, because I am that same ignorant shepherd."
Rachel's father was delighted to learn that his son-in-law was now a distinguished scholar.

Akiba never failed to give credit to Rachel for his achievements. When asked who was really a rich man, he always answered, "He who has a good wife."

Rabbi Akiba ben Joseph was the most respected and beloved of the talmudic sages. Most of the scholars of the following generations were his disciples. His decisions were widely accepted, and later talmudists declared that his opinions must be granted preference over all others. Because of the great importance of the Mishnah of Rabbi Akiba, the rabbis declared that he had kept the Torah from disappearing.

Holy tombs in Tiberias, from a 1598 manuscript written in Italy. The large tomb, upper right, is that of Rabbi Akiba. The tomb in the upper left is that of Rabbi Akiba's wife. She is buried in the cave below the tomb. In between and below are tombs of other rabbis.

ABBA ARIKHA, 3rd CENTURY C.E.

Babylonia was a rich, fertile country situated between the Tigris and Euphrates rivers. Jews had lived there for hundreds of years, dating back to the exile following Nebuchadnezzar's capture of Jerusalem in the sixth century B.C.E. At the time of the Second Temple, more Jews lived in Babylonia than in Judea.

The Babylonian Jewish community was rich and properous. It generously contributed toward the rebuilding of Palestine after the return from the exile. For centuries, Jews in every part of Babylonia volutaly paid a Temple tax for this purpose which was collectd in Nehardea and sent to Judea.

Magic bowl with Hebrew inscription found in the ruins of Babylon.

Some of the Babylonian Jews lived on the great fertile plains, and were farmers and cattle ranchers. Others worked in the cities as craftsmen, merchants, bankers, and traders. The Jews of Babylonia maintained their own synagogues, houses of study, and courts, although they turned for guidance to the Great Sanhedrin in Jerusalem.

Palestine–the Spiritual Center

Like Jews everywhere, the Jews of Babylonia regarded Palestine as the spiritual center of Judaism. Babylonian students, among them the great Hillel, flocked to Jerusalem to study Torah. After the destruction of the Second Temple, Babylonian Jews studied with the tanaim at the academies in Yavneh, Tiberias, and Sepphoris.

In Roman times, Babylonia was ruled by the Parthians, who were tolerant of the Jews in their land. After the two revolts, refugees from Judea streamed into Parthia's Babylonian provinces to begin a new life there. Thus the Jewish community of Babylonia grew in numbers and strength.

Rosh Galuta–the Exilarch

Babylonian Jewry was headed by an official called the rosh galuta ("leader of the exile" or "exilarch"). The exilarch ruled over all the Jewish communities in Babylonia. He collected taxes for the government as well as the taxes that the Jews levied on themselves to support their communal institutions.

The exilarch was the highest authority in the Jewish courts of justice and in all the affairs of the Babylonian Jewish community. When his carriage appeared on the streets, a runner would announce his coming. The Jews were proud of the exilarch, and showed him great respect.

Because there was often a lack of able leaders and teachers, Jewish educational and legal institutions in Babylonia eventually began to deteriorate. As a result, talented students from Babylonia went to study in the academies in Palestine, as Hillel had done centuries earlier. Two of these young Babylonians, Abba Arikha and Mar Samuel, were among the most gifted students of Judah HaNasi, head of the Sanhedrin.

Abba Arikha

In the early centuries, Babylonian Jewry's brightest young men went to study in Palestine. One of these young Babylonians was Abba Arikha ("Abba the Tall").

Because of his brilliance, Abba Arikha is usually known simply as Rav, meaning "Master." The word rav eventually became the title of all ordained rabbis.

This page from a manuscript of the Mishnah was writen between the twelfth and fourteenth centuries.

When Rav returned to Babylonia, he brought with him a copy of the newly composed Mishnah.

The exilarch appointed him inspector of markets and of weights and measures for the Jewish communities of Babylonia. As he journeyed through the land, Rav saw how slack the people's spiritual life had become. He began to reorganize the schools and synagogues.

This drinking bowl dates from the seventh century. It depicts King Shapur II on a hunt. Rav was on friendly terms with the exilarch of Persia, King Shapur II's intermediary in dealing with the Jewish community. He also enjoyed the special protection of Shapur because he had secretly contributed large sums of money to the king. As a result, Rav succeeded in easing the oppression against the Jews of Babylonia.

Eventually, Rav was appointed head of the academy at Nehardea, but he declined this post so that it could be given to another gifted student of Judah HaNasi, his colleague Mar Samuel, also known as Samuel Yarhina'ah ("Samuel the Astronomer").

Rav went on to found an academy of his own in Sura, near the city of Pumpeditha. His new school attracted many scholars and students.

The Months of Kallah

Rav instituted a revolutionary new plan of study, open to anyone who wanted to take advantage of it. Every year, during the months of Adar (March–April) and Elul (September), when the farmers could he spared from their work and when artisans and merchants could take a rest during their slack season, Rav would give a special course in Jewish law. These months were called the months of Kallah ("Assembly").

During the Kallah months and the weeks preceding the holidays, people would stream into Sura from all the provinces to attend the popular courses at the acamy. A thirst for learning took hold of Babylonian Jewry. Throughout the land synagogues and schoolhouses were improved and Jews met in great numbers to study and learn.

With the help of the Mishnah, Babylonian scholars were able to apply the Torah's teachings to life in exile. By introducing the Mishnah to their students, Rav and Samuel succeeded in making the Torah a living guide that enabled the Jews of Babylonia to deal with the many problems they faced. Samuel and Rav remained close friends and collaborators throughout their lives. Together, they revised the siddur (prayerbook). Rav wrote the beautiful Alenu prayer for Rosh Hashanah; it is still part of our daily service.

Samuel wrote a shorter version of the Shemoneh Esreh (Amidah), the Eighteen Benedictions.

The Zoroastrians

Samuel's last years were darkened by trouble.

In 226 C.E., the Parthians were overthrown by the Persians. The new rulers of Babylonia were Zoroastrians. Their priests tried to force this religion on all the inhabitants of the territories they had coquered. Since the Jews were not willing to accept Zoroastrianism, a time of persecution began.

After Samuel's death, Nehardea was plundered by desert raiders. It never regained its former importance. Now the main centers of Jewish learning shifted to Sura and Pumpeditha.

A relief from Persepolis dating from the early Second Temple period depicts Ahura Mazda, god of Zoroastrianism, the religion of ancient Persia. Zoroastrianism taught that the world was torn between two deities: Ahura Mazda, the Wise Lord, crator of heaven and earth, light, and life, who embodied the spirit of goodness, truth, and law; and Ahriman, the evil Spirit, whose essence was falsehood and death.

Fragment of an ancient manuscript siddur showing the Ahavath Rabbah prayer.

EZRA AND NEHEMIAH, 5th CENTURY B.C.E.

In 539 B.C.E. the Persians, led by Cyrus, defeated the Babylonian army. Cyrus was an enlightened conqueror and granted religious freedom to all the peoples in his huge empire, which extended From India to Egypt.

The exiled Jews of Babylon gained new hope from Cyrus's wise and tolerant policies. He gave them permission to return to Jerusalem and rebuild the Temple. To help restore the Temple's beauty, he gave them the golden bowls and other holy items which Nebuchadnezzar had stolen.

Inscribed cylinder recording the capture of Babylon by Cyrus. It tells how "without battle and without fighting, Marduk (the god of Babylon) made him (Cyrus) enter into his city of Babylon; who feared him not, he delivered into his hand." Nabonidus, the Chaldean king of Babylon, was not in favor with the priest and assisted in delivering the city to Cyrus.

The Torah of the Samaritans is housed in the synagogue in Nablus. It is written in ancient Hebrew and is extremely old.

From the biblical Book of Ezra we learn that 42,000 Jews eagerly joined the return. They were led by Zerubbabel, the grandson of one of the last kings of Judea, Jehoiachim. Now they would once again be able to live a Jewish life in their own Holy Land. Sadly, they found their once beautiful land in ruins. Fields and vineyards were overgrown with weeds. Towns that had once been busy and prosperous were deserted, with wild animals living in the ruined houses.

The pioneers did not waste time worrying about the present situation. They quickly cleared the fields, replanted the vineyards, and began to rebuild their homes.

The Samaritans

1n 586 B.C.E., when Babylon conquered Judea and destroyed the Temple, a number of Jews had been allowed to remain in the land. North of Judea, in what had been the kingdom of Israel until the Assyrian conquest in the eighth century B.C.E., lived many descendants of the tribes of' Ephraim and Manasseh. Over the years they had intermarried with the pagan peo-ples brought in by the Assyrians after they deported the Ten Lost Tribes. Their religion was a mixture of idol worship and Judaism.

The people who lived in this area called themselves Samaritans because the city of Samaria, once the capital of Israel, was their main city. Considering themselves Israelites, they wanted to be a part of the restored nation. When the exiles returned, they offered to help rebuild the Temple. The Jews from Babylon were determined to establesh a commonwealth based on the Torah. Since the Samaritans were really pagans with an Israelite veneer, the Jews refused their offer.

The Samaritans now became their bitter enemies. They attacked the Judean settlements and burned their crops. They sent false reports to Cyrus alleging that the Jews were planning a revolt against him. The king believed them and called a halt to the rebuilding of the Temple. The Samaritans were not the only enemy of the returning exiles. Edomite and Moabite raiders attacked their farms, kidnapped the inhabitants, and stole the harvest.

For the Zionists of the First Return, the future was dark. Over the next fifty years, the dwindling number of colonists suffered enemy attacks, poor harvests, and heavy Persian taxes. The tiny state of Judea was in deep trouble.

Ezra the Teacher

Among the exiles in Babylonia who were distressed by the news from Judea was Ezra, a learned man of priestly descent. Ezra was a dedicated teacher and had many students to whom he taught the Torah. Because he was highly skilled in the art of writing Torah scrolls, he is often referred to as Ezra the Scribe (Ezra HaSofer).

When Ezra asked King Artaxerxes I of Persia for permission to go to Jerusalem with his disciples, his request was granted. The king and the Jewish community of Babylonia generously gave Ezra many gifts for the Temple and also the supplies he needed for the long journey. Artaxerxes even sent along soldiers to protect the returnees.

Hebrew coin dating back to the fourth century B.C.E, the period of Ezra the Scribe. The coin is inscribed YHD (in ancient Hebrrew script), which stands for Yehud, the Persian name of Judea.

The Second Return

The Second Return consisted of about 1,300 settlers eager to rebuild their homeland. They arrived in Jerusalem in the summer of 458 B.C.E. and were warmly welcomed by the tiny Jewish community.

Ezra began his task without delay. He was saddened and disturbed to find that the people lacked any knowledge of the Torah.

Patiently Ezra and his disciples encouraged them to resume the great struggle to regain their homeland and rebuild the Temple.

Nehemiah, Governor of Judea

The next major task was to fortify Jerusalem against the hostile bands of raiders rebuilding its walls. Help came in 445 B.C.E. when Nehemiah, a Babylonian Jew, was appointed governor of Judea. Nehemiah had been the trusted cupbearer of King Artaxerxes I in Shushan (Susa), the Persian capital. A dedicated Zionist, he immediately set out for Judea, armed with royal credentials. The two great leaders of the returnees, Ezra and Nehemiah, combined their efforts to restore the commonwealth of Judea. Ezra was Judea's spiritual guide, and Nehemiah, its political leader. His enthusiasm energized the people to rebuild the walls of Jerusalem.

The walls and fortifications were completed in just 52 days. Because of the constant threat of Samaritan attacks, the workers" did the work with one hand and held a weapon with the other." The people of Judea defended the walls fiercely, and the raiders soon began to think twice before they attacked.

Nehemiah and Ezra laid the foundations of the new Jewish commonwealth The Torah was its constitution. Ezra and his students traveled throughout the land, teaching the people to live by its laws.

On the day before Sukkot in the year 444 B.C.E., thousands of Judeans made their way to Jerusalem. They built their sukkot in the ancient city of David, then assembled to hear from their two great leaders. Nehemiah and the priests and Levites of the Second Temple stood before the assembled Judeans, while Ezra read aloud from the Torah. The people, listening attentively, raised their hands and shouted, "Amen, Amen." They promised to obey the laws of the Torah. The work of Ezra and Nehemiah was followed by an era of peace for Judea. Towns and villages were rebuilt, land was tilled and cultivated. Many towns built their own marketplaces and houses of prayer.

Later on, these houses of prayer evolved into the synagogues which have become the centers of Jewish communal and religious life throughout the world.

Official seal of the province of Judah during the fifth-fourth centuries B.C.E.

JUDAH HANASI, 2nd CENTURY C.E.

After the defeat of Bar Kochba in 135 C.E., the Jewish population of Palestine sharply decreased. A huge number had been killed in the revolt or sold into slavery in other lands. Many of those who remained alive fled the Roman sword to safer parts of the world. After a while, however, a new administration in Rome made life safer for the Jews who still lived in their traditional homeland.

In 138, Emperor Antoninus Pius granted permission to reopen the schools and reestablish the Bet Din (Jewish court). During his reign Roman rule was much less harsh. The rabbis who had hidden from the Romans were now able to resume their leadership roles.

The stone cathedra (chair) of Moses from the third-century synagogue at Korazim, in Galilee. Chairs of this kind were installed in ancient synagogues for the principal teacher of the law, or for a person the community wished to honor.

With the end of the persecutions in Palestine, a new religious center was founded in the town of Usha. Rabbi Judah ben Ilai, a student of Rabbi Akiba, established an academy there. Once again the Sanhedrin was reestablished and a nasi was chosen as the spiritual head of the Jewish community.

The New Sanhedrin

The new Sanhedrin reopened schools and synagogues throughout the land. It began to ordain rabbis and set up schools where children were taught Hebrew and learned their heritage. Voluntary taxes were collected to support religious and educational institutions and help the poor.

Until this time the legal decisions of the sages had not been written down. Over the centuries a huge body of material had accumulated, known as the Oral Tradition. The Oral Tradition explained what the Written Torah meant. It consisted of lectures, questions and answers, legal opinions, discussions by the sages, and much more.

Although the Mishnah of Rabbi Akiba was an invaluable first step in systematically organizing this vast collection, there was still the problem of remembering it and handing it down. Every year, as more material accumulated, the problem became more serious. As a result, there was a great fear that the Oral Tradition and the work of the previous generations would be lost.

After the destruction of Jerusalem in 70 C.E., the center of the Jewish religious and national life shifted to the Galilee. Beth She'arim, about 10 miles from Haifa, became an important Jewish city. Rabbi Judah HaNasi made it the seat of the Sanhedrin. He also compiled the Mishnah there, and in 220 C.E. was buried there in the family tomb.

In 1953, Israeli archaeologists discovered a giant necropolis, an underground city of the dead. The numerous vaulted catacombs are cut out of the soft limestone hills around which the city was built.

After the destruction of Jerusalem, Jews could not use the traditional cemetery of the Mount of Olives, so the necropolis became the central burial ground. The necropolis is a series of long, vaulted interconnected catacombs with thousands of marble and stone coffins, some of which weigh up to five tons. The entrance to the underground city is from stone courtyards dug out of the hills. One of the catacombs contains burial sites with inscriptions that mention the talmudic sages Gamliel and Hanina.

The Six Sections of the Mishnah

1. Zeraim (Seeds): Laws of agriculture and prayer.
2. Mo'ed (Festivals): The observance of the Sabbath, festivals, and fast days.
3. Nashim (Women): Marriage and divorce.
4. Nezikin (Damages): Civil and criminal laws.
5. Kodashim (Holy matters): Temple services, and shehitah (Kosher slaughter).
6. Tohorot (Purities): Ritual purity and cleanliness.

JudahHaNasi–Judah the Prince

The task of preserving this body of knowledge fell to the genius of Rabbi Judah HaNasi–Judah the Prince. Judah the Prince succeeded his father, Simon, who had become *nasi* after the second revolt in 132 C.E. He held the office for almost 50 years.

An outstanding scholar, Judah HaNasi moved the Sanhedrin and the academy to Beth She'arim, and later to Sepphoris. As *nasi,* he had the sole authority to ordain rabbis and judges even for posts in other countries.

In Judah HaNasi's time, most Jews, even in the land of Israel, spoke Aramaic. Judah was greatly concerned about the survival of Hebrew. He wanted it to be a living language, used every day in Jewish homes. To set an example, he and his household spoke only Hebrew. It was said that Judah's servants spoke better Hebrew than many scholars. Judah used Hebrew when he compiled his great law code, the Mishnah.

Judah's love of the Torah and of Hebrew went hand in hand with wide cultural interests. He knew several languages and was learned in many subjects. He had many non-Jewish friends, including Marcus Aurelius (121-180 C.E.), a Roman emperor who was interested in philosophy.

The academy established by Rabbi Judah the Prince was a great success. Students from Babylonia and other distant places came there to study. He used to say, "I have learned much from my teachers, more from my colleagues, but most of all from my students." Judah HaNasi gave freely of his wealth to needy students and scholars.

The Mishnah–The Oral Tradition

The Oral Tradition had grown so big that some scholars could not remember all of it. The rabbis wisely decided that it was time to write everything down if the Oral Tradition was to survive. Judah set to work on the great task. The entire Oral Tradition was arranged logically according to subject. In about 200 C.E. it was put into written form that would ensure its survival.

The work that resulted from these labors is called the Mishnah. It consists of six sections, called orders (*sedarim*), *each of which is subdivided into several tractates (masechot).* All together, there are 63 tractates. The Mishnah is written in Hebrew. Several centuries later, it became the basis for the vast encyclopedia of Jewish law and lore known as the Talmud.

The Tannaitic Period Ends

When Rabbi Judah the Prince died, in about 220 C.E., he was deeply mourned by his friends, colleagues, and students. He was one of those rare men who embodied the spirit of a kind father for an entire people. "Not since Moses," the people said, "has there been a man like Judah, who so combined leadership with Torah." Judah's body was brought to burial at Beth She'arim. Everyone seemed to feel that a great era of Jewish history had come to an end.

With the death of Judah HaNasi, the tannaitic period ended. He is traditionally regarded as the last of the *tannain* (teachers).

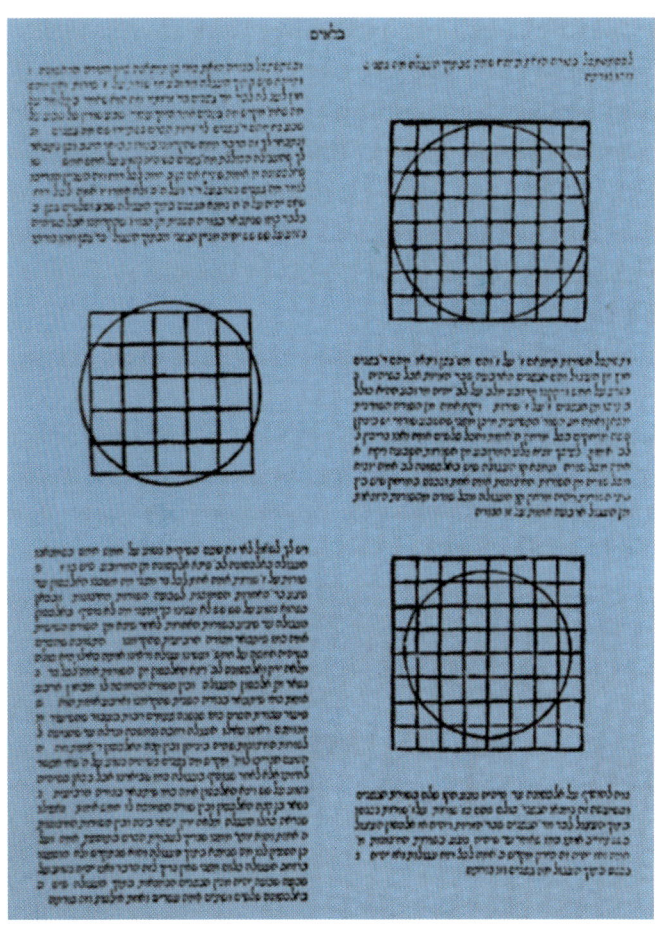

A page from the Mishnah Tractate Kilayim with explanatory diagrams. This complete edition of the Mishnah was printed by Soncino in Naples, Italy, in 1492.

SAADIA GAON, 882-942

An ancient painting showing Mohammed with the leader of a Jewish tribe in Arabia. He condemned the whole tribe to death because they refused to convert to the Muslim religion.

The Birth of Islam

An Arab named Mohammed proclaimed a new religion and called it Islam, meaning "submission" to the will of God. After his death in 632 C.E., he was succeeded by Caliph Abu Bakr and then by Caliph Omar.

Omar and his army of Bedouin horsemen conquered Egypt, Palestine, Syria, and Persia, spreading the faith of Islam to all of these lands. In 638 Omar captured Jerusalem and established a Moslem sanctuary there. Once again Jews were permitted to enter the city and to pray at the Western Wall. Soon there was a small Jewish community in Jerusalem.

Although Jewish life in Palestine revived after the Moslem conquest, Babylonia remained the main center of world Jewry. After the Arabs conquered Babylonia in 660, the situation rapidly improved. The schools of Sura and Pumpeditha reopened and were presided over by the geonim.

Under the Arabs, the Jewish community regained its autonomy. It was once again led by the exilarch, who now was authorized to collect taxes both for the caliph and for the Jewish community. The gaonim were given the right to select the exilarch, but their choice had to be approved by the caliph.

Geonim and Responsa

Whenever Jews anywhere were in doubt on questions of Jewish law, they would send messengers to the geonim in Babylonia. The Babylonian scholars sent their answers and legal decisions in clear, concise letters known as *teshuvot* (responsa). Ever since, decisions on halachic questions by Jewish scholars have been set down in accordance with the form used in the gaonic responsa. Nowadays responsa are still written by prominent rabbis who are experts on the halachah.

To teach the alefbet to young Hebrew scholars, this book was produced in tenth century Egypt. This page was found in the Cairo genizah.

The gaonic period extended from the seventh to the eleventh century. During this era the geonim sent teachers to acquaint Jews in far-off communities with developments in Sura and Pumpeditha, and to teach the Talmud.

By this means, knowledge of the Talmud was spread far and wide, and a bond was established among the many groups that made up world Jewry. Jewish communities thousands of miles away in Spain learned Talmud under teachers from Babylonia and sent teshuvot to the Babylonian academies.

Over the centuries of exile, Jews were becoming confused and divided by many issues. Some doubted their religion. Others believed in magic, or waited for the Messiah, or refused to accept the authority of the gaonim. There was no strong leader to guide them in this time of turmoil and confusion. Fortunately, in the midst of the crisis, a leader stepped forward who was not afraid to battle for traditional Judaism. That man was Saadia Gaon.

Saadia Gaon

Saadia Gaon was a scholar, an author, and the leader of Babylonian Jewry. His achievements marked him as one of the most important personalities of the period. Saadia was born in 882 in a village in Egypt. Even when he was a young man, his brilliance was apparent. He mastered the entire range of Jewish literature and also studied Moslem literary and scientific writings.

Eventually, Saadia settled in Babylonia, where he became the gaon (head) of the yeshiva in Sura. Saadia felt that the best way to improve the quality of Jewish learning was by applying the methods of science and philosophy. Since there were as yet no Hebrew grammars or Bible dictionaries, he set to work to provide some of these important tools.

Saadia Gaon was a profound religious philosopher. One of his greatest works was Sefer ha-Emunot ve-De'ot ("The Book of Beliefs and Opinions"), which explains Judaism's fundamental beliefs and ideas. Written in Arabic, it was helpful to the many Jews in Arabic-speaking countries who no longer spoke or read Hebrew.

Saadia was an accomplished poet in both Arabic and Hebrew. He translated the Bible into Arabic and put together one of the first Jewish prayer books. It was called the Siddur, meaning "order" (of prayer).

The First Hebrew Prayer Book

Saadia's Siddur was a very important achievement. Until this time the synagogue service had no fixed order or content. Now a more or less standardized service came into use among Jews everywhere. He wrote books on Jewish law, and his halachic decisions had been studied and quoted by generations of Jewish scholars.

In the days of Saadia Gaon, the prestige and power of the geonirn reached their high point. Saadia Gaon died at the age of 60. In his relatively short life his talent and personality made him one of the dominant figures in the development of Judaism and its literature.

After the death of the great master, the importance of the Babylonian schools diminished, and with it the influence of the geonim.

Page from a commentary by Saadia Gaon on Sefer Yezirah ("The Book of Creation"). The illustration shows the division of the universe into the four basic elements of water, air, fire, and earth.

Title page of the Emunot ve-De'ot by Saadia Gaon. The edition was printed in 1562, in Constantinople.

RABBI SHLOMO BEN ITZHAK (RASHI), 1040-1105

Christian Europe felt threatened by the rise of Islam and was concerned about the Moslem control of Jerusalem. To Christians as to Jews, Palestine was the Holy Land. It was holy because Jesus, the father of their faith, had lived and preached there.

Edict of Louis VI banishing the Jews from France in 1145. He appropriated their homes, money, and personal property. By exiling the Jews, he cancelled his large debt to the Jewish money lenders. The clever king also collected all the debts owed to the Jews by his Christian subjects.

The First Crusade

In 1095, a church council met in France and announced the First Crusade. This was to be a holy war to liberate Palestine from the Moslem unbelievers. The Crusader armies assembled to march to the Holy Land. Inflammatory sermons by the clergy raised the anger of the Crusaders against aliens and infidels.

Painting by Engelbert of Haselback showing the massacre of Jews, the poisoners of wells.

Victims of the Holy War

Throughout the eleventh century, the Jewish communities of the Rhineland in western Germany had been great centers of rabbinic scholarship. The yeshiva in the cities of Mainz, Worms, and Cologne had been crowded with hundreds of young and old Talmud students. Unfortunately, these cities were on the line of march of the Crusaders, and their Jewish inhabitants became the first victims of the "Holy War." In May 1096, the soldiers of the First Crusade killed or forcibly converted the Jews of Worms, Mainz, and Cologne. The destruction of these centers of learning increased the importance of a yeshiva in France headed by the scholar Rashi. Rashi and his students assumed the leadership in Jewish scholarship. Like lights glowing in the darkness, they kept the flame of Jewish learning alight.

Rashi the Scholar

Despite the grim situation in the Middle Ages, Jewish scholarship was ensured by the birth of a child in the year 1040 in the French city of Troyes. This child was destined to become the most popular and important figure in Ashkenazic rabbinic Judaism-Rabbi Shlomo ben Itzhak, popularly know as Rashi.

As a young man, Rashi studied at the academy in Worms, Germany. The parents and relatives of many of the students at the academy were engaged in international trade. They discussed their journeys in far-away lands with their children. In this way the students obtained a great deal of knowhow about business, agriculture, manufacturing and crafts, foreign countries, modes of travel, and other matters.

Rashi's knowledge of the world was greatly enriched by what he learned from his fellow students. On his return to Troyes, he earned his living from his vineyards, but devoted most of his time to teaching and

Rashi's Cursive Script

Mem Sofit	ם	ם	**Alef**	א	ﬡ
Nun	נ	ﬡ	**Beit**	ב	ב
Nun Sofit	ן	ן	**Gimel**	ג	ג
Samech	ס	ס	**Daled**	ד	ד
Ayin	ע	ﬠ	**Hay**	ה	ה
Fay	פ	פ	**Vav**	ו	ו
Fay Sofit	ף	ף	**Zayin**	ז	ז
Tzadi	צ	ﬞ	**Chet**	ח	ח
Tzadi Sofit	ץ	ץ	**Tet**	ט	ט
Quf	ק	ק	**Yud**	י	י
Resh	ר	ר	**Khaf**	כ	כ
Sin	ש	ש	**Khaf Sofit**	ך	ך
Tav	ת	ת	**Lamed**	ל	ל

Rashi was constantly writing new commentaries. It was very time-consuming to use the regular Hebrew alefbet so Rashi used a script that was much faster to write.

The Rashi chapel in the city of Worms, the synagogue where the great commentator worshipped and taught.

writing.

When the Holocaust of 1096–the First Crusade destroyed the yeshivot of the Rhineland, Rashi's tiny yeshiva became the most important center for tal-mudic study in Germany and France.

The Jews were forced to become the most despised of money lenders and collectors of rags, old clothes, and junk. They were shut up into ghettos and lived in a world where they were hated. Yet in the midst of this dangerous world of darkness and hatred, the Jews at home kept the light of learning burning bright. Learning flourished under the most adverse circumstances. The Jews built no cathedrals but they did establish academies of higher learning.

The responsibility of one Jew for the welfare of his fellow Jews was a primary principle of Jewish ghetto life. The poor were supported, the captives were ransomed, and the dead were given dignified burials. Religious and community duties were carried on with a sense of dignity and concern.

Rashi the Commentator

Before long Rashi's influence spread throughout the Jewish world. Students flocked to his yeshiva, and scholars everywhere corresponded with him, asking his advice on questions that confused them.

Rashi was the first commentator to help the ordinary Jew understand biblical and talmudic texts. His Torah commentary made it possible for everyone, even those who were not full-time scholars, to study the Bible with understanding.

There are two aspects to most biblical passages: the *peshat*, the simple, plain meaning, and the *derash*, the poetic meaning. In writing his commentary, Rashi first looked for the *peshat*, searching the body of Jewish literature to see what earlier scholars had suggested; if he couldn't find a satisfactory *peshat* meaning, he took the *derash* route and looked for a fanciful explanation.

In his commentary, Rashi quotes every biblical word or phrase that requires explanation, and then briefly clarifies it by reference to the Jewish sources or on the basis of his own knowledge. Since he lived in France, and his students were all familiar with the language of the country, he sometimes used French words in order to make the Bible's meaning as clear as possible. When he uses a French word, he prefaces it with the phrase *b'laaz*, meaning "in a foreign tongue." It was very time-consuming to write the regular Hebrew *alefbet*. So Rashi used the cursive script that was much easier and faster to write. Most of the early commentaries of the Torah and the Talmud are printed in Rashi script.

Rashi's Family

In addition to his commentary on the Torah, Rashi produced a commentary on the Talmud. His genius lay in his ability to simplify and edit the explanations offered by generations of scholars.

Rashi's work of commenting on the Bible and Talmud was continued by his grandsons. The most prominent of them were Rabbi Shmuel ben Meir (1080-1174), known as Rashbam, and Rabbi Jacob ben Meir (1100-1171), known as Rabbenu Tam. Rashi's daughters were also famous for their great wisdom and knowledge.

A study holl in the Rashi chaptel .

MAIMONIDES (RAMBAM), 1135-1204

The Golden Age of Spanish Jewry lasted for three centuries, starting around the year 900. The situation began to change when the Almohades, a fanatical Moslem sect from North Africa, invaded Andalusia. With the fall of Cordova in 1149, the Almohades became the new rulers of Moslem Spain.

Portrait of Maimonides.

The Spanish Jews Escaped

Unlike the earlier Moslem rulers, the Almohades sought to convert everyone to Islam. They persecuted Jews and Christians alike, forcing them to become Moslems or leave the land. Many Spanish Jews set out for North Africa.

Among them was Moses Maimonides. When he was 13 years old, his family fled to North Africa to escape persecution. There, as in Spain, Moses studied with his father, who was a judge to the Jewish community.

A page from a Hebrew bible with Rashi's commentary.

Several years later the family moved to Jerusalem. Because of the crusaders in Palestine, the family was once again forced to flee. This time they went to Egypt.

Moses Maimonides is often called Rambam in Hebrew, an acronym for Rabbenu Mosheh ben Maimon. Maimonides was well versed in Hebrew, the Bible, the Talmud, and other Jewish writings. He also studied mathematics and astronomy, Arabic literature and Greek philosophy. Moses even managed to study medicine and became a skilled physician.

The reason we know so much about Maimonides and his family is the *genizah* in Fostat, a town in Egypt. Every ancient synagogue had a storeroom called a *genizah*. In it were placed old prayer books and religious objects that could not be destroyed because they contained God's name. Often the genizah was also the storehouse for business documents and personal correspondence.

The Genizah

Around the beginning of the twentieth century, Professor Solomon Schechter began to catalogue and

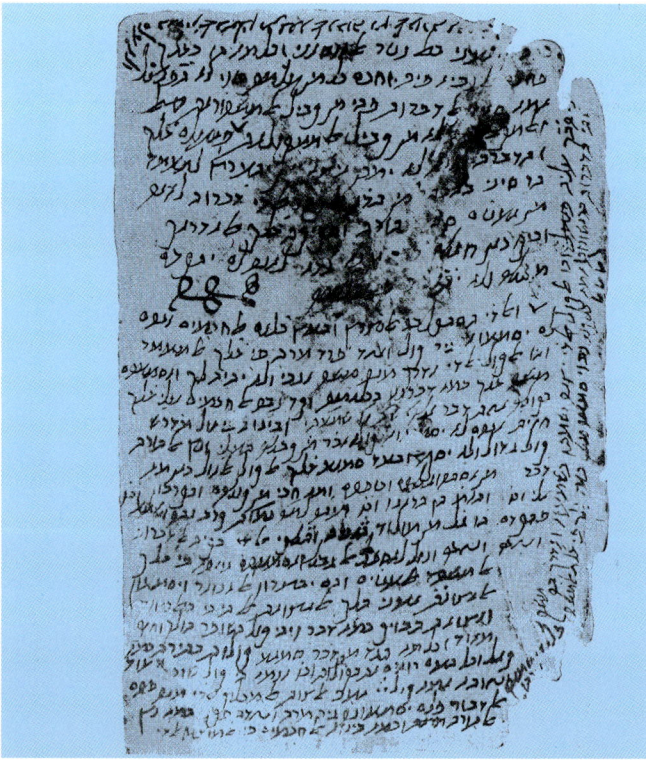

Holograph (a page written in the original handwriting of the author) of Maimonides. This is a page of the Guide to the Perplexed, written in Arabic in Hebrew letters by the Rambam himself.

translate the 200,000 Hebrew and Arabic documents in the genizah of the Ezra Synagogue in Fostat. This was the very synagogue where Maimonides had taught and prayed.

The treasure trove included hundreds of business letters from Moses Maimonides' younger brother, David. The letters give many details about his travels and business activities, as well as about the family.

The genizah documents tell us much about Maimonides' personal life. In one letter he writes, "The ordinary people find it difficult to visit me in Fostat, so I am forced to greet them in Cairo. When I get home I am too tired to study."

Even as a young man, Maimonides wrote brilliant books and essays. When the Jews of Morocco were hard pressed by the Almohades to become Moslems, they asked Maimonides what they should do. He advised them to leave the place of forced conversion; "Whoever remains in such a place," he said, "desecrates the Divine Name and is nearly as bad as a willful sinner."

Maimonides in Egypt

After much wandering, Maimonides and his family went to Egypt. He set up a medical practice in the city of Fostat, near Cairo. His fame spread, and before long he became the personal physician of Sultan Saladin and the royal family. Rich and poor, Jews and Moslems alike, patients of every background consulted him, and the great physician found time to see them all. The wealthy paid for his services, but the poor were treated free of charge.

The city of Cordova, in 1964, honored the memory of Maimonides by errecting a statue in his honor.

At the request of the *nagid*, the leader of the Jewish community, Maimonides also took on the responsibility of providing religious guidance to the Jews of Egypt. He became a greatly beloved teacher. After Sabbath services each week, he gave public lectures on Talmud and Torah.

Maimonides the Author

Despite his many duties, Maimonides managed to write the most important code of Jewish law since the completion of the Talmud. This great halachic code is called the Mishneh Torah ("Repetition of the Torah") or Yad HaChazakah ("The Strong Hand").

The Mishneh Torah codifies all the laws in the Mishnah and the Talmud, together with the commentaries of the gaonim and the scholars in the generations following them. Maimonides' best-known philosophical work is the Moreh Nevukhim ("Guide to the Perplexed"), written in Arabic. In it he clearly explains the principles and ideas of Judaism.

When Maimonides died in Fostat in 1204, he was mourned throughout the Jewish world. People compared him to the great leader who had led the Israelites out of Egypt in ancient times, saying, "From Moses to Moses, there was none like Moses."

Manuscript of Guide to the Perplexed (Barcelona, 1384).

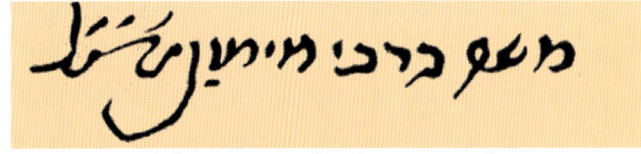

The autograph of Maimonides.

RABBI MOSES BEN NACHMAN (NACHMANIDES), 1194-1270

As Spain's Christians gradually began reconquering the country, more and more Jews came under their rule. The Christians made an all-out effort to convert them. Children were kidnapped and baptized. Enraged mobs rampaged through Jewish neighborhoods, offering the residents a choice between the church and the cross or death and the Torah. In the end, about a third of Spain's Jews chose Christianity just to save their lives. Reduced taxes and economic opportunity created an ideal environment for conversion.

Torture chamber of the Inquisition. Engraving from the Atlas van Stolk, Rotterdam, 1783.

The Marranos

The forced converts were known as Marranos, and also as New Christians, in contrast to Old Christians, who had been born into the Christian faith. By forcing the Marranos to convert, the Old Christians had unwittingly opened up areas of activity for them from which they had been excluded as Jews.

Because they proved to be so successful in these areas, the Marranos soon aroused much Old Christian resentment. Before long Marranos were advancing to positions of great political and financial influence. The Old Christians did not like this; their envy aroused, they began seeking a way to eliminate their Marrano competitors.

The Inquisition

The weapon they adopted was the Inquisition. During the twelfth century, the leaders of the Catholic Church had become concerned about the spread of heresy-beliefs and practices not in strict accordance with Catholic teachings. In 1233, Pope Gregory IV set up a special commission called the Inquisition to stamp out heresy by identifying and punishing heretics.

The Inquisition was originally established to deal with Christian heretics, but now it turned its attention to the Jews of Spain. Some of them had returned to Judaism after their forced conversions to Christianity; many others pretended outwardly to be Christians, but continued to observe Judaism secretly.

Jews were required by law to wear pointed hats and yellow badges.

Jews of both types were technically regarded as heretics and therefore came under the Inquisition's jurisdiction. Marranos who were observed changing bedsheets on Friday or leaving a candle burning were arrested. Those whom the Inquisition could not persuade to abandon Judaism were burned at the stake in a public ceremony known as an auto-da-fé. In the years that followed, thousands of Marranos were tortured and burned to death.

In an effort to persuade Spain's Jews and Marranos that Christianity was the only true religion, a convert appropriately named Pablo Christiani persuaded the king of Aragon to force Spanish Jewry's foremost scholar to debate him publicly on the belief in Jesus.

Rabbi Moses Ben Nachman

The rabbi chosen to defend Judaism in the debate between the royal court and high-ranking church dignitaries was Moses ben Nachman, also known as Nachmanides and as Ramban.

Nachmanides was Spanish Jewry's most important scholar and rabbinic leader. He earned his living as a doctor and also served as rabbi to the Jews of Gerona. Nachmanides proudly stood before the court and the king, facing the fanatical Pablo and the other church officials. In the debate Pablo tried to prove that Jesus was the Messiah, quoting isolated talmudic statements to support his claim.

Medieval Jewish scholars, distinguishable by their knobbed hats, dispute a point of faith with their Christian counterparts. From a woodcut by Johann von Armssheim, 1483.

Nahmanides' synagogue in Jerusalem. From the Casale Pilgrim, a sixteenth-century guide to the holy places of Palestine.

Nachmanides easily contradicted him. The statements quoted by Pablo, he explained, were legends and tales that had no historical bearing on what Jews believed. The important part of the Talmud was its legal portion, the halachah, and this contained nothing to support Pablo's arguments.

The wisdom of the aged Nachmanides impressed the king, who ended the debate without declaring Pablo the victor. On parting with Nachmanides, the king gave him a generous gift.

Not long afterwards Nachmanides published a transcript of the debate. Although the debate would have been publicized if the Christian spokesman had won, church officials were not eager to have Nachmanides' spirited defense of Judaism circulated.

When Pablo heard what Nachmanides had done, he reported it to the king. Once again Nachmanides was summoned to appear before the king. At the insistence of church officials, he was sentenced to two years in exile.

Nachmanides in Palestine

Nachmanides left Spain and went to Palestine. The aged scholar devoted the last years of his life to the Jews of Palestine. He built a synagogue in Jerusalem and opened a school. Scholars and students gathered around him. Before his death Nachmanides saw the results of his work. The religious life of the Jews in the land of Israel had been enriched and revitalized through his efforts.

Today in Jerusalem there is a synagogue in the Old City called the Ramban Synagogue. It is believed to have originally been situated on Mount Zion. However, it was moved to its present site around 1400. A letter written by Nachmanides about the miserable state of the Jewish community is displayed there.

In the sixteenth century the Turkish government prohibited Jews from praying in the Ramban Synagogue and it became a workshop. During the British Mandate it was converted into a store.

After the First World War, the mandates for Palestine, Syria, and Iraq were detached from Turkey. At a conference at San Remo in 1920, the Palestine mandate was granted to Great Britain, which had militarily occupied the country since 1917.

When the Israelis captured the Old City during the Six-Day War in 1967 it was rebuilt, and it is now used as a synagogue again.

Seal of Nachmanides found near the city of Acre.

GERSONIDES, LEVI BEN GERSON (RALBAG), 1288 – 1345

In the year 800, Pope Leo III crowned Charlemagne, or Charles the Great, as the Emperor of the Romans. Charlemagne's lands were later called the Holy Roman Empire to show that they were Christian and that they recognized the authority of the Pope.

Charlemagne the Ruler

In 1249 the seventh crusade was headed by Louis the Pious.

Charlemagne was a Frank by nationality. The Frankish civilization had grown and its people had adopted many Roman ways and converted to Christianity. Charlemagne was a brilliant man and a great ruler. His kingdom consisted of the lands that eventually would become France and Germany. He realized that his Jewish subjects could contribute much to the growth of trade. Ignoring the advice of the bishops, Charlemagne protected the Jews in his empire and put no restrictions on them.

Charlemagne also managed Church affairs by himself and reserved the right to appoint bishops and other church officials independent of Rome. After his death, there were long and bitter struggles for power between the popes and the emperors.

During the reign of Louis the Pious, the son of Charlemagne who adhered to his father's policies, the Jewish communities prospered. The bishops tried in vain to influence the new emperor to restrict the rights of the Jews. Louis the Pious continued to protect his Jewish subjects as his father had done before him.

Byzantine coin of Emperor Heraclius.

Meanwhile in the Byzantine Empire, Christian emperor Heraclius, who ruled from 610 to 641, feared the rising power of the Mohammedan religion. To safeguard the Christian faith, Heraclius had declared all religions except Christianity forbidden within his dominions. Thus the practice of Judaism, too, was outlawed in the Byzantine Empire.

Philip the Fair, the king of France, orders the expulsion of the Jews.

The Expulsions

Many kings followed the example of the Byzantine emperor. A king of Gaul had expelled from his domain all Jews who resisted conversion to Christianity. The kings of Burgundy and Lombardy did the same. In 1306, the Jews of France were expelled by King Phillip the Fair. In 1315 the Jews were recalled but were required to live in four principal cities, Avignon, Carpentra, Isle-sur-Seqund, and Cavallon. In the Jewish world this region was known as "The Four Communities."

Levi Ben Gerson–Leon de Bagnols

Levi Ben Gerson, or Leon de Bagnols, was also called Leo the Hebrew, but more usually by his literary name, Gersonides (born 1288, died about 1345). He was a man of universal knowledge, a living encyclopedia of his age. A famous Talmudist and Bible scholar, Gersonides was also a natural scientist, a physician, an astronomer, a mathematician, and above all a profound thinker.

Maestro Leon de Bagnols, as he was called as a physician, lived in Orange, Perpignan, and in Avignon, at that time the home of the popedom who protected the Jews. Therefore, he had not been a sufferer in the expulsion of his co-religionists from this land; but his heart bled at the sight of the suffering, which the exiles were made to undergo.

Although Levi lived in Provence, where, under the protection of the popes, the Jews suffered less than in other provinces of France, he sometimes lamented over the suffering of the Jews, which he said was "so intense that they render meditation impossible."

In an epilogue to his commentary on Deuteronomy written in 1338, he says he was unable to revise his commentary on the Pentateuch at Avignon, because he could not obtain there a copy of the Talmud.

Two pages from the "Birkat Hamazon" (1514) by Gersonides.

Ralbag the Scientist

Gersonides' major scientific work was the book *Milhamot Adonai,* "Adonai's Wars." It is an astronomical Hebrew text of 136 chapters. The text covers trigonometry, construction of astronomical instruments, as well as solar, lunar, and planetary motion. Pope Clement V had the book translated into Latin. Levi's best-known invention was the Jacob's Staff. It was an important navigational tool and was popular by navigators including Columbus, Magellan, and Basco de Gama. Levi also invented the camera obscura, which was an optical apparatus consisting of a darkened chamber into which light is admitted through a convex lens. This invention eventually developed into the modern camera.

Though he was a distinguished Hebrew scholar, Gersonides never held rabbinical office. He made his living practicing medicine.

Tittle page of Adonai's Wars, the chief work of Levi Ben Gershon, published in Italy in 1560.

Page from the first edition of Levi ben Gershom's commentary to the Torah, Mantua, 1480.

RABBI OBADIAH SFORNO, 1475 – 1550

The Jews first came into contact with the Greek and Roman world when they began expanding into the Near East. After the destruction of the Second Temple in Jerusalem by Titus in 70 B.C.E. the Jews lived under the political and cultural world of the Greeks and Romans.

The Diaspora

It was during this period that the Jews were dispersed throughout the European territories. The dispersion (diaspora) was advanced by voluntary immigrants and also by large masses of Jews sold as slaves by their Roman conquerors. These Jews were soon freed by their masters. The scattering of Jews throughout Greek and Roman Europe took place because of economic and commercial factors.

A Jewish inscription found in the catacombs in Rome, Italy.

Wherever Jews settled, they set up close-knit communities and established synagogues, making it easier to continue their traditional ways of life.
There were Jewish communities in Egypt, Greece, and Italy, and the majority of Italian Jews lived in Rome. By the second century there were twelve synagogues in Rome.

In the catacombs, there are Jewish inscriptions.
At the end of the thirteenth century, Jews were attracted to the self-governing towns of northern Italy.
Although ghetto walls had been erected in Rome, the Jews fared better there than in other parts of Europe.

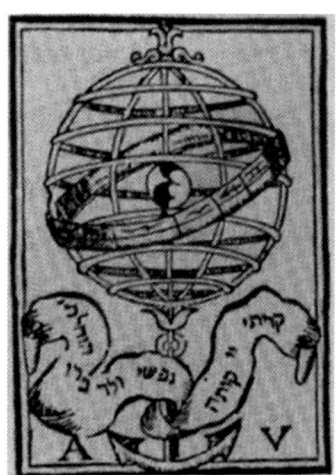
Hebrew emblem of the Italian printer Abraham Usque.

Bull of Pope John, May 29, 1554, ordering the burning of the Talmud.

Italy attracted the persecuted Jews from Spain, Germany, France, and England. Jewish traders, printers, bankers, seafarers, mapmakers, doctors, and scholars flooded to Italy.

A Pariah Caste

In the sixteenth century, the diaspora Jews were turned into a pariah caste by the legislation of the popes and princes. The Roman Inquisition,

A street in the Jewish ghetto in Venice, Italy.

the burning of the Talmud, creation of the Rome ghetto, and expulsion of the Jews from the Papal state were signposts of a virulent anti-Semitism that has persisted into the twenty-first century and was one of the causes of the Holocaust.

Obadiah Sforno

Obadiah Sforno was an example of the type of universal man who enriched the Renaissance era in Italy. Born in the town of Cesena in 1475, he studied medicine in Rome

Doctor bleeding a patient, a primitive form of medical treatment.

and soon acquired renown as a physician. In the Hebrew literature of that period, he is mentioned as "the great doctor" *(abir ha-rofeim)*.

Sforno was also proficient in Talmudic literature, mathematics, and philosophy. In Bologna he established a Talmudic academy, and he himself served as the head of an academy all his life until his death in 1550. During the time of the Reformation, many Christians became interested in Hebrew literature. Sforno moved with ease among the intellectuals of the Christian community and was retained by Cardinal Johann Reuchlin to teach him the Hebrew language. However, despite the interest in Judaism, the position of the Jews behind the ghetto walls did not change for the better.

Italian Renaissance society was devoutly Christian and mostly hostile to Jews. However, the Jews of Trent lived on the best of terms with their Christian neighbors. They owned homes, built a special school for their children, and participated in communal activities.

In 1475, the unfortunate murder of the child Simon of Trent provided an opportunity for the priest Bernadinos to ignite anti-Jewish sentiments with the accusation of ritual murder. Even Pope Sixtus IV sanctioned the proceedings, which as usual were based on a web of lies.

As a result, the Jewish community was totally destroyed, Many Jews were murdered and the pitiful remainder of survivors were expelled.

Sforno the Commentator

Sforno composed a commentary on Euclid's mathematics, but obtained his fame chiefly through his commentaries on Scripture. He wrote a commentary to the whole Pentateuch, the Book of Psalms, the Song of Songs, Ecclesiastes, Job, and other biblical books and as well as a commentary on *Pirkei Avot* ("Sayings of the Fathers").

This versatile and cultured man battled with extreme determination against the widely accepted notion that the Torah is based merely on belief and not on knowledge. Only from the Bible, Sforno asserts, do we learn of the central role of man in the structure of the universe. Only from the Torah do we become aware that the whole extent of the universe, all the spheres and planets, were created for the sake of man, and that man is endowed with free will so that he can strive to become like his Creator. Only the divine Torah illuminates our eyes with true knowledge.

Two pages from the fifteenth century manuscript of a prayer book in Judeo-Italy.

JOSEPH KARO, 1488-1575

Starting in the thirteenth century, the Ottoman Turks expanded militarily and conquered many territories. Hordes of galloping Turkish cavalrymen carved out a large state in Asia Minor and parts of Europe. Their unstoppable advance brought an end to the decadent, thousand-year-old Byzantine Empire. On May 13, 1453, the armies of Sultan Mahomet II completed the Turkish victory by capturing the Byzantine capital of Constantinople.

View of Constantinople, seventeenth century.

The Sultan and Jews

Proud of his victory, the sultan realized that his warriors knew how to fight a war, but lacked the skills and education to run a great empire. Mahomet did not trust the political reliability of the Greek and Armenian middle class in the newly conquered lands. He realized that the Jews expelled from Spain were just what were needed for the economic and cultural development of his empire.

Suleiman the Magnificent receiving Christian vassals as his army besieges the Hungarian town of Szigetvar.

Mahomet II invited the Jewish exiles to settle in Turkey, guaranteeing them protection and religious freedom. In a short time, a tremendous number accepted his invitation and began flooding into the Ottoman domains. The sultan welcomed the newcomers with open arms. One Turkish official exclaimed, "How can you consider King Ferdinand a wise ruler when he has impoverished his own land and enriched ours?"

The influx of highly educated, enterprising Sephardic Jews brought rich seeds of culture, commerce, and industry to the Ottoman world. Among the refugees were scientists who familiarized the Turks with the latest inventions in military science and established factories to manufacture gun powder and cannons.

One of the wanderers who found a home in the Turkish Empire was a young scholar named Joseph ben Ephraim Karo.

Title page of the Shulchan Aruch. It lists 20 different commentators. Included is the commentary by Moses Isserles.

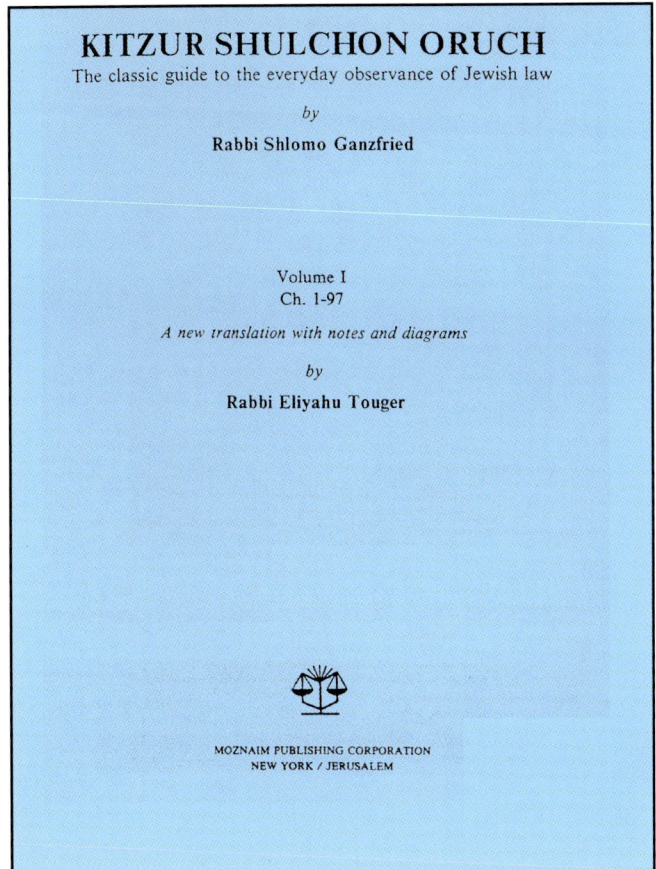

English translation of the Kitzur Shulchan Aruch.

Joseph Karo

Born in Spain in 1488, Joseph Karo lived through the great expulsion as a four-year-old. After long wanderings his family settled in Turkey.

Even as a child Karo was recognized as a genius, and his fame spread rapidly. While still a young man, he was appointed rabbi of Nicopolis, in what is now Bulgaria. Eventually he settled Palestine in city of Safed, where he became the head of an academy of Jewish learning.

In 1522 Joseph Karo began writing the Bet Yosef ("House of Joseph"). This monumental four-volume work was an encyclopedic code of talmudic law. Karo spent more than twenty years on it.

The Shulchan Aruch

After finishing the Bet Yosef, Rabbi Joseph Karo spent another ten years preparing a shorter code, the Shulchan Aruch ("Prepared Table"). This was intended as a handy reference for those seeking detailed halachic guidance on Jewish practices and customs. The Shulchan Aruch quickly became popular because it consisted of short, simple statements that explained what to do in any given situation without complicated elaborations or digressions.

Initially the Shulchan Aruch met with opposition from Ashkenazic scholars because it was based on halachic decisions by Sephardic rabbis and sometimes disregarded French and German traditions. This problem was overcome by Rabbi Moses Isserles (1525-1572), also known as Rema, of Cracow, Poland. Rema added explanations of Ashkenazic practice to Rabbi Karo's text, making it suitable for use by all Jews everywhere.

The Bet Yosef was Rabbi Joseph Karo's beloved child, and the Shulchan Aruch was secondary, a stepchild. Nevertheless, it was the Shulchan Aruch that came to play a most important role in Judaism.

It became a cornerstone of rabbinic Judaism.

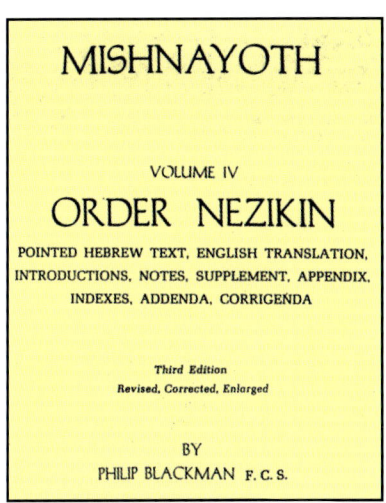

English tittle page of a translation of the Mishnah.

The Marrano Mystic

Rabbi Karo was, in a way, a two-sided personality. Although he had a methodical, down-to-earth, encyclopedic mind, he was, at the same time, a believer in the mystical teachings of the Kabbalah. In fact he was a follower of Solomon Molcho, a Marrano mystic whose Christian name was Diego Pires.

Joseph Karo was hypnotized by Molcho's fiery speeches and prophetic visions, and the two men became fast friends. Solomon Molcho's influence on Karo was so great that he began seeing visions of a higher being called a Maggid who revealed heavenly secrets to him. He claimed that the Maggid visited him every Shabbat and on holidays.

Rabbi Joseph Karo was regarded as Safed's leading halachic scholar, and his yeshiva had more than 200 students. In addition to his duties, he also found time to write hundreds of responsa to halachic inquiries.

Joseph Karo died in Safed at the age of 87. His name has been immortalized by his most famous book, the Shulchan Aruch . It is the authoritative book of Jewish law for Jewry throughout the world.

ISAAC ABRABANEL, 1437-1508

The Marranos were constantly watched by spies and informers. Anyone suspected of practicing Judaism was arrested by the Inquisition. The property of those arrested was confiscated. Most of them were tortured. Many were burned at the stake in a ceremony called the *auto-da-fé*.

Finding Marranos was a huge money-making project. Very often people were arrested and tortured simply because they were well-to-do. Their confiscated property was divided between the church and the crown. Sometimes people were accused of being secret Jews and arrested simply because someone had a grudge against them.

The Inquisition

Queen Isabella and King Ferdinand witness the conversion of a Jew. Note that the kneeling Jew has crossed his arms into the shape of a cross.

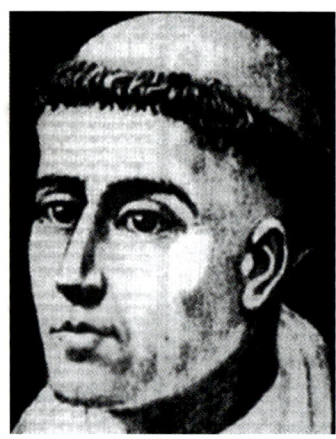

The infamous Torquemada.

Tomás de Torquemada, who led the Inquisition, warned Queen Isabella and King Ferdinand that the presence of Jews in Spain was bad for the church and would weaken the country. If the Jews were forced to leave Spain, he said, it would be much easier to control the Marranos.

The king and queen agreed, but put off doing anything because the Jews were still needed for their important political and economic contribution to Spain's national power. Spain was at war with Granada, the last Moslem outpost in Spanish territory, and it would have weakened the war effort if the many thousands of Jewish army officers, mapmakers, doctors, ammunition makers, and businessmen were driven out of the country.

However, Granada surrendered on January 2, 1492. King Ferdinand and Queen Isabella triumphantly entered the city. Now in control of all of Spain, they gave in and agreed to banish the Jews.

The Expulsion

The date of the expulsion on the Hebrew calendar was the ninth day of the month of Av in the year 1492. This was the very same day on which the First Temple had been destroyed by the Babylonians in 586 B.C.E. and the Second Temple had been destroyed by the Romans in 70 C.E.

Everything had to be left behind. Jews who had property traded it for sturdy traveling clothes. Precious jewels were exchanged for food for the long, perilous journey. Like vultures feasting on a dead body, the priests surrounded the exiles and even invaded the synagogues. They urged the hapless victims to convert and save their lives and their property. A few consented, but the majority chose to go into exile.

Don Isaac Abrabanel

On August 2, 1492, 300,000 Jews left Spain. One of them was Don Isaac Abrabanel, one of Spain's most important officials.

Don Isaac Abrabanel was born in Portugal in 1437, to a family that was socially and politically prominent. His education included Hebrew, Talmud, mathematics, science, Greek literature, and the writings of Christian and Moslem scholars.

Isaac's father, Judah, had been the royal treasurer of Portugal. His parents' home was a meeting place for Jewish, Christian, and Moslem scholars, politicians, and financiers. From them Isaac learned the arts of diplomacy and high finance.

King Alfonso V of Portugal, under whom Jews enjoyed freedom and prosperity, had appointed Isaac as his treasurer when his father died. Isaac helped his people whenever he could. When Jewish captives in Morocco were being sold as slaves, he personally intervened and managed to ransom and free all of them.

After Alfonso's death in 1482, Isaac Abrabanel's enemies accused him of plotting against the crown and he was forced to flee to Spain.

After his escape, Abrabanel settled in the city of Toledo. Now, at the age of 40, he devoted himself to his first love, writing a commentary on the Bible. This work was interrupted when Isaac was summoned to appear at the court of King Ferdinand and Queen Isabella.

At that moment in history, Spain had many political, economic, and military problems. The rulers needed a miracle worker who could pull the country out of its troubles. In a short time Abrabanel managed to replenish the Spanish treasury, mobilize the country's resources, and resupply the army with food and arms.

When Ferdinand and Isabella issued the order expelling the Jews from Spain, Abrabanel tried to get them to change their minds. He offered an enormous sum of money if the expulsion order was cancelled.

King Ferdinand, who took more interest in his treasury than in the Catholic faith, wanted to accept the bribe and rescind the order. Then the fanatical grand inquisitor Torquemada shouted, "Judas Iscariot sold Christ for 30 pieces of silver; now your highnesses are about to sell him for 300,000 ducats. Here he is, take him and sell him!"

Isaac Abrabanel.

Abrabanel Leaves Spain

Although Abrabanel's plea was unsuccessful, he could have stayed in Spain if he wished, because Ferdinand and Isabella offered to exempt him from the expulsion order. Instead he cast his lot with his friends and brethren, the Jewish people. Like Moses leading the children of Israel out of Egypt, he led the exodus from Spain.

After much wandering, Abrabanel found a refuge in a town near Naples, Italy. Notwithstanding his advanced years, Don Isaac managed to complete his commentary on most of the Bible. His discussions of the kings of Judah and Israel are extremely illuminat-ing, because he intimately knew the ways of kings, governments, and their intrigues.

Abrabanel died in 1508, at a ripe old age, and was buried in Padua, Italy. In 1904, the Jews of Padua erected a monument in the cemetery in memory of Don Isaac Abrabanel.

Two Jews await thir fate at an auto-da-fé. Note the holiday atmosphere and notables in the viewing stands.

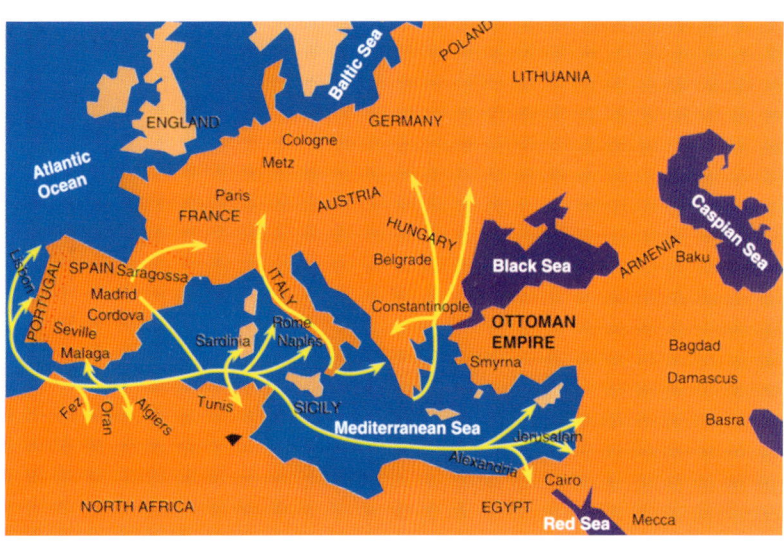

The expulsion from Spain in 1492. The map shows how the first exiles went to Portugal and southern Italy; persecution followed and many fled eastward to countries of the Ottoman Empire.

RABBI ISAAC LURIA, 1534-1572

The body of mystical knowledge comprising the Kabbalah developed over hundreds of years. In the thirteenth century most of these teachings were compiled in a book called the *Zohar*, by Moses de Leon of Castile, Spain. Written in Aramaic and organized as a commentary on the Torah, it expounded sacred mysteries hidden from ordinary readers of the Bible.

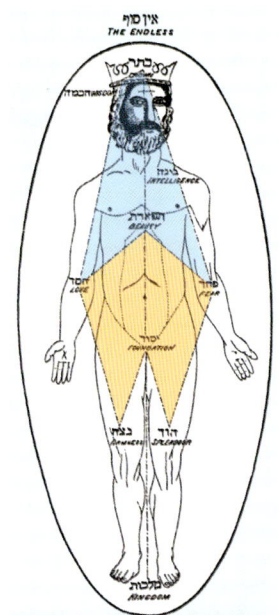

According to the Kabbalah, each of the Sefirot of the Tree of life corresponds to a part of the human body. These power centers are energy spheres which control the physical, mental, and psychological functions of the human being. When they are operating properly they provide the individual with special abilities of perception and creativity.

Title page of the first edition of the Zohar, Mantua, 1558.

The Zohar

According to Moses de Leon, the Zohar dated back to the second century C.E. and had been written by Simeon bar Yochai, a colleague of Rabbi Akiba. Moses de Leon claimed to have found it in a cave in which Simeon bar Yochai and his son Eliezer had hidden for thirteen years during the Roman persecution in the time of Hadrian. Throughout this period, the Talmud records, Simeon and his son ate the fruit of a carob tree and spent their time studying the mysteries of the Torah.

The Zohar fascinated Jewish scholars, and in the next few centuries interest in Kabbalah spread from Spain to other countries. The kabbalists maintained that every aspect of the Torah, even including the shapes of the letters and variations in spelling that sometimes look like errors, had a secret meaning that could be uncovered through intensive study. All these hidden meanings were set forth in the Zohar, for those who knew how to find them.

The Zohar also teaches that every act of every human being has an effect on the world above. When we perform good deeds, we crown the day with goodness, and it becomes our protection in the world to come. But if we perform a cruel deed, it has a negative effect on the day and will destroy us in the world to come. Thus good and bad deeds can build or destroy the balance of the earth.

Rabbi Isaac Luria in Safed

Some of the formulas and symbols developed by the mystics are utilized in the prayer book. The blowing of the shofar, for instance, is introduced with a kabbalistic prayer. The prayer before reading the Torah is also introduced with a passage from the Zohar.

The expulsion from Spain in 1492 helped increase interest in mystical lore. Jews of Spanish origin became the leaders in the study of the Kabbalah. It attracted them because they were seeking an explanation for their past misfortunes. Safed became the center of the kabbalistic movement. The beauty of the surrounding hills and the mysterious echoes which reverberated through the valleys inspired the saintliness of the Safed kabbalists. One of the most important kabbalists who settled there was Isaac Luria

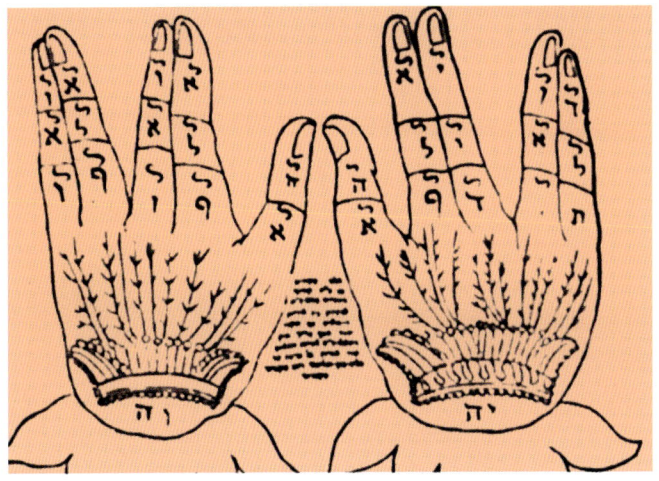

Most Jews believed that Hebrew letters and the Hebrew language were sacred, since they were used by God to create the world. The kabbalist Abraham Abulafia (1240–1300) believed that combinations of letters could help an individual achieve prophetic vision and knowledge of God. The above is a kabbalistic drawing showing the channels of divine emanation and letter combinations in the form of hands.

The Ari

When Rabbi Isaac Luria settled in Safed, he found many enthusiastic students there. By devoting themselves to the joys of mysticism and prayer, they hoped to hasten the coming of the Messiah and the time of eternal peace.

Rabbi Luria's saintly way of life, personality, and approach to kabbalistic study soon won him the affection and loyalty of Safed's mystical community. After he died at the young age of 38, they preserved his teachings and transmitted them to later generations.

Luria's students referred to him as the Ari, an acronym for Adoneinu Rabbi Yitzchak ("Our master, Rabbi Isaac"). *Ari* is the Hebrew word meaning "lion." The disciples of Rabbi Isaac thought him as courageous, strong, and mighty as a lion, the ancient symbol of the tribe of Judah.

Rabbi Isaac Luria

The greatest teacher of Kabbalah in Safed was the brilliant young Rabbi Isaac Luria. Born in Jerusalem, he lost his father when he was a child. He was brought to Cairo, where he was educated under the care of his uncle. Luria made rapid progress in his rabbinic studies and became acquainted with the Kabbalah, to which he vigorously applied himself.

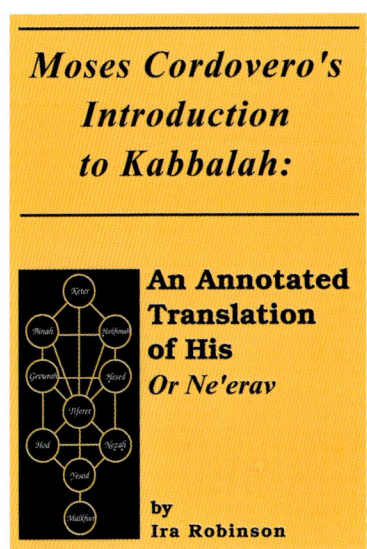

Moses Cordovero (1522–1570) is abbreviated as Re MaK. In his short life he authored more than thirty books, including commentaries on the Torah and works on the Kabbalah.

"How awesome is this place," reads the inscription over the entrance to the synagogue of the ARI.

ISRAEL BEN ELIEZER (BAAL SHEM TOV), 1698-1760

Toward the end of the Middle Ages, large numbers of Jews from Germany settled in Poland, which at that time included much of Lithuania and Ukraine. They came at the invitation of the Polish kings, who needed them because of their advanced commercial and technical skills. In the years that followed, Polish Jewry prospered. Governed by a body of rabbis known as the Council of Four Lands, Polish Jews were able to live under their own laws and spoke their own language, Yiddish. There was always a certain amount of anti-semitism.

Meeting place of the Council of the Four Lands, Lublin, sixteenth and seventeenth centuries.

The Pogroms

The Cossack leader Bogdan Chmielnicki killed thousands of Ukrainian Jews in the revolt he led in 1648.

Jewish hostility among Poland's peasants and Christian clergy, but by and large Polish Jewry prospered. The situation changed radically after 1648, when the Cossacks of Ukraine rose up in revolt under the leadership of Bogdan Chmielnicki.

The Cossacks killed thousands of Jews in brutal pogroms. Jewish communities were destroyed, and Jewish property was looted. In the aftermath of the revolt, conditions for the Jews steadily deteriorated. The Council of Four Lands was abolished by the government. Communities that had been rebuilt after the Chemielnicki pogroms went into a decline. Many communities were so poor that they could not even maintain their school systems.

The Polish government was also gravely weakened. Three times the land was invaded and partitioned by its more powerful neighbors. By 1796, nothing remained and Poland lost its independence. Depending upon where they lived, the Jews of Poland now became subjects of either Russia, Prussia, or Austria. The ruler of Russia in 1796 was Catherine the Great. She regarded herself as a liberal empress, but her subjects lived under primitive conditions. The partitions of Poland brought Catherine the lion's share of Polish Jewry. In order to prevent this mass of Jews from expanding into other parts of her empire, she restricted their right of residence to the areas taken from Poland in which they were already living.

This area was known as the Pale of Settlement. It included eastern Poland, Ukraine, and Lithuania. In addition to its Jewish residents, it had a much larger population of Christians who hated their Jewish neighbors.

It was here, in the little towns and villages of the Pale, in a few crowded cities and lonely inns along the highway, that most of Europe's Jews were to live for the next 200 years. The Russian government imposed many harsh restrictions upon them. They had to pay high taxes and could not move or travel without permission; they could not attend Russian schools or academies of higher learning and were barred from many other public institutions.

Nonetheless, Jewish life in the Pale was active and full. While all but a few Russian nobles were illiterate, even the humblest Jewish family sent its sons to the one-room cheder to learn to read and write and

Catherine the Great was the daughter of a minor German ruler. In 1745 she married the Russian Tsar Peter lll and soon after his mysterious death, in 1761, made herself the ruler of the greatest state in Europe. Domestically, she ruled with an iron hand and militarily advanced Russian power. She enlarged the kingdom by acquiring the Black Sea territories from the Ottoman Empire. Envious statesmen saw Catherine's success as the work of the devil.

Hasidic scholar wearing a streimel, a fur hat worn by some Hasidic sects on holidays and special occasions.

The synagogue of the Baal Shem Tov.

engage in studying the Torah. The very restrictions that had been imposed upon them served to knit the Jews of the Pale to a way of life based on brotherhood, neighborliness, and genuine concern for one another. This period was to produce two great religious leaders, each quite different from the other and each concerned with a different way of life. One was Israel ben Eliezer, known as the Baal Shem Tov; the other was Elijah ben Solomon, the Gaon of Vilna.

Israel Ben Eliezer

Israel Ben Eliezer was born in a small town in Ukraine about 1698. When still a small child, he lost both his parents and was cared for by the community. After graduating from the cheder he became the assistant to the teacher.

Israel liked children, and they, in turn, loved to listen to his stories. He took great delight in roaming the woods around the town and often would take his pupils with him. There, amidst the wonders of nature, teacher and pupils would chant the psalms and the melodies of the prayers. Israel married a young woman called Hannah, and the two moved to a village in the Carpathian Mountains, where Israel earned his living as a lime digger. He enjoyed his work, for while it brought him very little money, it left him time to study and to meditate on God and life. For seven years Israel and Hannah lived in solitude in the mountains. All around him Israel could behold the beauty God had created. The humble lime digger was convinced that the holiness, or Shechinah, of God dwelt within every living thing. Everyone, scholar and simple laborer alike, could reach spiritual heights by prayer and by being kind and loving to all creatures.

The Worship of the Heart

The "worship of the heart" through joy and ecstasy, Israel taught, was of greater importance than dry, routine, ritual observance. Some of his famous stories illustrate this point.

In one story, a shepherd boy who does not know how to read the siddur prays, one solemn Yom Kippur, by blowing his whistle. It is the only way he has to express his intense love for God. Because it is sincere and genuine, it is a legitimate way for him to pray.

In another story, a lad who knows only the letters of the Hebrew alphabet recites them as his prayer, feeling sure that God will put them together in the right combinations.

Israel ben Eliezer's teachings appealed to many people, especially those who were poor and uneducated. He wrote no books; his wisdom was spread by word of mouth among rabbis and among the tradesmen, artisans, and laborers who were his followers.

Baal Shem Tov–The Besht

His followers told many wonderful tales about the good deeds he performed, and before long the kindly Israel ben Eliezer was known as the Baal Shem Tov, the "Master of the Good Name," for it was said that he could heal people by merely pronouncing the Holy Name of God. He is also known as the Besht, an acronym made up of the first letters of Baal Shem Tov. The followers of the Baal Shem Tov, who called themselves Hasidim ("pious ones"), would dance with joy in their synagogues when they welcomed the Sabbath. Even in the midst of prayers they would dance and sing wordless melodies in praise of God. The leaders of the Hasidim in the generations after the Baal Shem Tov were known as Tzaddikim ("righteous ones"), and their disciples followed them with great fervor.

Israel ben Eliezer died in 1760 at the age of 62.

THE GAON OF VILNA, 1720-1797

In the fifteenth and sixteenth centuries, the Jews succeeded in performing an important service in central Europe. In those centuries the rulers of Poland underestimated the value of their raw materials. Enterprising Jewish traders carried the raw materials, such as wood and metals, to Germany and exchanged them for manufactured products.

Jewish Traders

Jews were also important in the cloth and wool trades. They had connections with Jewish wool and cloth manufacturers in England, France, and Germany. Jews also took an active role in the manufacture of wine. They entered into this activity because they were forbidden to drink wine prepared by a non-Jew.

The Jewish community enjoyed a self-sufficient economy and had its own merchants, farms, and tradesmen. These paintings by Arthur Szyk picture a Jewish blacksmith and baker at work.

Jews conducted their business according to talmudic law and developed their own community organizations. Each town had its own organization called the Kahal. Each Kahal collected its own taxes and dealt with civil matters in its own local courts. The Kahal also had its own president, its charity institutions, its synagogues, its hospitals, and whatever was needed for its survival. By the eighteenth century, Jewish traders and manufacturers were restricted by the government and lost most of their markets. The restrictions were very beneficial for the Christian traders and manufacturers, who now took over the markets developed by the Jews.

After the death of the Baal Shem Tov in 1760, Hasidism spread throughout Poland and Ukraine, and began to make inroads into Lithuania. There it met with opposition, because Polish Jewry and Lithuanian Jewry had quite different cultures and lifestyles. Because of their poverty, Polish Jews placed their faith in Kabbalah and believed in secret incantations, faith healing, and religious amulets. The Lithuanians, who were better educated, focused on the rigors of halachic study and formal worship.

The Vilna Gaon.

Lithuanian Jewry

Unlike Polish Jewry, Lithuanian Jewry maintained the tradition of talmudic scholarship. In the eighteenth century, Vilna, the capital of Lithuania, had a population of only 5,000 Jews, yet it produced numerous sages with the highest level of scholarship. As a result, Vilna came to be called the Jerusalem of Lithuania.

Elijah, the Gaon of Vilna, was a product of this scholarly community. He emphasized the importance of scholarship, while the Baal Shem Tov stressed emotional mysticism. Both men, each in his own way, met the needs, hopes, and aspirations of their communities. Each raised the spiritual level of Jewish life in Eastern Europe.

The Gaon of Vilna

The Rabbis who fought against Hasidism were called *Mitnagdim* ("opponents.") Their leader was the Gaon of Vilna, Elijah ben Solomon, the greatest of Vilna's many scholars also known as the Vilna Gaon.

Even when he was a young man everyone recognized that Elijah was an *ilui*, a child prodigy. By the age of ten he had outgrown the knowledge of his teachers and began studying independently. By the time he became bar mitzvah, Elijah had already gone through all 24 volumes of the Talmud. In addition, without a teacher, he studied mathematics, astronomy, science, and anatomy.

Elijah never accepted an official position as a rabbi. He spent many hours in his study, quietly engaged in scholarly work and teaching a small circle of advanced scholars who wanted to acquire his approach to the Talmud. His method was one of precise detail. He would first read each passage thoroughly and then refer to its original sources in the Mishnah and in the Torah itself. This exacting method made for a much clearer understanding of the halachah.

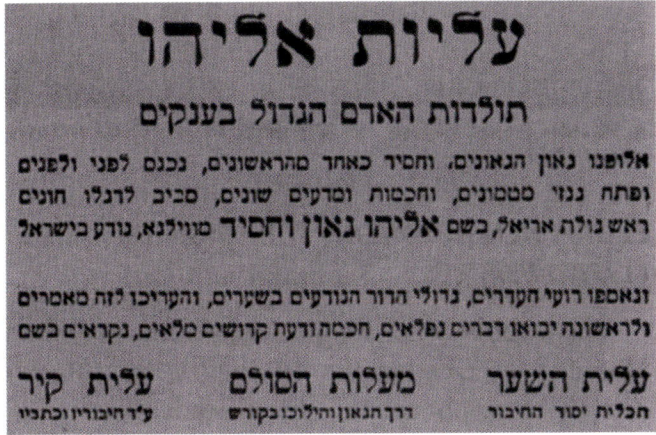

A page of one many learned works about the Vilna Gaon.

Like the great scholars of earlier days, the Vilna Gaon mastered mathematics and astronomy in addition to the works of Jewish philosophy. He and his disciples encouraged the study of science as essential for a proper understanding of the Torah. This approach was quite unusual, for in those days most yeshiva scholars confined themselves strictly to the Talmud and the commentaries of Rashi and the Tosafists.

Many people came to the kindly Rabbi Elijah with their personal problems. He always advised them and, when necessary, quietly arranged for financial assistance to help them out of their difficulties.

Hasidism and Mitnagdim

In the days of the Vilna Gaon the conflict between Hasidism and Mitnagdim became very bitter. One source of difficulty was the Hasidic claim that the Tzaddikim were intermediaries between the ordinary Hasidim and God. The Mitnagdim maintained that all human beings were personally responsible to God and therefore no intermediary was needed.

The Vilna Gaon took up the fight against Hasidism, going so far as to forbid his followers to intermarry with them. In time, this ban was lifted, as it became evident that the Hasidic approach fully followed the laws and commandments of the Torah.

Hasidim and Mitnagdim persisted in their different ways, as they do today, but each group learned to respect and appreciate the other's contribution to Judaism.

Until his death, when he was almost 80, the Gaon of Vilna spent his days in study and writing. Hard as it may be to believe, he wrote more than 80 books. Among them were commentaries on almost every important work of Jewish literature, including several on the Kabbalah.

Tombstone of the Gaon of Vilna.

BIBLIOGRAPHY

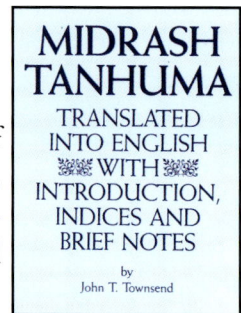

Midrash
Form of commentary on a biblical passage, much like a sermon. There are two kinds of midrashim: the midrash halachah, which tries to clarify a point of law, and the midrash aggadah, which illustrates a spiritual or ethical point. Both kinds of midrashim seek to interpret the deeper meaning of a biblical passage. Midrashic writings on all parts of the Bible have been collected over a thousand-year span.

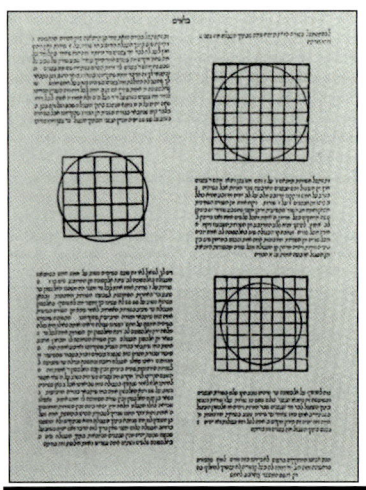

Mishnah
Side by side with the Written Law in the Bible, there developed the Oral Law, which expanded upon the ordinances of the Pentateuch. The Oral Law was handed down from master to disciple, discussed in academies of learning, and applied in courts of law. Judah the Prince compiled, systematized, and reduced to writing the Oral Law. This compendium of laws, legal opinions, and decisions and comments upon them is the Mishnah. It is not a code of law, but rather a digest of opinions which invite further study and discussion.

A page from the Mishnah Tractate Kilayim with explanatory diagrams. This complete edition of the Mishnah was printed by Soncino in Naples, Italy, in 1492.

Pirké Avot
At the end of the third century C.E. Rabbi Judah the Prince compiled the legal and moral traditions of the Jewish people into an authoritative code called the Mishnah. It became the legal-religious guidebook of Judaism and ultimately served as the foundation of the Talmud. Not long after the main body of the Mishnah was completed, a tractate called *Pirké Avot*, meaning Sayings of the Fathers, was added to this code. It was devoted not to matters of law but to the pursuit and practice of wisdom and ethics. It quickly became the best-known and best-loved tractate of the Mishnah and was eventually included in the prayer book; to this day, it is read and studied with devotion.

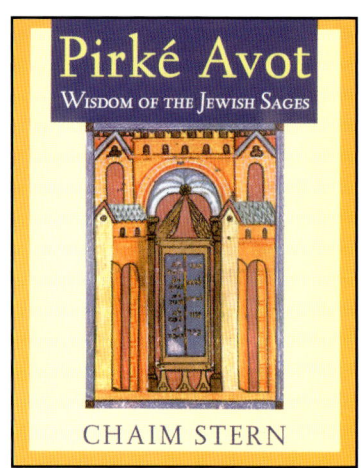

Shulchan Aruch
Famous code of Jewish law, first published about 1565 in Safed, Palestine. It was written by Joseph Karo (born in Toledo Spain, in 1488 and died in Safed in 1575). The Shulchan Aruch (based on the Arba Turim by Jacob ben Asher) deals with ritual and legal matters and is arranged simply so that it can be used by everyone. Shulchan Aruch means the "set table"–the laws are arranged so that everyone can help himself to them, as he would to food at a prepared table.

Title page of the Shulchan Aruch. It lists 20 different commentators. Included is the commentary by Moses Isserles.

Talmud, Babylonian

One of the two versions of the Talmud. It consists of the Mishnah, the Tosefta (supplement to the Mishnah), and the Babylonian Gemara. It was edited by Rabina and Ashi and was completed by the Saboraim at the beginning of the sixth century C.E. It is longer and more complete than the Palestinian Talmud and is more frequently used.

Talmud, Palestinian

Consists of the Mishnah and the Palestinian Gemara, completed by the Palestinian Amoraim by the middle of the fourth century C.E.. It is older and shorter than the Babylonian Talmud. Though it was not compiled in Jerusalem, its Hebrew name is "Talmud Yerushalmi."

A page of the Talmud with some of the commentaries. This selection is from tractate Berachot. Tosafot means "commentaries." The tosafot are in yellow color.

The Targum

Throughout the Near East, and especially in Babylonia and Syria, Aramaic was the dominant language. After the return from the Babylonian exile, it also became the everyday spoken language of Judea. Since the Torah was written in Hebrew, it was necessary to provide a translation for the many people who were no longer able to understand it.

Ezra solved the problem by providing a translator who stood right next to the Torah reader during services and translated the Hebrew into Aramaic for the congregants. Eventually the oral translations provided in this manner were set down in writing. The Aramaic translation of the Torah is called the *Targum*. Note the close similarity between the name Targum and the word *meturgeman* (translator). The Talmud mentions that in some synagogues the Torah was read twice, once in Hebrew and once in Aramaic.

There are three major Aramaic translations of the Torah: Targum Onkelos, Targum Jonathan, and the Palestinian Targum (Targum Yerushalmi).

Page from a Hebrew Bible with commentaries. The narrow column at the upper left is the Aramaic translation by Onkelos, the most widely-used Targum. It is still printed side by side with the original Hebrew text in modern editions of the Torah. In some synagogues it is recited with the regular weekly portion. Onkelos was a convert to Judaism.

Tze-enah Ure'nah

The *Tze-enah Ure'nah* is a sixteenth-century paraphrase in Yiddish of the Five Books of Moses, and includes the haftarot and the five meggilot. The title Tze-enah Ure'nah means, "Go forth and See!"

Isaac Yanover compiled the book, which was first published in Prague. It became a standard religious book among Yiddish–speaking women in Europe. Its original title was *Teitsh Chaumash,* meaning "Translation Torah." It filled the gap in the religious and cultural life of Jewish women. The simple translation is filled with inspirational, moral, and ethical reflections. The text is still in use among Orthodox Yiddish–speaking women today. An English translation is also available.

Title page of a *Tze-enah Ure'nah*.

The Zohar

The classic of Jewish mysticism, the Kabbalah. Traditionally attributed to Simeon ben Yohai, it was no doubt the product of the thirteenth-century. Most scholars attribute its authorship to Moses de Leon.

In form, it is a commentary on sections of the Pentateuch and the megillot and is in Aramaic. It has justly been called "The Bible of Jewish Mysticism." All later works of mysticism are based on it, and it has exerted great influence on Jewish belief and custom.

Title page of the first edition of the Zohar, Mantua, 1558.

Yalkut Shimoni

Yalkut Shimoni, often called "the Yalkut," is a collection of halachic and aggadic ethical and historical statements, compiled by Simeon Kara Hadarshan of Frankfort, Germany, in the thirteenth century. This material is arranged according to the biblical books to which it refers, and it covers the entire twenty-four books of the Tanak.

The compiler collected interpretations and explanations of the biblical passages and arranged them in proper order, at the same time indicating the sources from which they were derived. The collection is a convenient reference work for midrash.

BIOGRAPHICAL VIGNETTES

Aviezer, Nathan
Professor Aviezer (formerly Wiser) received his doctorate in physics from the University of Chicago and held a research position at the IBM Watson Research Center near New York.

In 1967, Nathan and his wife, Dvora, made aliyah to Israel, where he joined Bar-Ilan University as Professor of Physics and Chairman of the Physics Department.

Aviezer is the author of more than 100 scientific articles on solid-state physics and in 1984 was elected as a Fellow of the American Physical Society in recognition of his important research contributions to the theory of the electrical resistivity of metals. The Aviezers have four children and live in Petach Tikva.

Bechor Shor, Joseph ben Isaac of Orleans
Bechor Shor was a French talmudic and Torah scholar who was active in the twelfth century. Besides tosafot (Talmudic commentaries), he also authored a commentary on the Torah. He confined himself to literary interpretations *(peshat)* and tried to provide rational explanations for biblical miracles. In addition, Bechor Shor was the author of a number of liturgical poems. His writings indicate that he was familiar with theology.

Arthur A. Chiel (1920–1983)
Born in 1920, Rabbi Arthur Chiel was a spiritual leader, Director of B'nai Brith Hillel Foundation at the University of Manitoba where he established the Department of Judaic Studies. He subsequently became Rabbi of Congregation B'nai Jacob in Woodbridge, CT. and served as a Fellow at Ezra Stiles College at Yale University. He wrote several books and numerous articles on the history of Jews in Manitoba and his most prominent work was *The Guide to Sidrot and Haftarot.*

Hizkuni, Hezekiah ben Manoah
Hizkuni was a 13th century French scholar who write a cabalistic commentary on the Five Books of Moses.

His commentary was based primarily on Rashi, but he also quotes about twenty other biblical authorities. He dedicated the text to his father, who lost his hand during a pogrom.

Hirsch, Samson Raphael (1801–1888)
Rabbi Hirsch, a German rabbi, lived in an era when challenges were being raised against traditional Jewry. He had a traditional Jewish education and also spent a year studying philosophy and history at the University of Bonn. Hirsch's basic argument was that Jews, not Judaism, was in need of reform. Hirsch's most important contribution was his commentary on the Torah. His book *The Nineteen Letters of Ben Uziel* was written in the form of a series of letters between a questioning young Jewish intellectual and a traditional believer.

Ibn Ezra, Abraham (1065-1164)
Abraham Ibn Ezra was an expert in Torah, literature, philosophy, astronomy, and medicine. He was born in Toledo, Spain, and lived in that area until 1140. Then he left Spain and spent the rest of his life as a wandering scholar. Wherever he went, Jews and non-Jews regarded this strange visitor as if he were a planetary alien who passed on superior wisdom. His commentaries on the Tanak set a scholarly standard and his poetry is full of wit and spiritual devotion. Ibn Ezra wrote commentaries on the Five Books of Moses, Job, Daniel, Isaiah, Psalms, and Song of Songs, as well as astrological and grammatical works.

Jacob, Benno
Benno Jacob (1862-1945) devoted a major portion of his life to biblical studies, yet until his retirement in 1929 he was rabbi of the large Jewish community of Dortmund with its 3,500 members and played a leading role in German Jewish life.

He was a colorful, courageous, original personality. While at the university, he organized a dueling fraternity of Jewish students, so that they could defend themselves against insults. Later he vigorously fought anti-Semitism through his writings and confrontations.

His main work was The Pentateuch: Critical and Exegetic Studies (Der Pentateuch Exegetisch-Kritische Forschungen [Leipzig, 1905), set the pattern for his later studies. It dealt with some of the most difficult and neglected sections of the Pentateuch. Each segment contained many original ideas. He understood the biblical sections on chronology, genealogy, the desert sanctuary and the sacrificial cult to deal with matters basic to an understanding of Biblical religion and treated these segments of the Bible eschewed by most readers.

Kimhi, David
David Kimhi, known under the abbreviation of RaDaK, was born in Narbonne, France, in about 1160 and died in 1235. His field of interest was Hebrew grammar, and in 1132 he published an encyclopedia of Hebrew grammar called *Michlol.*

Kimhi also wrote commentaries on the Prophets, Psalms, and Chronicles as well as the Torah. Commentaries on Proverbs and Ruth are also ascribed to him. His commentaries are characterized by interpretations based on reason and grammatical rules and by his frequent allusions to the Aramaic version (Targum).

Onkelos and Aquila (second century C.E.)
Both Onkelos and Aquila were proselytes and both translated the Torah. Onkelos' translation was in Aramaic and Aquila's was in Greek.

The similarity in facts has caused confusion, and identical stories are told about both of them.

Onkelos is referred to as a relative of the emperor Hadrian. Fearing the anger and opposition of Hadrian, he traveled from Rome to Israel for his conversion. According to the Talmud, the emperor opposed his conversion and sent four successive groups of soldiers to arrest him, but Onkelos succeeded in converting them all to Judaism. He was a disciple of Rabban Gamaliel and conducted himself with utmost piety. The rabbis ruled that everyone should review the weekly Torah portion twice in the original and once in the Targum, which is, the Aramaic translation of Onkelos.

Rashbam
Rashbam (1080–1174) is an acronym for Rabbi Samuel ben Meir. He was the son of Rashi's daughter Jocheved, and brother of Jacob ben Meir, Rabbenu Tam. He supplemented the commentary of his grandfather, Rashi, and often disagreed with his interpretations. On his own he wrote a commentary on the Torah and on several volumes of the Talmud. Rashbam writes simply and explains the rational meaning *(peshat)* of the text. He used his extensive secular knowledge of politics and science to clarify his commentaries.

Rosner, Fred
Dr. Fred Rosner is Professor of Medicine at New York's Mount Sinai School of Medicine. An internationally known authority on medical ethics, he has lectured widely on Jewish medical ethics. He is a member of the Medical Advisory Board of the Kennedy Institute of Ethics at Georgetown University and is chairman of the Medical Ethics Committee of the Medical Society of the State of New York.

He is the author of many widely acclaimed books on Jewish medical ethics.

Scharfstein (Shenash,) Sol (1921–)

Shenash (Shlomo ben Asher) is the pen name of Sol Scharfstein. Shenash was born in 1921 in the Russian city of Dinivetz. His parents, Asher and Fanny, immigrated to America, where they founded the Ktav Publishing House in New York City. He received a rigorous Jewish education at the Herzilyah Hebrew Teachers College. His Hebrew and English education was interrupted by the outbreak of World War II. He served in the European Theatre of Operations and was discharged in 1946. He graduated from New York University, married Edythe Shore from Boston, Massachusetts and is the father of three children, Joel, Alan, and Janet, and the proud grandfather of seven. Mr. Scharfstein has written more that seventy-five Jewish books in Hebrew and English. His textbooks are used worldwide. Haveri I, and II, his first textbooks, were published in 1948 with his wife Edythe and have sold close to a million copies. Some of his books are *The Five Books of Moses: And Easy-To-Read Torah Translation; The Book of Haftorot for Shabbat, Festivals, and Fast Days; Chronicles of Jewish History; Understanding Jewish Holidays and Customs; L'Shonee I and II; The Story Hagadah; Understanding Israel; A Reading and Prayer Primer,* and much more. In addition he has authored numerous children's books and designed educational devices, which are used in preschool programs.

Mr. Scharfstein received a honorary doctorate from Yeshiva University in 2006 for his contribution to Jewish education.

Soloveitchik, Rabbi Joseph B. (1903-1993)

Rabbi Joseph B. Soloveitchik was born in Poland in 1903 to a family noted for outstanding Torah scholarship. His grandfather, Rav Chaim of Brisk, and his father, Rav Moshe, had revitalized talmudic study through a renewed emphasis on scientific clarification and rigorous analysis. The young Rabbi Joseph absorbed this method of talmudic study through the instruction and training which he received from his father.

He pursued his secular studies at the University of Berlin, where he concentrated on logic and metaphysics, and he was awarded his Ph.D. degree in 1931. Arriving in America in 1932, he settled in Boston, where he guided the growth and development of the Maimonides Day School. In 1941 he succeeded his late father as Rosh Yeshiva and as professor of philosophy at Yeshiva University, where it had been his practice to deliver weekly *shiurim* to senior students and lectures in philosophy to graduate students.

Rabbi Soloveitchik had a profound hold upon the minds and views of thousands of Jewish leaders throughout the United States. His mastery of halachah and his broad knowledge of general subjects, combined with his incisive understanding of modern problems, render him one of the unique Torah personalities of our time.

Sturm, Edward (1919-2008)

After serving in the American army during World War II, he took advantage of the G.I. Bill to complete his education, including a PhD in geology from Rutgers University. In the early stages of the State of Israel, he volunteered his talents to develop the legendary King Solomon copper mines. Later, he initiated what became the worldwide custom of examining personal baggage at airports and contributed articles on security to prominent journals. As a professor of geology, he taught mineralogy and crystallography at Texas Tech and the City University of New York. At present, he is professor Emeritus of Brooklyn College. He takes pride in his wife's accomplishments, a Ph.D in psychology, and his three children's achievements, all Ph.Ds, who teach at various universities.

Index

Aaron
  blossoming of staff, 383–384
  death of, 392
  death of sons, 302
  descendants of, 342–343
  forgiven by Moses, 284
  and the Levites, 359
  ordination of, 234–236
  ordination of, with sons, 278–279
  sons of, 282–283
Abel, 40–41
Abimelech
  and Abraham, 72, 75–78
  and Isaac, 89–90
Abraham (Abram)
  and Abimelech, 72, 75–78
  Adonai's covenant with, 61–64
  ancestry of, 18
  commanded to leave Ur, 55–56, 58
  death and burial of, 85 in Egypt, 55, 57
  finding wife for Isaac, 78
  and Lot, 56, 58
  name changed to, 65
  promise of land to, 55
  promise of son to, 61–62
  and Sodom, 61, 67–71
Abram. See Abraham
Adam, descendants of, 43
Adonai
  anger at Israelites, 456–458
  anger of, 512–514
  appearance of, 66–67
  choice of sanctuary, 463–465
  command not to forget, 455–456
  dedication of plunder to, 420–421
  forgiveness denied to wicked, 502–503
  glory revealed, 282
  image of, 35
  Israel as God's special people, 452
  Israelites as children of, 467–468
  laws given to Moses by, 443–445
  Moses pleads with, 382
  Moses' song of praise to, 510
  penalties for disobeying, 312
  punishment for cursing, 323
  reassures Moses, 171
  rebellion against, 456–458
  rejection of, 511–512
  as rescuer, 503–504
  rests after creation, 36–37
  as shelter, 519
  speaks to Moses, 164–165, 357–358
  vows made to, 417
adultery, 350–351
aliyah (pl. aliyot), 26
aliyot, order of, 26
altar, 229–230
  for Tabernacle, 255
Amalek, 491
  Adonai's promise to destroy, 211
Amidah, 166
Amorites
  Israelites defeated by, 437
  Israelites' defeat of, 394–395
Amram, 162, 172
anav, 165
anger, of Adonai, 512–514
animals
  forbidden, 334–335
  tithes for, 335
Aramaic language, 22
Ararat Mountains, 47–48
  ark, of Noah, 45–48
Ark
  of the Covenant, 225–226, 363–364
  scroll placed in, 509
  of Torah, 25
Aron Ha–Kodesh (Holy Ark), 25
See also Ark
Asherites, Moses' blessing on, 518–519
assembly, 362, 508
astrologers, 167
atonement, 383
  Day of. *See* Yom Kippur
  sacrifices for, 237
  for unclean discharge, 300
Atzei Chayyim (trees of life), 25, 27
Avaris, 160
Avihu, 282–283
Azazel goat, 302–303

ba'al koreh, 26
ba'al maftir, 27
Babel, Tower of, 53
Balaam, 397–405
    prophecies against Moab, 398–399
Balak, 397–405
baldness, 291
Bamidbar, introduction and
    summary, 336
Bar Mitzvah, 27
basket of reeds, 162
Bat Mitzvah, 27
"Be strong and courageous," 506
beginning, 34–35
Benjaminites, Moses' blessing on, 517
Bereshit, introduction and summary, 32
Beth El, 96, 115–116
Betzalel, 239
    builds Tabernacle, 158, 250–251
bimah (platform), 23
birth, uncleanness from, 288
blessings, 496–498
    on Israelites by Moses, 517–519
    for obedience, 443–461
blood, eating of, forbidden, 304, 311
Book of the Law, 213–221
breastplate
    for priest, 232–233, 257–259
    for Torah, 25
bugles, for assembly, 362
burning bush, 164–165
burns, 290

Cain, 40–42
Caleb, 372
calendar, Hebrew, 30–31
camp, purification of, 349–350
Canaan, 165
    scouting out, 370–372
Canaanites, Israel to drive out, 426–427
celestial bodies, creation of, 34–35
census, 406–409
    of first-born, 345
    of Israelites, 238, 339–340
    of Levites, 343–344
children, teaching commandments to, 449–450, 514
choice of life or death, 505

choshen (breastplate), 25. *See* also
    breastplate
circumcision, 64–65, 74
cities, 327
cities of refuge, 429, 445, 478
cloud over Tabernacle, 262, 361
commandments, 309–312
    near to Israel, 504
    obedience to, 493–494
complaints of the Israelites, 365–367
contagious diseases, 292–293
courtyard for Tabernacle, 230
Covenant, obedience to, 501–502
covenants with Abraham, 61–64
creation account, 34–37
crops, tithing for, 335
crown of the Torah, 25
curses, for disobedience, 495–496
curtain
    entrance, for Tabernacle, 256
    of Torah, 25

Danites, Moses' blessing on, 518–519
debts cancelled. See Shmittah defects
    in priests, 315
    in sacrifices, 316–317
defilement, laws against, 314
Deuteronomy. See Devarim
Devarim, introduction and
    summary, 434–435
Dinah, rape of, 112–114
donations, 333–334
donkey speaks to Balaam, 398–399
"Do not be afraid," 440

earth
    creation of, 34
    dominion over, 35–36
Edomites, no hate for, 486–487
Edom's refusal of passage to Israel, 391
Egypt
    Adonai's victory over, 195–197
    promised deliverance from, 165–169
Egyptians, no hate for, 486–487
Ehyeh Asher Ehyeh (I Will Be
    Who I Will Be), 165
Eleazar, 388–389
Eliezer, 168

Elim, 199
Elisheva, 172
Elohim, 29, 161, 166, 176
enclosure for Tabernacle, 230
ephod, 257–259
Esau
    birth of, 87
    birthright sold to Jacob, 88
    descendants of, 116–118
    marries Ishmaelite, 95
    reconciliation with Jacob, 110–112
Etz Chayyim (tree of life), Torah as, 25
excuses for disobedience not
    tolerated, 508
Exodus, 201–202. *See also* Shemot
    child's question about, 191
    from Egypt, 18–19
    route, 19
    Song of Moses about, 195–198

faithfulness, 476
festivals, 321–322, 412–415
fighters, 441
fire over Tabernacle, 262, 361
first-born
    of animals, dedication of, 471–472
    census of, 345
    death of, 183–186
    dedication of, 186–187
First Temple, destruction of, 21
Five Books of Moses. *See* Torah
fluid discharges, 299–300
forty years, 374–375
fruit, dedication of fourth year, 311

gabbai (pl. *gabbaim*), 26
Gabriel, 167
Gadites
    Moses' blessing on, 518
    petition to Moses, 422–423
Garden of Eden, expulsion from, 40
    garments
        fringes required, 378–379, 485
        priestly, sanctification of, 280
gelilah, 26
Genesis. *See* Bereshit
Gershom
    circumcision of, 168
Gershonites
    descendants of, 349
    priestly duties of, 348–349
goat, Azazel, 303
God, names of, 29
Golden Calf, 158, 240–243
Gomorrah, destruction of, 67–71
grapes, cluster of, from Canaan, 371
Greek language, 22
guilt, cleansing from, 481

Haftarah, 27
Hagar, 62–63
hagbah, 26
hand as Torah ornament, 25
Heaven, 36
Herod, 524
Hillel, 184, 524–525
Hizkuni, 164
holidays. *See* festivals
holiness, 287, 308, 313
honors of Torah, 26–27
houses
    safety for, 484
    in walled cities, 327
humanity
    creation of, 35–37
    dominion given to, 35–36
    fall of, 38–40
Hyksos, 160

idolatry, 329
    destroying, in the land, 465–466
    forbidden, 465–466
incense altar, 237
infections, 292–293
inhabitants of Canaan
    untrustworthy, 246
inheritance for daughters, 409–410
Isaac
    and Abimelech, 89–90
    Abraham finds wife for, 78
    birth of, 74
    blesses Jacob, 93–94
    deceived by Jacob, 90–93
    sacrifice of, 76–78
Ishmael
    birth of, 63
    descendants of, 63

Israel. *See also* Jacob
    at Beth El, 115–117
    blessing of sons, 151–153
    in Canaan, 119–122
    death and burial of, 148, 154–155
    sons in Egypt, 132–142
Israelites
    as Adonai's nation, 502
    assembly of, 509
    complaining in wilderness, 365–367
    defeated by Amorites, 437
    Edom, journey around, 391
    instructions for, 231–237
    marching order of, in wilderness, 340–341
    rebellion of, 372–374
    settle in Goshen, 145–146
    at Sinai, 208
    tribal leaders appointed, 435
    victories in wilderness, 394–396
    wanderings, 437–439
Issacharites, Moses' blessing on, 518

Jacob. *See also* Israel
    agreement with Laban, 101–102
    birth of, 87
    birth of children, 99–101
    and Heaven's ladder, 96
    Isaac's blessing upon, 93–94
    and Leah, 98–99
    at Machanayim, 106
    in Padan Aram, 95
    and Rachel, 97–105
    reconciles with Esau, 110–112
    renamed Israel, 109
    treaty with Laban, 105–106
    wrestles with angel, 109–110
Jair, 423
Jerusalem
    siege of, 522–523
Jethro. See Yitro
Jochebed (Shifra), 161
Joseph (Yosef)
    birth of, 101
    death of, 160
    interprets dreams, 126–130
    Moses' blessing on, 517–518
    in Potiphar's house, 125
    in prison, 126–127
    reconciles with brothers, 156
    rises to power in Egypt, 160
    and reunion with family, 132–137, 142
    and salvation of Egypt, 147
    sold to Ishmaelites, 120–121
Joshua
    and Caleb, 372
    as successor to Moses, 508
Jubilee Year, 325
judges, appointment of, 474–475

Kehothites, 172, 344
    priestly duties of, 346–347
keter Torah (crown of the Torah), 25
Keturah, 163
Ketuvim (Writings), 28
king, appointment of, 475–476
Knowledge, Tree of, 38
Korach, rebellion of, 158, 380–381

Laban, 101–106
laws
    authority and justice, 219
    command to study, 452
    criminal activities and abuse, 216–218
    about dead animals, 286–287
    against defilement, 314
    dietary, 285–287
    equality under, 323
    of family relationships, 486
    given to Moses by Adonai, 443–445
    for infections, 292–293
    injuries and penalties, 214–216
    obedience to, 454–455, 461–463
    for pregnancy and birth, 288
    purity, 221
    Sabbath, 220–221, 249
    about sexual acts, 306–307
    for skin diseases, 289–291
    slaves and slavery, 213–214
    various, 308–312
    written on stone, 494
Leah, 98–99
Lemech, 44
leprosy, 167, 300–302
    healing of, 295
    poor person's offering for, 296

"Let My people go", 169
Levites
   and Aaron, 359
   descendants of, 343–345
   Gershonite duties, 348–349
   Kehothite duties, 346–347
   land for, 428
   Moses' blessing on, 517
   sanctuary, responsibilities of, 384–386
Leviticus. *See* Vayikra
life or death, choice of, 505
loans, 488
Lot, 56, 58

Machir, 423
Machpelah, cave of, 66, 79–80
magicians, 173, 176, 178
Maimonides, 173, 182
Manna, in the wilderness, 157, 200–202
Mantle of the Law, 25
Ma'ot Chittim, 183
marriage, regulations regarding, 488
Masoretes, 22
Matriarchs, 18, 166
meat, promise of, in wilderness, 365–367
Meeting Tent, 158, 338
Melchi-tzedek, 60
menorah, 226–227, 322
   lighting of, 358–359
Merneptah, 161
Midianites, 163
   revenge against, 418
mildew, 293
   in houses, 296–297
   and skin infections, 298–299
minyan (quorum), 27
Miriam (Puah), 161
   curing of, 369
   cursing of, 369
Mishnah, 12, 525, 556
mitzvot, 158, 183
Moses
   addresses Israelites, 434, 446, 501
   before Adonai, 243–245
   Adonai speaks to, 357
   birth of, 162
   death of, 519–520
   forgives Aaron, 284
   inspects Tabernacle, 259–260
   on Jordan's east bank, 434–520
   as judge, 206–207
   in Midian, 163–164
   modesty of, 165
   before Pharaoh, 18, 169–170, 172–173, 180–182
   pleads for mercy, 382
   at Sinai, 239–240
   Song of, 195–198
   and Torah, 19
   veiled face of, 248
   view of Promised Land, 515
   and Yitro, 205–206
Mount Sinai, 24, 157, 165
   Moses at, 324
   Moses returns from, 240–241
murder, finding victim of, 481

Nachmanides (Ramban), 160
   See also Ramban
Nachor, descendants of, 54–55
Nadav, 282–283
Naphtalites, Moses' blessing on, 518–519
Nazarite vow, 351–353
Nevi'im (Prophets), 28
Nile River, 174
Noah
   birth of, 43
   descendants of, 43–44, 50–51
   and flood, 46–48
Novah, 423
Numbers. See Bamidbar

obedience
   blessing for, 453–455, 460–461
   commanded, 504
   to commandments, 493–494
   to covenant, 501
offerings. See also sacrifices
   for anointing, 274–275
   burnt, 274
   dishonesty, 273
   dough, 376–377
   grain, 376
   guilt, 275

of high priest, 274–275
peace, 276–278
Shemini Atzeret, 416
sin, 272–273
for sin, individual, 377–378
of tribal leaders, 354–357
Og, Israelites' defeat of, 396, 440–441
Oholiav, 239
oil, sacred, for anointing, 239
ordination
    of Aaron and family, 234–236
    of Aaron and sons, 278–279
    rams for, 279–280
    seven days for, 280

parochet (curtain), 25
partition for Tabernacle, 229
Passover, 18, 183–187, 413
    in the wilderness, 360–361
past, remembrance of,
    commanded, 510–511
Patriarchs, 18, 58, 166
Pentecost. See Shavuot
people, Israel as Adonai's, 331–333
petichah, 26
Pharaoh
    dreams of, 129–130
    Israelites in bondage to, 157
    and promotion of Joseph, 130–131
    refusal to release Israel, 179, 182
    "who did not know", 157
Pinchas, plague stopped by, 405–406
Pithom, 161
plagues, 157
    boils on cattle, 176–178
    frogs and lice, 175–176
    hail, 178–179
    locusts and darkness, 181–182
platform for Torah reading, 26
plunder for Adonai, 420–421
pomegranates, 25
poor, wages for, 489
pregnancy, laws for, 288
priests, 476
    with defects, 315
    garments for, 257–259
    kingdom of, 207
produce, eating a neighbor's, 487–488

Promised Land
    Adonai's blessing of, 330–331
    Adonai's ownership of, 326
    cities of refuge in, 429
    for daughters of Tzelafechad, 410
    division of, 408–409, 427–428
    entering, 494
    for farming, 334–335
    inheritance for women, 431
    instructions to depart for, 244–245
    for Levites, 428
    redemption of, 326
    victory in, for obedience, 464
property, laws regarding lost, 483–484
prophets, false, 477
Ptolemy II (Philadelphus), 22
purification, 389–390
    after war, 419

quail
    Adonai's provision of,
        157, 367–368
    in the wilderness, 200–202
quorum for assembly (minyan), 27

Rabbi Akiba, 526–527
Rachel, 97–105
    Laban's idol stolen by, 104–105
rainbow, 50
Ramban (Nachmanides), 160
    See also Nachmanides
Rashi, 163
Rebecca
    marriage to Isaac, 84–85
    at the well, 81–82
redemption
    of land, 326
    of poor, 328
Reubenites, 160
    petition to Moses, 422–423
Reuel, 163, 164
rimonim (pomegranates), 25
ritual purity, 314–315
robe, 259
    for priests, 233–234
rock, water from, 202–203, 390–391
Rosh Hashanah, 320, 414

Sabbath, 31
    of Sabbaths, 303–304
sacrifices. See also offerings
    for anointing of priests, 274–275
    for atonement, 237
    burnt offerings, 274
    daily, 411–412
    defective, forbidden, 474–475
    grain offerings, 265–268
    guilt offerings, 275
    for high priest's sins, 268–270
    incense, 237
    instructions for, 265
    for Israel's sins, 270–272
    morning and evening, 236
    official, 304
    peace offerings, 267–268, 276–278
    wave offering, 235–236
safety for houses, 484
sanctuary, Adonai's choice for, 463–465
Sanhedrin, 524
Sarah (Sarai)
    barrenness of, 61–62
    death and burial of, 79
    name changed to, 65
scapegoat. See goat, Azazel
scouts, 436–437
    sent to Canaan, 370–372
Sea of Reeds, crossing of, 157, 194–195
seder, 184, 185
Seir, descendants of, 117–118
Sephardic system of Torah reading, 27
Septuagint (LXX), 22
sexual acts, unlawful, 306–307
Shabbat, 157
Shammai, 525
Shavuot (Weeks), 23
Shem, descendants of, 52
Shemot, introduction and summary, 157–158
Shmittah, year of, 469–470
Sichon, Israelites' defeat of, 395–396, 440
Simchat Torah, 23
skin diseases, 289–291
slaves, Israelite, 329

snake
    curse upon, 39
    image of, for redemption, 394
Sodom
    destruction of, 67–71
    wickedness of, 67–69
Song of Moses, 195–198
spies. See scouts
staff
    of Aaron, as warning, 384
    of Aaron blossoms, 383–384
    of Moses, turns into snake, 173
Sukkot, 321–322, 415–417, 473

Tabernacle
    cloud and fire over, 361
    constructed, 251–255
    erected, 261
    frames for, 228
    furnishings for, 254–256
    inspected by Moses, 259–260
    instructions for, 227–230
    offerings for, 249
Tamar, 122–124
Tanak, 28
Targum, 22
taryag mitzvot, 29
Ten Commandments, 24
    Israelites' awe at, 157, 212
    Israelites commit to follow, 448–449
    received at Sinai, 157, 209–211
    second reading of, 446–448
    second tablets cut, 245–246, 458
Terach, descendants of, 54–55
testimony of heaven and earth, 505
tetragrammaton (YHWH), 29
tithe, 335
    second, 468–469
    third-year, 493
    tithing of, 387
Torah
    in Babylon, 21
    ceremonies and honors, 26–27
    contents of, 28–29
    division of, 19, 21, 28–29
    history in, 18–21
    holidays, 21
    introduction to, 12–13

in Israel, 21
and Moses, 19
ornaments and settings of, 25
procession, 23
reading of, commanded, 507–508
reading of, in assembly, 26–27
reading of, Sephardic, 27
scholarship, 22
writing the scroll, 28
Tree of Knowledge, 38
trees of life, 25, 27
trope, 26
Tzelafechad
   daughters of, land for, 410
   daughters of, marry, 431
Tzipporah, 168
uncleanness
   from discharge, 300
   separation from clean, 300
unfaithfulness, 350–351

Vayikra, introduction and summary, 263
vegetation, creation of, 35
vengeance on Adonai's enemies, 514
vineyards, 484
virgins, 485–486

wages for the poor, 489
war, 482–483
   dividing plunder, 419–420
washbasin for ritual cleansing, 238
water from the rock, 202–203, 390–391
Weeks, Feast of, 23
weights and measures, 312
wells
   Beer-sheva, 75–76, 90
   Isaac's quarrels over, 89
wicked, Adonai's displeasure with, 44
wilderness wanderings, 424–426
   from Sinai to Paran, 363–364
witchcraft forbidden, 313
witnesses, false, 479
women, inheritance of land for, 431

yad (hand), 25
YHWH (Yahweh), 29
Vilna Gaon, 46
Yitro, advice to Moses from, 205–207
Yom Kippur, 320, 415
Yosef. See Joseph

Zebulunites, Moses' blessing on, 518
zechut avot, 166